FOOD & WINE

annual cookbook 2010

an entire year of recipes

FOOD & WINE ANNUAL COOKBOOK 2010

EDITOR **Kate Heddings**
DESIGNER **Ethan Cornell**
SENIOR EDITOR **Zoe Singer**
ASSOCIATE FOOD EDITOR **Melissa Rubel Jacobson**
COPY EDITOR **Lisa Leventer**
EDITORIAL ASSISTANT **Olivia Young**
PRODUCTION MANAGER **Matt Carson**
DEPUTY PHOTO EDITOR **Anthony LaSala**

FRONT COVER

Cheddar BLT Burger with Tarragon Russian Dressing, P. 154
PHOTOGRAPH Quentin Bacon
FOOD STYLING Simon Andrews
PROP STYLING Jessica Romm

BACK COVER

PHOTOGRAPH (SOUP) Frances Janisch
PHOTOGRAPH (PORK) Ditte Isager
FOOD STYLING (SOUP, PORK) Alison Attenborough
PHOTOGRAPH (TART) John Kernick
FOOD STYLING (TART) Susie Theodorou

FLAP PHOTOGRAPHS

PORTRAITS Andrew French

AMERICAN EXPRESS PUBLISHING CORPORATION

PRESIDENT/C.E.O. **Ed Kelly**
S.V.P./CHIEF MARKETING OFFICER **Mark V. Stanich**
C.F.O./S.V.P./CORPORATE DEVELOPMENT & OPERATIONS **Paul B. Francis**
V.P./GENERAL MANAGER **Frank Bland, Keith Strohmeier**

V.P., BOOKS & PRODUCTS/PUBLISHER **Marshall Corey**
DIRECTOR, BOOK PROGRAMS **Bruce Spanier**
SENIOR MARKETING MANAGER, BRANDED BOOKS **Eric Lucie**
ASSISTANT MARKETING MANAGER **Lizabeth Clark**
DIRECTOR OF FULFILLMENT & PREMIUM VALUE **Phil Black**
MANAGER OF CUSTOMER EXPERIENCE &
PRODUCT DEVELOPMENT **Charles Graver**
DIRECTOR OF FINANCE **Thomas Noonan**
ASSOCIATE BUSINESS MANAGER **Uma Mahabir**
OPERATIONS DIRECTOR (PREPRESS) **Rosalie Abatemarco Samat**
OPERATIONS DIRECTOR (MANUFACTURING) **Anthony White**

ISBN 978-1-60320-120-9
ISSN 1097-1564

Published by American Express Publishing Corporation
1120 Avenue of the Americas, New York, New York 10036

Manufactured in the United States of America

FOOD & WINE MAGAZINE

S.V.P./EDITOR IN CHIEF **Dana Cowin**
CREATIVE DIRECTOR **Stephen Scoble**
MANAGING EDITOR **Mary Ellen Ward**
EXECUTIVE EDITOR **Pamela Kaufman**
EXECUTIVE FOOD EDITOR **Tina Ujlaki**
EXECUTIVE ONLINE EDITOR **Rebecca Bauer**

FEATURES

FEATURES EDITOR **Michelle Shih**
RESTAURANT EDITOR **Kate Krader**
SENIOR EDITOR **Christine Quinlan**
SENIOR ONLINE EDITORS **Ratha Tep, Tracy Ziemer**
TRAVEL EDITOR **Jen Murphy**
STYLE EDITOR **Jessica Romm**
ASSISTANT EDITORS **Alessandra Bulow, Kerianne Hansen,
Kelly Snowden**

FOOD

SENIOR EDITOR **Kate Heddings**
ASSOCIATE EDITORS **Kristin Donnelly, Emily Kaiser**
TEST KITCHEN SUPERVISOR **Marcia Kiesel**
SENIOR RECIPE DEVELOPER **Grace Parisi**
SENIOR ASSOCIATE RECIPE DEVELOPER **Melissa Rubel Jacobson**
KITCHEN ASSISTANT **Brian Malik**

WINE

WINE EDITOR **Ray Isle**
ASSISTANT EDITOR **Megan Krigbaum**

ART

ART DIRECTOR **Courtney Waddell Eckersley**
SENIOR DESIGNER **Michael Patti**
DESIGNER **James Maikowski**

PHOTO

DIRECTOR OF PHOTOGRAPHY **Fredrika Stjärne**
DEPUTY PHOTO EDITOR **Anthony LaSala**
PHOTO ASSISTANT **Rebecca Stepler**

PRODUCTION

PRODUCTION MANAGER **Matt Carson**
DESIGN/PRODUCTION ASSISTANT **Carl Hesler**

COPY & RESEARCH

COPY CHIEF **Michele Berkover Petry**
SENIOR COPY EDITOR **Ann Lien**
ASSISTANT RESEARCH EDITORS **John Mantia, Emily McKenna**

FOOD&WINE

annual cookbook
an entire year of recipes
2010

American Express Publishing Corporation, New York

FOOD&WINE
BOOKS

contents

GREEN GODDESS
CHICKEN SALAD (P. 55)

CHIPOTLE-MARINATED FLATIRON
STEAK WITH AVOCADO-CORN
RELISH (P. 136)

50 healthy & fast favorites

Every single recipe in this book is delicious and satisfying, but over the course of the year, some stand out. Here are our 50 healthy and fast favorites.

HEALTHY

FAST

foreword

In the January 2009 issue of FOOD & WINE we announced the year's biggest trend: the rise of home cooking. We followed that proclamation with twelve months of extraordinary recipes to satisfy anyone who spends a lot of time at the stove. Many of our recipes were inspired by the innovative Italian restaurants opening up all across the U.S.—from an elegant Los Angeles dining room to a cheese-centric spot in Chicago. Some of their best dishes include a mozzarella-rich Frittata Sandwich (p. 278), a clever Antipasto Salad loaded with vegetables, spicy salami and provolone (p. 41) and a delectable Pasta with Sizzled Sage (p. 82). Chef-driven burger joints also popped up everywhere, providing a great jumping-off point for the home cook. Definitely worth trying are the Green-Chile Bacon Burgers with Goat Cheese from Bobby Flay (p. 150) and Laurent Tourondel's Cheddar BLT Burger (p. 154), pictured on the cover of this book.

In '09 American home cooks became even more obsessed with wine pairings, so throughout this book you'll find recipes designed to go beautifully with wine. Leek-and-Pecorino Pizza is great with Pinot Noir (p. 256); Sour-Orange Yucatán Chicken is terrific with Pinot Gris (p. 98). For more guidance, we've provided a wine glossary (p. 367) and a wine-pairing cheat sheet (p. 377).

New additions to this book include an opinionated list of F&W editors' favorite fast and healthy recipes of the year (p. 7). One smash hit was chef Joanne Chang's Spicy Peanut Noodles (p. 93)—a recipe that Chang proposed to us after we solicited ideas on Twitter for great Americanized ethnic dishes. Indeed, Chang had so many good suggestions that we decided to print them all. And F&W editors took home bootleg copies of those recipes even before the issue went to press. Also new in this edition are simple menus offering ideas for dinner parties, holiday gatherings and other special occasions.

Whether you're craving pasta, burgers or Chinese noodles, we hope you'll enjoy cooking and eating every day from this amazing collection of recipes.

Dana Cowin

Editor in Chief
FOOD & WINE Magazine

Kate Heddings

Editor
FOOD & WINE Cookbooks

GRILLED SHRIMP
SATAY (P. 32)

starters

The world's best party food, from
grilled shrimp satay to fried peanuts.

CRISPY UDON NOODLES WITH NORI SALT

DEVILED-EGG SPREAD

Crispy Udon Noodles with Nori Salt

 **TOTAL: 35 MIN**
8 SERVINGS ● ●

Inspired by a snack served at Japanese restaurants, F&W's Marcia Kiesel boils udon noodles until they are nearly al dente, then ties them into small bundles and quickly fries them in a shallow layer of oil. They are addictively crunchy.

4 ounces dried udon noodles
Vegetable oil, for tossing and frying
1 sheet nori
1 tablespoon kosher salt

1. Bring a medium saucepan of water to a boil. Add the udon noodles and cook until they are almost al dente, about 4 minutes. Drain thoroughly and transfer the udon to a medium bowl. Gently toss the noodles with vegetable oil to help keep them from sticking together.

2. Using a pair of sturdy metal tongs, hold the nori over an open flame and toast about 4 inches from the heat until the nori is darkened and crisp, about 5 seconds per side. Let cool, then crumble and transfer the nori to a spice grinder. Add the salt and grind to a powder.

3. Take 4 udon strands and carefully tie them in a loose knot near one end. Repeat with the remaining udon. In a large skillet, heat ¼ inch of vegetable oil until shimmering. Fry 4 of the udon bundles at a time over moderately high heat, spreading the udon out in a fan, until golden and crisp, about 1 minute per side. Transfer the bundles to paper towels to drain; dust with the nori salt and serve. —*Marcia Kiesel*

MAKE AHEAD The fried udon bundles can be stored in an airtight container for up to 3 hours. The nori salt can be stored in an airtight container for up to 2 weeks.

Deviled-Egg Spread

 **TOTAL: 40 MIN**
10 SERVINGS ● ●

"I can't have a party without deviled eggs," says cookbook author Katie Lee, whose cooking often reflects her Southern roots (she was born in West Virginia). Here, she deconstructs the retro hors d'oeuvre, blending hard-boiled eggs with mustard and mayonnaise to create a sort of egg salad that she can spread on toasts. "Simplicity is key," she says. "To me, it's more about tasting the egg."

1 dozen large eggs
2 tablespoons white vinegar
½ pound sliced white sandwich bread
1 cup mayonnaise
1 tablespoon yellow mustard
Kosher salt and freshly ground pepper
Paprika, for dusting

1. Preheat the oven to 450°. In a large saucepan, cover the eggs with water, add the vinegar and bring to a rapid boil. Cover the saucepan and remove it from the heat; let stand for 15 minutes. Drain the eggs and cool them under cold running water, shaking the pan vigorously to crack the shells. Let the eggs cool in the water.

2. Meanwhile, quarter the bread slices on the diagonal and arrange them in a single layer on a large baking sheet. Toast the bread in the oven for about 6 minutes, turning once, until barely browned.

3. Peel the eggs and halve them lengthwise. Coarsely chop half the egg whites and transfer to a bowl. Add the remaining whites and all of the yolks to a food processor along with the mayonnaise and mustard; process until smooth. Scrape the mixture into the bowl and blend with the chopped whites. Season with salt and pepper.

4. Top the toast points with the egg spread and dust lightly with paprika. Arrange the toasts on a platter and serve. Alternatively, serve the egg spread in a bowl with the toast points alongside. —Katie Lee

MAKE AHEAD The Deviled-Egg Spread can be refrigerated overnight.

Maple-Soy Snack Mix

ACTIVE: 10 MIN; TOTAL: 45 MIN
20 SERVINGS ● ○

12 cups Rice Chex cereal (12 ounces)
1½ pounds roasted mixed salted nuts, such as almonds, cashews, pistachios and peanuts (6 cups)
3 cups Asian rice cracker mix (7 ounces)
3 cups sesame sticks (8 ounces)
3 cups pretzel nuggets or mini pretzels (8 ounces)
2 sticks unsalted butter
½ cup Grade B pure maple syrup
⅓ cup soy sauce
1 tablespoon Thai red curry paste or *sambal oelek*
Kosher salt and freshly ground pepper

1. Preheat the oven to 275°. In a large bowl, combine the cereal with the nuts, rice cracker mix, sesame sticks and pretzels.

2. In a medium saucepan, combine the butter, maple syrup, soy sauce and curry paste and bring to a simmer, whisking to dissolve the curry paste. Pour the mixture over the snack mix and toss to coat completely. Season generously with salt and pepper and spread on 3 large rimmed baking sheets. Bake for 35 minutes, stirring 2 or 3 times and shifting the sheets, until nearly dry and toasted. Let cool completely, stirring occasionally. Serve the snack mix in bowls. —Grace Parisi

MAKE AHEAD The snack mix can be stored in airtight containers at room temperature for up to 2 weeks. Recrisp if necessary.

Spicy Lime Leaf Beer Nuts

 TOTAL: 30 MIN
MAKES 6 CUPS ● ● ○

This dish is one of many *kap klaem* (drinking snacks) on the menu at Pok Pok's Whiskey Soda Lounge in Portland, Oregon.

1 cup peanut oil, for frying
10 large fresh kaffir lime leaves (see Note)
8 small dried red chiles
6 cups raw peanuts (2 pounds)
1 tablespoon kosher salt
4 large garlic cloves, minced

1. In a very large skillet, heat the peanut oil. Line a plate with paper towels. Add the lime leaves and chiles to the skillet and fry over moderate heat until the lime leaves are crisp and the chiles turn deep red, about 1 minute. Using a slotted spoon, transfer the lime leaves and chiles to the paper towels to drain.

2. Line a large rimmed baking sheet with paper towels. Add the peanuts to the skillet and stir-fry over moderate heat until golden brown, about 10 minutes. Using a slotted spoon, transfer the peanuts to the paper towels to drain. Transfer the hot peanuts to a bowl and toss with the salt.

3. Add the garlic to the skillet and fry over moderate heat until golden, about 2 minutes. Using a slotted spoon or fine-mesh skimmer, transfer the garlic to the plate with the lime leaves and chiles and pat dry.

4. Using your hands, finely crush the lime leaves and chiles over the peanuts. Add the garlic and toss to combine. Transfer the peanuts to small bowls and serve warm or at room temperature. —Andy Ricker

NOTE It is important to use fresh (not dried) kaffir lime leaves here. They are available at Asian supermarkets; if sold frozen, defrost before using.

MAKE AHEAD The peanuts can be stored in an airtight container for up to 1 week.

Fried Peanuts with Asian Flavors

ACTIVE: 15 MIN; TOTAL: 1 HR 15 MIN
10 SERVINGS ● ● ● ●

1 pound raw peanuts (2½ cups)
½ cup fresh lime juice or lemon juice
½ cup vegetable oil
2 medium shallots, thinly sliced
Salt
2 kaffir lime leaves, very thinly sliced, or finely grated zest of 1 lime
Cilantro sprigs, for garnish

1. In a bowl, toss the peanuts and lime juice; let stand for 1 hour, tossing occasionally.

2. Drain the peanuts and pat dry on paper towels. In a large nonstick skillet, heat the vegetable oil until shimmering. Add the shallots and cook over moderately high heat, stirring, until browned and crisp, about 2 minutes. Using a slotted spoon, transfer the shallots to a plate.

3. Add half of the peanuts to the hot oil and cook over moderate heat, stirring, until golden, about 5 minutes. Using a slotted spoon, transfer the nuts to paper towels. Season with salt and let cool. Repeat with the remaining peanuts. In a bowl, toss the peanuts with the lime leaves, garnish with the shallots and cilantro and serve. —Chris Yeo

starters

Chicken-Liver Crostini

ACTIVE: 30 MIN; TOTAL: 1 HR
MAKES ABOUT 32 CROSTINI ● ●

- 1 pound chicken livers
- 2 tablespoons unsalted butter
- ¼ cup extra-virgin olive oil
- 1 white onion, finely chopped
- 2 sage sprigs
- 1 rosemary sprig
- 1 anchovy fillet, minced
- 1 tablespoon drained capers

Salt and freshly ground pepper

- ¼ cup Cognac
- 1 large baguette, thinly sliced

1. Trim the chicken livers of any sinews and veins and set them on paper towels to dry for about 20 minutes.

2. Preheat the oven to 350°. In a large skillet, melt the butter in 1 tablespoon of the olive oil. Add the chopped onion, sage and rosemary and cook over moderately high heat, stirring occasionally, until the onion is softened, about 5 minutes. Stir in the minced anchovy and capers and cook over low heat until the onion is lightly browned, about 8 minutes longer. Scrape the mixture into a medium bowl.

3. Add the remaining 3 tablespoons of olive oil to the skillet. Season the chicken livers with salt and pepper, add them to the skillet and cook over high heat until browned, about 2 minutes. Flip and cook the chicken livers for 1 minute longer. Stir in the chopped onion and anchovy mixture. Add the Cognac and carefully ignite it with a long match. Cook the livers until the flames subside.

4. Discard the herb sprigs and scrape the contents of the skillet into a food processor; let cool slightly. Pulse until chunky, then season with salt and pepper.

5. Place the baguette slices on a large baking sheet and toast them for about 15 minutes, until they are golden and crisp. Spread the baguette toasts with the chicken-liver mixture and serve.
—*Marco Canora*

Chicken-Liver Mousse with Bacon and Apple

ACTIVE: 35 MIN; TOTAL: 2 HR PLUS
COOLING AND OVERNIGHT CHILLING
10 TO 12 SERVINGS ● ●

- 2 tablespoons unsalted butter
- 2 slices of bacon, cut into
  ½-inch dice
- 1 pound chicken livers, trimmed

Salt and freshly ground white pepper

- ½ small onion, finely diced
- 1 small Granny Smith apple—
  peeled, cored and finely diced
- ¼ teaspoon ground allspice
- ¼ cup Calvados or other brandy
- 1½ cups half-and-half
- 5 large egg yolks

Toasted baguette slices and Pickled
  Red Onion (p. 354), for serving

1. Preheat the oven to 300°. Butter four 1-cup ramekins. In a large skillet, melt the butter. Add the bacon and cook over moderate heat until lightly browned, 4 minutes. With a slotted spoon, transfer the bacon to a plate. Add the livers to the skillet, season with salt and white pepper and cook over moderate heat until browned, 2 minutes per side. Transfer to the plate.

2. Add the onion, apple and allspice to the skillet and cook over low heat, stirring occasionally, until the onion and apple are softened, about 5 minutes. Add the Calvados and carefully ignite it with a long match. When the flames subside, scrape the apple-onion mixture into a blender and let cool to room temperature.

3. Add the bacon and chicken livers to the blender along with the half-and-half, egg yolks and 1 teaspoon of salt. Blend until very smooth. Pass the mixture through a coarse sieve into a large glass measuring cup. Pour into the prepared ramekins and transfer to a small roasting pan. Add enough hot water to reach halfway up the sides of the ramekins, cover loosely with foil and bake for about 1½ hours, until an instant-read thermometer inserted in the mousse registers 155°. Remove the ramekins from the water bath and let cool to room temperature.

4. Cover and refrigerate the ramekins until the mousse is chilled, preferably overnight. Serve with toasted baguette slices and Pickled Red Onion. —*Shawn McClain*

Creamy Chicken-Liver Mousse

TOTAL: 40 MIN PLUS OVERNIGHT
CHILLING
8 TO 10 SERVINGS ●

- 4 teaspoons yellow mustard seeds
- 2½ sticks unsalted butter, softened
- 3 large shallots, thinly sliced
- 2 pounds chicken livers, halved

Kosher salt and freshly ground pepper

- ¼ cup Cognac
- ¼ cup chopped flat-leaf parsley
- 10 caperberries, thinly sliced

1. In a large skillet, toss the mustard seeds over moderately high heat until toasted, about 1 minute. Transfer to a plate. Heat 4 tablespoons of the butter in the skillet. Add the shallots and cook over moderate heat until softened. Add the livers, season with salt and pepper and cook until barely pink inside, about 8 minutes. Add the Cognac and simmer for 1 minute. Scrape into a food processor; let cool.

2. Add 1½ sticks of the butter to the livers and puree until smooth. Transfer to a bowl. Fold in 3 teaspoons of the mustard seeds, 3 tablespoons of the parsley and 8 of the sliced caperberries and season with ½ teaspoon each of salt and pepper. Spread the mousse in a 6-cup soufflé dish and top with the remaining parsley, mustard seeds and caperberries.

3. In a small bowl, gently melt the remaining 4 tablespoons of butter in the microwave. Skim the foam from the surface. Spoon the clear butter evenly over the mousse, leaving behind the milk solids; tilt to distribute the butter. Cover and refrigerate overnight. —*Marcia Kiesel*
SERVE WITH Baguette toasts.

starters

Savory Tomato Parfaits

ACTIVE: 15 MIN; TOTAL: 1 HR 30 MIN

4 SERVINGS ● ●

For this multihued starter, Norwegian farmer-chef Andreas Viestad creates thick purees with three colors of tomatoes, seasoning each with salt but little else. "Nothing masks the flavors of the tomatoes," he says. You can try this recipe with any three tomato varieties depending on availability. "There is a certain pleasure in using different types of tomatoes for the same recipe," Viestad says. "It makes you less inclined to think, This is the way a dish should taste."

- ½ pound medium dark heirloom tomatoes, such as Black Krim, cored and chopped
- Salt
- ½ pound yellow plum tomatoes, cored and chopped
- 1 teaspoon chopped parsley
- ¼ teaspoon thyme leaves
- A few drops of white wine vinegar
- ½ pound red cherry tomatoes, halved
- Breadsticks, for garnish

1. In a blender, puree the dark tomatoes at high speed until very smooth, about 2 minutes; scrape down the side as necessary. Season the puree with salt and carefully pour it into 4 tall, narrow glasses. Refrigerate for about 30 minutes, until the puree has firmed up slightly.
2. Rinse and dry the blender. Repeat the pureeing process with the yellow tomatoes. Add the parsley, thyme and vinegar; season with salt. Carefully pour the yellow tomato puree on top of the chilled puree in the glasses and refrigerate for about 15 minutes, until the yellow puree is set.
3. Rinse and dry the blender and repeat the process with the cherry tomatoes to make the top layer of the parfaits. Refrigerate for at least 30 minutes, until set. Garnish the parfaits with breadsticks and serve. —Andreas Viestad

Chawan Mushi

ACTIVE: 20 MIN; TOTAL: 50 MIN

PLUS 3 HR CHILLING

4 SERVINGS ● ●

Wildly creative New York City chef David Chang (an F&W Best New Chef 2006) is obsessed with Asian flavors, as in this steamed Japanese egg custard with mushrooms and crabmeat.

- 2 teaspoons instant dashi powder (see Note)
- 2 cups warm water
- 3 large eggs
- ¼ cup salted roasted cashews, coarsely chopped
- 4 ounces lump crabmeat, broken up
- 1 scallion, cut into fine matchsticks (2 inches)
- 4 small shiitake mushrooms, stemmed and caps very thinly sliced

1. In a medium bowl, whisk the dashi powder into the warm water until it is dissolved. Let the sediment settle, then pour the clear dashi into a large measuring cup; rinse out the bowl. In the same bowl, using chopsticks, very gently stir the eggs until blended, without incorporating too much air. Stir in the dashi, then strain the mixture back into the measuring cup.
2. Divide the cashews between 4 shallow 1-cup bowls. Top with the egg mixture and wrap each bowl in plastic. Carefully set the bowls in a steamer basket set over boiling water and steam for 14 minutes, or until the custards are set. Immediately transfer the bowls to the refrigerator to chill for at least 3 hours or overnight.
3. Unwrap the custards. Top with the crabmeat, scallion and shiitake and serve. —David Chang

NOTE Dashi powder is a flavorful instant Japanese stock powder made with smoky dried bonito fish flakes and savory konbu seaweed. Look for it at Japanese markets and natural food stores.

Sorrel Mousse with Lemon Cream

TOTAL: 30 MIN PLUS 4 HR CHILLING

6 SERVINGS ● ●

When chef Patrick O'Connell opened the Inn at Little Washington in Washington, Virginia, he experimented with sorrel in lots of different ways, eventually creating this exquisite, tangy mousse.

- 1½ cups stemmed sorrel leaves
- 1 cup chicken stock or vegetable broth
- ¾ teaspoon unflavored gelatin
- 3 tablespoons fresh lemon juice
- 1 tablespoon red wine vinegar
- Salt and freshly ground white pepper
- 1¼ cups heavy cream
- ¼ cup crème fraîche
- 1 ounce caviar (optional)

1. In a blender, puree the sorrel leaves with ¾ cup of the chicken stock until smooth. In a small bowl, sprinkle the gelatin over the remaining ¼ cup of chicken stock and let stand until softened, about 2 minutes. Microwave the gelatin mixture at medium power just until melted, 5 to 10 seconds. Add the gelatin mixture to the sorrel in the blender along with 2 tablespoons of the lemon juice and the red wine vinegar. Season with salt and white pepper and puree until very smooth. Add 1 cup of the heavy cream and pulse just until very lightly whipped, about 1 minute. Transfer the sorrel mousse to a measuring cup with a spout and pour into 6 small glasses. Refrigerate the mousse until set, about 4 hours.
2. Meanwhile, in a bowl, whisk the remaining ¼ cup of heavy cream and 1 tablespoon of lemon juice with the crème fraîche to soft peaks. Season the cream with salt and white pepper. Top each mousse with a dollop of the lemon cream and top the cream with the caviar if using. Serve chilled. —Patrick O'Connell

MAKE AHEAD The mousse can be made up to 1 day ahead. Refrigerate in serving glasses, topped with plastic wrap.

CHAWAN MUSHI

SORREL MOUSSE WITH LEMON CREAM

Artichoke Custards with Fava Bean Sauce

ACTIVE: 40 MIN; TOTAL: 1 HR 30 MIN
6 SERVINGS ● ●

Made with fresh artichokes, these lush custards are an homage to spring.

- ½ lemon
- 4 artichokes (about 8 ounces each)
- 1 cup plus 2 tablespoons heavy cream
- 3 large eggs, at room temperature, beaten

Kosher salt and freshly ground white pepper

- ¾ cup frozen fava beans
- ¼ cup extra-virgin olive oil
- 1 garlic clove, minced
- ½ teaspoon chopped sage
- ½ teaspoon chopped rosemary
- 1 tomato—peeled, seeded and chopped

1. Preheat the oven to 325°. Butter six 4-ounce ramekins and set them in a medium baking dish. Fill a bowl with cold water and squeeze the lemon juice into it. Working with 1 artichoke at a time, snap off the outer leaves and trim off all but 1 inch of the stem. Cut off the remaining leaves at the top of the heart and peel the base and stem. Halve the artichoke and scoop out the furry choke. Add the heart to the lemon water and repeat with the remaining artichokes.

2. In a medium saucepan of boiling water, cook the artichokes until tender, about 10 minutes; drain and transfer to a food processor. Add 2 tablespoons of the cream; puree until smooth. Press the puree through a fine-mesh sieve into a bowl. Whisk in the remaining cream along with the eggs and season with ½ teaspoon of salt and a pinch of white pepper.

3. Pour the custard into the ramekins. Fill the dish with enough boiling water to reach halfway up the sides of the ramekins. Bake the custards for 45 minutes, until a knife inserted in the centers comes out clean. Remove the ramekins from the water.

4. Meanwhile, in a small saucepan of boiling water, cook the fava beans for 5 minutes. Drain, reserving ¼ cup of the water. Transfer the favas and the reserved water to a food processor and puree until smooth.

5. In a skillet, heat the oil. Add the garlic, sage and rosemary; cook over moderate heat for 1 minute. Add the tomato and cook, stirring and mashing, for 5 minutes. Add the puree and cook until heated through. Season with salt and white pepper.

6. Run the blade of a thin knife around each custard and invert onto plates. Spoon the sauce around the custards and serve.
—*Rolando Beramendi*

●HEALTHY ●MAKE AHEAD ● VEGETARIAN ● STAFF FAVORITE

17

Artichoke-and-Spinach Dip with Spiced Pita Chips

TOTAL: 30 MIN
8 SERVINGS ● ●

- 1 tablespoon extra-virgin olive oil
- 1 small onion, finely chopped
- 3 garlic cloves, minced
- 16 ounces marinated artichokes, drained and coarsely chopped
- ¼ cup dry white wine
- Two 10-ounce boxes frozen chopped spinach, thawed and squeezed dry
- 12 ounces cream cheese, at room temperature
- ½ cup freshly grated Parmigiano-Reggiano cheese
- 1 teaspoon finely grated lemon zest
- Tabasco
- Spiced Pita Chips (recipe follows), for serving

In a large skillet, heat the oil until shimmering. Add the onion and garlic; cook over moderate heat, stirring, until softened, 5 minutes. Add the artichokes and cook, stirring occasionally, until lightly browned, 5 minutes. Add the wine and cook until nearly evaporated. Add the spinach and cook, stirring, for 1 minute. Add the cream cheese, Parmesan and lemon zest; season with Tabasco. Cook until creamy, 2 minutes. Serve warm or at room temperature, with pita chips. —*Ken Oringer*

---

piquillo peppers

Sweet, smoky Spanish piquillos are perfect for parties.

Hors d'oeuvre Spread peppers with ricotta and minced herbs. Roll up and slice into pinwheels.

Dip Puree peppers with canned chickpeas and chopped garlic.

Salad Chop; add to potato salad.

SPICED PITA CHIPS

ACTIVE: 5 MIN; TOTAL: 25 MIN
8 SERVINGS ● ●

These crunchy chips are sprinkled with za'atar, the Middle Eastern spice blend of sumac, sesame seeds and dried herbs.

- 1 package 6-inch pocket pitas, split horizontally
- ¼ cup olive oil
- 1 tablespoon za'atar (see Note)
- 1 teaspoon sweet paprika
- Salt

Preheat the oven to 350°. Brush the split pitas all over with the olive oil and sprinkle with the za'atar and paprika; season with salt. Cut each pita into 6 wedges. Arrange the wedges on a baking sheet and bake for about 20 minutes, until golden and crisp. Let cool. —*KO*

NOTE Za'atar can also be rubbed on meat and vegetables or mixed into marinades. Look for it at kalustyans.com.

MAKE AHEAD The chips can be stored in an airtight container for up to 3 days.

Tomato Salsa with Cucumber "Chips"

TOTAL: 20 MIN
6 SERVINGS ● ● ●

This healthy take on the traditional chips-and-salsa combo is nearly fat-free and super-refreshing. The salsa is delicious served right after it's made, but the flavors meld nicely after a day or two of chilling.

- 1¼ pounds tomatoes, finely chopped
- ½ cup finely chopped sweet onion
- ½ cup finely chopped cilantro
- 1 small jalapeño, seeded and minced
- 2 tablespoons fresh lime juice
- Salt and freshly ground pepper
- 1 large seedless cucumber, sliced ¼ inch thick

In a bowl, toss the tomatoes with the onion, cilantro, jalapeño and lime juice and season with salt and pepper. Serve the salsa with the cucumber chips for dipping. —*Doris Esther Ayola Orozco*

Curried Tofu-and-Avocado Dip with Rosemary Pita Chips

TOTAL: 45 MIN
6 SERVINGS ● ● ●

To create this tasty—and healthy—dip, *Top Chef* culinary producer Lee Anne Wong blends soft or silken tofu (which has an especially custardy texture) with avocado and a little bit of low-fat sour cream and yogurt. She serves the dip with raw vegetables and rosemary pita chips.

- 4 whole wheat pitas, split
- 2 tablespoons extra-virgin olive oil
- 1 tablespoon chopped rosemary
- Salt
- 7 ounces soft or silken tofu, drained
- 1 Hass avocado—peeled, pitted and coarsely chopped
- ¼ cup low-fat sour cream
- ¼ cup plain fat-free Greek yogurt
- 1 teaspoon finely grated lime zest
- 2 tablespoons freshly squeezed lime juice
- 1 garlic clove
- 1½ teaspoons honey
- 1 teaspoon curry powder
- 2 tablespoons chopped fresh mint leaves
- Freshly ground pepper
- Grape tomatoes, cucumber slices and radishes, for serving

1. Preheat the oven to 325°. Stack the pita halves and cut them into 6 wedges; transfer to a bowl and add the olive oil and rosemary. Season with salt and toss. Spread the pita wedges on a baking sheet in a single layer and bake until crisp, about 30 minutes. Let them cool.

2. Meanwhile, in a food processor, puree the tofu, avocado, sour cream, yogurt, lime zest, lime juice, garlic, honey, curry powder and mint until smooth. Season the dip with salt and pepper and refrigerate until chilled. Serve the dip with the pita chips, tomatoes, cucumbers and radishes. —*Lee Anne Wong*

Ful Medammes

ACTIVE: 15 MIN; TOTAL: 1 HR PLUS
OVERNIGHT SOAKING

6 SERVINGS ● ●

Similar to hummus, this creamy fava bean dip is often served for breakfast in Syria. It consists of tender cooked dried favas mixed with either tahini or lemon juice (or both), then topped with a swirl of olive oil and Aleppo pepper paste. In Aleppo, entire cafés are devoted to it. One of cookbook author Anissa Helou's favorites is Abu Abdo's, in the Christian quarter. "Abu works nonstop from 7 a.m. to 3 p.m., deftly ladling *ful* from a large copper jar into bowls or plastic bags for takeout," she says. This is her adaptation.

- 1 cup dried small fava beans (7 ounces)
- 1 teaspoon baking soda
- 1 tablespoon Aleppo pepper flakes (see Note)

Kosher salt

- 1 small garlic clove, smashed
- ¼ cup tahini paste, at room temperature
- 1½ tablespoons fresh lemon juice
- ¼ cup extra-virgin olive oil

1. In a medium bowl, cover the fava beans with 2 inches of water and add the baking soda; stir to dissolve. In a small bowl, combine the Aleppo pepper flakes with 2 tablespoons of water. Refrigerate the beans and Aleppo pepper overnight.
2. Drain and rinse the fava beans and add them to a medium saucepan. Cover with 2 inches of fresh water and bring to a boil. Simmer over moderately low heat for about 20 minutes, until the beans are just tender. Season with a generous pinch of salt and cook for 10 minutes longer, until softened. Drain the beans, reserving ¼ cup of the cooking liquid.
3. In a medium bowl, using a pestle or the back of a spoon, crush the garlic to a paste with a pinch of salt. Whisk in the tahini and lemon juice. Whisk in ¼ cup of water.
4. Pour the tahini into a wide serving bowl. Mound the warm fava beans in the center and pour the reserved cooking liquid on top. Drizzle with the Aleppo pepper paste and the oil and serve. —*Anissa Helou*

SERVE WITH Warm pita.

NOTE Mildly hot Aleppo peppers are sun-dried and ground to a powder. They're available at penzeys.com.

Tangy Red-Pepper-and-Nut Dip

TOTAL: 30 MIN
MAKES 3 CUPS ● ● ● ●

The classic Syrian nut dip *muhammara* typically contains walnuts, bread crumbs, Aleppo pepper paste and pomegranate syrup, but there are endless variations. In this bright-flavored take, pistachios, cashews and freshly toasted pine nuts, almonds and walnuts provide a chunky texture, while onions and red bell peppers make the dip tangy-sweet.

- ¼ cup vegetable oil
- ¼ cup pine nuts
- ¼ cup sliced almonds
- ½ cup walnuts
- ¼ cup unsalted roasted pistachios
- ¼ cup unsalted roasted cashews
- 3 medium red bell peppers (1 pound), cut into 2-inch pieces
- 1 medium sweet onion, coarsely chopped
- ⅓ cup toasted bread crumbs
- ½ cup extra-virgin olive oil

Salt

Cayenne pepper

1. In a small skillet, heat the vegetable oil. Add the pine nuts and almonds and cook over moderately high heat, stirring, until lightly golden, about 2 minutes. Using a slotted spoon, transfer the nuts to a plate.
2. Add the walnuts to the skillet and cook, stirring, until toasted, about 3 minutes. Transfer to a food processor and let cool completely. Add the pistachios and cashews and pulse until the nuts are finely chopped. Scrape into a medium bowl.
3. Add the bell peppers and onion to the food processor and pulse until finely chopped. Transfer the pepper mixture to a fine-mesh sieve and press to extract as much liquid as possible. Add the mixture to the chopped nuts. Stir in the pine nuts, almonds, bread crumbs and olive oil. Season with salt and cayenne and serve. —*Anissa Helou*

SERVE WITH Warm pita.

Curried Crab Dip

TOTAL: 25 MIN
20 SERVINGS ●

- 2 tablespoons unsalted butter
- 1 sweet onion, finely chopped
- 2 tablespoons minced fresh ginger
- 2 teaspoons Madras curry powder
- 3 tablespoons mango chutney (preferably Major Gray), chopped
- 8 ounces cream cheese, softened
- 1 cup mayonnaise
- 2 tablespoons fresh lime juice
- 2 scallions, thinly sliced
- ¼ cup finely chopped cilantro
- 1 pound lump crabmeat, picked over

Salt and freshly ground pepper

Mixed sweet potato, vegetable and pita chips, for serving

In a deep, medium skillet, melt the butter. Add the onion and ginger and cook over moderate heat, stirring occasionally, until softened, about 7 minutes. Add the curry powder and cook, stirring, for 1 minute. Add the chutney, cream cheese, mayonnaise and lime juice and cook, stirring, until smooth and creamy, about 1 minute. Stir in the scallions, cilantro and crab, breaking up the crab slightly with the spoon. Season with salt and pepper and cook until the dip is heated through, about 1 minute. Transfer to a shallow bowl and serve with chips. —*Grace Parisi*

MAKE AHEAD The Curried Crab Dip can be refrigerated overnight. Reheat gently before serving.

starters

Cheese-Topped Guacamole

TOTAL: 30 MIN
4 TO 6 SERVINGS ●

In this play on nachos, gooey melted cheese tops chunky guacamole.

- 2 Hass avocados, diced
- 1 medium tomato, diced
- ¼ small red onion, minced
- ¼ cup finely chopped cilantro
- 2 tablespoons finely chopped mint leaves
- 1 jalapeño, seeded and minced
- 2 tablespoons fresh lime juice

Salt and freshly ground pepper

- 1 cup shredded *queso oaxaca* or Monterey Jack

Tortilla chips, for serving

In a shallow bowl, mix the avocados, tomato, onion, cilantro, mint, jalapeño and lime juice; season with salt and pepper. Melt the cheese in a microwave-safe bowl, pour over the guacamole and serve with tortilla chips.
—*Gonzalo Martinez*

Griddled Goat Cheese with Spicy Olives

TOTAL: 25 MIN
10 SERVINGS ● ●

Argentine chef Francis Mallmann prepares this dish on a *chapa* (griddle) placed over a hot fire; a large flat-bottomed skillet on the grill or stovetop also works well. Mallmann cooks fresh goat cheese until it develops a delectable brown crust, then places the warm cheese on toasts and tops them with spicy olives.

Ten 1-inch-thick slices of peasant bread, cut from a long loaf
- ½ cup extra-virgin olive oil, plus more for the griddle
- 1 cup pitted kalamata olives
- 1 teaspoon crushed red pepper
- 2 tablespoons chopped oregano, plus oregano leaves for garnish

One 9-ounce log fresh goat cheese, cut into 10 slices

Sea salt, for sprinkling

1. Light a grill or preheat the oven to 400°. Toast the bread on a rack over moderately high heat for 3 minutes or on a baking sheet in the oven for 5 minutes.

2. Heat a griddle or cast-iron skillet over a moderate fire or moderately low heat on the stove. In a bowl, combine the ½ cup of olive oil with the olives, crushed red pepper and chopped oregano. Lightly oil the griddle. Add the cheese slices and cook until browned and crusty on the bottom, about 45 seconds over the fire or about 3 minutes on the stove.

3. Place the toasts on plates and carefully set the goat cheese on top, browned side up. Spoon the marinated olives over the cheese, sprinkle with salt and the oregano leaves and serve right away.
—*Francis Mallmann*

Katie's Pimento Goat Cheese

TOTAL: 25 MIN
10 SERVINGS ● ● ●

"My grandpa always used to make pimento cheese for me with sharp cheddar, or even Velveeta," says West Virginia–born cookbook author Katie Lee. "I wanted to make it more grown-up." Her goat-cheese version of the sweet-pepper-studded spread—a Southern classic—is light and silky.

One 11-ounce log fresh goat cheese, softened
- 4 ounces smoked cheddar cheese, coarsely shredded (1 packed cup)
- ½ cup mayonnaise
- ¼ cup drained jarred pimientos, coarsely chopped
- 2 scallions, thinly sliced
- 1 tablespoon sweet pickle relish from a jar
- 1 teaspoon onion powder
- 1 teaspoon Tabasco

Salt and freshly ground pepper

Whole radishes and celery ribs, for serving

In a medium bowl, using a wooden spoon, blend the goat cheese with the cheddar, mayonnaise, pimientos, scallions, pickle relish, onion powder and Tabasco and season with salt and pepper. Transfer the pimento cheese to a bowl and serve with radishes and celery ribs.
—*Katie Lee*

MAKE AHEAD The pimento cheese dip can be stored in an airtight container and refrigerated for up to 4 days.

Pimento Cheese– and–Bacon Crostini

TOTAL: 30 MIN PLUS 2 HR CHILLING
MAKES 40 CROSTINI ● ●

These crostini come from *Down Home with the Neelys*, the first cookbook from Food Network duo Gina and Patrick.

- 2½ cups shredded extra-sharp white cheddar cheese
- 2½ cups shredded extra-sharp orange cheddar cheese

One 7-ounce jar pimientos, drained and finely chopped
- ¾ cup mayonnaise
- ½ teaspoon freshly ground black pepper
- ½ teaspoon garlic powder

Cayenne pepper
- 40 toasted baguette slices
- 4 strips of cooked bacon, crumbled

1. In a mixer fitted with the paddle, combine the white and orange cheddar cheeses. Add the chopped pimientos, mayonnaise, black pepper and garlic powder; blend at low speed. Season the pimento cheese with cayenne pepper to taste. Cover and refrigerate for 2 hours.

2. Preheat the oven to 400°. Spread the pimento cheese on the toasts, top with the bacon and bake until the cheese is melted and browned, about 2 minutes. Serve. —*Gina and Patrick Neely*

MAKE AHEAD The pimento cheese can be prepared through Step 1 and refrigerated for up to 3 days.

KATIE'S PIMENTO GOAT CHEESE

CHEESE-TOPPED GUACAMOLE

starters

Whiskey-Cheese Fondue

TOTAL: 25 MIN
8 SERVINGS ● ●

Matt Lewis of Baked in Brooklyn, New York, and Charleston, South Carolina, is enamored of fondue—in fact, he had a special pot made for dessert fondues at his former Manhattan shop, Chocolate Bar. His terrific cheddar-Jack cheese fondue includes whiskey, which adds a great kick.

- 1 **pound extra-sharp cheddar cheese, shredded**
- ½ **pound Monterey Jack cheese, shredded**
- 2 **tablespoons cornstarch**
- 2 **garlic cloves, halved**
- 1 **cup dry white wine**
- 3 **tablespoons whiskey**

Salt and freshly ground pepper
Crusty bread, breadsticks and carrot sticks, for serving

In a medium bowl, toss the cheeses with the cornstarch. Rub the garlic on the inside of a medium saucepan, then discard. Add the wine to the saucepan and bring to a simmer. Add the cheese mixture in 4 batches, whisking constantly over moderate heat and letting it melt completely between additions. Pour in the whiskey and stir just until the fondue begins to bubble, about 3 minutes. Season with salt and pepper. Serve hot, with bread, breadsticks and carrots. —*Matt Lewis*

---

fast trout pâté

Chef April Bloomfield (an F&W Best New Chef 2007) of New York City's Spotted Pig and The Breslin makes this great starter: Mix flaked skinless smoked trout with crème fraîche, cottage cheese, sliced scallions, olive oil and salt. Serve on grilled bread.

Asparagus-and-Ricotta Toasts

TOTAL: 30 MIN
8 SERVINGS ● ●

Gerard Craft (an F&W Best New Chef 2008) likes using fresh ricotta cheese for his toasts; his favorite kind is from Di Palo Selects in Manhattan (dipaloselects.com). He tops the cheese with lemon-scented asparagus, which brightens the flavors.

- 2 **tablespoons extra-virgin olive oil, plus more for drizzling and brushing**
- 8 **slices packaged thin white bread**
- ¾ **pound pencil-thin asparagus, cut into 2-inch lengths**

Salt and freshly ground pepper

- 2 **teaspoons freshly squeezed lemon juice**
- ¼ **teaspoon finely grated lemon zest**
- ½ **cup fresh ricotta (5 ounces)**

1. Preheat the oven to 350° and lightly brush a baking sheet with olive oil. Using a 2-inch round biscuit cutter, stamp 4 rounds out of each slice of white bread and transfer the rounds to the baking sheet. Lightly brush them with olive oil and toast for about 15 minutes, until lightly golden and slightly crisp.

2. Meanwhile, in a medium skillet, heat the 2 tablespoons of olive oil. Add the asparagus, season with salt and pepper and cook over high heat, stirring occasionally, until the stalks are just crisp-tender, about 1 minute. Stir the fresh lemon juice into the asparagus, take the skillet off the heat and let the asparagus cool slightly.

3. In a small bowl, stir the lemon zest into the fresh ricotta and season the cheese with salt and pepper. Spread the lemon ricotta on the toast rounds and top each toast with some of the sautéed asparagus. Drizzle the asparagus toasts lightly with olive oil and sprinkle them with a little salt. Serve the toasts right away.
—*Gerard Craft*

Crab-and-Avocado Toasts

TOTAL: 30 MIN
8 SERVINGS ●

Tossing sweet crabmeat with fresh mint and lime juice, then spooning it over mashed avocado on toast, makes for a very simple and delicious starter. You can make the toasts or buy store-bought canapé toasts to save time.

- 2 **tablespoons extra-virgin olive oil, plus more for brushing**
- 8 **slices packaged thin white bread**
- 2 **Hass avocados**

Salt and cayenne pepper

- 4 **ounces lump crabmeat, picked over**
- 1 **tablespoon chopped mint**
- 2 **teaspoons fresh lime juice**

1. Preheat the oven to 350° and lightly brush a large baking sheet with olive oil. Using a 2-inch round biscuit cutter, stamp 4 rounds out of each slice of bread and transfer to the baking sheet. Lightly brush the rounds with olive oil and toast for about 15 minutes, until they are lightly golden and slightly crisp.

2. Halve the avocados and scoop out their flesh into a small bowl. Use a fork to mash the avocados with a pinch each of salt and cayenne pepper. In another small bowl, gently stir the crabmeat with the mint and lime juice and season with salt. Spread the mashed avocado on the toasts, top with the crab mixture and serve right away.
—*Gerard Craft*

MAKE AHEAD The toasts can be stored in an airtight container overnight.

Broiled Mussels with Hot Paprika Crumbs

TOTAL: 35 MIN
8 SERVINGS ● ●

- ½ **cup dry white wine**
- 2 **pounds mussels, scrubbed**
- 3 **cups coarse fresh bread crumbs (see Note)**

2 tablespoons unsalted butter

2 tablespoons extra-virgin
olive oil

1 large garlic clove, very
finely chopped

2 teaspoons hot paprika

1 tablespoon chopped thyme

½ teaspoon finely grated
lemon zest

Salt and freshly ground pepper

1. In a pot, bring the wine to a boil. Add the mussels. Cover and cook over high heat, shaking the pot, until the mussels open, 4 minutes. Using a skimmer, transfer the mussels to a rimmed baking sheet and let cool. Pour the mussel cooking liquid into a bowl. Loosen the mussels in their shells and discard the empty half of each shell. Spoon the cooking liquid over the mussels to keep them moist. Cover with plastic wrap.

2. Put the bread crumbs in a medium bowl. In a small skillet, melt the butter in the oil. Add the garlic and paprika and cook over moderate heat until fragrant. Scrape the contents of the skillet over the crumbs. Add the thyme and lemon zest, season with salt and pepper and toss well.

3. Preheat the broiler. Remove the plastic wrap from the mussels and top them with the bread crumbs. Broil 6 inches from the heat for about 2 minutes, rotating the pan as necessary, until the bread crumbs are browned and crisp. Serve right away.
—*Marcia Kiesel*

NOTE To make fresh bread crumbs, pulse slices of fresh country bread in a food processor until light, fluffy crumbs form.

Tuna with Roasted Peppers and Pine Nuts

TOTAL: 35 MIN
4 SERVINGS ● ●

Spanish chef Raul Molina Fernandez mixes a *sofrito* of roasted red peppers, tomato and pine nuts with cubes of salted tuna belly. The version here calls for top-quality canned tuna instead.

1 red bell pepper

3 tablespoons pine nuts

3 tablespoons extra-virgin
olive oil

1 medium onion, cut into
½-inch dice

1 large tomato, coarsely chopped

One 8-ounce can tuna packed in olive
oil, drained and broken into
chunks (see Note)

Salt and freshly ground pepper

1. Roast the red pepper directly over a gas flame or under a preheated broiler, turning occasionally, until the pepper skin is charred all over. Transfer the hot pepper to a bowl, cover the bowl tightly with plastic wrap and let cool. When the pepper is cool enough to handle, scrape off and discard the charred skin, seeds and stem. Cut the pepper into ½-inch pieces.

2. In a large skillet, toast the pine nuts over moderate heat, shaking the skillet a few times, until the nuts are golden brown and fragrant, about 2 minutes. Transfer the pine nuts to a plate.

3. Add the olive oil and diced onion to the skillet and cook over moderate heat until the onion is softened, about 5 minutes. Add the red pepper pieces and the chopped tomato and cook, stirring occasionally, until the tomato is softened, about 3 minutes. Transfer the vegetable mixture to a large serving bowl and let cool to room temperature.

4. Add the tuna and toasted pine nuts to the vegetable mixture in the bowl and gently toss to combine. Season with salt and pepper and serve.
—*Raul Molina Fernandez*

SERVE WITH Toasted baguette slices or thickly sliced country bread.

NOTE High-quality olive oil–packed tuna is available at specialty food stores and tienda.com.

MAKE AHEAD The salad can be refrigerated, covered, overnight. Bring to room temperature before serving.

Red Snapper Crudo with Watercress Pesto

TOTAL: 30 MIN
4 SERVINGS ● ●

While traveling on the Adriatic coast of Italy, L.A. chef Matt Molina tried slivers of raw *orata*, a meaty local white fish, embellished with a fresh green pesto. Since *orata* is harder to find in the U.S., this recipe calls for red snapper.

2 tablespoons pine nuts

2 cups watercress, thick stems
discarded, plus 1 cup small
watercress sprigs (from one
6-ounce bunch)

1 small garlic clove, chopped

2 teaspoons fresh lemon juice

¼ cup plus 1 teaspoon
extra-virgin olive oil,
plus more for drizzling

Kosher salt

½ pound skinless red snapper
fillet, sliced on the bias
⅛ inch thick

Maldon salt, for sprinkling

1. Preheat the oven to 350°. Spread the pine nuts in a pie plate and bake for about 3 minutes, until golden brown. Let cool completely. In a food processor, combine the 2 cups of watercress with the toasted pine nuts, garlic and 1 teaspoon of the lemon juice and process to a coarse puree. With the machine on, gradually stream in ¼ cup of the olive oil and process until smooth. Season the pesto with kosher salt.

2. Spread 1 tablespoon of the watercress pesto in the center of each plate. Arrange the red snapper slices over the pesto, overlapping them slightly. In a small bowl, toss the small watercress sprigs with the remaining 1 teaspoon each of lemon juice and olive oil and season with kosher salt. Mound the watercress salad on the plates next to the snapper. Lightly drizzle the snapper with olive oil and sprinkle with Maldon salt. Serve right away.
—*Matt Molina*

Mini Corn Cakes with Seared Salmon

⏱ TOTAL: 45 MIN
10 SERVINGS ●

Argentine chef Francis Mallmann cooks salmon on one side only, charring it lightly, while the other side stays tender, sweet and fresh-tasting.

- 6 ears of corn, shucked
- 2 large eggs
- ½ cup milk
- ½ cup all-purpose flour
- Salt
- Extra-virgin olive oil, for frying and brushing
- 1½ pounds skinless center-cut salmon fillet, cut crosswise into ten ⅓-inch-thick slices
- Freshly ground pepper
- Flat-leaf parsley leaves, for garnish

1. Bring a large saucepan of water to a boil. Add the shucked corn and boil over moderately high heat until just tender, about 4 minutes; drain. When cool enough to handle, cut the corn kernels from the cobs; you will need 2 cups.

2. Preheat the oven to 225°. In a medium bowl, whisk the eggs with the milk. Stir in the corn kernels, flour and ½ teaspoon of salt. In a large nonstick skillet, heat ⅛ inch of olive oil until hot. Drop tablespoons of the corn cake batter into the skillet and cook over moderately high heat, turning once, until golden brown, 4 minutes. Transfer the cakes to a baking sheet and keep them warm in the oven. Repeat with the remaining batter.

3. Heat a griddle over high heat or on a preheated grill. Brush the salmon with oil and season with salt and pepper. Lay the fish on the griddle and cook undisturbed over high heat until browned on the bottom and barely cooked, 3 minutes.

4. Place the corn cakes on plates and top with a salmon slice. Garnish with the parsley and serve right away.
—Francis Mallmann

Cilantro-Flecked Corn Fritters with Chile-Mint Sauce

ACTIVE: 40 MIN; TOTAL: 1 HR
MAKES SIXTEEN 2-INCH FRITTERS ●

- 4 medium ears of corn, shucked, or 2½ cups frozen corn
- 2 tablespoons vegetable oil, plus more for pan-frying
- 1½ tablespoons minced fresh ginger
- 3 garlic cloves, minced
- 2 tablespoons whole cilantro leaves
- Salt and freshly ground pepper
- 1 packed cup mint leaves
- 1 serrano chile, seeded and minced
- ¼ cup water
- All-purpose flour, for dusting
- Chat masala, for sprinkling (optional; see Note)

1. In a large saucepan of boiling salted water, cook the ears of corn over moderately high heat just until tender, about 4 minutes. Drain and, when cool enough to handle, cut the kernels off the cobs; you should have 2½ cups. If you're using frozen corn, boil it for 2 minutes, then drain.

2. In a medium skillet, heat the 2 tablespoons of vegetable oil. Add the ginger and two-thirds of the garlic and cook over moderate heat, stirring, until fragrant, about 2 minutes. Add the corn and cook, stirring, for 2 minutes. Transfer to a food processor and puree. Scrape into a bowl. Stir in the cilantro and season with salt and pepper. Form into 2-inch patties and refrigerate for at least 20 minutes.

3. Preheat the oven to 350°. In a mini food processor, combine the mint leaves, chile, water and the remaining garlic; process to a coarse puree. Season with salt.

4. In a large nonstick skillet, heat ¼ inch of oil until shimmering. Dust the fritters with flour and tap off the excess. Add half of the fritters to the skillet and cook over moderately high heat until browned and crisp, about 2 minutes per side. Drain the fritters on paper towels. Transfer to a baking sheet and keep warm in the oven while you fry the remaining fritters. Arrange the fritters on a platter. Sprinkle with *chat masala,* top with a small dollop of the chile-mint sauce and serve right away.
—Peggy Markel

NOTE *Chat masala* spice blend is available at Indian markets and kalustyans.com.

Seafood Tostada Bites

⏱ TOTAL: 30 MIN
MAKES 24 HORS D'OEUVRES ●

- Two 8-inch flour tortillas
- 1 cup vegetable oil
- 4 tablespoons unsalted butter
- 1 leek, white and pale green parts, halved lengthwise and thinly sliced crosswise
- 24 shelled and deveined small shrimp (about ½ pound)
- ½ pound sea scallops, cut into ½-inch pieces
- ½ pound lump crabmeat
- Salt and freshly ground pepper
- ¾ cup dry white wine
- 2 tablespoons minced parsley

1. On a cutting board, cut the tortillas into 24 equal triangles. In a medium skillet, heat the oil over moderately high heat. Add the tortilla triangles; fry until golden, 1 minute. Using a slotted spoon, transfer the tortillas to a paper towel–lined plate.

2. In a large, deep skillet, melt 1 tablespoon of the butter. Add the leek and cook over moderate heat, stirring occasionally, until softened, about 4 minutes. Stir in the shrimp, scallops and crab and season with salt and pepper. Add the wine and simmer just until the shrimp are pink, about 2 minutes. Using a slotted spoon, transfer the seafood to a bowl. Add the parsley and the remaining 3 tablespoons of butter to the skillet and simmer until the liquid is reduced to a few tablespoons, about 3 minutes. Return the seafood to the pan and toss to coat.

3. Spoon the seafood into Chinese soup spoons or shot glasses, garnish with the tortillas and serve. —Grace Parisi

SEAFOOD TOSTADA BITES

Paneer-and-Pepper Fritters

TOTAL: 40 MIN
4 SERVINGS ●

½ pound *paneer* (see Note) or
  farmer cheese, crumbled
¼ cup finely diced red bell pepper
¼ cup finely diced green bell pepper
1 garlic clove, minced
1 teaspoon finely grated
  fresh ginger
½ cup plus 3 tablespoons
  crème fraîche
½ teaspoon ground cumin
½ teaspoon ground coriander
½ teaspoon garam masala
¼ to ½ teaspoon cayenne pepper
Salt and freshly ground black pepper
All-purpose flour, for dredging
2 large eggs, lightly beaten
2 cups *panko* (Japanese
  bread crumbs)
Vegetable oil, for frying
Lemon wedges, for serving

1. In a bowl, combine the paneer, bell peppers, garlic, ginger and crème fraîche. Add the cumin, coriander, garam masala and cayenne and season with salt and black pepper. Shape into 12 balls and flatten each into a 2½-inch patty.
2. Put the flour, beaten eggs and *panko* in 3 separate shallow dishes. Dredge the patties in the flour, then dip them in the beaten eggs; let any excess egg drip off. Coat the patties with the *panko*.
3. Preheat the oven to 325°. In a large saucepan, heat 1¼ inches of vegetable oil to 350°. Fry 4 patties at a time, turning once, until golden brown and crisp, about 1 minute. Using a slotted spoon, transfer the fritters to a paper towel–lined platter and season with salt. Keep warm in the oven while you fry the remaining fritters. Serve right away, with lemon wedges.
—*Rajat Parr*
NOTE *Paneer*, a firm-textured fresh Indian cheese, is available at large supermarkets and Indian groceries.

Mashed-Potato Spring Rolls

TOTAL: 30 MIN
4 TO 6 SERVINGS
David Chang, the force behind New York City's Momofuku restaurants, took an F&W challenge by improvising a feast from basic Thanksgiving leftovers. He turned mashed potatoes and green beans into this clever canapé, a salute to the 1950s. Leftover gravy serves as a savory dipping sauce.

16 slices of packaged white
  sandwich bread
1 cup mashed potatoes
½ cup thinly sliced cooked
  green beans
¼ teaspoon *togarashi* (see Note)
  or cayenne pepper
Kosher salt and freshly ground
  black pepper
1 large egg yolk mixed with
  1 tablespoon of water
2 cups vegetable oil, for frying
Warm turkey gravy and Sriracha chile
  sauce, for serving

1. Stack the bread in 4 piles and trim the crusts. Using a rolling pin, roll out each bread slice to a 3-by-5-inch rectangle.
2. In a large bowl, combine the mashed potatoes, green beans and *togarashi* and season with salt and black pepper. Brush the edges of 4 bread rectangles with the egg yolk mixture. Shape 1 tablespoon of the potato mixture into a log along a long edge of a rectangle, leaving ½ inch on each end. Tightly roll up the bread to form a cylinder; press the ends together to seal. Repeat with the remaining bread and potato mixture.
3. In a skillet, heat the oil to 325°. Add half of the rolls and fry, turning occasionally, until well-browned, about 1½ minutes. Transfer to paper towels. Repeat with the remaining rolls. Serve with gravy and Sriracha.
—*David Chang*
NOTE *Togarashi*, a Japanese blend of dried ground chiles and sesame seeds, is available at Asian markets.

Pistachio-Cheese Arancini

TOTAL: 1 HR
MAKES 16 ARANCINI ● ● ●
These *arancini* (fried risotto balls) are filled with creamy, cheesy rice, studded with nuts and peas and encased in a crunchy crust.

2½ tablespoons unsalted butter
1 small onion, minced
1½ cups arborio rice
½ cup dry white wine
Pinch of saffron threads, crumbled
Salt and freshly ground pepper
3 cups chicken stock or low-sodium
  broth, warmed
3 tablespoons freshly grated
  Parmigiano-Reggiano cheese
½ tablespoon all-purpose flour, plus
  more for dusting
¼ cup plus 2 tablespoons milk
Pinch of freshly grated nutmeg
4 ounces fresh mozzarella, diced
¼ cup plus 2 tablespoons chopped
  salted pistachios
2 tablespoons frozen peas, thawed
2 large eggs, beaten
1½ cups *panko* (Japanese
  bread crumbs)
Vegetable oil, for frying

1. In a large saucepan, melt 2 tablespoons of the butter. Add the onion; cook over moderate heat, stirring, until lightly browned, 7 minutes. Add the rice; cook, stirring, until well coated. Add the wine and saffron, season with salt and pepper and cook, stirring, until the wine is absorbed, 2 minutes. Add the stock ½ cup at a time and cook, stirring constantly between additions, until it is absorbed. The risotto is done when the rice is al dente, 25 minutes total. Stir in the grated cheese, transfer to a bowl and let cool.
2. Melt the remaining ½ tablespoon of butter in a saucepan. Add the ½ tablespoon of flour and whisk constantly over moderate heat for 1 minute. Add the milk and whisk until thickened. Season with nutmeg, salt and pepper; transfer to a bowl to cool. Add the mozzarella, pistachios and peas.

MASHED-POTATO SPRING ROLLS

PISTACHIO-CHEESE ARANCINI

3. Line a large baking sheet with wax paper. Put the eggs, *panko* and flour for dusting in 3 shallow bowls. Using lightly moistened hands, shape the rice into 16 equal balls. Make an indentation in the center of each ball with your finger and press the sides to make the hollow larger. Spoon a scant tablespoon of the pistachio filling into the hollow and press the risotto around it. Transfer each ball to the baking sheet. Dust the *arancini* with flour, tapping off the excess. Coat them with the egg and roll in the *panko*.

4. In a large, deep skillet, heat 1 inch of vegetable oil to 350°. Fry the *arancini* over moderate heat, turning occasionally, until golden and heated through, 8 minutes. Drain the *arancini* on paper towels and serve hot. —*Renato Poliafito*

MAKE AHEAD The fried *arancini* can be refrigerated overnight; reheat them in a low oven until crispy.

Lamb Pizzettes

⏱ **TOTAL: 40 MIN**

MAKES 5 DOZEN PIZZETTES ●

Extra-virgin olive oil, for brushing

30 mini 2-inch pitas, separated into 2 rounds each

¼ cup chopped mint leaves

2 scallions, finely chopped

1½ teaspoons ground cumin

¼ teaspoon cinnamon

2 tablespoons pine nuts

1 large egg

Kosher salt and freshly ground pepper

1 pound ground lamb

1 cup plain Greek yogurt

1½ teaspoons chile oil, plus more for drizzling

1. Preheat the oven to 425°. Brush 2 large baking sheets with oil. Arrange the pitas cut side up on the baking sheets and brush with olive oil. Bake in the upper and lower thirds of the oven, shifting the sheets, for 8 to 10 minutes, until lightly toasted and crisp.

2. Meanwhile, in a large bowl, combine 2 tablespoons of the mint with the scallions, cumin, cinnamon, pine nuts, egg, 1½ teaspoons of salt and ½ teaspoon of pepper. Add the ground lamb and knead until evenly combined. Spread each pita with a slightly rounded teaspoon of the meat mixture and bake for about 8 minutes, shifting the baking sheets, until the lamb is cooked through.

3. Meanwhile, in a small bowl, whisk the yogurt with the 1½ teaspoons of chile oil and the remaining 2 tablespoons of mint and season with salt and pepper. Spoon small dollops of the yogurt onto the pizzettes and garnish with a drop of chile oil. Serve right away. —*Grace Parisi*

MAKE AHEAD The pizzettes can be baked earlier in the day and reheated gently.

starters

Hush Puppies with Remoulade

TOTAL: 30 MIN PLUS 1 HR CHILLING

MAKES 3 DOZEN HUSH PUPPIES ●

F&W's Emily Kaiser created these crispy hush puppies—cornmeal dumplings—by adapting a recipe from chef Susan McCreight Lindeborg. (Lindeborg ran the kitchen at Washington, DC's Morrison-Clark Inn when Emily worked there as a cook.)

HUSH PUPPIES

- 1 cup coarse yellow cornmeal
- 1 cup all-purpose flour
- 2 tablespoons sugar
- 1 tablespoon baking soda
- 2 teaspoons kosher salt
- 2 teaspoons dried oregano
- 1 teaspoon cayenne pepper
- ½ teaspoon freshly ground black pepper
- 3 large eggs, lightly beaten
- ¾ cup milk
- 2 scallions, finely chopped
- 1 tablespoon vegetable oil, plus more for frying

REMOULADE

- ¾ cup mayonnaise
- 2 tablespoons whole-grain mustard
- 1 tablespoon ketchup
- 1 tablespoon cider vinegar
- 1 medium shallot, minced
- 1 scallion, finely chopped

Tabasco sauce

Salt and freshly ground black pepper

1. PREPARE THE HUSH PUPPIES: In a large bowl, whisk the cornmeal with the flour, sugar, baking soda, salt, oregano, cayenne pepper and black pepper. In a medium bowl, whisk the eggs with the milk, scallions and the 1 tablespoon of vegetable oil. Stir the wet ingredients into the cornmeal mixture until just blended. Cover and refrigerate the batter for 1 hour.

2. MEANWHILE, MAKE THE REMOULADE: In a medium bowl, whisk the mayonnaise with the mustard, ketchup, cider vinegar, shallot and scallion. Season the remoulade with Tabasco, salt and black pepper.

3. In a medium saucepan, heat 2 inches of oil to 325°. Set a large rack over a baking sheet. Drop 6 rounded tablespoons of batter at a time into the hot oil and fry, turning once, until the hush puppies are browned and crisp, 2 minutes. Using a slotted spoon, transfer the hush puppies to the rack to drain. Serve the hush puppies hot, with the remoulade. *—Emily Kaiser*

Natchitoches Meat Pies with Spicy Buttermilk Dip

ACTIVE: 1 HR; TOTAL: 1 HR 40 MIN

MAKES 12 PIES ●

Natchitoches, Louisiana, is renowned for its meat pies. Kelly English (an F&W Best New Chef 2009) serves his mini version with a great dipping sauce that combines two quintessential Southern ingredients: buttermilk and hot sauce.

DOUGH

- 2½ cups all-purpose flour
- 2 teaspoons salt
- ½ cup vegetable oil
- ½ cup ice water

FILLING

- 2 tablespoons unsalted butter
- ½ pound ground beef chuck
- 1 large garlic clove, minced
- ½ onion, finely diced
- ¼ green bell pepper, finely diced
- 1 bay leaf
- 1 tablespoon tomato paste
- ¼ teaspoon cayenne pepper
- ¼ teaspoon ground cloves
- ¼ teaspoon chopped thyme
- ⅛ teaspoon ground coriander
- ⅛ teaspoon ground allspice

Salt

Hot sauce, preferably Tabasco

- 1 egg beaten with 2 tablespoons of milk

BUTTERMILK DIP

- ½ cup mayonnaise
- ½ cup buttermilk
- ¼ cup plus 1 tablespoon sour cream
- 1½ teaspoons celery salt
- 1 teaspoon fresh lemon juice

Salt

Hot sauce, preferably Tabasco

- 1 scallion, thinly sliced

1. MAKE THE DOUGH: In a food processor, combine the flour and salt. With the machine on, add the oil and process until the flour is moistened. Sprinkle on the ice water and pulse 5 or 6 times, just until the dough is moistened. Transfer the dough to a work surface and knead just until smooth. Form the dough into 2 disks, wrap in plastic and refrigerate for 30 minutes.

2. MEANWHILE, MAKE THE FILLING: In a large skillet, melt the butter. Add the ground beef and cook over moderately high heat until no pink remains, breaking up the meat with a spoon, about 5 minutes. Add the garlic, onion, bell pepper and bay leaf and cook over moderate heat, stirring occasionally, until the onion is translucent, 7 minutes. Stir in the tomato paste, cayenne, cloves, thyme, coriander and allspice; cook over moderately low heat for 3 minutes. Season with salt and hot sauce and let cool.

3. Discard the bay leaf. Transfer the filling to a food processor and pulse until chopped.

4. Preheat the oven to 350° and line a large baking sheet with parchment paper. On a floured work surface, roll out each disk of dough to a 12-inch round. Using a 4-inch biscuit cutter, stamp out 6 rounds from each piece of dough. Brush the edges of the rounds with some of the egg wash and place a rounded tablespoon of filling to one side of each circle. Fold the other half of the dough over the filling and press to seal. Crimp the edges with a fork. Transfer the pies to the baking sheet and brush with the egg wash. Bake for 25 minutes, until golden brown.

5. MAKE THE BUTTERMILK DIP: In a bowl, combine the mayonnaise, buttermilk, sour cream, celery salt and lemon juice. Season with salt and hot sauce. Transfer to a serving bowl and top with the scallion. Serve the pies with the buttermilk dip.
—Kelly English

NATCHITOCHES MEAT PIES
WITH SPICY BUTTERMILK DIP

starters

Mini Panamanian Beef Empanadas

ACTIVE: 1 HR 15 MIN;
TOTAL: 2 HR 15 MIN
MAKES ABOUT 24 EMPANADAS ● ●

At the Panamonte Inn & Spa in Boquete, Panama, chef-owner Charlie Collins shows guests how to prepare this perfectly flaky empanada dough.

DOUGH

- 2 cups all-purpose flour
- 1 tablespoon sugar
- 1 teaspoon salt
- 1 stick cold unsalted butter, cut into small pieces
- 2 large eggs, lightly beaten
- ¼ cup dry white wine
- 1 teaspoon white vinegar

FILLING

- 1 tablespoon vegetable oil
- ½ teaspoon achiote seeds (also called annatto seeds)
- ¼ pound ground beef
- 1 garlic clove, minced
- 1 small onion, finely diced
- ¼ cup finely diced red bell pepper
- ¼ cup chopped, seeded tomato
- ½ tablespoon tomato paste
- ¼ cup chicken stock or low-sodium broth
- 2 tablespoons chopped cilantro

Salt and freshly ground pepper
Vegetable oil, for frying

1. MAKE THE DOUGH: In a food processor, pulse the flour with the sugar and salt. Add the butter and pulse until the mixture resembles coarse meal. Beat the eggs with the wine and vinegar and drizzle over the flour mixture. Pulse until the dough just comes together. On a lightly floured work surface, gently knead the dough until smooth. Wrap the dough in plastic and refrigerate until firm, about 1 hour.

2. PREPARE THE FILLING: In a medium skillet, heat the oil. Add the achiote seeds and cook over moderately high heat until the seeds darken and the oil is orange,

about 1 minute. Discard the seeds. Add the ground beef to the skillet and cook, breaking up the meat with a wooden spoon, until no traces of pink remain, about 3 minutes. Add the garlic, onion and bell pepper and cook over moderate heat until the onion is softened, about 5 minutes. Add the tomato, tomato paste and chicken stock and simmer over moderate heat until the liquid has nearly evaporated, about 3 minutes. Stir in the cilantro and season with salt and pepper. Let cool.

3. On a generously floured work surface, roll out the dough ⅛ inch thick. With a 3-inch round biscuit cutter, stamp out as many rounds as possible (you should have about 24). Reroll the dough scraps and stamp out additional rounds if possible. Brush the excess flour off the rounds. Working with 1 round at a time and keeping the rest covered with plastic wrap, form the empanadas: Spoon 2 teaspoons of the filling on one side of the dough round. Fold the dough over to enclose the filling and crimp the edges with a fork to seal. Cover with plastic wrap while you form the remaining empanadas.

4. Preheat the oven to 350°. In a deep skillet, heat ½ inch of oil to 350°. Fry 4 empanadas at a time, turning once, until browned and crisp, 2 minutes. Drain on paper towels and transfer to a baking sheet. When all of the empanadas have been fried, reheat them in the oven and serve.
—*Charlie Collins*

VARIATION Rather than frying, you can bake the empanadas: Preheat the oven to 350°. Beat 1 egg with 1 tablespoon of milk. Evenly space the uncooked empanadas on 2 baking sheets lined with parchment paper and brush with the egg wash. Bake in the upper and lower thirds of the oven for 25 minutes, until golden brown.

MAKE AHEAD The filled, uncooked empanadas can be frozen on a baking sheet, then transferred to an airtight bag. Bake them in a 350° oven without thawing.

Spinach-and-Pork Wontons

TOTAL: 1 HR
6 SERVINGS ●

- 2 cups baby spinach, rinsed
- 1 tablespoon plus 1½ teaspoons soy sauce
- 1 teaspoon Asian sesame oil
- 1 teaspoon dry sherry
- ¼ teaspoon salt
- ¼ teaspoon sugar

Pinch of freshly ground white pepper

- ¼ pound ground pork
- 1 small scallion, minced
- ¾ teaspoon minced fresh ginger

Cornstarch, for sprinkling

- 30 thin wonton wrappers
- 2 tablespoons chile oil
- 2 tablespoons peanut oil
- 1 small garlic clove, minced
- 2 tablespoons chopped cilantro

1. In a skillet, cook the spinach, stirring, until wilted; transfer to a colander and squeeze dry. Finely chop the spinach.

2. In a bowl, combine 1½ teaspoons of the soy sauce with the sesame oil, sherry, salt, sugar and white pepper. Mix in the pork, scallion, ginger and spinach. Chill the filling for 10 minutes.

3. Dust a large baking sheet with cornstarch. Arrange 4 wonton wrappers on a work surface, keeping the other wrappers covered with plastic wrap. Brush the edges of the wrappers with water and spoon 1 teaspoon of filling in the center of each. Fold the wrappers diagonally over the filling to form triangles; seal. Bring the two opposite corners of the triangle together; press to seal. Transfer to the baking sheet and cover. Repeat.

4. In a large saucepan of boiling water, simmer the wontons over moderate heat, stirring occasionally. When they float, cook for 3 minutes longer. Drain the wontons well.

5. In a large bowl, combine the remaining soy sauce with the chile oil, peanut oil and garlic. Add the wontons and toss. Sprinkle with the cilantro and serve.
—*Andrea Nguyen*

SPINACH-AND-PORK WONTONS

KUNG PAO CHICKEN DRUMSTICK (AND REDHEAD IN BED, P. 361)

Kung Pao Chicken Drumsticks

ACTIVE: 30 MIN; TOTAL: 2 HR

10 SERVINGS ●

These succulent, crispy drumettes (called "lollipops" at rap star Ludacris's Straits Atlanta restaurant) are chef Chris Yeo's riff on kung pao, a Szechuan dish made with stir-fried diced chicken and chiles. Yeo uses the cooked chiles as the base for a rich dipping sauce.

- ¼   cup vegetable oil, plus more for frying
- 1   garlic clove, minced
- 1   tablespoon finely grated fresh ginger
- ¼   cup dried red chiles, such as *chile de árbol*
- ½   cup sugar
- ¼   cup soy sauce
- ¼   cup tamari or soy sauce (see Note)
- ¼   cup dry sherry
- ½   teaspoon red wine vinegar
- 2   tablespoons cornstarch dissolved in 3 tablespoons of water
- ½   teaspoon Asian sesame oil
- ½   cup chopped scallions
- 3½ pounds chicken drumettes

Salt and freshly ground pepper

All-purpose flour, for dusting

Chopped roasted peanuts, for garnish

1. In a medium saucepan, heat the ¼ cup of vegetable oil. Add the garlic and ginger and cook over moderately high heat, stirring, until fragrant, about 1 minute. Add the chiles and cook until they turn dark red, about 2 minutes. Lower the heat to moderate, add the sugar, soy sauce, tamari, sherry and vinegar and simmer until the sugar dissolves, about 5 minutes. Remove the sauce from the heat, cover and let stand for 1 hour.

2. Strain the sauce and return it to the saucepan. Bring to a boil over moderately high heat. Whisk in the cornstarch mixture and bring back to a boil. Remove from the heat, stir in the sesame oil and scallions and transfer to a bowl.

3. Preheat the oven to 400°. In a large pot, bring 3 inches of oil to 325°. Season the chicken with salt and pepper and dust well with flour. Set a rack over a rimmed baking sheet near the stove. Working in batches, fry the drumettes until browned and crisp, about 7 minutes. Drain the drumettes on the rack and keep warm on a platter in the oven while you fry the rest. Sprinkle with the chopped peanuts and serve with the kung pao sauce. *—Chris Yeo*

NOTE Like soy sauce, tamari is made from soy beans, but it has a richer, cleaner flavor. It's available at some grocery stores and at Asian markets.

● HEALTHY ● MAKE AHEAD ● VEGETARIAN ● STAFF FAVORITE

31

Goat Cheese–Chorizo Rolls

 TOTAL: 45 MIN
MAKES 18 ROLLS ● ●

These crispy rolls are a riff on Argentinean street food.

- 8 ounces fresh goat cheese
- 1 cup chopped dry chorizo
- 1½ tablespoons minced chives
- Salt and freshly ground pepper
- Nine 12-by-16-inch sheets of thawed phyllo dough
- Melted butter, for brushing

1. Preheat the oven to 400° and line 2 large baking sheets with parchment paper. In a bowl, combine the goat cheese, chorizo and chives; season with salt and pepper.
2. Lay a sheet of phyllo on a clean, dry work surface and brush it with melted butter. Top with 2 more phyllo sheets, lightly buttering each sheet as you go. Cut the phyllo into 6 rectangles. Place a tablespoon of the goat cheese filling at the base of each rectangle and roll up the phyllo, folding in the sides. Set the rolls on the prepared baking sheets. Repeat twice more to make 18 rolls total. Brush the rolls with butter; bake for 10 minutes, until golden. Serve hot.
—*Nirmala Narine*

COCKTAIL PARTY

Caesar Salad Spears,
p. 37

Tangy Red-Pepper-
and-Nut Dip, p. 19

Lamb Pizzettes, p. 27

Goat Cheese–
Chorizo Rolls (above)

Pistachio-
Cheese Arancini,
p. 26

Round, deep-flavored Syrah

Sausage-Stuffed Peppadews

 TOTAL: 35 MIN
MAKES 5 DOZEN STUFFED PEPPADEWS ●

Little peppers that have been marinated in vinegar and sugar, peppadews are delightful when stuffed with spicy sausage and rice, then baked.

- 1 pound hot Italian sausages, casings removed
- ½ cup cooked white rice
- 2 tablespoons olive tapenade
- 60 yellow or red peppadew peppers (from two 14-ounce jars), drained (see Note)
- 2 tablespoons extra-virgin olive oil
- 2 tablespoons freshly grated Parmigiano-Reggiano cheese

1. Preheat the oven to 450°. In a medium bowl, knead the sausage meat with the cooked rice and olive tapenade. Fill the peppadew peppers with the meat mixture, pressing to compact it. Arrange the peppadews meat side up on a lightly oiled baking sheet; lightly press down on them so they don't wobble. Drizzle the peppadews all over with olive oil and sprinkle with the grated Parmigiano-Reggiano.
2. Bake the peppadews in the upper third of the oven for about 15 minutes, until the sausage meat is cooked through. Transfer to a platter and serve warm or at room temperature. —*Grace Parisi*

NOTE Look for peppadews at delis or in jars at the supermarket.

MAKE AHEAD The unbaked stuffed peppadews can be refrigerated overnight. Bring to room temperature before baking. The baked stuffed peppadews can be covered loosely and kept at room temperature for up to 2 hours.

Grilled Shrimp Satay

photo, page 10

TOTAL: 1 HR 30 MIN PLUS 3 HR CHILLING
10 SERVINGS ● ●

In Singapore, satays are usually made with chicken or lamb. But for parties, Atlanta chef Chris Yeo likes to use shrimp because he thinks it's more festive. He marinates the shellfish in an alluring mixture of sautéed garlic, ginger and ground spices, then threads each shrimp on its own skewer and grills them until they're lightly charred.

- 1 small onion, coarsely chopped
- 4 garlic cloves, coarsely chopped
- 3 large stalks of fresh lemongrass, bottom third of the tender white inner bulb only, thinly sliced
- ¼ cup minced fresh ginger
- ½ cup vegetable oil
- 1 tablespoon ground coriander
- 1 tablespoon sugar
- 1 teaspoon ground fennel seeds
- 1 teaspoon ground cumin
- 1 teaspoon turmeric
- 1 teaspoon kosher salt
- 30 large shrimp (about 1¾ pounds), shelled and deveined
- Garlic Peanut Sauce (recipe follows), for serving

1. In a mini food processor, combine the onion, garlic, lemongrass and ginger and process to a smooth paste. In a large skillet, heat the vegetable oil. Add the onion paste to the skillet and cook over moderately low heat, stirring occasionally, until it is browned, about 25 minutes.
2. Add the ground coriander, sugar, ground fennel seeds, cumin, turmeric and salt to the skillet and cook over moderately high heat, stirring constantly, until the spices are fragrant, about 1 minute. Scrape the spice paste into a small bowl and let it cool completely.
3. In a large, shallow dish, coat the shrimp with the spice paste. Cover and refrigerate for at least 3 hours or overnight.

4. Soak 30 bamboo skewers in water for 30 minutes. Light a grill. Thread 1 shrimp lengthwise onto each bamboo skewer and stretch each one out on the skewer. Grill over high heat for about 1½ minutes per side, until the shrimp are nicely charred and just cooked through. Transfer the shrimp skewers to a platter and serve them immediately, with the Garlic Peanut Sauce. —*Chris Yeo*

MAKE AHEAD The spice paste can be refrigerated for up to 2 days. Bring to room temperature before using.

GARLIC PEANUT SAUCE

TOTAL: 25 MIN
MAKES ABOUT 1½ CUPS ● ●
Unlike most versions of this Asian condiment, which taste like overly sweet peanut butter, this one is spicy, nutty and just slightly fruity thanks to the addition of coconut milk and tamarind. The peanut sauce is terrific with the shrimp satay but just as good with almost any grilled or roasted meat or poultry.

- ½ small onion, coarsely chopped
- 2 garlic cloves, coarsely chopped
- 1 large stalk of fresh lemongrass, bottom third of the tender white inner bulb only, thinly sliced
- 1 tablespoon vegetable oil
- 1 tablespoon ground coriander
- 2 tablespoons *sambal oelek* (see Note)
- ½ cup unsweetened coconut milk
- 1 tablespoon tamarind concentrate (see Note)
- 1 tablespoon sugar
- 2½ tablespoons smooth or chunky peanut butter

Salt

1. In a mini food processor, combine the onion, garlic and lemongrass and process to a paste.

2. In a large nonstick skillet, heat the vegetable oil. Add the onion paste; cook over moderately low heat, stirring occasionally, until golden brown, about 8 minutes. Add the ground coriander and cook until fragrant, about 2 minutes. Add the *sambal oelek* and cook, stirring, for 2 minutes. Add the coconut milk and boil over high heat until thickened, about 2 minutes. Stir in the tamarind concentrate, sugar and peanut butter until smooth. Remove from the heat and season with salt. Let cool, then transfer to a small bowl. —*CY*

NOTE *Sambal oelek,* a spicy Indonesian chile sauce, and tamarind concentrate are both available at Asian markets and at specialty food stores.

MAKE AHEAD The Garlic Peanut Sauce can be refrigerated, covered, for up to 2 days. Let the sauce return to room temperature before serving.

Hazelnut Profiteroles with Blue Cheese and Grapes

ACTIVE: 30 MIN; TOTAL: 1 HR 30 MIN
MAKES 48 PROFITEROLES ● ●
Chicago chef Shawn McClain loves to serve these savory cream puffs with drinks. To keep them from getting soggy, he pokes a hole in the sides of the puffs as soon as they come out of the oven to release the steam. Then he fills them with a creamy mixture of blue cheese and mascarpone.

- ½ cup hazelnuts
- 1 cup milk
- 1 stick plus 1 tablespoon unsalted butter
- 2 tablespoons Frangelico or other nut-flavored liqueur
- 2 teaspoons sugar
- ¾ teaspoon salt
- 1 cup all-purpose flour
- 4 large eggs
- 1 large egg yolk mixed with 2 tablespoons of water
- ¼ pound blue cheese, such as Maytag, at room temperature
- ½ cup mascarpone
- ½ cup heavy cream

Seedless red grapes, for serving

1. Preheat the oven to 375° and position racks in the upper and middle thirds. Line 2 large baking sheets with parchment paper. Spread the hazelnuts in a pie plate and toast for about 12 minutes, until the nuts are fragrant and the skins are blistered. Transfer the nuts to a clean kitchen towel and rub vigorously to remove the skins. Let the hazelnuts cool completely. Transfer the hazelnuts to a food processor and finely grind them.

2. In a large saucepan, combine the milk with the butter, Frangelico, sugar and salt and bring to a simmer over moderate heat. Remove from the heat. Add the flour and ¼ cup plus 2 tablespoons of the hazelnuts; stir with a wooden spoon until a mass forms. Return the saucepan to moderate heat and cook, stirring, for 1 minute. Transfer to a bowl and let cool for 2 minutes. Using an electric mixer, beat in the eggs one at a time, beating well between additions.

3. Transfer the dough to a pastry bag fitted with a ½-inch plain tip. Pipe 1-inch mounds of the dough onto the prepared baking sheets about 1 inch apart. Brush the tops with the egg wash and sprinkle with the remaining ground hazelnuts. Bake for about 25 minutes, until the profiteroles are puffed and golden; shift the pans from top to bottom and front to back halfway through baking. Poke a hole in the side of each puff to release the steam. Let the puffs cool completely.

4. In a bowl, using an electric mixer, beat the blue cheese with the mascarpone and cream at medium speed until firm and fluffy. Using a serrated knife, split each puff horizontally; remove any doughy centers. Fill each puff with ½ tablespoon of the blue cheese cream and replace the tops. Serve with the grapes. —*Shawn McClain*

MAKE AHEAD The filling can be refrigerated for up to 4 hours. The baked puffs can be covered and stored at room temperature for up to 2 days. Recrisp in the oven before splitting, filling and serving.

starters

Grilled Eggplant Involtini with Goat Cheese and Green Beans

TOTAL: 40 MIN
6 SERVINGS ● ●

In this updated version of classic eggplant *involtini* (stuffed rolls), grilled eggplant rolls are stuffed with thin green beans and topped with a goat cheese vinaigrette. The dressing would also be great on a salad of peppery greens like arugula.

Two 1-pound eggplants, cut
    lengthwise into thirds
Extra-virgin olive oil
Salt and freshly ground black pepper
36 thin green beans
1 tablespoon sun-dried tomato
    paste or pesto
½ cup fresh goat cheese, softened
3 tablespoons rice vinegar
6 cups packed watercress,
    thick stems discarded
6 sun-dried tomato halves,
    coarsely chopped

1. Light a grill. Brush the eggplant with olive oil and season with salt and pepper. Grill over moderate heat until lightly charred and just tender, about 10 minutes.
2. In a saucepan of boiling salted water, cook the beans until they are crisp-tender, 3 minutes. Drain and pat dry. In a bowl, toss the beans with the sun-dried tomato paste and season with salt and pepper. Arrange the eggplant slices on a work surface. Bundle 6 green beans at one end of each slice and roll into cylinders. Transfer the *involtini* to plates, seam side down.
3. In a small bowl, whisk the goat cheese with the vinegar. Add 5 tablespoons of olive oil, whisking until smooth. Season the dressing with salt and pepper.
4. In a large bowl, toss the watercress with the sun-dried tomatoes. Add ¼ cup of the goat cheese dressing and toss to coat. Mound the salad beside the *involtini*. Spoon the remaining goat cheese dressing over the *involtini* and serve.
—Giorgio Locatelli and Rosita Missoni

Pan-Fried Scamorza with Arugula Salad and Two Pestos

ACTIVE: 35 MIN; TOTAL: 1 HR 10 MIN
6 SERVINGS ● ●

Scamorza, a firm Italian cow's milk cheese, develops an irresistible crust when fried. Provolone would also work here.

12 plum tomatoes, sliced 1 inch thick
¾ cup plus 1½ tablespoons extra-
    virgin olive oil, more for drizzling
Salt
Sugar
4 oregano sprigs
12 cups packed arugula leaves
½ cup oil-packed sun-dried tomato
    halves, chopped
1 tablespoon red wine vinegar
1 tablespoon white wine vinegar
1½ tablespoons vegetable oil
9 ounces *scamorza,* sliced
    ½ inch thick (about 6 slices)

1. Preheat the oven to 325°. On a rimmed baking sheet, arrange the tomatoes in a single layer. Drizzle with olive oil, season with salt and sugar and top with the oregano. Bake for 1 hour, until the tomatoes are soft but still hold their shape. Discard the oregano.
2. Meanwhile, in a food processor, puree 3 cups of the arugula with ¼ cup of the olive oil until smooth. Season with salt and scrape into a bowl. Wipe out the food processor.
3. Add the sun-dried tomatoes and ½ cup of the olive oil to the processor; process to a coarse puree and season with salt.
4. In a bowl, whisk the vinegars with the vegetable oil and 1½ tablespoons of the olive oil. Season the dressing with salt.
5. Heat a nonstick skillet. Pan-fry the cheese over high heat, turning once, until well-browned and just starting to melt, 2 minutes. Transfer the *scamorza* to plates.
6. In a bowl, toss the remaining arugula with the dressing. Mound the salad alongside the cheese. Dot the cheese with the pestos. Arrange the tomato slices around the salad, drizzle with olive oil and serve.
—Giorgio Locatelli and Rosita Missoni

Pinzimonio with Tonnato Sauce

TOTAL: 20 MIN
6 SERVINGS ● ● ●

Pinzimonio is a supersimple Italian dish of raw vegetables served with seasoned olive oil for dipping. In his clever variation, Nate Appleman (an F&W Best New Chef 2009) replaces the olive oil with *tonnato,* a creamy sauce made with tuna and lemon.

¼ cup extra-virgin olive oil, plus
    more for drizzling
One 8-ounce jar Italian tuna
    in olive oil, drained
3 tablespoons fresh lemon juice
4 oil-packed anchovies, drained
2 tablespoons capers, rinsed
¼ cup mayonnaise
¼ pound green, Roma or wax beans
8 Parisian round carrots or
    baby carrots
4 tender celery ribs with leaves
    attached, quartered crosswise
2 lemon, Persian or Kirby
    cucumbers, peeled and
    quartered lengthwise
2 small watermelon radishes,
    cut into 8 wedges each, or
    10 small radishes, halved
1 fennel bulb, cored and
    cut into 16 wedges
½ teaspoon coarse sea salt

1. In a food processor, combine the ¼ cup of olive oil with the tuna, lemon juice, anchovies, capers and mayonnaise. Process until smooth. Scrape the *tonnato* sauce into a serving bowl, cover and refrigerate.
2. In a pot of boiling salted water, cook the beans until crisp-tender, 2 minutes. Drain and rinse under cold water; pat dry.
3. Arrange the beans, carrots, celery, cucumbers, radishes and fennel on a platter; sprinkle with the sea salt. Drizzle the *tonnato* sauce with olive oil and serve with the vegetables. *—Nate Appleman*
MAKE AHEAD The *tonnato* sauce can be refrigerated overnight.

PINZIMONIO WITH TONNATO SAUCE

TOMATO TARTLETS

FREE-FORM ONION TART

Tomato Tartlets

TOTAL: 45 MIN

MAKES 5 DOZEN PIECES ● ●

These luscious little rectangular tarts consist of flaky pastry topped with fresh ricotta and oven-roasted cherry tomatoes. To make the cheese silky, whirl it in a food processor until smooth.

All-purpose flour, for rolling

½ **pound all-butter puff pastry**

30 **cherry tomatoes (about 1 pound), halved crosswise**

2 **tablespoons extra-virgin olive oil**

2 **teaspoons fresh thyme leaves, plus more for garnish**

Kosher salt and freshly ground pepper

½ **pound fresh ricotta cheese**

1. Preheat the oven to 425° and line a large baking sheet with parchment paper. Position racks in the middle and upper thirds of the oven. On a lightly floured surface,

roll out the puff pastry to a 9½-by-17½-inch rectangle. Using a straight edge, trim the pastry to a 9-by-17-inch rectangle. Transfer the pastry to the baking sheet and poke all over with a fork. Top the pastry with another sheet of parchment and another baking sheet and bake for 25 minutes on the middle rack, until golden. Remove the top baking sheet and parchment paper and continue to bake the pastry until lightly browned and dry, about 10 minutes longer. Slide the paper and pastry onto a rack and let cool.

2. Meanwhile, in a large bowl, toss the halved cherry tomatoes with the olive oil and the 2 teaspoons of fresh thyme leaves and season with salt and pepper. Spread the cherry tomatoes on a large rimmed baking sheet, cut side up, and bake on the upper rack for about 15 minutes, until softened slightly. Let cool.

3. In a food processor, puree the ricotta cheese until very creamy. Spread the ricotta over the baked and cooled pastry and season with salt and pepper. Arrange the roasted cherry tomatoes cut side up on the ricotta in 5 rows of 12. Sprinkle lightly with fresh thyme. Using a long knife, cut the pastry between the tomatoes into 60 squares. Transfer the tartlets to platters and serve at once. *—Grace Parisi*

MAKE AHEAD The recipe can be prepared through Step 2 and kept at room temperature for up to 8 hours.

Free-Form Onion Tart

ACTIVE: 40 MIN; TOTAL: 2 HR 15 MIN

4 TO 6 SERVINGS ● ● ●

At Cavallo Point, an eco-lodge in Sausalito, California, cooking school director Kelsie Kerr teaches the basics of preparing seasonal recipes. The buttery dough for her savory onion tart, for instance, is great with all kinds of fillings, including fruit. To create the flakiest crust possible, Kerr stresses the importance of keeping both the butter and the dough cold

DOUGH

- 1 cup all-purpose flour
- ¼ teaspoon salt
- 6 tablespoons unsalted butter, cut into small pieces and chilled
- 5 tablespoons ice-cold water

FILLING

- 4 tablespoons unsalted butter
- 2½ pounds sweet onions, very thinly sliced
- 6 thyme sprigs
- 2 tablespoons crème fraîche

Salt and freshly ground pepper

- 1 egg beaten with 1 tablespoon of milk

1. MAKE THE DOUGH: In a bowl, whisk the flour with the salt. Using your fingers, rub the butter into the flour until the mixture resembles coarse meal. Drizzle the water over the flour and stir gently just until incorporated; gently press to form a dough. Flatten the dough into a disk, wrap in plastic and refrigerate for 1 hour.

2. MEANWHILE, PREPARE THE FILLING: In a skillet, melt the butter. Add the onions and thyme and cook over moderately high heat until softened, about 10 minutes. Reduce the heat to moderately low; cook until the onions are golden, 20 minutes longer. Remove from the heat and discard the thyme. Stir in the crème fraîche and season with salt and pepper. Let cool.

3. Set a pizza stone on the bottom of the oven or position a rack on the lowest rung and preheat the oven to 375°. Line a large baking sheet with parchment paper. On a floured work surface, roll out the dough to a 12-inch round and transfer to the baking sheet. Spread the onions on the round, leaving a 1½-inch border. Fold the edge of the dough up and over the filling and brush the edge with the egg wash.

4. Bake the tart on the stone or on the bottom shelf for about 40 minutes, until the dough is richly browned on the bottom.

5. Transfer the tart to the top shelf of the oven and bake for about 5 minutes longer, until the top of the crust is browned. Transfer to a rack and let cool slightly. Cut the warm tart into wedges and serve.

—Kelsie Kerr

SERVE WITH Watercress-asparagus salad.
MAKE AHEAD The onion tart can be baked up to 2 hours in advance. Reheat in a 350° oven before serving.

Caesar Salad Spears

TOTAL: 30 MIN
MAKES 5 DOZEN SPEARS ● ●

Salads usually require forks, but F&W's Grace Parisi transforms a classic Caesar into an elegant finger food. She tosses chopped endives with a creamy, lemony dressing, then spoons the dressed mixture inside endive spears, topping the leaves with grated Parmigiano-Reggiano cheese and crunchy mini croutons.

- 2 cups ¼-inch-diced white bread
- ¼ cup extra-virgin olive oil

Kosher salt and freshly ground black pepper

- 3 anchovy fillets, mashed
- 1 small garlic clove, smashed
- ¼ cup mayonnaise
- ½ teaspoon finely grated lemon zest
- 2 tablespoons fresh lemon juice
- ¼ cup freshly grated Parmigiano-Reggiano cheese, plus more for garnish
- 7 Belgian endives

1. Preheat the oven to 350°. In a medium bowl, toss the diced white bread with 2 tablespoons of the olive oil and season with salt and pepper. Spread the seasoned bread on a large rimmed baking sheet and toast in the oven for about 10 minutes, stirring halfway through, until the croutons are golden and crisp.

2. Meanwhile, in the same bowl, using a wooden spoon, mash the anchovies to a paste with the smashed garlic and a pinch of salt. Whisk in the mayonnaise, lemon zest and lemon juice, then whisk in the remaining 2 tablespoons of olive oil and season with salt and pepper. Stir in the ¼ cup of grated cheese.

3. Trim the endives and remove the 60 largest leaves from 6 of the heads. Stack the leaves and trim them to about 4 inches. Thinly slice the remaining endive, along with the trimmings of the other 6 heads (you should have about 3 cups), and toss with the dressing. Spoon the salad onto each spear and garnish with the croutons and grated cheese. Serve immediately.

—Grace Parisi

Melon-and-Peach Salad with Prosciutto and Mozzarella

TOTAL: 30 MIN
4 SERVINGS

Andy Glover, the chef at Mission Estate Winery on New Zealand's North Island, makes this gorgeous salad with smoked pork. Prosciutto is a tasty stand-in.

One 1½-pound ripe honeydew melon—seeded, peeled and thinly sliced

- 1 ripe peach, peeled and thinly sliced
- 1 tablespoon extra-virgin olive oil
- 2 teaspoons vin cotto or balsamic vinegar

Salt and freshly ground pepper

- 2 tablespoons chopped fresh basil leaves
- 2 tablespoons chopped fresh marjoram leaves
- ½ pound fresh mozzarella, chopped
- 8 thin slices of prosciutto (2 ounces)

In a bowl, toss the melon and peach with the oil and vin cotto; season with salt and pepper. Let stand for 5 minutes. Stir in the herbs and cheese. Transfer the salad to a platter, top with the prosciutto and serve.

—Andy Glover

CHOPPED SALAD WITH
GRAPES AND MINT (P. 45)

salads

Simple and spectacular
ideas for all kinds of vegetables—
including lettuce.

HERB-AND-ENDIVE SALAD WITH CREAMY LIME DRESSING

BLT BREAD SALAD

Herb-and-Endive Salad with Creamy Lime Dressing

 TOTAL: 20 MIN
6 SERVINGS ● ●

Herb salads can be bold, but crisp endive leaves keep this one delicate.

- ¼ cup plus 1 tablespoon mayonnaise
- 1 tablespoon fresh lime juice
- 1 teaspoon finely grated lime zest

Salt and freshly ground pepper

- 2 cups packed flat-leaf parsley
- 1 cup packed small basil leaves
- 1 cup packed 1-inch chive pieces
- ½ cup small mint leaves
- ¼ cup tarragon leaves
- 2 Belgian endives, separated into leaves or halved lengthwise and sliced crosswise ½ inch thick

Chive or sage blossoms, for garnish (optional)

In a small bowl, combine the mayonnaise with the lime juice and zest; season with salt and pepper. In a large bowl, mix the herbs with the endives. Add the dressing, toss and garnish with the chive blossoms; serve.
—*Marcia Kiesel*

BLT Bread Salad

 TOTAL: 25 MIN
4 SERVINGS ●

To make this Italian-style salad, Philadelphia restaurant reviewer Joy Manning tosses cubes of bread with just a little B (bacon) and lots of L (soft butter lettuce) and T (small yellow and red tomatoes). Instead of using mayonnaise, she blends the basil-inflected dressing with protein-rich soft tofu.

Three ¾-inch-thick slices of rustic white bread, cubed (4 cups)

- 3 ounces soft silken tofu
- ¼ cup basil leaves
- 2 tablespoons canola oil
- 1 tablespoon Champagne vinegar
- ½ small shallot, coarsely chopped

Kosher salt and freshly ground black pepper

- 4 thick slices of bacon (4 ounces), cut crosswise into ½-inch strips
- 1 head of butter lettuce, torn into bite-size pieces (about 5 cups)
- 1 cup red cherry tomatoes, halved
- 1 cup yellow pear tomatoes, halved

1. Preheat the oven to 250°. Spread the bread cubes on a rimmed baking sheet and toast in the oven for about 15 minutes, until the bread cubes are dry.

2. Meanwhile, in a blender, combine the tofu with the basil leaves, canola oil, Champagne vinegar and chopped shallot and puree until very smooth. Season the dressing with salt and pepper.

3. In a medium skillet, cook the bacon over moderate heat, stirring occasionally, until crisp, about 6 minutes. Transfer the bacon to paper towels and let drain.

4. In a large bowl, toss the toasted bread cubes with the bacon, lettuce and tomatoes. Add the basil dressing, toss the salad until evenly coated and serve.

—Joy Manning

Heirloom Tomato Salad

 TOTAL: 10 MIN
4 TO 6 SERVINGS ● ●

"This is the tomato salad I make almost every day," says Norwegian television chef–turned–farmer Andreas Viestad. Although he seasons it with little more than salt, olive oil and basil, he always uses different varieties of tomatoes, so the salad tastes different each time.

2 pounds heirloom tomatoes,
    cored—large ones sliced ¼ inch
    thick, small ones halved
Salt
Extra virgin olive oil, for drizzling
2 tablespoons very finely
    chopped chives
2 tablespoons chopped basil
1 tablespoon freshly grated
    Parmigiano-Reggiano cheese

Arrange the tomatoes on a platter. Sprinkle them with salt and drizzle with oil. Scatter the chives, basil and Parmigiano-Reggiano over the tomatoes and serve.

—Andreas Viestad

SERVE WITH Crusty bread.

Tangy Tomato and Mango Salad

 TOTAL: 25 MIN
10 SERVINGS ● ● ●

In chef Jean-Georges Vongerichten's version of a dish from his friend Maya Gurley's St. Bart's restaurant, Maya's, he dresses plump tomatoes, fresh basil leaves and sweet, juicy mango slices with a simple red wine vinaigrette.

¼ cup plus 1 tablespoon
    red wine vinegar
¼ cup extra-virgin olive oil
Salt
3 large shallots, thinly sliced
2 cups thinly sliced basil leaves
10 medium tomatoes (3 pounds),
    sliced ¼ inch thick
3 large, ripe mangoes—peeled,
    pitted and sliced ¼ inch thick

In a small bowl, combine the red wine vinegar with the olive oil; season the dressing with salt. Add the sliced shallots and 1 cup of the basil and toss well. Arrange the tomatoes on a platter and top with the mango slices. Drizzle with the dressing, garnish with the remaining 1 cup of basil leaves and serve.

—Jean-Georges Vongerichten

Antipasto Salad

 TOTAL: 30 MIN
6 SERVINGS ●

Lachlan Mackinnon-Patterson, the chef at Frasca Food and Wine in Boulder, Colorado, and an active champion of the Slow Food movement, makes this chopped salad with locally grown greens.

¼ cup plus 2 tablespoons
    extra-virgin olive oil
3 tablespoons red
    wine vinegar
1 tablespoon very finely
    chopped shallot
2 tablespoons very finely
    chopped oregano
Salt and freshly ground pepper
4 ounces sliced provolone cheese,
    cut into thin strips
4 ounces thickly sliced Genoa
    salami, cut into thin strips
½ medium red onion,
    thinly sliced
½ cup pitted olives,
    coarsely chopped
½ medium head of radicchio,
    cored and coarsely chopped

½ medium head of frisée,
    coarsely chopped
1 cup finely chopped red cabbage
2 cups baby arugula (2 ounces)

In a bowl, whisk the olive oil with the red wine vinegar. Whisk in the chopped shallot and oregano and season with salt and pepper. Add the provolone cheese, Genoa salami, sliced red onion, chopped olives, radicchio, frisée, red cabbage and baby arugula. Toss well and serve.

—Lachlan Mackinnon-Patterson

MAKE AHEAD The dressed salad can be refrigerated for up to 1 hour.

Green Bean–Tomato Salad with Herbs

 TOTAL: 20 MIN
10 SERVINGS ● ● ●

2 pounds green beans
1½ teaspoons Dijon mustard
2 tablespoons red
    wine vinegar
¼ cup plus 1 tablespoon
    extra-virgin olive oil
Kosher salt and freshly
    ground pepper
1 tablespoon chopped
    fresh tarragon
1 tablespoon snipped chives
½ teaspoon chopped fresh
    thyme leaves
½ pound cherry tomatoes, halved

1. Bring a large pot of salted water to a boil. Add the green beans and cook until crisp-tender, 5 minutes. Drain and rinse the green beans under cold water until they are chilled; pat the green beans dry.

2. In a large bowl, whisk the mustard with the vinegar. Gradually whisk in the olive oil and season with salt and pepper. Add the green beans, tarragon, chives and thyme and toss to coat. Add the tomatoes, toss gently and serve.

—Melissa Rubel Jacobson

MAKE AHEAD The salad can be refrigerated for up to 4 hours.

Tomato, Cucumber and Sweet Onion Salad with Cumin Salt

TOTAL: 15 MIN
4 TO 6 SERVINGS ● ● ●

A sprinkle of toasted cumin seeds ground with coarse sea salt gives this summery tomato salad its warm depth of flavor. Any leftover cumin salt is terrific on grilled chicken or roasted potatoes.

- 1 tablespoon cumin seeds
- 1½ tablespoons coarse sea salt
- 2¼ pounds tomatoes, cored and sliced ¼ inch thick
- 1 pound cucumbers, peeled and sliced ⅛ inch thick
- 1 large sweet onion, very thinly sliced
- ¼ cup extra-virgin olive oil
- 3 tablespoons freshly squeezed lemon juice

1. In a small skillet, toast the cumin seeds over moderately high heat, stirring, until fragrant, about 30 seconds; transfer the seeds to a mortar and let cool. Add the salt to the cumin seeds and grind to a coarse powder.
2. In a large bowl, toss together the sliced tomatoes, cucumbers, sweet onion, olive oil and fresh lemon juice. Sprinkle 2 teaspoons of the cumin salt over the salad and toss well. Transfer to a large platter and serve. —Andreas Viestad

Tomato-and-Anchovy Salad with Garlic Cream

TOTAL: 30 MIN
4 SERVINGS ●

At New York City's Eleven Madison Park, chef Daniel Humm varies the ingredients for this lovely salad depending on what he finds at the farmers' market—on good days, beautiful heirloom tomatoes. He tosses them with briny oil-and-vinegar-marinated white anchovies, also known by the Spanish name *boquerones,* which are available at the deli counter of many specialty food stores.

- 6 small garlic cloves, halved
- ¼ cup milk
- Salt and freshly ground pepper
- 2 pounds assorted heirloom tomatoes, cut into wedges and slices
- ¼ cup small basil leaves
- ¼ cup extra-virgin olive oil
- 12 white anchovy fillets
- 2 teaspoons aged balsamic vinegar

1. In a small saucepan, cover the garlic with cold water and bring to a boil. Boil for 2 minutes, then drain. Repeat two more times, blanching the garlic until tender; drain and transfer to a mini food processor. Add the milk and puree until smooth. Season the garlic cream with salt and pepper.
2. In a large bowl, toss the tomatoes and basil with 2 tablespoons of the olive oil and season with salt and pepper. Gently stir in the anchovies to combine.
3. Spoon the garlic cream onto plates and top with the tomato salad. Drizzle with the vinegar and the remaining 2 tablespoons of oil and serve. —Daniel Humm

Japanese-Cucumber Salad

TOTAL: 25 MIN
6 SERVINGS ● ●

- ¼ cup shoyu (see Note) or soy sauce
- ¼ cup rice vinegar
- 1½ teaspoons Asian sesame oil
- 2½ pounds Japanese cucumbers
- 2 scallions, thinly sliced
- Freshly ground pepper
- 1 tablespoon bonito flakes (see Note)

In a bowl, combine the shoyu with the vinegar and sesame oil. Using a vegetable peeler, remove strips of skin from the cucumbers. Halve the cucumbers lengthwise and cut crosswise into ½-inch half moons. Add the cucumbers and scallions to the bowl, season with pepper and toss to coat. Refrigerate for 15 minutes. Sprinkle with the bonito flakes and serve. —Michael Black

NOTE Shoyu is less salty than Chinese soy sauce. Both shoyu and bonito flakes are available at Asian specialty food stores.

Bitter Greens with Almonds and Goat Cheese

TOTAL: 30 MIN
4 SERVINGS ●

Apricot jam warmed and mixed with olive oil, vinegar and herbs makes an irresistible sweet-tart dressing for bitter greens.

- ½ cup whole unsalted almonds
- 1 large shallot, thinly sliced
- 3 tablespoons raspberry vinegar
- 6 cups baby arugula (6 ounces)
- 2 Belgian endives, thinly sliced crosswise
- ½ small head of radicchio, cored and finely shredded
- 3 tablespoons extra-virgin olive oil
- 1 teaspoon rosemary leaves
- ½ teaspoon thyme leaves
- 3 tablespoons apricot jam
- Kosher salt and freshly ground black pepper
- One 8-ounce log of fresh goat cheese, cut into 8 rounds

1. Preheat the oven to 350°. Spread the almonds in a pie plate and toast for 10 minutes, until golden. Let the nuts cool, then coarsely chop them.
2. In a small bowl, mix together the sliced shallot and raspberry vinegar; let stand for about 10 minutes. In a large bowl, toss the baby arugula, endives, radicchio and toasted almonds. In a skillet, heat the oil, rosemary and thyme over moderate heat for 2 minutes, until the herbs sizzle. Stir in the jam and cook until melted, 30 seconds. Add the shallot and vinegar and cook over low heat until warmed, 30 seconds. Season with salt and pepper. Pour the dressing over the greens and toss. Mound the salad on plates, arrange 2 rounds of goat cheese on each plate and serve. —Melissa Rubel Jacobson

TOMATO-AND-ANCHOVY
SALAD WITH GARLIC CREAM

BITTER GREENS WITH
ALMONDS AND GOAT CHEESE

Crisp Escarole Salad with Garlicky Anchovy Dressing

TOTAL: 35 MIN
4 SERVINGS ● ●

Bagna cauda ("hot bath"), a classic Piedmontese sauce made with anchovies, garlic, butter and olive oil, is generally served warm, with raw vegetables for dipping. F&W's Melissa Rubel Jacobson transforms most of bagna cauda's ingredients into a salad dressing that she tosses with a nicely crunchy mix of escarole, radishes, celery and cucumber.

Two ¾-inch-thick slices of
    sourdough bread, cut into
    ¾-inch dice (3 cups)
  1 large head of escarole, light green
    and white leaves only, cut
    crosswise into 1-inch strips
  6 radishes, thinly sliced
  4 celery ribs with leaves,
    thinly sliced
  1 cup grape tomatoes, halved
  ½ seedless cucumber, halved
    lengthwise and thinly sliced
    crosswise
  ½ cup extra-virgin olive oil
  8 oil-packed anchovy fillets,
    drained and coarsely chopped
  6 large garlic cloves, minced
2½ tablespoons fresh lemon juice
Freshly ground pepper
Kosher salt

---

easy italian salad

From chef Marc Vetri of Vetri in Philadelphia: Make a vinaigrette with olive oil, sherry vinegar, honey, chopped rosemary, salt and pepper. Drizzle the vinaigrette on sliced radicchio and top with shaved pecorino.

---

1. Preheat the oven to 350°. On a baking sheet, toast the bread for 15 minutes, tossing once, until lightly golden; let cool.
2. Meanwhile, in a large bowl, toss the escarole strips with the radishes, celery, tomatoes and cucumber.
3. In a small saucepan, combine the olive oil, chopped anchovies and garlic and cook over moderate heat, stirring occasionally, until the garlic is lightly golden, about 7 minutes. Add the lemon juice and season generously with pepper.
4. Add the croutons to the salad and toss. Pour the dressing over the salad, season lightly with salt and toss again. Serve at once. —*Melissa Rubel Jacobson*

Spinach Salad with Kimchi and Sesame

TOTAL: 5 MIN
6 SERVINGS ● ● ○

Kimchi, the Korean pickled cabbage, is salty, spicy and pungent. F&W's Marcia Kiesel uses it to create a quick, easy and terrific variation on spinach salad.

1½ tablespoons soy sauce
1½ teaspoons sherry vinegar
  ½ teaspoon Asian sesame oil
  5 ounces baby spinach
  ½ cup kimchi, coarsely chopped
  2 teaspoons toasted sesame seeds

In a small bowl, combine the soy sauce with the vinegar and sesame oil. In a medium bowl, toss the spinach with the kimchi and sesame seeds. Add the dressing, toss well and serve. —*Marcia Kiesel*

Iceberg Salad with Blue Cheese Dressing

TOTAL: 30 MIN
6 SERVINGS ● ●

New Orleans restaurateur Donald Link makes fresh mayonnaise for his delightfully creamy blue cheese dressing. To speed up the recipe, use prepared mayo in this easy-to-eat version of the classic iceberg wedge salad.

  3 cups 1-inch-cubed crusty
    white bread
  ½ cup plus 1 tablespoon
    vegetable oil
  ¾ pound sliced bacon
  1 garlic clove, crushed
Salt
  2 tablespoons mayonnaise
  3 tablespoons buttermilk
1½ tablespoons red wine vinegar
  1 teaspoon Dijon mustard
Cayenne pepper
  ¼ pound blue cheese,
    preferably Maytag, crumbled
    (¾ cup)
  1 head of iceberg lettuce,
    cut into 1-inch pieces
  ½ small red onion, very
    thinly sliced
  1 celery rib, thinly sliced

1. Preheat the oven to 350°. On a large rimmed baking sheet, toss the bread cubes with 1 tablespoon of the vegetable oil and toast for about 15 minutes, stirring once or twice, until the croutons are golden and crisp all over.
2. Meanwhile, in a large skillet, cook the bacon over moderately high heat, turning the slices once, until they are crisp, about 6 minutes. Drain the slices on paper towels, let cool slightly and crumble.
3. In a small bowl, using the back of a spoon, mash the crushed garlic clove to a paste with a pinch of salt. Whisk in the mayonnaise, buttermilk, red wine vinegar and Dijon mustard. Gradually whisk in the remaining ½ cup of vegetable oil and season with salt and cayenne pepper. Stir in the crumbled blue cheese.
4. In a large bowl, toss the iceberg lettuce, sliced red onion, celery, crumbled bacon and croutons with the dressing and serve right away. —*Donald Link*

MAKE AHEAD The bacon and dressing can be refrigerated separately overnight. The croutons can be stored overnight in an airtight container.

Fennel and Aged Pecorino Salad

TOTAL: 20 MIN
6 SERVINGS ○

This crisp salad combines fennel, scallions and parsley with shavings of sharp, salty aged pecorino cheese; the pecorino from the small Tuscan town of Pienza is especially tasty.

1½ tablespoons red wine vinegar
¼ cup extra-virgin olive oil
Salt and freshly ground pepper
2 large fennel bulbs (2 pounds)— halved, cored and very thinly sliced, fronds reserved
2 scallions, white and green parts, thinly sliced
½ cup flat-leaf parsley leaves
5 ounces aged pecorino, shaved (2 cups)

In a large bowl, whisk the red wine vinegar with the olive oil; season generously with salt and pepper. Add the sliced fennel, scallions, parsley leaves and shaved pecorino and toss the salad gently. Transfer the salad to plates, garnish with the fennel fronds and serve right away.
—*Rolando Beramendi*

Green Bean–and–Roasted Red Pepper Salad

TOTAL: 50 MIN
10 SERVINGS ● ● ○ ○

5 red bell peppers
3 medium shallots, thinly sliced
2 garlic cloves, minced
¼ cup red wine vinegar
1 tablespoon sherry vinegar
Salt
½ cup extra-virgin olive oil
Freshly ground pepper
1½ pounds green beans
1 pound cherry tomatoes, halved
2 tablespoons chopped mint
2 tablespoons chopped parsley
½ cup roasted almonds, chopped

1. Preheat the broiler. Roast the peppers under the broiler or over a gas flame, turning a few times, until charred all over; transfer to a work surface and let cool. Discard the skin, stems and seeds and cut the peppers into 2-by-1-inch strips.
2. In a small bowl, combine the shallots with the garlic, red wine and sherry vinegars and a large pinch of salt. Let stand for 10 minutes. Stir in the olive oil and season with salt and pepper.
3. Meanwhile, bring a large pot of salted water to a boil. Add the beans and cook until crisp-tender, about 4 minutes. Drain and spread out on a large baking sheet. Let cool to room temperature.
4. In a large bowl, combine the peppers with the beans, tomatoes, mint and parsley. Add the shallot dressing and toss well. Sprinkle with the almonds and serve.
—*Michael Emanuel*

Chopped Salad with Grapes and Mint

photo, page 38

TOTAL: 30 MIN
4 TO 6 SERVINGS

1 heart of romaine, coarsely chopped
1 pint grape tomatoes, halved
1 medium seedless cucumber, peeled and cut into ½-inch dice
1 small red onion, cut into ¼-inch dice
1 cup corn kernels
1 cup diced cooked chicken
½ cup halved green grapes
3 ounces feta cheese, crumbled (½ cup)
3 tablespoons extra-virgin olive oil
2 tablespoons finely chopped fresh mint leaves
2 tablespoons finely chopped fresh basil leaves
2 tablespoons red wine vinegar
1 tablespoon fresh lime juice
Salt and freshly ground pepper

In a large bowl, toss all of the ingredients together. Season with salt and freshly ground pepper and serve immediately.
—*Emily Kaiser*

Beet Salad with Tangerines

ACTIVE: 35 MIN; TOTAL: 1 HR 35 MIN
8 SERVINGS ● ● ●

This clever recipe uses sweet-tart tangerines two ways: Sections of fruit are tossed into the salad, and tangerine juice flavors the vinaigrette.

24 baby orange beets
2 tablespoons pine nuts
¼ cup plus 1 teaspoon vegetable oil
8 tangerines
4 small shallots, thinly sliced
3 tablespoons raspberry vinegar
Salt

1. Preheat the oven to 375°. Put the beets in a roasting pan, cover with foil and bake them for about 1 hour, until they are tender. When they are cool enough to handle, peel and quarter the beets.
2. In a pie plate, toss the pine nuts with 1 teaspoon of the vegetable oil and toast them in the oven for about 3 minutes, until they are golden brown.
3. Using a sharp knife, peel the tangerines. Working over a medium bowl, slice in between the membranes to release the tangerine sections. Squeeze the juice from the membranes into a small bowl; you should have ½ cup.
4. In another small bowl, toss the sliced shallots and raspberry vinegar with a pinch of salt and let stand for 5 minutes. Stir in the ½ cup of tangerine juice and the remaining ¼ cup of vegetable oil and season the dressing with salt.
5. Arrange the beets and tangerine sections on plates and drizzle with the dressing. Top with the toasted pine nuts and serve. —*Marcia Kiesel*

MAKE AHEAD The roasted beets can be refrigerated overnight. Bring to room temperature before proceeding.

salads

Watermelon Salad with Feta and Mint

TOTAL: 25 MIN
12 SERVINGS ● ●

⅓ cup extra-virgin olive oil
3 tablespoons fresh lemon juice
2 teaspoons kosher salt
1 teaspoon Tabasco
½ teaspoon freshly ground pepper
One 8-pound seedless watermelon, scooped into balls with a melon baller or cut into 1½-inch chunks (10 cups), chilled
½ pound feta cheese, crumbled (2 cups)
1¼ cups pitted kalamata olives, coarsely chopped (optional)
1 small sweet onion, cut into ½-inch dice
1 cup coarsely chopped mint leaves

In a large bowl, whisk the oil, lemon juice, salt, Tabasco and pepper. Add the watermelon, feta, olives and onion and toss gently. Garnish with the mint and serve.
—*Jacques Pépin*

Asian Pear–Arugula Salad with Goat Cheese

TOTAL: 20 MIN
10 SERVINGS ● ○

This salad has a perfect mix of bitter (arugula), sweet (Asian pear), tangy (lemon) and crunchy (pumpkin seeds).

¼ cup extra-virgin olive oil
2 tablespoons fresh lemon juice
1 teaspoon honey
½ teaspoon chopped thyme
Salt and freshly ground pepper
5 ounces baby arugula
3 Asian pears (1½ pounds)— peeled and very thinly sliced on a mandoline, cores discarded
½ cup salted roasted pumpkin seeds
3 ounces fresh goat cheese, crumbled
Sea salt, for sprinkling

1. In a small bowl, whisk the olive oil with the lemon juice, honey and chopped thyme. Season the salad dressing with salt and pepper.
2. In a large bowl, toss the arugula with the pear slices and pumpkin seeds. Add the dressing and toss well. Top with the goat cheese, sprinkle lightly with sea salt and serve right away.
—*Randolph Dudley*

MAKE AHEAD The salad dressing can be refrigerated overnight.

Grilled Apricot, Arugula and Goat Cheese Salad

TOTAL: 30 MIN
4 SERVINGS ○

6 fresh apricots, halved and pitted
3 tablespoons extra-virgin olive oil
1 teaspoon thyme leaves
Salt and freshly ground pepper
2 tablespoons pine nuts
1½ teaspoons aged balsamic vinegar
1 bunch of arugula (4 ounces), stemmed
One 4-ounce log of fresh goat cheese, cut into 12 slices

1. Light a grill. In a medium bowl, toss the apricots with 1 tablespoon of the olive oil and the thyme and season with salt and pepper. Let stand for 10 minutes.
2. Grill the apricot halves over high heat for about 5 minutes, turning once, until lightly charred and softened.
3. Meanwhile, in a small skillet, toast the pine nuts over moderate heat, stirring, until golden, about 3 minutes. Transfer the nuts to a cutting board and finely chop.
4. Put the pine nuts in a medium bowl. Whisk in the vinegar and the remaining 2 tablespoons of olive oil and season with salt and pepper. Add the arugula and toss. Arrange the goat cheese slices on plates. Top with the apricot halves and arugula salad and serve right away.
—*Daniel Humm*

Beet-and-Sorrel Salad with Pistachio

ACTIVE: 30 MIN; TOTAL: 2 HR
6 SERVINGS ● ●

Sorrel is a leafy green that gives dishes a tart, almost sour flavor. For this salad, Paul Liebrandt (an F&W Best New Chef 2009) likes using red ribbon sorrel—a European variety with bright green leaves and intense red veins—because it's so pretty with the beets and its tang is so nice with the nutty pistachio sauce.

2 pounds baby beets, preferably a mix of golden, Chioggia and red
4 ounces brioche, cut into ¾-inch cubes (2 cups) or thin slices
¼ cup roasted pistachios
Salt and freshly ground pepper
1½ tablespoons extra-virgin olive oil
1½ tablespoons pistachio oil
1½ tablespoons balsamic vinegar
3 cups sorrel, preferably red ribbon (see Note)

1. Preheat the oven to 350°. Spread the beets in a baking dish. Add ½ cup of water and cover with foil. Roast for 1½ hours, until tender. Let cool, then peel and cut into wedges and slices. Transfer to a bowl.
2. Meanwhile, spread the brioche cubes on a baking sheet and toast for about 8 minutes, until golden.
3. In a blender, combine the pistachios with ¾ cup of water; blend at high speed for 1 minute. Strain into a bowl and refrigerate until chilled. (It will thicken slightly.) Season the sauce with salt and pepper.
4. In a small bowl, whisk the olive oil with the pistachio oil and balsamic vinegar. Season with salt and pepper. Toss 3 tablespoons of the vinaigrette with the beets. Spoon the pistachio sauce onto plates. Mound the beets in the center; top with the sorrel. Drizzle with the remaining vinaigrette; garnish with the brioche croutons. Serve right away. —*Paul Liebrandt*
NOTE Red ribbon sorrel is available at chefsgarden.com.

BEET-AND-SORREL
SALAD WITH PISTACHIO

salads

Spicy Green Papaya Salad

TOTAL: 30 MIN
8 SERVINGS ●

For this Thai classic, Andy Ricker of Pok Pok in Portland, Oregon, uses a mortar and pestle to pound crunchy raw green beans with a piquant mix of chiles, garlic, fish sauce and lime juice. He then tosses in crisp strips of unripened papaya.

- 6 medium dried shrimp
- One 1½-pound green papaya
- 2 small Thai chiles, coarsely chopped (see Note)
- 1 large garlic clove, halved
- ¼ cup plus 3 tablespoons palm sugar or light brown sugar
- ¼ pound thin green beans, halved crosswise
- 3 tablespoons fresh lime juice
- 2 tablespoons Asian fish sauce
- 2 dozen cherry tomatoes, halved
- ⅓ cup coarsely chopped roasted, salted peanuts

1. In a small bowl, cover the dried shrimp with hot water. Let stand for 5 minutes, then drain. Cut the shrimp into thirds.
2. Using a serrated knife, halve the papaya crosswise and peel the skin. Scrape out the seeds. Using a mandoline, julienne the flesh (you should have about 6 cups).
3. In a large mortar, pound the chopped Thai chiles to a coarse paste with the garlic clove. Add the palm sugar and soaked shrimp and pound until blended. Add the green beans and lightly pound them. Pour in the lime juice and fish sauce and stir until the sugar is dissolved. Add the tomatoes and lightly pound them. Scrape the mixture into a large bowl. Add the papaya and peanuts, toss well and serve.
—*Andy Ricker*

NOTE When chopping incendiary peppers like tiny Thai chiles, it's a good idea to wear latex gloves. Be sure to wash the knife and board well afterward, since anything touched by the spicy oils from the chiles can also transfer the heat to your skin.

Baby Spinach and Papaya Salad with Curry Vinaigrette

TOTAL: 20 MIN
6 SERVINGS ● ●

- ¼ cup plus 2 tablespoons extra-virgin olive oil
- 3 tablespoons low-sodium soy sauce
- 2 tablespoons honey
- 1 tablespoon balsamic vinegar
- 1 teaspoon mild curry powder
- Salt and freshly ground pepper
- 1¼ pounds peeled, seeded papaya, cut into 1-inch cubes (4 cups)
- 10 ounces baby spinach
- ¼ cup salted roasted pumpkin seeds

In a blender, combine the oil, soy sauce, honey, vinegar and curry powder and blend until emulsified. Season the dressing with salt and pepper and pour into a large bowl. Add the papaya and spinach to the dressing and toss well. Sprinkle the salad with the pumpkin seeds and serve.
—*Doris Esther Ayola Orozco*

Mushroom Salad with Mint

TOTAL: 10 MIN
4 SERVINGS ● ●

Restaurateur and winemaker Joe Bastianich drizzles sliced mushrooms with lemon juice and olive oil for a salad he calls "soulful but still filling." He adds, "Raw mushrooms are a great conduit for good oil."

- 16 medium white or cremini mushrooms (½ pound), trimmed and very thinly sliced
- ¼ cup extra-virgin olive oil
- 1 tablespoon plus 1 teaspoon fresh lemon juice
- Salt and freshly ground pepper
- Finely grated zest of 1 small lemon
- ¼ cup thinly sliced mint leaves

Arrange the mushrooms on a platter. Drizzle with the oil and lemon juice and season with salt and pepper. Scatter the lemon zest and mint over the mushrooms; serve right away. —*Joe Bastianich*

Green Mango Salad

TOTAL: 15 MIN
6 SERVINGS ● ● ●

Be sure to use firm, underripe fruit for this jalapeño-spiced salad: They add an essential tang to the recipe.

- 2 very large, green (unripe) mangoes, peeled and cut into 2-by-½-inch batons
- ½ large sweet onion, sliced lengthwise
- 1 jalapeño, seeded and very finely chopped
- 2 tablespoons fresh lime juice
- Salt and freshly ground black pepper

In a bowl, toss the green mangoes, sweet onion and chopped jalapeño with the lime juice. Season the mango salad with salt and pepper and serve right away.
—*Doris Esther Ayola Orozco*

SERVE WITH Grilled chicken or shrimp.

MAKE AHEAD The mango salad can be refrigerated for up to 1 hour.

Arugula-Fennel Salad

TOTAL: 15 MIN
4 SERVINGS ● ● ●

Eugenia Bone, prolific home cook, writer and author of *Well-Preserved,* serves this simple green salad with plenty of rustic bread and a cheese plate. She always includes Taleggio and aged Parmigiano-Reggiano, as well as fresh imported sheep's-milk ricotta whenever she can find it at the market.

- 1 tablespoon very finely chopped shallot
- 2 teaspoons fresh lemon juice
- ½ teaspoon Dijon mustard
- 3 tablespoons canola oil
- 6 ounces baby arugula leaves, washed and spun dry
- ½ fennel bulb, cored and very thinly sliced
- Kosher salt and freshly ground black pepper

GREEN MANGO SALAD

ARUGULA-FENNEL SALAD

In a large salad bowl, whisk together the chopped shallot, lemon juice and mustard. Gradually add the oil, whisking constantly, until the vinaigrette is emulsified and creamy-looking. Add the baby arugula and sliced fennel to the salad bowl, season the salad with salt and black pepper and toss well. Serve. —*Eugenia Bone*

SERVE WITH Assorted cheeses and crusty peasant bread.

MAKE AHEAD The vinaigrette can be prepared up to 4 hours in advance and kept in the salad bowl at room temperature. Whisk the dressing well before tossing with the arugula and fennel.

Fall Harvest Salad

TOTAL: 40 MIN
10 TO 12 SERVINGS ● ● ● ●
With its chunks of butternut squash, pumpkin seeds, pecans and greens, this salad epitomizes fall flavors. The easiest way to peel the butternut squash is with a sturdy U-peeler (named for its wide, U-shaped handle), which is available at kitchenware shops.

¼ cup plus 3 tablespoons vegetable oil, preferably peanut
2 cups peeled butternut squash (10 ounces), cut into 1-inch cubes
Salt and freshly ground pepper
2 tablespoons sherry vinegar
1 tablespoon chopped tarragon
1 tablespoon chopped parsley
10 ounces mixed salad greens or mesclun
1 cup coarsely chopped pecans
½ cup roasted pumpkin seeds

1. In a large nonstick skillet, heat 2 tablespoons of the vegetable oil. Add the butternut squash cubes in an even layer, season with salt and pepper and cook over moderately high heat until the cubes are browned on the bottom, about 5 minutes. Turn the squash cubes with a spatula and cook over moderately low heat until they are browned on the other side and just tender, about 7 minutes.

2. In a small bowl, combine the sherry vinegar with the chopped tarragon, parsley and the remaining 5 tablespoons of vegetable oil; season the dressing with salt and pepper. In a large bowl, toss the mixed salad greens with the chopped pecans, pumpkin seeds and roasted squash. Pour the dressing over the salad and toss well. Serve right away. —*Shawn McClain*

MAKE AHEAD The dressing can be kept at room temperature for up to 2 hours. The cooked squash can be refrigerated overnight. Bring to room temperature before using in the salad.

●HEALTHY ●MAKE AHEAD ● VEGETARIAN ● STAFF FAVORITE

49

salads

Butternut Squash Salad with Hazelnuts

⏱ TOTAL: 30 MIN
4 SERVINGS ●●

This lovely winter salad gets a double hit of hazelnut: hazelnut oil in the rich dressing and toasted hazelnuts in the salad.

3½ cups diced butternut squash
3 tablespoons extra-virgin olive oil
Kosher salt and freshly ground
    black pepper
½ cup blanched hazelnuts
3 cups baby arugula (3 ounces)
1 medium head of frisée, torn into
    bite-size pieces
3 ounces prosciutto, torn into
    bite-size pieces
1½ tablespoons snipped chives
2½ tablespoons balsamic vinegar
2 tablespoons hazelnut oil

1. Preheat the oven to 425°. On a baking sheet, toss the squash with 2 tablespoons of the olive oil; season with salt and pepper.

Roast for 20 minutes, until tender. Spread the hazelnuts in a pie plate and toast for about 6 minutes, until golden. Let cool, then chop the hazelnuts.

2. In a large bowl, toss the arugula, frisée, prosciutto, chives, hazelnuts and squash. In a small microwave-safe bowl, mix the remaining 1 tablespoon of olive oil with the vinegar and hazelnut oil and season with salt and pepper. Microwave the dressing until hot, about 1 minute. Pour the dressing over the salad, toss well and serve.
—*Melissa Rubel Jacobson*

Spaghetti Squash Salad with Pine Nuts and Tarragon

ACTIVE: 30 MIN; TOTAL: 1 HR 20 MIN
10 SERVINGS ●●

Spaghetti squash, which separates into spaghetti-like strands when cooked, is an excellent base for this easy salad. The recipe would also be good with roasted cubes of butternut squash.

½ cup pine nuts
3 large spaghetti squash
    (9 pounds), halved lengthwise
    and seeds scraped
⅔ cup extra-virgin olive oil,
    plus more for drizzling
Salt and freshly ground
    black pepper
1 cup water
½ cup dry white wine
3 tablespoons white wine
    vinegar
Finely grated zest of 1 lemon
1 tablespoon fresh lemon juice
1 teaspoon chopped fresh
    thyme leaves
Pinch of crushed red pepper
2 tablespoons chopped tarragon
4 ounces *queso fresco* or *ricotta
    salata,* crumbled (1 cup)

1. Preheat the oven to 350°. Spread the pine nuts in a pie plate and bake for about 5 minutes, until golden brown. Transfer to a plate and let cool.

2. Arrange the spaghetti squash halves cut side up on 2 large rimmed baking sheets. Drizzle with extra-virgin olive oil and season with salt and pepper. Flip the squash cut side down and pour the water and wine into the pans. Bake for about 50 minutes, until the squash is barely tender. Flip the squash cut side up and let cool until warm.

3. In a small bowl, combine the white wine vinegar with the lemon zest and lemon juice, thyme and crushed red pepper. Whisk in the ⅔ cup of olive oil; season with salt and pepper.

4. Working over large a bowl, using a fork, scrape out the spaghetti squash, separating the strands. Pour the dressing over the squash and toss to coat. Add the tarragon, *queso fresco* and pine nuts and toss again. Serve right away.
—*Patrick Stubbers*

MAKE AHEAD The cooked spaghetti squash can be prepared through Step 2 and refrigerated overnight. Bring to room temperature before dressing.

Spicy Chickpea Salad

ACTIVE: 15 MIN; TOTAL: 2 HR 15 MIN
PLUS OVERNIGHT SOAKING
4 SERVINGS ●●●

San Francisco wine director Rajat Parr was born in Kolkata (formerly Calcutta) in 1972 and didn't leave until he was 22, which explains why Indian flavors are such a big part of his cooking. This tart and spicy salad, for instance, is a twist on the classic Indian street food called *chana chaat.*

1 cup dried chickpeas (about
    5 ounces), soaked overnight
    and drained
1 tomato, cut into ½-inch dice
½ cup diced cucumber (½ inch)
½ small red onion, finely diced
½ jalapeño, seeded and minced
2 tablespoons extra-virgin olive oil
1 tablespoon vegetable oil
2 tablespoons fresh lemon juice

seasonal salads

Winter Fennel-and-Orange Salad
Toss shaved fennel with sliced oranges, olive oil and lemon juice. Top with shaved Parmesan cheese.

Spring Sugar Snap Pea Salad
Toss steamed sugar snaps with sliced radish, minced shallot, salt, pepper and crème fraîche.

Summer Corn Salad
Slice kernels from steamed corn; toss with chopped tomatoes, steamed green beans and pesto.

Autumn Roasted Root Salad
Toss sliced carrots, sunchokes and red onions with olive oil, salt and pepper. Roast at 400° until soft. Serve over arugula dressed with olive oil and balsamic vinegar.

1 teaspoon ground cumin
¼ teaspoon cayenne pepper
1 teaspoon dried mango powder,
    optional (see Note)
Salt

1. In a large saucepan, cover the chickpeas with 4 inches of water. Bring to a boil and simmer over moderate heat, stirring occasionally, until tender, about 2 hours; drain.
2. In a large bowl, combine the tomato, cucumber, red onion, jalapeño, olive oil, vegetable oil, lemon juice, cumin, cayenne and mango powder. Add the chickpeas and season with salt. Serve the chickpea salad at room temperature or slightly chilled. —*Rajat Parr*

NOTE Used as a tart seasoning in Indian dishes, dried mango powder (also known as *amchoor*) is made from sun-dried green mangoes. It's available at Indian markets and kalustyans.com.

MAKE AHEAD The chickpea salad can be refrigerated for up to 4 hours.

Barley-and-Spinach Salad with Tofu Dressing
TOTAL: 1 HR
6 SERVINGS ●

1 cup pearl barley (7½ ounces)
3 cups chicken stock
4 thyme sprigs
2 garlic cloves, minced
Salt
2 tablespoons extra-virgin olive oil
10 ounces cremini mushrooms,
    quartered (4 cups)
Freshly ground pepper
2 shallots, thinly sliced
7 ounces baby spinach
¼ cup basil leaves, torn
3 tablespoons chopped mint
¼ cup sherry vinegar
1 tablespoon fresh lemon juice
2 tablespoons light brown sugar
1 cup grape tomatoes, halved
7 ounces firm tofu, drained
    and crumbled

1. In a medium saucepan, combine the barley, stock, thyme and half of the garlic. Add a generous pinch of salt and bring to a boil. Cover and cook over moderately low heat until the barley is tender, 25 minutes. Discard the thyme. Drain the barley and transfer to a large bowl; cover and keep warm.
2. Meanwhile, in a large skillet, heat 1 tablespoon of the oil. Add the mushrooms, season with salt and pepper and cook over high heat, stirring, until lightly browned, 5 minutes. Add the shallots and cook, stirring, until softened, 3 minutes longer. Scrape the mushrooms into the barley and toss. Add the spinach, basil and mint, but do not stir.
3. Heat the remaining 1 tablespoon of oil in the skillet. Add the remaining garlic and cook over moderate heat until softened. Add the vinegar, lemon juice and sugar and bring to a boil. Cook until slightly thickened, 1 minute. Add the tomatoes; cook to heat through. Stir in the tofu; season with salt and pepper. Scrape the dressing over the salad, toss and serve. —*Lee Anne Wong*

Spinach-and-Shrimp Salad with Chile Dressing

TOTAL: 25 MIN
4 SERVINGS ●

8 ounces baby spinach
1 cup frozen baby peas,
    thawed and drained
½ cup grape tomatoes, halved
¼ cup plus 2 tablespoons
    vegetable oil
1 onion, finely chopped
1 Holland or serrano chile, minced
1 teaspoon finely grated ginger
½ teaspoon cumin seeds
¼ teaspoon turmeric
2½ tablespoons fresh lemon juice
Kosher salt and freshly ground pepper
1 pound cooked large shrimp

1. In a large bowl, toss the spinach, peas and tomatoes. In a medium skillet, heat the oil. Add the onion and cook over moderately high heat until lightly golden,

4 minutes. Add the chile, ginger, cumin and turmeric and cook for 2 minutes. Add the lemon juice and season the dressing with salt and pepper.
2. Add the shrimp to the salad. Pour the dressing over the salad, toss well and serve. —*Melissa Rubel Jacobson*

Crab, Avocado and Asparagus Salad

TOTAL: 45 MIN
8 SERVINGS ● ●

1 pound thick asparagus
7 tablespoons extra-virgin olive oil
3 tablespoons fresh lemon juice
6 medium basil leaves
1 small shallot, coarsely chopped
½ cup flat-leaf parsley leaves
Kosher salt and freshly ground pepper
3½ ounces pea shoots, trimmed
¼ cup salted roasted pistachios,
    coarsely chopped
1 pound jumbo lump crabmeat
2 Hass avocados, each cut
    into 8 wedges

1. Bring a saucepan of salted water to a boil. Fill a bowl with ice water. Cut off 1 inch of the asparagus tips and cut each tip in half lengthwise. Using a peeler or mandoline, shave the asparagus spears lengthwise. Blanch the asparagus tips and strands in the boiling water until just heated through, 10 seconds. Drain and transfer to the ice water to chill; drain well. Pat dry and transfer to a bowl.
2. In a blender, blend the olive oil, lemon juice, basil leaves, chopped shallot and ¼ cup of the parsley. Season the dressing with salt and pepper.
3. Add the pea shoots, pistachios and the remaining ¼ cup of parsley leaves to the blanched asparagus. Toss with half of the dressing and season with salt and pepper. Add the crabmeat, avocado wedges and the remaining dressing, toss the salad gently and serve at once.
—*Melissa Rubel Jacobson*

salads

Tuna–and–White Bean Salad with Herb-Caper Pesto

 TOTAL: 20 MIN
6 SERVINGS ● ●

Excellent jarred Italian tuna makes all the difference in this hearty salad. The versatile herb-caper pesto can also be used on chicken, fish or pasta.

- 1 small garlic clove
- ½ cup packed flat-leaf parsley leaves
- ¼ cup packed basil leaves
- 1½ tablespoons fresh oregano leaves
- ¼ cup capers, drained
- 2 tablespoons pine nuts
- ¼ cup extra-virgin olive oil
- 1 teaspoon fresh lemon juice

Kosher salt and freshly ground black pepper

Three 7-ounce jars high-quality Italian tuna packed in olive oil, drained

Two 15-ounce cans cannellini beans, drained and rinsed

- 3 Belgian endives, thinly sliced crosswise

1. In a food processor, combine the garlic clove with the flat-leaf parsley, basil and oregano leaves and pulse until the herbs are coarsely chopped. Add the drained capers and pine nuts and pulse until they are coarsely chopped. Add the olive oil and fresh lemon juice and pulse until the mixture comes together but is still chunky. Season the herb-caper pesto with salt and black pepper.

2. In a large bowl, break up the tuna into bite-size chunks. Add the cannellini beans, sliced endives and the herb-caper pesto and toss gently until the salad is evenly coated with the pesto. Season the tuna salad with salt and pepper and serve.
—*Melissa Rubel Jacobson*

MAKE AHEAD The tossed salad can be refrigerated for up to 4 hours.

Warm Duck-and-Cabbage Salad

 TOTAL: 35 MIN
4 SERVINGS ●

More and more specialty food stores are selling duck confit legs, but in a pinch, rotisserie chicken works well, too.

- 3 duck confit legs (see Note)
- 5 tablespoons extra-virgin olive oil

One 10-ounce Yukon Gold potato, peeled and cut into ⅓-inch dice

- 1 small shallot, minced
- 2 teaspoons capers, drained and coarsely chopped
- ¼ teaspoon chopped fresh thyme
- 3 tablespoons red wine vinegar
- 2 teaspoons Dijon mustard

Kosher salt and freshly ground black pepper

- ½ large head of napa cabbage, finely shredded (8 cups)

1. Preheat the broiler and set an oven rack 3 inches from the heat. Set the duck confit legs on a rimmed baking sheet and broil for about 10 minutes, rotating the baking sheet halfway through and watching closely, until the duck skin is crisp and browned all over.

2. Meanwhile, in a large skillet, heat the oil. Add the potato and cook over moderately high heat until golden, about 8 minutes. Add the shallot and cook over moderately low heat for 1 minute. Add the capers and thyme and cook for 30 seconds. Stir in the vinegar and mustard; season with salt and pepper.

3. Remove the meat and skin from the duck; discard the bones. Scrape away any fat that remains on the underside of the skin. Cut the skin into strips and shred the meat. In a bowl, toss the duck, cabbage and dressing. Season with salt and pepper and serve. —*Melissa Rubel Jacobson*

NOTE Duck confit, which is cured in salt, then poached in fat, is available at many specialty markets and dartagnan.com.

Thai Green Salad with Duck Cracklings

 TOTAL: 45 MIN
8 SERVINGS ●

This zippy salad is a great way to use incredibly moist and flavorful duck confit. Tossing the salad with cracklings (duck skin crisped in a pan) adds superb crunch.

- 8 duck confit legs—skin cut into fine strips, meat shredded (see Note for previous recipe)
- 1 tablespoon finely chopped fresh ginger
- 1 large garlic clove, very finely chopped
- 1 serrano chile, seeded and very finely chopped
- 2 tablespoons light brown sugar
- 3 tablespoons Asian fish sauce
- 2 tablespoons fresh lime juice
- 2 tablespoons water
- 1¼ pounds baby Bibb lettuce, leaves separated
- ½ cup mint leaves
- ½ cup cilantro leaves

1. In a large nonstick skillet, cook the strips of duck confit skin over moderate heat until they are golden and crisp, about 8 minutes. Using a slotted spoon, transfer the cracklings to a plate. Pour off all but 2 tablespoons of the duck fat in the skillet and add the shredded duck meat. Cook over moderate heat, stirring occasionally, until tender and crispy in spots, about 7 minutes. Let cool slightly.

2. Meanwhile, in a mortar (or using a mini food processor), pound the chopped ginger, garlic, chile and brown sugar to a coarse paste, then stir in the fish sauce, lime juice and water.

3. In a large bowl, toss the lettuce with the mint, cilantro, duck, cracklings and dressing. Transfer the salad to plates and serve.
—*Grace Parisi*

MAKE AHEAD The dressing can be refrigerated overnight.

THAI GREEN SALAD WITH
DUCK CRACKLINGS

LEMONY WALDORF SALAD

AVOCADO-AND-ONION SALAD

Lemony Waldorf Salad

 TOTAL: 25 MIN
6 SERVINGS ● ●

½ cup walnut halves (2 ounces)
1 tablespoon minced shallot
½ teaspoon finely grated lemon zest
2 tablespoons fresh lemon juice
1 tablespoon white wine vinegar
¼ cup plus 2 tablespoons canola oil
2 tablespoons walnut oil
½ teaspoon ground cumin
Salt and freshly ground pepper
2 cups shredded romaine lettuce
4 large radishes, halved lengthwise and thinly sliced crosswise (1 cup)
1 cup thinly sliced celery hearts plus ¼ cup chopped celery leaves
1 small head of frisée, chopped
¼ cup golden raisins
1 Fuji apple—peeled, quartered, cored and thinly sliced crosswise

1. Preheat the oven to 350°. Spread the walnuts in a pie plate and toast for about 8 minutes, until golden and fragrant. Let the nuts cool, then break into pieces.
2. Meanwhile, in a large bowl, combine the shallot and lemon zest with the lemon juice and vinegar. Whisk in the canola and walnut oils and the cumin. Season the dressing with salt and pepper.
3. Add the lettuce to the bowl along with the walnuts, radishes, celery hearts and leaves, frisée, raisins and apple. Toss well and serve. —*Mark Peel*

Avocado-and-Onion Salad

 TOTAL: 10 MIN
6 SERVINGS ● ●

Since Cubans don't usually have ready access to salad greens, cooking teacher Lourdes Castro says, many start a meal with this simple salad instead.

1 Florida avocado or 3 Hass avocados, thinly sliced
¼ small red onion, very thinly sliced
1 tablespoon extra-virgin olive oil
1 tablespoon red wine vinegar
Salt and freshly ground pepper

Arrange the avocado slices on a platter and top with the onion. Drizzle with the olive oil and vinegar and season with salt and pepper. Serve right away.
—*Lourdes Castro*

Waldorf Chicken Salad

ACTIVE: 35 MIN; TOTAL: 2 HR 15 MIN
4 SERVINGS ●

3 chicken breast halves on the bone, with skin (about 14 ounces each)
2 large garlic cloves, minced
1 teaspoon ground fennel seeds
Kosher salt and freshly ground pepper
7 tablespoons extra-virgin olive oil

1 cup walnut halves (4 ounces)

1 tablespoon red wine vinegar

½ teaspoon Dijon mustard

2 ounces blue cheese, crumbled (¼ cup)

¼ cup buttermilk

½ teaspoon finely grated lemon zest

1 cup red seedless grapes, halved

2 Fuji apples, cored and thinly sliced

2 celery ribs, thinly sliced

5 ounces mesclun salad greens

2 tablespoons chopped parsley

2 tablespoons chopped tarragon

2 tablespoons snipped chives

1. Make 3 deep slashes in each chicken breast. In a small bowl, mash the garlic, fennel, 2 teaspoons of salt and ½ teaspoon of pepper. Stir in 3 tablespoons of the oil. Rub the mixture all over the chicken and into the slashes. Transfer to a small roasting pan, cover and let stand for 1 hour.

2. Preheat the oven to 350°. Spread the walnuts in a pie plate and toast for 10 minutes, until browned and fragrant. Let cool.

3. Roast the chicken for about 40 minutes, until cooked through. Let cool slightly, then discard the skin and thinly slice the meat.

4. In a food processor, blend the vinegar with the mustard and the remaining ¼ cup of oil. Blend in the cheese and buttermilk. Transfer to a bowl, stir in the lemon zest and season the dressing with salt and pepper.

5. In a bowl, combine the chicken with the walnuts, grapes, apples, celery, mesclun, parsley, tarragon and chives. Add the dressing, toss well and serve. —*Mark Sullivan*

Green Goddess Chicken Salad

TOTAL: 35 MIN

6 SERVINGS ● ●

2 oil-packed anchovies, drained

1 small garlic clove

½ cup packed flat-leaf parsley leaves

¼ cup packed basil leaves

¼ cup coarsely chopped dill

1 tablespoon oregano leaves

¾ cup mayonnaise

2½ tablespoons fresh lemon juice

2 tablespoons snipped chives

Kosher salt and freshly ground pepper

One 1-pound loaf of ciabatta—bottom crust reserved for another use, bread cut into 1-inch cubes

One 2-pound rotisserie chicken—skin and bones discarded, meat pulled into large bite-size pieces

8 piquillo peppers (from a 9.8-ounce jar), drained and quartered lengthwise

3 inner celery ribs with leaves, thinly sliced

½ cup pitted kalamata olives, halved

1. In a food processor, pulse the anchovies, garlic, parsley, basil, dill and oregano until coarsely chopped. Add the mayonnaise and lemon juice and process until smooth. Fold in the chives; season with salt and pepper.

2. In a large bowl, toss the ciabatta with the chicken, piquillo peppers, celery and olives. Add the dressing and toss to coat. Season with salt and pepper and serve. —*Melissa Rubel Jacobson*

Avocado, Grapefruit and Hearts of Palm Salad

TOTAL: 30 MIN

8 SERVINGS ●

4 red grapefruits

1 tablespoon tamarind concentrate

1 tablespoon fresh lime juice

1 tablespoon sugar

½ teaspoon Asian fish sauce

¼ teaspoon ground cumin

½ cup canola oil

Salt

Tabasco

4 Hass avocados, cut into 1-inch pieces

1 small red onion, thinly sliced

Two 14-ounce cans hearts of palm, drained and sliced ½ inch thick on the diagonal

½ cup coarsely chopped cilantro

---

1. Using a sharp knife, peel the grapefruits, removing all of the bitter white pith. Working over a cutting board, cut in between the membranes to release the sections. Cut the sections into bite-size pieces.

2. Squeeze the grapefruit membranes over a small bowl and reserve ¼ cup of the grapefruit juice. Whisk in the tamarind concentrate, fresh lime juice, sugar, fish sauce and cumin. Whisk in the canola oil in a thin stream. Season the salad dressing with salt and Tabasco.

3. Transfer the grapefruit pieces to a large bowl. Add the avocados, onion, hearts of palm, cilantro and dressing. Toss gently and serve right away. —*Ken Oringer*

MAKE AHEAD The dressing can be refrigerated for up to 3 days.

Watercress, Avocado and Walnut Salad

TOTAL: 25 MIN

4 SERVINGS ● ●

2 tablespoons fresh lemon juice

1 medium shallot, minced

3 tablespoons extra-virgin olive oil

Salt and freshly ground pepper

½ cup walnut halves

2 firm, ripe Hass avocados, each cut into 8 wedges

Two 12-ounce bunches of watercress, thick stems discarded

1. Preheat the oven to 350°. In a large bowl, combine the lemon juice and minced shallot and let stand for 10 minutes. Gradually whisk in the olive oil and season the dressing with salt and pepper.

2. Meanwhile, spread the walnuts in a pie plate and toast until golden brown and fragrant, 6 minutes. Let cool, then transfer to a work surface and coarsely chop.

3. Lightly season the avocado wedges with salt. Add the avocado, chopped toasted walnuts and watercress to the dressing and toss well. Season the salad with salt and pepper and serve right away. —*Joe Marcos*

CHILLED TOMATO SOUP
WITH TARRAGON
CRÈME FRAÎCHE (P. 75)

soups

Soups in every style, from elegant
starters to hearty main courses.

SPINACH SOUP WITH HORSERADISH GRANITÉ

WATERCRESS SOUP WITH PICKLED CUCUMBERS

Spinach Soup with Horseradish Granité

ACTIVE: 40 MIN; TOTAL: 2 HR

8 SERVINGS ● ●

Chef Tristan Welch's passion for old English cookbooks inspired him to give the historically Francophile menu at London's Launceston Place an Anglo-Saxon makeover. He recasts horseradish (the traditional accompaniment to roast beef) as a spicy *granité* to garnish this creamy soup.

- 1 quart chicken stock
- 2 cups whole milk
- 2 large thyme sprigs
- 2 bay leaves
- 3 tablespoons vegetable oil
- 1 pound red potatoes, peeled and thinly sliced
- 2 large leeks, white and tender green parts only, halved lengthwise and thinly sliced

Salt

- 5 ounces spinach leaves

Freshly ground pepper

Horseradish Granité (recipe follows), for serving

- 8 baguette slices, toasted

1. In a large saucepan, combine the chicken stock with the whole milk, thyme sprigs and bay leaves. Cover and bring to a simmer over low heat.

2. In a large saucepan, heat the vegetable oil. Add the potatoes and leeks and season lightly with salt. Cover and cook over moderately low heat until the vegetables are softened, about 7 minutes. Pour the stock mixture over the potatoes and leeks, cover and simmer over moderately low heat until the potatoes are tender, about 15 minutes. Discard the thyme and bay leaves.

3. Bring the soup to a boil. Add the spinach and wilt over moderately high heat, about 1 minute. Working in batches, puree the soup in a blender. Return the soup to the saucepan; season with salt and pepper.

4. Ladle the soup into bowls. Scoop a rounded tablespoon of the Horseradish Granité onto each toast. Float the toasts in the soup and serve right away.
—*Tristan Welch*

HORSERADISH GRANITÉ

TOTAL: 15 MIN PLUS 1 HR FREEZING

MAKES ¾ CUP ● ○

- ½ cup milk
- 2 tablespoons prepared horseradish, drained

Salt

In a blender, puree the milk with the horseradish. Transfer to a small glass baking dish and season with salt. Freeze for about 1 hour, until firm. Using a fork, scrape the *granité* until snow-like; serve. —*TW*

Watercress Soup with Pickled Cucumbers

ACTIVE: 30 MIN; TOTAL: 1 HR

8 SERVINGS ● ●

Quick-pickled cucumber slices give this delicate, fresh-tasting soup a little zing.

- 3 tablespoons extra-virgin olive oil
- 1 large leek, white and tender green parts only, thinly sliced
- 2 cups low-sodium chicken broth
- 2 cups water

One 8-ounce Yukon Gold potato, peeled and sliced ⅓ inch thick

- ½ pound watercress, coarsely chopped (5 cups)
- 1 cup whole milk
- 1 cup skim milk

Salt and freshly ground pepper

- ½ European cucumber, peeled
- 1 tablespoon unseasoned rice vinegar

1. In a large saucepan, heat the olive oil. Add the leek and cook over moderate heat, stirring, until softened, about 3 minutes. Add the broth and water and bring to a boil. Add the potato, cover and simmer over low heat until tender, about 15 minutes. Add the watercress and cook until bright green, about 2 minutes.

2. Working in batches, puree the soup in a blender. Return the soup to the saucepan. Add the whole and skim milks and season with salt and pepper; keep warm.

3. Meanwhile, trim the peeled cucumber to form a rectangle. Cut the cucumber crosswise into very thin slices. In a medium bowl, combine the rice vinegar with a large pinch of salt. Add the cucumber slices and toss well. Let stand until they have softened, about 5 minutes.

4. Ladle the soup into bowls. Garnish with cucumber slices and serve.
—Marcia Kiesel

MAKE AHEAD The soup can be refrigerated for up to 2 days.

Pea Consommé with Mint

ACTIVE: 25 MIN; TOTAL: 2 HR 25 MIN

4 SERVINGS ● ● ●

Napa chef Jeremy Fox (an F&W Best New Chef 2008) tops this healthy consommé with shards of white chocolate. He likes the way the chocolate brings out the peas' sweetness while adding only a little fat.

- 2 pounds English peas in the pod, peas shelled and pods reserved, or 1 pound snow peas plus one 9-ounce box frozen peas, thawed
- 1 garlic clove, smashed
- 1 medium shallot, thinly sliced
- ⅓ cup small mint leaves
- 1 quart water
- 2 teaspoons Champagne vinegar
- 2 teaspoons fresh lemon juice

Salt

- 1 tablespoon extra-virgin olive oil
- 2 tablespoons roasted macadamia nuts, chopped
- 2 tablespoons chopped white chocolate
- ½ cup pea shoots

1. In a 12-inch piece of cheesecloth, wrap the pea pods or snow peas with the smashed garlic clove, thinly sliced shallot and 1 tablespoon of the mint leaves into a flat bundle; tie with kitchen twine. In a large saucepan, cover the bundle with the water and bring to a simmer. Cover and cook over very low heat for 2 hours.

2. Strain the consommé into a bowl, pressing on the bundle. Return the consommé to the saucepan. Add the peas, Champagne vinegar and fresh lemon juice and season with salt. Cover and reheat gently. Ladle the pea consommé into soup bowls and drizzle with the olive oil. Garnish with the macadamia nuts, white chocolate, pea shoots and the remaining mint leaves and serve. —Jeremy Fox

MAKE AHEAD The soup can be refrigerated for up to 2 days. Reheat gently.

Zucchini-and-Fennel Soup

TOTAL: 55 MIN

8 SERVINGS ● ●

This soothing, mellow soup from Peter Ting, a London-based ceramicist and cook, is terrific served hot or cold.

- 1 large fennel bulb—8 small fronds reserved, bulb cored and sliced ½ inch thick
- 2 tablespoons fresh lemon juice

Salt

- 2 tablespoons extra-virgin olive oil
- 1¾ pounds zucchini, sliced crosswise ¼ inch thick
- 1 large onion, thinly sliced
- 1 large garlic clove, smashed
- 1 quart chicken stock

Freshly ground pepper

- ½ cup crème fraîche

1. In a medium saucepan, cover the sliced fennel with water. Add the lemon juice and a large pinch of salt and bring to a boil. Cover and simmer over low heat until the fennel is tender when pierced with a knife, about 20 minutes. Drain the fennel.

2. In a large pot, heat the olive oil. Add the zucchini, onion and garlic, season with salt and cook over moderate heat, stirring occasionally, until the vegetables are just softened, about 10 minutes. Add the chicken stock and cooked fennel and bring to a boil. Cover partially and simmer over moderate heat, stirring a few times, until the vegetables have softened completely, about 8 minutes.

3. Working in batches, puree the soup in a blender. Return the soup to the pot and season with salt and pepper. Ladle the soup into shallow bowls. Dollop 1 tablespoon of the crème fraîche into each serving and swirl in. Garnish with the fennel fronds and serve the soup right away.
—Peter Ting

MAKE AHEAD The soup can be refrigerated for up to 2 days. Reheat gently or serve the soup cold.

soups

Smoky Tomato Soup with Maple-Candied Bacon

TOTAL: 30 MIN
4 SERVINGS ● ●

- 8 slices of thick-cut applewood-smoked bacon (8 ounces)
- 2 tablespoons maple sugar or light brown sugar (see Note)
- 2 tablespoons unsalted butter
- ¼ cup extra-virgin olive oil
- 1 small onion, finely chopped
- 3 large garlic cloves, minced
- 1½ tablespoons tomato paste
- 3 tablespoons granulated sugar
- 1 teaspoon smoked paprika
- 1 teaspoon grated orange zest
- ½ teaspoon piment d'Espelette (see Note on p. 106)

Kosher salt and freshly ground pepper

- ½ cup dry rosé wine

Two 15-ounce cans chopped tomatoes

- 2 cups water
- ¼ cup fresh orange juice
- 3 tablespoons sour cream

1. Preheat the oven to 400°. Line a rimmed baking sheet with parchment. Arrange the bacon on the paper and bake for 8 minutes, until almost crisp. Drain the oil from the baking sheet. Sprinkle the bacon with the sugar and bake for 8 minutes, until glazed; cool.

2. Meanwhile, in a saucepan, melt the butter in the olive oil. Add the chopped onion and cook over moderately high heat until softened, 5 minutes. Add the garlic and cook over moderate heat for 30 seconds. Add the tomato paste and cook, stirring, until darkened, about 2 minutes. Stir in the granulated sugar, smoked paprika, orange zest, piment d'Espelette, 1 tablespoon of salt and ¼ teaspoon of pepper and cook for 30 seconds. Add the rosé and bring to a boil. Add the tomatoes with their juices; bring to a simmer. Remove from the heat.

3. Stir the water, orange juice and sour cream into the saucepan. Working in batches, puree the soup until smooth. Return the soup to the saucepan; season with salt and pepper. Reheat, ladle into bowls and serve with the bacon. The soup can be served chilled. —*Naomi Pomeroy*

NOTE Maple sugar, which is made from the boiled sap of the sugar maple tree, is available at health-food stores.

Celery Root Soup with Clementine-Relish Toasts

ACTIVE: 30 MIN; TOTAL: 50 MIN
4 SERVINGS ●

- 1 tablespoon unsalted butter
- 1 medium leek, white and tender green parts only, thinly sliced
- 1½ pounds celery root, peeled and cut into 1-inch cubes
- 2 cups low-sodium chicken broth
- 1 cup water
- ¼ cup heavy cream

Salt and freshly ground white pepper

- 2 firm clementines
- 1 medium shallot, minced
- ½ teaspoon white wine vinegar
- ¼ teaspoon yellow mustard seeds
- ½ teaspoon minced tarragon

Four ½-inch-thick baguette toasts

1. Preheat the oven to 350°. In a saucepan, melt the butter. Add the leek and cook over moderately low heat, stirring, until softened. Add the celery root, broth and water. Bring to a simmer; cook until the celery root is tender, 20 minutes. Puree the soup in a blender; return to the saucepan and stir in the cream. Season with salt and pepper.

2. Meanwhile, remove the peel and white pith from the clementines. Working over a skillet, cut between the membranes to release the sections. Squeeze the juice from the membranes into the skillet; add the shallot, vinegar and mustard seeds. Cook over moderately high heat, stirring, until most of the juice has evaporated and the fruit has started to break down, 2 minutes. Let cool to room temperature. Stir in the tarragon; season with salt. Spread the relish over the toasts and serve with the soup. —*Laura Adrian and Braden Perkins*

Mushroom Soup with Toasted Bread

ACTIVE: 30 MIN; TOTAL: 2 HR 10 MIN
12 SERVINGS ● ● ●

To thicken the texture and deepen the flavor of this lush mushroom soup, legendary chef Michel Bras purees it with bread toasted to a dark brown. He learned the trick from his mother growing up in the Aubrac mountains, one of France's poorest regions. "I used to mix bread crumbs with sugar for a little treat," Bras says. "We were happy with very little."

Three ½-inch slices of sourdough bread (6 ounces), crusts removed

- 4 tablespoons unsalted butter
- 1½ pounds white mushrooms, coarsely chopped
- 2 portobello mushrooms—stems discarded, black gills reserved for garnish, caps coarsely chopped
- 2 large garlic cloves, thinly sliced

Salt and freshly ground white pepper

- 6 cups vegetable broth or water
- ¾ cup heavy cream
- 12 dill sprigs

1. Preheat the oven to 300°. Bake the bread slices on a baking sheet for about 1 hour and 40 minutes, until deeply browned.

2. In a pot, melt the butter. Add the mushrooms and garlic; season with salt and pepper. Cover and cook over moderate heat until the mushrooms are softened, 5 minutes. Add the broth and ½ cup of the cream; bring to a boil. Cover and simmer until the mushrooms are tender, 10 minutes.

3. Add the toasted bread to the soup; simmer until softened, 5 minutes. Working in batches, puree the soup in a food processor. Return the soup to the pot, season with salt and pepper and keep warm.

4. In a saucepan, bring the remaining ¼ cup of cream to a boil. Remove from the heat; whisk until frothy. Ladle the soup into bowls, top with the frothed cream, garnish with the dill and portobello gills and serve. —*Michel Bras*

MUSHROOM SOUP
WITH TOASTED BREAD

soups

Roasted Squash Soup with Maple-Glazed Bananas

ACTIVE: 30 MIN; TOTAL: 1 HR 30 MIN
8 SERVINGS ● ● ●

Tim Hollingsworth of the French Laundry in Yountville, California, recently represented the United States at the prestigious Bocuse d'Or international chef competition. He made this fabulous butternut squash soup for a special F&W challenge: to create a gorgeous menu that even a novice cook could prepare.

One 2-pound butternut squash, halved lengthwise and seeded
Kosher salt
½ cup pecans
1 banana, scooped into balls with a melon baller or sliced ½ inch thick
1 tablespoon pure maple syrup
1 cup water
½ cup crème fraîche
Pinch of cinnamon
8 small watercress sprigs, for garnish

1. Preheat the oven to 375°. Butter a medium baking dish. Season the squash with salt and set it cut side down in the baking dish. Bake for about 1 hour and 10 minutes, until very tender. Let cool slightly.
2. Meanwhile, spread the pecans in a pie plate and toast for about 7 minutes, or until fragrant. Let cool, then coarsely chop and transfer to a medium bowl. Add the banana and maple syrup and stir to coat.
3. Peel the roasted squash. In a blender, puree the squash, water, crème fraîche and cinnamon until very smooth. Transfer to a medium saucepan and warm over low heat. Ladle the soup into shallow bowls and garnish with the banana-nut topping and watercress sprigs. Serve hot or at room temperature.
—Timothy Hollingsworth

MAKE AHEAD The soup can be refrigerated for up to 2 days. Reheat it gently and make the garnish just before serving.

Creamy Spring Onion Soup

ACTIVE: 30 MIN; TOTAL: 1 HR
8 SERVINGS ● ●

2 tablespoons extra-virgin olive oil
4 bunches of scallions—white and tender green parts cut into 1-inch lengths, green tops thinly sliced
4 leeks, white and tender green parts only, thinly sliced
1 fennel bulb, thinly sliced
1 onion, thinly sliced
Salt and freshly ground white pepper
2 cups dry white wine
3 cups water
2 cups heavy cream
¾ cup buttermilk
2 ounces fresh goat cheese (¼ cup), softened

1. In a large pot, heat the olive oil. Add the white and tender green parts of the scallions along with the leeks, fennel and onion; season the vegetables with salt and white pepper. Cook over low heat, stirring frequently, until the vegetables begin to soften, about 15 minutes. Add the white wine and boil over high heat until reduced to a few tablespoons, about 12 minutes. Add the water and cream and bring to a simmer. Cook until the vegetables are very tender and pale green, about 15 minutes longer. Add the scallion tops and cook just until softened, about 2 minutes.
2. Working in batches, puree the soup in a blender and return it to the pot. Season with salt and white pepper.
3. In a medium bowl, whisk the buttermilk with the fresh goat cheese. Ladle the soup into shallow bowls, drizzle with the goat cheese and buttermilk mixture and serve.
—Gerard Craft

VARIATION In the spring, you can use green garlic (which is harvested before the cloves have matured and has a subtle garlic flavor) in place of the scallions.

MAKE AHEAD The spring onion soup and creamy goat cheese mixture can be refrigerated separately overnight.

Black Lentil Soup

ACTIVE: 20 MIN; TOTAL: 1 HR 15 MIN
4 SERVINGS ● ● ●

This earthy lentil soup is San Francisco wine expert Rajat Parr's take on dal, the ubiquitous Indian side dish. He gives the staple unexpected richness by whisking in butter just before serving.

1 cup black lentils (6 ounces)
2 cardamom pods
One 1-inch piece of fresh ginger, peeled and thinly sliced, plus 2 tablespoons minced ginger
5 tablespoons unsalted butter
1 onion, cut into ½-inch dice
2 garlic cloves, minced
½ teaspoon ground coriander
½ teaspoon ground cumin
¼ teaspoon cayenne pepper
¼ teaspoon garam masala
2 quarts vegetable stock or low-sodium broth
1 cup canned crushed tomatoes
Salt

1. In a pot, cover the lentils, cardamom and sliced ginger with 1 inch of water. Bring to a boil and cook over moderately high heat until the lentils start to soften, about 10 minutes. Drain the lentils and transfer to a bowl; discard the cardamom and ginger.
2. Melt 3 tablespoons of the butter in the pot. Add the onion, garlic and minced ginger and cook over moderate heat, stirring occasionally, until softened, 8 minutes. Reduce the heat to low. Add the coriander, cumin, cayenne and garam masala and cook, stirring, until fragrant, 4 minutes.
3. Add the stock, tomatoes and lentils to the pot and bring to a boil over high heat. Simmer over moderate heat until the lentils are softened and the soup has thickened, about 1 hour. Stir in the remaining 2 tablespoons of butter and season with salt. Ladle into bowls and serve.
—Rajat Parr

MAKE AHEAD The lentil soup can be refrigerated for up to 2 days; rewarm gently.

perfecting creamy soup

These luxuriously creamy soups from F&W's **Marcia Kiesel** *are the perfect starters for a dinner party because they can be made in advance, then reheated and garnished just before serving.*

Creamy Carrot Soup with Scallions and Poppy Seeds

ACTIVE: 35 MIN; TOTAL: 1 HR

12 SERVINGS ● ● ● ●

- 2 tablespoons unsalted butter
- 3 tablespoons extra-virgin olive oil
- 1 large onion, coarsely chopped
- 1 quart low-sodium vegetable broth
- 1 quart water
- 2 pounds carrots, sliced ⅓ inch thick
- 6 large scallions, thinly sliced crosswise
- 2 teaspoons poppy seeds
- ½ cup heavy cream
- ½ cup milk

Salt and freshly ground pepper

1. In a large pot, melt the butter in 1 tablespoon of the olive oil. Add the onion, cover and cook over low heat, stirring occasionally, until softened, about 5 minutes. Add the broth and water along with the carrots and bring to a boil over high heat. Cover and simmer over low heat until the carrots are tender, about 30 minutes.

2. Meanwhile, in a small saucepan, heat the remaining 2 tablespoons of olive oil. Add the scallions and poppy seeds and cook over moderately high heat, stirring, until the scallions are softened, about 1 minute.

3. Working in batches, puree the carrot soup in a blender until completely smooth; transfer to a clean saucepan. Stir in the cream and milk and simmer over moderate heat, stirring. Season the soup with salt and pepper and ladle into bowls. Garnish with the sliced scallions and poppy seeds and serve the soup right away.

MAKE AHEAD The carrot soup can be refrigerated overnight. Reheat gently.

TWO GREAT VARIATIONS

---

1 Creamy Parsnip Soup with Prosciutto

Replace the carrots with 2½ pounds parsnips. Peel the parsnips and cut them into 2-inch chunks. Add to the broth and simmer the soup for about 30 minutes, until tender. Puree the soup in batches as directed. For the garnish, cut 2 ounces thinly sliced prosciutto into ¼-inch-wide strips. Cook the prosciutto in 1 tablespoon olive oil until crisp; drain the strips on paper towels. Garnish the parsnip soup with the crispy prosciutto strips and 1 tablespoon fresh thyme leaves.

2 Creamy Broccoli Soup with Croutons

Replace the carrots with 2 heads of broccoli, stems peeled. Reserve 3 cups of florets. Chop the remaining broccoli and add to the onion in Step 1. Simmer the soup for 20 minutes, then add 2 cups of the reserved broccoli florets; cover and simmer until the broccoli is barely tender. Puree in batches as directed. Cook the remaining 1 cup broccoli florets in 2 tablespoons olive oil in a covered skillet until browned. Garnish the soup with the browned florets and small croutons.

soups

Lentil Soup with Smoked Turkey

ACTIVE: 30 MIN; TOTAL: 1 HR 45 MIN

4 TO 6 SERVINGS ● ● ●

Simmering a Parmesan rind in the broth along with the smoked turkey and lentils would give this soup an even richer taste.

 1 tablespoon extra-virgin olive oil
 3 garlic cloves, peeled
 2 celery ribs, finely chopped
 2 carrots, finely chopped
 1 onion, finely chopped
One 16-ounce can whole tomatoes, chopped and juices reserved
 1 bay leaf
 1 cup green or brown lentils
 ¾ pound smoked turkey wing and thigh
 2 quarts water
 4 small red potatoes, peeled and sliced ¼ inch thick
 ¼ cup chopped flat-leaf parsley
Salt and freshly ground pepper
Freshly grated Parmigiano-Reggiano cheese, for serving

1. In a large soup pot, heat the olive oil. Add the garlic, celery, carrots and onion and cook over moderate heat, stirring occasionally, until softened, 7 minutes. Add the tomatoes, bay leaf, lentils, smoked turkey and water and bring to a boil. Cover partially and simmer, stirring occasionally, until the lentils are very tender, 1 hour. Add the potatoes and simmer until tender, about 10 minutes longer.

2. Remove the turkey meat from the bones and add the meat to the soup; discard the turkey skin, bones and bay leaf. Add the chopped parsley and season the soup with salt and pepper. Ladle into bowls and serve hot, passing the grated Parmigiano-Reggiano cheese at the table.
—Eugenia Bone

MAKE AHEAD The lentil soup can be refrigerated for up to 3 days.

Minestrone with Black-Eyed Peas and Kidney Beans

ACTIVE: 30 MIN; TOTAL: 1 HR 30 MIN

6 SERVINGS ● ●

 3 tablespoons extra-virgin olive oil
 2 ounces pancetta, finely diced
 1 large onion, finely chopped
 2 celery ribs, thinly sliced
 4 garlic cloves, thinly sliced
 1 leek, white and tender green parts thinly sliced, 1 dark top reserved
Salt and freshly ground pepper
 ½ pound Savoy or other green cabbage, coarsely shredded
One 14-ounce can diced tomatoes
 1 cup dried black-eyed peas
 2 quarts water
 3 parsley sprigs
 1 bay leaf
 3 thyme sprigs
One 15-ounce can red kidney beans, drained and rinsed
 2 ounces penne
 ½ cup shredded basil
 ¼ cup plus 2 tablespoons freshly grated Parmigiano-Reggiano cheese

1. In a large soup pot, heat 2 tablespoons of the olive oil. Add the pancetta, onion, celery, garlic and sliced leek and season with salt and pepper. Cook over moderate heat until the vegetables are softened, 10 minutes. Add the cabbage and cook until slightly wilted, 1 minute. Add the tomatoes and cook for about 5 minutes. Add the black-eyed peas and water; bring to a boil. Wrap the parsley, bay leaf and thyme in the reserved leek top and secure with kitchen twine. Add to the pot.

2. Cover the pot and simmer over low heat until the black-eyed peas are tender, 45 minutes. Discard the herbs. Add the kidney beans and simmer for 10 minutes longer.

3. Meanwhile, in a pot of boiling salted water, cook the penne until al dente. Drain and cool under running water. Slice the penne crosswise into ¼-inch rings.

4. In a nonstick skillet, heat the remaining 1 tablespoon of oil. Add the penne in a single layer and cook over moderately high heat, turning once, until golden, 5 minutes. Drain the penne rings on paper towels.

5. Stir the pasta and basil into the soup. Ladle the soup into bowls, sprinkle each with 1 tablespoon of the cheese and serve.
—Mark Peel

Hearty Minestrone Soup

ACTIVE: 30 MIN; TOTAL: 2 HR 30 MIN PLUS OVERNIGHT SOAKING

4 SERVINGS ● ●

 1¼ cups dried white beans (8 ounces), such as cannellini or navy, soaked overnight and drained
 3 tablespoons extra-virgin olive oil
 2 ounces pancetta, finely diced
 2 medium shallots, minced
 2 large celery ribs, finely diced
 1 medium onion, finely diced
 1 large carrot, finely diced
 ½ fennel bulb, cored and diced
 4 garlic cloves, minced
 ½ teaspoon crushed red pepper
 2 bay leaves
 2 tablespoons tomato paste
One 14-ounce can plum tomatoes, chopped, juices reserved
 1 quart low-sodium chicken broth
Salt and freshly ground pepper
 1 cup baby arugula
 ½ cup flat-leaf parsley leaves
 1 tablespoon fresh lemon juice

1. In a large pot, cover the beans with 2 inches of water and bring to a boil. Simmer over low heat, stirring occasionally, until tender, about 2 hours; add water as necessary to keep the beans covered. Drain the beans and reserve the cooking liquid.

2. Meanwhile, in another large pot, heat 2 tablespoons of the olive oil. Add the pancetta and cook over moderate heat until the fat has rendered and the pancetta is

MINESTRONE WITH BLACK-EYED PEAS AND KIDNEY BEANS

BLACK BEAN SOUP WITH CRISPY TORTILLAS

crisp, about 4 minutes. Add the shallots, celery, onion, carrot and fennel and cook, stirring occasionally, until the vegetables are softened, about 6 minutes. Add the garlic, crushed red pepper and bay leaves and cook, stirring, until fragrant, about 2 minutes. Add the tomato paste and cook, stirring, until it sticks to the bottom of the pot, about 2 minutes. Stir in the plum tomatoes and chicken broth; bring to a boil. Simmer over low heat until the vegetables are very tender and the soup is flavorful, about 1 hour. Add the beans and enough of the reserved cooking liquid to thin out the soup. Discard the bay leaves; season with salt and pepper.

3. In a bowl, toss the arugula and parsley with the lemon juice and remaining 1 tablespoon of oil. Season with salt and pepper. Serve the soup in bowls; top with the salad. —David Bull

Black Bean Soup with Crispy Tortillas

TOTAL: 35 MIN
4 SERVINGS ● ● ○ ○

This hearty, ultrasimple soup requires little more than a couple of cans of black beans, some chopped onion and a bit of ground cumin. A topping of fried tortilla wedges (or store-bought chips if you prefer to skip the frying) adds crunch.

Vegetable oil, for frying
Three 6-inch corn tortillas,
    cut into narrow wedges
Kosher salt
  1 medium onion, cut into
      ¼-inch dice
  1 teaspoon ground cumin
Two 15-ounce cans black beans
  2 tablespoons chopped
      fresh cilantro
Freshly ground pepper

1. In a medium saucepan, heat ½ inch of vegetable oil over moderately high heat until a deep-fry thermometer registers 350°. Add the tortillas and fry, stirring occasionally, until crisp and lightly golden, about 1½ minutes. Using a slotted spoon, transfer the tortillas to paper towels to drain; season with salt.

2. In a medium soup pot, heat 2 tablespoons of the oil used to fry the tortillas. Add the onion and cook over moderate heat until softened, about 6 minutes. Add the cumin and cook for 1 minute. Add the beans and their liquid and 1½ cups of water. Bring to a simmer and cook until slightly thickened, about 15 minutes. Stir in 1 tablespoon of the cilantro and season with salt and pepper. Ladle the soup into bowls and top with a few tortillas. Sprinkle with the remaining 1 tablespoon of cilantro and serve. —Melissa Rubel Jacobson

● HEALTHY ● MAKE AHEAD ○ VEGETARIAN ● STAFF FAVORITE

soups

Cranberry Bean Soup

ACTIVE: 45 MIN; TOTAL: 1 HR 45 MIN

6 SERVINGS ● ●

Fresh cranberry beans (also known as shell beans or *borlotti*) have a delicate, nutty taste. Simmered for an hour in this soup, they become soft and creamy.

- 1 tablespoon extra-virgin olive oil
- ½ cup chopped pancetta (3 ounces)
- 3 garlic cloves, minced
- 2 large celery ribs, finely chopped
- 2 carrots, finely chopped
- 1 onion, finely chopped
- 6 cups water
- 3 cups fresh cranberry beans (from 2½ pounds in the shell)
- 1 cup chopped canned tomatoes
- 1 bay leaf

One 3-inch-wide Parmigiano-Reggiano cheese rind, plus ½ cup freshly grated cheese for serving

Salt

- ½ pound small-cut pasta, such as elbows

Freshly ground pepper

- 3 tablespoons chopped flat-leaf parsley

1. In a large pot, heat the olive oil. Add the pancetta and cook over moderate heat until the fat has rendered, about 4 minutes. Add the garlic, celery, carrots and onion and cook over moderate heat, stirring occasionally, until softened, about 7 minutes. Add the water, beans, tomatoes, bay leaf and cheese rind, cover and bring to a boil. Reduce the heat to low and simmer until the beans are tender, about 1 hour.
2. Meanwhile, in a medium saucepan of boiling salted water, cook the pasta until it is al dente. Drain.
3. Discard the bay leaf and cheese rind from the soup. Season the soup with salt and pepper and stir in the parsley. Spoon the pasta into 6 bowls and ladle the soup on top. Serve with the grated cheese.
—*Eugenia Bone*

Chickpeas and Swiss Chard in Sun-Dried-Tomato Broth

TOTAL: 30 MIN

4 SERVINGS ● ●

- 6 cups low-sodium chicken broth

One 2-inch-wide Parmigiano-Reggiano cheese rind, plus ½ cup freshly grated cheese for serving

Two 15-ounce cans chickpeas, rinsed and drained

- 1 bunch of Swiss chard (¾ pound), stems discarded and leaves cut into 1-inch ribbons
- ¼ cup plus 1½ tablespoons store-bought sun-dried-tomato pesto

Kosher salt and freshly ground black pepper

1. In a medium soup pot, bring the broth to a simmer with the cheese rind and the chickpeas. Cook over low heat until the broth is flavorful, about 10 minutes; discard the rind. Add the Swiss chard and simmer until wilted, about 4 minutes.
2. Remove from the heat and stir in ¼ cup of the sun-dried-tomato pesto. Season the soup with salt and pepper. Ladle into bowls and sprinkle with the grated cheese. Garnish each bowl with a dollop of the remaining pesto and serve.
—*Melissa Rubel Jacobson*

Colombian Chicken Soup

TOTAL: 1 HR

6 SERVINGS ● ● ●

Stirring plenty of chicken breast and brown rice into this version of *ajiaco*—the cilantro-scented chicken soup that's virtually Colombia's national dish—turns it into a satisfying one-dish meal.

- ⅔ cup short-grain brown rice
- 1⅓ cups water

Salt

- 1 whole skinless chicken breast, on the bone (about 1½ pounds)
- ½ cup thinly sliced scallions
- 2 garlic cloves, smashed
- 2 shucked ears of corn, each cut into 6 rounds
- ½ teaspoon ground cumin
- ½ cup plus 2 tablespoons chopped cilantro
- 8 cups low-sodium chicken broth

Freshly ground pepper

- ½ pound white potatoes, peeled and cut into ¾-inch cubes
- ½ pound thick asparagus, cut into 1-inch lengths
- 1 Hass avocado, diced
- ¼ cup plus 2 tablespoons fat-free yogurt
- 1 tablespoon drained small capers

1. In a small saucepan, cover the rice with the water and bring to a boil. Reduce the heat, cover and simmer until the rice is tender, 35 to 45 minutes. Remove from the heat and let stand for 10 minutes, then season with salt and fluff with a fork.
2. Meanwhile, in a large saucepan, combine the chicken, scallions, garlic, corn, cumin and ½ cup of the cilantro with the chicken broth. Season with salt and pepper and bring to a boil. Simmer the broth over moderately high heat until the chicken is cooked through, about 12 minutes. Transfer the chicken to a plate and let cool slightly. Pull the meat off the bones and shred.
3. Strain the broth and return it to the saucepan. Return the corn to the broth and discard the remaining solids. Bring the broth to a boil. Add the potatoes and simmer over moderately high heat until nearly tender, about 8 minutes. Add the asparagus and simmer until the potatoes and asparagus are tender, about 5 minutes longer. Return the shredded chicken to the pot and season the soup with salt and pepper.
4. Ladle the soup into bowls; garnish with the avocado, yogurt, capers, rice and remaining chopped cilantro and serve.
—*Doris Esther Ayola Orozco*

MAKE AHEAD The cooked brown rice and the soup without the garnishes can be refrigerated separately overnight.

soups

Avgolemono Chicken Soup with Rice

TOTAL: 30 MIN
4 SERVINGS ● ●

Avgolemono is a classic Greek sauce of chicken broth, egg yolks and lemon juice. With the addition of a bit more chicken broth, cooked white rice and shredded chicken, it becomes a comforting soup.

- 4 cups homemade chicken stock or low-sodium broth
- Salt and freshly ground pepper
- 2 cups cooked white rice, warmed
- 2 large egg yolks
- ¼ cup plus 2 tablespoons fresh lemon juice
- 1 rotisserie chicken, meat pulled from the bones and coarsely shredded (1 pound)
- ¼ cup chopped fresh dill

In a large saucepan, season the chicken stock with salt and pepper and bring to a simmer. Transfer 1 cup of the hot stock to a blender. Add ½ cup of the warm white rice, the egg yolks and the fresh lemon juice and puree until smooth. Stir the puree into the simmering stock along with the chicken and the remaining 1½ cups of rice and simmer until thickened slightly, about 10 minutes. Stir in the dill and serve.

—*Grace Parisi*

amp up your soup

To give soups more flavor and style, be creative. Top vegetable or bean soups with sour cream and crumbled bacon; float cheese crostini on creamy purees; or brighten Asian broths with hot sauce, scallions and cilantro.

Chicken Meatball Soup with Orzo

TOTAL: 30 MIN
4 SERVINGS ● ● ●

- 1 cup orzo
- 1 tablespoon extra-virgin olive oil
- 1 pound fresh chicken sausage, such as sweet Italian, casings discarded and meat rolled into twenty 1-inch meatballs
- 1 large garlic clove, very finely chopped
- 6 cups chicken stock or low-sodium broth
- Kosher salt and freshly ground black pepper
- One 5-ounce bag baby spinach (5 cups)

1. In a large saucepan of boiling salted water, cook the orzo until it is al dente, about 8 minutes. Drain and rinse the orzo under cold water until cool.

2. Meanwhile, in a medium soup pot, heat the olive oil until shimmering. Add the chicken meatballs and cook over moderately high heat until they are lightly browned, about 4 minutes. Using a slotted spoon, transfer the meatballs to a plate. Add the garlic to the pot and cook over moderate heat until lightly golden, about 1 minute. Add the chicken stock, bring to a simmer and season with salt and pepper. Add the chicken meatballs to the broth and simmer until they are cooked through, about 3 minutes.

3. Add the baby spinach and cooled orzo to the simmering chicken broth and cook, stirring, until the spinach is wilted and the soup is piping hot, about 1 minute. Ladle the meatball-and-orzo soup into shallow bowls and serve.

—*Melissa Rubel Jacobson*

MAKE AHEAD The chicken soup and cooked orzo can be refrigerated separately overnight. Add the cooked orzo and baby spinach just before heating and serving.

Smoky Ham-and-Corn Chowder

TOTAL: 35 MIN
4 SERVINGS ● ●

Simmering the ham rind and corn cobs in water makes a tasty stock for this luxurious ham-and-corn chowder.

- 4 ears of corn, kernels cut off and cobs reserved
- 1 tablespoon vegetable oil
- 1 onion, cut into ¼-inch dice
- One ½-pound piece of ham—rind removed and reserved, ham cut into ¼-inch dice
- 2 cups heavy cream
- 1 pound baking potatoes, peeled and cut into ½-inch dice
- Kosher salt and freshly ground pepper

1. Using the back of a knife and working over a bowl, scrape the corn cobs to release any pulp and juices; reserve the cobs.

2. In a medium soup pot, heat the vegetable oil. Add the onion and cook over moderate heat until softened, about 6 minutes. Add 3 cups of water, the ham rind and the corn cobs, pulp and juices and bring to a simmer. Cook over moderately low heat for 5 minutes; discard the cobs and ham rind. Add the heavy cream and potatoes, bring to a simmer and cook until the potatoes are almost tender, about 5 minutes. Add the corn kernels and ham and simmer until the corn and potatoes are tender, about 5 minutes longer. Season the soup with salt and pepper, ladle into bowls and serve hot.

—*Melissa Rubel Jacobson*

Cabbage, Kielbasa and Rice Soup

TOTAL: 30 MIN
4 SERVINGS ●

Good sausage is an excellent time-saver because the links are already spiced and seasoned. The slices of Polish kielbasa in this soup add a wonderfully smoky, peppery, garlicky flavor.

7¾ cups low-sodium chicken broth
1 cup long-grain white rice, such as
   basmati or jasmine
1 tablespoon vegetable oil
¾ pound kielbasa, halved lengthwise
   and thinly sliced
1 onion, halved and thinly sliced
½ medium green cabbage, cored
   and finely shredded
Kosher salt and freshly ground pepper

1. In a medium saucepan, combine 1¾ cups of the chicken broth with the rice and bring to a simmer. Cover and cook over low heat for about 18 minutes, until the rice is tender.

2. Meanwhile, in a soup pot, heat the oil. Add the kielbasa and cook over moderately high heat until lightly browned, about 4 minutes. Add the onion and cabbage and cook until softened, about 6 minutes. Add the remaining 6 cups of broth and bring to a simmer. Cook over moderately low heat until the cabbage is tender, 10 minutes. Season with salt and pepper, stir in the rice and serve.
—*Melissa Rubel Jacobson*

MAKE AHEAD The soup and the rice can be refrigerated separately overnight.

Country Potato-and-Cabbage Soup

ACTIVE: 30 MIN; TOTAL: 1 HR
4 SERVINGS ●
3 tablespoons extra-virgin olive oil
4 ounces thick-cut bacon, diced
1 large onion, thinly sliced
1 leek, white and tender
   green parts only, thinly sliced
½ cup dry white wine
6 parsley sprigs
6 thyme sprigs
1 bay leaf
1 pound small red
   potatoes, thinly sliced
6 cups chicken stock
1 pound green cabbage,
   finely shredded (4 cups)

Salt and freshly ground pepper
2 tablespoons snipped chives
Three ½-inch-thick slices of country
   bread, cut into cubes
2 garlic cloves, lightly smashed
2 tablespoons minced parsley

1. In a soup pot, heat 1 tablespoon of the oil. Add the bacon and cook over moderately high heat until crisp, 5 minutes. Add the onion and leek and cook over low heat until softened, 10 minutes. Add the wine and simmer until nearly evaporated, 5 minutes.

2. Tie the parsley sprigs, thyme sprigs and bay leaf with string; add to the pot along with the potatoes and stock. Bring to a boil, then simmer until the potatoes are tender, 10 minutes. Add the cabbage, season with salt and pepper and simmer until the cabbage is tender, 10 to 15 minutes longer. Discard the herb bundle. Stir in the chives.

3. Meanwhile, in a medium skillet, heat the remaining 2 tablespoons of oil. Add the bread and garlic and cook over moderate heat, stirring, until the croutons are golden brown, 6 minutes; discard the garlic. Season with salt and sprinkle with the parsley.

4. Ladle the soup into deep bowls. Sprinkle with the croutons and serve.
—*Mark Sullivan*

Fish-and-Shellfish Chowder

TOTAL: 1 HR
4 SERVINGS ● ●
To deepen the flavor of this lightly creamy, bacon-studded seafood chowder, chef Wade Murphy of the Lisloughrey Lodge in Cong, Ireland, adds the briny cooking liquid from the mussels and clams.
2 medium red potatoes, peeled
   and cut into ½-inch dice
2 cups water
2 tablespoons extra-virgin olive oil
1 medium onion, finely diced
2 garlic cloves, minced
½ cup dry white wine
2 dozen mussels, scrubbed
16 littleneck clams, scrubbed

2 slices of bacon, finely diced
1 celery rib, finely diced
1 tablespoon all-purpose flour
1 cup heavy cream
6 ounces skinless salmon fillet,
   cut into 1-inch cubes
6 ounces cleaned monkfish
   fillet, cut into 1-inch cubes
Salt and freshly ground pepper
2 tablespoons chopped
   flat-leaf parsley

1. In a saucepan, cover the potatoes with the water and bring to a boil. Cover and cook over moderate heat until the potatoes are tender, about 6 minutes. Remove from the heat and let stand, covered.

2. Meanwhile, in a large saucepan, heat 1 tablespoon of the oil. Add half of the onion and garlic and cook over moderate heat until softened, 5 minutes. Add the wine and bring to a boil. Add the mussels, cover and cook over moderately high heat until they open, 3 minutes; transfer to a bowl. Add the clams to the saucepan, cover and cook. As the clams open, transfer them to the bowl. Strain and reserve the cooking liquid. Remove the mussels and clams from their shells and coarsely chop them.

3. Wipe out the saucepan. Add the remaining 1 tablespoon of olive oil and the bacon and cook over moderate heat until crisp, 4 minutes. Add the celery and the remaining onion and garlic. Cover and cook over moderately low heat until softened, 7 minutes. Stir in the flour, then gradually whisk in the potato cooking water. Bring to a boil, whisking, and cook until thickened slightly. Add the potatoes and the cream and bring to a simmer. Add the salmon and monkfish and simmer over moderate heat, stirring a few times, until the fish is just cooked, 3 minutes. Add the mussels and clams and pour in their reserved cooking liquid, stopping before you reach the grit at the bottom; stir until heated through. Season with salt and pepper and add the parsley. Serve the chowder in bowls. —*Wade Murphy*

soups

Smoky Shrimp-and-Chorizo Soup

ACTIVE: 30 MIN; TOTAL: 1 HR 15 MIN
8 SERVINGS

- 2 pounds medium shrimp—shelled and deveined, shells reserved
- 2 quarts low-sodium chicken broth
- 8 ounces dry chorizo, peeled and thinly sliced
- 1 large sweet onion, diced
- 1 large carrot, cut into fine matchsticks
- 1 garlic clove, minced
- 1 teaspoon sweet smoked paprika
- One 28-ounce can diced tomatoes, drained
- 1 tablespoon all-purpose flour mixed with 2 tablespoons of water

Salt and freshly ground pepper
Avocado slices, for garnish
Garlic-rubbed toasts, for serving

1. In a medium saucepan, simmer the shrimp shells in the chicken broth, covered, for 10 minutes. Strain the broth and discard the shells.

2. In a large soup pot, cook the chorizo over moderate heat, stirring occasionally, until browned, about 5 minutes. Using a slotted spoon, transfer the chorizo to a plate. Add the onion, carrot, garlic and paprika to the pot and cook over moderate heat until softened, about 5 minutes. Add the tomatoes and cook until the liquid has evaporated, about 5 minutes. Return the chorizo to the pot, add the shrimp broth and bring to a boil. Simmer over moderate heat for 25 minutes. Stir the flour mixture, whisk it into the soup and boil for 2 minutes. Season with salt and pepper. Add the shrimp to the soup and cook just until pink and curled, about 2 minutes. Ladle the soup into bowls and top with the avocado. Serve with the toasts. —*Grace Parisi*

Provençal Fish Soup

ACTIVE: 40 MIN; TOTAL: 1 HR 30 MIN
4 SERVINGS ● ●

- ¼ cup extra-virgin olive oil
- 1 large onion, finely chopped
- 2 celery ribs, finely chopped
- 1 small carrot, finely chopped
- 6 garlic cloves, coarsely chopped
- Four 3-inch strips of orange zest
- 4 thyme sprigs
- 2 teaspoons fennel seeds
- 2 teaspoons coriander seeds
- Pinch of saffron threads
- 1 tablespoon tomato paste
- One 16-ounce can whole tomatoes, chopped and juices reserved
- Two 8-ounce bottles clam juice
- ¾ cup dry red wine
- ½ cup ruby port
- 1¾ pounds skinless grouper or red snapper fillets, coarsely chopped
- ½ pound medium shrimp in the shell
- 1 tablespoon Pernod

Salt and coarsely ground pepper

1. In a large pot, heat the oil. Add the onion, celery and carrot and cook over moderately high heat until softened, 5 minutes. Add the garlic, orange zest, thyme, fennel, coriander and saffron and cook over moderate heat, stirring, until fragrant, about 5 minutes. Stir in the tomato paste and cook over high heat until glossy, about 1 minute. Add the tomatoes, clam juice, red wine and port and bring to a boil. Add the grouper and shrimp, cover partially and simmer for 45 minutes. Discard the zest and thyme.

2. Working in batches, transfer the soup to a food processor and pulse until coarsely chopped. Rinse the pot. Set a food mill fitted with a coarse blade over the pot and run the soup through it; bring to a simmer. Stir in the Pernod and season with salt and pepper. Serve hot. —*Sara Simpson*

SERVE WITH Creamy Anchovy Rouille (recipe follows), baguette toasts and shredded Gruyère cheese.

CREAMY ANCHOVY ROUILLE

 TOTAL: 15 MIN
MAKES 1 CUP ●

- 1 small red bell pepper
- ½ cup mayonnaise
- 2 oil-packed anchovy fillets, drained and chopped
- 2 teaspoons Dijon mustard
- 2 teaspoons fresh lemon juice
- 2 garlic cloves, chopped
- Pinch of saffron threads
- 2 tablespoons extra-virgin olive oil

Salt and freshly ground pepper
Tabasco

Roast the bell pepper over a gas flame or under a preheated broiler, turning occasionally, until charred all over. Transfer to a plate to cool. Discard the skin, stem and seeds. Coarsely chop the pepper and transfer to a blender. Add the mayonnaise, anchovies, mustard, lemon juice, garlic and saffron and puree. With the machine on, add the oil. Season with salt, pepper and Tabasco; serve. —*SS*

Shoyu Ramen

ACTIVE: 1 HR; TOTAL: 5 HR PLUS OVERNIGHT CHILLING
8 SERVINGS ●
BROTH

- 4 pounds chicken necks and backs
- One 3-pound rack of pork baby back ribs, cut into 4 sections
- 1 large leek, halved lengthwise
- 2 ounces fresh ginger, thinly sliced (½ cup)
- 4 garlic cloves
- 4 quarts water
- ¼ cup plus 2 tablespoons shoyu or other soy sauce
- 1 tablespoon vegetable oil
- One 3½-pound boneless pork shoulder butt, trimmed and tied

Salt

- One 12-by-2-inch piece of kombu (seaweed; see Note)

PROVENÇAL FISH SOUP

SHOYU RAMEN

RAMEN

Shoyu or other soy sauce, for seasoning and brushing

24 **ounces fresh or 16 ounces dried** *chuka* **soba (curly noodles), boiled until al dente (see Note)**

5 **ounces baby spinach, steamed**

4 **large soft-boiled eggs, peeled and soaked for 1 hour in equal parts soy sauce and mirin (sweet rice wine)**

2 **thinly sliced scallions, 2 sheets of quartered nori (dried seaweed), rice vinegar and togarashi (Japanese chile powder), for garnishing and seasoning (see Note)**

1. MAKE THE BROTH: In a large stockpot, combine the chicken necks and backs, pork ribs, leek, ginger, garlic, water and shoyu. Bring to a boil.

2. Meanwhile, in a large skillet, heat the oil. Season the pork butt with salt and brown it well on all sides over high heat, 12 minutes; transfer to the stockpot. Simmer the broth over moderately low heat for 2 hours, until the pork butt and ribs are just tender; skim any scum that rises to the surface. Transfer the meat to a platter and refrigerate. Strain the broth.

3. Return the broth to the pot. Add the kombu and simmer over moderately low heat for 1 hour and 30 minutes. Let cool, then refrigerate the broth overnight.

4. THE NEXT DAY, PREPARE THE RAMEN: Preheat the broiler. Skim the fat off of the broth and discard the kombu. Bring to a simmer. Season with shoyu and keep hot.

5. Untie the pork butt and slice it across the grain ⅓ inch thick. Cut the ribs between the bones. Arrange the pork slices and ribs on a large baking sheet and brush with shoyu. Broil 8 inches from the heat for about 3 minutes, turning once, until the meat is crisp; keep warm.

6. Divide the noodles among 8 bowls; ladle 1½ cups of broth into each one. Add the spinach in piles. Drain the eggs, cut them in half and set a half in each bowl. Arrange 2 slices of pork butt and 1 rib in each bowl; garnish with the scallions and nori. Serve immediately, passing the vinegar and togarashi. —*Grace Parisi*

VARIATIONS Stir ½ teaspoon white miso, ½ teaspoon Madras curry paste or 2 teaspoons coarsely ground toasted sesame seeds into each serving of broth before adding the toppings.

MAKE AHEAD The broth can be refrigerated for up to 3 days or frozen for up to 2 months; discard the kombu after 1 day.

NOTE Japanese ingredients are available at asianfoodgrocer.com.

soups

Hot-and-Sour Soup

TOTAL: 30 MIN
4 SERVINGS ●

Boston chef Joanne Chang's version of the Chinese take-out standby has all of the tangy, peppery flavors of the traditional recipe but none of the gloppiness. Chang uses ground pork instead of thin strips of meat, which is a little unorthodox but a great time-saver.

- 2 tablespoons canola oil
- ½ pound ground pork
- 4 scallions—3 minced,
  1 thinly sliced
- One 1-inch piece of fresh ginger,
  peeled and minced
- 1 small garlic clove, minced
- 3½ cups low-sodium
  chicken broth
- 12 ounces medium-soft tofu,
  drained and diced
- 4 white button mushrooms,
  thinly sliced
- ¼ cup rice vinegar
- ¼ cup soy sauce
- 1 tablespoon sugar
- 2 teaspoons Tabasco
- 1 teaspoon freshly ground
  black pepper
- 1 tablespoon Asian sesame oil
- 2 teaspoons cornstarch
- 2 eggs, lightly beaten

1. In a large saucepan, heat the canola oil. Add the ground pork, minced scallions, ginger and garlic and stir-fry over moderately high heat until the pork is cooked through. Add the chicken broth and bring to a simmer. Add the tofu, mushrooms, rice vinegar, soy sauce, sugar, Tabasco, pepper and 2 teaspoons of the sesame oil and return the soup to a simmer.

2. Whisk the cornstarch with 2 teaspoons of water; whisk into the soup. Whisk in the eggs and simmer for 1 minute. Drizzle with the remaining 1 teaspoon of sesame oil, sprinkle with the sliced scallion and serve.
—*Joanne Chang*

Chilled Zucchini Soup with Purslane

TOTAL: 45 MIN PLUS 3 HR CHILLING
12 SERVINGS ● ● ○

This cool vegan soup from Alain Coumont, founder of the café chain Le Pain Quotidien, gets its creaminess from pureed zucchini, sautéed onion and garlic. It's brightened with purslane, a lemony weed that Coumont plucks from his country garden in the Languedoc region of southern France. If purslane is not available at your local farmers' market, substitute baby arugula leaves.

- 2 tablespoons extra-virgin
  olive oil, plus more for drizzling
- 1 small onion, thinly sliced
- 2 garlic cloves, thinly sliced
- 1 teaspoon thyme leaves
- 1 bay leaf
- 8 small zucchini (3 pounds),
  thinly sliced, plus long
  zucchini shavings for garnish
- Kosher salt
- 3 cups water
- 2 tablespoons finely shredded
  basil leaves
- 2 cups ice
- Freshly ground pepper
- 2 cups purslane or baby
  arugula leaves

1. In a large saucepan, heat the 2 tablespoons of olive oil. Add the onion and garlic and cook over moderate heat until translucent, about 8 minutes. Stir in the thyme and bay leaf and cook until fragrant, about 1 minute. Add the sliced zucchini, season with salt and cook, stirring occasionally, until tender, about 10 minutes. Add the water and bring to a boil. Remove the saucepan from the heat. Discard the bay leaf and stir in the shredded basil.

2. Working in batches, puree the soup in a blender until very smooth. Transfer the zucchini puree to a large bowl. Stir in the ice. Refrigerate the zucchini soup for at least 3 hours, until thoroughly chilled.

3. Season the soup with salt and pepper. Ladle into shallow bowls and top with a small handful of purslane and zucchini shavings. Drizzle with olive oil and serve.
—*Alain Coumont*

MAKE AHEAD The soup can be refrigerated for up to 1 day.

Cucumber-Yogurt Soup with Peperoncini

ACTIVE: 15 MIN; TOTAL: 45 MIN
6 SERVINGS ● ● ● ○

F&W's Marcia Kiesel serves peperoncini (long, thin Italian pickled chiles) with this otherwise mild soup to add an appealingly piquant flavor.

- 1 pound cucumbers—
  peeled, seeded and coarsely
  chopped, plus cucumber
  spears for serving
- 10 small peperoncini—
  4 stemmed, seeded and
  chopped, plus ¼ cup
  of liquid from the jar
- ¼ cup plus 2 tablespoons
  chopped fresh dill
- 1 cup plain whole-milk yogurt
- 1 cup buttermilk
- ¼ teaspoon ground cumin
- Salt

1. In a blender, puree the chopped cucumbers with the chopped peperoncini, the pickling liquid, 2 tablespoons of the dill, the yogurt and buttermilk until very smooth. Stir in the cumin and the remaining dill and season with salt. Refrigerate until chilled, about 30 minutes.

2. Ladle the soup into 6 bowls. Serve each bowl with a whole peperoncini and cucumber spears on the side.
—*Marcia Kiesel*

NOTE For a passed hors d'oeuvre, this soup can also be served in cups topped with a toothpick-speared peperoncino.

MAKE AHEAD The cucumber-yogurt soup can be refrigerated for up to 1 day. Stir before serving.

Chilled Red Bell Pepper Shooters

TOTAL: 30 MIN PLUS 1 HR CHILLING

6 SERVINGS ● ●

This cool, savory red pepper soup would be great for a picnic. Or pass it in shot glasses as an unusual hors d'oeuvre.

- 2 tablespoons extra-virgin olive oil
- 2 large red bell peppers (1 pound), thinly sliced
- 1 large garlic clove, very finely chopped
- 1 small onion, thinly sliced

Salt

- 1 teaspoon tomato paste
- 1 cup water
- ½ cup low-sodium chicken broth

Freshly ground black pepper

Vegetable oil, for frying

Two 6-inch corn tortillas, cut into 1-inch-wide strips

Freshly grated Parmigiano-Reggiano cheese, for dusting

1. In a large saucepan, heat the olive oil. Add the sliced red bell peppers, chopped garlic, sliced onion and a pinch of salt. Cover and cook over moderately low heat until the bell peppers are softened, about 8 minutes. Stir in the tomato paste, water and chicken broth and bring to a boil. Cover and simmer over low heat until the peppers are very tender, about 10 minutes.

cold soup tips

Make soups supersmooth by pureeing, then straining them.

Enrich soups by swirling in heavy cream or crème fraîche.

Add ice cubes to each soup bowl on very hot days.

Top bowls with a refreshing garnish like cucumber slices or a few lightly dressed salad leaves.

2. Transfer the red pepper soup to a blender and puree until smooth. Season with salt and pepper and refrigerate for about 1 hour, until lightly chilled.

3. Meanwhile, in a large skillet, heat ¼ inch of vegetable oil until shimmering. Add the tortilla strips and fry over moderately high heat until crisp. Use a slotted spoon to transfer the tortilla strips to paper towels to drain. Dust the warm tortilla strips with the grated Parmigiano-Reggiano cheese. Serve the chilled red bell pepper soup in shot glasses with the tortilla strips.
—*Marcia Kiesel*

White Gazpacho

TOTAL: 25 MIN PLUS 1 HR CHILLING

6 SERVINGS ● ● ○ ○

- ½ medium head of cauliflower, cut into 1-inch florets
- 2 slices of white bread, crusts trimmed off
- ¼ cup pine nuts (1½ ounces)
- 2 medium garlic cloves, coarsely chopped
- 2 tablespoons sherry vinegar
- 1 large shallot, coarsely chopped
- 1¼ cups blanched slivered almonds (about 6½ ounces)
- ½ medium seedless cucumber, peeled and coarsely chopped, plus ¼ cup finely diced cucumber for garnish
- ⅓ cup extra-virgin olive oil

Kosher salt

1. In a large saucepan of boiling salted water, cook the cauliflower until tender, about 8 minutes. Drain, rinse under cold water until cool and drain well.

2. In a blender, combine 1½ cups of cold water with the cooked cauliflower, bread, pine nuts, chopped garlic, sherry vinegar, chopped shallot, 1 cup of the slivered almonds and the coarsely chopped cucumber; blend until smooth. Add the olive oil

and pulse just until incorporated. If necessary, add more water to thin the gazpacho. Season the soup with salt and refrigerate until chilled, about 1 hour.

3. Preheat the oven to 350°. Spread the remaining ¼ cup of slivered almonds in a pie plate and toast for about 6 minutes, until fragrant and lightly golden. Ladle the gazpacho into bowls. Garnish the soup with the toasted almonds and the finely diced cucumber and serve.
—*Joy Manning*

MAKE AHEAD The gazpacho can be refrigerated overnight. Garnish with the almonds and diced cucumber just before serving.

Cherry Gazpacho with Basil

ACTIVE: 45 MIN; TOTAL: 3 HR

4 SERVINGS ● ● ○

Chef Daniel Humm's ingenious gazpacho—a simplified version of a soup he serves at his haute New York City restaurant, Eleven Madison Park—combines pureed juicy bing cherries with red wine vinegar and Tabasco, all topped with elegant croutons.

Two 1-inch-thick slices of white Pullman bread

- ½ cup extra-virgin olive oil, plus more for drizzling
- 3 garlic cloves, 1 thinly sliced
- 1 red bell pepper, coarsely chopped
- 1 yellow bell pepper, coarsely chopped
- 1 seedless cucumber, peeled and coarsely chopped
- 1 pound bing cherries, pitted, 12 cherries finely diced
- 3 ounces tomato juice
- 1½ ounces red wine vinegar

Salt and freshly ground pepper

- 1 thyme sprig

Tabasco

- 4 basil leaves, torn, for garnish

1. Drizzle 1 slice of the bread with olive oil on both sides. In a medium skillet, fry the bread over moderate heat, turning once or twice, until golden, about 4 minutes.

Rub the fried bread on one side with 1 whole garlic clove. Cut the bread into 1-inch cubes and transfer to a medium bowl. Add the sliced garlic, red and yellow bell peppers, cucumber, whole pitted cherries, tomato juice, red wine vinegar and ¼ cup of the olive oil. Season lightly with salt and pepper and let stand at room temperature for about 2 hours.

2. Meanwhile, remove the crust from the remaining bread slice. Cut the bread into ½-inch cubes and toss with the remaining ¼ cup of olive oil. Add the bread cubes to the skillet along with the thyme sprig and the remaining whole garlic clove and cook over moderate heat, stirring frequently, until the croutons are browned and crisp, about 4 minutes. Transfer the croutons to paper towels to drain. Discard the garlic clove and thyme sprig and season the croutons with salt.

3. Working in batches, puree the cherry and bell pepper mixture in a blender until completely smooth. Strain the gazpacho through a fine-mesh sieve into a medium bowl. Season the soup with salt, pepper and Tabasco.

4. Ladle the cherry gazpacho into shallow bowls. Garnish with the diced cherries, croutons and torn basil leaves. Drizzle with olive oil and serve the soup right away. —Daniel Humm

MAKE AHEAD The cherry gazpacho can be prepared through Step 3 up to 1 day ahead. Refrigerate the gazpacho and store the croutons in an airtight container at room temperature.

Tangy Green Zebra Gazpacho

TOTAL: 30 MIN PLUS 1 HR CHILLING
10 SERVINGS ● ● ○

Green Zebras are striped heirloom tomatoes; they are sweet like red tomatoes but give this gazpacho a lovely jade hue. To make the chilled soup extra tangy, use tomatillos or unripe red tomatoes instead of Green Zebras.

2 pounds Green Zebra tomatoes, cored and coarsely chopped, plus 1 Green Zebra tomato cut into small wedges for garnish

1 seedless cucumber, unpeeled and coarsely chopped, plus finely diced unpeeled cucumber for garnish

1 medium sweet onion, coarsely chopped

1 Hass avocado—halved, pitted and peeled

1 small jalapeño, stemmed and seeded

2 medium garlic cloves

2 tablespoons fresh lime juice

2 tablespoons mint leaves, plus more for garnish

2 tablespoons cilantro leaves

¼ cup extra-virgin olive oil, plus more for drizzling

Salt and freshly ground black pepper

1. In a blender, combine half each of the coarsely chopped green tomatoes, cucumber and onion with the avocado, jalapeño, garlic, lime juice and 1 cup of cold water and puree until smooth. Transfer the puree to a large bowl.

2. Add the remaining coarsely chopped green tomatoes, cucumber and onion to the blender along with the 2 tablespoons of mint, the cilantro and ¼ cup of olive oil and pulse to a chunky puree. Add the puree to the bowl and stir well. Refrigerate the soup until well chilled, about 1 hour. Season the gazpacho with salt and black pepper and ladle it into chilled bowls. Garnish the cold soup with the tomato wedges, diced cucumber, mint leaves and a drizzle of olive oil and serve. —Katie Lee

MAKE AHEAD The green gazpacho can be stored in an airtight container and refrigerated overnight. Just before serving, stir the gazpacho and garnish with the tomato, cucumber, mint and olive oil.

Chilled Tomato Soup with Tarragon Crème Fraîche

photo, page 56
TOTAL: 20 MIN PLUS 2 HR CHILLING
6 SERVINGS ● ○

Supersweet summer tomatoes will make this cold soup especially delicious. But to enhance the flavor of even less-than-perfect produce, F&W's Melissa Rubel Jacobson uses some tomato paste, which adds a rich, concentrated taste.

4 pounds tomatoes, quartered and seeded

2 cups low-sodium vegetable broth

½ cup extra-virgin olive oil

¼ cup tomato paste

1 tablespoon red wine vinegar

2 teaspoons sugar

Kosher salt and freshly ground black pepper

½ cup crème fraîche

1½ tablespoons chopped tarragon, plus tarragon leaves for garnish

1. Working in a blender in 2 batches, puree the quartered tomatoes with the vegetable broth, olive oil, tomato paste, red wine vinegar and sugar until very smooth. Transfer the mixture to a large bowl and season with salt and black pepper. Cover the soup and refrigerate until completely chilled, about 2 hours.

2. In a small bowl, mix the crème fraîche with the chopped tarragon and season with black pepper. Ladle the chilled tomato soup into soup bowls. Top the soup with dollops of the tarragon crème fraîche, garnish with the tarragon leaves and serve right away. —Melissa Rubel Jacobson

MAKE AHEAD The tomato soup can be refrigerated for up to 1 day. The tarragon crème fraîche can be refrigerated for up to 2 days; bring to room temperature before serving. Just before serving, stir the soup and garnish with the tarragon crème fraîche and tarragon leaves.

PAPPARDELLE WITH
VEAL RAGÙ (P. 86)

pasta

Brilliant ways to serve noodles of all kinds—
Italian, Asian and beyond.

BUCATINI CARBONARA

WHOLE WHEAT RIGATONI WITH ROASTED VEGETABLES

Bucatini Carbonara

 TOTAL: 30 MIN
4 FIRST-COURSE SERVINGS ●

6 ounces bucatini or *perciatelli*
1 tablespoon extra-virgin
   olive oil
4 ounces pancetta, sliced
   ¼ inch thick and cut into
   ¼-inch dice
1 shallot, very finely chopped
1 garlic clove, very finely
   chopped
1 cup heavy cream
2 tablespoons freshly grated
   Parmigiano-Reggiano cheese,
   plus more for serving
4 large egg yolks
Salt
2 tablespoons coarsely
   chopped parsley
Freshly ground pepper

1. In a large pot of boiling salted water, cook the bucatini until al dente. Drain, reserving 3 tablespoons of the pasta cooking water.

2. Meanwhile, in a large skillet, heat the oil. Add the pancetta and cook over moderate heat until most of the fat has been rendered, 7 minutes. Add the shallot and garlic and cook over moderate heat for 1 minute. Add the cream and simmer over moderate heat until slightly thickened, about 2 minutes. Add the hot pasta to the skillet and stir to coat, 1 minute. Remove from the heat. Stir in the reserved pasta cooking water, the 2 tablespoons of grated cheese and the egg yolks. Season with salt. Divide the pasta into bowls and sprinkle with parsley and pepper. Serve, passing more grated cheese at the table.
—*Linton Hopkins*

WINE Cherry-inflected, earthy Sangiovese.

Whole Wheat Rigatoni with Roasted Vegetables

ACTIVE: 35 MIN; TOTAL: 1 HR 30 MIN
4 SERVINGS ● ●

One 1½-pound acorn squash—
   scrubbed, cut crosswise
   into ⅓-inch-thick rings, seeds
   discarded
1 small red onion, cut into
   ¼-inch-thick slices
¼ cup extra-virgin olive oil
Salt and freshly ground pepper
6 large plum tomatoes,
   halved and cored
12 unpeeled garlic cloves
½ pound whole wheat rigatoni
2 tablespoons pine nuts
¼ teaspoon crushed red pepper
4 kalamata olives, pitted
   and sliced
¼ cup thinly sliced basil leaves

2 tablespoons chopped
   flat-leaf parsley
2 tablespoons freshly grated
   pecorino cheese

1. Preheat the oven to 350°. On a large rimmed baking sheet, toss the acorn squash and red onion slices with 1 tablespoon of the olive oil; season with salt and pepper and spread in a single layer. Drizzle 2 tablespoons of the olive oil on another large rimmed baking sheet; add the tomato halves and whole garlic cloves and roll to coat with olive oil. Season the halved tomatoes with salt and pepper and turn them cut side down.

2. Transfer both sheets to the oven. Roast the garlic for about 40 minutes, until tender. Using tongs, transfer the garlic to a bowl; continue roasting the tomatoes for about 20 minutes longer, until very soft. Roast the squash and onion for about 45 minutes total, until tender and golden brown. Cut the squash into bite-size pieces and transfer to a large bowl along with the onions. Discard the tomato skins and coarsely chop the flesh. Add the tomatoes and their juices to the squash. Squeeze the garlic out of the skins into the bowl.

3. Bring a large pot of salted water to a boil. Add the rigatoni and cook until al dente. Drain, reserving ½ cup of the pasta cooking water. Return the drained rigatoni to the pasta pot.

4. Meanwhile, in a large skillet, heat the remaining 1 tablespoon of oil. Add the pine nuts and toast over moderate heat until golden. Add the crushed red pepper and olives and cook for 1 minute. Add the roasted vegetables and stir over moderately high heat until heated through, about 2 minutes. Season with salt and pepper and scrape into the pasta; add the reserved cooking water, basil and parsley and toss. Serve the pasta in bowls, topping each with ½ tablespoon of the grated pecorino.
—*Eric Chopin*
WINE Fresh, lively Soave.

Creamy Buckwheat Pasta with Wild Mushrooms

TOTAL: 30 MIN
6 SERVINGS ● ●

½ pound wild mushrooms, such as oysters and chanterelles, sliced ¼ inch thick
2 tablespoons extra-virgin olive oil
Salt and freshly ground black pepper
6 large eggs
1 pound buckwheat pappardelle (see Note)
1 leek, white and light green parts only, halved and sliced ⅛ inch thick
¼ cup plus 2 tablespoons mascarpone cheese
¼ cup heavy cream
3 tablespoons unsalted butter
1½ cups baby spinach
Freshly grated Parmigiano-Reggiano cheese, for sprinkling

1. Preheat the oven to 400°. On a nonstick baking sheet, toss the mushrooms with 1 tablespoon of the olive oil and season with salt and black pepper. Roast the mushrooms for 15 minutes.

2. Meanwhile, in a medium pot of boiling salted water, cook the eggs for 5 minutes. Drain the eggs and cool under cold running water. In another pot of boiling salted water, cook the buckwheat pappardelle until al dente; drain well.

3. In a medium skillet, heat the remaining 1 tablespoon of olive oil. Add the leek and cook over moderate heat until translucent, 3 minutes. Reduce the heat to low and stir in the mascarpone and cream, then stir in the butter. Season with salt and pepper and remove from the heat.

4. Add the roasted mushrooms, cooked pasta and spinach to the skillet and toss to coat. Season with salt and pepper and mound the pasta into shallow bowls. Peel and halve the eggs, adding one to each bowl. Sprinkle the pasta with Parmigiano-Reggiano cheese and serve immediately.
—*Matthew Accarrino*
NOTE Buckwheat pasta (called *pizzoccheri* in Italian) is available at specialty and health-food shops.
WINE Bright, tart Barbera.

Linguine with Tomatoes, Baby Zucchini and Herbs

TOTAL: 25 MIN
4 SERVINGS ● ● ●

"This dish makes you understand the less-is-more approach of Italian cooking," says Norwegian TV chef–turned–farmer Andreas Viestad about his pasta served with a raw tomato and zucchini sauce.

1 pound tomatoes, cored and finely chopped
1 tablespoon chopped basil
1 tablespoon chopped flat-leaf parsley
2 medium garlic cloves, very finely chopped
2 teaspoons kosher salt
1 small red chile, seeded and minced
⅓ cup extra-virgin olive oil
12 ounces linguine
3 baby zucchini, thinly sliced
¼ cup freshly grated Parmigiano-Reggiano cheese, plus more for serving

1. In a large bowl, toss the chopped tomatoes with the basil, parsley, garlic, salt, red chile and olive oil.

2. In a large pot of boiling salted water, cook the linguine until it is al dente; drain well. Add the linguine to the bowl along with the thinly sliced zucchini and toss well. Add the ¼ cup of grated cheese, toss again and serve in wide bowls, passing more grated cheese at the table.
—*Andreas Viestad*
WINE Fresh, fruity rosé.

pasta

Spaghetti with Tomatoes and Capers

TOTAL: 30 MIN
6 SERVINGS ●

"This dish is so simple, even my granddaughter Margherita can make it," jokes design matriarch and avid home cook Rosita Missoni. The recipe also lends itself to countless variations. Missoni likes to add zucchini and hot peppers in the summer.

- ¾ pound spaghetti
- 6 tablespoons extra-virgin olive oil
- 1 pint cherry tomatoes, halved
- ½ cup black olives, chopped
- 4 anchovy fillets, chopped
- 1 tablespoon small capers
- Salt and freshly ground pepper
- ¼ cup chopped basil

1. Bring a pot of salted water to a boil. Add the spaghetti and cook until al dente; drain, reserving ⅓ cup of the cooking water.

2. Meanwhile, in a large, deep skillet, heat the oil. Add the tomatoes, olives, anchovies and capers and cook over moderate heat, stirring, until just hot, about 3 minutes.

3. Add the pasta to the skillet along with the reserved cooking water and toss. Season with salt and pepper and transfer to a large bowl. Sprinkle with the basil and serve. —*Giorgio Locatelli and Rosita Missoni*
WINE Fresh, minerally Vermentino.

Summery Fettuccine Alfredo

TOTAL: 20 MIN
4 TO 6 SERVINGS ●

The extra-light Alfredo sauce for the pasta here gets its silkiness from fresh ricotta and grated pecorino cheese.

- ¾ pound fettuccine
- 1 cup thick whole-milk ricotta cheese
- ½ cup finely grated pecorino cheese (1½ ounces), plus more for serving
- ¼ cup chopped basil leaves
- Salt and freshly ground black pepper

1. In a large pot of boiling salted water, cook the fettuccine until al dente. Reserve ¾ cup of the pasta cooking water and drain the fettuccine well.

2. Add the ricotta and the ½ cup of pecorino to the pot along with the reserved cooking water; stir until smooth. Add the fettuccine and basil, season with salt and pepper and toss. Serve, passing additional grated pecorino at the table. —*Emily Kaiser*
WINE Juicy, fresh Dolcetto.

Linguine with Red Cabbage

ACTIVE: 20 MIN; TOTAL: 50 MIN
8 SERVINGS ● ● ●

F&W's Marcia Kiesel tops linguine and red cabbage with a scattering of crumbled feta cheese, which melts on the warm pasta to give the dish a creamy tang.

- ¼ cup plus 2 tablespoons extra-virgin olive oil
- 2 medium red onions, very thinly sliced
- 4 garlic cloves, minced
- 2 pounds red cabbage, thinly sliced (8 cups)
- 1 pound linguine
- Salt and freshly ground pepper
- 4 ounces Greek feta cheese, crumbled (1 cup)

1. In a large, deep skillet, heat the olive oil. Add the onions, cover and cook over moderately low heat, stirring occasionally, until very soft, 10 minutes. Add the garlic and cook, stirring, until fragrant, about 3 minutes. Add the sliced red cabbage, cover and cook, stirring occasionally, until the cabbage is tender, about 20 minutes.

2. Meanwhile, in a large pot of boiling salted water, cook the linguine until al dente. Drain the pasta well, reserving 1 cup of the cooking water. Return the pasta to the pot.

3. Toss the cabbage with the pasta and reserved cooking water and season with salt and pepper. Transfer to bowls, top with the feta and serve. —*Marcia Kiesel*
WINE Juicy, fresh Dolcetto.

Red Wine Spaghetti with Walnuts and Parsley

TOTAL: 40 MIN
4 SERVINGS ● ●

Adapted from a recipe by New York City pastry chef Gina DePalma, this spaghetti dish is greater than the sum of its parts. Who knew that basic dried pasta, simply boiled in red wine, could develop such complex flavor?

- 5 cups water
- 3¼ cups dry red wine
- Salt
- ¾ pound spaghetti
- ¼ cup extra-virgin olive oil
- 4 small garlic cloves, thinly sliced
- ¼ teaspoon crushed red pepper
- ½ cup finely chopped flat-leaf parsley
- 1 cup walnuts (4 ounces), toasted and coarsely chopped
- ½ cup grated Parmigiano-Reggiano cheese, plus more for serving
- Freshly ground black pepper

1. In a saucepan, combine the water with 3 cups of the red wine and a large pinch of salt and bring to a boil. Add the spaghetti and cook, stirring, until al dente. Drain the spaghetti, reserving ¼ cup of the pasta cooking liquid.

2. In a skillet, heat 2 tablespoons of the olive oil. Add the sliced garlic and crushed red pepper and season with salt. Cook over moderate heat for 1 minute. Add the remaining ¼ cup of red wine and the reserved pasta cooking liquid and bring to a simmer. Stir in the drained spaghetti and cook until the liquid is nearly absorbed, about 2 minutes. Add the chopped parsley, walnuts, the ½ cup of grated cheese and the remaining 2 tablespoons of olive oil and toss. Season the pasta with salt and black pepper and serve, passing extra grated cheese at the table.
—*Kristin Donnelly*
WINE Cherry-inflected, earthy Sangiovese.

LINGUINE WITH RED CABBAGE

pasta

Pasta with Sizzled Sage

ACTIVE: 45 MIN; TOTAL: 1 HR 15 MIN
4 TO 6 SERVINGS ● ●

1¼ cups plus 2 tablespoons
   all-purpose flour

Kosher salt

7 large egg yolks

4 tablespoons unsalted butter

½ cup sage leaves

Freshly ground pepper

¼ cup grated Parmigiano-Reggiano
   cheese, plus more for serving

1. In the bowl of a mixer fitted with the paddle, mix the flour with 1 teaspoon of salt. Add the egg yolks and mix at medium speed until the dough is blended and resembles wet sand, about 1½ minutes. Transfer to a work surface and knead until a firm dough forms. Cover with plastic wrap and let stand at room temperature for 30 minutes.

2. Cut the pasta dough into 3 equal pieces and keep covered with plastic wrap. Working with one piece at a time, flatten the dough and run it through a pasta machine: Begin at the widest setting and work your way through consecutively narrower settings until you reach the thinnest one. Cut the sheet into 3 equal pieces. Run each piece through the spaghetti setting and transfer to a large rimmed baking sheet; toss the strands to keep them separate. Repeat with the remaining pasta dough.

3. In a large skillet, melt the butter. Add the sage and cook over moderate heat, turning once, until crisp, 3 minutes. Season with salt and pepper. With a slotted spoon, transfer the sage to a plate; reserve the butter.

4. In a large pot of boiling salted water, cook the pasta, stirring, until al dente, about 1 minute. Drain, reserving ¼ cup of the cooking water. Return the pasta to the pot, toss with the reserved butter and cooking water and season with salt and pepper. Transfer to a bowl and scatter the sage and cheese on top. Serve, passing more cheese at the table. —*Justin Neidermeyer*
WINE Dry, fruity sparkling wine.

Fusilli alla Crazy Bastard

TOTAL: 40 MIN
4 SERVINGS ● ●

This pasta is an ode to Charles Barsotti's 1994 *New Yorker* cartoon of a rigatoni noodle on the phone to a friend, exclaiming, "Fusilli, you crazy bastard!"

½ cup walnut halves

1 pint cherry tomatoes

2 tablespoons plus 1 teaspoon
   olive oil

Salt and freshly ground black pepper

1 pound fusilli

3 garlic cloves, sliced

½ pound beet greens, rinsed and
   coarsely chopped

Pinch of crushed red pepper

½ pound soft goat cheese, sliced

¼ cup freshly grated Parmigiano-
   Reggiano cheese

1. Preheat the oven to 350°. On a rimmed baking sheet, toast the walnuts for 7 minutes, until lightly browned; let cool slightly. Coarsely chop and transfer to a bowl.

2. Raise the oven temperature to 450°. On the rimmed baking sheet, toss the cherry tomatoes with 1 teaspoon of the olive oil and ½ teaspoon each of salt and pepper. Roast the tomatoes for about 10 minutes, until browned in spots.

3. In a large pot of boiling salted water, cook the fusilli. Meanwhile, heat the remaining 2 tablespoons of olive oil in a large skillet. Add the garlic and cook over moderate heat, stirring constantly, until golden, 2 minutes. Add the roasted tomatoes, beet greens and crushed red pepper and cook, crushing the tomatoes slightly, until the greens are just wilted, 3 minutes.

4. Drain the fusilli, reserving ½ cup of the cooking water. Add the pasta, cooking water and goat cheese to the skillet and cook over moderate heat, tossing to coat. Season with salt and pepper. Transfer to a bowl, garnish with the walnuts, top with the Parmesan and serve. —*Andy Nusser*
WINE Fresh, lively Soave.

Zucchini Linguine with Herbs

TOTAL: 30 MIN
8 SERVINGS ●

4 pounds small zucchini

6 tablespoons unsalted butter

4 scallions, thinly sliced lengthwise

Salt and freshly ground pepper

1½ pounds fresh linguine or spaghetti

2 tablespoons chopped tarragon
   or chervil, plus more for garnish

1 tablespoon chopped lemon thyme

1 teaspoon finely grated lemon zest

8 ounces young pecorino cheese,
   grated, plus more for garnish

1. Using a mandoline, julienne the zucchini lengthwise, stopping when you reach the seedy centers.

2. In a large, deep skillet, melt the butter. Add the zucchini and scallions, season with salt and pepper and cook over moderately high heat until just softened, 8 minutes.

3. Boil the pasta in salted water until al dente. Drain, reserving 1 cup of the water.

4. Add the pasta to the skillet along with the herbs, lemon zest and cheese; toss. Add the reserved water; cook over moderately high heat, stirring, until the sauce is slightly thickened, 3 minutes. Garnish with tarragon and cheese and serve. —*Grace Parisi*
WINE Peppery, refreshing Grüner Veltliner.

Rigatoni with Spicy Italian Salami, Cherry Tomatoes, Olives and Capers

TOTAL: 30 MIN
4 SERVINGS

20 cherry tomatoes

5 teaspoons extra-virgin olive oil

Kosher salt and freshly ground pepper

½ pound spicy soppressata,
   halved and thinly sliced

2 garlic cloves, minced

¼ cup dry white wine

¼ cup pitted kalamata olives, halved

¼ cup drained capers

¼ cup chopped flat-leaf parsley

½ pound rigatoni

FUSILLI ALLA CRAZY BASTARD

ZUCCHINI LINGUINE WITH HERBS

1. Preheat the oven to 375°. Bring a large pot of salted water to a boil. In a small baking dish, toss the tomatoes with 2 teaspoons of the oil and season with salt and pepper. Roast the tomatoes for about 10 minutes, until their skins begin to split.
2. In a large skillet, heat the remaining 3 teaspoons of oil. Add the soppressata and cook over moderately high heat for 2 minutes. Using a slotted spoon, transfer the soppressata to paper towels to drain.
3. Add the garlic to the skillet and cook over moderate heat until fragrant, 30 seconds. Add the tomatoes and lightly smash them. Add the wine and simmer over moderate heat until reduced by half, 3 minutes. Remove the skillet from the heat; stir in the soppressata, olives, capers and parsley.
4. Meanwhile, cook the rigatoni in the boiling water until al dente. Drain, reserving ½ cup of the pasta cooking water.

5. Add the rigatoni and cooking water to the sauce and toss over moderate heat until the pasta is thoroughly coated, about 2 minutes. Season with salt and pepper and serve in shallow bowls. —*Curtis Stone*
WINE Intense, fruity Zinfandel.

Angel Hair Pasta with Crab and Country Ham

TOTAL: 25 MIN
4 SERVINGS

- 1 tablespoon extra-virgin olive oil
- 2 thin slices of country ham or prosciutto, cut into thin strips
- 3 tablespoons unsalted butter
- ½ cup sliced shallots
- 1 small garlic clove, minced
- ¾ cup dry white wine
- ½ pound lump crabmeat
- 1½ teaspoons chopped thyme

- ½ pound dried angel hair pasta
- Salt and freshly ground pepper
- 2 tablespoons chopped parsley

1. In a deep skillet, heat the oil. Add the ham and cook over moderate heat, tossing, until hot; using tongs, transfer to a plate.
2. Melt 1 tablespoon of butter in the skillet. Add the shallots and cook over moderate heat until softened, 4 minutes. Add the garlic and cook until fragrant. Add the wine and boil until reduced by half, 2 minutes. Add the crab and thyme and toss until hot.
3. Meanwhile, cook the pasta in a large pot of boiling salted water until al dente. Drain, reserving ⅔ cup of the cooking water.
4. Add the ham, pasta, reserved cooking water and remaining 2 tablespoons of butter to the skillet; toss. Season with salt and pepper. Garnish with the parsley and serve in bowls. —*Marcia Kiesel*
WINE Fresh, minerally Vermentino.

●HEALTHY ●MAKE AHEAD ●VEGETARIAN ●STAFF FAVORITE

pasta

Spinach-and-Ricotta Tortelli with Browned Butter

ACTIVE: 1 HR 30 MIN; TOTAL: 2 HR

MAKES ABOUT 80 TORTELLI;

6 SERVINGS ●●

The pasta for this tortelli (a larger version of tortellini) is extremely silky and supple, which makes it excellent with the creamy ricotta-and-spinach filling. If there's any dough left over, cut it into noodles, as New York chef Marco Canora does, then dry it and store it in bags in the refrigerator to have on hand for last-minute dinners.

1¾   cups all-purpose flour,
      plus more for dusting
Kosher salt
  1   large egg
  7   large egg yolks
  ¾   cup fresh ricotta
  ⅓   cup plus ¼ cup freshly
      grated Parmigiano-
      Reggiano cheese
  ¼   cup thawed frozen spinach,
      squeezed dry
  2   teaspoons extra-virgin
      olive oil
Pinch of freshly grated nutmeg
Freshly ground pepper
  4   tablespoons unsalted butter

1. In a food processor, combine the 1¾ cups of flour with a pinch of salt. Add the whole egg, 5 of the egg yolks and 1 table-spoon of water and process until a crumbly dough forms, about 2 minutes. Turn the dough out onto a work surface and knead until smooth; if the dough is too tough to knead, sprinkle it with another tablespoon of water as you knead. Wrap the pasta dough in plastic and let it rest at room temperature for 30 minutes.

2. Unwrap the dough and divide it into 3 pieces. Work with one piece at a time and keep the rest covered. Press the dough to flatten it slightly. Using a hand-cranked pasta machine set at the widest setting, roll the dough through successively narrower settings to the thinnest one. Lay the pasta on a lightly floured work surface, sprinkle with flour and cover with wax paper. Repeat with the remaining dough, dusting with flour and layering between wax paper.

3. Using a 2¼-inch fluted biscuit cutter, stamp out rounds from the pasta sheets. Cover with plastic wrap.

4. In a medium bowl, combine the ricotta with ⅓ cup of the Parmigiano-Reggiano, the spinach, oil and nutmeg and season with salt and pepper. Transfer the filling to a pastry bag fitted with a ¼-inch round tip or to a sturdy plastic bag with a corner snipped off.

5. In a small bowl, combine the 2 remaining yolks with ¼ cup of water. Working with one dough round at a time, lightly brush the edge with the egg wash. Pipe a scant ½ teaspoon of the filling in the center and fold the dough over the filling to form a half moon; press the edge to seal. Lightly brush the dough with water if dry. Bring the ends of the half moon together around your finger, overlapping them slightly and pressing them together. Fill and shape the remaining tortelli, transferring them to a tray lined with floured wax paper.

6. Bring a large pot of salted water to a boil. Add the tortelli and cook, stirring occasionally, until they rise to the surface and the pasta is cooked through, 7 to 8 minutes, then drain, reserving ¼ cup of the water. Transfer the tortelli to a large bowl.

7. In a large skillet, cook the butter over moderately high heat until it is lightly browned, about 5 minutes. Stir in the tortelli, the reserved pasta cooking water and the remaining ¼ cup of grated cheese. Serve the tortelli right away.

—*Marco Canora*

MAKE AHEAD Freeze the uncooked tortelli in a single layer, then transfer to a resealable plastic bag; freeze for up to 1 month. Boil the tortelli directly from the freezer without thawing.

WINE Ripe, luxurious Chardonnay.

Penne with Asparagus, Sage and Peas

 TOTAL: 35 MIN
4 SERVINGS

For a simple spring dish, chef Cindy Pawlcyn folds penne with asparagus and sweet peas, then adds a little cream for richness.

  ½   pound penne
  2   tablespoons extra-virgin
      olive oil
  3   medium garlic cloves, very
      finely chopped
  1   pound thick asparagus, cut
      into 1-inch lengths
  2   cups chicken stock
  2   cups (10 ounces) shelled
      English peas or frozen baby
      peas, thawed
  ¼   cup heavy cream
  2   tablespoons unsalted butter
  1   tablespoon finely chopped
      fresh sage
  ½   cup freshly grated
      Parmigiano-Reggiano cheese,
      plus more for serving
Salt and freshly ground black
      pepper

1. Bring a large pot of salted water to a boil. Add the penne and cook, stirring occasionally, until al dente. Drain.

2. Meanwhile, in a large skillet, heat the olive oil. Add the garlic and asparagus and cook over moderately low heat, stirring occasionally, until the garlic is fragrant, about 3 minutes. Add the stock and boil over high heat until reduced by half and the asparagus are tender, about 5 minutes.

3. Add the peas and cream to the skillet and boil over high heat until the sauce has thickened, 3 minutes. Stir in the penne and cook until heated through. Remove from the heat and stir in the butter, sage and the ½ cup of cheese. Season with salt and pepper. Transfer the pasta to bowls and serve right away, passing additional cheese at the table.

—*Cindy Pawlcyn*

WINE Fresh, lively Soave.

PENNE WITH ASPARAGUS,
SAGE AND PEAS

pasta

Pappardelle with Veal Ragù

photo, page 76

ACTIVE: 30 MIN; TOTAL: 2 HR 45 MIN

8 SERVINGS ● ●

3½ to 4 pounds boneless veal
    shoulder, cut into 3-inch chunks
Salt and freshly ground pepper
All-purpose flour, for dusting
  ½ cup extra-virgin olive oil
   1 large sweet onion, finely
    chopped
   4 garlic cloves, minced
1½ teaspoons ground coriander
1½ teaspoons ground fennel
1½ cups dry red wine
Two 28-ounce cans Italian whole
    tomatoes, drained and chopped
   4 cups chicken or veal stock
1½ tablespoons minced rosemary
   2 pounds fresh pappardelle
Freshly grated Parmigiano-Reggiano
    cheese

1. Season the veal with salt and pepper and dust with flour, tapping off the excess. In a large enameled cast-iron casserole, heat ¼ cup of the olive oil. Add the veal and cook over moderately high heat until browned all over, about 12 minutes. Transfer the veal to a plate.

2. Add the remaining ¼ cup of oil to the casserole. Stir in the onion, garlic, coriander and fennel and cook over low heat for 5 minutes. Add the wine and boil until reduced to ⅓ cup, 5 minutes. Add the tomatoes and cook over moderately high heat for 5 minutes. Add the stock and rosemary and bring to a boil. Add the veal, cover partially and cook over low heat until very tender, 2 hours.

3. Remove the meat and shred it. Boil the sauce until slightly reduced, about 10 minutes. Stir in the meat.

4. Cook the pappardelle in boiling salted water until al dente. Drain and return to the pot. Add the ragù and toss over low heat until the pasta is coated. Serve with cheese at the table. —*Grace Parisi*

WINE Complex, aromatic Nebbiolo.

Macaroni and Many Cheeses

TOTAL: 35 MIN

4 TO 6 SERVINGS ● ● ●

At the end of their wine-and-cheese tastings, Napa party hosts Helen Jane Hearn and Natalie Wassum—a.k.a. the Cheesewhizzes—gather any leftovers to make an incredible mac and cheese later in the week. The adaptation below, based on a recipe from Marion Cunningham's *The Supper Book,* works beautifully with any semihard cheese but is particularly good with an international blend of French Mimolette, Dutch Gouda and American Vella dry Jack. A layer of Italian Parmigiano-Reggiano forms a crisp topping.

   2 cups elbow macaroni
   4 tablespoons unsalted butter
  ¼ cup all-purpose flour
   3 cups milk
   2 cups mixed shredded semihard
    cheeses, such as Mimolette,
    aged Gouda and Vella dry Jack
    (½ pound)
Salt and freshly ground
    black pepper
 ⅔ cup freshly grated Parmigiano-
    Reggiano cheese

1. Preheat the broiler. In a medium saucepan of boiling salted water, cook the macaroni until al dente; drain well.

2. Meanwhile, in another medium saucepan, melt the butter over low heat. Whisk in the flour until a paste forms. Gradually whisk in the milk until smooth. Bring the sauce to a boil over moderately high heat, whisking, until thickened. Off the heat, stir in the mixed shredded cheeses until melted. Season with salt and pepper.

3. Stir the macaroni into the cheese sauce; transfer to a 9-by-13-inch glass or ceramic baking dish; sprinkle on the Parmigiano-Reggiano. Broil 4 inches from the heat for 4 minutes, until richly browned. Let rest for 5 minutes before serving.

—*Helen Jane Hearn and Natalie Wassum*

WINE Bright, tart Barbera.

Carrot Macaroni and Cheese

ACTIVE: 30 MIN; TOTAL: 1 HR 20 MIN

4 SERVINGS ● ● ●

  ¾ pound carrots, peeled and
    thinly sliced
Zest and juice of 1 navel orange,
    zest removed in strips with
    a vegetable peeler
Salt
   3 cups *penne rigate*
    (9 ounces)
   3 ounces sharp cheddar cheese,
    shredded (1½ cups)
   1 tablespoon chopped fresh
    tarragon leaves
Freshly ground white pepper

1. Preheat the oven to 350°. In a medium saucepan, combine the sliced carrots with the orange zest and juice and ¼ cup of water. Season with salt and bring to a boil. Cover and simmer over moderate heat until the carrots are very soft, about 30 minutes. Discard the strips of orange zest. Transfer the cooked carrots and any liquid to a blender and puree until the mixture is very smooth.

2. Meanwhile, in a large saucepan of boiling salted water, cook the pasta until al dente. Drain the pasta, reserving 1 cup of the cooking water.

3. Return the cooked penne to the pot. Add the reserved cooking water and the carrot puree and cook over moderate heat, stirring frequently, until the the pasta is coated with a thickened sauce, about 5 minutes. Stir in three-fourths of the shredded cheddar cheese and cook, stirring, until the sauce is very creamy, 2 to 3 minutes longer. Stir in the tarragon and season with salt and white pepper.

4. Transfer the pasta to a medium baking dish and top with the remaining shredded cheddar cheese. Bake until the cheese is melted and lightly browned, about 20 minutes. Let stand for 5 minutes before serving. —*Jeremy Fox*

WINE Dry, light Champagne.

pasta

Modern Turkey Tetrazzini

ACTIVE: 1 HR; TOTAL: 1 HR 30 MIN

6 TO 8 SERVINGS ●

This creamy classic is updated with whole-grain pasta and wild mushrooms.

- 3 turkey drumsticks
  (2¾ pounds total)
- 1 tablespoon vegetable oil

Kosher salt and freshly
  ground pepper

- 1 pound whole-grain rotini
  or fusilli
- 1 stick plus 2 tablespoons
  unsalted butter
- 6 medium shallots,
  cut into ½-inch dice
- ½ pound shiitake mushrooms,
  stems discarded and caps
  cut into 1-inch pieces
- ½ pound oyster mushrooms,
  cut into 1-inch pieces
- 1 teaspoon finely chopped sage
- ½ teaspoon chopped thyme
- ½ cup dry white wine
- ½ cup all-purpose flour
- 3½ cups chicken stock or
  low-sodium broth
- 2 tablespoons heavy cream
- ½ cup frozen baby peas
- 2 slices of whole wheat
  sandwich bread
- ½ cup freshly grated Parmigiano-
  Reggiano cheese

---

best whole wheat pasta

We love the nutty flavor of De Cecco brand's whole wheat pasta. Founded in 1886, the company shapes all its pastas in handmade bronze dies and dries them slowly, which results in a particularly nice texture.

---

1. Preheat the oven to 375°. In a medium roasting pan, rub the turkey drumsticks with the vegetable oil and season with salt and pepper. Roast the turkey for about 45 minutes, until cooked through. Let stand until cool enough to handle, about 10 minutes. Cut the turkey meat into ½-inch pieces; discard the skin and bones.

2. Bring a large pot of salted water to a boil. Add the rotini and cook until it is al dente. Drain the pasta well.

3. Meanwhile, in a large, deep skillet, melt 1 stick of the butter. Add the diced shallots and cook over moderate heat until softened, about 4 minutes. Add the shiitake and oyster mushrooms and cook until softened, about 5 minutes. Add the sage and thyme and cook until fragrant. Add the wine, bring to a boil and cook over high heat until reduced by half, about 3 minutes. Add the flour and cook over moderate heat, stirring constantly, until moistened, about 1 minute. Add the chicken stock, bring to a simmer and cook over low heat until thickened, about 3 minutes. Stir in the cream, turkey, peas and pasta and season with salt and pepper.

4. Spread the contents of the skillet in a deep 9-by-13-inch baking dish.

5. In a medium microwave-safe bowl, melt the remaining 2 tablespoons of butter. In a food processor, pulse the slices of whole wheat sandwich bread until fine crumbs form. Add the fresh bread crumbs and grated Parmigiano-Reggiano cheese to the melted butter and toss until thoroughly combined. Season the bread crumbs with salt and pepper and sprinkle the crumbs evenly over the casserole. Bake the casserole for about 30 minutes, until golden brown on top. Serve hot.

—*Melissa Rubel Jacobson*

MAKE AHEAD The cooked turkey Tetrazzini can be cooled, covered and refrigerated in its baking dish for up to 2 days. Reheat the casserole at 350° and serve hot.

WINE Fruity, light-bodied Beaujolais.

Shiitake-and-Scallion Lo Mein

TOTAL: 40 MIN

8 SERVINGS ● ●

Asian street-food vendors sometimes serve food in banana leaves instead of using plates or bowls. Look for the leaves at Asian markets. Here, F&W's Melissa Rubel Jacobson wraps banana leaves around silky Chinese lo mein noodles.

- 1 pound wide lo mein noodles
- ¼ pound snow peas,
  halved diagonally
- ¼ cup soy sauce
- ¼ cup mirin
- 2 teaspoons Asian sesame oil
- 3 tablespoons canola oil
- 1 pound shiitake mushrooms,
  stems discarded and caps
  thinly sliced
- 6 scallions, cut into 1-inch lengths
- 1 tablespoon minced fresh ginger
- 2 tablespoons water
- 2 tablespoons chopped cilantro

1. In a large pot of boiling salted water, cook the noodles until tender; add the snow peas to the noodles in the last 2 minutes of cooking. Drain the noodles and snow peas and rinse under cold water until cool. In a small bowl, mix the soy sauce with the mirin and sesame oil.

2. In a very large, deep skillet, heat 2 tablespoons of the canola oil until shimmering. Add the shiitake and cook over moderately high heat, undisturbed, until browned, about 5 minutes. Add the remaining 1 tablespoon of canola oil, the scallions and ginger and stir-fry until the scallions soften, about 3 minutes. Add the water and cook over moderate heat, scraping up the browned bits from the bottom of the pan, 1 minute. Add the noodles, snow peas and soy sauce mixture to the skillet and cook, tossing the noodles until heated through, about 2 minutes. Add the cilantro, transfer to banana leaf cones or bowls and serve.

—*Melissa Rubel Jacobson*

WINE Fruity, light-bodied Beaujolais.

GREEK BAKED PASTA

PASTA WITH SMOTHERED
BROCCOLI RABE AND OLIVES

pasta

Pasta with Smothered Broccoli Rabe and Olives

ACTIVE: 20 MIN; TOTAL: 1 HR 40 MIN

4 SERVINGS ● ●

Many Mediterranean cooks use clay pots to cook foods without added liquid. In Sicily, the method is called *affogato* and the pot is an earthenware *tegame*. In author Paula Wolfert's adaptation of a specialty she enjoyed many years ago at the Ristorante Circolo Uliveto, in the Sicilian town of Trecastagni, she substitutes an easier-to-find *cazuela* for the *tegame*. She uses it to cook coarsely chopped broccoli rabe (ideally the young, leafy kind) with grated pecorino cheese, briny olives and meaty anchovies, then folds the mixture into boiled pasta and bakes it.

- 5 oil-cured black olives, pitted
- 4 anchovy fillets
- 2 tablespoons golden raisins
- ½ cup chopped flat-leaf parsley
- 2 large scallions, coarsely chopped
- 1 medium garlic clove, very finely chopped
- 2 tablespoons freshly grated pecorino cheese, plus more for sprinkling
- ¼ cup extra-virgin olive oil
- 1¼ pounds broccoli rabe, thick stems discarded and the rest coarsely chopped
- 1 tablespoon dry red wine
- Salt and freshly ground black pepper
- ½ pound pasta, such as *garganelli*, fusilli or pasta shells

1. In separate small bowls, cover the olives, anchovies and raisins with hot water and let soak for 10 minutes. Drain well. Coarsely chop the olives and finely chop the anchovies. In a small bowl, combine the olives, anchovies and raisins with the parsley, scallions, garlic and the 2 tablespoons of grated pecorino cheese.

2. Coat a 10- or 12-inch *cazuela* or oven-proof skillet with 2 tablespoons of the olive oil. Spread half of the broccoli rabe in the *cazuela* in an even layer. Sprinkle with the olive mixture and cover with the remaining broccoli rabe. Press a piece of parchment paper on top of the broccoli rabe and cover the *cazuela* lightly. Cook over low heat until the broccoli rabe is tender, about 40 minutes. Add the wine, cover and cook for 10 minutes longer. Transfer the *cazuela* to a padded or wooden surface. (To avoid thermal shock, do not place it on a cold stone or metal surface.) Uncover, season with salt and pepper and let stand.

3. Meanwhile, preheat the oven to 400°. Bring a large saucepan of salted water to a boil. Add the pasta and cook until al dente. Drain the pasta and return it to the saucepan. Toss with the remaining 2 tablespoons of olive oil and season with salt and black pepper. Gently fold the drained pasta into the broccoli rabe. Sprinkle with grated pecorino and bake until bubbling, about 10 minutes. Serve hot or warm.
—*Paula Wolfert*

MAKE AHEAD The broccoli rabe can be prepared through Step 2 and refrigerated overnight in the *cazuela*. Bring to room temperature before proceeding.

WINE Fresh, minerally Vermentino.

Greek Baked Pasta

ACTIVE: 25 MIN; TOTAL: 45 MIN

6 SERVINGS ● ●

The moist and fragrant baked pasta casserole pastitsio is like a Greek version of lasagna. It combines béchamel (a creamy white sauce of butter, flour and milk), pasta, ground lamb, tomato sauce, cheese, cinnamon and nutmeg. Instead of using béchamel, F&W's Grace Parisi layers the pasta with lamb ragù and a simple egg yolk and ricotta mixture before baking.

- 2 tablespoons extra-virgin olive oil
- 1½ pounds lean ground lamb
- 1 onion, finely chopped
- 1 teaspoon dried oregano, crumbled
- ¾ teaspoon cinnamon
- Pinch of ground cloves
- Salt and freshly ground pepper
- 3 cups jarred marinara sauce
- 1 pound ziti or penne
- 3 cups fresh ricotta (1½ pounds)
- 4 large egg yolks
- ½ teaspoon ground nutmeg
- ¾ cup freshly grated Parmigiano-Reggiano cheese

1. Preheat the oven to 350°. Bring a large pot of salted water to a boil. In a large saucepan, heat the olive oil until shimmering. Add the lamb, onion, oregano, cinnamon, cloves and a generous pinch each of salt and pepper. Cook over high heat, stirring frequently, until the lamb is no longer pink and any liquid has evaporated, about 8 minutes. Add the marinara sauce and bring to a boil. Boil over high heat, stirring occasionally, until the sauce has reduced slightly, about 5 minutes.

2. Cook the pasta until barely al dente; drain and return to the pot. Meanwhile, in a blender, blend 2 cups of the ricotta with the yolks, nutmeg and ½ cup of the Parmigiano-Reggiano until smooth. Season with salt and pepper. Pulse in the remaining ricotta.

3. Add the lamb ragù to the pasta and toss. Transfer to a 9-by-13-inch baking dish. Pour the ricotta mixture on top and sprinkle with the remaining ¼ cup of Parmigiano-Reggiano. Bake in the center of the oven for about 20 minutes, until heated through. Turn the broiler on and broil until the top is golden brown. Let stand for a few minutes before serving. —*Grace Parisi*

MAKE AHEAD The casserole can be covered and refrigerated for up to 2 days. Reheat at 350° and serve hot.

WINE Intense, spicy Syrah.

perfecting gnocchi

American chefs are busy riffing on this Italian classic. F&W's **Grace Parisi** *shares one traditional recipe and three tasty variations.*

Potato Gnocchi with Butter and Cheese

ACTIVE: 30 MIN; TOTAL: 1 HR 30 MIN

4 TO 6 SERVINGS ● ○ ○

- 2 pounds baking potatoes (about 4)
- 2 large egg yolks

Salt

- ½ cup all-purpose flour, plus more for dusting
- 4 tablespoons unsalted butter

Freshly ground black pepper

Freshly grated Parmigiano-Reggiano cheese

1. Preheat the oven to 400°. Pierce the potatoes all over with a fork. Bake in a microwave oven at high power for 10 minutes, then flip the potatoes and microwave for 5 minutes longer. Transfer the potatoes to the oven and bake for 15 minutes. Alternatively, bake the potatoes in the oven for about 1 hour, until tender.

2. Halve the potatoes. Scoop the flesh into a ricer and rice the potatoes. Transfer 2 slightly packed cups of riced potatoes to a bowl. Stir in the egg yolks and 1 teaspoon of salt. Add the ½ cup of flour; stir until a stiff dough forms. Knead the dough gently until smooth but slightly sticky.

3. Line a baking sheet with wax paper and dust with flour. On a floured surface, cut the dough into 4 pieces; roll each into a ¾-inch-thick rope. Cut the ropes into ¾-inch pieces. Roll each piece against the tines of a fork to make ridges; transfer to the baking sheet.

CARROT-POTATO GNOCCHI

4. In a large, deep skillet of simmering salted water, cook the gnocchi until they float, then simmer for 2 minutes longer. In a large nonstick skillet, melt the butter. Using a slotted spoon, add the gnocchi to the butter. Season with salt and pepper; cook over high heat for 1 minute. Sprinkle with the cheese and serve.

MAKE AHEAD The uncooked gnocchi pieces can be frozen on the prepared baking sheet, then transferred to a resealable plastic bag and frozen for up to 1 month. Boil without defrosting.

WINE Juicy, fresh Dolcetto.

THREE GREAT VARIATIONS

1 Carrot-Potato Gnocchi

Sauté 4 sliced carrots in 1 tablespoon olive oil over moderate heat for 2 minutes. Add ¼ cup water and a pinch of salt. Cook, covered, until tender, 15 minutes. Puree; add ½ cup carrot puree and an extra 2 tablespoons flour to the dough in Step 2.

2 Garlic-Potato Gnocchi

On a sheet of foil, drizzle 10 unpeeled garlic cloves with olive oil. Wrap up the garlic and roast at 450° for 30 minutes, until tender. Squeeze out the garlic and add to the dough along with 2 additional tablespoons flour in Step 2.

3 Rye-Potato Gnocchi

Substitute ½ cup plus 2 tablespoons dark rye flour in place of the ½ cup all-purpose flour. (Stone-ground dark rye flour, milled from the whole grain, is available at natural food markets and from bobsredmill.com.)

SUPERFAST GNOCCHI SAUCES

Brown Butter and Sage In a medium skillet, cook 4 tablespoons unsalted butter with 10 small sage leaves until the butter is fragrant and nutty, about 3 minutes. Add the simmered gnocchi and cook for 1 minute. Sprinkle the gnocchi with grated Parmigiano-Reggiano cheese and freshly ground pepper.

Parmigiano-Reggiano Cream In a large skillet, bring ¾ cup heavy cream to a boil over moderate heat and simmer gently for 2 minutes. Carefully add the gnocchi and ¼ cup finely grated Parmigiano-Reggiano. Cook over low heat, stirring gently, until the cheese is melted, about 1 minute.

SHIITAKE-AND-SCALLION LO MEIN

Soba Noodle Salad with Thai Red Curry Sauce

 TOTAL: 45 MIN
4 SERVINGS

At the Farm at Cape Kidnappers, a resort on New Zealand's North Island, chef Dale Gartland makes his incredible Thai dressing with a bright-flavored blend of kaffir lime leaves, red chiles, shallots and coriander root; store-bought red Thai curry paste is a fine shortcut.

1 tablespoon vegetable oil
1 tablespoon red Thai curry paste
One 14-ounce can whole tomatoes—drained and chopped, juices reserved
¾ cup chicken stock or low-sodium broth
¾ cup unsweetened coconut milk
2 tablespoons light brown sugar
1 tablespoon fresh lime juice
1 teaspoon Asian fish sauce

OPEN HOUSE BUFFET

1 pound bok choy—stems thinly sliced, leaves coarsely chopped
6 ounces soba noodles
2 tablespoons thinly sliced pickled ginger
1 tablespoon toasted sesame seeds
½ cup roasted cashews
½ cup mung bean sprouts
1 scallion, thinly sliced

1. Bring a large saucepan of salted water to a boil. In a medium saucepan, heat the vegetable oil. Add the red curry paste and cook over moderately high heat, stirring, until fragrant, about 30 seconds. Add the tomatoes and their juices and boil over moderately high heat until reduced to ¾ cup, about 4 minutes. Add the chicken stock, coconut milk and brown sugar and simmer over moderate heat, stirring occasionally, until reduced to 1½ cups, about 7 minutes. Remove from the heat and stir in the lime juice and fish sauce.

2. Line a plate with paper towels. Add the bok choy stems and leaves to the boiling water and cook until crisp-tender, about 1 minute. Using a slotted spoon, transfer the bok choy to the paper towels and pat dry.

3. Add the soba to the boiling water and cook, stirring occasionally, until al dente. Drain the soba and rinse in a colander under cold water. Let stand for 5 minutes, tossing occasionally, until dry.

4. Transfer the soba to a large bowl. Add the pickled ginger, sesame seeds, 1 cup of the curry sauce and all but ½ cup of the bok choy leaves; toss well. Arrange the soba salad in shallow bowls and drizzle with the remaining sauce. Garnish the salad with the cashews, bean sprouts, scallion and the remaining bok choy and serve. —*Dale Gartland*

MAKE AHEAD The red curry sauce can be refrigerated for up to 2 days. Bring to room temperature before serving.

WINE Vivid, lightly sweet Riesling.

Stir-Fried Udon Noodles

 TOTAL: 45 MIN
4 SERVINGS ● ●

3 tablespoons vegetable oil
½ pound large shrimp, shelled and deveined
¼ pound skinless, boneless chicken breast, thinly sliced
2½ cups chopped napa cabbage
1 small onion, thinly sliced
1 medium carrot, thinly sliced on the bias
7 ounces enoki mushrooms
4 ounces oyster mushrooms
¼ cup dried wood ear mushrooms, soaked in warm water for 10 minutes and drained
½ cup chicken stock
3 tablespoons soy sauce
1 teaspoon Asian sesame oil
18 ounces frozen precooked udon noodles, thawed
Kosher salt and freshly ground black pepper
Chopped scallions, for garnish

1. In a skillet, heat 1 tablespoon of the vegetable oil. Add the shrimp and stir-fry over moderately high heat until curled, 2 minutes; transfer to a plate. Add 1 tablespoon of oil to the skillet. Add the chicken and stir-fry until white throughout, 3 minutes; transfer to the plate with the shrimp.

2. Add the remaining 1 tablespoon of vegetable oil to the skillet. Add the cabbage, onion, carrot and the mushrooms and stir-fry for 4 minutes. Add the stock, soy sauce, sesame oil, shrimp and chicken; remove from the heat.

3. Meanwhile, cook the udon in a pot of boiling salted water for 1 minute. Drain and add to the skillet. Stir-fry over high heat until heated through. Season with salt and pepper, garnish with scallions and serve. —*Takashi Yagihashi*

WINE Ripe, juicy Pinot Noir.

Glass Noodle Stir-Fry

 **TOTAL: 30 MIN**
6 SERVINGS ● ●

Made from the starch of vegetables like mung beans, translucent glass noodles (a.k.a. cellophane noodles) are ubiquitous at pan-Asian restaurants. *Top Chef* Season 5 winner Hosea Rosenberg gives the noodles extra care, stir-frying them in Asian sesame oil with a generous array of vegetables—sugar snaps, carrots, zucchini and yellow squash, to name a few—then tossing them with tangy rice vinegar.

Four 1¾-ounce packages glass
    (cellophane) noodles
¼ cup vegetable oil
2 teaspoons Asian sesame oil
6 ounces sugar snap peas,
    cut into thin matchsticks
    (about 2 cups)
2 small carrots, cut into thin
    matchsticks
1 red bell pepper, cut into thin
    matchsticks
1 small red onion, thinly sliced
1 small yellow squash, cut into
    thin matchsticks
1 small zucchini, cut into thin
    matchsticks
4 scallions, thinly sliced
Salt and freshly ground pepper
2 tablespoons rice vinegar
2 tablespoons fresh orange juice

1. In a large bowl of hot water, soak the glass noodles until pliable, about 15 minutes. Drain well, shaking off any excess water. Using kitchen scissors, cut the glass noodles into 4-inch lengths.

2. In a large nonstick skillet, heat the vegetable oil with the sesame oil. Add the snap peas, carrots, red pepper, red onion, yellow squash, zucchini and scallions and season with salt and pepper. Stir-fry the vegetables over high heat until lightly browned in spots but still crisp-tender, about 3 minutes.

3. Add the noodles to the skillet and stir-fry over high heat until softened, 2 minutes.

Add the rice vinegar and orange juice and continue stir-frying until the glass noodles are translucent, about 2 minutes. Transfer the noodle stir-fry to plates and serve hot. —*Hosea Rosenberg*

WINE Lively, tart Sauvignon Blanc.

Rice-Noodle Salad with Chicken and Herbs

 TOTAL: 40 MIN
4 TO 6 SERVINGS ● ●

½ pound dried rice noodles,
    about ¼ inch wide
¾ cup fresh grapefruit juice
2 large garlic cloves, minced
2 tablespoons sugar
¼ cup plus 1 tablespoon
    Asian fish sauce
½ pound cabbage, finely shredded
    (4 cups)
3 large scallions, thinly sliced
½ pound cooked chicken,
    cut into long strips
½ cup chopped cilantro
¼ cup chopped mint
Sriracha chile sauce, for serving

1. In a bowl, cover the noodles with cold water and let stand until pliable, 25 minutes. Drain. Bring a saucepan of water to a boil. Add the noodles and cook, stirring, until al dente, 1 minute. Drain the noodles in a colander and return them to the pan. Fill the saucepan with cold water and swish the noodles around. Drain and repeat 2 more times. Drain the noodles in the colander, lifting and tossing, until dry.

2. In a small bowl, stir the grapefruit juice with the garlic, sugar and fish sauce until the sugar is dissolved.

3. In a large bowl, toss the rice noodles with the cabbage and scallions. Add the dressing and toss well. Add the chicken, cilantro and mint and toss. Serve, passing Sriracha sauce at the table. —*Marcia Kiesel*

MAKE AHEAD The dressing can be refrigerated overnight.

WINE Light, fresh Pinot Grigio.

Spicy Peanut Noodles

 TOTAL: 20 MIN
6 SERVINGS ● ●

"My mother used to make this," says Boston chef Joanne Chang. "I learned to re-create it in college, far away from any Chinese markets." Pantry staples like spaghetti and peanut butter are perfect stand-ins for the traditional ingredients. To give spaghetti the soft texture of Chinese noodles, cook it a few minutes longer than the box advises.

1 pound spaghetti
¾ cup smooth peanut butter
½ cup unseasoned rice vinegar
3 tablespoons plus 1 teaspoon
    sugar
6 tablespoons soy sauce
¼ cup water
1 tablespoon Asian sesame oil
2 teaspoons crushed red pepper
One 2-inch piece of fresh ginger
    root, peeled and coarsely
    chopped
1 large garlic clove
3 celery ribs, thinly sliced
½ cup coarsely chopped cilantro
    leaves and tender stems
Lime wedges, for serving

1. In a pot of boiling salted water, cook the spaghetti until tender. Drain and rinse under cold water until cooled. Drain well.

2. In a blender, puree the peanut butter with 6 tablespoons of the vinegar, 3 tablespoons of the sugar, the soy sauce, water, sesame oil, crushed red pepper, ginger and garlic. Transfer ½ cup of the peanut dressing to a bowl and toss with the noodles.

3. In another bowl, toss the celery with the cilantro and the remaining 2 tablespoons of vinegar and 1 teaspoon of sugar.

4. Transfer the noodles to bowls and drizzle with the remaining peanut dressing. Top with the celery and serve with lime wedges. —*Joanne Chang*

MAKE AHEAD The peanut dressing can be refrigerated for 2 days.

WINE Tart, citrusy Riesling.

SOUR-ORANGE
YUCATÁN
CHICKEN (P. 98)

poultry

Exciting new ideas for
chicken and other birds—roasted,
baked, fried or braised.

ROAST CHICKEN WITH TANGERINES

PANKO-COATED CHICKEN SCHNITZEL

Roast Chicken with Tangerines

ACTIVE: 20 MIN; TOTAL: 2 HR 30 MIN

6 SERVINGS

After serving this crisp-skinned roast chicken stuffed with tangerine halves and glazed with honey, white wine and fresh tangerine juice, writer and cookbook author Eugenia Bone likes to make a big pot of chicken soup with the bones and fruit. She simmers the soup for hours on very low heat.

One 6-pound roasting chicken

- 2 medium garlic cloves, thinly sliced
- 6 rosemary sprigs
- 3 tangerines, washed and halved
- 2 tablespoons extra-virgin olive oil
- ½ cup dry white wine
- ¼ cup honey

Salt and freshly ground black pepper

- 1¾ cups chicken stock or low-sodium broth

1. Preheat the oven to 425°. Set the chicken on a rack in a large roasting pan and stuff the cavity with the sliced garlic cloves, rosemary sprigs and 4 of the tangerine halves. Tie the chicken legs together with kitchen twine. Juice the remaining 2 tangerine halves. Rub the olive oil over the chicken. Pour the white wine and fresh tangerine juice over the chicken, drizzle on the honey and season the bird all over with salt and pepper.

2. Roast the chicken for 20 minutes. Add 1 cup of the chicken stock to the roasting pan, cover the pan with foil and reduce the oven temperature to 375°. Roast the chicken for 40 minutes longer, then add the remaining ¾ cup of chicken stock to the roasting pan. Cover and roast for 50 minutes longer, or until an instant-read thermometer inserted in an inner thigh registers 165°.

3. Transfer the chicken to a large carving board and let rest for 15 minutes. Strain the pan juices through a mesh sieve set over a medium saucepan. Use a wide spoon to skim the fat. Carve the chicken and serve right away, passing the pan juices at the table.
—*Eugenia Bone*

WINE Fruity, low-oak Chardonnay.

Panko-Coated Chicken Schnitzel

 **TOTAL: 15 MIN**

4 SERVINGS ●

Star chef Thomas Keller of the French Laundry in Yountville, California, uses Japanese *panko* bread crumbs to give his schnitzel an extra-crunchy crust.

Four ¼-inch-thick skinless,
    boneless chicken cutlets
Salt and freshly ground
    black pepper
  2 cups _panko_ bread crumbs
  1 cup all-purpose flour
  3 eggs, beaten
  ¼ cup canola oil
  6 tablespoons unsalted butter
  2 tablespoons fresh lemon juice
  1 tablespoon chopped flat-leaf
    parsley leaves
  2 teaspoons capers

1. Season the chicken cutlets with salt and pepper. Put the _panko_ bread crumbs, flour and eggs in 3 large, shallow bowls. Dredge the chicken cutlets in the flour, shaking off any excess. Dip the chicken in the eggs, then dredge in the _panko_ bread crumbs, pressing to help the crumbs adhere.

2. In a large, deep skillet, heat the canola oil to 365°. When the oil is ready, carefully add the chicken breasts and fry over moderately high heat, turning once, until the chicken is cooked, about 6 minutes. Transfer the fried chicken breasts to a paper towel–lined plate to drain.

3. In a small saucepan, cook the butter over moderately high heat until browned, about 6 minutes. Stir in the lemon juice, parsley and capers; spoon the pan sauce over the chicken and serve.
—_Thomas Keller_
WINE Dry, earthy sparkling wine.

Super-Crispy Fried Chicken
TOTAL: 50 MIN PLUS OVERNIGHT SOAKING
4 SERVINGS ●

Meg Grace's stellar fried chicken is the specialty at the regional-American Redhead in Manhattan's East Village.

  1 quart water
  ⅓ cup plus 1 teaspoon kosher salt
  ¼ cup packed light brown sugar
  4 large garlic cloves, smashed
  4 thyme sprigs

  1 tablespoon cracked
    black peppercorns
One 3½-pound chicken,
    cut into 8 pieces
Vegetable oil, for frying
  2 cups all-purpose flour
1½ teaspoons baking powder
1½ teaspoons cornstarch
  ½ teaspoon freshly ground
    black pepper
  ¼ teaspoon cayenne pepper

1. In a large, deep bowl, combine the water with ⅓ cup of the salt, the brown sugar, garlic, thyme sprigs and black peppercorns and stir to dissolve the salt. Add the chicken pieces, submerging them in the brine. Refrigerate the chicken overnight.

2. Preheat the oven to 300°. In a large, heavy pot, heat 2 inches of vegetable oil to 325°. Drain the chicken pieces and pat them dry with paper towels.

3. In a large bowl, combine the flour, baking powder, cornstarch, black pepper, cayenne and the remaining 1 teaspoon of salt. Set a rack over a large rimmed baking sheet near the stove. Dredge half of the chicken in the spiced flour, then shake off the excess. Fry the chicken for about 10 minutes, or until an instant-read thermometer inserted into the thickest part of a thigh registers 160°. Reduce the heat if the chicken browns too quickly. Transfer the chicken pieces to the rack and keep warm in the oven while you coat and fry the remaining chicken. Serve hot.
—_Meg Grace_
WINE Light, crisp white Burgundy.

Chicken with Slow-Roasted Tomatoes and Cheesy Grits
ACTIVE: 30 MIN; TOTAL: 2 HR
4 SERVINGS

Sweet, tender slow-roasted tomatoes accompany this exceptionally crisp-skinned chicken. Some of the tomatoes are cleverly mashed into the pan juices to enrich the savory jus.

  8 plum tomatoes, halved
    lengthwise
  ¼ cup extra-virgin olive oil
Salt and freshly ground pepper
  4 large rosemary sprigs
One 3½-pound chicken
  2 medium white onions,
    cut into wedges
  ½ cup dry white wine
Creamy Cheese Grits (p. 236),
    for serving

1. Preheat the oven to 350°. On a rimmed baking sheet, toss the tomatoes with 2 tablespoons of the oil and season with salt and pepper. Turn the tomatoes cut side down and scatter the rosemary sprigs around; bake on the bottom shelf of the oven for 1 hour and 15 minutes, or until the tomatoes are very soft and starting to brown. Let cool, then discard the skins.

2. Meanwhile, in a roasting pan, rub the chicken all over with 1 tablespoon of the oil and season with salt and pepper. Scatter the onion wedges around the chicken, drizzle with the remaining 1 tablespoon of oil and season with salt and pepper. Roast the chicken and onions in the upper third of the oven for 1 hour and 10 minutes.

3. Increase the oven temperature to 450°. Add the wine to the pan and roast the chicken for about 20 minutes longer, until the onions are well browned, the chicken is golden and the cavity juices run clear. Pour the cavity juices into the pan. Transfer the chicken and onions to a platter; let the chicken rest for 10 minutes.

4. Set the roasting pan over moderately high heat and add 4 of the tomato halves and ½ cup of water. Simmer, scraping up any browned bits and mashing the tomatoes, until reduced by one-third. Strain the jus into a saucepan and season with salt and pepper. Carve the chicken and serve with the tomatoes, onions, tomato jus and Creamy Cheese Grits. —_Marcia Kiesel_
SERVE WITH Sautéed zucchini chunks.
WINE Lush, fragrant Viognier.

poultry

Sour-Orange Yucatán Chickens

photo, page 94

ACTIVE: 40 MIN; TOTAL: 3 HR PLUS
OVERNIGHT MARINATING

8 SERVINGS

- 20 garlic cloves, halved
- ¼ cup vegetable oil
- 1⅓ cups fresh orange juice
- ½ cup fresh lemon juice
- ¼ cup pure ancho chile powder
- 2 tablespoons hot paprika
- 4 teaspoons kosher salt, plus
  more for seasoning
- 2 teaspoons ground cumin
- Two 3½-pound chickens
- ¼ cup plus 1 tablespoon honey

1. In a food processor, mince the garlic with the vegetable oil. Add the orange and lemon juices, chile powder, paprika, salt and cumin and blend well.

2. Loosen the skin on the chicken breasts and around the legs. Put each chicken in a bowl and cover with the citrus marinade. Rub the marinade under the skin and in the cavity. Turn the chickens breast side up, cover and refrigerate overnight.

3. Preheat the oven to 350°. Set the chickens breast side up in a large roasting pan and season with salt. Add the citrus marinade to the roasting pan, along with 1 cup of water. Bake for 1 hour. Spoon ¼ cup of the pan juices into a small bowl and stir in 3 tablespoons of the honey; pour this mixture over the chickens and bake for about 1 hour and 15 minutes, until an instant-read thermometer inserted in the inner thighs registers 160°.

4. Carefully drain the juices from the chicken cavities into the roasting pan. Transfer the chickens to a carving board and let rest for 10 minutes. Pour the pan juices into a saucepan. Add the remaining 2 tablespoons of honey, bring to a boil and season with salt. Carve the chickens and serve with the pan sauce.

—Marcia Kiesel

WINE Full-bodied, rich Pinot Gris.

Roasted Herb Chicken with Morels and Watercress Salad

ACTIVE: 40 MIN; TOTAL: 2 HR 30 MIN
4 SERVINGS

Kevin O'Connor, former wine director at Spago restaurant in Beverly Hills, roasts chicken with white wine, whole garlic cloves and plenty of herbs. Then he takes the fragrant juices left in the pan and mixes some into a lush vinaigrette for watercress and the rest into sautéed morel mushrooms.

- One 3½-pound chicken
- 3 tablespoons extra-virgin
  olive oil
- Salt and freshly ground pepper
- ½ cup chopped mixed herbs,
  such as thyme, rosemary,
  oregano and parsley
- 2 heads of garlic, separated into
  unpeeled cloves
- 1 cup dry white wine
- 1½ ounces dried morel mushrooms
  (see Note)
- 1 cup boiling water
- 2 tablespoons unsalted butter
- 1 tablespoon sherry vinegar
- ½ pound watercress,
  thick stems discarded

1. Preheat the oven to 450°. Rub the chicken all over with 2 tablespoons of the olive oil. Season the chicken inside and out with salt and pepper and set it in a roasting pan, breast side up. Rub all but 1 tablespoon of the chopped mixed herbs over the chicken, covering it well. Scatter the unpeeled garlic cloves in the roasting pan and roast for 15 minutes.

2. Reduce the oven temperature to 350°. Slowly pour ½ cup of the white wine over the top of the chicken, being careful not to disturb the herb crust, and roast the chicken for 15 minutes longer. Reduce the oven temperature to 300° and roast for 30 minutes more. Slowly pour the remaining ½ cup of white wine over the chicken; continue to roast for about 40 minutes

longer, until an instant-read thermometer inserted in the chicken's inner thigh registers 165°.

3. Meanwhile, in a heatproof bowl, soak the dried morel mushrooms in the boiling water until softened, about 10 minutes. Drain the morels and rinse well to dislodge any grit in their crevices; reserve the morel soaking liquid.

4. In a large skillet, melt the butter in the remaining 1 tablespoon of olive oil. Add the drained morels and season with salt and pepper. Cover and cook over moderate heat until the mushrooms are glazed, about 3 minutes. Carefully pour in the reserved morel soaking liquid, stopping before you reach the grit at the bottom of the bowl. Boil until the mushroom liquid is reduced to 2 tablespoons and stir in the 1 tablespoon of remaining mixed herbs. Cover the morels and set aside.

5. Carefully tilt the chicken to drain the cavity juices back into the roasting pan and transfer the chicken to a large carving board. Peel the roasted garlic cloves and transfer them to a small plate. Pour the juices from the roasting pan into a small saucepan and use a spoon to skim off the fat. Transfer ¼ cup of the skimmed pan juices to a large bowl. Stir in the sherry vinegar and season with salt and pepper. Add the watercress and toss well. Add the remaining pan juices and the roasted garlic to the sautéed morels and reheat over moderate heat, stirring; season the mushrooms with salt and pepper.

6. Carve the chicken and serve with the watercress salad and morels.

—Kevin O'Connor

NOTE Alternatively, cut 1 pound of fresh morels or other wild mushrooms into 2-inch pieces, cleaning them carefully to dislodge any grit. Cook the mushrooms in the butter and olive oil over moderate heat, covered, for 5 minutes, then uncovered for 3 minutes, until browned.

WINE Ripe, luxurious Chardonnay.

ROASTED HERB CHICKEN WITH
MORELS AND WATERCRESS SALAD

poultry

Grill-Smoked Whole Chicken

ACTIVE: 30 MIN; TOTAL: 2 HR 30 MIN

4 SERVINGS

One 3½-pound chicken
1   lemon, halved
10   thyme sprigs
Salt and freshly ground pepper
1   cup applewood chips

1. Light a charcoal grill, and when the coals are covered with white ash, push them to one side. Alternatively, preheat only one zone of a gas grill. Carefully lift the grate and set a foil drip pan in the unheated zone; replace the grate. Stuff the chicken cavity with the lemon halves and thyme sprigs and season the chicken all over with salt and pepper.

2. If using a charcoal grill, thoroughly soak the wood chips, then drain. For a gas grill, wrap the chips in foil and puncture the foil all over. Add the chips to the fire or gas flames and heat until they begin to smoke. Set the chicken on the grate over the drip pan. Cover the grill and smoke the chicken

over low heat until golden and an instant-read thermometer inserted into the thigh registers 165°, about 1 hour 15 minutes. Let the chicken rest for 10 minutes before carving, then serve. —*Kerry Simon*
WINE Juicy, spicy Grenache.

Hainan Chicken with Rice and Two Sauces

ACTIVE: 45 MIN; TOTAL: 2 HR 20 MIN

8 SERVINGS ● ●

One 6- to 7-pound chicken
6   large scallions, coarsely chopped
One 3-inch piece of fresh ginger, thinly sliced
2   tablespoons vegetable oil
1½   cups long-grain white rice, rinsed
2   garlic cloves, minced
2¼   cups chicken stock or low-sodium broth
Salt

1. Set the chicken in a large pot, breast side down, and cover with water. Add the scallions and ginger and bring to a boil. Simmer over low heat for 20 minutes, skimming occasionally. Turn the chicken breast side up and simmer for an additional 40 minutes. Remove from the heat, cover and let stand for 1 hour, until cooked through.

2. Meanwhile, in a medium saucepan, heat the oil. Stir in the rice and garlic and cook over moderately high heat until fragrant, about 2 minutes. Add the stock and bring to a boil. Cover, reduce the heat to low and cook for about 13 minutes, until the rice is tender and the stock has been absorbed. Remove from the heat and let stand, covered, for 5 minutes. Fluff the rice and season it with salt. Cover and keep warm.

3. Transfer the chicken to a work surface. Reserve the stock for another use. Discard the chicken skin; remove the meat from the bones, slice into thin strips and arrange on a platter. Serve with the rice. —*Peter Ting*
SERVE WITH Chile Dipping Sauce and Scallion Dipping Sauce (recipes follow).
WINE Dry, fruity sparkling wine.

CHILE DIPPING SAUCE

 TOTAL: 10 MIN
MAKES ½ CUP ●

3   medium fresh hot red chiles, such as Holland or cayenne, seeded and coarsely chopped
1   tablespoon finely grated fresh ginger
1   tablespoon chicken stock or low-sodium broth
1   garlic clove, smashed
2   teaspoons sugar
1   teaspoon salt
1   teaspoon fresh lime juice
1   teaspoon Sriracha chile sauce

In a mini food processor, process the chiles, ginger, stock, garlic, sugar, salt, lime juice and Sriracha until smooth. Transfer to a small bowl and serve. —*PT*

SCALLION DIPPING SAUCE

TOTAL: 15 MIN
MAKES 1 CUP ● ●

6   large scallions, finely chopped
2   tablespoons finely grated fresh ginger
2   teaspoons kosher salt
¼   cup vegetable oil

In a medium heatproof bowl, combine the scallions with the ginger and salt. In a small saucepan, heat the vegetable oil until shimmering. Pour the oil over the scallions and stir to combine. Serve. —*PT*

Roasted-Chicken-and-Potato Salad with Béarnaise Dressing

ACTIVE: 50 MIN; TOTAL: 1 HR 15 MIN

4 SERVINGS ●

2   tablespoons unsalted butter
¾   cup vegetable oil
½   pound small red potatoes, halved
Salt and freshly ground pepper
½   pound shiitake mushrooms, stems discarded and caps quartered
½   teaspoon chopped rosemary
½   teaspoon chopped thyme
½   teaspoon chopped oregano

fast ideas for cooked chicken

Use Grill-Smoked Chicken (recipe above) or store-bought rotisserie chicken to make these dishes:

Barbecued-Chicken Sandwiches
Simmer shredded chicken with barbecue sauce and serve in rolls.

Pulled-Chicken Tacos
Serve shredded chicken in corn tortillas with avocado, salsa and fresh lime juice.

Smoked-Chicken Frittata
Sauté shredded chicken with onions, then add beaten eggs. Cook until the bottom sets, then broil until cooked through.

Four 6-ounce boneless chicken
   breast halves with skin

1½ tablespoons dry white wine

1½ tablespoons white wine vinegar

1 small shallot, minced

2 large egg yolks

3½ teaspoons fresh lemon juice

1 teaspoon dry mustard powder

2 tablespoons chopped tarragon

2 tablespoons extra-virgin
   olive oil

6 ounces watercress,
   stems discarded

6 ounces arugula, stems discarded

4 ounces cucumber—peeled,
   quartered and thinly sliced

½ small red onion, thinly sliced

1. Preheat the oven to 375°. In an ovenproof skillet, melt the butter in 2 tablespoons of the vegetable oil. Add the potatoes, cut side down, season with salt and pepper and cook over high heat until browned, 3 minutes. Turn the potatoes and roast in the oven for 20 minutes. Add the mushrooms, season with salt and pepper and roast, stirring a few times, for 25 minutes. Stir in the rosemary, thyme and oregano; keep warm.

2. Meanwhile, in another ovenproof skillet, heat 2 tablespoons of the vegetable oil. Season the chicken with salt and pepper and add to the skillet, skin side down. Cook over high heat until browned, 3 minutes. Turn the chicken and transfer to the oven. Roast for 10 minutes, until just cooked through. Transfer the chicken to a carving board; let rest.

3. In a nonreactive saucepan, combine the wine, vinegar and shallot and boil until reduced to 1 tablespoon, 2 minutes; scrape into a blender. Add the yolks and blend. Add ½ teaspoon of the lemon juice and the mustard and blend. With the machine on, slowly pour in the remaining ½ cup of vegetable oil; blend until smooth. Season with salt and pepper; stir in the tarragon.

4. In a large bowl, combine the olive oil with the remaining 3 teaspoons of lemon juice and season with salt and pepper. Add the

watercress, arugula, cucumber and onion and toss. Add the warm potatoes and mushrooms and toss. Slice each chicken breast crosswise and serve with the salad, passing the dressing at the table. —*Wade Murphy*
WINE Full-bodied, rich Pinot Gris.

Chinese Chicken Salad

TOTAL: 35 MIN
4 SERVINGS ●

¼ cup mayonnaise

¼ cup plus 2 tablespoons
   unseasoned rice vinegar

3 tablespoons plus
   1½ teaspoons sugar

¼ cup soy sauce

2 tablespoons Asian sesame oil

1 tablespoon Tabasco

One ½-inch piece of ginger, very
   finely chopped

1 small garlic clove, minced

One 2½-pound rotisserie chicken,
   meat shredded

3 scallions, thinly sliced

2 celery ribs, thinly sliced

1 cup unsalted roasted peanuts,
   coarsely chopped

¾ cup coarsely chopped cilantro

1 small head of romaine, cut into
   ½-inch ribbons

1 tablespoon extra-virgin olive oil

2 oranges, peeled with a knife and
   cut into sections

Lime wedges, for serving

1. In a large bowl, whisk the mayonnaise with ¼ cup of the vinegar, 3 tablespoons of the sugar and the soy sauce, sesame oil, Tabasco, ginger and garlic. Add the chicken, scallions, celery, peanuts and cilantro and toss until coated.

2. In another bowl, toss the romaine with the remaining 2 tablespoons of vinegar, 1½ teaspoons of sugar and the olive oil. Spread the romaine in 4 bowls. Top with the chicken and oranges and serve with lime wedges. —*Joanne Chang*
WINE Tart, citrusy Riesling.

Chicken Smothered in Gravy

TOTAL: 45 MIN
4 SERVINGS ● ●

2½ tablespoons canola oil

Eight 3-ounce skinless
   chicken drumsticks

Salt and freshly ground pepper

1 ounce bacon (1 thick slice) cut
   crosswise into ¼-inch strips

1½ tablespoons all-purpose flour

1 medium onion, thinly sliced

1 garlic clove, thinly sliced

1 large tomato—peeled, seeded
   and coarsely chopped

1 teaspoon tomato paste

1 cup 2-percent milk

¼ cup low-sodium chicken broth

2 parsley sprigs plus 2 teaspoons
   chopped parsley

1. Preheat the oven to 375°. In an ovenproof nonstick skillet, heat 1 tablespoon of the oil. Season the chicken with salt and pepper and add to the pan. Cook over moderately high heat until browned all over, 8 minutes. Transfer the chicken to a plate.

2. Add the bacon to the skillet and cook, stirring, until the fat is rendered, 2 minutes. Drain off the fat. Add the remaining 1½ tablespoons of oil to the skillet and stir in the flour until incorporated. Add the onion and garlic and cook over moderate heat, stirring, until slightly softened, 3 minutes. Add the tomato and tomato paste and cook, stirring, until the tomato softens slightly, 5 minutes. Add the milk and broth and bring to a boil, stirring, until slightly thickened, 3 minutes. Return the chicken and any accumulated juices to the skillet; add the parsley sprigs.

3. Cover; braise in the oven until cooked through, 20 minutes. Using tongs, transfer chicken to a platter; remove the parsley.

4. Return the skillet to moderate heat and cook the gravy, whisking constantly, until smooth, about 2 minutes. Whisk in the chopped parsley, pour the gravy over the chicken and serve. —*Mark Peel*
WINE Deep, velvety Merlot.

Chicken Salad with Zucchini, Lemon and Pine Nuts

TOTAL: 40 MIN PLUS 2 HR MARINATING

4 SERVINGS ●

Chef Armand Arnal of La Chassagnette, outside of the southern French city of Arles, uses ingredients from his restaurant's enormous organic garden to create seasonal Provençal dishes like this salad of chicken tossed with toasted pine nuts and lemon-marinated zucchini.

⅓ cup dried currants

¼ cup plus 2 tablespoons extra-virgin olive oil

1 garlic clove, thinly sliced

⅛ teaspoon ground cumin

Finely grated zest of 1 lemon

Juice of 2 lemons

Kosher salt and freshly ground pepper

3 medium zucchini (2 pounds), cut into 3-by-½-inch sticks

1 large shallot, minced

1½ pounds skinless, boneless chicken breast halves

3 tablespoons pine nuts

2 cups lightly packed baby arugula leaves

One 1-inch piece preserved lemon, peel only, slivered (optional)

1. In a small bowl, cover the currants with hot water and let stand until softened, about 10 minutes. Drain.

2. In a large nonreactive bowl, combine 2 tablespoons of the olive oil with the garlic, cumin, lemon zest, half of the lemon juice, ½ teaspoon of salt and ¼ teaspoon of pepper. Add the zucchini and currants and toss to coat. Let stand at room temperature for 2 hours, stirring occasionally.

3. Meanwhile, in a large, shallow glass or ceramic dish, combine the minced shallot with 2 tablespoons of the olive oil and the remaining lemon juice. Add the chicken breast halves, turning to coat thoroughly with the marinade. Cover and refrigerate for 1 hour, turning a few times.

4. In a small skillet, toast the pine nuts over moderate heat, tossing a few times, until golden brown, about 2 minutes. Transfer the pine nuts to a plate and let cool.

5. Remove the chicken breast halves from the marinade, scraping off the shallot. Slice the chicken on the bias 1½ inches thick and season with salt and pepper. In a large skillet, heat the remaining 2 tablespoons of olive oil. Add the chicken slices and cook over moderately high heat, turning a few times, until lightly browned and cooked through, about 8 minutes.

6. Transfer the chicken to a large, shallow serving bowl and let cool slightly. Add the marinated zucchini and currants, toasted pine nuts, arugula and preserved lemon and toss lightly. Serve right away.
—*Armand Arnal*

WINE Creamy, supple Pinot Blanc.

Fried Chicken Liver, Bacon and Tomato Salad with Ranch Dressing

TOTAL: 1 HR

6 SERVINGS ●

This carnivore's salad is filled with bold ingredients like bacon and pickled onion, but the star ingredient is chicken livers. L.A. chefs Jon Shook and Vinny Dotolo (F&W Best New Chefs 2009) soak the livers in buttermilk and coat them in flour, then repeat the process before frying for extra-crispy results.

PICKLED RED ONION

1 small red onion, halved and thinly sliced

½ cup red wine vinegar

2 tablespoons sugar

DRESSING

¼ cup sour cream

¼ cup mayonnaise

1½ tablespoons buttermilk

1¼ teaspoons fresh lemon juice

¾ teaspoon hot sauce

½ teaspoon Dijon mustard

½ teaspoon red wine vinegar

¼ teaspoon Worcestershire sauce

1 small garlic clove, minced

½ teaspoon chopped parsley

½ teaspoon snipped chives

Kosher salt and freshly ground pepper

SALAD

6 slices of thick-cut applewood-smoked bacon (6 ounces)

3 cups self-rising flour (see Note)

1 tablespoon garlic powder

2½ teaspoons cayenne pepper

2 teaspoons onion powder

1 teaspoon smoked paprika

Kosher salt and freshly ground pepper

1 pound chicken livers, trimmed and rinsed

2½ cups buttermilk

Vegetable oil, for frying

¾ pound heirloom cherry tomatoes, halved

½ cup whole flat-leaf parsley leaves

4 tender celery ribs, thinly sliced on the bias, leaves reserved

1. MAKE THE PICKLED RED ONION: Put the sliced red onion in a medium bowl. In a small saucepan, heat the red wine vinegar with the sugar over moderately high heat until just beginning to simmer and the sugar is dissolved. Pour the hot vinegar over the sliced red onion and let stand for 30 minutes. Drain, reserving 1½ teaspoons of the onion pickling liquid.

2. MEANWHILE, MAKE THE DRESSING: In a medium bowl, whisk all of the ingredients together and season with salt and pepper. Cover and refrigerate.

3. ASSEMBLE THE SALAD: In a large skillet, cook the bacon over moderate heat until crisp, about 10 minutes; drain on paper towels. Cut each piece of bacon in half.

4. In a large bowl, mix the flour with the garlic powder, cayenne, onion powder, smoked paprika, 2 teaspoons of salt and ¼ teaspoon of pepper.

5. In a bowl, soak the livers in 1 cup of the buttermilk for 10 minutes; drain. Add the remaining 1½ cups of buttermilk. Dredge

FRIED CHICKEN LIVER, BACON AND TOMATO SALAD

GRILLED RED CURRY CHICKEN

the chicken livers in the seasoned flour until coated, then redip the chicken livers in the buttermilk and dredge again in the flour to double-coat.

6. In a large, deep skillet, heat ½ inch of vegetable oil to 325°. Fry the livers until golden, about 2 minutes per side. Drain the chicken livers on paper towels and immediately season with salt.

7. In a bowl, toss the tomatoes, parsley and celery ribs and leaves. Add the pickled onion and the reserved 1½ teaspoons of pickling liquid. Spoon the ranch dressing onto plates. Top with the tomato salad, chicken livers and bacon and serve at once.

—Vinny Dotolo and Jon Shook

NOTE You can buy self-rising flour or make it yourself: Combine 3 cups of all-purpose flour with 1½ tablespoons of baking powder and 1½ teaspoons of salt.

WINE Ripe, juicy Pinot Noir.

Grilled Red Curry Chicken

ACTIVE: 15 MIN; TOTAL: 50 MIN

4 SERVINGS

Roasting a whole chicken takes about an hour, but cut out the backbone and flatten the bird and it will grill perfectly in 30 minutes. F&W's Melissa Rubel Jacobson rubs the chicken all over with a very simple Thai-inspired mix of red curry paste, coconut milk and brown sugar.

One 3-pound chicken,
    wing tips removed
¼ cup unsweetened coconut milk
2 tablespoons red curry paste
1 teaspoon dark brown sugar
Salt and freshly ground pepper

1. Light a grill. Using kitchen shears, cut along both sides of the chicken backbone; discard the backbone. Turn the chicken breast side up and press down firmly on the breast bone to crack and flatten it.

Using a sharp knife, cut deep slits to the bone ½ inch apart along the chicken legs and thighs. Transfer the flattened chicken to a medium baking dish.

2. In a small bowl, whisk the coconut milk with the curry paste and brown sugar until smooth. Rub the curry mixture all over the chicken, into the slits and under the skin; season with salt and pepper.

3. Grill the chicken skin side down over moderate heat until the skin is browned and crisp, about 10 minutes. Turn the chicken skin side up, cover and grill over moderate heat until cooked through, about 20 minutes. Transfer the chicken to a cutting board and let rest for 5 minutes. Carve the chicken and serve.

—Melissa Rubel Jacobson

SERVE WITH Sautéed napa cabbage and grilled eggplant.

WINE Rich Alsace Gewürztraminer.

poultry

Honey–Soy Sauce Chicken with Mâche-and-Citrus Salad

ACTIVE: 45 MIN; TOTAL: 1 HR 45 MIN
4 SERVINGS

- ¼ cup plus 1 tablespoon soy sauce
- ¼ cup honey
- 3 garlic cloves, minced
- 1 tablespoon grated fresh ginger
- 12 chicken drumsticks (3½ pounds)
- 1 teaspoon finely grated lime zest
- 1 tablespoon fresh lime juice
- 3 navel oranges
- 3 tablespoons canola oil

Salt and freshly ground pepper
- 5 cups mâche (5 ounces)
- 1 small head of frisée, torn into bite-size pieces
- 1 small cucumber—peeled, seeded and thinly sliced
- 1 tablespoon toasted sesame seeds

1. In a large, resealable plastic bag, mix ¼ cup of the soy sauce with the honey, garlic and ginger. Add the chicken and turn to coat. Refrigerate for at least 1 hour.
2. Preheat the broiler with a rack set 10 inches from the heat. Line a large rimmed baking sheet with foil. Arrange the chicken on the sheet and pour the marinade on top. Broil for about 25 minutes, turning the chicken frequently, until cooked through.
3. Meanwhile, in a small bowl, combine the lime zest, lime juice and the remaining soy sauce. Finely grate the zest of 1 orange into the bowl and whisk in the canola oil.
4. Using a knife, peel the oranges, removing all of the white pith. Working over a bowl, cut in between the membranes to release the sections. Squeeze 1 tablespoon of juice into the dressing; season with salt and pepper.
5. Toss the oranges with the mâche, frisée and cucumber. Add the dressing and toss. Transfer the salad and chicken to plates and drizzle with any juices from the baking sheet. Sprinkle with the sesame seeds and serve. —Curtis Stone

WINE Fruity, low-oak Chardonnay.

Butter-Basted Chicken Skewers

TOTAL: 40 MIN PLUS 3 HR MARINATING
6 SERVINGS ● ●

- 2 tablespoons vegetable oil
- 1 small onion, thinly sliced
- 1 cup cottage cheese
- 2 garlic cloves, coarsely chopped
- 2 tablespoons chopped fresh ginger
- 2 tablespoons fresh lemon juice
- 1½ teaspoons ground coriander
- 1 teaspoon garam masala
- 1 teaspoon kosher salt
- ¼ teaspoon cayenne pepper
- 3 pounds skinless, boneless chicken breasts, cut into 1½-inch pieces
- 2 tablespoons ghee or unsalted butter, melted

Chat masala, for sprinkling (see Note)
- 2 tablespoons chopped cilantro

1. In a small skillet, heat the oil until shimmering. Add the onion and cook over moderately low heat, stirring occasionally, until browned, about 12 minutes. Transfer to a mini food processor. Add the cottage cheese, garlic, ginger, lemon juice, coriander, garam masala, salt and cayenne and process until smooth.
2. In a large bowl, toss the chicken with the cottage cheese mixture. Cover and refrigerate for 3 hours.
3. Preheat the broiler. Thread the chicken pieces onto 6 long metal skewers. Place the skewers on a large baking sheet and brush the chicken generously with the ghee. Broil 3 inches from the heat, turning and basting twice with ghee, until richly browned and cooked through, 7 minutes.
4. Transfer the skewers to a platter. Sprinkle generously with chat masala, garnish with the cilantro and serve right away. —Peggy Markel

NOTE Chat masala is a tangy spice blend that usually contains ground green mango, chile and mint. Look for it at Indian markets or order it from kalustyans.com.

WINE Ripe, luxurious Chardonnay.

Chicken Drumsticks with Asian Barbecue Sauce

ACTIVE: 20 MIN; TOTAL: 1 HR
8 SERVINGS ●

Instead of making a traditional American barbecue sauce, F&W's Grace Parisi prepares a sweet, sticky, slightly fiery version using Asian ingredients like chile sauce, hoisin sauce, rice vinegar and ginger.

- 2 tablespoons vegetable oil
- 1 teaspoon Chinese five-spice powder
- 16 chicken drumsticks (3 pounds)

Salt and freshly ground pepper
- ¾ cup hoisin sauce
- ¼ cup sweet Asian chile sauce or hot pepper jelly
- ¼ cup unseasoned rice vinegar
- ¼ cup chicken stock or broth
- 2 tablespoons very finely chopped fresh ginger
- 2 large garlic cloves
- 1 teaspoon Asian sesame oil
- 1 cup toasted sesame seeds

1. Preheat the oven to 425°. In a large bowl, mix the vegetable oil with the five-spice powder. Add the chicken, season with salt and pepper and toss. Arrange the chicken on a foil-lined baking sheet. Roast for about 35 minutes, turning twice, until cooked.
2. Meanwhile, in a blender, combine the hoisin sauce, chile sauce, rice vinegar, stock, ginger, garlic and sesame oil and puree until very smooth. Transfer to a saucepan and simmer until slightly thickened, 5 minutes.
3. Transfer the chicken to a bowl and toss with the sauce until completely coated.
4. Preheat the broiler and position a rack 8 inches from the heat. Return the chicken to the baking sheet and broil for about 10 minutes, brushing with the sauce and turning occasionally, until glazed and sticky.
5. Add the sesame seeds to a bowl. Dip the chicken in the seeds to coat; serve. —Grace Parisi

WINE Rustic, peppery Malbec.

CHICKEN DRUMSTICKS WITH
ASIAN BARBECUE SAUCE

Chicken Thighs with Spicy Tomato-Pepper Sauce

ACTIVE: 1 HR; TOTAL: 1 HR 30 MIN

10 SERVINGS ●●

Chef-winemaker Gerald Hirigoyen (an F&W Best New Chef 1994), who was born in the Basque region that straddles France and Spain, named his San Francisco restaurant after *pipérade,* a Basque vegetable stew that combines tomatoes, bell peppers and onions. Here Hirigoyen uses a *pipérade* puree to braise chicken. He says that children love this lightly sweet sauce: "Anytime I'm cooking for my son and need to get him to eat something, I use *pipérade* and call it ketchup."

- 1 cup extra-virgin olive oil
- 2 small onions, thinly sliced
- 2 red bell peppers, thinly sliced
- 2 yellow bell peppers, thinly sliced
- 12 medium garlic cloves, thinly sliced (½ cup)
- 2 pounds plum tomatoes, seeded and coarsely chopped

Kosher salt

Piment d'Espelette or hot paprika (see Note)

- 20 chicken thighs (about 8 pounds)

Freshly ground pepper

- ½ cup light brown sugar
- 1 cup sherry vinegar

---

basting with fresh herbs

Chef Robert Del Grande swears by his grandmother's trick: "I saw her do this when I was a kid. She would tie fresh herbs to a brush and baste chicken on the grill with it. Some things just stick in your mind."

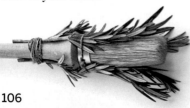

1. In a very large ovenproof skillet, heat ½ cup plus 2 tablespoons of the olive oil. Add the onions, bell peppers and garlic and cook over moderately high heat, stirring occasionally, until softened and lightly browned, about 10 minutes. Add the tomatoes and cook until softened and all of the liquid has evaporated, about 10 minutes longer.

2. Transfer the vegetables to a blender and puree until smooth. Season the vegetable puree with salt and piment d'Espelette.

3. Wash and dry the skillet. Heat 3 tablespoons of the oil in each of 2 very large ovenproof skillets. Season the chicken with salt and pepper. Add 10 of the thighs to each skillet, skin side down. Cook over moderately high heat, turning once, until the chicken is golden brown, about 12 minutes. Remove from the heat. Transfer the chicken to a platter and pour off the fat in the skillets.

4. Add ¼ cup of the brown sugar to one of the skillets and cook over high heat, whisking constantly, until melted, about 1 minute. Off the heat, carefully whisk in ½ cup of the vinegar; turn away to avoid the fumes. Cook over moderate heat, whisking and scraping up any browned bits from the bottom of the skillet, until thick and syrupy, about 1 minute. Add half of the vegetable puree; bring to a boil. Return 10 of the chicken thighs to the skillet, skin side up. Repeat with the second skillet and the remaining ¼ cup sugar, ½ cup of vinegar, puree and chicken. Cover both skillets and simmer the chicken over low heat until cooked through, 12 minutes.

5. Preheat the broiler and position a rack 8 inches from the heat. Uncover the skillets and broil the chicken until the skin is lightly browned and crisp, about 2 minutes. Transfer to a platter, spoon the sauce on top and serve. —*Gerald Hirigoyen*

NOTE Piment d'Espelette, a smoky, mildly spicy ground chile native to the Basque region, is available at specialty food shops, spice shops and piperade.com.

WINE Juicy, spicy Grenache.

Herb-Marinated Chicken Skewers with Harissa

TOTAL: 45 MIN PLUS 2 HR MARINATING

4 SERVINGS ●

Chef Andres Barrera of Manhattan's City Winery briefly marinates chicken in herbs and cumin before skewering and grilling it; then he serves it with a cool chickpea puree and fiery harissa. Scented with toasted and ground cumin, coriander and caraway seeds, his harissa is a knockout, but jarred harissa also works.

CHICKEN

- ¼ cup extra-virgin olive oil
- 1 tablespoon rosemary leaves
- 1 teaspoon chopped thyme
- 1 teaspoon chopped oregano
- 1 teaspoon ground cumin
- 1½ pounds skinless, boneless chicken breast halves, cut into 1½-inch cubes

Salt

HARISSA

- 1 teaspoon cumin seeds
- 1 teaspoon coriander seeds
- 1 teaspoon caraway seeds
- 2 roasted red peppers from a jar, coarsely chopped
- 1 red Thai chile, with seeds, chopped
- 1 garlic clove, chopped
- 3 tablespoons extra-virgin olive oil
- 1 tablespoon fresh lemon juice

Salt

Hummus, for serving

1. MARINATE THE CHICKEN: In a large bowl, mix the olive oil with the rosemary, thyme, oregano and ground cumin. Add the chicken and toss well. Cover and refrigerate for at least 2 hours or overnight.

2. MEANWHILE, MAKE THE HARISSA: In a small skillet, toast the cumin, coriander and caraway seeds over moderately high heat, shaking the skillet a few times, until the spices are fragrant, about 2 minutes. Transfer to a spice grinder and let cool completely. Grind to a powder.

3. In a blender, combine the roasted peppers with the chile, garlic, olive oil, lemon juice and ground spices and puree. Season the harissa with salt.

4. Light a grill. Thread the chicken pieces onto 8 metal skewers. Season with salt and grill over moderately high heat, turning, until nicely charred and just cooked, about 14 minutes. Serve the skewers with the harissa and hummus.

—*Andres Barrera*

MAKE AHEAD The harissa can be refrigerated for up to 5 days. Let come to room temperature before serving.

WINE Zippy, fresh Pinot Bianco.

Crispy Baked Red Chile Chicken Wings

ACTIVE: 15 MIN; TOTAL: 1 HR
12 FIRST-COURSE SERVINGS

- 4 pounds chicken wings
- 2 tablespoons vegetable oil

Kosher salt and freshly
  ground black pepper

- 1 tablespoon plus 1 teaspoon ancho chile powder
- 1 tablespoon plus 1 teaspoon chile powder

Pinch of cayenne pepper

- 1½ cups sour cream
- 3 pickled jalapeños, seeded and minced, plus 3 tablespoons jalapeño pickling liquid from the jar
- 3 tablespoons coarsely chopped cilantro leaves

1. Preheat the oven to 425°. In a large bowl, toss the chicken wings with the vegetable oil and season them liberally with kosher salt and black pepper. Sprinkle the chicken wings with the ancho chile powder, chile powder and cayenne pepper and toss to coat the chicken evenly in the seasonings. Transfer the chicken wings skin side up to 2 large rimmed baking sheets and bake them for about 45 minutes, until the wings are cooked through and crisp.

2. Meanwhile, in a medium bowl, mix the sour cream with the minced jalapeños, the jalapeño pickling liquid and the chopped cilantro and season the dip with salt. Transfer the crispy baked wings to a serving platter and serve at once, with the jalapeño–sour cream dip.

—*Melissa Rubel Jacobson*

MAKE AHEAD The jalapeño–sour cream dip can be covered and refrigerated for up to 2 days. Stir before serving.

WINE Fresh, fruity rosé.

Chicken, Wild Mushroom and Roasted-Garlic Sauté

ACTIVE: 40 MIN; TOTAL: 1 HR 45 MIN
4 SERVINGS ●

F&W's Marcia Kiesel, a self-described mushroom freak, uses fresh mushrooms and dried porcini to make her delicious, earthy chicken thigh sauté with roasted garlic cloves. She finishes the dish with a sprinkle of chopped tarragon, which adds a light, herbal sweetness.

- 1 large head of garlic, top fourth cut off
- 3 tablespoons extra-virgin olive oil, plus more for drizzling
- ½ cup dried porcini mushrooms
- ¾ cup boiling water
- 1½ pounds skinless, boneless chicken thighs, cut into 2-inch pieces

Salt and freshly ground pepper

- ½ pound assorted fresh mushrooms, such as stemmed shiitake, cremini and oyster, quartered
- 1 tablespoon unsalted butter, plus 2 tablespoons chilled
- 2 large shallots, thinly sliced
- ¼ cup dry red wine
- ½ cup chicken stock
- 2 medium tomatoes, cut into 1-inch dice
- 1 tablespoon chopped fresh tarragon

Crusty bread, for serving

1. Preheat the oven to 350°. Set the head of garlic on a double layer of foil, cut side up. Drizzle with olive oil, then wrap in the foil. Roast the garlic until very soft, about 1 hour and 30 minutes. Let cool, then peel, keeping the cloves intact.

2. Meanwhile, in a medium heatproof bowl, cover the dried porcini mushrooms with the boiling water and let stand until softened, about 15 minutes. Rinse the soaked porcini and coarsely chop them; reserve the soaking liquid.

3. In a large skillet, heat 1 tablespoon of the olive oil. Season the chicken thighs with salt and pepper and spread the thighs in a single layer in the skillet. Cook over high heat until the chicken pieces are browned on the bottom, about 4 minutes. Use tongs to transfer the chicken thighs to a large bowl.

4. Add 1 tablespoon of the olive oil to the skillet. Add the assorted fresh mushrooms and season with salt and pepper. Cover the skillet and cook over moderate heat, stirring a few times, until the mushrooms have browned and their liquid has evaporated, about 5 minutes. Transfer the mushrooms to a plate.

5. In the skillet, melt the 1 tablespoon of butter in the remaining 1 tablespoon of olive oil. Add the thinly sliced shallots to the skillet and cook over moderate heat, stirring, until softened, about 3 minutes. Add the red wine and boil over moderately high heat until reduced by half, about 2 minutes. Pour in the reserved porcini soaking liquid, stopping before you reach the grit at the bottom of the bowl. Add the chicken stock, diced tomatoes, fresh mushrooms, porcini, roasted garlic and chicken thighs and bring to a simmer. Remove from the heat. Add the chopped tarragon and season with salt and pepper. Swirl in the 2 tablespoons of chilled butter, 1 tablespoon at a time. Serve with crusty bread. —*Marcia Kiesel*

WINE Complex, elegant Pinot Noir.

Miso-Ginger Chicken and Cabbage

TOTAL: 25 MIN
4 SERVINGS ●

- 3 tablespoons light miso paste
- 2 garlic cloves, minced
- 1 teaspoon Asian sesame oil
- ¾ cup chicken stock or low-sodium broth
- 3 tablespoons vegetable oil
- 1¼ pounds skinless, boneless chicken thighs, cut into 1½-inch pieces

Salt and freshly ground pepper

- ½ pound shiitake mushrooms, stemmed, caps quartered
- 2 tablespoons minced ginger
- ¾ pound napa cabbage, coarsely chopped (4 cups)
- 3 ounces daikon radish, peeled and thinly sliced (½ cup)
- 2 scallions, thinly sliced

1. In a bowl, whisk the miso, garlic, sesame oil and ½ cup of the stock. In a large skillet, heat the vegetable oil. Add the chicken, season with salt and pepper; cook over high heat until just cooked through, 4 minutes. Using a slotted spoon, transfer to a plate.
2. Add the shiitake, ginger and the remaining stock to the skillet. Cover and cook over moderate heat until the shiitake are tender, 2 minutes. Add the cabbage and chicken and stir-fry over high heat for 1 minute. Add the miso sauce and bring to a simmer. Stir in the daikon and scallions. Transfer to bowls and serve. —*Marcia Kiesel*
WINE Dry, earthy sparkling wine.

Chicken Shawarma with Green Beans and Zucchini

ACTIVE: 30 MIN; TOTAL: 1 HR
6 SERVINGS ●●

- 1 pound zucchini, sliced ¼ inch thick
- ½ pound green beans
- ½ cup extra-virgin olive oil

Kosher salt

- 1½ teaspoons ground allspice
- 1½ teaspoons ground black pepper
- ½ teaspoon ground white pepper
- ¼ teaspoon cinnamon
- ¼ teaspoon ground cumin
- ¼ teaspoon ground coriander
- 6 skinless, boneless chicken thighs
- 1 garlic clove, minced
- 1 cup plain low-fat yogurt
- 2 tablespoons fresh lemon juice

Six 6-inch pitas, split horizontally

- ½ small red onion, thinly sliced

1. Preheat the oven to 425°. In a medium bowl, toss the zucchini and green beans with 2 tablespoons of the olive oil and season with salt; spread on a baking sheet. In the same bowl, combine the allspice, black pepper, white pepper, cinnamon, cumin and coriander with 2 tablespoons of the olive oil. Rub the spice paste all over the chicken and season with salt. Arrange the chicken on another baking sheet.
2. Roast the chicken on the lower rack and the vegetables on the upper rack of the oven for 15 minutes, until the vegetables are tender and the chicken is nearly cooked through. Remove the vegetables. Preheat the broiler and broil the chicken, turning once, until crisp and browned, 10 minutes; cut into strips.
3. Meanwhile, heat the remaining ¼ cup of olive oil in a small skillet. Add the garlic and cook over moderate heat until lightly browned, about 30 seconds. Remove from the heat and whisk in the yogurt and lemon juice; season with salt.
4. Arrange the pitas cut side up on a work surface and brush each round with about 1½ teaspoons of the yogurt sauce. Divide the chicken, roasted vegetables and red onion among the pitas and roll the bread around the filling into tight cylinders.
5. Heat a griddle over moderately high heat. Cook the rolls seam side down until golden and crisp, 2 minutes. Turn and toast the other side. Halve each roll; serve with the remaining yogurt sauce. —*Ana Sortun*
WINE Round, deep-flavored Syrah.

Chicken Sofrito

ACTIVE: 25 MIN; TOTAL: 1 HR 15 MIN
4 SERVINGS ●

For this sublime version of everyday chicken and rice, the chicken is dusted in chile powder and the rice is cooked with *sofrito*—a Spanish mixture of chopped onion, garlic and bell pepper. Everything then bakes together in a skillet so that the delectable chicken juices flavor the rice. Broiling the dish at the last minute turns the chicken skin enticingly brown.

- 1 tablespoon vegetable oil
- 4 whole chicken legs, separated into drumsticks and thighs

Salt and freshly ground black pepper

- ½ teaspoon chile powder, plus more for dusting
- 1 medium onion, cut into ½-inch dice
- 3 garlic cloves, minced
- 1 jalapeño, seeded and minced
- 2 large thyme sprigs
- 1 red bell pepper, cut into ½-inch-wide strips

Rounded ¼ teaspoon anise seeds

Pinch of cayenne pepper

- 1 cup chopped canned tomatoes
- 3 cups chicken stock or low-sodium broth
- 1 cup short-grain white rice
- 2 tablespoons fresh lemon juice
- ½ cup roasted almonds

1. Preheat the oven to 375°. In a large oven-proof skillet, heat the vegetable oil. Season the chicken with salt and pepper and dust lightly with chile powder. Add the chicken to the skillet and cook over moderate heat until well browned, about 4 minutes per side. Transfer to a plate.
2. Add the onion, garlic, jalapeño and thyme sprigs to the skillet and cook over moderately low heat, stirring occasionally, until the onion is softened, about 8 minutes.

CHICKEN SOFRITO

CHICKEN PAPRIKASH

Add the bell pepper, anise seeds, cayenne and the ½ teaspoon of chile powder and cook, stirring, until fragrant, about 1 minute. Add the chopped tomatoes, raise the heat to high and cook until bubbling. Add the chicken stock and bring to a boil. Stir in the rice and ½ teaspoon of salt and bring to a simmer. Arrange the chicken pieces on the rice, skin side up. Bake in the upper third of the oven for about 25 minutes, until the chicken is just cooked through and the rice is tender and has absorbed the stock.

3. Preheat the broiler. Broil the *sofrito* 6 inches from the heat for about 2 minutes, until the chicken skin is crisp. Transfer the chicken to a plate. Discard the thyme sprigs, stir the lemon juice into the rice and scatter the almonds on top. Spoon the rice onto plates, add the chicken and serve.

—*Marcia Kiesel*

WINE Earthy, medium-bodied Tempranillo.

Chicken Paprikash

ACTIVE: 30 MIN; TOTAL: 1 HR 30 MIN

8 SERVINGS ● ●

- ¼ cup canola oil
- 1 large onion, thinly sliced
- 2 red bell peppers, thinly sliced
- 3 large garlic cloves, thinly sliced
- ¼ cup sweet Hungarian paprika, plus more for sprinkling
- 1½ teaspoons caraway seeds, ground
- 3 tablespoons all-purpose flour
- 6 cups chicken stock or low-sodium broth
- 2 bay leaves
- 2 thyme sprigs

Salt and freshly ground pepper

- 2 pounds skinless, boneless chicken breasts, cut into 1-inch pieces
- ½ cup fat-free sour cream

1. In a large enameled cast-iron casserole or Dutch oven, heat the oil until shimmering. Add the onion, bell peppers and garlic and cook over moderate heat, stirring occasionally, until just beginning to brown, about 8 minutes. Add the paprika, caraway and flour and cook, stirring, for 2 minutes. Add the stock, bay leaves and thyme sprigs, season with salt and pepper and bring to a boil. Simmer over moderately low heat, stirring occasionally, until the peppers are very tender and the sauce is thickened, about 1 hour.

2. Add the chicken pieces to the sauce and cook over high heat until just white throughout, about 6 minutes. Discard the bay leaves and thyme sprigs. Spoon the chicken into bowls and top with sour cream. Sprinkle with paprika and serve.

—*Grace Parisi*

WINE Complex, aromatic Chenin Blanc.

poultry

Chicken Legs with Roasted Garlic–Ancho Sauce

ACTIVE: 40 MIN; TOTAL: 2 HR
4 SERVINGS ●

These roasted chicken legs taste like more than the sum of their parts. Only five ingredients, including pleasantly bitter ancho chiles (dried poblanos), make a luscious sauce that you'd swear has butter in it (it doesn't). The secret is the slow-roasted garlic, which becomes silky in the blender. The smoky sauce is fabulous with the juicy chicken legs here, but it would be equally good with anything from grilled corn on the cob to lamb chops.

- 1 head of garlic
- Extra-virgin olive oil
- 1 medium ancho chile
- ¼ cup plus 2 tablespoons chicken stock or low-sodium broth
- 2 teaspoons soy sauce
- Salt and freshly ground black pepper
- 4 whole chicken legs, split into drumsticks and thighs

1. Preheat the oven to 375°. Cut off the top quarter of the garlic and set it on a sheet of foil. Drizzle the garlic with olive oil, wrap it in the foil and roast for about 1 hour and 20 minutes, until tender.

2. Meanwhile, in a small saucepan, cover the ancho chile with water and bring to a boil. Cover the saucepan and simmer over low heat, turning the ancho a few times, until the chile is soft, about 10 minutes. Drain the chile. Discard the ancho stem and seeds. Coarsely chop the chile and transfer it to a blender.

3. Squeeze the roasted garlic cloves from the skins into the blender. Add the chicken stock and puree until smooth. With the machine running, gradually pour in ¼ cup of olive oil and puree until it's incorporated. Pour the sauce into the small saucepan, stir in the soy sauce and season with salt and black pepper.

4. Light a grill. Rub the chicken with olive oil and season with salt and pepper. Grill over moderate heat, turning frequently, until nicely charred and cooked through, 30 minutes total. Reheat the sauce and serve with the chicken. —*Marcia Kiesel*
MAKE AHEAD The ancho sauce can be refrigerated in an airtight container for up to 3 days. Reheat gently.
WINE Earthy, medium-bodied Tempranillo.

Chilaquiles-Style Roasted Chicken Legs

ACTIVE: 15 MIN; TOTAL: 45 MIN
4 SERVINGS

Chilaquiles is a baked Mexican dish that's often made with leftover shredded chicken, tortilla strips and cheese. In her more substantial and refined version, F&W's Grace Parisi bakes whole chicken legs with tomatoes, hominy, jalapeños and tortilla chips.

- 2 garlic cloves, smashed
- Kosher salt
- 1½ teaspoons ground cumin
- 1½ teaspoons chile powder
- 2 tablespoons extra-virgin olive oil
- One 28-ounce can diced tomatoes, drained well
- 1 cup canned hominy, drained
- ¼ cup sliced pickled jalapeños
- 6 cups lightly crushed thick corn tortilla chips (6 ounces)
- 4 whole chicken legs (about 12 ounces each)
- Chopped cilantro and sour cream, for serving

1. Preheat the oven to 450°. On a work surface, mash the garlic to a paste with a pinch of salt. Transfer the garlic paste to a small bowl and stir in the ground cumin, chile powder and 1 tablespoon of the oil.

2. In a 9-by-13-inch glass or ceramic baking dish, toss the drained diced tomatoes with the hominy, sliced pickled jalapeños, half of the spice paste and the remaining 1 tablespoon of olive oil. Gently mix in the crushed tortilla chips.

3. On a work surface, cut halfway through the joint between the thigh and drumstick on the underside of each chicken leg. Score the top of each leg 3 or 4 times, cutting to the bone. Rub the remaining spice paste over and into the chicken and arrange skin side up in the baking dish. Roast in the center of the oven for about 30 minutes, until the chicken is cooked through.

4. Leave the chicken in the oven and turn on the broiler. Broil for about 3 minutes, just until the chicken skin is golden and crispy. Transfer to a large plate and return the baking dish to the oven. Broil for about 3 minutes, until the tortilla chips are lightly browned. Return the chicken to the baking dish, sprinkle with cilantro and serve with sour cream. —*Grace Parisi*
WINE Juicy, fresh Dolcetto.

Pan-Roasted Chicken Breasts with Mole Negro

ACTIVE: 20 MIN; TOTAL: 1 HR
4 SERVINGS ●

The Mexican city of Oaxaca is famous for its complex mole sauces, often made with more than 20 ingredients. Since moles are so time-consuming to make, most Mexican cooks rely on prepared pastes sold at outdoor markets, and Oaxacan chef Alejandro Ruíz Olmedo is no exception. Instead of stewing chicken in the mole sauce, Olmedo takes a more elegant approach: He roasts chicken breasts until the skin is crisp and serves the mole alongside.

- 1 cup black mole paste (see Note)
- 3 cups chicken stock
- Salt and freshly ground pepper
- 2 tablespoons vegetable oil
- 4 bone-in chicken breast halves with skin
- Toasted sesame seeds, for garnish

1. Preheat the oven to 400°. In a saucepan, whisk the mole paste with the stock. Boil the mole sauce over high heat, whisking occasionally, until reduced to 2 cups, 25 minutes. Season with salt and pepper.

2. In an ovenproof skillet, heat the oil until shimmering. Season the chicken breasts with salt and pepper and add them to the skillet, skin side down. Cook over moderately high heat until browned and crisp, 4 minutes. Turn the chicken and cook for 3 minutes. Transfer the skillet to the oven and roast the chicken for 20 minutes, until just cooked through. Let the chicken rest in the skillet for 5 minutes, then transfer to plates. Spoon the mole sauce alongside, garnish with sesame seeds and serve.
—Alejandro Ruíz Olmedo

NOTE Black mole paste is available at Latin markets or mexgrocer.com.

WINE Intense, fruity Zinfandel.

Chicken Breasts with Potatoes and Mashed Peas

ACTIVE: 30 MIN; TOTAL: 1 HR 45 MIN
4 SERVINGS

F&W's Marcia Kiesel likes to brown chicken breasts in butter on the stove before roasting them in the oven; the butter enriches both the chicken and the pan juices, which become the base for a flavorful sauce. As a delicious accompaniment, she mashes green peas and mixes them in with whole peas and fresh mint.

- 2 **pounds fingerling potatoes, scrubbed and halved lengthwise**
- 2 **tablespoons extra-virgin olive oil**
- **Salt and freshly ground pepper**
- 3 **tablespoons unsalted butter, plus 2 tablespoons chilled**
- **Four ¾-pound chicken breast halves on the bone**
- 2 **large thyme sprigs, plus 2 teaspoons chopped thyme**
- ½ **cup plus 2 tablespoons dry white wine**
- ½ **cup chicken stock or low-sodium broth**
- **Two 10-ounce packages of frozen baby peas**
- 1 **tablespoon finely chopped mint**

1. Preheat the oven to 425°. On a large rimmed baking sheet, toss the potatoes with the olive oil and season with salt and pepper. Roast the potatoes for about 35 minutes, or until tender and browned. Set the potatoes aside. Reduce the oven temperature to 350°.

2. Meanwhile, in a large ovenproof skillet, melt the 3 tablespoons of butter. Season the chicken breast halves with salt and pepper and add to the skillet, skin side down, along with the thyme sprigs. Cook over moderately low heat until the skin is well browned, about 15 minutes. Turn and cook for 5 minutes longer, basting occasionally with the pan juices.

3. Transfer the chicken to the oven and roast for about 15 minutes, until cooked through. Add the chicken to the potatoes and keep warm. Reserve 3 tablespoons of the melted fat from the skillet.

4. Pour off the remaining fat from the skillet and discard the thyme sprigs. Add ½ cup of the wine to the skillet and boil over moderately high heat, scraping up the browned bits, until reduced by half, about 2 minutes. Add the stock and boil until slightly thickened, about 3 minutes. Remove from the heat and stir in the chopped thyme and 2 tablespoons of chilled butter, 1 tablespoon at a time. Season the pan sauce with salt and pepper.

5. Bring a large saucepan of water to a boil. Add the peas, cover and cook over moderate heat, stirring occasionally, until tender, about 3 minutes. Drain the peas, transfer half to a food processor and coarsely puree. Stir the puree back into the remaining peas. Add the reserved fat from the skillet along with the remaining 2 tablespoons of wine and the mint. Season with salt and pepper.

6. Transfer the chicken breasts and potatoes to plates. Spoon the mashed peas alongside and serve with the pan sauce.
—Marcia Kiesel

WINE Rich, complex white Burgundy.

Chicken Breasts with Walnuts, Leeks and Candied Lemon

TOTAL: 45 MIN
4 SERVINGS ● ●

- ¼ **cup extra-virgin olive oil**
- 2 **leeks, white and tender green parts only, sliced 1 inch thick**
- **Salt**
- 1 **tablespoon sugar**
- ½ **preserved lemon, pulp discarded and peel thinly sliced**
- 2 **tablespoons white wine vinegar**
- 1 **tablespoon minced chives**
- 2 **teaspoons minced dill**
- 1 **teaspoon minced tarragon**
- **Freshly ground pepper**
- **Four 6-ounce skinless, boneless chicken breast halves**
- ½ **cup toasted walnuts, for garnish**

1. In a medium skillet, heat 1 tablespoon of the olive oil. Add the leeks and a pinch of salt; cook over moderate heat, stirring, until softened, about 2 minutes. Add 2 tablespoons of water, cover the skillet and cook over low heat for 4 minutes. Remove from the heat.

2. In a small saucepan, combine the sugar with 1 tablespoon of water and simmer over moderate heat until syrupy, 2 minutes. Add the preserved lemon and simmer for 1 minute; add to the leeks and keep warm.

3. In a bowl, whisk the vinegar, chives, dill and tarragon with 2 tablespoons of the olive oil. Season with salt and pepper.

4. In a large skillet, heat the remaining 1 tablespoon of olive oil until shimmering. Season the chicken with salt and pepper and add to the skillet. Cook over moderately high heat until golden, 3 minutes. Reduce the heat to moderate; cook for 2 minutes longer. Turn the breasts; cook until just white throughout, 4 minutes.

5. Spoon the leeks and candied lemon onto plates. Top with the chicken. Drizzle with the vinaigrette, garnish with the walnuts and serve. *—Angela Hartnett*

WINE Ripe, luxurious Chardonnay.

Mustard-Glazed Chicken with Arugula and Bok Choy

 TOTAL: 40 MIN
4 SERVINGS ●

Takashi Yagihashi (an F&W Best New Chef 2000) glazes chicken breasts in a vibrant mustard sauce; on the side he serves an arugula salad dressed lightly with soy sauce and rice wine vinegar.

- 4 teaspoons dry mustard powder
- 4 teaspoons water
- ½ teaspoon mirin
- 1½ teaspoons low-sodium soy sauce
- ¾ teaspoon sugar
- ¼ cup canola oil
- 4 skinless, boneless chicken breast halves (about 6 ounces each)

Salt and freshly ground pepper

- 2 medium heads of bok choy (about 1¼ pounds), halved lengthwise
- 1 tablespoon rice vinegar

One 5-ounce bag baby arugula

1. Preheat the oven to 425°. In a bowl, stir the mustard, water, mirin, 1 teaspoon of the soy sauce and ½ teaspoon of the sugar.
2. In an ovenproof skillet, heat 1 tablespoon of the oil. Season the chicken with salt and pepper and cook over high heat until golden, 2 minutes. Flip the chicken and brush with the mustard; transfer to the oven and roast for 8 minutes, or until cooked through. Transfer the chicken to a cutting board and let rest for 5 minutes; slice. Wipe out the skillet.
3. Meanwhile, steam the bok choy for 5 minutes. Drain; pat dry. In the same skillet, heat 1 tablespoon of the oil. Add the bok choy cut side down and cook over high heat, turning once, until browned, 3 minutes. Transfer to a platter; season with salt and pepper. Arrange the chicken over the bok choy.
4. In a bowl, whisk the vinegar with the remaining oil, soy sauce and sugar; season with salt and pepper. Add the arugula and toss; arrange over the chicken and serve.
—*Takashi Yagihashi*

WINE Light, crisp white Burgundy.

Spicy Asian-Chicken-Salad Lettuce Cups

 TOTAL: 20 MIN
MAKES 12 LETTUCE CUPS ● ●

- ½ cup mayonnaise
- 2 teaspoons *sambal oelek* or Chinese chile-garlic sauce
- 1 teaspoon Dijon mustard
- ½ teaspoon Asian sesame oil

One 2-pound rotisserie chicken—skin and bones discarded, meat pulled into bite-size pieces

- ⅓ cup water chestnuts, coarsely chopped
- 2 scallions, white and green parts, thinly sliced

Kosher salt and freshly ground pepper

- 12 Bibb or iceberg lettuce leaves
- 1 Hass avocado, peeled and cut into 12 slices

Lime wedges, for serving

In a medium bowl, mix the mayonnaise with the *sambal oelek,* mustard and sesame oil. Stir in the chicken, water chestnuts and scallions and season with salt and pepper. Spoon the chicken salad into the lettuce leaves and top with a slice of avocado. Serve with lime wedges.
—*Melissa Rubel Jacobson*

WINE Tart, citrusy Riesling.

Chicken Salad with Piquillo Dressing

 TOTAL: 30 MIN
4 SERVINGS ●

- 4 boneless chicken breast halves with skin (about 2 pounds)

Salt and freshly ground pepper

- ¼ cup plus 1 tablespoon extra-virgin olive oil
- 12 ounces red-skinned potatoes, cut into 1-inch pieces
- ½ cup jarred piquillo peppers (4 ounces)
- 1 small garlic clove
- 2 tablespoons sherry vinegar
- 1 tablespoon honey

- 1 tablespoon fresh lemon juice
- ¼ cup pitted kalamata olives, sliced
- 1 carrot, shaved into ribbons with a vegetable peeler
- 12 ounces mesclun (4 packed cups)

1. Preheat the oven to 425°. Season the chicken with salt and pepper. In a large ovenproof skillet, heat 1 tablespoon of the olive oil over moderately high heat. Add the chicken skin side down and cook until very lightly browned, about 3 minutes. Turn the chicken skin side up and transfer the skillet to the oven; roast the chicken for about 10 minutes, until it is cooked through. Transfer the roasted chicken to a work surface and let cool.
2. Meanwhile, bring a medium saucepan of salted water to a boil. Add the potatoes and cook until tender, about 10 minutes. Drain the potatoes and let cool.
3. In a blender, combine the piquillo peppers with the garlic, vinegar, honey and lemon juice and puree until very smooth. With the machine on, add the remaining ¼ cup of olive oil in a thin stream and blend until the dressing is emulsified. Season the dressing with salt and pepper.
4. Discard the chicken skin and thinly slice the breasts crosswise. In a large bowl, toss the chicken with the potatoes, olives and carrot and toss with the dressing. Add the mesclun, toss gently and serve.
—*Seamus Mullen*

MAKE AHEAD The salad can be prepared through Step 3 and refrigerated overnight.
WINE Full-bodied, rich Pinot Gris.

Updated Chicken Chow Mein

 TOTAL: 45 MIN
4 SERVINGS

- 5 tablespoons vegetable oil
- 1 pound fresh plain chicken sausages, cut into ½-inch pieces
- 4 garlic cloves, very finely chopped
- 2 tablespoons minced ginger
- 4 ounces snow peas, cut in half

MUSTARD-GLAZED CHICKEN WITH ARUGULA AND BOK CHOY

SPICY ASIAN-CHICKEN-SALAD LETTUCE CUPS

2 fresh, hot long red chiles, seeded and thinly sliced

⅓ cup fresh orange juice

½ pound fresh or dried Chinese egg noodles, cooked

1 cup chicken stock mixed with 3 tablespoons of hoisin sauce and 2 teaspoons of cornstarch

Salt

½ cup slivered basil leaves

1. In a wok, heat 2 tablespoons of the oil. Add the chicken sausage and stir-fry over high heat, breaking it up, until just cooked through, 3 minutes. Transfer to a plate.

2. Heat the remaining 3 tablespoons of oil in the wok. Add the garlic and ginger and stir-fry over moderately high heat until golden, 1½ minutes. Off the heat, stir in the snow peas and chiles for 1 minute. Add the orange juice and stir over moderately high heat for 30 seconds. Add the sausage, noodles and stock mixture, season with salt and stir-fry until the sauce is thickened, about 2 minutes. Remove from the heat, stir in the basil and serve.
—*Marcia Kiesel*

WINE Vivid, lightly sweet Riesling.

Thai Chicken, Zucchini and Tomato Curry

TOTAL: 30 MIN
4 SERVINGS ●

3 tablespoons vegetable oil

1¼ pounds skinless, boneless chicken breasts, sliced crosswise ⅓ inch thick

Salt and freshly ground pepper

1 onion, sliced ¼ inch thick

2 zucchini (1 pound), cut into 2-by-½-inch sticks

1½ cups cherry tomatoes

1 tablespoon Thai red curry paste

½ cup unsweetened coconut milk

2 tablespoons water

Finely grated zest of 1 lime

1 tablespoon fresh lime juice

½ cup chopped cilantro

Rice, for serving

1. In a large skillet, heat 2 tablespoons of the oil. Add the chicken, season with salt and pepper and cook over high heat until just white throughout, 2 minutes. Transfer the chicken to a plate.

2. Add the remaining oil to the skillet. Add the onion and stir-fry over moderately high heat for 2 minutes. Add the zucchini and cherry tomatoes and stir-fry for 2 minutes. Stir in the curry paste, coconut milk, water, lime zest and lime juice and bring to a simmer. Add the chicken and stir for 20 seconds. Stir in the cilantro. Transfer to bowls and serve with rice. —*Marcia Kiesel*

WINE Vivid, lightly sweet Riesling.

●HEALTHY ●MAKE AHEAD ●VEGETARIAN ●STAFF FAVORITE

poultry

Corn, Chicken and Beef Gratins

ACTIVE: 45 MIN; TOTAL: 1 HR 15 MIN

4 SERVINGS ●

- 4 whole chicken legs, split into drumsticks and thighs
- Salt and freshly ground pepper
- 2 tablespoons vegetable oil
- 1 small onion, finely chopped
- ½ pound lean ground beef
- 1 garlic clove, minced
- ½ teaspoon ground cumin
- ½ teaspoon hot paprika
- 5 cups fresh corn kernels
- 1 cup chopped basil leaves
- 4 large hard-cooked eggs, peeled and halved lengthwise
- ½ cup pitted kalamata olives
- ½ cup raisins

1. Preheat the oven to 400°. On a large rimmed baking sheet, season the chicken with salt and pepper. Roast on the top shelf of the oven for 25 minutes, until the skin is golden and crisp and the meat is cooked through. Transfer the chicken to a platter. Increase the oven temperature to 450°.

2. Meanwhile, in a skillet, heat the oil. Add the onion; cook over moderately high heat until softened, 3 minutes. Add the beef, garlic, cumin and paprika; cook, breaking up the meat, until no pink remains, 5 minutes. Season with salt and pepper.

3. In a food processor, puree the corn and basil. Scrape into a saucepan; stir over high heat until thickened. Season with salt.

4. Spread the beef in four 12-ounce gratin dishes. Set the chicken and eggs on the meat and sprinkle with the olives and raisins. Spread a 1-inch-thick layer of the corn on top of each dish. Bake on the top shelf for 10 minutes, until bubbling and heated through. Serve. —*Alex Aguilera*

SERVE WITH Tomato salsa.

MAKE AHEAD The assembled gratins can be refrigerated overnight. Bring to room temperature before baking.

WINE Cherry-inflected, earthy Sangiovese.

Chicken-and-Leek Pie

ACTIVE: 25 MIN; TOTAL: 2 HR 45 MIN

4 SERVINGS ● ●

- 3 whole chicken legs
- Kosher salt and freshly ground pepper
- 1 teaspoon extra-virgin olive oil
- 2 tablespoons unsalted butter
- 1 onion, cut into ¼-inch dice
- 1 large leek, white and pale green parts only, halved lengthwise and cut crosswise into ½-inch pieces
- 1 tablespoon grainy mustard
- ¼ cup all-purpose flour
- 1 cup low-sodium chicken broth
- ¾ cup plus 1 tablespoon whole milk
- ¼ cup heavy cream
- 2 tablespoons chopped tarragon
- One 14-ounce package all-butter puff pastry
- 1 large egg, lightly beaten
- 1 tablespoon sesame seeds

1. Preheat the oven to 400°. On a rimmed baking sheet, season the chicken legs with salt and pepper and drizzle with the olive oil. Roast the chicken for about 30 minutes, until browned and cooked through. Let stand until cool enough to handle. Shred the chicken, discarding the skin and bones. Reserve the pan drippings. Reduce the oven temperature to 375°.

2. In a large saucepan, melt the butter. Add the onion and leek and cook over moderate heat until tender, about 5 minutes. Stir in the mustard and flour and cook until pasty, about 1 minute. Whisk in the chicken broth, ¾ cup of the milk, the cream and the chicken pan drippings and bring to a simmer. Cook over moderate heat, stirring frequently, until thick, about 5 minutes. Stir in the shredded chicken and the tarragon and season with salt and pepper. Let stand until cool, about 30 minutes.

3. Spread the chicken in an 8-by-11½-inch baking dish. On a lightly floured work surface, roll out the puff pastry to a 9-by-13-inch rectangle. Lay the pastry over the baking dish; gently tuck in the overhanging pastry. Using a sharp knife, cut 3 slits in the top of the pastry. In a small bowl, beat the egg with the remaining 1 tablespoon of milk. Brush the egg wash over the pastry and sprinkle with the sesame seeds. Set the pie on a rimmed baking sheet and bake for about 1 hour, until the puff pastry is golden brown and the filling is bubbly. Let stand for 30 minutes before serving. —*Curtis Stone*

WINE Complex, aromatic Chenin Blanc.

Chicken Curry with Squash

TOTAL: 50 MIN

8 SERVINGS ●

- ¼ cup canola oil
- 1 large onion, finely chopped
- 2 large garlic cloves, minced
- 2 tablespoons minced fresh ginger
- 2 hot chiles with seeds, minced
- 2 tablespoons Madras curry powder
- 1½ teaspoons turmeric
- 5 cups low-sodium chicken broth
- ½ cup coconut milk
- Salt and freshly ground pepper
- 2 pounds Yukon Gold potatoes, peeled and cut into 1½-inch pieces
- 1 pound cauliflower, cut into florets
- 2 yellow squash, cut into 1-inch pieces
- 1½ pounds skinless, boneless chicken breasts, cut into 1-inch pieces
- Rice and lemon wedges, for serving

1. In a large enameled cast-iron casserole, heat the oil until shimmering. Add the onion, garlic, ginger and chiles and cook over moderate heat, stirring occasionally, until softened, about 5 minutes. Stir in the curry powder and turmeric and cook for 2 minutes. Add the broth and coconut milk and season with salt and pepper. Bring to a boil and simmer for 5 minutes. Add the potatoes and cook over moderate heat until barely tender, 5 minutes. Add the cauliflower and squash, cover partially and cook over moderately low heat, stirring occasionally, until the vegetables are tender, 15 minutes.

2. Add the chicken to the casserole, season with salt and pepper and cook just until white throughout, 5 minutes. Serve over rice, with lemon wedges. —*Grace Parisi*
WINE Vivid, lightly sweet Riesling.

Grilled Chicken Breasts with Sautéed Mushrooms

TOTAL: 1 HR
10 SERVINGS

- 10 boneless chicken breast halves with skin
- 40 small, tender oregano sprigs
- 1 tablespoon grated orange zest
- Vegetable oil, for rubbing
- Salt and freshly ground pepper
- 1 stick unsalted butter
- 4 garlic cloves, minced
- 3 pounds assorted wild mushrooms, large mushrooms thickly sliced
- ½ cup chopped flat-leaf parsley
- 2 tablespoons fresh lemon juice

1. Light a grill. Gently loosen the skin from the chicken breasts and stuff 4 oregano sprigs and a pinch of orange zest under the skin. Smooth the skin over the filling. Rub the chicken with oil and season with salt and pepper. Grill over low heat, skin side down, until browned and crisp, 12 minutes. Turn and grill until just cooked through, 15 minutes longer. Transfer the chicken to plates and let rest for 5 minutes.
2. Meanwhile, in a large skillet, melt the butter. Add the garlic and cook over low heat until golden, 2 minutes. Add the mushrooms and season with salt and pepper. Cover and cook over moderate heat, stirring a few times, until the mushrooms release their liquid, 4 minutes. Carefully pour off the liquid; you should have ½ cup. Continue to cook, uncovered, over moderately high heat, stirring, until browned, 15 minutes. Add the parsley, lemon juice and reserved liquid and season with salt and pepper.
3. Spoon the mushrooms over and around the chicken; serve. —*Francis Mallmann*
WINE Ripe, juicy Pinot Noir.

Cheese-Stuffed Chicken Cutlets with Mustard Sauce

TOTAL: 50 MIN
4 SERVINGS

- Four 6-ounce chicken cutlets, about ½ inch thick
- 4 thin slices of plain havarti cheese, about 4-by-3 inches
- 4 teaspoons chopped thyme
- ½ cup chicken stock or low-sodium broth
- ¼ cup heavy cream
- 1 tablespoon plus 1 teaspoon Dijon mustard
- Salt and freshly ground pepper
- 2 large eggs
- 2 tablespoons freshly grated Parmigiano-Reggiano cheese
- All-purpose flour, for dredging
- Extra-virgin olive oil, for frying

1. Preheat the oven to 350°. Using a small knife, cut a 4-by-3-inch pocket in the side of each chicken cutlet. Insert a havarti slice and spread 1 teaspoon of thyme in each pocket; press gently to close.
2. In a small saucepan, boil the stock and cream over moderately high heat until reduced to ½ cup, about 5 minutes. Whisk in the mustard and boil for 30 seconds, whisking a few times. Season with salt and pepper and remove from the heat.
3. In a shallow bowl, beat the eggs. Beat in the Parmigiano-Reggiano. Put the flour in another shallow bowl.
4. In a large nonstick skillet, heat ¼ inch of olive oil. Season the cutlets with salt and pepper. Dredge 2 cutlets in flour, shaking off the excess, then coat with the beaten egg. Fry over moderately high heat until golden, about 2 minutes per side. Transfer to a large rimmed baking sheet. Coat and fry the remaining cutlets.
5. Bake the chicken for about 12 minutes, until just cooked through. Reheat the sauce and pour onto plates. Set the cutlets on the sauce and serve. —*Marcia Kiesel*
WINE Dry, fruity sparkling wine.

Grilled Spiced Duck Breasts with Blackberries

TOTAL: 40 MIN
10 SERVINGS

- 1 cup balsamic vinegar
- 1 quart blackberries
- Salt and freshly ground pepper
- Ten 6-ounce boneless Pekin duck breast halves with skin
- 1 tablespoon ancho chile powder
- 1½ teaspoons ground coriander
- 1 teaspoon ground cumin
- 1 teaspoon dry mustard powder

1. In a medium saucepan, boil the vinegar over high heat until reduced by half, about 7 minutes. Add the blackberries and cook, stirring very gently, until they are just softened, about 2 minutes. Using a slotted spoon, transfer the blackberries to a bowl. Boil the liquid over high heat until reduced to ⅓ cup, about 3 minutes. Carefully pour the accumulated juices from the blackberries into the saucepan and boil for about 30 seconds longer. Season the reduction with salt and pepper and pour it over the softened blackberries.
2. Light a grill or preheat a grill pan. Using a sharp knife, score the duck skin in a crosshatch pattern. In a small bowl, mix the ancho powder with the coriander, cumin and mustard powder. Season the duck breasts with salt and pepper and rub the spice mixture into the skin. Grill the duck breasts skin side down over moderate heat until lightly charred and crisp, about 3 minutes. Turn the breasts and cook for about 4 minutes longer for medium-rare meat. Transfer the duck to a carving board and let rest for 5 minutes.
3. Thinly slice the duck on the diagonal and transfer to plates. Serve with the blackberry sauce. —*Katie Lee*
MAKE AHEAD The sauce can be refrigerated overnight; reheat gently. The spice-rubbed duck can be refrigerated overnight; bring to room temperature before grilling.
WINE Complex, elegant Pinot Noir.

poultry

Duck Breast with Fig Sauce

TOTAL: 40 MIN PLUS 2 HR MARINATING

4 SERVINGS

DUCK

Two 12-ounce Moulard duck breasts
　　with skin

¼ cup extra-virgin olive oil

One 2-inch strip of lemon peel

Juice of 1 lemon

1 tablespoon thyme leaves

1 tablespoon rosemary leaves

1 large shallot, thinly sliced

1 tablespoon prepared
　　horseradish, drained

1 large garlic clove, smashed

FIG SAUCE

12 small dried Black Mission figs,
　　stems trimmed

1½ cups chicken stock or
　　low-sodium broth

1 tablespoon unsalted butter

1 garlic clove, minced

2 tablespoons brandy

1 rosemary sprig

Salt and freshly ground pepper

1. PREPARE THE DUCK: Score the skin of the duck breasts in a crosshatch pattern. In a shallow dish, combine the oil with the lemon peel, lemon juice, thyme, rosemary, shallot, horseradish and garlic. Add the duck and turn to coat. Let stand at room temperature for 2 hours, turning a few times.

2. MAKE THE FIG SAUCE: In a saucepan, combine the figs with the stock; bring to a boil. Cover and simmer over moderately low heat until tender, 10 minutes. Remove the figs from the stock, chop coarsely and return them to the saucepan.

3. In a small skillet, melt the butter. Add the garlic and cook over moderate heat until fragrant, about 30 seconds. Add the brandy; simmer for 1 minute. Add the rosemary sprig, figs and fig stock and simmer over moderate heat until the sauce is slightly thickened, about 3 minutes. Season the fig sauce with salt and pepper, cover and keep warm.

4. Scrape the marinade from the duck and season with salt and pepper. Put the duck in a large cast-iron skillet, skin side down, and cook over moderately low heat until most of the fat has been rendered, 10 minutes. Increase the heat to moderate and cook until the skin is browned and crisp, 4 minutes. Turn and cook until medium-rare, 3 minutes longer. Transfer the duck to a board, skin side up; let rest 5 minutes.

5. Slice the duck breasts crosswise and transfer to plates. Discard the rosemary, spoon the sauce over the duck and serve.
—Eugenia Bone

WINE Complex, aromatic Nebbiolo.

Braised Duck with Pinot Noir, Cherry Tomatoes and Grapes

ACTIVE: 25 MIN; TOTAL: 2 HR 40 MIN

4 SERVINGS ●

One 5-pound duck,
　　giblets removed

Salt and freshly ground pepper

One 750-milliliter bottle Pinot Noir

10 black peppercorns

2 medium garlic cloves,
　　crushed and peeled

1 bay leaf

1 pound cherry tomatoes

½ pound red or black seedless
　　grapes, stems discarded

1. Preheat the oven to 450°. Rub the duck inside and out with salt. Let stand at room temperature for 30 minutes.

2. Set the duck breast side down in a very large enameled cast-iron casserole. Pour the wine on top and add the peppercorns, garlic and bay leaf. Braise the duck uncovered in the oven for 20 minutes, until it starts to brown. Turn the duck breast side up, sprinkle with salt and add the tomatoes and grapes. Braise uncovered for 20 minutes. Reduce the oven temperature to 300°. Cover the casserole and braise the duck for about 45 minutes longer, until an instant-read thermometer inserted in the thickest part of the thigh registers 160°.

3. Transfer the duck to a rimmed baking sheet. Strain the pan juices into a saucepan; reserve the tomatoes and grapes and discard the remaining solids. Skim off the fat and boil the juices until reduced to 1 cup, 20 minutes. Add the cherry tomatoes and grapes; season with salt and pepper.

4. Preheat the broiler. Using poultry shears or a large, sharp knife, cut the duck in half. Arrange the duck halves on the baking sheet, skin side up. Broil the duck 6 inches from the heat for about 4 minutes, rotating the pan as necessary, until the skin is crisp. Carve the duck and serve with the pan sauce.
—Andreas Viestad

WINE Complex, elegant Pinot Noir.

Coriander-Crusted Duck Breasts

TOTAL: 20 MIN

4 SERVINGS

2 teaspoons coriander seeds

Two 1-pound Muscovy or
　　moulard duck breasts,
　　excess fat trimmed

Salt and freshly ground pepper

Grandma's Crushed Potatoes (p. 238),
　　for serving

1. In a large skillet, toast the coriander seeds over moderately high heat, shaking the pan, until fragrant, about 1½ minutes. Transfer to a spice grinder and let cool completely. Grind to a powder.

2. Using a sharp knife, score the duck skin in a crosshatch pattern; season with salt and pepper. Heat the skillet. Add the duck skin side down and cook over moderate heat until the skin is browned and crisp, about 5 minutes. Turn the breasts skin side up and sprinkle with the ground coriander. Cook until medium-rare, about 4 minutes longer. Transfer the duck to a carving board and let rest for 5 minutes. Thinly slice the duck breasts crosswise and serve with Grandma's Crushed Potatoes.
—Rajat Parr

WINE Ripe, juicy Pinot Noir.

CORIANDER-CRUSTED DUCK
BREASTS (WITH GRANDMA'S
CRUSHED POTATOES, P. 238)

Turkey Burgers with Smoked Gouda

TOTAL: 30 MIN
4 SERVINGS

By adding two flourishes to a simple grilled turkey burger, grill-meister Bobby Flay makes it fantastic. First he melts slices of smoky Gouda cheese onto the turkey, then he spreads toasted buns with a sweet-spicy sauce of whole-grain and Dijon mustard, horseradish and honey.

- 1 red onion, cut into ⅓-inch-thick slabs
- Vegetable oil, for brushing
- 4 hamburger buns, split
- 1½ pounds ground turkey
- Salt and freshly ground black pepper
- 4 slices of smoked Gouda cheese (4 ounces)
- 3 tablespoons Dijon mustard
- 2 tablespoons whole-grain mustard
- 1 tablespoon drained prepared horseradish
- 1 tablespoon honey

1. Light a grill or preheat a grill pan. Brush the red onion slabs with vegetable oil and grill until charred and softened, about 5 minutes. Brush the cut sides of the hamburger buns with oil and grill until toasted, about 30 seconds.
2. Form the ground turkey into four 1-inch-thick patties and brush with oil. Season with salt and pepper and grill over high heat, turning once, until nearly cooked through, about 10 minutes. Top with the Gouda, close the grill and cook until the cheese is melted and the burgers are cooked through, about 1 minute longer.
3. Meanwhile, in a small bowl, combine the mustards, horseradish and honey and spread on the bottom half of the buns. Top with the burgers and onions. Close the burgers and serve right away.
—*Bobby Flay*
WINE Fresh, fruity rosé.

Turkey Burgers with Spicy Pickle Sauce

TOTAL: 30 MIN
6 SERVINGS ● ●

- ½ cup plain fat-free Greek yogurt
- ½ cup chopped dill pickles
- 2 tablespoons chopped pickled hot peppers
- Kosher salt and freshly ground black pepper
- 2¼ pounds lean ground turkey
- 1 teaspoon smoked sweet paprika
- Extra-virgin olive oil, for brushing
- 6 whole wheat English muffins or hamburger buns, split
- Lettuce and sliced red onion and tomatoes, for serving

1. Light a grill or preheat a grill pan. In a bowl, mix the yogurt with the pickles and peppers and season with salt and pepper.
2. In a bowl, knead the turkey with the paprika and 1½ teaspoons of salt. Form the meat into 6 patties about ¾ inch thick. Brush the patties with oil; season them salt and pepper. Grill over moderately high heat, turning once or twice, until cooked through, 12 minutes. Grill the English muffins on both sides until toasted, 2 minutes.
3. Spread the pickle sauce on the tops and bottoms of the English muffins. Layer the bottom halves of the English muffins with the burgers, lettuce, onion and tomatoes. Close the sandwiches and serve the turkey burgers right away. —*Grace Parisi*
MAKE AHEAD The pickle sauce can be refrigerated overnight.
WINE Dry, earthy sparkling wine.

Soy-Braised Turkey with Turkey Rice

ACTIVE: 25 MIN; TOTAL: 1 HR 10 MIN
6 SERVINGS ●

Simmering dark turkey meat in a deeply savory combination of brown sugar and soy sauce adds flavor, while cooking jasmine rice with rendered turkey fat adds a wonderful richness. The topping—pickled shallot rings—provides a lovely pink color and piquancy.

- 1 medium shallot, thinly sliced, plus 1 small shallot, quartered
- 1 tablespoon red wine vinegar
- ½ teaspoon sugar
- Salt
- ⅓ cup light or low-sodium soy sauce
- 2 cups water
- 2 tablespoons light brown sugar
- 2 garlic cloves, coarsely chopped
- 2 tablespoons coarsely chopped fresh ginger
- 3 cups shredded cooked dark turkey meat
- 2½ cups Turkey Stock (p. 120) or chicken stock
- 1½ cups uncooked jasmine rice
- ¼ cup rendered turkey fat

1. In a small bowl, combine the sliced shallot, vinegar, sugar and ¼ teaspoon of salt. Let stand, stirring occasionally, until the shallot is softened, about 1 hour.
2. In a saucepan, mix the soy sauce, water, brown sugar, quartered shallot, garlic and ginger; bring to a boil. Add the turkey meat and cook over low heat, stirring, until the liquid is reduced by half, 1 hour.
3. Meanwhile, in a medium saucepan, combine the Turkey Stock with the rice, turkey fat and a pinch of salt and bring to a boil. Cover and simmer over low heat until the rice is tender and the stock is absorbed, about 20 minutes.
4. Cover the saucepan with a kitchen towel, then cover with the lid; let the rice steam for 20 minutes off the heat. Fluff the rice with a fork. Spoon the soy-braised turkey into bowls, add the turkey rice and garnish with the pickled shallot. —*David Chang*
MAKE AHEAD The soy-braised turkey can be refrigerated, covered, for up to 2 days; reheat before serving.
WINE Minerally, complex Sauvignon Blanc.

perfecting roast turkey

To create crisp skin and flavorful meat, F&W's **Grace Parisi** *blends ingredients like lemons or pecans into a butter that she rubs all over the turkey. The added ingredients, along with homemade turkey stock, make for spectacular gravy.*

Roast Turkey with Lemon and Chives

ACTIVE: 45 MIN; TOTAL: 4 HR 30 MIN

12 SERVINGS

¼ cup plus 2 tablespoons snipped chives

2 sticks unsalted butter, softened

Finely grated zest and juice of ½ lemon,
    plus 1 lemon thinly sliced

Kosher salt and freshly ground pepper

¼ cup all-purpose flour

One 18-pound turkey

1 carrot, cut into 1-inch pieces

1 onion, cut into 1-inch wedges

4 cups Turkey Stock (p. 120)

1. Preheat the oven to 350°. In a food processor, combine ¼ cup of the chives with the butter, the lemon zest and juice, 1 tablespoon of kosher salt and 1 teaspoon of pepper and pulse until smooth. Transfer ¼ cup of the lemon-chive butter to a small bowl and stir in the flour; reserve.

2. Beginning at the neck, gently separate the turkey skin from the breast and legs using your fingers. Season the turkey cavity with salt. Rub half of the lemon-chive butter from the food processor under the skin, spreading it over the breast and thighs.

3. Set the turkey on a rack in a large roasting pan and scatter the carrot, onion and lemon slices in the pan; add 1½ cups of water. Rub the remaining lemon-chive butter from the food processor all over the outside of the turkey. Roast on the bottom rack of the oven for 3½ to 4 hours, adding 1½ cups of water to the roasting pan and tenting the turkey with foil halfway through roasting. The turkey is done when an instant-read thermometer inserted deep in the thigh registers 170°. Uncover the turkey and transfer to a carving board; let rest for 30 minutes.

4. Meanwhile, strain the pan juices into a large measuring cup; discard the solids. Spoon off the fat and discard it. (You should have about 2 cups of defatted pan juices.) In a large saucepan, boil the Turkey Stock until it is reduced to 3 cups, about 15 minutes. Set the roasting pan over 2 burners on high heat; add the reduced stock and scrape up any browned bits stuck to the bottom and sides of the pan. Strain the stock back into the saucepan. Add the pan juices and bring to a simmer. Whisk in the reserved butter-and-flour mixture and simmer over moderate heat, whisking constantly. Cook until thickened, about 4 minutes, and season the gravy with salt. Add the remaining 2 tablespoons of chives. Carve the turkey and serve, passing the gravy at the table.

WINE Ripe, juicy Pinot Noir.

TWO GREAT VARIATIONS

1 Roast Turkey with Fried Sage & Pecans

Omit the chives, lemon zest and juice. Toast 1 cup pecans. Cook 1 smashed garlic clove in 1 cup canola oil for 1 minute. Add 1 cup sage leaves and fry, stirring gently, until crisp. Drain the garlic and sage on paper towels. Blend the butter with half of the sage, the garlic, pecans, salt and pepper. Use the butter, roast the turkey; make gravy as directed. Garnish with the remaining sage.

WINE Ripe, luxurious Chardonnay.

2 Roast Turkey with Jalapeño-Paprika Gravy

In the butter, replace the snipped chives, lemon zest and lemon juice with 3 whole pickled jalapeños, 2 large garlic cloves and 1 tablespoon sweet paprika. Season the butter with salt and black pepper. Use the jalapeño butter, roast the turkey and make the gravy as directed. Carve the turkey and serve, passing the jalapeño-paprika gravy at the table.

WINE Rich Alsace Gewürztraminer.

TURKEY STOCK

ACTIVE: 20 MIN; TOTAL: 4 HR 30 MIN
MAKES ABOUT 3 QUARTS ●

- 7 pounds turkey parts, such as wings, thighs and drumsticks
- 4 quarts water
- 1 large onion, thickly sliced
- 1 large carrot, thickly sliced
- 1 large celery rib, thickly sliced
- 2 garlic cloves, smashed
- 1 teaspoon kosher salt

Freshly ground pepper

1. Preheat the oven to 400°. In a large roasting pan, roast the turkey for 1½ hours, until well browned. Transfer to a stock pot.

2. Set the roasting pan over 2 burners. Add 1 quart of the water and bring to a boil, scraping up the browned bits from the bottom. Add the liquid to the pot.

3. Add the onion, carrot, celery, garlic, salt and several pinches of pepper to the pot with the remaining 3 quarts of water and bring to a boil. Reduce the heat to moderately low, cover partially and simmer the stock for about 2½ hours. Strain; skim the fat before using or freezing. —GP

Turkey Breast with Ginger-Scallion Sauce

ACTIVE: 45 MIN; TOTAL: 1 HR 30 MIN
6 SERVINGS ●

- 1½ cups thinly sliced scallions
- 6 tablespoons minced ginger
- ¼ cup vegetable oil
- 1 teaspoon sherry vinegar
- 1½ teaspoons light or low-sodium soy sauce

Kosher salt

- ¾ pound cooked turkey breast

Turkey Cracklings (recipe follows)

1. In a bowl, combine the scallions with the ginger, oil, vinegar and soy sauce. Season with kosher salt.

2. Cut the turkey into 6 slices. Arrange on plates and spoon the sauce on top. Garnish with cracklings; serve. —David Chang

WINE Full-bodied, rich Pinot Gris.

TURKEY CRACKLINGS

◔ **TOTAL: 35 MIN**
6 SERVINGS ●

Skin from about ¼ of a roast turkey

Preheat the oven to 375° and line a baking sheet with parchment paper. Spread the turkey skin on it and cover with parchment and another baking sheet. Set a heavy ovenproof pot on top. Bake for about 30 minutes, until crisp and golden. Let cool slightly; break into pieces. —DC

Herb-Roasted Turkey with Gravy

ACTIVE: 1 HR; TOTAL: 4 HR 30 MIN
PLUS OVERNIGHT BRINING
12 SERVINGS

- 2 tablespoons fennel seeds
- 2 tablespoons mustard seeds
- 2 tablespoons coriander seeds
- 6 bay leaves
- 1½ cups kosher salt
- 1 cup sugar
- 8 quarts cold water

One 18-pound turkey

- 2 sticks plus 2 tablespoons unsalted butter, softened
- 3 tablespoons chopped parsley
- 1 tablespoon chopped sage
- 1 tablespoon chopped thyme

Freshly ground pepper

- 2 tablespoons all-purpose flour
- 3 quarts chicken stock or low-sodium broth
- ½ small onion, finely chopped
- 1 small carrot, finely chopped
- 1 celery rib, finely chopped
- 1 cup diced peasant bread

1. In a large saucepan, combine the fennel, mustard and coriander seeds with the bay leaves, salt, sugar and 1 quart of the water. Bring to a boil, stirring to dissolve the salt and sugar. Transfer the mixture to a very large bowl or pot and add the remaining 7 quarts of cold water. Add the turkey, breast side down. Cover and refrigerate for at least 8 hours or overnight.

2. Preheat the oven to 450°. Drain and rinse the turkey and pat dry; discard the brine. Starting at the neck end of the bird, slip your hand between the skin and meat to loosen the turkey skin.

3. In a medium bowl, combine the 2 sticks of butter with the parsley, sage and thyme and season with pepper. Spoon ¼ cup of the herb butter into a small bowl and stir in the flour; cover and chill. Spread the remaining herb butter all over and under the skin of the turkey and set it on a rack in a roasting pan. Add 2 cups of the stock to the pan and roast for 30 minutes. Lower the oven temperature to 325° and roast the turkey for about 2½ hours longer, basting occasionally; the turkey is done when an instant-read thermometer inserted in the thigh registers 170°. Transfer the turkey to a cutting board and let rest for 30 minutes.

4. Meanwhile, in a large saucepan, melt the remaining 2 tablespoons of butter. Add the onion, carrot and celery and cook over moderate heat, stirring occasionally, until softened, about 5 minutes. Stir in the bread and cook for 1 minute. Add 2 quarts of the stock and bring to a boil. Simmer over moderate heat until the liquid is reduced to 3 cups, about 1 hour and 15 minutes. Whisk to break up the bread. Strain the stock through a fine sieve and return it to the saucepan. Whisk in the chilled reserved herb butter and bring the gravy to a boil. Cook, whisking, until thickened, about 5 minutes.

5. Pour off the fat from the roasting pan; place over high heat. Add the remaining 2 cups of stock and cook, scraping up any browned bits stuck to the pan, until boiling. Strain the pan drippings into the gravy and season with salt and pepper.

6. Carve the turkey and serve on a platter, passing the gravy at the table.
—Shawn McClain

SERVE WITH Glazed carrots.

WINE Ripe, juicy Pinot Noir.

HERB-ROASTED TURKEY

TURKEY BREAST
WITH GINGER-SCALLION
SAUCE AND TURKEY
CRACKLINGS

poultry

Mango-Glazed Turkey Breast

TOTAL: 45 MIN

8 SERVINGS ● ●

One 7-pound whole boneless
  turkey breast

Kosher salt and freshly ground
  black pepper

1¼ cups mango chutney, plus
  more for serving

3 cups cilantro leaves and
  tender stems

2 cups fresh mint leaves

¾ cup water

½ cup extra-virgin olive oil

1. Light a grill or heat a grill pan. Set the turkey breast skin side down on a work surface. Working with your knife parallel to the work surface, cut through the breast, leaving about 1 inch of meat attached at one side, then open it up like a book; the goal is to have meat that is of even thickness. Season the meat all over with salt and black pepper. Grill the turkey breast over moderate heat, turning once, until the skin is crisp and the meat is just cooked through, about 25 minutes.

2. Meanwhile, microwave 1 cup of the mango chutney at medium power until it melts slightly, about 1 minute; scrape the melted chutney into a food processor and puree until completely smooth. Transfer the pureed mango chutney to a bowl. In the same food processor, puree the remaining ¼ cup of chutney with the cilantro, mint, water and oil until smooth; season with salt and pepper.

3. Once the turkey breast is just cooked through, brush it with the plain pureed chutney and grill, turning once, until the chutney forms a sticky glaze, about 2 minutes per side. Transfer the turkey to a cutting board, cover with foil and let rest for 10 minutes. Carve the turkey breast and serve right away, with the cilantro-mint sauce and chutney.

—*Melissa Rubel Jacobson*

WINE Fruity, low-oak Chardonnay.

Focaccia-Stuffed Squab with Bean Stew

ACTIVE: 45 MIN; TOTAL: 2 HR 45 MIN

2 SERVINGS

Celestino Drago (an F&W Best New Chef 1993) serves updated Italian food like this squab at Drago Centro in downtown L.A. "It's traditional to stuff birds with plain bread," Drago says, "but I like to use focaccia with herbs; it's nicer."

⅔ cup dried cannellini beans

5½ tablespoons extra-virgin
  olive oil

1 small onion, cut into
  ¼-inch dice

1 carrot, cut into ¼-inch dice

1 celery rib, cut into ¼-inch dice

1 garlic clove, minced

3 cups chicken stock or
  low-sodium broth

1 small red bell pepper

4 ounces green beans,
  cut into ½-inch lengths

Salt and freshly ground
  black pepper

2 cups ½-inch-cubed
  plain focaccia

2 squab—neck and wing tips
  removed, livers reserved

1 medium shallot, minced

1 teaspoon finely chopped
  fresh thyme

2 tablespoons unsalted
  butter, softened

1. In a medium saucepan, cover the cannellini beans with water and bring to a boil. Remove from the heat, cover and let stand for 1 hour. Drain the beans.

2. In the same saucepan, heat 2 tablespoons of the oil. Add the onion, carrot, celery and garlic and cook over moderate heat, stirring, until the vegetables are softened, 5 minutes. Add the cannellini beans and chicken stock and bring to a boil. Cover and simmer over low heat, stirring occasionally, until the beans are tender, about 1 hour and 15 minutes.

3. Meanwhile, roast the red pepper directly over a gas flame or under a preheated broiler until charred all over. Let cool slightly, then discard the charred skin, stem and seeds. Cut the pepper into ½-inch dice. Add the green beans to the cannellini beans and simmer over moderate heat until tender, about 5 minutes. Stir in the roasted red pepper and season with salt and pepper.

4. Preheat the oven to 375°. On a rimmed baking sheet, toss the focaccia with 1 tablespoon of the oil. Bake for 7 minutes, or until crisp; let cool. Leave the oven on.

5. In a small skillet, heat ½ tablespoon of the oil. Season the squab livers with salt and pepper and cook over moderately high heat until lightly browned, about 1 minute per side. Add the shallot and cook over low heat until softened, about 3 minutes. Finely dice the livers and add them to the focaccia along with the shallot. Stir in the thyme and season with salt and pepper.

6. Stuff the squab with the focaccia. Rub the butter all over the squab and season with salt and pepper. In a large ovenproof skillet, heat the remaining 2 tablespoons of oil. Add the squab, breast side up. Roast the squab in the upper third of the oven for about 20 minutes, basting every 5 minutes, until an instant-read thermometer inserted in the breast registers 130° for medium-rare. Transfer the squab to a carving board and let rest for 5 minutes. Mound the stuffing from each bird onto each plate. Carve the breast halves and whole legs and transfer to the plates. Spoon the bean stew alongside and serve.

—*Celestino Drago*

WINE Complex, aromatic Nebbiolo.

Cornish Hens with Plum-and-Leek Stuffing and Celery Root

ACTIVE: 1 HR; TOTAL: 2 HR 30 MIN

10 SERVINGS ●

The best part of this dish may be the pan juices, which are flavored by the celery root and plums that roast with the hens.

¼ cup plus 2 tablespoons extra-virgin olive oil, plus more for drizzling

¼ pound pancetta, finely chopped (1 cup)

3 medium leeks, white and pale green parts only, chopped

2 garlic cloves, minced

¼ cup dry white wine

6 red plums (1 pound), pitted and cut into ½-inch dice (2 cups)

2 cups fresh bread crumbs

½ tablespoon chopped thyme

½ cup chopped parsley

Salt and freshly ground pepper

Five 1-pound Cornish hens

6 pounds celery root, peeled and cut into ½-inch dice

2 cups chicken stock

1. Preheat the oven to 400°. In a large, deep skillet, heat 2 tablespoons of the olive oil. Add the pancetta and cook over moderate heat until crisp, about 6 minutes. Add the leeks and garlic, cover and cook, stirring occasionally, until the leeks are softened and starting to brown, about 10 minutes.

2. Add the wine to the skillet and cook over moderately high heat until reduced by one-third, about 5 minutes. Add the plums, cover and cook, stirring occasionally, until just softened, about 5 minutes. Transfer the contents of the skillet to a large bowl and let cool to room temperature. Stir in the bread crumbs, thyme and ¼ cup of the parsley. Season with salt and pepper.

3. Fill the cavities of the hens with the plum stuffing. Twist the wings behind the backs and tie the legs together. Spread the celery root in a single layer on 2 large rimmed baking sheets. Drizzle with the remaining ¼ cup of olive oil and season with salt and pepper. Arrange the hens on top of the celery root breast side up, drizzle with olive oil and season with salt and pepper. Turn the hens breast side down. Carefully pour the chicken stock into the baking sheets, cover with foil and roast in the oven for 45 minutes.

4. Turn the hens breast side up and roast, uncovered, for about 30 minutes longer, switching the baking sheets halfway through. The hens are done when they're golden brown and an instant-read thermometer inserted in the inner thighs registers 160°. Transfer the hens to a work surface and let rest for 10 minutes.

5. Meanwhile, using a slotted spoon, transfer the celery root to a platter and garnish with the remaining ¼ cup of parsley. Transfer the pan juices to a bowl and skim off any fat; season with salt and pepper. Transfer the hens to plates and serve with the stuffing, celery root and pan juices.
—Damien Schaefer

MAKE AHEAD The plum-and-leek stuffing can be refrigerated overnight.

WINE Deep, velvety Merlot.

Lemony Spiced Tandoor Quail

TOTAL: 50 MIN PLUS 4 HR MARINATING
6 SERVINGS ●●

At Samode, a 400-year-old palace-hotel in northern India, chef Krishna Kumar has a secret for especially juicy and tender quail: marinating the bird first in fresh lemon juice and hot paprika, then in a mixture of yogurt, ginger and the spice blend garam masala. Cooking the quail on a grill pan, then popping them into a Western-style oven, gives the birds a nicely smoky flavor similar to that created by a tandoor oven.

12 whole quail, necks and wing tips removed

¼ cup fresh lemon juice, plus lemon wedges for serving

Salt

1 tablespoon plus 1 teaspoon hot paprika

1 cup whole-milk yogurt

¼ cup coarsely chopped ginger

4 medium garlic cloves, coarsely chopped

1 tablespoon unsweetened toasted wheat germ

1 teaspoon garam masala

2 tablespoons vegetable oil, plus more for grilling

1 tablespoon extra-virgin olive oil

Freshly ground pepper

1 head of romaine, cut into bite-size pieces

½ small red onion, very thinly sliced

1. Using a sharp knife, make a ¼-inch-deep slash in each breast half and thigh of each quail. Transfer the quail to a large rimmed baking sheet and drizzle with 2 tablespoons of the lemon juice; rub to coat thoroughly. Season the quail with salt and sprinkle 2 teaspoons of the hot paprika over the quail, rubbing the seasonings into the slashes. Cover and refrigerate the spiced quail for 1 hour.

2. In a mini food processor, combine the yogurt, chopped ginger, garlic, wheat germ, garam masala, the 2 tablespoons of vegetable oil, 1 tablespoon of fresh lemon juice and remaining 2 teaspoons of paprika and process until smooth. Coat the quail with the marinade, cover and refrigerate for 3 hours.

3. Preheat the oven to 400°. Heat a large grill pan and coat it with vegetable oil. Grill 4 quail at a time over moderately high heat until nicely charred all over, about 5 minutes total. Transfer the grilled quail to a large rimmed baking sheet. Repeat with the remaining quail.

4. Transfer the quail to the oven and roast for about 12 minutes, until an instant-read thermometer inserted in the breasts reads 130° for medium-rare.

5. In a large bowl, combine the remaining 1 tablespoon of lemon juice with the olive oil and season with salt and pepper. Add the romaine and red onion and toss. Mound the salad on plates and top with the quail. Serve, passing lemon wedges at the table.
—Peggy Markel

WINE Dry, fruity sparkling wine.

THREE-INGREDIENT
PRIME RIB ROAST (P. 132)

beef, lamb & game

The ultimate carnivore's guide,
from a three-ingredient prime rib roast
to a chef's perfect cheeseburger.

GRILLED BEEF-TENDERLOIN SKEWERS WITH RED-MISO GLAZE

HANGER STEAK WITH HERB-NUT SALSA

Grilled Beef-Tenderloin Skewers with Red-Miso Glaze

 TOTAL: 30 MIN
4 SERVINGS ●

Tangy and salty-sweet, these skewers are also delicious made with chicken breast or pork tenderloin.

- ¼ cup plus 2 tablespoons vegetable oil
- 4 garlic cloves, thinly sliced
- ¼ cup low-sodium soy sauce
- 2 tablespoons red miso paste
- 1 teaspoon Asian sesame oil

Pinch of sugar

Pinch of salt

- 1¼ pounds beef tenderloin, sliced ¼ inch thick

1. Preheat a grill. In a saucepan, heat the vegetable oil. Add the garlic; stir over low heat until crisp, 3 minutes. With a slotted spoon, transfer to a blender; reserve the oil for another use. Add the soy sauce, miso, sesame oil, sugar and salt; puree.

2. Thread the meat on skewers. Lightly brush with the miso glaze. Grill over high heat for 1 minute. Brush with the glaze again. Grill, turning, until charred, 2 minutes, then serve. —*Jean-Georges Vongerichten*
WINE Ripe, juicy Pinot Noir.

Hanger Steak with Herb-Nut Salsa

TOTAL: 40 MIN
6 TO 8 SERVINGS ●

- ¼ cup hazelnuts
- ½ cup minced flat-leaf parsley
- ¼ cup snipped chives
- 2 teaspoons minced tarragon
- 1 teaspoon minced chervil
- 2 oil-packed anchovy fillets, minced
- 2 teaspoons chopped rinsed capers
- 1 medium shallot, minced
- 2 tablespoons sherry vinegar
- ¾ cup extra-virgin olive oil, plus more for brushing

Salt and freshly ground pepper

- 2 trimmed 1-pound hanger steaks

1. Preheat the oven to 375°. Toast the hazelnuts in a pie plate until the skins are blistered, 12 minutes. Transfer the nuts to a towel; let cool slightly, then rub off the skins. Finely chop and transfer to a bowl. Add the parsley, chives, tarragon, chervil, anchovies, capers and shallot. Stir in the vinegar and ¾ cup oil; season with salt and pepper.

2. Light a grill or preheat a grill pan. Brush the steaks with oil and season generously with salt and pepper. Grill over moderately high heat, turning occasionally, 12 minutes for medium-rare meat. Let rest for 5 minutes. Slice the meat across the grain and serve with the salsa. —*Naomi Pomeroy*
WINE Lively, fruity Merlot.

Hanger Steak with Warm Bulgur Salad

ACTIVE: 30 MIN; TOTAL: 1 HR 45 MIN
4 SERVINGS

- 2 garlic cloves, minced
- 1 tablespoon ground cumin

Kosher salt and freshly ground pepper

- ½ cup extra-virgin olive oil

One 2-pound hanger steak

- 1½ cups bulgur (9 ounces), rinsed
- ¼ teaspoon cinnamon
- 1½ cups boiling water
- 1 tablespoon unsalted butter
- ½ large white onion, chopped
- 2 carrots, cut into ½-inch pieces
- 1 turnip (8 ounces), peeled and cut into ½-inch pieces
- ½ cup chicken stock
- 1½ tablespoons fresh lemon juice
- ½ cup chopped flat-leaf parsley
- 2 tablespoons chopped mint

1. Preheat the oven to 350°. In a small bowl, mash the garlic, cumin, 1 tablespoon of salt and 1 teaspoon of pepper with 2 tablespoons of the oil; rub all over the steak. Cover and let stand at room temperature for 1 hour.
2. Meanwhile, in a medium baking dish, mix the bulgur and cinnamon. Stir in 2 tablespoons of the oil and the boiling water and season with salt and pepper. Cover tightly with foil and bake for 20 minutes, until the water is completely absorbed. Fluff the bulgur with a fork, then cover and keep warm.
3. In a large saucepan, melt the butter in 1 tablespoon of the oil. Add the onion and cook over moderate heat until barely softened, about 2 minutes. Add the carrots and turnip, season with salt and pepper and cook for 2 minutes, until just softened. Add the stock and bring to a simmer. Cover and cook over low heat until the vegetables are tender, 10 minutes. Stir the vegetables and liquid into the bulgur with the lemon juice, parsley, mint and 2 tablespoons of the oil.
4. In an ovenproof skillet, heat the remaining 1 tablespoon of oil and swirl to coat the pan. Add the steak; cook over high heat, turning once, until browned, 8 minutes. Transfer the skillet to the oven and roast for 25 minutes, turning once, until an instant-read thermometer inserted into the thickest part registers 135°. Transfer the steak to a cutting board and let rest for 10 minutes. Thinly slice the steak and serve with the bulgur.
—*Mark Sullivan*
WINE Deep, velvety Merlot.

Warm Flank Steak Salad with Mint and Cilantro

ACTIVE: 30 MIN; TOTAL: 1 HR
8 SERVINGS ● ●

- ¼ cup soy sauce
- 2 teaspoons freshly ground pepper
- ¼ cup minced fresh lemongrass

One 2½-pound flank steak

- 3 tablespoons fresh lime juice
- 2 tablespoons Asian fish sauce
- 1 tablespoon crushed red pepper
- ½ teaspoon sugar
- 2 medium shallots, thinly sliced
- ½ cup mint leaves
- ¼ cup cilantro leaves
- 2 teaspoons roasted rice powder (optional; see Note)

1. In a glass baking dish, mix the soy sauce with the pepper and 2 tablespoons of the lemongrass. Add the steak and turn to coat. Let stand for 30 minutes.
2. Light a grill. Grill the flank steak over moderately high heat, turning once, until charred on the outside but still pink within, about 8 minutes. Transfer the steak to a carving board and let stand for 5 minutes. Cut the steak in half lengthwise. Slice the halves across the grain ¼ inch thick.
3. In a large wok or nonreactive skillet, combine the lime juice with the fish sauce, crushed red pepper, sugar and the remaining 2 tablespoons of lemongrass. Cook over moderate heat until hot. Stir in the steak along with 1 tablespoon of the marinade. Add the shallots, mint, cilantro and rice powder, stirring to coat. Transfer the salad to plates and serve. —*Andy Ricker*

NOTE Rice powder is available at Asian markets. To make it, in a skillet, toast raw glutinous rice over low heat, stirring occasionally, for 40 minutes. Transfer to a mortar or spice grinder; let cool. Grind finely.
WINE Fresh, fruity rosé.

Wasabi Flank Steak and Miso-Glazed Potatoes

 TOTAL: 40 MIN
6 SERVINGS ●

- 2 tablespoons wasabi powder
- 2 tablespoons water
- 2 tablespoons drained horseradish
- 1 teaspoon low-sodium soy sauce

One 2-pound flank steak

- 4 teaspoons canola oil

Salt and freshly ground pepper

- 1 pound fingerling potatoes
- 1 tablespoon miso
- 1 tablespoon mirin
- 1 bunch of watercress, stemmed

1. Preheat the oven to 450° and preheat a cast-iron grill pan. In a bowl, combine the wasabi and water. Stir in the horseradish and soy sauce. Rub the steak with 1 teaspoon of the oil and season with salt and pepper. Grill the steak over high heat until lightly charred, 5 minutes. Flip the steak and spread the wasabi over the charred side.
2. Transfer the pan to the oven and roast the steak for 10 minutes, until an instant-read thermometer inserted in the thickest part registers 135° for medium-rare; transfer to a cutting board and let rest for 10 minutes.
3. Meanwhile, in a saucepan of boiling water, cook the potatoes for 15 minutes. Drain and let cool, then peel. Wipe out the saucepan. Add the remaining oil and the potatoes and cook over moderate heat, stirring occasionally, until golden, 5 minutes. Combine the miso and mirin; add to the potatoes and cook, stirring, until glazed, 2 minutes.
4. Thinly slice the steak across the grain serve with the potatoes and watercress.
—*Takashi Yagihashi*
WINE Fruity, light-bodied Beaujolais.

beef, lamb & game

Vaca Frita

ACTIVE: 30 MIN; TOTAL: 2 HR
6 SERVINGS ● ●

Sautéing shredded beef in small batches until it turns crisp and delectable is the secret to Cuba's *vaca frita* ("fried cow").

1½ pounds flank steak,
      cut into 4 pieces
  1 green bell pepper, cored
      and quartered
  2 large onions—1 halved,
      1 thinly sliced
  1 bay leaf
  2 garlic cloves, smashed
Salt and freshly ground pepper
  ¼ cup plus 2 tablespoons
      fresh lime juice
  3 tablespoons extra-virgin olive oil

1. In a saucepan, combine the steak with the bell pepper, halved onion and bay leaf. Add water to cover and bring to a boil. Simmer over moderate heat for 20 minutes. Transfer the steak to a surface; let cool. Strain the broth for another use. Shred the meat and transfer it to a bowl.
2. Using the side of a large knife, mash the garlic to a paste with ½ teaspoon of salt. Stir the paste into the meat along with the lime juice, oil and sliced onion. Let stand for at least 30 minutes or up to 1½ hours.
3. Heat a large, flat griddle until very hot. Working in batches, spread the beef on the griddle in a thin layer; season with salt and pepper. Cook over high heat, turning once or twice, until sizzling and crispy in spots, 6 minutes per batch. Transfer to a platter and serve. —*Lourdes Castro*
WINE Ripe, juicy Pinot Noir.

Korean Sizzling Beef

TOTAL: 30 MIN PLUS 4 HR MARINATING
8 SERVINGS ● ●

  ¼ cup soy sauce
  2 tablespoons sugar
  2 tablespoons dry white wine
  2 large garlic cloves, minced
  1 tablespoon Asian sesame oil

  2 teaspoons crushed red pepper
One 2½-pound beef flank steak, cut
      across the grain into twenty
      ¼-inch-thick slices
  16 scallions
Vegetable oil, for rubbing
Salt
Steamed rice, for serving

1. In a large, shallow dish, combine the soy sauce with the sugar, white wine, garlic, sesame oil and crushed red pepper, stirring to dissolve the sugar. Add the sliced flank steak and coat thoroughly in the marinade. Cover and refrigerate the steak for at least 4 hours or overnight.
2. Light a grill or heat a griddle. Rub the scallions all over with vegetable oil and grill them over high heat, turning once, until the scallions are just softened, about 2 minutes. Season with salt.
3. Working in batches, grill the flank steak over high heat until the slices are richly browned and medium-rare, about 30 seconds per side. Transfer the steak to a serving platter and serve with the grilled scallions and steamed rice. —*Marcia Kiesel*
WINE Rich, ripe Cabernet Sauvignon.

Grilled Flank Steak with Corn, Tomato and Asparagus Salad

ACTIVE: 50 MIN; TOTAL: 2 HR 30 MIN
4 SERVINGS ●

1½ cups dry red wine
  ½ cup Dijon mustard
  ¼ cup packed dark brown sugar
  8 garlic cloves, crushed and peeled
  3 large shallots, coarsely chopped
  2 tablespoons chopped
      flat-leaf parsley
  1 tablespoon chopped thyme
Kosher salt and freshly ground pepper
One 1½-pound flank steak
  2 tablespoons cider vinegar
  1 tablespoon honey
  6 ounces cherry tomatoes,
      preferably Sweet 100 tomatoes,
      quartered (about 1½ cups)

  ¼ small sweet onion, such as
      Walla Walla, thinly sliced
  6 ounces thin asparagus
  2 ears of corn, shucked
  1 tablespoon extra-virgin olive oil
  6 basil leaves, finely shredded
  1 tablespoon unsalted butter
  6 ounces fresh morel mushrooms,
      cleaned and halved if large, or
      a scant ½ ounce dried morels,
      reconstituted in boiling water
      for 10 minutes

1. In a large glass baking dish, whisk the wine, mustard, brown sugar, garlic, shallots, parsley, thyme, 1 tablespoon of salt and 1 teaspoon of pepper. Add the steak and turn to coat. Let stand at room temperature for 2 hours or refrigerate for up to 8 hours.
2. Meanwhile, in a medium bowl, whisk the cider vinegar and honey. Add the tomatoes and onion and toss. Let stand for 1 hour.
3. Light a grill. Coat the asparagus and corn with olive oil and season with salt and pepper. Grill over moderately high heat, turning occasionally, until tender and browned in spots, about 3 minutes for the asparagus and 6 minutes for the corn. Transfer to a work surface; when cool enough to handle, cut the asparagus into pieces and cut the corn from the cobs. Add the asparagus, corn and basil to the tomatoes and toss.
4. Remove the steak from the marinade and pat dry with paper towels; season lightly with salt and pepper. Grill the steak, turning once, until medium-rare, about 10 minutes total. Transfer the steak to a work surface and let rest for 10 minutes.
5. Meanwhile, in a skillet, melt the butter. Add the morels and cook over moderately high heat until browned, about 3 minutes. Season with salt and pepper.
6. Thinly slice the steak against the grain and transfer to plates. Season the tomato salad with salt and pepper and spoon alongside the steak. Top the steak with the morels and serve. —*Mark Fuller*
WINE Earthy, medium-bodied Tempranillo.

GRILLED FLANK STEAK WITH CORN,
TOMATO AND ASPARAGUS SALAD

beef, lamb & game

Roast Beef Summer Rolls

TOTAL: 40 MIN

6 SERVINGS ● ●

Vietnamese summer rolls are often filled with chicken or shrimp, but F&W's Grace Parisi makes her speedy ones with thin slices of roast beef from the deli counter.

- 1 large garlic clove, smashed
- 1½ tablespoons light brown sugar
- 1 teaspoon Thai green curry paste
- 2 tablespoons fresh lime juice
- 2 tablespoons Asian fish sauce
- ¼ cup chopped cilantro
- ¼ cup chopped mint
- ⅓ cup mayonnaise
- 4 cups coleslaw mix
- ½ pound rare deli roast beef, thinly sliced and cut into ½-inch strips

Twenty-four 6-inch round rice paper wrappers, plus more in case of breakage

1. In a mortar, pound the garlic to a paste with the brown sugar and green curry paste. Add the lime juice, fish sauce and 3 tablespoons of water. Stir in half of the cilantro and mint. In a small bowl, whisk the mayonnaise with 1 tablespoon of the green curry dipping sauce.

2. In a large bowl, toss the coleslaw mix with the roast beef and the remaining cilantro and mint.

3. Fill a pie plate with warm water. Dip 2 or 3 rice paper wrappers at a time in the water, then set them on a work surface to soften, about 1 minute. Spread a scant teaspoon of the curry mayonnaise on the bottom third of each wrapper and top with a scant 3 tablespoons of the roast beef filling. Roll the wrappers into tight cylinders, tucking in the sides as you go. Transfer the rolls to a plastic wrap–lined baking sheet and repeat with the remaining wrappers, curry mayonnaise and filling.

4. Just before serving, cut each roll in half and serve with the dipping sauce.
—*Grace Parisi*

WINE Fresh, fruity rosé.

Tamarind Beef

ACTIVE: 30 MIN; TOTAL: 1 HR 15 MIN

10 SERVINGS ●

"I made up this dish to have one thing on my menu that wasn't spicy," says chef Chris Yeo of his Singaporean menu at Straits Atlanta. He marinates cubes of beef tenderloin in a sesame oil mixture so it's even more tender, then adds flavor to the mild beef by searing the pieces in shallot-infused oil. The crispy shallots fried beforehand in the oil are a terrific garnish.

- ½ cup Asian sesame oil
- ½ cup sugar

Kosher salt

- 3 pounds trimmed beef tenderloin, cut into 1-inch cubes
- 1½ cups water
- ⅔ cup tamarind concentrate
- ¼ cup Asian fish sauce
- 3 tablespoons vegetable oil
- 2 large shallots, thinly sliced

1. In a large, shallow bowl, combine the sesame oil with ¼ cup of the sugar and 2 tablespoons of salt. Add the beef and stir to coat with the marinade. Let stand at room temperature for 1 hour.

2. In a medium saucepan, combine the water with the tamarind concentrate, fish sauce and the remaining ¼ cup of sugar and bring to a boil. Cook over high heat, stirring occasionally, until the sugar is dissolved and the sauce is reduced to 1 cup, about 12 minutes. Season with salt and remove from the heat; keep warm.

3. In a large skillet, heat the vegetable oil until shimmering. Add the shallots; cook over moderately high heat until browned and crisp, about 2 minutes. Using a slotted spoon, transfer the shallots to a plate.

4. Add half of the shallot oil to another large skillet and heat both skillets. Drain the meat and add one-fourth to each skillet in an even layer without crowding. Cook over high heat, turning once, until browned, about 2 minutes. Using a slotted spoon, transfer the meat to a platter. Repeat with

the remaining meat. Pour the warm tamarind sauce over the meat, top with the fried shallots and serve. —*Chris Yeo*

SERVE WITH Steamed brussels sprouts.

WINE Complex, elegant Pinot Noir.

Beef Tenderloin with Aromatic Thai Spices

ACTIVE: 30 MIN; TOTAL: 3 HR 15 MIN

4 SERVINGS ●

Star chef Jean-Georges Vongerichten loves to cook beef tenderloin sous vide—a restaurant technique that home cooks can easily replicate by simmering the steaks in a resealable plastic bag at a low temperature (a thermometer is essential).

- ¼ cup plus 2 tablespoons vegetable oil
- 4 garlic cloves, thinly sliced

Four 8-ounce beef tenderloin steaks (about 1½ inches thick)

- 2 shallots, thinly sliced

Eight 1-inch rosemary sprigs

- 10 thyme sprigs
- 7 kaffir lime leaves, chopped

Six 1-inch strips of orange zest

- 2 tablespoons Asian fish sauce
- ⅓ cup low-sodium soy sauce
- 10 dried Thai chiles, coarsely chopped
- 1 tablespoon unsalted butter
- 1 tablespoon extra-virgin olive oil

1. In a small saucepan, heat the vegetable oil. Add the garlic and cook over low heat until pale golden and crisp, stirring constantly, about 3 minutes. Drain the garlic chips on paper towels and reserve the oil; let both cool to room temperature.

2. Using a sharp paring knife, make 1-inch slits all over the tenderloin steaks. Stuff the slits with the garlic chips.

3. Fill a large, sturdy resealable plastic freezer bag with the shallots, rosemary, thyme, lime leaves, orange zest, fish sauce, soy sauce, dried chiles and the reserved garlic oil. Add the steaks and seal, turning to coat the meat with the marinade. Let stand at room temperature for 2 hours.

ROAST BEEF SUMMER ROLLS

TAMARIND BEEF

4. Bring a large pot of water barely to a simmer; the water should register 135° on a candy or instant-read thermometer. Discard most of the marinade and reseal the plastic bag, pressing out any air. Add the bag to the water and cover with a rack or plate to keep it submerged. Cook the meat in the bag at 135° for 45 minutes, adjusting the heat as necessary to maintain the temperature. Remove from the water. Transfer the steaks to a plate; scrape off the marinade.

5. In a skillet, melt the butter in the olive oil and heat until nearly smoking. Add the steaks and cook over high heat, turning once, until browned and an instant-read thermometer inserted in the thickest part of the steaks registers 130° for medium-rare, 6 minutes. Serve right away.
—*Jean-Georges Vongerichten*

SERVE WITH Sautéed Swiss chard.
WINE Cherry-inflected, earthy Sangiovese.

Garlic Salt–Crusted Bistecca

ACTIVE: 45 MIN; TOTAL: 5 HR PLUS
OVERNIGHT STANDING
4 SERVINGS

 1 large garlic clove, very
    finely chopped
⅓ cup kosher salt
 2 teaspoons cracked
    black peppercorns
 1 large rosemary sprig, leaves
    very finely chopped
 1 large sage sprig, leaves very
    finely chopped
One 4-pound porterhouse steak
    (about 3 inches thick)
Extra-virgin olive oil

1. In a mortar or using the side of a large knife, crush the chopped garlic with 2 tablespoons of the kosher salt to a paste. Stir in the peppercorns, rosemary, sage and the remaining salt. Spread the mixture

on a plate and let stand overnight at room temperature, stirring occasionally, until dry and crumbly.

2. Generously rub the salt mixture all over the steak. Let the steak stand at room temperature for 4 hours or refrigerate it for 6 hours.

3. Preheat the oven to 425°. Light a grill or preheat a grill pan. Scrape the salt from the steak and brush lightly with olive oil; grill over high heat for about 10 minutes, turning, until crusty all over. Transfer the steak to a shallow roasting pan and roast for about 10 minutes longer, turning once or twice, until an instant-read thermometer inserted into the thickest part of the meat registers 125°. Transfer the steak to a cutting board and let rest for 10 minutes. Slice the meat from the bone and serve.
—*David Myers*

WINE Complex, aromatic Nebbiolo.

beef, lamb & game

Rib Eye Roast with Chestnuts and Brussels Sprout Leaves

TOTAL: 1 HR

8 SERVINGS ●

One 3½-pound boneless
    rib eye roast, tied

1½ tablespoons extra-virgin
    olive oil

Salt and freshly ground pepper

1 stick unsalted butter

2 garlic cloves, smashed

2 thyme sprigs

8 brussels sprouts, leaves
    separated

8 cooked chestnuts from a
    vacuum-packed jar, sliced

¼ Asian pear, cored and
    cut into thin wedges

¼ teaspoon Sichuan
    peppercorns, ground

1. Preheat the oven to 350°. Rub the rib eye roast with ½ tablespoon of the olive oil and season with salt and pepper. Heat a large ovenproof skillet until very hot. Add the roast and cook over high heat, turning occasionally, until well-browned all over, about 12 minutes. Remove from the heat and add the butter, garlic and thyme. Spoon the butter mixture over the meat and roast, basting, for about 20 minutes, or until an instant-read thermometer inserted in the center registers 125°. Let rest for 20 minutes.

2. In a medium saucepan of boiling water, blanch the brussels sprout leaves for 20 seconds. Drain and pat dry. In a skillet, heat the remaining 1 tablespoon of oil. Add the chestnuts and cook over moderate heat, stirring, until golden, 3 minutes. Add the pear and sprout leaves and cook, stirring, for 1 minute. Sprinkle with the Sichuan peppercorns and season with salt.

3. Untie the roast and carve it across the grain into thin slices. Garnish with the chestnuts, pear and brussels sprouts.

—Timothy Hollingsworth

WINE Firm, complex Cabernet Sauvignon.

Three-Ingredient Prime Rib Roast

photo, page 124

ACTIVE: 15 MIN; TOTAL: 4 HR

10 SERVINGS ●

At first glance, coffee and prime rib roast would seem to be unlikely partners, but this inspired recipe from Ryan Farr of 4505 Meats in San Francisco reveals that they both have an earthy quality that makes them a natural match. Just be sure to scrape off any excess coffee rub from the roast before carving and serving.

⅓ cup finely ground coffee

2 tablespoons kosher salt

1 tablespoon freshly ground pepper

¼ vanilla bean, split, seeds scraped

One 12-pound, bone-in prime rib
    roast (5 bones)

1. In a small bowl, thoroughly blend the ground coffee with the kosher salt, pepper and scraped vanilla bean seeds. Set the rib roast in a large roasting pan and rub it all over with the coffee mixture, concentrating most of the rub on the fatty part of the meat. Turn the roast bone side down and let the beef stand at room temperature for about 30 minutes.

2. Preheat the oven to 450°. Roast the meat for 15 minutes. Reduce the oven temperature to 325° and roast for about 2½ hours longer, until an instant-read thermometer inserted in the thickest part of the meat registers 125° for medium-rare.

3. Transfer the prime rib roast to a large carving board and let the meat rest for 20 minutes. Use a knife to scrape away any excess coffee rub. Carve the meat in ½-inch-thick slices and serve.

—Ryan Farr

MAKE AHEAD The prime rib roast can be rubbed with the coffee mixture, wrapped well in plastic wrap and refrigerated overnight. Take the roast out at least an hour before cooking to allow the meat to come to room temperature.

WINE Juicy, spicy Grenache.

Beef Tenderloin with Pickled Onions and Pink Peppercorns

ACTIVE: 25 MIN; TOTAL: 1 HR 30 MIN

8 SERVINGS ●

1 cup raspberry vinegar

¼ cup plus 2 tablespoons sugar

Kosher salt

2 large red onions, very
    thinly sliced

1¾ pounds center-cut beef
    tenderloin in one piece, tied

2 teaspoons canola oil

2 tablespoons pink peppercorns

One 750-milliliter bottle
    light-bodied rosé

¼ teaspoon cornstarch dissolved
    in 2 teaspoons of water

1. Preheat the oven to 350°. In a large bowl, stir the raspberry vinegar with ¼ cup of the sugar and 1 tablespoon of salt until the sugar and salt are dissolved. Add the sliced onions and let stand at room temperature, stirring occasionally, until they are softened, about 1 hour. Drain the onions, reserving the pickling liquid.

2. Meanwhile, rub the beef tenderloin with the canola oil and set it in a small roasting pan. Season with salt and pat with 1 tablespoon of the peppercorns. Roast on the lowest rack of the oven for about 40 minutes, until an instant-read thermometer inserted in the center registers 125° for medium-rare. Transfer the roast to a board and let rest for 30 minutes.

3. Meanwhile, in a large saucepan, combine the rosé with the remaining 2 tablespoons of sugar and boil over high heat until reduced to ½ cup, about 20 minutes. Add ¼ cup of the pickling liquid and bring to a simmer. Add the cornstarch slurry and the remaining 1 tablespoon of peppercorns and cook until thickened, about 1 minute.

4. Slice the meat, removing the strings. Transfer to plates and top with the onions. Drizzle with the sauce and serve.

—Grace Parisi

WINE Rich, ripe Cabernet Sauvignon.

perfecting roast beef

F&W's **Grace Parisi** *creates a delectable and affordable roast beef, then offers three different recipes that transform the leftovers into a second meal.*

Coriander-Dusted Roast Beef

ACTIVE: 15 MIN; TOTAL: 1 HR 20 MIN

8 TO 10 SERVINGS ●

To make the stroganoff, salad or fajitas below (which serve four), save half of this roast and some of the gravy.

One 3¾-pound beef eye of round roast

   2   **tablespoons extra-virgin olive oil**

   1   **tablespoon whole coriander seeds,**
       coarsely ground

   1   **teaspoon sweet paprika**

Kosher salt and freshly ground pepper

1½ **tablespoons all-purpose flour**

   2   **cups beef stock, preferably homemade,**
       or canned, low-sodium broth

1. Preheat the oven to 350°. Rub the roast with 1 tablespoon of the olive oil. In a small bowl, combine the ground coriander seeds and paprika with 2 teaspoons of kosher salt and 1 teaspoon of pepper. Rub the spice blend all over the roast.

2. In a medium roasting pan, heat the remaining 1 tablespoon of olive oil. Add the roast and brown it well on all sides over moderate heat, turning with tongs, about 5 minutes. Turn the roast fat side up. Transfer the pan to the oven and roast the meat for 35 minutes, or until an instant-read thermometer inserted in the thinner end registers 120° for medium-rare meat. Transfer the roast to a cutting board and let rest for 20 minutes.

3. Set the roasting pan on the stove over high heat. Sprinkle in the flour and cook for 2 minutes, whisking constantly. Add the beef stock and bring to a boil. Simmer, whisking constantly, until

the gravy has thickened, about 2 minutes. Season with salt and pepper. Transfer to a gravy boat or bowl and keep warm. Slice the roast beef ¼ inch thick and serve with the gravy.

WINE Intense, fruity Zinfandel.

THREE DELICIOUS IDEAS FOR LEFTOVERS

1 Beef Stroganoff

Slice the leftover roast ¼ inch thick and cut into strips. In a skillet, combine 2 tablespoons olive oil, 1 sliced onion, 8 ounces sliced cremini mushrooms and 1 teaspoon thyme. Season with salt and pepper and cook over moderate heat until the vegetables are tender, 8 minutes. Add 1 cup of the gravy and boil. Stir in ¼ cup sour cream. Add the meat and simmer until hot.

WINE Deep, velvety Merlot.

2 Ginger-Beef Salad

Slice the leftover roast ¼ inch thick and finely shred. In a large bowl, whisk 2 tablespoons each of rice vinegar, Asian fish sauce and canola oil with 1½ tablespoons minced fresh ginger and 1 tablespoon sugar. Add the shredded roast beef, 8 cups salad greens, 1 cup fried chow mein noodles, 6 sliced radishes and ¼ cup each of chopped mint and cilantro. Toss the salad and serve.

WINE Fresh, fruity rosé.

3 Fajitas

Slice the leftover roast ¼ inch thick and cut into strips. In a skillet, combine 2 tablespoons canola oil, 1 sliced large onion, 1 sliced red bell pepper and 2 sliced garlic cloves. Season with salt, pepper and 1 tablespoon chile powder; sauté until browned in spots, 5 minutes. Add the meat and ¼ cup of the gravy; cook for 1 minute. Serve in warm tortillas with salsa, sour cream and cilantro.

WINE Rustic, peppery Malbec.

beef, lamb & game

Paprika-Rubbed Tenderloin with Citrus-Mustard Butter

ACTIVE: 30 MIN; TOTAL: 1 HR 45 MIN

4 SERVINGS

Four 7-ounce beef tenderloin steaks
    (about 1½ inches thick)

Olive oil

1½ tablespoons hot smoked paprika

Kosher salt

  2 tablespoons yellow miso paste

  2 tablespoons low-sodium soy sauce

1½ tablespoons fresh lime juice

  ½ teaspoon finely grated lime zest

  ½ tablespoon dry mustard powder

  ½ tablespoon fresh orange juice

  ¼ teaspoon *kecap manis*
     (see Note)

  ¼ teaspoon sweet smoked paprika

  1 stick unsalted butter

1. Preheat the oven to 200°. Rub the steaks with olive oil and sprinkle them with the hot paprika, rubbing to coat. Season the steaks with salt and transfer them to a small roasting pan. Roast for about 1½ hours, until an instant-read thermometer inserted in the thickest part of the steaks registers 125° for medium-rare.

2. Meanwhile, in a mini food processor, puree the miso with the soy sauce, lime juice and zest, mustard powder, orange juice, *kecap manis* and sweet paprika.

---

secret to juicy grilled steak

When grilling steaks, Texas chef Tim Love likes to leave some fat on the meat. "Be sure there's at least a quarter-inch of fat around steaks and chops to keep them moist," he recommends, "and score the fat in advance so that the meat doesn't curl up on the grill."

---

3. In a medium saucepan, melt the butter. Add the miso mixture and whisk over moderate heat until smooth and creamy, about 1 minute. Keep warm over low heat.

4. In a skillet, heat 1 tablespoon of oil. Add the steaks; cook over high heat, turning once, until browned, 4 minutes total. Transfer to plates; serve with the citrus-mustard butter. —*Jean-Georges Vongerichten*

NOTE *Kecap manis* is a sweet Indonesian soy-based sauce sold at Asian markets.

WINE Round, deep-flavored Shiraz.

Grilled Beef Medallions with Cauliflower-Broccoli Hash

ACTIVE: 45 MIN; TOTAL: 1 HR 15 MIN
PLUS 2 HR MARINATING

4 SERVINGS

  ½ cup parsley leaves

  2 tablespoons chopped rosemary

  1 tablespoon light brown sugar

  3 tablespoons extra-virgin olive oil

One 1¾-pound beef tenderloin
    in one piece

  2 cups coarsely chopped broccoli
    florets (½ pound)

  2 cups coarsely chopped cauliflower
    florets (½ pound)

1½ pounds baking potatoes, peeled
    and cut into 2-inch chunks

Salt and freshly ground pepper

  3 ounces minced pancetta

  3 tablespoons vegetable oil

  ¼ cup beef stock or
    low-sodium broth

  2 teaspoons Dijon mustard

  1 teaspoon white truffle oil
    (optional)

1. In a mini food processor, combine the parsley with the rosemary, brown sugar and 2 tablespoons of the olive oil; process to a paste. Coat the tenderloin with the paste, cover tightly with plastic wrap and refrigerate for at least 2 hours or overnight.

2. Bring a large saucepan of salted water to a boil. Line a large bowl with paper towels. Add the broccoli and cauliflower to the

saucepan and boil until crisp-tender, about 2 minutes. Using a slotted spoon, transfer the broccoli and cauliflower to the bowl and pat dry. Discard the paper towels.

3. Add the potatoes to the saucepan and cook over moderately high heat until tender, about 10 minutes. Drain the potatoes and return to the saucepan. Shake the saucepan over moderately high heat for about 20 seconds to dry the potatoes. Mash the potatoes and add them to the bowl with the broccoli and cauliflower. Mix well and season with salt and pepper.

4. In a large nonstick skillet, heat the remaining 1 tablespoon of olive oil. Add the pancetta and cook over moderately low heat, stirring a few times, until crisp, about 5 minutes. Stir the pancetta and olive oil into the potato hash.

5. In the same skillet, heat 2 tablespoons of the vegetable oil. Spread the hash in an even layer; cook over high heat until browned and crisp on the bottom, 3 minutes. Using a spatula, flip the hash over in sections. Carefully pour the remaining 1 tablespoon vegetable oil around the edge of the hash; cook until browned on the other side, 3 minutes. Remove from the heat.

6. Light a grill. Unwrap the tenderloin and cut it crosswise into four 1½-inch-thick medallions. Season with salt and pepper and grill over moderately high heat, turning once, until charred on the outside and an instant-read thermometer inserted in the thickest part of the medallion registers 125° for medium-rare, about 8 minutes. Transfer to a platter and let rest for 5 minutes.

7. In a small saucepan, bring the beef stock to a boil and stir in the mustard. Pour in any accumulated meat juices and season the jus with salt and pepper.

8. Reheat the hash until sizzling. Transfer the hash to plates and drizzle with the truffle oil, if using. Arrange the beef medallions alongside the hash. Drizzle with the jus and serve right away. —*Andy Glover*

WINE Complex, elegant Pinot Noir.

beef, lamb & game

Peppered Beef Tenderloin with Roasted Garlic-Herb Butter

ACTIVE: 30 MIN; TOTAL: 1 HR 40 MIN
6 SERVINGS

- 2 tablespoons coarsely ground black pepper
- 1 teaspoon kosher salt
- 1 teaspoon dark brown sugar
- 1 teaspoon soy sauce
- ½ teaspoon apple cider vinegar
- 1 tablespoon plus 1 teaspoon extra-virgin olive oil
- 6 tenderloin steaks (about 1½ inches thick)
- 4 garlic cloves, unpeeled
- ¼ teaspoon each of fresh thyme, rosemary and oregano
- 4 tablespoons unsalted butter, softened

1. Preheat the oven to 275°. In a bowl, mix the pepper, salt, brown sugar, soy sauce, vinegar and 1 teaspoon of the olive oil. Rub 2 teaspoons of the paste all over each steak. Wrap the steaks individually in plastic and let stand at room temperature for 1 hour.
2. Meanwhile, on a double-layer square of aluminum foil, toss the garlic with the herbs; drizzle the remaining 1 tablespoon of oil on top. Fold the foil to enclose the garlic and transfer to a baking sheet. Roast for 45 minutes, until the garlic is very soft.
3. When the garlic is cool, squeeze the cloves from their skins into a bowl; add the herbs. Using a fork, mash the garlic with the herbs and butter. Spoon the garlic butter onto a sheet of plastic wrap, roll into a log and refrigerate until firm, 30 minutes.
4. Build a very hot fire on one side of a charcoal grill or light a gas grill. Unwrap each steak; grill over high heat for about 7 minutes, turning once, for rare. For medium-rare, transfer the steaks to the cool side of the grill, close the lid and cook 4 more minutes, turning halfway through. Top with the garlic-herb butter; let stand 5 minutes, then serve. —*Chris Lilly*
WINE Firm, complex Cabernet Sauvignon.

Balsamic-and-Rosemary-Marinated Florentine Steak

ACTIVE: 20 MIN; TOTAL: 1 HOUR PLUS OVERNIGHT MARINATING
4 TO 6 SERVINGS ●

- 1 cup balsamic vinegar
- ½ cup plus 2 tablespoons extra-virgin olive oil
- ¼ cup finely chopped fresh rosemary
- One 3-pound porterhouse steak (about 4 inches thick)
- 2 teaspoons kosher salt
- 2 teaspoons coarsely ground black pepper

1. In a sturdy resealable plastic bag, combine the vinegar with ½ cup of the olive oil and the rosemary. Add the steak, seal the bag and refrigerate overnight, turning the bag several times.
2. Preheat the oven to 425° and bring the porterhouse to room temperature. Heat a large grill pan. Remove the steak from the marinade and season with the salt and pepper. Rub the side with the remaining 2 tablespoons of olive oil. Grill the steak over moderately high heat until nicely charred on the top and bottom, about 5 minutes per side. Transfer the steak to a rimmed baking sheet and roast for about 30 minutes, until an instant-read thermometer inserted into the tenderloin (the smaller section) registers 125°. Alternatively, build a fire on one side of a charcoal grill or light a gas grill. Grill the steak over moderate heat for 5 minutes on each side. Transfer the steak to the cool side of the grill, close the lid and cook for 30 minutes longer. Transfer the steak to a large carving board and let the meat rest for about 10 minutes. Slice the porterhouse across the grain and serve immediately. —*Matt Molina*
SERVE WITH Roasted Cipollini Onions with Sherry Vinegar (p. 218) and Giant Grilled Hunks of Bread (p. 255).
WINE Cherry-inflected, earthy Sangiovese.

Grilled Porterhouse Steak with Summer Vegetables

 TOTAL: 45 MIN
4 SERVINGS

- ½ cup extra-virgin olive oil
- 2 tablespoons fresh lemon juice
- 1 tablespoon red wine vinegar
- 1 tablespoon Dijon mustard
- 1 tablespoon chopped fresh oregano leaves
- Salt and freshly ground pepper
- 2 medium zucchini, sliced on the diagonal ⅓ inch thick
- 1 medium red onion, sliced ⅓ inch thick
- 1 red bell pepper, cored and quartered
- ¼ pound shiitake mushrooms, stemmed
- 1 pound asparagus
- 1 bunch of scallions, roots trimmed and bottom 6 inches only
- Two 1-pound porterhouse steaks (about 1 inch thick)

1. Light a charcoal grill. In a small bowl, whisk the olive oil with the lemon juice, red wine vinegar, mustard and oregano and season with salt and pepper. Transfer half of the dressing to a large bowl. Add the zucchini, onion, red bell pepper, mushrooms, asparagus and scallions. Season the vegetables with salt and pepper and toss.
2. In a perforated grill pan, grill the vegetables over high heat, tossing, until charred in spots, about 10 minutes; return the vegetables to the bowl, add the remaining dressing and toss.
3. Season the steaks generously with salt and pepper. Grill the steaks over high heat, turning occasionally, about 11 minutes for medium-rare meat. Transfer the steaks to a carving board and let rest for 5 minutes. Slice the meat from the bones and serve with the grilled vegetables. —*Kerry Simon*
WINE Complex, aromatic Nebbiolo.

●HEALTHY ●MAKE AHEAD ●VEGETARIAN ●STAFF FAVORITE

beef, lamb & game

T-Bone Churrasco a la Plancha

ACTIVE: 30 MIN; TOTAL: 1 HR

2 SERVINGS

Chef Francis Mallmann delves into Argentine grilling methods like *a la plancha*—on a griddle—in his 2009 book *Seven Fires: Grilling the Argentine Way*.

Two ¾-pound T-bone steaks
    (cut ½ inch thick)
6 tablespoons extra-virgin
    olive oil
2 tablespoons chopped oregano
1 large roasted red bell pepper,
    cut into 1-inch strips (¾ cup)
¾ pound fingerling potatoes
2 small onions, thinly sliced
2 fresh bay leaves
2 cups chicken stock
2 cups water
Kosher salt
2 cups chopped beet greens
Freshly ground black pepper
Crushed red pepper

1. Rub the steaks with 2 tablespoons of the oil and the oregano and let stand for 30 minutes. In a medium saucepan, combine the pepper, potatoes, onions, bay leaves, stock, water and 2 tablespoons of the oil. Season with salt and bring to a boil. Cook over moderately high heat for 30 minutes. Drain, discard the bay leaves and return the vegetables to the saucepan. Coarsely mash the potatoes with a fork. Fold in the beet greens and season with salt, black pepper and crushed red pepper.
2. Heat a cast-iron skillet; add the remaining oil. Add the potato hash; press into a round. Cook over moderately high heat until crusty on the bottom, 5 minutes. Carefully flip (in parts if necessary); cook until browned on the other side. Transfer to a plate.
3. Preheat a griddle. Add the steaks, season with salt and pepper and cook over high heat until well-browned, 3 minutes. Flip and cook for 2 minutes. Serve right away, with the hash. —*Francis Mallmann*
WINE Rustic, peppery Malbec.

Grilled Skirt Steaks

TOTAL: 20 MIN
10 SERVINGS

Sides of fresh tomatoes and lemony pureed avocado lighten this dish, while crispy potatoes soak up the meat juices.

5 Hass avocados—halved, pitted
    and peeled
½ cup extra-virgin olive oil
¼ cup fresh lemon juice
½ teaspoon crushed red pepper
Sea salt and freshly ground
    black pepper
Five 1-pound skirt steaks
40 cherry tomatoes, halved
Rösti Potatoes (p. 237),
    for serving

1. Light a grill. In a food processor, puree the avocados with the olive oil, lemon juice and crushed red pepper. Season the puree with sea salt and black pepper.
2. Season the steaks with sea salt and black pepper and grill over high heat, turning once, until charred outside and medium-rare within, about 5 minutes. Transfer to a carving board and let rest for 5 minutes.
3. Cut each steak in half crosswise; transfer to plates. Spoon the tomatoes and avocado puree alongside. Place the Rösti Potatoes next to the avocado puree and serve.
—*Francis Mallmann*
WINE Deep, velvety Merlot.

Chipotle-Marinated Flatiron Steak with Avocado-Corn Relish

TOTAL: 40 MIN
4 SERVINGS ●

The flatiron steak, a.k.a. the top blade steak, is a marbled cut of beef from the shoulder. Uniform in thickness and rectangular in shape (just like an old-fashioned iron), it's easy to butterfly for quick cooking on the grill. Here, F&W's Melissa Rubel Jacobson flavors the meat with a bold Southwestern-style marinade made with smoky chipotle and fresh orange juice.

One 1½-pound flatiron steak
    (about ¾ inch thick)
¼ cup fresh orange juice
1 canned chipotle in adobo,
    plus 1 tablespoon adobo sauce
    from the can
1 large garlic clove
2 tablespoons extra-virgin olive oil
2 Hass avocados, cut into
    ½-inch dice
½ cup fresh corn kernels
    (from 1 ear of corn)
¼ cup minced red onion
1 small jalapeño, seeded and minced
1 tablespoon fresh lime juice
Kosher salt and freshly ground pepper

1. Light a grill or heat a grill pan. Set the steak flat on a work surface. Using a sharp knife, carefully cut through the center of the steak (parallel to the work surface), leaving ½ inch of the meat attached at the side so it can be opened like a book. Set the butterflied flatiron steak in a medium bowl or baking dish.
2. In a blender, combine the orange juice with the chipotle, adobo sauce, garlic and 1 tablespoon of the olive oil and puree until smooth. Pour the marinade over the steak and let stand for 10 minutes.
3. Meanwhile, in another medium bowl, gently mix the avocados with the corn, red onion, jalapeño, lime juice and the remaining 1 tablespoon of olive oil. Season the relish with salt and pepper.
4. Remove the steak from the marinade, letting the excess drip back into the bowl; do not wipe off the marinade. Season with salt and pepper. Grill the steak flat over moderately high heat, turning once, until medium, about 6 minutes on each side. Transfer to a cutting board, cover with foil and let rest for 5 minutes. Thinly slice the steak across the grain and serve with the relish. —*Melissa Rubel Jacobson*
SERVE WITH Tortillas or black beans and lime wedges.
WINE Intense, fruity Zinfandel.

GRILLED SKIRT STEAK (AND
RÖSTI POTATOES, P. 237)

CHIPOTLE-MARINATED
FLATIRON STEAK WITH
AVOCADO-CORN RELISH

beef, lamb & game

Grilled Steak Tacos with Avocado Salsa

TOTAL: 50 MIN

4 TO 6 SERVINGS

The cilantro, the cheese and even the chiles in the salsa are grilled for these tacos.

- 3 jalapeños
- Extra-virgin olive oil
- 1 large onion—half cut into ½-inch dice, half sliced ¼ inch thick
- 1 garlic clove, minced
- 1 pound tomatillos, husked and chopped
- 1 Hass avocado, diced
- ½ cup chopped cilantro
- 1 tablespoon fresh lime juice
- Salt and freshly ground pepper
- 2 links of fresh chorizo
- ½ pound *queso panela* or halloumi cheese, cut into squares
- One 1½-pound flank steak

HOLIDAY DINNER PARTY

Celery Root Soup with
Clementine Toasts, p. 60

Fresh, lively Soave

. . . .

Syrah-Braised Lamb with
Olives and Endives, right

Rosemary-Roasted Potatoes,
p. 237

Fennel and Pecorino Salad,
p. 45

Round, deep-flavored Syrah

. . . .

Almond-Orange Cake with
Lemon Semifreddo, p. 317

---

1. Heat a grill pan. Grill the jalapeños until charred. Stem and seed the jalapeños; finely dice 2 of them. Thinly slice the remaining jalapeño and reserve on a platter.
2. In a saucepan, heat 2 tablespoons of olive oil. Add the diced jalapeños and onion and the garlic and cook over moderate heat until golden, 10 minutes. Add the tomatillos and cook until softened. Transfer to a bowl and let cool. Stir in the avocado, cilantro and lime juice; season with salt and pepper.
3. Oil the chorizo; grill over moderate heat until cooked through. Remove the casings; crumble the meat into a bowl. Lightly brush the cheese with oil; grill for 1 minute per side; oil the pan and grill the sliced onion until charred. Transfer both to the platter.
4. Oil the steak and season with salt and pepper. Grill over moderately high heat, turning once, 8 minutes for medium-rare. Transfer to a board and let rest for 5 minutes. Thinly slice the steak and serve with the accompaniments. —*Gonzalo Martinez*

SERVE WITH Warm flour tortillas.

WINE Earthy, medium-bodied Tempranillo.

Syrah-Braised Short Ribs

ACTIVE: 30 MIN; TOTAL: 5 HR 10 MIN

4 SERVINGS ●

Sommelier Clint Sloan of McCrady's in Charleston, South Carolina, loves this recipe, adapted from the *Joy of Cooking*, because it brings out the flavors in the braising wine.

- Eight 1-inch-thick flanken-style beef short ribs
- Salt and freshly ground pepper
- ½ tablespoon chopped parsley
- ½ tablespoon chopped oregano
- ½ tablespoon chopped rosemary
- 1 tablespoon vegetable oil
- ½ pound chopped bacon
- 2 cups chopped onion
- ½ cup chopped carrots
- ½ cup chopped celery
- 1½ cups Syrah
- 1 cup beef broth

1. Season the short ribs with salt and pepper; sprinkle with the chopped parsley, oregano and rosemary.
2. In a skillet, heat the vegetable oil. Add the bacon and cook until crisp; transfer to a roasting pan. Brown the ribs in the skillet; transfer to the pan. Add the onion, carrots and celery to the skillet and brown over moderately high heat. Add the Syrah and beef broth, bring to a boil and pour over the ribs.
3. Cover the pan and braise in a 325° oven for 4 hours, until the meat is tender. Transfer the ribs to a platter. Strain the sauce, skim off the fat and boil over high heat until reduced to 2 cups. Season with salt and pepper, pour over the ribs and serve. —*Clint Sloan*

WINE Fruity, luscious Syrah.

Syrah-Braised Lamb with Olives, Cherries and Endives

ACTIVE: 1 HR; TOTAL: 4 HR

6 TO 8 SERVINGS ● ●

Rajat Parr, the sommelier and partner at RN74 in San Francisco, braises succulent lamb shoulder in Syrah, then adds olives and dried cherries that he's soaked in red wine. The unusual combination makes the sauce deliciously sweet and savory.

- 1 cup pitted kalamata olives
- ¾ cup dried sour cherries
- 2 bottles Syrah or other dry red wine
- 1 tablespoon extra-virgin olive oil
- 5 thick slices of applewood-smoked bacon, cut into 1-inch pieces
- One 5-pound boneless lamb shoulder roast, tied
- Salt and freshly ground pepper
- 1 cup beef stock, preferably homemade
- 8 garlic cloves, smashed and peeled
- 8 thyme sprigs
- 2 carrots, thinly sliced
- 2 medium onions, coarsely chopped

2 bay leaves
1 teaspoon whole black peppercorns
4 Belgian endives, halved lengthwise
2 tablespoons sugar
1½ tablespoons fresh lemon juice
4 tablespoons unsalted butter, 3 softened
¼ cup all-purpose flour

1. Preheat the oven to 300°. In a medium saucepan, combine the olives with the sour cherries and 1½ cups of the wine. Bring to a boil and simmer over low heat for 5 minutes. Cover and set aside.
2. In a large enameled cast-iron casserole, heat the olive oil. Add the bacon and cook over moderate heat until the fat has rendered, about 7 minutes. Using a slotted spoon, transfer the bacon to a plate.
3. Season the lamb all over with salt and pepper. Add the roast to the casserole and brown it well on all sides over moderately high heat, about 8 minutes. Transfer the lamb to the plate with the bacon. Add the beef stock and the remaining red wine to the casserole and bring to a boil, scraping up the browned bits from the bottom.
4. Return the lamb and the bacon to the casserole. Add the garlic, thyme, carrots, onions, bay leaves and peppercorns. Cover the casserole and braise the lamb in the oven for about 2 hours and 45 minutes, until the meat is very tender and an instant-read thermometer inserted in the center of the roast registers 180°.
5. Meanwhile, arrange the endives cut side down in a large skillet. Add the sugar, lemon juice, the 1 tablespoon of unsoftened butter and 1½ cups of water and bring to a boil. Cover and cook over moderate heat until the endives are tender, about 15 minutes. Uncover and cook over moderate heat until the endives are caramelized on the bottom, about 8 minutes longer. Season with salt and pepper and keep warm.

6. In a small bowl, blend the 3 tablespoons of softened butter with the flour to make a paste and set aside.
7. Transfer the lamb to a carving board and cover loosely with foil. Strain the braising liquid into a medium saucepan and skim off the fat. Boil over high heat until reduced to 4 cups, about 30 minutes. Add the olives, cherries and red wine and simmer over moderate heat for 3 minutes. Whisk some of the braising liquid into the flour paste until smooth, then whisk the paste into the simmering sauce and cook over low heat, stirring occasionally, until no floury taste remains, about 10 minutes. Season with salt and pepper. Discard the strings and carve the lamb in thick slices. Serve with the sauce and the endives.
—Rajat Parr

MAKE AHEAD The sliced braised lamb can be kept in the sauce and refrigerated overnight. Reheat, covered, in a 350° oven.
WINE Round, deep-flavored Syrah.

Braised Lamb Shanks with Garlic and Indian Spices
ACTIVE: 45 MIN; TOTAL: 3 HR
4 SERVINGS ●
These ultratender lamb shanks are braised in a rich mix of red wine and tomatoes scented with cinnamon.

3 tablespoons vegetable oil
4 lamb shanks (5 pounds total)
Salt and freshly ground pepper
1 medium onion, coarsely chopped
1 head of garlic, separated into cloves and peeled
½ cup coarsely chopped fresh ginger
One 14-ounce can crushed tomatoes
3 cups dry red wine, such as Syrah
1 quart chicken stock
4 whole cloves
2 cardamom pods

2 teaspoons coriander seeds
1 teaspoon cumin seeds
One ½-inch cinnamon stick
¼ cup thinly sliced mint leaves, for garnish
Cheesy Farro-and-Tomato Risotto (p. 240), for serving

1. Preheat the oven to 325°. In an enameled cast-iron casserole, heat the oil. Season the lamb with salt and pepper and cook over moderately high heat until browned, about 4 minutes per side. Transfer to a bowl.
2. Add the chopped onion to the casserole and cook over moderate heat, stirring, until softened, about 7 minutes. Add the peeled garlic cloves and chopped ginger and cook over moderately high heat, stirring, until fragrant, 2 minutes. Add the crushed tomatoes and simmer the sauce until very thick, about 2 minutes. Pour in the red wine and boil for 3 more minutes. Add the chicken stock, cloves, cardamom, coriander, cumin and cinnamon and bring to a boil. Add the lamb shanks and any accumulated juices and cover. Braise in the oven for about 2 hours, turning once, until the meat is very tender.
3. Transfer the lamb to a large bowl and cover with foil to keep warm. Strain the braising liquid through a sieve into a large skillet and use a large spoon to skim off the fat. Bring the braising liquid to a simmer and boil over high heat until reduced to 2 cups, 20 minutes; season with salt and pepper. Add the lamb to the skillet, cover and simmer over low heat, turning the shanks a few times, until heated through, 3 minutes. Transfer the shanks and sauce to shallow bowls, garnish with the mint and serve with Cheesy Farro-and-Tomato Risotto. —Rajat Parr
MAKE AHEAD The recipe can be prepared through Step 2 and refrigerated overnight. Add an additional ½ cup of chicken stock or water to the braised lamb and reheat gently before proceeding.
WINE Intense, spicy Syrah.

beef, lamb & game

Slow-Roasted Lamb Shoulder with Almond-Mint Pesto

ACTIVE: 30 MIN; TOTAL: 3 HR PLUS OVERNIGHT SEASONING

8 SERVINGS ●

Gerard Craft (an F&W Best New Chef 2008) recommends seasoning lamb with salt and pepper, covering it with plastic wrap and letting it sit overnight in the refrigerator; easier than brining, this method helps keep the meat succulent.

Four 1½-pound lamb shoulder roasts, tied (have your butcher do this)

Salt and freshly ground pepper

3 ounces slivered almonds

1 garlic clove, smashed

2 cups mint leaves (from one 3-ounce bunch)

¼ cup freshly grated Parmigiano-Reggiano cheese

¾ cup plus 2 tablespoons extra-virgin olive oil

Lemon wedges, for serving

Potato Puree (recipe follows), for serving

1. Season the lamb roasts generously with salt and pepper, wrap in plastic and refrigerate overnight. Bring the roasts to room temperature before cooking.

2. Preheat the oven to 325°. In a food processor, pulse the slivered almonds with the smashed garlic clove until finely chopped. Add the mint leaves, grated Parmigiano-Reggiano cheese and ¾ cup of the olive oil and process until smooth. Season the almond-mint pesto with salt.

3. In a large skillet, heat the remaining 2 tablespoons of olive oil until shimmering. Add the lamb roasts and cook over high heat, turning, until they are browned all over, about 10 minutes total. Transfer the roasts to a large roasting pan and spread half of the almond-mint pesto all over them. Cover tightly with foil and roast for about 2 hours, until an instant-read thermometer inserted in the center of

each roast registers 170°. Remove the foil, increase the oven temperature to 425° and roast for 30 minutes longer, until the meat is browned on top. Transfer the lamb roasts to a large cutting board and let rest for about 10 minutes.

4. Remove the strings and carve each roast into ½-inch-thick slices. Serve with the remaining almond-mint pesto, lemon wedges and the Potato Puree.
—*Gerard Craft*

WINE Round, deep-flavored Syrah.

POTATO PUREE

 TOTAL: 45 MIN

8 SERVINGS ●

Putting potatoes through a ricer makes them perfectly fluffy.

3 pounds large baking potatoes, peeled

1 stick unsalted butter

1 cup milk

Kosher salt

1. Bring a large saucepan of water to a boil. Add the whole potatoes and cook over moderate heat until tender, about 20 minutes. Drain the potatoes and wipe out the saucepan. Working with 1 potato at a time, pass the potatoes through a ricer back into the saucepan.

2. In a small saucepan, melt the butter in the milk over moderate heat. Gradually whisk the hot milk into the riced potatoes and season generously with kosher salt. Cook the potatoes over moderate heat, whisking, until hot. Serve immediately.
—*GC*

Lamb Chops with Frizzled Herbs

 TOTAL: 40 MIN

8 SERVINGS ●

Quickly frying fresh herbs like rosemary, parsley and sage in half an inch of olive oil makes them addictively tasty and ultra-crispy. It's a nice way to dress up tender lamb chops.

½ cup extra-virgin olive oil

¼ cup red wine vinegar

8 large garlic cloves, roughly chopped

¼ cup plus 2 tablespoons rosemary leaves

24 frenched lamb chops (about 5½ pounds)

Vegetable oil, for frying

16 sage leaves

¼ cup loosely packed flat-leaf parsley leaves

Kosher salt and freshly ground pepper

1. In a large glass baking dish, whisk together the olive oil, red wine vinegar, chopped garlic and 2 tablespoons of the rosemary leaves. Add the frenched lamb chops to the marinade and turn to coat. Let the lamb marinate at room temperature for 30 minutes.

2. Meanwhile, in a small saucepan, heat ½ inch of vegetable oil until shimmering. Add the remaining ¼ cup of rosemary leaves to the hot oil and fry for 15 seconds. Using a slotted spoon, transfer the fried rosemary leaves to paper towels to drain. Add the sage leaves to the oil and fry until the bubbles in the oil subside, about 45 seconds; with a slotted spoon, transfer the sage to the paper towels. Add the parsley leaves to the hot oil and cover the pan immediately to avoid splattering; fry the parsley for 15 seconds, then add to the other herbs on the paper towels. Season the herbs with salt.

3. Heat a grill pan. Scrape the marinade off the lamb chops and season the chops with kosher salt and pepper. Working in batches, grill the chops over moderately high heat, turning once, just until they are pink in the center, about 6 minutes total. Transfer the lamb chops to dinner plates, sprinkle them with the frizzled herbs and serve immediately.
—*Melissa Rubel Jacobson*

WINE Firm, complex Cabernet Sauvignon.

LAMB CHOPS WITH
FRIZZLED HERBS

beef, lamb & game

Moroccan Spiced Lamb Patties with Peppers and Halloumi

 ACTIVE: 10 MIN; TOTAL: 35 MIN
4 SERVINGS

This excellent recipe combines Moroccan lamb—spiced with cumin, cinnamon and cloves—with the Greek cheese halloumi. Made from sheep's milk, halloumi is very versatile because it doesn't melt when it's roasted, grilled or pan-fried.

- 12 ounces roasted red peppers, cut into ½-inch strips (2 cups)
- 1 large, sweet onion, thinly sliced
- 8 ounces halloumi cheese, cut into ⅓-inch-thick slices (see Note)
- ½ teaspoon crushed red pepper
- 3 tablespoons extra-virgin olive oil
- Kosher salt and freshly ground black pepper
- 1½ pounds ground lamb
- 2 teaspoons ground cumin
- ¼ teaspoon cinnamon
- ⅛ teaspoon ground cloves
- 2 tablespoons chopped flat-leaf parsley leaves
- Warm pita, for serving

1. Preheat the oven to 450°. In a large roasting pan, toss the peppers, onion, halloumi and crushed red pepper with 2½ tablespoons of the olive oil. Season with salt and black pepper.

2. In a medium bowl, knead the lamb with the cumin, cinnamon, cloves, 1½ teaspoons of salt and ½ teaspoon of black pepper and form into four 4-inch patties. Arrange the patties over the vegetables and rub lightly with the remaining ½ tablespoon of olive oil. Roast for about 25 minutes, until the vegetables are very tender and the patties are cooked through. Sprinkle the parsley on top and serve with warm pita. —*Grace Parisi*

NOTE Halloumi is available at some supermarkets. Feta cheese is a fine substitute.
WINE Juicy, spicy Grenache.

Wine-Marinated Lamb Chops with Fennel Salad

ACTIVE: 40 MIN; TOTAL: 1 HR 30 MIN
4 SERVINGS

F&W's Kristin Donnelly loves making fennel salads as a weeknight side dish. Instead of throwing out the tough yet fragrant stalks of the fennel bulb, she uses them to infuse a white wine marinade for lamb chops.

- 2 large fennel bulbs—fronds and stalks reserved, bulbs quartered, cored and thinly sliced on a mandoline
- One 750-milliliter bottle dry white wine
- 2 medium garlic cloves, very thinly sliced
- Zest of 1 lemon, peeled in strips
- ¼ teaspoon crushed red pepper flakes
- 8 loin lamb chops
- ¼ cup extra-virgin olive oil
- Kosher salt and freshly ground black pepper
- ½ cup chicken stock or low-sodium broth
- 1 tablespoon crème fraîche
- 2 tablespoons fresh lemon juice

1. Thinly slice the fennel stalks. Finely chop enough of the fronds to make 3 tablespoons. In a shallow dish, combine the fennel stalks, white wine, sliced garlic, lemon zest and red pepper flakes. Add the lamb chops and turn to coat. Let stand at room temperature for 1 hour, turning the chops once halfway through.

2. Pat the lamb chops dry. Strain ½ cup of the marinade and reserve. In a very large skillet, heat 2 tablespoons of the olive oil. Season the lamb chops with salt and pepper, add them to the skillet and cook over moderately high heat until browned, about 4 minutes. Turn the chops, reduce the heat to moderate and cook until medium-rare, about 4 minutes longer; transfer the chops to a plate and let rest.

3. Pour off the fat in the skillet. Add the reserved ½ cup of strained marinade and boil over high heat, scraping up the browned bits from the bottom of the skillet, until the liquid is reduced by half, about 2 minutes. Add the chicken stock and boil until reduced to ¼ cup, about 4 more minutes. Reduce the heat to low and stir in the crème fraîche. Remove the skillet from the heat. Add 1 tablespoon of the chopped fennel fronds and season with salt.

4. In a medium bowl, toss the sliced fennel bulb with the fresh lemon juice and the remaining 2 tablespoons each of olive oil and chopped fennel fronds. Season the fennel salad with salt and pepper. Transfer the salad to plates and top with the lamb chops. Spoon the pan sauce over the chops and serve right away.
—*Kristin Donnelly*
WINE Lush, fragrant Viognier.

Chopped Lamb Steak with Garlicky Spinach

 TOTAL: 45 MIN
4 SERVINGS ●

"Chopped steaks are really just glorified hamburgers," says F&W's Marcia Kiesel. "It's a ground meat patty, but you eat it with a fork and knife like a steak—with or without bread." Marcia updates the old-fashioned diner staple by using ground lamb instead of beef and serving it with garlicky wilted spinach and warm fresh goat cheese. "This is such a good lazy summer meal," she says.

- ½ pound spinach, stems discarded and leaves rinsed
- 3 tablespoons extra-virgin olive oil, plus more for brushing
- 1 small red onion, finely diced
- 1½ pounds ground lamb
- 2 tablespoons dry red wine, preferably Pinot Noir
- ½ teaspoon ground cumin
- ¼ teaspoon cinnamon

WINE-MARINATED LAMB CHOPS WITH FENNEL SALAD

CHOPPED LAMB STEAK WITH GARLICKY SPINACH

Kosher salt and freshly ground
   black pepper
1 large garlic clove, very
   finely chopped
4 slices of peasant bread
4 ounces fresh goat cheese,
   cut into 4 pieces
Fresh marjoram leaves, for
   garnish

1. Heat a medium skillet over moderately high heat. Add a large handful of spinach and cook, stirring, until the leaves are wilted. Transfer the wilted spinach to a colander and repeat with the remaining leaves. Gently squeeze the spinach dry, coarsely chop and reserve.

2. In the same skillet, heat 1 tablespoon of olive oil. Add the diced red onion and cook over moderate heat, stirring frequently, until softened, about 7 minutes. Transfer the sautéed onion to a large bowl

and let cool. Add the ground lamb to the bowl and break it up slightly. Add the red wine, cumin, cinnamon, ½ teaspoon of salt and ½ teaspoon of black pepper and blend well. Gently form the lamb mixture into four 4-inch patties.

3. In the same skillet, heat the remaining 2 tablespoons of olive oil. Add the chopped garlic and cook over moderate heat until the garlic is fragrant, about 40 seconds. Add the wilted chopped spinach and cook, stirring, until hot. Season the garlicky spinach with salt and black pepper, cover and keep warm.

4. Light a grill. Lightly brush the peasant bread slices on both sides with olive oil and grill, turning once, until the slices are lightly browned, about 1 minute per side. Spread some of the fresh goat cheese on each slice of grilled peasant bread and top with the garlicky spinach.

5. Brush the lamb patties with olive oil and season them lightly with salt and black pepper. Grill the lamb steaks over moderately high heat, turning once, until the patties are nicely charred outside and medium-rare within, about 4 minutes per side. Transfer the chopped lamb steaks to the spinach-topped grilled bread, garnish the steaks with fresh marjoram leaves and serve with a fork and knife.
—*Marcia Kiesel*

NOTE You can also serve the chopped steaks without bread by piling the spinach and goat cheese on top.

MAKE AHEAD The garlicky spinach and uncooked lamb patties can be covered and refrigerated overnight. Gently rewarm the spinach before serving. Take the lamb patties out an hour before grilling to bring them to room temperature.

WINE Complex, elegant Pinot Noir.

●HEALTHY ●MAKE AHEAD ●VEGETARIAN ●STAFF FAVORITE

beef, lamb & game

Grilled Lamb Chops with Roasted Garlic

ACTIVE: 30 MIN; TOTAL: 1 HR 30 MIN PLUS OVERNIGHT MARINATING

4 SERVINGS

The little bit of cumin in the garlicky marinade for these chops highlights the lamb's slightly gamey flavor.

- ¼ cup extra-virgin olive oil, plus more for drizzling
- 4 thyme sprigs
- 1 garlic clove, minced, plus 2 heads of garlic, halved crosswise
- 2 teaspoons chopped rosemary leaves
- ¼ teaspoon ground cumin

---

japanese knives

American cooks have taken to lightweight, supersharp Japanese chef's knives.

Gyuto The equivalent of the Western chef's knife, *gyuto* means "large meat knife" in Japanese but is a great all-purpose knife for all kinds of chopping and slicing.

Santoku The word *santoku* roughly translates to "three uses"—designed for meat, fish and produce, the knife is essentially a smaller, more user-friendly version of a cleaver.

Petty With a blade that's usually four to six inches long, this is the Japanese version of the Western utility knife—great for small jobs like peeling citrus and mincing herbs.

- 8 lamb loin chops
- Salt and freshly ground black pepper
- White Bean Puree (recipe follows), for serving

1. In a large, shallow dish, combine the ¼ cup of olive oil with the thyme, minced garlic, rosemary and cumin. Add the lamb chops and turn to coat with the marinade. Refrigerate overnight.

2. Preheat the oven to 350°. Set the halved heads of garlic cut side up on a large sheet of foil and drizzle with oil. Wrap the garlic in the foil and roast for 1 hour, until tender.

3. Light a grill. Remove the chops from the marinade; discard the thyme and scrape off the garlic. Season the chops with salt and pepper and grill over moderate heat until lightly charred and medium-rare, 5 minutes per side. Serve the chops with the roasted garlic and White Bean Puree. —*Robert Wiedmaier*

WINE Round, deep-flavored Syrah.

WHITE BEAN PUREE

TOTAL: 25 MIN

4 SERVINGS ●

- 3 tablespoons unsalted butter
- 1 small onion, finely diced
- 1 garlic clove, minced
- 1 thyme sprig
- Two 15-ounce cans cannellini beans, drained and rinsed
- 1 cup low-sodium chicken broth
- Salt and freshly ground pepper

In a medium saucepan, melt the butter. Add the onion, garlic and thyme sprig and cook over moderate heat, stirring a few times, until the onion is softened, about 7 minutes. Add the beans and broth and simmer over moderately high heat until the broth is reduced by half, about 5 minutes; discard the thyme sprig. Puree the bean mixture in a blender. Season with salt and pepper and serve hot. —*RW*

MAKE AHEAD The puree can be refrigerated for up to 3 days. Reheat gently.

Cumin-Rubbed Leg of Lamb with Black Olive–Yogurt Sauce

 TOTAL: 40 MIN

8 SERVINGS ● ●

- One 3¾-pound piece of boneless leg of lamb, trimmed
- 1 tablespoon ground cumin
- 2 teaspoons hot paprika
- Kosher salt and freshly ground pepper
- 2 tablespoons extra-virgin olive oil
- 4 bell peppers, quartered and seeded
- 2 cups 2-percent plain Greek yogurt
- 1 cup pitted kalamata olives, coarsely chopped
- ½ cup coarsely chopped flat-leaf parsley leaves
- 1 small garlic clove, minced

1. Light a grill. Set the lamb fat side down on a work surface. Using a large, sharp knife and holding it parallel to the work surface, cut through the thickest part of the meat, leaving it attached at one side so it can be opened like a book.

2. In a small bowl, mix the cumin with the paprika, 2 teaspoons of salt, ½ teaspoon of pepper and 1 tablespoon of the olive oil. Rub the cumin paste all over the lamb.

3. In a large bowl, toss the peppers with the remaining 1 tablespoon of olive oil and season with salt and pepper. Grill the lamb and peppers over moderately high heat, turning once, until the meat is medium and the peppers are crisp-tender, about 8 minutes per side. Transfer the lamb to a cutting board and let rest for 10 minutes. Transfer the peppers to a bowl and cover with foil.

4. In a medium bowl, mix the yogurt with the olives, parsley and garlic and season with salt and pepper. Slice the lamb and serve with the grilled peppers and olive-yogurt sauce. —*Melissa Rubel Jacobson*

SERVE WITH Grilled pita or couscous.

MAKE AHEAD The black olive–yogurt sauce can be refrigerated for up to 2 days.

WINE Round, deep-flavored Shiraz.

Vadouvan-Spiced Leg of Lamb

ACTIVE: 30 MIN; TOTAL: 4 HR
8 SERVINGS ●

Vadouvan is an Indian-style spice blend from France that can include fried onion, garlic, curry leaves, cardamom, fenugreek and mustard seeds. If you can't find *vadouvan*, curry powder is a fine substitute.

- 2 sticks unsalted butter
- 3 tablespoons *vadouvan* (see Note) or curry powder
- 2 tablespoons coarsely grated orange zest
- 2 tablespoons chopped rosemary
- 2 tablespoons kosher salt
- 1 tablespoon crushed pink peppercorns
- 1 teaspoon freshly ground black pepper

One 8½- to 9-pound semi-boneless leg of lamb (shank bone in)

- 1 cup water

1. In a saucepan, combine the butter, *vadouvan*, zest, rosemary, salt, pink peppercorns and black pepper. Cook over moderate heat until the butter is melted; let cool.

2. Rub the curry butter all over the lamb. Roll the boned portion of the lamb into a cylinder and tie it with butcher's twine at 3-inch intervals. Set the lamb on a rack in a roasting pan and let stand for 30 minutes.

3. Preheat the oven to 325°. Roast the lamb for about 2½ hours, basting it every hour, until an instant-read thermometer inserted into the thickest part registers 130° for medium-rare meat. Transfer the lamb to a carving board and let rest for 15 minutes.

4. Pour the pan juices into a small saucepan and skim off the fat. Set the roasting pan over moderately high heat. When the drippings sizzle, add the water and bring to a boil, scraping up the browned bits. Add the deglazed drippings to the pan juices and keep hot. Carve the lamb into ½-inch-thick slices and serve with the curried jus.
—*Ryan Farr*

NOTE *Vadouvan* is available at some specialty markets and spicehouse.com.
MAKE AHEAD The butter-coated tied roast can be refrigerated overnight. Bring to room temperature before roasting.
WINE Intense, spicy Syrah.

Herbed Roast Leg of Lamb

ACTIVE: 25 MIN; TOTAL: 1 HR 40 MIN
6 SERVINGS

Roasting large cuts of meat is simple as long as you have an instant-read thermometer to check for doneness. A great piece of meat like this leg of lamb needs little more than a drizzling of extra-virgin olive oil and a sprinkling of herbs.

One 3½-pound trimmed boneless leg of lamb, butterflied
Extra-virgin olive oil, for drizzling
- ¼ cup chopped parsley, plus 2 parsley sprigs
- ¼ cup minced chives
- 1 tablespoon chopped thyme, plus 2 thyme sprigs
- 2 teaspoons chopped marjoram, plus 1 marjoram sprig
Salt and freshly ground pepper
Fleur de sel, for sprinkling

1. Preheat the oven to 375°. Open the leg of lamb on a work surface, fat side down. Drizzle olive oil over the lamb, rub in the chopped herbs and season with salt and pepper. Roll up the lamb, fat side out, and tie with kitchen twine at 1-inch intervals. Season with salt and pepper.

2. Line the bottom of a small roasting pan with the herb sprigs. Add the lamb and roast in the top third of the oven for about 1 hour, until an instant-read thermometer inserted in the meat registers 125° for medium-rare. Transfer to a carving board and let rest for 15 minutes. Strain the roasting juices into a cup and skim off the fat. Discard the strings and thinly slice the roast. Drizzle with the juices, sprinkle with fleur de sel and serve.
—*Kelsie Kerr*

WINE Earthy, medium-bodied Tempranillo.

Mustard-Crusted Lamb

ACTIVE: 35 MIN; TOTAL: 1 HR 40 MIN
6 SERVINGS

- 3 tablespoons unsalted butter
- ¾ cup finely diced shallots
- 1 teaspoon chopped thyme
- ¾ cup dry vermouth
- ¾ cup Dijon mustard
- 1 large egg
- 1 tablespoon chopped tarragon
Salt and freshly ground pepper
One 5-pound boneless leg of lamb, trimmed and butterflied
- 2 tablespoons extra-virgin olive oil
- 2 cups bread crumbs mixed with 3 tablespoons browned butter (see Note), 2 tablespoons chopped parsley and 1 tablespoon chopped thyme

1. Preheat the oven to 350°. In a skillet, melt the butter. Add the shallots and thyme and cook over moderate heat for 2 minutes. Add the vermouth and reduce by half. Transfer to a bowl; whisk in the mustard, egg, tarragon and a pinch of salt and pepper.

2. Set the lamb fat side down and season with salt and pepper. Rub one-fourth of the mustard mixture on the meat. Roll up; tie at 2-inch intervals with kitchen string.

3. Heat the oil in a roasting pan. Add the lamb and sear over high heat until browned all over, 8 minutes. Transfer to a plate and remove the strings. Rub with the remaining mustard mixture and pat the bread crumb coating all over. Roast the lamb in the roasting pan for 50 minutes, until an instant-read thermometer inserted in the center registers 130° for medium-rare. Let rest for 15 minutes before carving.
—*Suzanne Goin*

NOTE To make 3 tablespoons of browned butter, in a medium skillet, cook 4 tablespoons of unsalted butter until fragrant, nutty and no longer sizzling, 3 minutes. Pour through a fine-mesh sieve into a small bowl and discard the solids.
WINE Firm, complex Cabernet Sauvignon.

beef, lamb & game

Kibbe in Yogurt Sauce

ACTIVE: 1 HR; TOTAL: 2 HR
5 TO 6 SERVINGS ● ●

A Syrian comfort food, kibbe (Middle Eastern stuffed meatballs) are braised in a tangy yogurt sauce, a staple of Syrian cuisine. "Many Syrian cooks do not flavor the yogurt," says cookbook author Anissa Helou, "but I prefer to lift it with herbs and garlic." She also suggests swapping in a few teaspoons of dried mint in place of the cilantro. Be sure to use very fine bulgur wheat, she adds, or else the kibbe mixture will be coarse and hard to shape.

FILLING

- 6 tablespoons unsalted butter
- ½ cup pine nuts
- 1 large white onion, finely chopped
- ½ pound ground lamb
- 1½ teaspoons cinnamon
- 1½ teaspoons ground allspice
- ½ teaspoon freshly ground pepper

Salt

KIBBE

- 1 medium onion, quartered
- 1 pound ground lamb
- 1 cup fine bulgur, rinsed
- 1 teaspoon cinnamon
- 1 teaspoon ground allspice
- ½ teaspoon freshly ground pepper
- 2 teaspoons kosher salt

YOGURT SAUCE

- 4 cups plain Greek-style yogurt
- 1½ cups water
- 2 large eggs, beaten

CILANTRO BUTTER

- 4 tablespoons unsalted butter
- 6 garlic cloves, smashed
- 1 cup chopped cilantro

1. **MAKE THE FILLING:** In a small skillet, melt the butter. Add the pine nuts and cook over moderate heat, stirring, until the nuts are golden and the butter is browned, 3 minutes. Using a slotted spoon, transfer the nuts to a bowl.
2. Add the onion to the skillet and cook over moderate heat until softened, 8 minutes.

Add the lamb and cook, stirring to break up any lumps, until no pink remains, 8 minutes. Stir in the cinnamon, allspice, pepper and pine nuts and season with salt. Let cool.
3. **MAKE THE KIBBE:** Fill a bowl with lightly salted water. In a food processor, pulse the onion until finely chopped. Add the lamb and pulse just to incorporate, then add the bulgur and pulse to blend. Transfer the mixture to a bowl. Moisten your hands with the salt water and knead in the cinnamon, allspice, pepper and salt.
4. Moisten your hands again and roll 3 tablespoons of the kibbe mixture into an egg shape. Using your index finger, poke a hole in 1 end of the egg; gently work your finger into the kibbe until you have a 3-inch-long egg-shaped shell with ¼-inch-thick walls. Cradling the kibbe in one hand so that the walls don't collapse, spoon 1 tablespoon of the filling into the cavity. Pinch the end to seal. Set the kibbe on a plate. Repeat with the remaining mixture and filling (you should have about 20 kibbe). Freeze for about 30 minutes, until firm.
5. **MAKE THE YOGURT SAUCE:** In a large saucepan, combine the yogurt with the water and eggs and cook over moderately low heat, whisking, until the yogurt just begins to simmer. Add the kibbe to the yogurt sauce and cook over low heat until the sauce is thickened and the kibbe are firm and cooked through, 15 minutes.
6. **MEANWHILE, MAKE THE CILANTRO BUTTER:** In a small skillet, melt the butter. Add the garlic; cook over moderate heat until lightly browned, about 2 minutes. Discard the garlic. Stir in the cilantro and remove from the heat.
7. Transfer the kibbe and sauce to a platter. Drizzle with the cilantro butter and serve.
—*Anissa Helou*

SERVE WITH Warm pita and rice.
MAKE AHEAD The assembled, uncooked kibbe can be frozen for up to 2 weeks. Defrost before proceeding.
WINE Juicy, spicy Grenache.

Middle Eastern Lamb Skewers

TOTAL: 30 MIN PLUS 6 HR MARINATING
4 SERVINGS ● ●

Chef Michael Solomonov of Zahav in Philadelphia adds onion juice or pureed onions to his Middle Eastern–style marinades to tenderize and caramelize the meat. The marinade is great on chicken breast as well as lamb.

- 1 medium onion, quartered
- 1 garlic clove, peeled
- 4 flat-leaf parsley sprigs
- ½ teaspoon finely grated lemon zest
- 3 tablespoons fresh lemon juice
- 1 teaspoon ground allspice
- 1 tablespoon kosher salt

Pinch of saffron threads

- 1¼ pounds trimmed lamb loin, cut into 1-inch cubes
- 2 tablespoons vegetable oil

Warm pita bread and plain Greek-style (strained) yogurt, for serving

1. In the jar of a blender, combine the quartered onion, peeled garlic clove, parsley sprigs, grated lemon zest, fresh lemon juice, ground allspice, kosher salt and saffron threads and puree until the mixture is very smooth. Transfer the marinade to a resealable plastic bag, add the cubed lamb loin and turn to coat the meat in the marinade. Seal the bag, pressing out any air. Refrigerate the lamb for at least 6 hours or preferably overnight.
2. Light a grill or preheat a grill pan. Drain the lamb cubes, shaking off the excess marinade. Thread the lamb onto 4 long skewers, leaving a bit of room between the cubes. Brush the lamb skewers all over with the vegetable oil and grill over high heat, turning occasionally, until lightly charred all over, about 5 minutes for medium-rare meat. Serve the lamb skewers with warm pita and Greek yogurt.
—*Michael Solomonov*

WINE Lively, fruity Merlot.

MIDDLE EASTERN
LAMB SKEWERS

beef, lamb & game

Lamb Skewers with Salsa Verde

ACTIVE: 30 MIN; TOTAL: 2 HR 30 MIN

4 SERVINGS ●

At New York City's Boqueria, chef Seamus Mullen marinates leg-of-lamb pieces in a mix of more than 10 ingredients (including saffron and Spanish paprika), many of which he also uses to make the accompanying salsa verde. In this streamlined version of the recipe, the lamb is simply marinated in a bit of the salsa verde to save a step.

¼ cup packed mint leaves
¼ cup packed flat-leaf parsley leaves
¼ cup snipped chives
2 tablespoons minced shallot
1 tablespoon fresh lemon juice
1 tablespoon sherry vinegar
1 teaspoon crushed red pepper
Salt
¾ cup extra-virgin olive oil
1½ teaspoons smoked sweet paprika
1 teaspoon ground cumin
1½ pounds leg of lamb, cut into 1-inch pieces

1. In a food processor, combine the mint, parsley and chives with the shallot, lemon juice, sherry vinegar, crushed red pepper and a pinch of salt and process until finely chopped. Add the olive oil and process the salsa verde until smooth.

2. Transfer half of the salsa verde to a small bowl. Transfer the remaining salsa verde to another bowl and stir in the paprika and cumin. Add the lamb pieces and turn to coat thoroughly. Thread the lamb onto 8 long skewers and refrigerate for at least 2 hours or up to 24 hours.

3. Light a grill or preheat a grill pan. Grill the lamb skewers over high heat, turning them occasionally, until the lamb is lightly charred in spots, about 6 minutes for medium meat. Serve the lamb skewers with the salsa verde. —*Seamus Mullen*

WINE Earthy, medium-bodied Tempranillo.

Yogurt-Marinated Lamb Kebabs with Lemon Butter

ACTIVE: 25 MIN; TOTAL: 45 MIN PLUS OVERNIGHT MARINATING

4 TO 6 SERVINGS ●

At Shahpura Bagh, a luxurious guesthouse in the Rajasthani countryside of northwestern India, chefs marinate lamb to make it exceptionally tender, then give it an extra burst of tangy flavor with a basting of lemon butter just before serving.

2 cups plain whole-milk yogurt
1½ cups water
2 pounds trimmed boneless leg of lamb, cut into 1½-inch cubes
1½ teaspoons pure chile powder, such as ancho
1 teaspoon turmeric
1 large garlic clove, minced
½ teaspoon cayenne pepper
Kosher salt
Six 1-by-2-inch strips of lemon peel
3 tablespoons ghee or unsalted butter, melted (see Note)
2 tablespoons fresh lemon juice

1. In a large bowl, whisk 1 cup of the yogurt with the water. Add the lamb cubes, toss to coat and refrigerate overnight.

2. Light a grill. Drain the lamb and pat dry with paper towels. In a large bowl, whisk the remaining 1 cup of yogurt with the chile powder, turmeric, garlic, cayenne and 1 teaspoon of salt. Add the lamb, toss to coat and let stand for 10 to 20 minutes.

3. On each of 6 metal skewers, thread a piece of the lemon peel. Thread the lamb cubes onto the skewers and season with salt. In a small bowl, combine the ghee with the lemon juice.

4. Grill the skewers over moderately high heat, turning, until starting to char all over, about 3 minutes. Continue to grill, turning and basting with the ghee and lemon juice, until medium-rare, about 4 minutes longer. Serve the lamb on or off the skewers. —*Peggy Markel*

SERVE WITH Basmati rice.

NOTE Prized for its high smoking point and rich flavor, ghee (clarified butter) is made by heating butter to separate the golden fat (the ghee) from the water and milk solids. You can make your own or buy it from Indian groceries.

WINE Intense, fruity Zinfandel.

Spicy Lamb Shish Kebabs

ACTIVE: 30 MIN; TOTAL: 1 HR 30 MIN

6 SERVINGS ●

¼ cup plain fat-free Greek yogurt
1 tablespoon hot paprika
1 teaspoon ground cumin
½ teaspoon ground allspice
2 garlic cloves, very finely chopped
1 tablespoon extra-virgin olive oil, plus more for brushing
Kosher salt and freshly ground black pepper
2 pounds trimmed lean leg of lamb, cut into 1-inch cubes
1 pound small zucchini, halved lengthwise and cut crosswise into 1-inch pieces
Warmed pita bread, for serving

1. In a large bowl, whisk the yogurt with the paprika, cumin, allspice, garlic and the 1 tablespoon of olive oil. Season with 1½ teaspoons of kosher salt and ½ teaspoon of black pepper. Add the lamb cubes and stir until evenly coated. Let stand at room temperature for 1 hour or refrigerate for up to 3 hours.

2. Light a grill or preheat a grill pan. Thread the lamb cubes and zucchini pieces onto 12 long metal skewers and brush with olive oil. Season lightly with salt and pepper. Grill the kebabs over moderately high heat, turning, until the lamb is browned outside and medium-rare inside, about 6 minutes. Serve the lamb kebabs with the pita. —*Grace Parisi*

WINE Fruity, luscious Syrah.

Rabbit Stew with Olives and Rosemary

ACTIVE: 30 MIN; TOTAL: 1 HR 30 MIN
6 SERVINGS ●

"This is one of my favorite things on the planet," says New York City chef Marco Canora about his savory, rustic rabbit stew. The base for the sauce is a *battuto*, a mixture of finely chopped onion, celery and carrots sautéed in olive oil that's at the heart of many Italian dishes.

¼ cup plus 2 tablespoons extra-virgin olive oil
Two 3-pound rabbits, each cut into 10 pieces (see Note)
Salt and freshly ground pepper
1 cup dry red wine
1 onion, finely chopped
1 carrot, finely chopped
2 celery ribs, finely chopped
2 tablespoons tomato paste
4 rosemary sprigs, tied into 2 bundles with kitchen string
4 cups chicken stock or low-sodium broth
½ pound Niçoise olives (1½ cups)

1. In a large, deep skillet, heat 2 tablespoons of the olive oil. Season the rabbit with salt and pepper. Working in 2 batches, brown the rabbit over moderately high heat, turning occasionally, until crusty all over, about 10 minutes; lower the heat to moderate for the second batch. Transfer the rabbit to a large plate.

2. Add the red wine to the skillet and cook over moderately high heat, using a wooden spoon to scrape up any browned bits on the bottom of the pan. Pour the wine into a cup; wipe out the skillet.

3. Add the remaining ¼ cup of olive oil to the skillet. Add the chopped onion, carrot and celery and cook over moderate heat, stirring occasionally, until the vegetables are softened, about 8 minutes. Add the tomato paste and rosemary bundles to the vegetables and cook, stirring, until the tomato paste begins to brown, about 5 minutes. Add the browned rabbit pieces and any accumulated juices along with the reserved wine to the skillet and cook, stirring occasionally, until sizzling, about 3 minutes. Add 2 cups of the chicken stock, season with salt and pepper and bring to a boil. Cover partially and cook over low heat for 30 minutes. Add the olives and the remaining 2 cups of chicken stock and cook until the sauce is slightly reduced and the rabbit is tender, about 20 minutes longer. Remove and discard the rosemary bundles. Serve the rabbit stew with its sauce in shallow bowls. —Marco Canora

SERVE WITH Crusty bread.
NOTE Rabbit is sold at butcher shops and farmers' markets, and by D'Artagnan (800-327-8246 or dartagnan.com).
MAKE AHEAD The stew can be refrigerated for up to 2 days.
WINE Juicy, fresh Dolcetto.

Rabbit Ragout with Soppressata and Pappardelle

ACTIVE: 1 HR; TOTAL: 2 HR 40 MIN
6 SERVINGS ●

Star chef and *Top Chef* judge Tom Colicchio perfected this rabbit—braised with sweet tomatoes, spicy soppressata and olives—while he was heading up the kitchen at Manhattan's Gramercy Tavern.

2¾ pounds plum tomatoes
2 tablespoons extra-virgin olive oil
6 rabbit legs (about 7 ounces each; see Note above)
Kosher salt and freshly ground black pepper
3 cups chicken stock or low-sodium broth
1 cup pitted Niçoise olives (4 ounces)
¼ cup sherry vinegar
1 tablespoon very finely chopped fresh rosemary
6 ounces thickly sliced soppressata, finely diced
¾ pound pappardelle

1. Bring a medium saucepan of water to a boil and fill a bowl with ice water. Using a sharp knife, core the bottom of each plum tomato with a shallow X. Blanch the tomatoes by plunging them into the boiling water for 30 seconds to loosen their skins. Transfer the tomatoes to the ice water bath to cool. Pull the peels off the blanched tomatoes and cut the tomatoes in half crosswise. Scoop the seeds and pulp into a mesh strainer set over a medium bowl. Press the pulp and juice through the strainer and discard the seeds. Coarsely chop the tomato flesh and add it to the strained pulp and juice.

2. Heat the olive oil in a large enameled cast-iron casserole or Dutch oven. Season the rabbit legs with salt and pepper. Add them to the casserole and cook over moderately high heat, turning once, until lightly browned all over, about 6 minutes. Transfer the rabbit to a plate.

3. Add the chicken stock to the casserole and bring to a boil, scraping up any browned bits stuck to the bottom of the casserole with a wooden spoon. Add the chopped tomatoes, olives, sherry vinegar, chopped fresh rosemary and the browned rabbit pieces and season lightly with salt and pepper. Cover partially and cook over moderately low heat, stirring occasionally, until the rabbit is tender, about 1 hour and 10 minutes. Transfer the rabbit pieces to a plate. Boil the sauce until thickened, about 20 minutes.

4. Pull the rabbit meat from the bones and shred it. Return the rabbit meat to the casserole, add the diced soppressata and simmer for 10 minutes.

5. Meanwhile, in a large pot of boiling, salted water, cook the pappardelle until al dente. Drain well and divide among shallow bowls. Spoon the ragout over the pappardelle and serve. —Tom Colicchio
MAKE AHEAD The ragout can be refrigerated for up to 2 days. Rewarm gently.
WINE Complex, aromatic Nebbiolo.

beef, lamb & game

Meatballs with Peas

ACTIVE: 25 MIN; TOTAL: 1 HR 25 MIN
4 SERVINGS ●●

MEATBALLS

½   pound ground beef chuck
½   pound ground pork
3   tablespoons golden raisins,
    soaked in hot water and drained
1   large egg, beaten
½   cup minced onion
2   tablespoons dry bread crumbs
2   tablespoons freshly grated
    Parmigiano-Reggiano cheese
1   tablespoon chopped thyme
1   tablespoon chopped parsley
1   tablespoon water
1¼ teaspoons salt
½   teaspoon freshly ground pepper
1   tablespoon extra-virgin olive oil
½   cup dry white wine

SAUCE

1   tablespoon extra-virgin olive oil
½   cup minced onion
1   garlic clove, minced
One 16-ounce can chopped tomatoes
1   teaspoon dried oregano
1½ cups frozen peas, thawed
Salt and freshly ground pepper

1. MAKE THE MEATBALLS: Preheat the broiler. In a large bowl, mix the ground beef chuck and pork with the raisins, egg, onion, bread crumbs, cheese, thyme, parsley, water, salt and pepper with your hands. Form the mixture into 24 meatballs.

2. Spread the olive oil on a baking sheet; add the meatballs and broil 3 inches from the heat for 7 minutes, rolling a few times, until lightly browned. Turn the oven to 400°. Bake the meatballs for 5 minutes, then transfer them to a baking dish and pour the white wine over them.

3. MAKE THE SAUCE: In a saucepan, heat the oil. Add the onion and garlic and cook over moderate heat for 5 minutes. Add the tomatoes and oregano and cook for 5 minutes. Add the peas and cook 5 minutes, until thickened. Season with salt and pepper.

4. Pour the sauce over the meatballs and bake for 30 minutes, until the sauce is bubbling. Let rest for 10 minutes, then serve. —*Eugenia Bone*

SERVE WITH Rice or mashed potatoes.
WINE Rich, ripe Cabernet Sauvignon.

Meat Loaf with Mustard Seeds and White Pepper

ACTIVE: 15 MIN; TOTAL: 1 HR 40 MIN
8 TO 10 SERVINGS ●●

1   cup seasoned dry bread crumbs
1   cup heavy cream
1   pound ground beef
1   pound ground veal
1   pound ground pork
3   large egg yolks
⅓   cup yellow mustard seeds
½   cup whole-grain mustard
½   cup chopped parsley
5   garlic cloves, minced
1   tablespoon freshly ground
    white pepper
2   teaspoons kosher salt

1. Preheat the oven to 325°. In a bowl, combine the bread crumbs and cream; let stand until the cream is absorbed, 2 minutes.

2. In a bowl, mix the ground beef, veal and pork with the egg yolks, mustard seeds, whole-grain mustard, parsley, garlic, white pepper and salt, blending thoroughly. Pack the mixture into a 2-quart loaf pan and bake for 1 hour and 15 minutes, until an instant-read thermometer inserted into the center of the meat loaf registers 155°. Let the meat loaf rest for 10 minutes before serving. —*Tom Mylan*

WINE Lively, fruity Merlot.

Green-Chile Bacon Burgers with Goat Cheese

TOTAL: 45 MIN
4 SERVINGS ●

Instead of frying strips of bacon, grill master Bobby Flay brushes them with mango chutney, then bakes them until they are sweet, crispy and smoky.

8   thick-cut slices of bacon
    (about ½ pound)
½   cup mango chutney,
    preferably Major Grey brand
1   poblano chile
Vegetable oil, for brushing
4   hamburger buns, split
1   large tomato, cut into
    4 thick slices
1½ pounds ground beef chuck
Salt and freshly ground pepper
3   ounces fresh goat cheese,
    cut into 4 slices
Watercress sprigs or lettuce,
    for serving

1. Preheat the oven to 375°. Line a large rimmed baking sheet with parchment paper. Arrange the bacon slices on the paper and brush both sides liberally with the chutney, leaving any chunks in the jar. Bake the bacon for about 30 minutes, turning once, until caramelized. Transfer the glazed bacon to a rack and let cool.

2. Meanwhile, light a grill or preheat a grill pan. Rub the chile with oil and grill until charred all over, about 5 minutes. Transfer to a bowl, cover with plastic wrap and let stand for 10 minutes. Peel the poblano and coarsely chop it.

3. Brush the cut sides of the buns with oil and grill until toasted, about 30 seconds. Brush the tomato slices with oil and grill just until lightly charred, about 1 minute. Place the grilled tomato slices on the bottom half of the buns.

4. Form the beef into four 1-inch-thick patties and brush with oil. Season with salt and pepper and grill over high heat, turning once, until nearly medium-rare, about 6 minutes. Top with the goat cheese and chopped poblano, close the grill and cook until the cheese is completely melted and the burgers are medium-rare, about 1 minute. Set the burgers on the buns, top with the bacon and watercress and serve right away. —*Bobby Flay*

WINE Intense, fruity Zinfandel.

perfecting meatballs

Food stylist **Alison Attenborough** *prepares much of the food in the pages of FOOD & WINE.*
She and her chef husband, **Jamie Kimm,** *wrote* Williams-Sonoma Cooking for Friends,
which is full of ideas for dressing up ordinary foods. Here, they play
with scale to transform the unglamorous meatball into the ideal party dish.

Basic Meatballs

TOTAL: 20 MIN
MAKES 28 MEATBALLS ●

Attenborough and Kimm use a mix of beef, pork and veal in their meatballs. The pork and veal help lighten the texture, while the mix of meats makes the meatballs super flavorful.

- ⅓ pound ground beef
- ⅓ pound ground pork
- ⅓ pound ground veal
- 1 garlic clove, minced
- 1½ teaspoons kosher salt
- ¼ teaspoon freshly ground pepper
- 2 tablespoons olive oil

In a large bowl, combine the meat, garlic, salt and pepper until mixed. Roll the mixture into 1-inch balls. In a large nonstick skillet, heat the olive oil. Brown the meatballs over moderately high heat, turning occasionally, until they are cooked all the way through, about 7 minutes.

MAKE AHEAD The meatballs can be cooked up to 2 days in advance.

WINE Bright, tart Barbera.

SUPERSIZE
MEATBALLS

....
THREE GREAT VARIATIONS
....

1 Meatball Spiedini

To turn meatballs into cocktail-friendly finger food, make *spiedini* (Italian-style skewers): Prepare Basic Meatballs. On each of 14 cocktail skewers, spear 2 just-fried meatballs with a cherry tomato half and 1 or 2 basil leaves. Transfer the *spiedini* to a large serving platter and sprinkle them liberally with freshly grated Parmigiano-Reggiano cheese. Serve the *spiedini* warm. Makes 14 skewers.

WINE Juicy, fresh Dolcetto.

2 Supersize Meatballs

Start with 1½ pounds mixed ground beef, pork and veal. Mix in ¼ cup bread crumbs soaked in ¼ cup milk, ½ small minced onion, 2 minced garlic cloves, 1 tablespoon chopped parsley, 1 teaspoon minced oregano, 1 egg, 1 tablespoon salt and ¼ teaspoon pepper. Form into 4 balls. Brown in olive oil. Add 3½ cups marinara, cover and simmer for 30 minutes. Serve with spaghetti. Makes 4 servings.

WINE Cherry-inflected, earthy Sangiovese.

3 Asian Meatball Wraps

Start with 1½ pounds mixed ground beef, pork and veal. Mix in 1 minced garlic clove, 1 minced shallot, 2 tablespoons Asian fish sauce, 1 teaspoon grated lime zest, ½ teaspoon salt and ¼ teaspoon pepper. Roll into 2-inch balls; brown in an ovenproof skillet; bake at 400° for 7 minutes. Set each meatball in a lettuce leaf. Garnish with mint. Serve with hot sauce and lime wedges. Makes 20 wraps.

WINE Fruity, luscious Syrah.

Kogi Dogs

TOTAL: 40 MIN
8 SERVINGS ●

L.A. chef Roy Choi created these kimchi hot dogs for his Korean taco truck, Kogi.

- 2 cups finely shredded cabbage
- 1 large scallion, finely chopped
- 1 tablespoon fresh lime juice

Salt and freshly ground pepper

- 1 tablespoon toasted sesame seeds
- ½ cup mayonnaise

Vegetable oil

- 1 cup kimchi, drained, patted dry
- 8 hot dog buns, split
- 8 all-beef hot dogs, partially split
- 1 cup shredded sharp cheddar
- 2 cups shredded romaine
- 1 small onion, thinly sliced
- 2 cups cilantro sprigs

Sriracha chile sauce, for drizzling

1. In a large bowl, toss the cabbage, scallion and lime juice; season with salt and pepper. In a mortar, pound the sesame seeds until crushed and transfer to a small bowl. Stir in the mayonnaise and season with salt.

2. In a nonstick skillet, heat 1 tablespoon of oil. Add the kimchi and cook over high heat until browned all over, 3 minutes.

3. Light a grill. Brush the insides of the buns with oil and grill over moderately high heat, cut side down, until crisp, 20 seconds. Turn and grill for 20 seconds longer. Spread the cut sides with the sesame mayonnaise.

4. Grill the dogs until charred, 3 minutes. Tuck them into the buns with kimchi, cheddar, cabbage salad, romaine, onion and cilantro. Drizzle with Sriracha. —*Roy Choi*
WINE Fresh, fruity rosé.

Cumin-Spiced Burgers with Harissa Mayo

TOTAL: 35 MIN
8 SERVINGS

- 3 pounds ground chuck

Kosher salt and freshly ground pepper

- ¼ cup plus 2 teaspoons harissa (see Note)

- 2½ teaspoons ground cumin
- 2 teaspoons garlic powder
- 1 teaspoon dried thyme
- 1 red onion, sliced ¼ inch thick
- 1 tablespoon extra-virgin olive oil

Eight 6-inch oval rolls, split

- 1 cup mayonnaise
- 1 teaspoon caraway seeds

Tomato and cucumber slices

1. In a large bowl, gently mix the ground chuck with 1 tablespoon of kosher salt, 1 teaspoon of pepper, 2 tablespoons plus 2 teaspoons of the harissa, the cumin, garlic powder and thyme. Form the meat into eight ¾-inch-thick oval patties. In a medium bowl, toss the onion slices with the olive oil and season with salt and pepper.

2. Heat a grill pan. Cook the onions over moderate heat, turning once, until tender, about 10 minutes. Transfer to a plate and keep warm. Grill the burgers over moderately high heat, turning once, until medium, about 8 minutes. Grill the rolls until lightly toasted, about 2 minutes.

3. Meanwhile, mix the mayonnaise with the caraway and the remaining 2 tablespoons of harissa; season with salt and pepper.

4. Spread the mayo on the rolls. Top with the patties, onions, tomato and cucumber; close the sandwiches and serve.
—*Melissa Rubel Jacobson*
NOTE Harissa, a pungent North African spice paste, is sold in specialty food stores.
WINE Intense, spicy Syrah.

Beef Burgers with Peanut-Chipotle Barbecue Sauce

ACTIVE: 30 MIN; TOTAL: 1 HR
4 SERVINGS

- 1 tablespoon vegetable oil, plus more for brushing
- 1 onion, finely chopped
- 2 tablespoons minced fresh ginger
- 2 garlic cloves, minced
- 1 cup tomato puree
- 2 tablespoons ketchup
- 1 tablespoon red wine vinegar

- 1 tablespoon Worcestershire sauce
- 1½ tablespoons Dijon mustard
- 2 tablespoons honey
- 2 tablespoons molasses
- 3 tablespoons pure ancho chile powder
- 1 canned chipotle in adobo, minced
- ½ cup water
- 2 tablespoons creamy peanut butter

Salt and freshly ground pepper

- 4 hamburger buns, split
- 1½ pounds ground beef chuck
- ½ cup shredded cheddar (3 ounces)
- 1 scallion, finely chopped

Lettuce and tomato slices

1. In a medium saucepan, heat the 1 tablespoon of oil. Add the onion and ginger and cook over moderate heat, stirring occasionally, until softened, about 5 minutes. Add the garlic and cook for 1 minute, stirring. Add the tomato puree, ketchup, vinegar, Worcestershire sauce, mustard, honey, molasses, ancho chile powder, chipotle and water. Bring to a simmer and cook over low heat, stirring occasionally, until thickened, about 30 minutes. Transfer the sauce to a blender. Add the peanut butter and puree until smooth. Season the barbecue sauce with salt and pepper.

2. Light a grill or preheat a grill pan. Brush the cut sides of the buns with oil and grill until toasted, about 30 seconds. Spread some of the barbecue sauce on the buns.

3. Form the meat into four 1-inch-thick patties and brush with oil. Season with salt and pepper and grill over high heat, turning once, until nearly cooked through, about 5 minutes. Brush the burgers with some of the sauce and grill until lightly glazed, about 2 minutes. Top with the cheddar and scallion, close the grill and cook just until the cheese is completely melted, about 1 minute. Set the burgers on the buns, top with lettuce and tomato and serve right away. —*Bobby Flay*
WINE Rich, ripe Cabernet Sauvignon.

BEEF BURGER WITH PEANUT-
CHIPOTLE BARBECUE SAUCE

CHEDDAR BLT BURGER WITH TARRAGON RUSSIAN DRESSING

SHEPHERD'S PIE

Cheddar BLT Burgers with Tarragon Russian Dressing

TOTAL: 30 MIN
6 SERVINGS ●

At BLT Burger in Las Vegas, chef Laurent Tourondel brushes burgers with melted butter while they're on the grill. The natural sugars in the butter caramelize, making the meat extra-delicious.

- ½ cup mayonnaise
- ⅓ cup ketchup
- 1 tablespoon red wine vinegar
- 1 tablespoon grated onion
- 1 tablespoon chopped parsley
- 1 tablespoon chopped tarragon
- 1 teaspoon Worcestershire sauce
- 12 ounces thickly sliced bacon
- 1⅓ pounds ground beef chuck
- 1⅓ pounds ground beef sirloin
- 1 teaspoon kosher salt
- ½ teaspoon freshly ground pepper
- 2 tablespoons unsalted butter, melted
- 3 ounces sharp cheddar cheese, cut into 6 slices
- 6 hamburger buns, split and toasted
- 6 iceberg lettuce leaves
- 6 slices of tomato
- 6 slices of red onion

1. In a medium bowl, whisk the mayonnaise with the ketchup, red wine vinegar, grated onion, chopped parsley and tarragon and the Worcestershire sauce. Cover and refrigerate the dressing.

2. In a large skillet, cook the bacon over moderately high heat, turning once, until crisp, about 6 minutes. Drain the bacon on paper towels and cut the strips into large pieces.

3. Light a grill and fill a large bowl with ice water. Gently mix the ground chuck with the ground sirloin, salt and pepper. Form the meat into six 4-inch patties about 1¼ inches thick. Submerge the patties in the cold water and let soak for 30 seconds. Immediately transfer the burgers to the grill and brush with some of the melted butter. Grill over high heat for 9 minutes for medium-rare meat, turning once or twice and brushing occasionally with more butter. Top the burgers with the cheddar cheese slices during the last minute of grilling and let melt.

4. Spread the tarragon Russian dressing on the toasted hamburger buns. Set the lettuce leaves and tomato slices on the bottom halves of the buns and top with the burgers, red onion slices and bacon pieces. Close the burgers, cut them in half and serve right away.

—*Laurent Tourondel*

WINE Deep, velvety Merlot.

Shepherd's Pie

ACTIVE: 1 HR; TOTAL: 2 HR 20 MIN

8 SERVINGS ●

London chef Tom Aikens infuses milk and cream with fresh rosemary and thyme before folding them into the potatoes to update this British classic.

LAMB FILLING

- 2 tablespoons vegetable oil
- 3 pounds ground lamb

Salt and freshly ground pepper

- 2 tablespoons unsalted butter
- 1 large onion, cut into ⅓-inch dice
- 2 medium turnips, peeled and cut into ⅓-inch dice
- 2 large carrots, cut into ⅓-inch dice
- 2 large celery ribs, cut into ⅓-inch dice
- 4 garlic cloves, minced
- 1 tablespoon thyme leaves
- ¼ cup water
- 2 tablespoons tomato paste
- ¼ cup plus 1 tablespoon all-purpose flour
- 1 quart beef stock

POTATO TOPPING

- ½ cup milk
- ½ cup heavy cream
- 3 tablespoons unsalted butter, softened
- 2 tablespoons extra-virgin olive oil

One 3-inch rosemary sprig

- 1 bay leaf
- 2 thyme sprigs

Freshly grated nutmeg

- 2½ pounds baking potatoes, peeled and cut into 2-inch chunks
- 3 large garlic cloves, halved

Salt and freshly ground pepper

1. MAKE THE FILLING: Set a colander over a bowl. In a large enameled cast-iron casserole, heat the oil until shimmering. Add the lamb, season with salt and pepper and brown over high heat, stirring occasionally, 8 minutes. Transfer the lamb to the colander; wipe out the casserole.

2. Melt the butter in the casserole. Add the onion, turnips, carrots, celery, garlic, thyme and water and season with salt and pepper. Cover and cook over moderately low heat, stirring occasionally, until the vegetables are just tender, about 15 minutes.

3. Return the lamb to the casserole. Stir in the tomato paste and cook for 1 minute. Sprinkle with the flour and cook for 1 minute. Pour in the stock and bring to a boil. Simmer over low heat, stirring, until the sauce has thickened, 10 minutes. Season with salt and pepper. Transfer the lamb to eight 1½-cup ramekins or gratin dishes. Let cool.

4. MAKE THE TOPPING: In a medium saucepan, combine the milk, cream, butter, oil, rosemary, bay leaf, thyme and a pinch of nutmeg and bring to a boil. Remove from the heat and let stand for 20 minutes.

5. Meanwhile, preheat the oven to 400°. In a large saucepan, cover the potatoes with water. Add the garlic and a large pinch of salt and bring to a boil. Cook over moderately high heat until the potatoes are tender, 12 minutes; drain. Return the potatoes and garlic to the saucepan and shake over high heat until dry. Pass the potatoes and garlic through a ricer into a large bowl. Strain the milk mixture over the potatoes and stir it in. Season with salt and pepper.

6. Spread the mashed potatoes over the lamb. Bake in the upper third of the oven for 20 minutes, until the filling is bubbling. Preheat the broiler. Broil 4 inches from the heat for 2 minutes, until browned. Let rest for at least 10 minutes before serving. *—Tom Aikens*

WINE Ripe, juicy Pinot Noir.

Chili with Guajillo and Ancho Chiles and Hominy

ACTIVE: 30 MIN; TOTAL: 2 HR 30 MIN

8 SERVINGS ●●

Butcher Tom Mylan of the Meat Hook in Brooklyn, New York, flavors his chili with three kinds of dried chiles: fruity *guajillos*, smoky anchos and a New Mexico chile.

- 8 *guajillo* chiles
- 2 ancho chiles
- 1 dried New Mexico chile
- 4 cups water
- 1½ tablespoons cumin seeds
- 2 tablespoons vegetable oil
- 2 large onions, coarsely chopped
- 8 medium garlic cloves, very finely chopped
- 2 pounds ground beef
- 1 pound ground pork
- ½ pound ground lamb

One 28-ounce can hominy

- ¼ cup finely ground cornmeal

Salt and freshly ground black pepper

1. Break open the chiles and discard the stems and seeds. In a medium saucepan, cover the chiles with the water and bring to a boil. Cover the saucepan and remove from the heat. Let the chiles stand, stirring a few times, until very soft, about 1 hour. Working in batches, puree the chiles with their soaking liquid in a blender.

2. In a large pot, toast the cumin seeds over moderately high heat until fragrant, about 1 minute. Transfer the cumin seeds to a spice grinder and let cool completely. Grind the cumin seeds to a powder.

3. In the same pot, heat the oil. Add the onions and garlic and cook over moderately high heat, stirring occasionally, until softened, about 6 minutes. Add the ground beef, pork and lamb and cook, breaking up the meat into coarse chunks, until starting to brown, about 10 minutes. Add the ground cumin and cook, stirring, for 1 minute. Add the chile puree and simmer over low heat for 1 hour, stirring occasionally.

4. Stir the hominy and its liquid into the chili. Gradually stir in the cornmeal. Simmer, stirring, until thickened, 5 minutes. Season the chili with salt and pepper and serve. *—Tom Mylan*

MAKE AHEAD The chili can be refrigerated for up to 3 days. Reheat gently.

WINE Rustic, peppery Malbec.

ASIAN SPICED PORK
SHOULDER (P. 159)

pork
& veal

Irresistible sweet-sticky
baby back ribs, supremely juicy
veal chops and more.

CHILE-BRINED FRESH HAM

GARLIC-RUBBED PORK SHOULDER WITH VEGETABLES

Chile-Brined Fresh Ham

ACTIVE: 30 MIN; TOTAL: 5 HR PLUS
24 HR BRINING

10 TO 12 SERVINGS

Butcher Ryan Farr of 4505 Meats in San Francisco likes to spike the brine for his fresh ham with chiles. Brining helps the pork skin turn crackly in the oven.

- 4 cups kosher salt
- 2 cups sugar
- 6 quarts cold water
- 1 cup black peppercorns, crushed
- 5 ounces Thai or serrano chiles, stemmed and finely chopped (see Note)
- 8 whole cloves
- 4 cups ice cubes
- One 18-pound bone-in fresh ham, with skin
- 2 cups low-sodium chicken broth

1. In a large saucepan, combine the salt and sugar with 2 quarts of the water. Bring to a boil over moderately high heat, stirring to dissolve the salt and sugar. Pour the brine into a very large pot. Stir in the crushed black peppercorns, finely chopped fresh chiles and whole cloves. Add the remaining 4 quarts of water and the ice and stir until the ice has melted and the brine is at room temperature. Add the ham, skin side up; the skin does not have to be submerged. Brine the ham in the refrigerator for 24 hours.

2. Preheat the oven to 400°. Remove the ham from the brine and brush off the peppercorns and cloves. Set the ham skin side up in a roasting pan and let stand for 30 minutes at room temperature.

3. Roast the ham for 1 hour; turn the pan and add 1 cup of water halfway through. Reduce the oven to 300°; roast the ham for 2½ hours longer, until an instant-read thermometer inserted into the thickest part of the meat registers 150°. Transfer the ham to a carving board and let rest for 30 minutes.

4. Strain the pan juices through a mesh sieve set over a medium saucepan and use a wide spoon to skim off most of the fat. Add the chicken broth and bring the liquid to a boil. Cut the skin off the ham and break it into pieces. Thinly slice the meat and serve with the jus and crisp skin.

—Ryan Farr

NOTE When chopping superhot chile peppers such as Thai or serrano chiles, wear gloves to protect your skin, and wash your board and knife well afterward, as capsaicin (the active component in chiles that irritates skin) transfers easily to everything it comes in contact with.

WINE Fruity, soft Chenin Blanc.

Garlic-Rubbed Pork Shoulder with Spring Vegetables

ACTIVE: 1 HR; TOTAL: 3 HR 30 MIN
6 SERVINGS ● ●

Most cooks braise or smoke pork shoulder. But Andrew Green, wine director for the Bacchus Management Group (which includes Spruce in San Francisco), rubs it with garlic and herbs, then slow-roasts the meat until it's juicy and crusty.

8 large garlic cloves, smashed and peeled

Kosher salt

2 tablespoons ground coriander

1½ tablespoons chopped fresh thyme leaves

1½ tablespoons chopped fresh oregano leaves

Freshly ground black pepper

½ cup plus 3 tablespoons extra-virgin olive oil

One 7½-pound butterflied boneless pork shoulder

2 pounds fava beans, shelled (2 cups), or 2 cups frozen shelled edamame

24 whole baby carrots or 4 medium carrots, sliced ¼ inch thick

4 pounds fresh English peas, shelled, or two 10-ounce packages frozen peas

2 tablespoons unsalted butter

3 tablespoons mixed finely chopped fresh herbs, such as flat-leaf parsley, chives and tarragon

1 tablespoon aged balsamic vinegar

1. Preheat the oven to 400°. With the side of a large knife, mash the garlic cloves with 1 tablespoon of kosher salt to make a coarse paste. Transfer the paste to a small bowl. Stir in the coriander, thyme, oregano, 1 tablespoon of salt, 2 tablespoons of coarsely ground black pepper and ½ cup of the olive oil until incorporated.

2. On a work surface, rub the garlic-herb oil all over the butterflied pork. With the fatty side up, fold the pork under itself into thirds and transfer to a roasting pan. Roast the pork for 40 minutes. Reduce the oven temperature to 300° and roast the pork for about 2 hours and 20 minutes longer, until an instant-read thermometer inserted in the center registers 160°.

3. Meanwhile, bring a large saucepan of salted water to a boil. Add the fava beans and boil until the skins loosen, about 2 minutes. Using a slotted spoon, transfer the favas to a work surface; peel off and discard the tough skins and transfer the favas to a bowl. Alternatively, boil the frozen edamame for 2 minutes and transfer to a bowl. Add the carrots to the saucepan and boil until tender, about 4 minutes. Using a slotted spoon, transfer the carrots to the bowl. Add the peas and cook until tender, about 2 minutes; if using frozen, boil just until hot, 30 seconds. Drain the peas and transfer to the bowl.

4. In the same saucepan, melt the butter in 1 tablespoon of the olive oil. Stir in the vegetables and season with salt and pepper. Cook over moderate heat until just heated through. Stir in the 3 tablespoons of chopped herbs.

5. Transfer the pork to a carving board and let rest for at least 10 minutes. Strain the pan juices into a small saucepan and skim off the fat. Add the remaining 2 tablespoons of olive oil and the balsamic vinegar and season with salt and pepper. Bring to a simmer, cover and keep hot.

6. Thickly slice the pork across the grain and transfer to plates. Serve with the vegetables, passing the sauce at the table.
—Andrew Green

MAKE AHEAD The blanched vegetables can be stored in an airtight container and refrigerated overnight. The sliced pork can be refrigerated in the pan sauce for up to 2 days. Reheat gently before serving.

WINE Deep, velvety Merlot.

Asian Spiced Pork Shoulder

photo, page 156

ACTIVE: 40 MIN; TOTAL: 4 HR
8 SERVINGS ● ●

2 teaspoons Chinese five-spice powder

2 teaspoons kosher salt

4 large garlic cloves—2 minced, 2 halved

1 teaspoon grated orange zest, plus four 3-inch-long strips of zest

One 6½-pound boneless pork butt

¾ cup soy sauce

¼ cup brandy

1 bunch of scallions, cut into 2-inch lengths

2 tablespoons coarsely cracked rock candy or granulated sugar

Steamed rice, for serving

1. Preheat the oven to 350°. In a bowl, combine 1 teaspoon of the five-spice with the salt, minced garlic and grated orange zest. Place the pork fat side down on a work surface and open up the meat. Rub all over with the spice mixture and fold up the meat.

2. Set the pork fat side up in a large roasting pan. Add the halved garlic, orange zest strips, soy sauce, brandy, scallions, sugar and the remaining 1 teaspoon of five-spice powder to the pan along with 1½ cups of water. Bake for 15 minutes, then lower the oven temperature to 325° and bake for 45 minutes, basting twice. Cover the pan with foil and bake for 1½ hours, basting every 20 minutes. Uncover and bake for about 45 minutes longer, basting twice, until the pork is richly glazed and an instant-read thermometer inserted in the thickest part registers 175°. Transfer the pork to a carving board, cover with foil and let rest for 15 minutes.

3. Strain the pan juices into a saucepan; skim off the fat. Boil over high heat until reduced to 2½ cups, 6 minutes. Slice the pork and serve with the pan juices and rice.
—Marcia Kiesel

WINE Fruity, luscious Syrah.

pork & veal

Braised Pork Shoulder with Chimichurri

ACTIVE: 45 MIN; TOTAL: 3 HR 15 MIN
8 SERVINGS ● ●

- 2 tablespoons unsalted butter
- 1 tablespoon vegetable oil
- 5 pounds pork shoulder, trimmed and cut into 5 equal pieces

Salt and freshly ground pepper

- 5 garlic cloves
- 2 large onions, coarsely chopped
- 3 thyme sprigs
- 1 bay leaf
- 2 cups chicken stock

Chimichurri sauce (see Note), for serving

Preheat the oven to 275°. In a skillet, melt the butter in the oil. Season the pork with salt and pepper; brown over high heat, 3 to 4 minutes per side. Transfer to an enameled cast-iron casserole and add the garlic,

onions, thyme, bay leaf, stock and 2 cups of water; bring to a boil. Cover with foil and bake for 2½ hours, until the pork is falling-apart tender. Transfer to a dish; keep warm. Strain the liquid, return to the casserole and reduce by half over moderately high heat. Season with salt and pepper, add to the pork and serve with chimichurri.
—*Vinny Dotolo and Jon Shook*

NOTE Purchase chimichurri or prepare Dotolo and Shook's excellent version: In a mortar, mash to a paste 1 chopped garlic clove with 1 seeded jalapeño. Season with 1 teaspoon of salt. Work in 1 bunch each of stemmed curly and flat-leaf parsley and ¼ cup of chopped fresh oregano leaves. Stir in ¾ cup of olive oil and 2 tablespoons of white wine vinegar; season with ½ teaspoon of crushed red pepper flakes.
WINE Rustic, peppery Malbec.

Pork Souvlaki with Tzatziki

TOTAL: 40 MIN
4 SERVINGS ●

Greeks make souvlaki by marinating chunks of meat (usually pork or lamb) in oil, lemon juice and oregano, then skewering and grilling them. F&W's Grace Parisi opts for pork shoulder because it's so tender and succulent. Instead of threading the meat onto skewers, she simply cooks it (with onions) in a grill pan until it's nicely charred, then serves it with store-bought pita and homemade tzatziki, a garlicky cucumber-yogurt sauce.

- 1¼ pounds trimmed pork shoulder, cut into 3-by-½-inch strips
- 1 large onion, cut through the root end into ½-inch wedges
- ¼ cup plus 2 tablespoons extra-virgin olive oil
- 3 tablespoons fresh lemon juice, plus lemon wedges for serving
- 2 tablespoons chopped fresh oregano
- 2 garlic cloves, mashed to a paste

Kosher salt and freshly ground pepper

- 1 cup plain whole-milk Greek yogurt
- ½ European cucumber, seeded and finely diced
- 2 tablespoons chopped fresh mint

Warm pita, for serving

1. In a medium bowl, toss the pork strips and onion wedges with the olive oil, lemon juice, chopped oregano and half of the garlic paste. Season with 1½ teaspoons of salt and ½ teaspoon of pepper and let stand for 20 minutes.

2. Meanwhile, in a bowl, mix the yogurt, diced cucumber, fresh mint and the remaining garlic paste. Season the tzatziki with salt and pepper.

3. Heat a large cast-iron griddle or grill pan until very hot. Add the pork strips and onion wedges along with any marinade and cook over high heat, turning once or twice, until the pork and onion are tender, about 10 minutes. Transfer the pork and onion to plates and serve right away, with the tzatziki, lemon wedges and pita.
—*Grace Parisi*

WINE Juicy, spicy Grenache.

Pork-and-Chile Stew

ACTIVE: 30 MIN; TOTAL: 2 HR 30 MIN
4 SERVINGS ●

- 6 pounds baby back ribs, membranes removed, cut into 3-rib sections
- 4 teaspoons salt
- 2 medium white onions, coarsely chopped
- 4 garlic cloves
- 4 serrano chiles, stemmed
- 4 poblano chiles—roasted, skinned, stemmed, seeded and chopped
- 4 white-corn tortillas, toasted and torn into small pieces
- 1 bunch of cilantro, finely chopped

Crumbled *cotija* or feta cheese, sliced radishes, lime wedges and cilantro sprigs, for serving

APRÈS-SKI DINNER

Whiskey-Cheese Fondue, p. 22

Fresh, minerally Vermentino
. . . .

Braised Pork Shoulder with Chimichurri, above

Maple-Ginger-Roasted Vegetables, p. 217

Mashed Potatoes with Crispy Shallots, p. 239

Rustic, peppery Malbec
. . . .

Ginger Cookies & Hot Cider, p. 332 & p. 365

1. In a large, deep pot, cover the rib sections with 10 cups of water and add the salt. Bring to a boil, then cover partially and simmer over low heat until the meat is tender, 1½ hours.

2. Transfer the ribs to a large plate; keep warm. Skim off excess fat from the cooking liquid; you should have about 6 cups of liquid. Add the onions, garlic and serranos to the pot and bring to a boil. Simmer over moderately low heat for 20 minutes. Add the poblanos and tortilla pieces; let cool. Working in batches, coarsely puree the cooking liquid.

3. Return the liquid to the pot. Add the ribs and simmer over moderately low heat until the stew is slightly thickened, about 15 minutes. Stir in the chopped cilantro and serve with the crumbled cheese, sliced radishes, lime wedges and cilantro sprigs.
—*Robert Del Grande*

MAKE AHEAD The pork stew can be prepared up to 2 days ahead. Rewarm before adding the cilantro.

WINE Fruity, light-bodied Beaujolais.

Grilled Pork Rib Roasts with Green Beans and Onions

ACTIVE: 1 HR; TOTAL: 2 HR 20 MIN
PLUS 2 HR BRINING
10 SERVINGS

To give pork rib roasts an irresistible sweet-salty crust, master chef Jean-Georges Vongerichten marinates them in a mix of soy sauce and maple syrup, then caramelizes them slowly on the grill. He serves the meat on a bed of crisp green beans and slow-braised onions in a fragrant broth of star anise, fennel and cumin.

PORK
- 1 quart water
- 2 cups soy sauce
- 1 cup pure Grade B maple syrup
- ¼ cup kosher salt
- Two 5-bone pork rib roasts (about 4 pounds each)

SPICE BROTH
- One 750-milliliter bottle floral white wine, such as Gewürztraminer
- ½ cup rice vinegar
- ½ cup soy sauce
- ⅓ cup pure Grade B maple syrup
- ¼ cup honey
- 4 star anise pods
- 3 whole cloves
- Three 3-inch cinnamon sticks, broken
- 1 tablespoon fennel seeds
- 1 tablespoon whole black peppercorns
- 2 teaspoons cumin seeds
- 6 large mint sprigs
- 1½ teaspoons cornstarch dissolved in 1 tablespoon of water
- Salt

ONIONS
- ⅔ cup extra-virgin olive oil
- 6 medium onions, sliced ¼ inch thick
- 1 large head of garlic, cloves peeled and thinly sliced
- 1 fresh red Thai chile with seeds, thinly sliced
- Salt and freshly ground pepper
- 1 pound thin green beans

1. PREPARE THE PORK: In a large non-reactive pot, mix the water with the soy sauce, maple syrup and salt, stirring to dissolve the salt. Add the pork rib roasts and refrigerate for 2 hours.

2. MEANWHILE, MAKE THE SPICE BROTH: In a large saucepan, mix the wine with the vinegar, soy sauce, maple syrup and honey. Add the star anise, cloves, cinnamon sticks, fennel seeds, peppercorns and cumin seeds and bring to a boil. Cook over moderately high heat until the spice broth is reduced to about 2 cups, about 25 minutes. Remove from the heat. Add the mint sprigs, cover and let the flavors infuse for about 30 minutes.

3. Strain the spice broth through a fine-mesh sieve into a medium saucepan and bring to a simmer over moderately high heat. Whisk the cornstarch-water mixture, then whisk it in and boil, whisking, until the spice broth is thickened, about 1 minute. Remove from the heat and season the broth with salt.

4. Light a grill. Preheat the oven to 350°. Remove the pork from the brine and pat dry with paper towels. Grill over medium heat, turning several times, until lightly charred all over, about 15 minutes. Transfer the pork to a large rimmed baking sheet and bake for about 50 minutes, until an instant-read thermometer registers 150° when inserted into the thickest part of the meat. Transfer the pork to a carving board to rest for about 10 minutes.

5. MEANWHILE, PREPARE THE ONIONS: In a large, deep skillet, heat the olive oil. Add the onions, garlic and chile, cover and cook over low heat, stirring occasionally, until the onions are softened but not browned, about 25 minutes. Season with salt and pepper.

6. Bring a large saucepan of salted water to a boil. Add the green beans and cook until crisp-tender, about 3 minutes. Drain and pat dry. Stir the green beans into the onions. Cover and cook over moderate heat until warmed through.

7. Reheat the spice broth. Transfer the green beans and onions to a platter. Using a sharp carving knife, slice the roasts from the racks, using the bones as your guide. Carve the roasts into 1-inch-thick slices and arrange them on top of the green beans and onions. Pour the spice broth over the pork and serve right away.
—*Jean-Georges Vongerichten*

MAKE AHEAD The strained spice broth and cooked onions can be refrigerated separately overnight. Gently reheat the onions and rewarm the spice broth before proceeding with the recipe.

WINE Complex, elegant Pinot Noir.

pork & veal

Mo's Sticky Ribs

ACTIVE: 20 MIN; TOTAL: 3 HR 20 MIN
4 TO 6 SERVINGS ● ●

2¼ pounds baby back ribs
Salt and freshly ground pepper
Granulated garlic, for sprinkling
Extra-virgin olive oil, for drizzling
 1 tablespoon whole cloves
One 12-ounce bottle lager
 1 cup ketchup
 1 cup peach or apricot jam
 3 tablespoons fresh lemon juice

1. Preheat the oven to 300°. On a rimmed baking sheet, season the ribs with salt, pepper and garlic. Drizzle with oil and scatter the cloves over the ribs and in the pan. Pour the beer over the ribs, cover with foil and bake for 2 hours, until the meat is tender.
2. Strain the pan juices into a saucepan. Whisk in the ketchup, jam and lemon juice and boil over high heat until reduced to 1½ cups, about 20 minutes.
3. Preheat the broiler. Set the ribs meaty side down on the baking sheet, brush with glaze and broil 4 inches from the heat for 7 minutes. Turn and brush with half of the remaining glaze. Broil for 10 minutes, until starting to char. Brush with the remaining glaze; broil until browned, 10 minutes. Let rest 10 minutes; serve. —*Fred Donnelly*
WINE Intense, fruity Zinfandel.

Honey-Glazed Baby Back Ribs with Whiskey Marinade

ACTIVE: 30 MIN; TOTAL: 6 HR 45 MIN
8 SERVINGS ● ●

MARINATED RIBS
 3 racks baby back ribs
    (about 5 pounds total)
¼ cup plus 2 tablespoons soy sauce
¼ cup plus 2 tablespoons whiskey
¼ cup honey
 2 tablespoons finely grated ginger
1½ teaspoons ground white pepper
 1 teaspoon Asian sesame oil
½ teaspoon cinnamon
¼ teaspoon freshly grated nutmeg

HONEY GLAZE AND
DIPPING SAUCE
¼ cup honey
 2 tablespoons hot water
½ cup fresh lime juice
¼ cup fish sauce
¼ cup soy sauce
¼ cup red pepper flakes,
    preferably Korean
¼ cup chopped cilantro
 2 tablespoons sugar

1. MARINATE THE RIBS: Arrange the rib racks in a large baking dish, overlapping slightly. In a bowl, whisk the soy sauce with the whiskey, honey, ginger, white pepper, sesame oil, cinnamon and nutmeg. Pour the marinade over the ribs and turn to coat. Cover and refrigerate for 4 hours.
2. MAKE THE GLAZE AND DIPPING SAUCE: In a small bowl, combine the honey with the hot water. In a medium bowl, combine the lime juice with the fish sauce, soy sauce, pepper flakes, cilantro and sugar; stir until the sugar is dissolved.
3. Preheat the oven to 300°. Line a rimmed baking sheet with foil. Arrange the ribs on the baking sheet, meaty side up. Roast for 2 hours, until tender. Baste the ribs with the honey mixture; roast for another 15 minutes, until browned and glossy. Remove from the oven and baste again.
4. Preheat a grill. Grill the racks over moderately high heat, turning once, until lightly charred, 4 minutes. Transfer to a cutting board; cut into individual ribs. Serve the dipping sauce alongside. —*Andy Ricker*
WINE Fruity, luscious Syrah.

Spicy and Sticky Baby Back Ribs

ACTIVE: 40 MIN; TOTAL: 4 HR PLUS
OVERNIGHT SEASONING
6 TO 8 SERVINGS ●

 1 cup dark brown sugar
 3 tablespoons kosher salt
 1 tablespoon dry mustard
 1 tablespoon ground fennel

 1 tablespoon freshly ground
    black pepper
 1 tablespoon cayenne pepper
 1 tablespoon sweet smoked paprika
 4 racks baby back ribs (about
    2½ pounds each), membrane
    removed from the underside
    of each rack
 1 tablespoon unsalted butter
 1 small onion, minced
 3 garlic cloves, minced
1½ teaspoons dried thyme
 1 cup ketchup
 1 cup cider vinegar
 1 cup beef broth
¼ cup hot sauce
¼ cup Worcestershire sauce
 2 tablespoons unsulfured molasses

1. In a small bowl, combine the brown sugar, salt, mustard, fennel, black pepper, cayenne and paprika. On 2 large rimmed baking sheets, sprinkle the spice mix all over the ribs, pressing and patting it. Cover with foil and refrigerate overnight.
2. Preheat the oven to 250°. Pour off any liquid on the baking sheets, cover the ribs with foil and roast for about 3 hours, until the meat is tender but not falling off the bone. Pour off any liquid on the baking sheets.
3. Meanwhile, in a saucepan, melt the butter. Add the onion, garlic and thyme; cook over moderate heat until the onion is softened, 5 minutes. Add the ketchup, vinegar, broth, hot sauce, Worcestershire and molasses; bring to a boil. Simmer over low heat, stirring occasionally, until thickened, 30 minutes.
4. Preheat the broiler and position a rack 10 inches from the heat. Brush the ribs liberally with the sauce and broil for about 10 minutes, turning and brushing occasionally with the sauce, until well browned and crispy in spots. Transfer the ribs to a work surface and let rest for 5 minutes. Cut in between the bones and mound the ribs on a platter. Pass any extra barbecue sauce on the side. —*Donald Link*
WINE Fruity, luscious Syrah.

MO'S
STICKY
RIBS

HONEY-GLAZED
BABY BACK RIBS WITH
WHISKEY MARINADE

pork & veal

Apple-Glazed Barbecued Baby Back Ribs

ACTIVE: 30 MIN; TOTAL: 4 HR 30 MIN
4 SERVINGS ●

These sticky ribs are roasted, then finished on the grill. They're a simpler version of a recipe by pit master Chris Lilly, who cooks his ribs entirely on the grill. To follow Lilly's example, use a thermometer to keep the temperature at a steady 250° and wrap the ribs in foil after adding the cider mixture.

½ cup dark brown sugar
4 teaspoons garlic salt
4 teaspoons pure ancho
   chile powder
2 teaspoons salt
1 teaspoon ground black pepper
½ teaspoon celery salt
¼ teaspoon cayenne pepper
¼ teaspoon cinnamon
¼ teaspoon freshly ground
   white pepper
½ cup apple cider
¼ cup apple jelly, melted
¼ cup honey
2 racks baby back ribs
   (about 4 pounds total)
1 cup prepared barbecue sauce

1. Preheat the oven to 250°. In a bowl, mix ¼ cup of the sugar with the garlic salt, chile powder, salt, black pepper, celery salt, cayenne, cinnamon and white pepper. Transfer 1 tablespoon of the spice mix to a medium bowl and whisk in the cider, apple jelly, honey and the remaining ¼ cup of sugar.

---

cooking ribs

Spareribs are fattier and more succulent than baby backs, which tend to be meatier and take longer to cook. The quickest way to cook both types is by separating the rack into individual ribs and roasting at a high temperature.

---

2. Pull the membrane off the underside of each rib rack using a towel to grasp the corner. On a rimmed baking sheet, rub the ribs with the remaining spice mix; bake, meaty side up, for 2½ hours. Pour the cider mixture over the ribs and turn to coat. Tightly cover with foil and bake for 1 hour.
3. Light a grill. Uncover the ribs and brush with the barbecue sauce; grill over moderate heat, turning and brushing, until glazed, 15 minutes. Let rest for 10 minutes, then cut between the bones and serve.
—*Chris Lilly*

WINE Juicy, spicy Grenache.

Maple Sugar–Ginger Roast Pork

ACTIVE: 20 MIN; TOTAL: 1 HR 20 MIN
PLUS OVERNIGHT MARINATING
8 SERVINGS

Cookbook editor Luisa Weiss marinates this pork loin roast with a sweet-and-spicy combination of maple sugar, grated fresh ginger and crushed red pepper; the sugar melts to form a luscious glaze as the meat roasts.

2½ pounds boneless pork loin
   roast, tied
2 garlic cloves, thinly sliced
2 tablespoons maple sugar
   (see Note)
1½ teaspoons finely grated
   fresh ginger
½ teaspoon kosher salt
¼ teaspoon crushed
   red pepper
2 tablespoons extra-virgin
   olive oil
Blood orange slices, red currants
   and sprigs of mint, for garnish
   (optional)

1. Using a small, sharp knife, make thin slits all over the pork loin roast and slip a garlic slice into each one. In a small bowl, mix the maple sugar with the ginger, salt, red pepper and olive oil. Rub the paste all over the pork, wrap it well in plastic and

---

refrigerate overnight in a small roasting pan; let stand at room temperature for 1 hour before roasting.
2. Preheat the oven to 450°. Roast the pork for 10 minutes. Lower the oven temperature to 400° and roast the pork for about 35 minutes longer, until an instant-read thermometer inserted in the thickest part registers 135°. Transfer the roast to a cutting board and let rest for 15 minutes before slicing. Discard the string and carve the pork into thin slices. Arrange on a platter, garnish with the orange slices, red currants and mint and serve.
—*Luisa Weiss*

NOTE Maple sugar, made from reduced maple syrup, is available at specialty food stores. Alternatively, use granulated brown sugar in this recipe.

WINE Juicy, spicy Grenache.

Roasted Pork Loin with Orange-Herb Sauce

ACTIVE: 20 MIN; TOTAL: 2 HR 15 MIN
4 SERVINGS

At Casa Oaxaca in Oaxaca, Mexico, chef Alejandro Ruíz Olmedo makes this recipe with suckling pigs; here he uses pork loin, roasting it in fresh orange juice steeped with herbs. When infused with pan drippings, the juice becomes the base for a tangy sauce.

3 tablespoons extra-virgin olive oil
2 garlic cloves, coarsely chopped
One 1½-pound boneless pork loin
Salt and freshly ground pepper
1 cup fresh orange juice
½ cup chicken stock
½ cup dry white wine
5 black peppercorns
1 rosemary sprig
1 oregano sprig
1 parsley sprig, plus 2 tablespoons
   chopped parsley leaves

1. In a large bowl, combine 2 tablespoons of the oil with the garlic. Add the pork, turn to coat and let stand for 1 hour.

ROASTED PORK LOIN WITH ORANGE-HERB SAUCE

SPICED PORK TENDERLOIN WITH HONEY MUSTARD

2. Set a rack in the upper third of the oven and preheat the oven to 400°. In a medium ovenproof skillet, heat the remaining oil. Season the pork with salt and pepper and add to the skillet, fat side down. Cook over moderately high heat until richly browned, 4 minutes. Brown the pork on the remaining sides, then turn it fat side up. Add the orange juice, stock, wine, peppercorns and herb sprigs and bring to a boil.

3. Transfer the skillet to the upper shelf of the oven and roast the pork for about 35 minutes, until an instant-read thermometer inserted in the center registers 145°. Transfer the pork to a carving board.

4. Strain the cooking liquid into a saucepan and boil until reduced to ½ cup, 15 minutes. Season with salt and pepper; stir in the chopped parsley. Carve the pork and serve with the sauce. —*Alejandro Ruíz Olmedo*
WINE Bright, tart Barbera.

Spiced Pork Tenderloin with Honey Mustard

⏱ **ACTIVE: 15 MIN; TOTAL: 45 MIN**
8 SERVINGS ●

Since pork tenderloin is low in fat, it tends to dry out, so be careful not to overcook this cut—these spice-coated tenderloins need just 20 minutes in the oven. F&W's Melissa Rubel Jacobson serves a stellar honey mustard alongside the pork to add moistness and sweet-spicy flavor.

- **3 tablespoons mustard seeds**
- **1 tablespoon fennel seeds**
- **½ teaspoon crushed red pepper**
- **Two 14-ounce pork tenderloins**
- **Kosher salt and freshly ground black pepper**
- **½ cup grainy Dijon mustard**
- **¼ cup traditional Dijon mustard**
- **¼ cup honey**

1. Preheat the oven to 375°. In a mortar, lightly crush the mustard and fennel seeds with the crushed red pepper. Set the pork tenderloins on a rimmed baking sheet and season them with salt and pepper. Spread the crushed spices on the baking sheet and roll the pork tenderloins in the crushed spices to coat them.

2. Roast the pork tenderloins for about 20 minutes, until an instant-read thermometer inserted in the thickest part of each tenderloin registers 145°. Transfer the pork tenderloins to a cutting board and let them rest for 10 minutes.

3. In a small bowl, mix the grainy and tradition Dijon mustards with the honey and season with salt and pepper. Slice the pork tenderloins ½ inch thick and serve with the honey mustard.
—*Melissa Rubel Jacobson*
WINE Juicy, fresh Dolcetto.

pork & veal

Pork Loin Roast with Herbs and Garlic

ACTIVE: 30 MIN; TOTAL: 2 HR 30 MIN PLUS OVERNIGHT MARINATING

10 SERVINGS ●

- 6 garlic cloves, peeled and very finely chopped
- ½ cup chopped mixed fresh herbs, such as parsley, thyme, sage and rosemary
- ¼ cup extra-virgin olive oil

One 5½-pound bone-in pork loin roast, chine bone removed (about 8 ribs)

Salt and freshly ground pepper

1. In a small bowl, combine the chopped garlic with the herbs and olive oil. To remove the loin in one piece while keeping the rib rack intact, run a long, sharp knife along the bones to release the meat. Season the loin and ribs with salt and pepper and coat them with the herb mixture. Using kitchen twine, tie the loin to the rack of ribs. Set the pork in a roasting pan, meat side up. Cover and refrigerate overnight or for up to 2 days. Bring the pork to room temperature before roasting.

2. Preheat the oven to 375°. Roast the pork in the upper third of the oven for 30 minutes. Reduce the oven temperature to 300° and roast for about 1 hour and 15 minutes longer, until an instant-read thermometer inserted in the thickest part of the meat registers 140°.

3. Transfer the pork to a work surface. Raise the oven temperature to 400°. Untie the loin and let it rest for 15 minutes.

4. Meanwhile, return the ribs to the pan. Roast the ribs in the oven for about 15 minutes, until browned and crisp on the outside and still moist within.

5. Carve the loin into ½-inch-thick slices. Cut the rack into individual ribs. Transfer the pork slices, along with the ribs, to plates and serve. —*Taylor Boetticher*

SERVE WITH Green Bean–and–Roasted Red Pepper Salad (p. 45).

WINE Rich, ripe Cabernet Sauvignon.

Pan-Roasted Pork Chops with Creamy Cabbage and Apples

ACTIVE: 40 MIN; TOTAL: 1 HR PLUS OVERNIGHT MARINATING

4 SERVINGS ●

- ¼ cup plus 1 tablespoon extra-virgin olive oil
- 4 thyme sprigs
- 1 garlic clove, coarsely chopped

Four 12-ounce bone-in pork loin chops

- 3 thick slices of applewood-smoked bacon, cut into ½-inch dice
- 2 tablespoons unsalted butter
- ½ head of Savoy cabbage, thinly sliced crosswise
- 1 Granny Smith apple—peeled, cored and cut into ½-inch dice
- 1 teaspoon white wine vinegar
- 1 tablespoon Dijon mustard
- ¾ cup heavy cream

Salt and freshly ground pepper

1. In a large, shallow dish, combine ¼ cup of the olive oil with the thyme sprigs and garlic. Add the pork chops and turn to coat with the marinade. Refrigerate overnight.

2. In a large skillet, cook the bacon over moderate heat, stirring a few times, until browned, about 4 minutes; pour off the fat. Add the butter and cabbage to the skillet, cover and cook, stirring occasionally, until the cabbage is tender, about 7 minutes. Add the apple and vinegar, cover and cook, stirring occasionally, until the apple is tender, about 5 minutes. Stir in the mustard and cream and simmer uncovered until the cream has thickened, about 3 minutes. Season with salt and pepper, cover and keep warm.

3. Preheat the oven to 325°. In a large ovenproof skillet, heat the remaining 1 tablespoon of olive oil until shimmering. Remove the pork chops from the marinade; discard the thyme sprigs and scrape off the garlic. Season the chops with salt and pepper and add to the skillet. Cook over moderately high heat until they are richly browned, about 3 minutes per side.

Transfer the skillet to the oven and roast the chops for about 12 minutes, turning once halfway through, until just pink in the center. Transfer the pork chops to plates and serve with the cabbage. —*Robert Wiedmaier*

MAKE AHEAD The cabbage can be refrigerated overnight. Reheat gently.

WINE Fresh, fruity rosé.

Pork-and-Tofu Stir-Fry

TOTAL: 25 MIN

4 SERVINGS ● ●

- 3 tablespoons vegetable oil
- 1 pound pork loin, cut into 1½-by-¼-inch strips

Salt and freshly ground black pepper

- 3 garlic cloves, minced

Large pinch of crushed red pepper flakes

- 1 large leek, halved and cut into 1-inch pieces
- 1 cup chicken stock or low-sodium broth
- ½ pound firm tofu, cut into 1-inch cubes
- ¼ cup hoisin sauce
- 2 teaspoons sherry vinegar
- ½ teaspoon Asian sesame oil

In a large skillet, heat 1 tablespoon of the vegetable oil. Add the pork strips, season with salt and pepper and stir-fry over high heat until the pork is cooked, 2 minutes. Transfer to a plate. Add the remaining vegetable oil to the skillet. Add the finely chopped garlic and crushed red pepper flakes and stir-fry for 1 minute. Add the leek pieces and ¼ cup of the chicken stock, cover and cook until the leek is softened, about 2 minutes. Add the remaining ¾ cup of chicken stock and bring the liquid to a simmer. Add the cubed tofu, then stir in the pork strips, hoisin sauce, sherry vinegar and sesame oil. Transfer the stir-fry to bowls and serve. —*Marcia Kiesel*

SERVE WITH Steamed white rice.

WINE Fruity, light-bodied Beaujolais.

pork & veal

Juicy Buttermilk Pork Chops

TOTAL: 20 MIN PLUS 4 HR SOAKING

4 SERVINGS

Chef Maria Hines of Tilth in Seattle uses pasture-raised Berkshire pork here. "It has the most wonderful flavor of all the pork I've ever tried," she says.

Four 1-inch-thick pork rib chops
1 quart buttermilk
Salt and freshly ground pepper
2 tablespoons olive oil

1. In a large bowl, cover the pork chops with the buttermilk, turning them to coat. Cover the bowl with plastic wrap and refrigerate for 4 hours.

---

grilling with smoke

Adam Perry Lang, chef at New York City's Daisy May's Barbecue USA and author of the book *Serious Barbecue*, likes to use wood to boost the smoky flavor of a charcoal fire. He recommends using wood chips for quick cooking and wood chunks for slow cooking (grillingwood.com and mainegrillingwoods.com are good sources). "Don't use freshly cut wood," he says, "because it smokes too heavily and makes food taste bitter."

Alder This wood gives off a light, mild smoke. Best for rich fish, especially salmon.

Oak A great all-purpose wood. It burns evenly and has a clean flavor.

Cherry or apple Sweet and fragrant but not overly strong. Best for mild meats like chicken and pork.

Mesquite Burns superhot and gives off an intense flavor. Best for full-flavored game meats.

---

2. Preheat the oven to 425°. Drain the chops, pat dry and season with salt and pepper.
3. In an ovenproof skillet, heat the olive oil. Add the pork chops and cook over high heat until the chops are browned on the bottom; turn the chops over. Transfer the skillet to the oven and roast the pork for 10 minutes, until an instant-read thermometer inserted into the thickest part of the meat (avoiding the bone) registers 135°. Let rest for 5 minutes, then serve. —*Maria Hines*

SERVE WITH Grits and collards.
WINE Ripe, juicy Pinot Noir.

Cocoa-and-Chile-Rubbed Pork Chops

ACTIVE: 30 MIN; TOTAL: 1 HR 30 MIN

4 SERVINGS

2 quarts water
1½ teaspoons crushed red pepper
Kosher salt
Four 1½-inch-thick boneless pork loin chops
1 tablespoon unsweetened cocoa powder
1 tablespoon light brown sugar
1 tablespoon pure ancho chile powder
Extra-virgin olive oil, for brushing

1. In a large bowl, combine the water with the red pepper and 1½ teaspoons of salt and stir until the salt dissolves. Add the pork chops and let brine at room temperature for 1 hour.
2. Light a grill and create a cool zone. (For a charcoal grill, rake the coals to one side; for a gas grill, leave one side unlit.) In a bowl, mix the cocoa, sugar and ancho powder with 1 tablespoon of salt.
3. Drain the pork chops and pat dry, removing any bits of crushed pepper. Brush generously with olive oil. Roll the pork chops in the cocoa rub and pat to help it adhere. Grill over moderately high heat for 4 minutes, turning the chops once or twice until lightly browned. Transfer the

chops to the cool zone, cover and grill for about 15 minutes, until an instant-read thermometer inserted in the center of the chops registers 135° for medium meat. Let the chops rest for 10 minutes before serving. —*Tim Love*

WINE Earthy, medium-bodied Tempranillo.

Pan-Seared Pork Chops with Green Peppercorn Sauce

ACTIVE: 45 MIN; TOTAL: 1 HR 45 MIN

4 SERVINGS ●

When L.A. chef Matt Molina visited Italy's Umbria region, he had succulent pork chops wrapped in thin layers of *lardo* (cured pork fat) at La Locanda della Ribollita in Chiusi. If *lardo* is hard to find, substitute pancetta (cured pork belly rolled into a log); unfurl the slices into long strips before wrapping the chops.

Eight 6-inch-long rosemary branches
4 garlic cloves—2 minced, 2 crushed
½ cup extra-virgin olive oil
Four ¾-inch-thick boneless pork chops
Salt and freshly ground black pepper
8 very thin slices of *lardo* (see Note) or unrolled pancetta
½ cup dry white wine
1 cup low-sodium chicken broth
Finely grated zest of 1 lemon
⅛ teaspoon crushed red pepper
2 tablespoons green peppercorns in brine, rinsed

1. Using your fingers, strip off the leaves from the bottom 4 inches of the rosemary branches and finely chop enough leaves to make 2 tablespoons. (Reserve the stripped rosemary branches.) In a large, shallow dish, mix the chopped rosemary with the minced garlic and ¼ cup of the olive oil. Season the pork chops with salt and black pepper, add them to the rosemary marinade and turn to coat. Let stand at room temperature for 1 hour.

2. Wrap 2 slices of the *lardo* around the edge of each pork chop and secure with a toothpick. On the side opposite the toothpick, skewer each of the chops with 2 stripped rosemary branches.

3. In a large skillet, heat 3 tablespoons of the olive oil. Add the pork chops and cook over moderately high heat until richly browned on the bottom, about 3 minutes. Turn the chops and cook over moderate heat until browned on the second side and just cooked through, about 4 minutes longer. Transfer to a platter; keep warm.

4. Pour off the fat in the skillet and add the remaining 1 tablespoon of olive oil. Add the crushed garlic and cook over moderately high heat until golden brown, about 1 minute. Add the wine and boil over high heat, scraping up the browned bits from the bottom of the skillet, until reduced to 2 tablespoons. Add the chicken broth, grated lemon zest and crushed red pepper and boil until reduced to ½ cup, about 8 minutes. Remove from the heat. Discard the crushed garlic and stir in the brined green peppercorns. Season with salt and black pepper. Remove the toothpicks from the pork. Spoon the sauce over the chops and serve. —*Matt Molina*

NOTE *Lardo,* pork fatback that has been cured in strips, is used to flavor soups and stews or to top bruschetta or pizza. It's available at Italian markets, specialty food shops and murrayscheese.com.

WINE Intense, spicy Syrah.

Pork Belly with Buckwheat Spaetzle and Collards

ACTIVE: 45 MIN; TOTAL: 3 HR PLUS OVERNIGHT CURING

4 SERVINGS ●

Chefs love pork belly because it's inexpensive yet tastes luxurious. Joseph Lenn, a chef at the Blackberry Farm resort in Walland, Tennessee, cures the meat overnight in salt and sugar to add flavor, then braises it until it's meltingly tender.

PORK BELLY

- 1 cup kosher salt
- ¼ cup sugar
- 1 pound lean pork belly, skin discarded
- 2 tablespoons vegetable oil
- 1 quart low-sodium chicken broth
- 4 thyme sprigs
- 1 large shallot, coarsely chopped
- 1 medium carrot, coarsely chopped
- 1 medium celery rib, chopped

SPAETZLE

- ¾ cup all-purpose flour
- ¼ cup buckwheat flour
- ½ teaspoon freshly grated nutmeg

Salt and freshly ground pepper

- 2 large eggs
- ¼ cup milk
- 1 tablespoon unsalted butter
- ½ tablespoon extra-virgin olive oil

GREENS

- ¼ cup extra-virgin olive oil
- 4 garlic cloves, halved
- 1 small onion, cut into ½-inch dice
- 1 tablespoon chopped thyme
- 1 cup low-sodium chicken broth
- 1 pound collard greens, center ribs discarded and leaves coarsely chopped

Salt and freshly ground pepper

1. PREPARE THE PORK BELLY: In a shallow dish, mix the salt with the sugar; add the pork belly and coat with the mixture. Cover the pork and refrigerate overnight.

2. The next day, rinse the pork belly and pat dry. Preheat the oven to 300°. In an ovenproof skillet, heat the vegetable oil until shimmering. Add the pork and cook over moderate heat, turning once, until richly browned, about 3 minutes per side. Add the chicken broth, thyme sprigs, shallot, carrot and celery and bring to a boil. Cover and braise in the oven until the pork is tender, 2 hours. Transfer the pork to a plate, cover with foil and keep warm. Boil the cooking liquid until reduced by two-thirds, about 15 minutes. Strain the liquid into a saucepan and skim off the fat.

3. MEANWHILE, PREPARE THE SPAETZLE: In a large bowl, combine the all-purpose flour and buckwheat flour with the nutmeg, 1 teaspoon of salt and ½ teaspoon of pepper. In a medium bowl, whisk the eggs with the milk, then whisk the mixture into the flour. Cover the batter and let rest at room temperature for 30 minutes.

4. Bring a large pot of salted water to a boil. Prepare a bowl of ice water. Carefully hold a colander with large holes over the boiling water. Gradually add the batter to the colander and press it through the holes with a spatula. Boil the spaetzle until tender, 1 minute. Using a slotted spoon, transfer the spaetzle to the ice water to cool completely, then drain on paper towels.

5. In a large nonstick skillet, melt the butter in the olive oil. Add the spaetzle and cook over high heat until browned on the bottom, 2 minutes. Stir and cook until browned all over, 1 minute longer. Season with salt and pepper and keep warm.

6. PREPARE THE GREENS: In a large, deep skillet, heat the olive oil. Add the garlic and onion and cook over moderate heat, stirring occasionally, until beginning to brown, about 7 minutes. Add the thyme and cook for 1 minute. Add the chicken broth and collards and bring to a boil. Cover and simmer over low heat, stirring occasionally, until the collards are tender, about 10 minutes. Season with salt and pepper.

7. Slice the pork lengthwise and transfer to plates. Spoon the greens and spaetzle alongside. Pour the reduced pork cooking liquid over the meat and serve.
—*Joseph Lenn*

MAKE AHEAD The braised pork can be refrigerated in its sauce overnight. The spaetzle batter and braised greens can be refrigerated separately overnight.

WINE Fruity, luscious Syrah.

THAI GROUND PORK SALAD

PAN-ROASTED VEAL CHOP WITH CABERNET SAUCE

Thai Ground Pork Salad

 TOTAL: 40 MIN
6 SERVINGS ● ●

- 2 pounds ground pork
- 2 garlic cloves, minced
- 2 small shallots, minced
- 1 jalapeño, seeded and minced, plus sliced jalapeño for garnish

Juice of 1 lime, plus lime wedges for serving

- 2 tablespoons Asian fish sauce
- 1 teaspoon light brown sugar
- 1 teaspoon Sriracha chile sauce, plus more for serving
- 1 tablespoon vegetable oil
- ½ cup chopped cilantro
- ½ cup chopped mint
- ½ cup chopped basil

Salt and freshly ground pepper

- 1 cup chopped salted peanuts
- 1 head Boston or other leafy lettuce

1. In a bowl, mix the pork, garlic, shallots and minced jalapeño. In a small bowl, whisk the lime juice, fish sauce, brown sugar and the 1 teaspoon of Sriracha.

2. In a skillet, heat the oil. Add the pork mixture; cook over high heat, stirring to break up the meat, until no pink remains, 5 minutes. Remove from the heat and stir in the lime mixture. Let stand 5 minutes. Transfer to a bowl; stir in the herbs. Season with salt and pepper. Top with peanuts and sliced jalapeños. Serve with lime wedges, Sriracha and lettuce for wrapping. —*Tom Mylan*
WINE Vivid, lightly sweet Riesling.

Sausage-and-Pepper Heros

 TOTAL: 30 MIN
6 SERVINGS

Extra-virgin olive oil

- 1 pound red bell peppers, sliced
- 1 large red onion, thinly sliced
- 2 garlic cloves, thinly sliced
- 1 teaspoon dried oregano, crumbled
- ½ teaspoon red pepper flakes

Kosher salt

- 6 pork sausages, about 5 ounces each (preferably with roasted pepper or parsley and cheese)
- 3 long hero rolls, split lengthwise

1. Heat a large cast-iron or nonstick griddle. Add 2 tablespoons of oil, the bell peppers, onion, garlic, oregano and pepper flakes; season with salt. Cook over moderate heat until beginning to brown, 6 minutes, then push to the back of the griddle, cover with a bowl and keep warm; stir occasionally.

2. Prick the sausages; cook over moderate heat until no pink remains, 10 minutes. Add to the vegetables; keep warm. Brush the rolls with oil; toast on griddle. Fill with sausages and peppers; serve. —*Grace Parisi*
WINE Rustic, peppery Malbec.

Sausage, Bread and Chicken Liver Spiedini

ACTIVE: 45 MIN; TOTAL: 2 HR

6 SERVINGS

Spiedini are skewers of meat and other ingredients that are grilled or broiled. "Sausages and chicken livers are staples of Tuscan cuisine," says Rolando Beramendi, who consulted on the all-Tuscan menu for Osteria Tornabuoni in Florence.

- ½ cup extra-virgin olive oil
- ½ cup dry red wine
- 2 medium garlic cloves, very finely chopped
- 1 teaspoon chopped rosemary
- ½ teaspoon juniper berries, crushed
- ½ pound chicken livers, trimmed and cut into 1½-inch pieces

Salt and freshly ground pepper

- 6 sweet Italian sausages
- 1 loaf crusty peasant bread, cut into 1½-inch cubes

About 36 small fresh bay leaves

1. In a medium bowl, combine ¼ cup of the olive oil with the red wine, garlic, rosemary, juniper berries and chicken livers. Season with salt and pepper and let stand at room temperature for 1 hour. Drain the livers, reserving the marinade.

2. Meanwhile, in a saucepan of boiling water, cook the sausages over high heat until cooked through, 10 minutes; let cool slightly. Cut each sausage into thirds.

3. Light a grill. On six 14-inch-long skewers, alternately thread the sausages, bread and livers very loosely, placing a bay leaf between each piece. Be sure to leave a tiny bit of space between each piece for even cooking.

4. Brush the skewers with the remaining ¼ cup of olive oil and some of the marinade; grill over moderately low heat, turning frequently, until the livers are cooked and the bread and sausages are lightly charred, about 10 minutes. Transfer the *spiedini* to plates and serve.
—Rolando Beramendi

WINE Complex, elegant Pinot Noir.

Pan-Roasted Veal Chops with Cabernet Sauce

ACTIVE: 20 MIN; TOTAL: 1 HR 20 MIN

PLUS OVERNIGHT MARINATING

4 SERVINGS

- ¼ cup plus 2 tablespoons extra-virgin olive oil
- 4 thyme sprigs
- 1 garlic clove, coarsely chopped

Four 12-ounce bone-in veal rib chops

- 2 cups Cabernet Sauvignon
- 2 large shallots, finely chopped
- 1 tablespoon unsalted butter
- 2 tablespoons all-purpose flour
- 2 cups beef stock

Salt and freshly ground pepper

Potato Puree (recipe follows)

1. In a large, shallow dish, combine ¼ cup of the olive oil with the thyme sprigs and garlic. Add the veal chops and turn to coat with the marinade. Refrigerate overnight.

2. In a medium saucepan, combine the wine with half of the shallots and boil until the wine has reduced to ½ cup, 15 minutes.

3. In a small saucepan, melt the butter. Add the remaining shallot and cook over moderately high heat, stirring, until golden, 3 minutes. Stir in the flour. Slowly whisk in the stock until smooth, then bring to a boil, whisking until thickened. Whisk in the reduced wine and simmer over low heat, whisking, for 30 minutes. Strain the sauce into the medium saucepan. Season with salt and pepper.

4. Preheat the oven to 325°. In a large skillet, heat the remaining 2 tablespoons of oil until shimmering. Remove the veal from the marinade; discard the thyme and scrape off the garlic. Season the chops with salt and pepper; add to the skillet. Cook over high heat until richly browned, 3 minutes per side. Transfer the skillet to the oven; roast the chops for about 10 minutes, turning once halfway; the veal should be just pink in the center. Transfer to plates; spoon the sauce on top. Serve with Potato Puree.
—Robert Wiedmaier

WINE Rich, ripe Cabernet Sauvignon.

POTATO PUREE

TOTAL: 25 MIN

4 SERVINGS ● ●

- 1 pound Yukon Gold potatoes, peeled and cut into 2-inch chunks
- 2 garlic cloves
- 4 tablespoons unsalted butter
- ¼ cup heavy cream

Salt and freshly ground pepper

1. In a pot, cover the potatoes and garlic with water. Bring to a boil; cook over moderately high heat until tender, 12 minutes. Drain.

2. Mash, adding the butter and cream. Season with salt and pepper; serve hot. —RW

Roast Veal with Marjoram

ACTIVE: 15 MIN; TOTAL: 1 HR 15 MIN

4 SERVINGS

One 2½-pound bone-in veal loin roast, bones frenched

Salt and freshly ground pepper

- 1 tablespoon extra-virgin olive oil
- 3 garlic cloves—2 thickly sliced, 1 minced
- 4 marjoram sprigs plus 1 tablespoon chopped marjoram
- 2 tablespoons fresh lemon juice
- ½ teaspoon finely grated lemon zest

Porcini Risotto (p. 246), for serving

1. Preheat the oven to 325°. Season the veal with salt and pepper. Heat the oil in a medium ovenproof skillet. Add the veal and cook over high heat, turning once or twice, until browned all over, 4 minutes. Add the sliced garlic and marjoram sprigs to the skillet and roast the veal for about 45 minutes, turning the meat once or twice, until an instant-read thermometer inserted in the center registers 135°. Let the meat rest for 15 minutes.

2. In a bowl, combine the lemon juice and zest with the chopped marjoram and minced garlic. Season with salt and pepper.

3. Carve the roast into ½-inch-thick slices and transfer to plates. Spoon the marjoram-lemon mixture over the veal and serve with Porcini Risotto. —Daniel Humm

WINE Firm, complex Cabernet Sauvignon.

CRISP SALMON WITH
AVOCADO SALAD (P. 178)

fish

Fast fillets, easy whole fish
and other delicious ideas.

GRILLED SALMON WITH PRESERVED LEMON AND GREEN OLIVES

SALMON WITH GINGERY VEGETABLES AND TURMERIC

Grilled Salmon with Preserved Lemon and Green Olives

 TOTAL: 30 MIN
6 SERVINGS ●

- ¼ preserved lemon, pulp discarded and peel minced (see Note)
- 1 small shallot, minced
- ¼ cup chopped parsley
- 3 tablespoons extra-virgin olive oil
- 3 tablespoons fresh lemon juice
- One 2-pound center-cut salmon fillet with skin
- Salt and freshly ground white pepper
- 8 large green olives, such as Cerignola, halved and pitted

1. Light a grill or heat a grill pan. In a bowl, mix the preserved lemon with the shallot, parsley and 1 tablespoon each of the oil and lemon juice. Using a knife, make 1-inch-deep slits in the salmon skin, 1 inch apart. Rub the preserved lemon mixture into the slits. Rub the remaining 2 tablespoons of oil all over the salmon, then drizzle the fish with the remaining 2 tablespoons of lemon juice; season with salt and white pepper.
2. Grill the salmon, skin side down, over moderate heat until lightly charred and crisp, 5 minutes. Turn and grill until just cooked through, 3 to 4 minutes more. Transfer to a platter, skin side up. Scatter the olives over the fish, cut it crosswise into 6 pieces and serve. —*Joe Bastianich*
NOTE Buy preserved lemons at specialty food shops or make your own (p. 354).
WINE Fresh, fruity rosé.

Salmon with Gingery Vegetables and Turmeric

 TOTAL: 30 MIN
4 SERVINGS ●

- ½ pound broccoli—cut into florets, stem peeled and sliced
- ½ pound cauliflower, cut into florets
- ¾ cup water
- 3 tablespoons vegetable oil, plus more for rubbing
- 1 medium onion, thinly sliced
- 1½ tablespoons minced fresh ginger
- Salt and freshly ground pepper
- ¼ teaspoon turmeric
- ½ cup unsweetened coconut milk
- 1 tablespoon chopped Indian lime pickle (see Note)
- Four 6-ounce salmon fillets with skin

1. In a deep skillet, simmer the broccoli and cauliflower, covered, in ½ cup of the water for 3 minutes; transfer to a bowl.
2. In the skillet, heat the 3 tablespoons of oil. Add the onion and ginger, season with salt and pepper and cook over moderate heat, stirring, until golden, 8 minutes. Add the turmeric; cook, stirring, until fragrant. Add the coconut milk, lime pickle and remaining water; bring to a simmer. Stir in the vegetables; season with salt and pepper. Cover; remove from the heat.

3. Preheat a grill pan. Rub the salmon with oil and season with salt and pepper. Grill, skin side down, over moderately high heat until crisp, 4 minutes. Turn and grill until just cooked through, 2 minutes longer. Serve the salmon with the vegetables.
—*Marcia Kiesel*

NOTE Tangy lime pickles can be found at Indian markets or kalustyans.com.

WINE Spicy American Gewürztraminer.

Black-Sesame Salmon Balls

ACTIVE: 25 MIN; TOTAL: 1 HR

MAKES 2 DOZEN SALMON BALLS ●

1½ pounds skinless salmon fillet, cut into 1 inch cubes

¼ cup plus 2 tablespoons finely chopped water chestnuts

1 large egg white

2 tablespoons cornstarch

1 teaspoon wasabi powder

4 small scallions, white and light green parts only, thinly sliced

2½ teaspoons finely grated ginger

Kosher salt and freshly ground pepper

½ cup black sesame seeds

2 tablespoons unseasoned rice vinegar

¼ cup low-sodium soy sauce

½ teaspoon Asian sesame oil

1. Spread the salmon cubes on a plate and freeze for 15 minutes. Transfer the salmon to a food processor. Add the water chestnuts, egg white, cornstarch, wasabi powder, three-fourths of the scallions, 1½ teaspoons of the ginger, 2 teaspoons of kosher salt and a pinch of pepper. Pulse 4 or 5 times, until the salmon is chopped and the mixture just comes together. Transfer to a bowl.

2. Spread the sesame seeds on a plate Scoop the salmon mixture into mounds of 2 tablespoons each and roll into 24 balls. Roll the balls in the seeds and transfer to 2 glass pie plates. Set one of the plates in a large steamer. Steam over boiling water until firm, about 6 minutes. Repeat with the remaining salmon balls.

3. Meanwhile, in a bowl, combine the vinegar, soy sauce and sesame oil with the remaining scallions and ginger. Serve the salmon balls with the dipping sauce.
—*Grace Parisi*

WINE Ripe, juicy Pinot Noir.

Poached Salmon with Corn and White Wine–Butter Sauce

TOTAL: 1 HR

4 SERVINGS

Poaching fish in wine is an easy way to infuse it with subtle flavor. Since some of the seasoning washes off, F&W's Kristin Donnelly likes to serve the salmon with a sprinkling of coarse salt.

4 medium zucchini (1½ pounds), coarsely shredded

Salt

2 tablespoons extra-virgin olive oil

3 medium shallots—2 finely chopped, 1 halved

Freshly ground pepper

2¾ cups dry white wine

1 cup fresh corn kernels

2 lemon thyme sprigs

1 bay leaf

Four 6-ounce skinless salmon fillets

1 stick cold unsalted butter, cut into tablespoons

¼ cup thinly sliced basil leaves

1. Set a colander over a bowl. Add the zucchini to the colander and toss with 1 teaspoon of salt. Let stand for 20 minutes. Squeeze the zucchini dry.

2. In a large, nonreactive skillet, heat the olive oil. Add the chopped shallots and season with salt and pepper. Cook over moderate heat until softened, about 3 minutes. Add ¼ cup of the wine and cook until evaporated, about 2 minutes. Stir in the corn and ½ cup of water. Cover and cook until the corn is tender, about 4 minutes. Stir in the zucchini and cook until heated through, about 2 minutes. Season with salt and pepper, cover and keep warm.

3. In a large nonreactive saucepan, combine 2 cups of the wine with the thyme, bay leaf, the halved shallot and 2 cups of water and bring to a simmer. Season the salmon with salt, add the fillets to the saucepan and cook at a bare simmer over low heat, turning once, about 6 minutes. Transfer the salmon to a plate and pat dry with paper towels. Discard the poaching liquid.

4. Add the remaining ½ cup of wine to the saucepan; bring to a simmer. Whisk in the butter, 1 tablespoon at a time, until incorporated. Season with salt. Stir the basil into the vegetables; transfer to plates. Nestle the salmon into the vegetables, top with the sauce and serve. —*Kristin Donnelly*

WINE Ripe, luxurious Chardonnay.

Salmon with Andouille Sausage and Green Olives

TOTAL: 30 MIN

4 SERVINGS

One 4-ounce link of andouille sausage, thinly sliced

¼ cup thinly sliced pitted green olives

2 tablespoons unsalted butter, softened

1 medium shallot, minced

Four 6-ounce skinless salmon fillets, preferably wild salmon

Extra-virgin olive oil, for rubbing

Salt and freshly ground pepper

1. Heat a small skillet over high heat. Add the andouille and cook, stirring, until sizzling, about 1 minute. Transfer to a bowl and let cool to room temperature. Mix the sausage with the olives, butter and shallot.

2. Light a grill. Rub the salmon fillets all over with olive oil and season lightly with salt and pepper. Grill the salmon over high heat, turning once, until nicely charred and just cooked through, about 3 minutes per side. Transfer the salmon to plates, top with the buttered andouille mixture and serve immediately. —*Marcia Kiesel*

WINE Ripe, juicy Pinot Noir.

fish

Pan-Roasted Salmon-and-Bread Salad

 ACTIVE: 15 MIN; TOTAL: 40 MIN
4 SERVINGS ● ●

This is a terrific all-in-one meal and an inventive use for salmon: Tender pieces of salmon fillet are nestled in hunks of crunchy ciabatta bread tossed with tomatoes, capers and superthin slices of lemon, then baked until the fish is just cooked.

Eight 1-inch-thick slices of ciabatta (from a 12-ounce loaf), cut into large chunks
5 tablespoons extra-virgin olive oil
2 pints grape tomatoes, halved
2 large garlic cloves, minced
2 tablespoons salted capers, rinsed and coarsely chopped
1 lemon, halved lengthwise and very thinly sliced
¼ cup chopped flat-leaf parsley
½ teaspoon crushed red pepper
Kosher salt and freshly ground pepper
2 pounds center-cut skinless salmon fillet, cut into 2-inch chunks

1. Preheat the oven to 450°. In a large roasting pan, toss the ciabatta chunks with 2 tablespoons of the olive oil. Roast for about 5 minutes, until the bread is lightly toasted.
2. In a large bowl, toss the tomato halves with the garlic, capers, lemon, parsley, crushed red pepper and 2 tablespoons of the olive oil; season with salt and pepper. Stir the tomatoes into the toasted bread. Roast for 10 to 12 minutes, until the tomatoes begin to soften and break down.
3. Meanwhile, in the same bowl, toss the salmon with the remaining 1 tablespoon of olive oil and season with salt and pepper. Nestle the salmon into the bread and tomatoes, spooning some of the tomatoes on top. Roast for about 6 minutes, until the salmon is just cooked through. Serve right away. —*Grace Parisi*
WINE Light, fresh Pinot Grigio.

Pomegranate-Glazed Salmon

TOTAL: 40 MIN PLUS 1 HR MARINATING
8 SERVINGS ●
SALMON
¼ cup soy sauce
2 tablespoons extra-virgin olive oil
2 tablespoons fresh lemon juice
2 tablespoons fresh lime juice
2 tablespoons agave nectar
4 garlic cloves, smashed
1 tablespoon finely grated ginger
1 teaspoon kosher salt
1 teaspoon freshly ground white pepper
Eight 6-ounce skinless salmon fillets
GLAZE
¼ cup pomegranate molasses
2 tablespoons agave nectar
2 tablespoons soy sauce
2 garlic cloves, minced
1 tablespoon finely grated ginger
1 tablespoon finely grated lime zest
Salt
1 cup shelled edamame, for garnish
½ cup pomegranate seeds, for garnish
Armenian Rice (p. 248), for serving

1. PREPARE THE SALMON: Combine the soy sauce, olive oil, lemon juice, lime juice, agave nectar, garlic, ginger, salt and white pepper in a large, shallow dish. Add the salmon fillets and turn to coat. Cover and refrigerate for 1 hour, turning a few times.
2. MAKE THE GLAZE: Meanwhile, in a medium bowl, whisk the pomegranate molasses with the agave nectar, soy sauce, garlic, ginger and lime zest.
3. Preheat the broiler. Transfer the salmon to a rimmed baking sheet. Season with salt; brush with half the glaze. Broil 4 inches from the heat for 3 minutes, until the fillets begin to brown. Brush with the remaining glaze; broil for 3 minutes longer, until richly glazed and just cooked through. Garnish with edamame and pomegranate seeds; serve with Armenian Rice. —*Lulu Powers*
WINE Fresh, fruity rosé.

Salmon with Shiitake and Red Wine Sauce

ACTIVE: 30 MIN; TOTAL: 1 HR 30 MIN
4 SERVINGS ●
5 tablespoons unsalted butter
1 large onion, coarsely chopped (about 1½ cups)
2 cups dry red wine
2 cups beef stock, preferably homemade
8 thyme sprigs
Salt and freshly ground pepper
1 cup wild rice, rinsed
½ pound shiitake mushrooms— stems discarded, caps cut into 1-inch pieces
Four 6- to 7-ounce skinless salmon fillets

1. In a saucepan, melt 3 tablespoons of the butter. Add the onion and cook over moderate heat until softened, 7 minutes. Add the red wine, beef stock and thyme and bring to a boil. Simmer until the liquid has reduced to ¾ cup, 1 hour and 15 minutes; strain into a clean saucepan. Season with salt and pepper, cover and keep hot.
2. Meanwhile, bring a medium saucepan of water to a boil. Add the wild rice and a pinch of salt, cover and simmer over low heat until tender, about 25 minutes. Drain the rice and return it to the saucepan. Season with salt, cover and keep warm.
3. Preheat the oven to 325°. In a medium skillet, melt the remaining 2 tablespoons of butter. Add the shiitake and season with salt and pepper. Cover and cook, stirring occasionally, until tender and browned, about 5 minutes.
4. Arrange the salmon on a rimmed baking sheet, skinned side down, and season with salt and pepper. Bake for about 15 minutes, until the fish is just cooked in the center.
5. Spoon the wild rice onto plates and set the salmon fillets on top. Spoon the shiitake mushrooms and red wine sauce over the fish and serve. —*Bernie Sun*
WINE Complex, elegant Pinot Noir.

SALMON WITH SHIITAKE
AND RED WINE SAUCE

Crisp Salmon with Avocado Salad

photo, page 172

 TOTAL: 30 MIN
8 SERVINGS ●

The wonderfully citrusy dressing for the salad here is made with fresh lemon and orange juices whisked with a little olive oil and mayonnaise until creamy.

2 tablespoons pine nuts
2½ tablespoons extra-virgin olive oil
2 tablespoons mayonnaise
1 tablespoon freshly squeezed lemon juice
1 tablespoon freshly squeezed orange juice
Kosher salt and freshly ground black pepper
Eight 6-ounce salmon fillets with skin
3 heads of Bibb lettuce—large leaves torn into bite-size pieces, small leaves left whole
2 Hass avocados, thinly sliced

1. In a small skillet, toast the pine nuts over moderate heat, tossing frequently, until golden, about 6 minutes. Transfer to a plate to cool. In a large bowl, whisk 1½ tablespoons of the olive oil with the mayonnaise, lemon juice and orange juice and season with salt and pepper.

---

tuna in olive oil

High-quality canned or jarred tuna in olive oil is a perfect staple for entertaining. Here are three superfast ways to use it:

Salad Toss with cubed country bread, chopped fresh tomatoes and vinaigrette.

Mousse Puree with softened butter and capers.

Dip Puree with lemon juice, capers, anchovies and olive oil.

---

2. Pat the salmon dry and season with salt and pepper. In a very large nonstick skillet, heat the remaining 1 tablespoon of oil over moderately high heat until shimmering. Add the fish skin side down and cook until crisp and golden, about 6 minutes. Turn and cook until just pink in the center, about 4 minutes longer. Transfer to plates.
3. Add the lettuce, avocados and pine nuts to the dressing and gently toss to coat. Mound the salad next to the salmon and serve. —*Melissa Rubel Jacobson*
WINE Lively, tart Sauvignon Blanc.

Tuna Scallopine with Parsley and Pomegranate Seeds

 TOTAL: 25 MIN
4 SERVINGS ● ●

1 tablespoon minced shallot
1 tablespoon red wine vinegar
1 tablespoon pure maple syrup
1 tablespoon drained capers
Salt and freshly ground pepper
3 tablespoons extra-virgin olive oil, plus more for rubbing
Four 5-ounce tuna steaks, about ½ inch thick
1 cup flat-leaf parsley leaves
½ cup pomegranate seeds
½ fennel bulb, cored and very thinly sliced
Hot sauce

1. In a bowl, mix the shallot, vinegar, maple syrup, capers and a pinch of salt and pepper; let stand for 15 minutes. Whisk in the oil.
2. Place the tuna between sheets of plastic wrap; pound the steaks ¼ inch thick. Rub with oil and season with salt and pepper.
3. Preheat a griddle. Add the tuna and cook on one side only until lightly seared, 1 minute. Transfer to plates, browned side up.
4. Add the parsley, pomegranate seeds and fennel to the dressing and season with hot sauce. Toss gently, mound the salad over the tuna and serve right away. —*Frank Stitt*
WINE Fresh, lively Soave.

Grilled Niçoise Tuna Steaks

ACTIVE: 15 MIN; TOTAL: 50 MIN
10 SERVINGS ●

½ cup extra-virgin olive oil
½ cup dry white wine
2½ tablespoons Dijon mustard
1 tablespoon coarsely chopped thyme leaves
1 tablespoon plus 1 teaspoon ground fennel
2 large shallots, coarsely chopped
Ten 8-ounce tuna steaks (about 1 inch thick)
Kosher salt and freshly ground pepper

1. In a medium bowl, whisk the olive oil with the wine, mustard, thyme, fennel and shallots. Arrange the tuna steaks on a large rimmed baking sheet and pour the marinade over them. Turn the tuna steaks to coat. Let stand for 30 minutes.
2. Light a grill or preheat a grill pan. Season the tuna with salt and pepper. Grill over moderately high heat, turning once, for 4 minutes per side, until medium. Thinly slice and serve. —*Melissa Rubel Jacobson*
SERVE WITH Green Bean–Tomato Salad with Herbs (p. 41).
WINE Fresh, fruity rosé.

Bluefish with Grape Leaves

 TOTAL: 30 MIN
2 SERVINGS ●

6 brined grape leaves, rinsed and stemmed (see Note)
Two 6-ounce skinless bluefish fillets
Salt and freshly ground pepper
6 tablespoons extra-virgin olive oil
2 tablespoons fresh lemon juice
1 garlic clove, mashed to a paste
1 anchovy fillet, mashed
1 tablespoon chopped chives
1 tablespoon chopped parsley
⅔ cup red seedless grapes, halved
½ small red onion, thinly sliced

1. Light a grill. Arrange 3 of the grape leaves so they're overlapping; repeat with the remaining leaves. Cut off the red flesh

GRILLED NIÇOISE TUNA (WITH GREEN BEAN SALAD, P. 41)

BLUEFISH WITH GRAPE LEAVES

from the underside of each fish fillet. Set the fish on the leaves and season with salt and pepper. Enclose the fish in the leaves and brush each fillet with ½ tablespoon of the olive oil.

2. In a bowl, whisk the lemon juice with the mashed garlic, anchovy, chives, parsley and 3 tablespoons of the olive oil; season with salt and pepper.

3. In a small bowl, toss the grapes with the onion and the remaining 2 tablespoons of olive oil. Season with salt and pepper. In a perforated grill pan, grill the grapes and onions until softened, 4 minutes; transfer to the lemon dressing and toss.

4. Grill the wrapped fish over high heat, turning once, until the fish is just cooked, 6 minutes. Serve with the grilled onions and grapes. —*Anita Lo*

NOTE Jarred grape leaves are sold in Middle Eastern markets.

WINE Dry, earthy sparkling wine.

Sesame-Crusted Tuna with Ginger Cream

⏱ TOTAL: 45 MIN
6 SERVINGS

Top Chef Season 5 winner Hosea Rosenberg created this quickly seared tuna recipe in 2001 when he was head chef at Dandelion in Boulder, Colorado. He spikes his ginger cream with Sriracha, the spicy red Thai chile sauce.

¼ cup vegetable oil
½ cup thinly sliced peeled ginger
½ small onion, finely chopped
2 garlic cloves, thinly sliced
¼ cup rice vinegar
¼ cup fresh orange juice
2 tablespoons mirin
2 tablespoons dry white wine
1 tablespoon Sriracha chile sauce
1½ cups heavy cream
Salt and freshly ground pepper
Six 6-ounce tuna steaks (1 inch thick)
½ cup sesame seeds
Glass Noodle Stir-Fry (p. 93),
    for serving

1. In a saucepan, heat 2 tablespoons of the oil. Add the ginger, onion and garlic and cook over moderate heat, stirring, until softened, 5 minutes. Add the vinegar, orange juice, mirin, wine and Sriracha and simmer until the liquid is almost evaporated, 10 minutes. Add the cream and simmer until reduced by half, 15 minutes. Strain the sauce, season with salt and pepper; keep warm.

2. Season the tuna with salt and pepper; coat both sides with sesame seeds. In a nonstick skillet, heat the remaining 2 tablespoons of oil. Add the tuna; cook over moderately high heat, turning once, until the seeds are browned and the tuna is medium-rare, 5 minutes. Slice the tuna ⅓ inch thick; serve with ginger cream and Glass Noodle Stir-Fry. —*Hosea Rosenberg*

WINE Lush, fragrant Viognier.

Mahimahi with Herbed White Wine Sauce

TOTAL: 30 MIN
4 SERVINGS ● ●

F&W's Marcia Kiesel likes to pair strongly flavored herbs such as thyme and marjoram with meaty mahimahi. For this easy, elegant dish, she cooks the fish in a combination of white wine and clam juice, which gives it a pleasantly briny edge.

- ¼ cup pine nuts
- 1 cup bottled clam juice
- ¼ cup dry white wine
- 1 medium shallot, very finely chopped
- 1 tablespoon finely chopped thyme
- 1 tablespoon finely chopped marjoram

Salt and freshly ground pepper
Four 6-ounce skinless mahimahi fillets
Extra-virgin olive oil, for rubbing
- 2 tablespoons finely chopped flat-leaf parsley

1. In a small saucepan, toast the pine nuts over moderate heat, shaking the pan a few times, until the nuts are fragrant, about 1 minute. Transfer to a plate.
2. Add the clam juice to the saucepan and boil over high heat until reduced by half, about 5 minutes. Add the wine and boil until reduced to ¼ cup, about 5 minutes. Add the shallot, thyme and marjoram and season with salt and pepper. Cover the sauce and keep warm.
3. Light a grill. Rub the fish fillets with olive oil; season with salt and pepper. Grill over high heat, turning once, until nicely charred and just cooked through, about 3 minutes per side. Transfer the fish to plates.
4. Stir the chopped parsley into the white wine sauce. Coarsely chop the toasted pine nuts. Spoon the sauce over the fish, sprinkle with the pine nuts and serve.
—*Marcia Kiesel*
WINE Zesty, fresh Albariño.

Stuffed Flounder with Frizzled Mint and Ginger

TOTAL: 50 MIN
4 SERVINGS

- 3 garlic cloves, minced
- 1 serrano chile, seeded and minced
- ½ cup chopped cilantro
- ¼ cup chopped mint, plus 24 mint leaves

Salt and freshly ground pepper
Four 6- to 8-ounce flounder fillets
- 2 tablespoons extra-virgin olive oil
- ½ cup heavy cream
- 2 tablespoons plain whole-milk yogurt, drained
- 1 tablespoon vegetable oil, plus more for pan-frying

One 2-inch piece of ginger, peeled and cut into very thin strips
All-purpose flour, for dredging

1. Preheat the oven to 300°. In a bowl, combine the garlic, serrano chile, cilantro and chopped mint. Season generously with salt and pepper. Cut a shallow 3-by-1½-inch pocket in the wide side of each flounder fillet. Spoon 1 teaspoon of the herb mixture into each pocket.
2. In a saucepan, heat the olive oil. Add the cream, yogurt and remaining herb mixture and simmer until slightly thickened, about 3 minutes. Remove from the heat.
3. In a large skillet, heat the 1 tablespoon of vegetable oil. Add the ginger in a single layer and cook over moderately high heat until browned and crisp, about 30 seconds. Tilt the skillet and transfer the ginger to a plate using a slotted spoon. Add the mint leaves to the skillet and cook until crisp, about 10 seconds. Add the mint to the ginger.
4. In the same skillet, heat ¼ inch of vegetable oil. Season the flounder with salt and pepper. Dredge 2 fillets in flour and shake off the excess. Fry over moderately high heat until golden brown, 3 minutes per side. Transfer to a baking sheet and repeat with the remaining fillets. Transfer the baking sheet to the oven to keep the fish warm.
5. Reheat the cream sauce and season with salt. Spoon the sauce onto plates and set the flounder on top. Scatter the fried ginger and mint over the fish and serve.
—*Peggy Markel*
WINE Complex, aromatic Chenin Blanc.

Sake-Steamed Halibut with Ginger and Cabbage

ACTIVE: 30 MIN; TOTAL: 1 HR
8 SERVINGS ●

F&W's Grace Parisi steams delicate halibut over cabbage that's been sautéed with ginger and leeks until soft and buttery.

- 1 cup thinly shaved cauliflower
- ½ cup pickled ginger juice from a jar of pickled ginger
- 2 tablespoons unsalted butter
- 2 tablespoons canola oil
- 2 pounds green cabbage, shredded
- 2 large leeks, white parts only, cut into 2-by-½-inch matchsticks

One 4-inch piece peeled fresh ginger, cut into fine matchsticks
Salt and freshly ground white pepper
- 1 cup sake
- 8 skinless halibut fillets (4 pounds)
- 2 scallions, white parts only, thinly sliced and separated into rings

1. Soak the cauliflower in the ginger juice at room temperature for 1 hour. Drain.
2. Meanwhile, in each of 2 medium skillets, melt 1 tablespoon of the butter in 1 tablespoon of the oil. Divide the cabbage, leeks and fresh ginger between the skillets and season with salt and pepper. Cover and cook over low heat, stirring frequently, until softened but not browned, about 8 minutes.
3. Divide the sake between the skillets and bring to a boil. Add 4 halibut fillets to each skillet and season with salt and pepper. Cover and cook over high heat until the fish is firm, about 10 minutes. Transfer the halibut and vegetables to shallow bowls. Garnish with the shaved cauliflower and sliced scallions and serve. —*Grace Parisi*
WINE Full-bodied, minerally Riesling.

SAKE-STEAMED HALIBUT
WITH GINGER AND CABBAGE

Grilled Halibut with Smashed Fingerlings and Tomato Butter

TOTAL: 40 MIN PLUS 2 HR MARINATING
4 SERVINGS

Caroline Styne, co-owner and sommelier of L.A.'s Lucques and A.O.C., likes to coat delicate halibut fillets in fresh herbs and grill them until lightly charred. To make a tangy sauce, she cooks cherry tomatoes in tarragon-infused browned butter until they burst with juice.

½   cup finely chopped
      flat-leaf parsley
¼   cup chopped tarragon,
      plus ¼ cup whole leaves
Finely grated zest of 1 lemon
Four 6- to 7-ounce skinless
      halibut fillets
2   pounds fingerling potatoes
Salt
¼   cup extra-virgin olive oil,
      plus more for drizzling
4   medium garlic cloves,
      very thinly sliced
2   medium shallots, thinly sliced
Freshly ground pepper
6   tablespoons unsalted butter
1   pint cherry tomatoes

1. In a medium bowl, toss the parsley with the chopped tarragon and lemon zest. Rub the herbs all over the halibut; cover and refrigerate for 2 hours.
2. In a large saucepan, cover the potatoes with water and bring to a boil. Salt generously and simmer over moderately high heat until tender, about 10 minutes. Drain and let cool to room temperature.
3. Light a grill. In a large nonstick skillet, heat the ¼ cup of olive oil. Add the garlic and shallots and cook over moderately high heat until golden, about 2 minutes. Add the potatoes and cook over low heat, smashing them gently with a spatula, until they start to break apart. Continue cooking, stirring a few times, until the potatoes are browned and crisp, about 5 minutes total. Season with salt and pepper.

4. In a medium skillet, melt the butter. Add the whole tarragon leaves and cook over moderate heat until the tarragon is fragrant, about 2 minutes. Add the tomatoes and cook over low heat, stirring occasionally, until the tomatoes burst and the butter is browned, about 7 minutes. Season the tomato butter with salt and pepper.
5. Drizzle the halibut with olive oil and season with salt and pepper. Grill the fillets over moderately high heat until nicely charred and just cooked, about 3 minutes per side. Transfer the fish to plates and spoon the tomato butter on top. Serve immediately, with the smashed potatoes.
—Caroline Styne

WINE Complex, elegant Pinot Noir.

Lemon-Stuffed Grilled Branzino

TOTAL: 30 MIN
4 SERVINGS ●

Branzino, a European sea bass, is low in fat but has a marvelous richness when cooked on the bone. Boston superchef Barbara Lynch stuffs the fish with lemon slices and herbs, then grills it until the skin is browned and crispy to add even more flavor.

Four 1-pound whole branzino—
      scaled and gutted, heads
      and tails removed
Salt and freshly ground pepper
4   thyme sprigs
4   bay leaves
2   lemons—1 thinly sliced,
      1 cut into wedges
1   tablespoon extra-virgin
      olive oil
Finely chopped parsley,
      for serving

1. Light a grill or preheat a grill pan. Season the fish cavities with salt and pepper. Stuff each cavity with a thyme sprig, a bay leaf and 2 lemon slices. Rub the outside of the branzino with the olive oil and season with salt and pepper.

2. Grill the stuffed branzino over high heat, turning the fish once, until their skin is browned and crisp and their flesh is just cooked through, about 7 minutes per side. Serve right away, passing salt, lemon wedges and parsley at the table.
—Barbara Lynch

WINE Fresh, minerally Vermentino.

Grilled Mackerel with Sicilian Caper-Tomato Salsa

 TOTAL: 45 MIN
4 SERVINGS ● ●

"Give mackerel a chance," begs Michael White, chef at the Italian seafood restaurant Marea in New York City. The Spanish fish he imports from Europe is grilled, which makes the skin enticingly crisp, and then topped with a bright, refreshing tomato-caper salsa.

1   pound new potatoes
3   tablespoons extra-virgin olive oil,
      plus more for brushing
1   large garlic clove, thinly sliced
Salt and freshly ground pepper
¾   pound ripe tomatoes—
      peeled, seeded and cut into
      ½-inch dice, or 3 cups cherry
      tomatoes, halved
3   tablespoons capers
1   tablespoon fresh lemon juice,
      plus 4 wedges for serving
4   Spanish mackerel fillets
      with skin (about 6 ounces each),
      pin bones removed

1. Bring a medium saucepan of water to a boil. Add the new potatoes and cook until the potatoes are tender when pierced with a sharp knife, about 20 minutes. Drain the potatoes and let cool slightly, then cut them into quarters.
2. In a medium skillet, heat the 3 tablespoons of olive oil. Add the boiled potatoes and cook over high heat, stirring occasionally, until the potatoes are lightly browned in spots, about 5 minutes. Add the garlic and continue cooking, stirring occasionally,

GRILLED HALIBUT WITH SMASHED FINGERLINGS

LEMON-STUFFED GRILLED BRANZINO

until the potatoes are browned and the garlic is crisp, about 3 minutes longer. Season with salt and pepper and keep warm.

3. Heat a grill pan. In a bowl, toss together the tomatoes, capers and lemon juice; season with salt and pepper. Brush the mackerel with olive oil and season with salt and pepper. Grill the fillets over high heat for 7 minutes, turning once, until they are lightly charred and cooked through. Transfer the grilled fish to plates and top with the salsa. Serve with the potatoes and lemon wedges. —*Michael White*

WINE Fresh, fruity rosé.

Spanish Mackerel Escabèche

TOTAL: 40 MIN PLUS 3 HR MARINATING
4 SERVINGS ●

In this light dish, Australian chef David Swain marinates fish fillets in red wine vinegar and olive oil along with sweet carrots and shallots.

- 2 medium carrots, cut into 2-inch lengths
- ¼ cup extra-virgin olive oil, plus more for frying
- 2 large shallots, very thinly sliced
- 4 thyme sprigs
- 4 bay leaves
- 1 large garlic clove, very thinly sliced
- ¼ cup plus 2 tablespoons red wine vinegar

Salt and freshly ground pepper
Four 6-ounce Spanish mackerel fillets with skin
- ¼ cup prepared black olive tapenade

1. Using a mandoline, cut the carrots into thin strips. In a small skillet, heat ¼ cup of the olive oil. Add the carrots, shallots, thyme sprigs, bay leaves and garlic and cook over moderate heat until the vegetables are softened, about 6 minutes. Remove from the heat. Stir in the vinegar and season with salt and pepper. Let stand for 10 minutes.

2. In a large nonstick skillet, heat ¼ inch of olive oil until shimmering. Season the mackerel fillets with salt and pepper and add them to the skillet skin side down. Cook over high heat until the skin is browned and crisp, about 4 minutes. Turn and cook the fillets for 1 minute longer, until almost cooked through. Transfer the fillets to a large, shallow glass or ceramic dish, skin side up. Top with the vegetables and their marinade. Let stand at room temperature for 3 hours, occasionally spooning the marinade over.

3. Discard the thyme and bay leaves. Arrange the fish on plates and spoon the vegetables and marinade on top. Dollop with the tapenade; serve. —*David Swain*

WINE Lively, tart Sauvignon Blanc.

fish

Scallion-and-Pecan-Crusted Catfish with Hominy Stew

ACTIVE: 40 MIN; TOTAL: 1 HR

4 SERVINGS

Most cooks fry catfish, but at the Blackberry Farm cooking school and retreat in Walland, Tennessee, chef Josh Feathers shows students how to bake fillets instead in a nutty crust of ground pecans. To determine whether the fish is done, he inserts a wire cake tester into the fillet, then removes it. If the tester is warm—not hot—to the touch, the fish is ready.

16 baby turnips, peeled
16 baby carrots, peeled
 1 tablespoon plus 1 teaspoon
    extra-virgin olive oil
 2 ounces pancetta or *guanciale*,
    finely chopped
12 large scallions or ramps,
    white bulbs separated from
    the greens
One 15-ounce can hominy,
    drained and rinsed
 1 cup vegetable stock or
    low-sodium broth
¼ cup finely chopped
    flat-leaf parsley
 2 teaspoons fresh
    lemon juice
½ teaspoon dried marjoram
½ teaspoon dried thyme
¼ teaspoon ground allspice
⅛ teaspoon cayenne pepper
 2 tablespoons
    unsalted butter
Salt and freshly ground
    black pepper
 1 cup dry bread crumbs
½ cup finely ground pecans
    (see Note)
Four 6-ounce skinless
    catfish fillets

1. Preheat the oven to 425°. In a medium saucepan of boiling salted water, cook the baby turnips and carrots until they are tender, about 5 minutes. Drain, transfer the vegetables to a bowl and wipe out the saucepan. In the saucepan, heat 1 teaspoon of the olive oil. Add the pancetta and cook over moderate heat, stirring occasionally, until the fat has rendered, about 4 minutes. Using a slotted spoon, transfer the cooked pancetta to a plate. Add the turnips, carrots, scallion bulbs and hominy to the saucepan and cook over moderate heat, stirring occasionally, until the vegetables are richly glazed, about 8 minutes.

2. Cut enough of the scallion greens into 2-inch lengths to make ½ cup; finely chop the remaining greens to make 1 cup. Add the vegetable stock, the ½ cup of scallion greens and the parsley to the saucepan. Cover and simmer over low heat until the scallion bulbs are tender, 2 minutes. Stir in the lemon juice, marjoram, thyme, allspice and cayenne. Stir in the butter, 1 tablespoon at a time, and season with salt and pepper. Cover the stew and remove from the heat.

3. In a skillet, heat the remaining 1 tablespoon of olive oil. Add the 1 cup of chopped scallion greens and cook over high heat until softened, about 1 minute. Scrape the scallion greens and oil into a medium bowl. Stir in the bread crumbs and pecans and season with salt and pepper. Arrange the catfish fillets on a large rimmed baking sheet and season with salt and pepper. Press the bread crumb mixture on each fillet to form a crust. Roast the fish on the top shelf of the oven for about 8 minutes, until the crust is crisp and the fish is just cooked through.

4. Gently reheat the hominy stew and spoon into shallow bowls. Scatter some reserved pancetta on top of each portion and serve with the pecan-crusted catfish.

—*Josh Feathers*

NOTE To grind nuts finely, pulse them in a food processor until they are fluffy; take care not to overprocess, as this will release the nuts' oils.

WINE Fruity, light-bodied Beaujolais.

Salt-Baked Trout

TOTAL: 55 MIN

8 SERVINGS ●

F&W's Marcia Kiesel uses pickled cocktail onions to make a fast, tart, crunchy sauce for this succulent salt-baked trout.

16 bay leaves
16 thyme sprigs
 8 boneless whole trout,
    tails cut off (about 8 ounces)
12 cups kosher salt (6 pounds),
    plus more for seasoning
 1 cup drained pickled cocktail
    onions, thinly sliced
¼ cup plus 2 tablespoons
    white wine vinegar
½ cup plus 2 tablespoons
    vegetable oil
Freshly ground pepper

1. Preheat the oven to 500°. Place 2 bay leaves and 2 thyme sprigs in the cavity of each trout; secure with toothpicks. On each of 2 large rimmed baking sheets, spread 2½ cups of kosher salt in a thick, even layer. Sprinkle the salt with water until damp. Place 4 of the stuffed trout on each baking sheet and cover each trout with about ¾ cup of salt, packing the salt to cover the fish completely. Use the remaining 1 cup of salt to fill in any gaps. Sprinkle the salt with water to dampen it. Bake the fish in the upper and lower thirds of the oven for 15 minutes.

2. Meanwhile, in a medium bowl, mix the drained pickled cocktail onions with the white wine vinegar and vegetable oil and season with salt and pepper.

3. Carefully break the salt crust off the trout and transfer the fish to dinner plates. Remove and discard the toothpicks and serve the trout at once, passing the pickled onion vinaigrette at the table.

—*Marcia Kiesel*

MAKE AHEAD The pickled onion vinaigrette can be refrigerated overnight. Serve at room temperature.

WINE Dry, fruity sparkling wine.

perfecting whole fish

Chefs love serving whole fish: It's easy to prepare and often much more delicious than fillets, because cooking fish on the bone helps keep it moist. Home cooks don't have to be intimidated by the technique, as F&W's **Grace Parisi** demonstrates with these three great rubs and simple cooking methods. She likes using red snapper here for its sweet, delicate flavor, but other firm, white-fleshed fish, such as striped bass, sea bass, porgy or small grouper, will also work beautifully in these versatile recipes.

CARIBBEAN-STYLE RED SNAPPER

STEP ONE *Pick your favorite flavor combination.*

For one whole cleaned and scaled 3-pound red snapper; 4 servings.

Asian
- ¼ cup chopped cilantro
- 2 tablespoons minced fresh ginger
- 2 scallions, finely chopped
- 1 garlic clove, minced
- 1 teaspoon Asian sesame oil
- 1 tablespoon canola oil

Mediterranean
- ¼ cup finely chopped parsley
- 2 tablespoons salted capers, rinsed and finely chopped
- 2 garlic cloves, minced
- ½ teaspoon crushed red pepper
- 1 tablespoon canola oil

Caribbean
- 2 tablespoons minced fresh ginger
- 1 garlic clove, minced
- 1 serrano chile, seeded and minced
- 1 teaspoon chopped thyme
- ⅛ teaspoon ground allspice
- 1 tablespoon canola oil

STEP TWO *Prepare the fish.*

Choose one of the flavor combinations above and chop all of the ingredients except the canola oil with a large pinch of salt. Transfer the paste to a small bowl and stir in the oil. Make 5 parallel 3-inch-long slashes on each side of the fish, slicing almost through to the bone. Lightly season the fish with salt and fill the slashes with the paste. Rub the fish all over with more canola oil.

STEP THREE *Cook the fish.*

Roast Preheat the oven to 425°. Transfer the fish to a heavy rimmed baking sheet so it stands upright. To keep the fish stable, splay the belly flaps and set a crumpled foil ball under the tail. Roast the fish for 30 minutes, until the flesh just flakes. Transfer the fish to a platter. Using 2 forks, lift the fillets off the bones and serve.

Steam Preheat the oven to 425°. Set the fish on a sheet of heavy-duty foil and set another sheet on top; fold up 3 of the sides. Add 1 tablespoon of water to the packet and seal completely. Transfer the fish to a rimmed baking sheet; steam in the oven for 30 minutes, until the flesh just flakes. Lift the fillets off the bones and serve.

Grill Light a grill and oil a grill basket that's large enough to hold the fish. Set the fish in the basket and grill over moderate heat, turning once, until the flesh just flakes with a fork, about 20 minutes. Carefully remove the fish from the basket and transfer to a platter. Using 2 forks, lift the fillets off the bones and serve.

fish

Salt-Crusted Tilapia with Lemongrass

ACTIVE: 20 MIN; TOTAL: 1 HR 20 MIN
8 SERVINGS ●

Thai cooks love tilapia, a mild white fish, for its versatility. "You can steam it, fry it or grill it," says Andy Ricker, chef at the fabulous Thai restaurant Pok Pok in Portland, Oregon. Here, he stuffs the whole fish with lemongrass, encases it in a salt crust and cooks it over a charcoal fire. Be sure the heat stays relatively low, or the crust will burn before the fish is ready to emerge moist and fragrant.

- 4 lemongrass stalks, tender inner bulbs only, cut into 2-inch lengths
- Four 2-pound tilapia, scaled and cleaned
- Slurry made with ½ cup cornstarch dissolved in 6 tablespoons of water
- ½ cup kosher salt
- Spicy Citrus Dipping Sauce (p. 193), for serving

1. In a mortar, lightly pound the lemongrass. Arrange the fish on a work surface and pat dry. Stuff the cavities with the lemongrass. Brush 3 tablespoons of the cornstarch slurry over one side of the fish. Spread ¼ cup of the salt over the slurry to form a thin crust. Let stand at room temperature until the crust is dry, about 20 minutes. Carefully turn the fish over and repeat with the remaining 3 tablespoons of slurry and ¼ cup of kosher salt. Let stand for another 20 minutes, until completely dry.
2. Light a grill. Carefully place the tilapia on the grill and cook over moderately low heat, turning once, until the fish is just cooked through, about 20 minutes. Transfer the tilapia to a work surface. Using your fingers or 2 forks, peel off the tilapia skin. Transfer the fish to plates and serve with the Spicy Citrus Dipping Sauce.
—Andy Ricker

WINE Dry, rich Champagne.

Cod with Artichokes and Chickpeas

 TOTAL: 45 MIN
4 SERVINGS

- 2 tablespoons unsalted butter
- ¼ cup extra-virgin olive oil
- 1 small white onion, sliced ½ inch thick
- One 9-ounce box frozen artichoke hearts, thawed and pressed dry
- ¼ pound shiitake mushrooms, stems discarded and caps quartered
- 2 carrots, cut into ½-inch pieces
- 2 garlic cloves, thinly sliced
- One 15-ounce can chickpeas, drained
- 1 cup chicken stock or low-sodium broth
- Salt and freshly ground pepper
- 2 tablespoons chopped flat-leaf parsley
- 2 tablespoons snipped chives
- Four 6-ounce skinless cod fillets
- Lemon wedges, for serving

1. In a large, deep skillet, melt the butter in 2 tablespoons of the olive oil. Add the onion, artichoke hearts, shiitake caps, carrots and garlic and cook over moderately high heat, stirring occasionally, until lightly browned, 7 minutes. Add the chickpeas and stock, season with salt and pepper and bring to a boil. Simmer over low heat until the vegetables are tender and the liquid is nearly evaporated, 5 minutes. Stir in the parsley and chives and keep warm.
2. In a large nonstick skillet, heat the remaining 2 tablespoons of olive oil until almost smoking. Season the cod fillets with salt and pepper, add to the skillet and cook over high heat until well browned on the bottom, about 6 minutes. Carefully flip the fillets and cook until they're white throughout, about 3 minutes longer.
3. Spoon the vegetables into shallow bowls and top with the seared cod fillets. Serve with lemon wedges. *—Mark Sullivan*

WINE Full-bodied, rich Pinot Gris.

Striped Bass with Sweet Carrots and Cider Glaze

 TOTAL: 40 MIN
4 SERVINGS ●

Chicago chef Bruce Sherman will cook only with sustainable fish. While in the Galápagos, he used wahoo in this recipe; back home he opts for striped bass or halibut.

- ½ cup apple cider
- ½ cup cider vinegar
- 1 tablespoon unsalted butter
- 3 tablespoons extra-virgin olive oil
- 1½ pounds carrots, peeled and sliced on the diagonal ⅛ inch thick
- 2 garlic cloves, crushed and peeled
- 2 rosemary sprigs
- Salt and freshly ground pepper
- 1 tablespoon chopped parsley
- 1 tablespoon vegetable oil
- Four 6-ounce skinless striped bass fillets or other sustainable meaty white fish fillets

1. In a nonreactive saucepan, boil the cider and cider vinegar over high heat until reduced to 2 tablespoons, 15 minutes. Remove from the heat and stir in the butter.
2. Meanwhile, in a nonstick skillet, heat the olive oil. Spread the carrots in an even layer and add the garlic and rosemary. Cook over moderately high heat, without stirring, for 3 minutes. Reduce the heat to moderate and cook, stirring, until the carrots are just tender and richly caramelized, 5 minutes longer. Discard the garlic and rosemary. Season the carrots with salt and pepper. Stir in the parsley and half of the cider glaze.
3. In a nonstick skillet, heat the vegetable oil. Season the fish with salt and pepper and add to the skillet. Cook over moderately high heat until the fillets are lightly browned, 4 minutes. Turn and cook until the fish is just white throughout, 2 minutes longer.
4. Transfer the caramelized carrots to plates and set the fish on top. Drizzle with the remaining cider glaze and serve.
—Bruce Sherman

WINE Tart, citrusy Riesling.

STRIPED BASS WITH SWEET
CARROTS AND CIDER GLAZE

COD WITH ARTICHOKES
AND CHICKPEAS

fish

Fennel-Baked Sea Bass with Fennel Two Ways

ACTIVE: 25 MIN; TOTAL: 1 HR

4 SERVINGS ●

Called *loup de mer* ("wolf of the sea") in French, Mediterranean sea bass is light enough to take on a delicate fennel flavor when baked over charred fennel stalks. For a more assertive flavor, swap in dried fennel stalks, available from specialty food shops.

- **2 large fennel bulbs with stalks**
- **2 tablespoons extra-virgin olive oil, plus more for rubbing**
- **½ cup chicken stock or low-sodium broth**
- **1 tablespoon unsalted butter**
- **Salt and freshly ground pepper**
- **Four 6-ounce sea bass fillets with skin**
- **1 tablespoon fresh lemon juice**

SPRING DINNER PARTY

Pea Consommé with Mint, p. 59

· · · · · · · · · · · · · · · · ·

Fennel-Baked Sea Bass with Fennel Two Ways, above

Rösti Potatoes, p. 237

Watercress, Avocado and Walnut Salad, p. 55

Zesty, fresh Albariño

· · · · · · · · · · · · · · · · ·

Warm Strawberry Crumb Cake, p. 290

---

1. Cut the stalks from the fennel bulbs; halve both the stalks and bulbs lengthwise. Using a mandoline, thinly slice one fennel bulb half. Transfer the slices to a small bowl of ice water and refrigerate for at least 30 minutes or up to 2 hours.

2. Meanwhile, cut the remaining 3 fennel bulb halves into 1-inch wedges. In a large skillet, heat 1 tablespoon of the olive oil. Add the fennel wedges in a single layer and add the chicken stock. Cover and cook over low heat, turning the fennel wedges a few times, until tender, about 25 minutes. Uncover, stir in the butter and season with salt and pepper. Keep warm.

3. Preheat the oven to 350°. In a large skillet, sear the fennel stalks over high heat, turning as necessary to char thoroughly on both sides, about 15 minutes.

4. Rub the fish fillets with oil, season with salt and pepper and arrange in the skillet on the charred fennel stalks. Bake on the top shelf of the oven for about 8 minutes, until the fish just flakes easily.

5. Drain the fennel slices and pat dry with a paper towel. Transfer them to a small bowl. Add the lemon juice and the remaining 1 tablespoon of olive oil, season with salt and pepper and toss.

6. Transfer the sea bass fillets to dinner plates; discard the fennel stalks. Top the sea bass with the fennel salad, arrange the braised fennel wedges alongside and serve the fish right away.
—*Armand Arnal*

WINE Zesty, fresh Albariño.

Pan-Seared Black Sea Bass with Endives and Grapes

 TOTAL: 35 MIN

10 FIRST-COURSE SERVINGS

Georgia chef Matt Palmerlee loves to use sustainable seafood like the line-caught sea bass in this recipe. In place of the red grapes, he makes the dish with sweeter, more complex Muscadine grapes when they're in season.

- **10 ounces sliced bacon, cut crosswise into ¼-inch strips**
- **10 Belgian endives, leaves coarsely chopped**
- **Salt and freshly ground black pepper**
- **2 tablespoons vegetable oil**
- **Ten 3-ounce black sea bass, black cod or sablefish fillets with skin**
- **1 cup seedless red grapes**

1. In a nonstick skillet, cook the bacon over moderate heat, stirring occasionally, until crisp, about 8 minutes. Using a slotted spoon, transfer the bacon to paper towels. Pour off all but 4 tablespoons of the fat.

2. Add the endives to the skillet. Cook over moderately high heat, stirring occasionally, until golden brown and softened, 6 minutes. Stir in the bacon; season with salt and pepper. Transfer the endives to a bowl and keep warm. Wipe out the skillet.

3. Heat the vegetable oil in each of 2 large nonstick skillets. Season the fish with salt and pepper and add the fillets to the skillets, skin side down. Cook over moderately high heat until the skin is browned and crisp, about 4 minutes. Turn and cook until the flesh is just white throughout, 2 minutes longer. Add the grapes to the skillets and cook, stirring, until hot, about 1 minute. Transfer the fish and grapes to plates on top of the endives and serve.
—*Matt Palmerlee*

WINE Light, fresh Pinot Grigio.

Grouper with Corn "Pudding" and Collard Greens

ACTIVE: 40 MIN; TOTAL: 1 HR 15 MIN

6 SERVINGS ●

At seafood-focused Reef in Houston, Bryan Caswell (an F&W Best New Chef 2009) serves grouper accompanied by a brilliantly simple corn pudding and collard greens. If you can't find grouper, substitute another moderately firm fish fillet such as tilefish, sea bass or cod.

CORN PUDDING

6 large ears of corn, shucked

1 tablespoon vegetable oil

2 tablespoons unsalted butter

1 tablespoon fresh lime juice

Salt

Cayenne pepper

COLLARD GREENS

1 tablespoon vegetable oil

2 ounces smoked andouille sausage, cut lengthwise into thin strips

½ pound young, tender collard greens, stems discarded and leaves cut into 1-inch-wide strips

1 small shallot, minced

1 small fresh red chile—halved, seeded and thinly sliced crosswise

2 red radishes, thinly sliced

2 small white icicle radishes, cut into thin sticks

1 large scallion, white part only, thinly sliced on the bias

1 tablespoon fresh lime juice

Salt

GROUPER

Six 7-ounce skinless grouper fillets

Vegetable oil, for rubbing

Salt

Cayenne pepper

3 tablespoons unsalted butter, softened

1. MAKE THE CORN PUDDING: Preheat the oven to 350° and place a 9- or 10-inch cast-iron skillet in it to heat. Using a box grater, coarsely grate the corn into a bowl, reserving all of the solids and juices. Add the oil to the hot skillet and swirl to coat. Spread the corn and juices in the skillet and bake for 45 minutes, until browned and crusty on the bottom. Scrape the corn into a saucepan and stir in the butter and lime juice. Season with salt and cayenne; keep warm.

2. MEANWHILE, PREPARE THE COLLARD GREENS: In a large cast-iron skillet, heat the oil. Add the andouille and cook over

moderate heat until browned, 2 minutes; transfer to a plate. Set the skillet over high heat, and when the oil is almost smoking, add the collards and cook, undisturbed, until slightly charred, 1 minute. Stir and cook for 30 seconds longer. Add the andouille, shallot and chile and cook over moderate heat, stirring, until the shallot is softened, 1 minute. Add the radishes and scallion and cook, stirring, for 30 seconds. Scrape the collards into a bowl and stir in the lime juice. Season with salt, cover and keep warm.

3. COOK THE GROUPER: Reduce the oven temperature to 325°. Heat a grill pan. Rub the grouper with oil and season with salt and cayenne. Grill over high heat, skinned side up, until lightly charred, 2 to 3 minutes. Turn and transfer to a large baking sheet. Top each fillet with ½ tablespoon of butter and bake for about 3 minutes, until cooked through.

4. Spoon the corn into small bowls. Spoon the collards onto plates and top with the grouper fillets and any pan juices. Serve right away, with the corn.

—Bryan Caswell

WINE Ripe, luxurious Chardonnay.

Grouper with Cucumber Salad and Soy-Mustard Dressing

 TOTAL: 40 MIN

4 SERVINGS ●

A refreshing salad of julienned cucumber, daikon and carrot tossed with a soy-mustard dressing makes this light fish dish incredibly vibrant.

3 tablespoons soy sauce

3 tablespoons rice vinegar

1 tablespoon mirin

1 tablespoon sake

2 teaspoons whole-grain mustard

3 garlic cloves, coarsely chopped

½ cup plus 1 tablespoon vegetable oil

1 medium seedless cucumber, peeled and halved crosswise

One 3-inch piece of carrot, peeled

One 3-inch piece of daikon, peeled

1 medium shallot, thinly sliced crosswise

Four 6-ounce skinless grouper fillets

Salt and freshly ground pepper

1 long red fresh chile, cut into long, fine strips

Toasted sesame seeds, cilantro leaves and finely chopped chives, for garnish

1. In a blender, puree the soy sauce with the rice vinegar, mirin, sake, mustard and one-third of the garlic. With the machine on, slowly pour in 6 tablespoons of the vegetable oil and blend until smooth.

2. Using a mandoline, thinly slice half of the cucumber lengthwise. Finely julienne the remaining cucumber half as well as the carrot and daikon. In a medium bowl, toss the julienned vegetables together.

3. In a large skillet, heat the remaining 3 tablespoons of vegetable oil. Add the sliced shallot and the remaining garlic and cook over moderate heat until golden brown, about 3 minutes. With a slotted spoon, transfer the shallot and garlic to a paper towel–lined plate to drain.

4. Season the grouper fillets with salt and pepper and add them to the skillet. Cook over moderately high heat until browned on the bottom, about 4 minutes. Turn and cook over moderate heat until just white throughout, about 2 minutes longer.

5. Spoon 1 tablespoon of the soy-mustard dressing in the center of each plate. Fold the cucumber slices and arrange them on the dressing. Set the grouper fillets on the cucumbers, browned sides up, and top with the julienned vegetables. Drizzle with the remaining dressing. Garnish with the fried garlic and shallot, the chile strips, toasted sesame seeds, cilantro leaves and chives and serve right away.

—Dale Gartland

MAKE AHEAD The soy-mustard dressing can be refrigerated overnight. Bring to room temperature before using.

WINE Minerally, complex Sauvignon Blanc.

ITALIAN SEAFOOD
STEW (P. 209)

shellfish

The definitive seafood stew, plus easy recipes
for shrimp, scallops and more.

ROSEMARY-SKEWERED SHRIMP

SHRIMP STIR-FRY WITH CRISPY NOODLES

Shrimp with Cheese-Grit Cakes and Bacon Vinaigrette

ACTIVE: 30 MIN TOTAL: 1 HR

6 SERVINGS

3½ cups milk

5 garlic cloves, minced

1 cup quick grits

½ cup shredded sharp cheddar

Salt and freshly ground pepper

Tabasco

2 tablespoons vegetable oil, plus more for brushing

4 ounces lean bacon, cut into ½-inch dice

2 small shallots, minced

1 small celery rib, minced

1 scallion, finely chopped

½ red bell pepper, minced

1 tablespoon chopped parsley

1 teaspoon chopped thyme

¼ cup balsamic vinegar

2 tablespoons Dijon mustard

1 tablespoon Worcestershire sauce

Barbecue spice mix or Cajun seasoning, for dusting

1 pound large shrimp, shelled and deveined

1. Lightly oil a 9-inch-square glass baking dish. In a medium saucepan, bring the milk to a simmer with half of the garlic. Slowly whisk in the grits over moderate heat until very thick, 3 minutes. Remove from the heat and whisk in the cheddar. Season with salt, pepper and Tabasco. Pour into the baking dish and press plastic wrap directly onto the surface. Let stand until firm, about 30 minutes.

2. Meanwhile, in a small skillet, heat the 2 tablespoons of oil. Add the bacon; cook over moderate heat until crisp. Add the shallots, celery, scallion, red pepper, parsley, thyme and the remaining garlic and cook, stirring, until the shallots are softened, about 2 minutes. Off the heat, stir in the vinegar, mustard, Worcestershire sauce and a few dashes of Tabasco. Season with salt and keep warm.

3. Heat a grill pan and brush with oil. Cut the grits into 12 squares and dust on both sides with barbecue spice mix. Cook over moderate heat until crisp, about 2 minutes per side. Keep the grit cakes warm in a low oven; keep the grill pan hot.

4. Brush the shrimp with oil, season with salt and pepper and dust with barbecue spice mix. Grill the shrimp in the pan over moderately high heat until lightly charred and just cooked through, about 1½ minutes per side. Arrange the shrimp and grit cakes on plates, drizzle the bacon vinaigrette on top and serve right away.

—Nathanial Zimet

WINE Fresh, fruity rosé.

Grilled Quick-Brined Jumbo Shrimp

TOTAL: 30 MIN PLUS 4 HR BRINING
8 SERVINGS ●

Andy Ricker, chef at the Thai grilling temple Pok Pok in Portland, Oregon, gives shrimp a quick brining to keep them firm and juicy when grilled.

10 cups water
½ cup kosher salt
¼ cup sugar
24 jumbo shrimp (2½ pounds)
Spicy Citrus Dipping Sauce
  (recipe follows), for serving

1. In a large bowl, combine the water, salt and sugar, stirring to dissolve the salt. Using a paring knife or scissors, slit each shrimp down the back through the shell; remove the dark veins. Add the shrimp to the brine, cover and refrigerate for 4 hours.
2. Light a grill. Drain the shrimp and pat dry. Grill the shrimp over moderately high heat, turning once, until the shells are lightly charred and the shrimp are just cooked through, about 5 minutes. Serve with the Spicy Citrus Dipping Sauce. —Andy Ricker

WINE Dry, fruity sparkling wine.

SPICY CITRUS DIPPING SAUCE

TOTAL: 25 MIN
MAKES 1½ CUPS ● ● ●

Since the Persian limes typically sold in America are tarter than Thai limes, Ricker sometimes sweetens their juice with a squeeze of fresh orange juice, as in this bright, superquick dipping sauce. It's delicious with Ricker's grilled shrimp (above) and salt-crusted tilapia (p. 186).

¾ cup water
¼ cup sugar
½ cup fresh lime juice
2 tablespoons fresh orange juice
4 Thai chiles, minced
3 large garlic cloves, minced
1½ teaspoons kosher salt
¼ cup finely chopped cilantro

In a medium bowl, combine the water with the sugar, stirring to dissolve the sugar. Add the lime juice, orange juice, chiles, garlic and salt, stirring to dissolve the salt. Stir in the cilantro and serve right away. —AR

MAKE AHEAD The sauce can be prepared up to 2 days ahead and refrigerated in a covered container. Stir in the chopped cilantro just before serving.

Rosemary-Skewered Shrimp

TOTAL: 30 MIN
10 FIRST-COURSE SERVINGS ●

These simple skewers are lovely because of their distinct rosemary flavor, which completely infuses the charred shrimp and sweet red peppers. They can be made on the grill or in a grill pan on the stovetop.

20 large shrimp (about 1½ pounds), shelled and deveined
1 large red bell pepper, cut into twenty 1-inch squares
10 thick rosemary branches (about 8 inches long), all but the top 2 inches of needles stripped off
⅓ cup extra-virgin olive oil
3 tablespoons fresh lemon juice
¼ cup chopped flat-leaf parsley
Salt and freshly ground black pepper

1. Light a grill or heat a grill pan. Alternately thread 2 shrimp and 2 red pepper squares onto each rosemary branch.
2. In a small bowl, combine the olive oil, lemon juice and parsley. Lightly brush the skewers with some of the olive oil mixture and season with salt and pepper.
3. Grill the skewers over high heat, brushing them with the olive oil and lemon juice mixture, until the shrimp are pink and just cooked through, about 1½ minutes per side. Serve the skewers right away. —Francis Mallmann

MAKE AHEAD The recipe can be prepared through Step 1 and refrigerated overnight.

WINE Zesty, fresh Albariño.

Shrimp–and–Bok Choy Stir-Fry with Crispy Noodles

TOTAL: 30 MIN
4 SERVINGS ●

¾ cup chicken stock or low-sodium broth
2 tablespoons low-sodium soy sauce
1 tablespoon mirin
1½ teaspoons cornstarch dissolved in 1 tablespoon of water
2 tablespoons canola oil
2 tablespoons finely julienned peeled fresh ginger
1 garlic clove, thinly sliced
½ teaspoon crushed red pepper
1 large onion, thinly sliced
¼ pound shiitake mushrooms, stemmed and caps thinly sliced
1 small head of bok choy (about 12 ounces), thinly sliced crosswise
1 pound medium shrimp, shelled and deveined
¼ package instant ramen noodles or fried Chinese noodles, crumbled
Brown rice, for serving

1. In a small bowl, whisk the stock with the soy sauce, mirin and cornstarch slurry.
2. Heat a nonstick wok or large, deep skillet until very hot, about 3 minutes. Add the canola oil, ginger, garlic and crushed red pepper and stir-fry until fragrant, about 20 seconds. Add the onion and shiitake and stir-fry until lightly browned and nearly tender, about 3 minutes. Add the bok choy and cook until the leaves are wilted and the stems are crisp-tender, about 2 minutes. Add the shrimp and stir-fry until they are pink and curled and nearly cooked through, about 3 minutes.
3. Stir the sauce, then add it to the wok; cook until slightly thickened, 2 minutes. Transfer the stir-fry to a bowl and garnish with the noodles. Serve with brown rice. —Takashi Yagihashi

WINE Peppery, refreshing Grüner Veltliner.

shellfish

Grilled Shrimp and Steamed Mussels in Coconut Broth

ACTIVE: 30 MIN; TOTAL: 1 HR 5 MIN
4 SERVINGS

Grilled shrimp and steamed mussels finish cooking in a terrific broth made with shrimp shells, coconut milk and pickled ginger for a piquant kick.

- 1 pound large shrimp, shelled and deveined, shells reserved
- 2 tablespoons extra-virgin olive oil

Finely grated zest of 1 lemon

Salt and freshly ground pepper

- 3 cups water
- ¼ cup pickled ginger from a jar
- 1 large onion, finely chopped
- 1 fennel bulb, cored and finely chopped
- 3 tablespoons unsalted butter
- 4 garlic cloves, minced
- 2 tablespoons minced ginger
- 1 medium carrot, thinly sliced crosswise on a mandoline
- ¾ cup unsweetened coconut milk
- ½ cup dry white wine
- 1 pound mussels, scrubbed
- 2 tablespoons chopped parsley

1. In a medium bowl, toss the shrimp with the olive oil and lemon zest and season with salt and pepper. Cover and refrigerate for 30 minutes.

2. In a medium saucepan, combine the water, shrimp shells, pickled ginger and half of the chopped onion and fennel. Cover and simmer over moderate heat for 15 minutes. Strain the broth and discard the solids.

3. In a large, deep skillet, melt the butter. Add the garlic, minced ginger, carrot and the remaining chopped onion and fennel and cook over moderately high heat, stirring occasionally, until the vegetables begin to brown, about 3 minutes. Add the shrimp broth and boil over high heat until slightly reduced, about 4 minutes. Add the coconut milk and boil over high heat until thickened, about 4 minutes.

4. Heat a grill pan. In a medium saucepan, bring the wine to a boil. Add the mussels, cover and cook over high heat until their shells open, about 3 minutes.

5. When the grill pan is very hot, grill the shrimp over high heat until lightly charred and barely cooked, about 1 minute per side. Transfer the shrimp to the coconut broth. Add the steamed mussels and their cooking liquid and simmer over moderate heat until the shrimp are just cooked through, about 2 minutes. Season with salt and pepper. Spoon the seafood and broth into bowls, sprinkle with the parsley and serve right away.
—*John Lancaster and Robert Perkins*

SERVE WITH Steamed rice.

WINE Full-bodied, minerally Riesling.

Salt-Roasted Shrimp

ACTIVE: 10 MIN; TOTAL: 30 MIN
4 SERVINGS ●

While traveling in Italy, chef Matt Molina of L.A.'s Osteria Mozza had ultrafresh shrimp in the town of Cesenatico on the Adriatic coast. His recipe here re-creates the dish. Roasting the shrimp in salt concentrates their sweet flavor.

- 4 cups kosher salt (2 pounds)
- 1½ pounds unshelled large shrimp, preferably head-on

Extra-virgin olive oil, for serving

1. Preheat the oven to 500°. Pour the kosher salt into a large, heavy ovenproof skillet and heat it in the oven for 15 minutes, until the salt is very hot.

2. Arrange the shrimp in a single layer in a deep metal baking pan. Pour the hot salt over the shrimp, covering them completely. Roast the shrimp for 5 minutes, until just cooked through. Rinse the shrimp briefly under hot water and pat dry. Serve immediately, with olive oil for dipping.
—*Matt Molina*

WINE Creamy, supple Pinot Blanc.

Sizzling Shrimp Scampi

TOTAL: 30 MIN
8 SERVINGS ●

Scampi refers to shrimp that are split lengthwise, brushed with garlicky butter and broiled. The recipe here calls for flavoring butter with lemon, garlic, parsley and fresh thyme, then dotting it liberally on shrimp and roasting the shellfish at high heat until the whole thing sizzles.

- 2 sticks unsalted butter, softened
- 3 large garlic cloves, very finely chopped
- 1 tablespoon plus 2 teaspoons chopped flat-leaf parsley
- 1½ teaspoons finely grated lemon zest
- 1 teaspoon fresh lemon juice
- ½ teaspoon chopped fresh thyme leaves

Kosher salt and freshly ground black pepper

- 3 pounds large shrimp—shelled and deveined, tails left on
- 1 tablespoon thinly sliced basil leaves

Crusty bread, for serving

1. Preheat the oven to 450°. In a medium bowl, mix the butter with the garlic, 2 teaspoons of the parsley, the lemon zest, lemon juice and thyme and season with salt and pepper.

2. In a large gratin dish, arrange the shrimp, tails up, in a circular pattern. Dot the shrimp with the flavored butter and roast for about 10 minutes, until the shrimp are pink and the butter is bubbling. Sprinkle the shrimp with the remaining 1 tablespoon of chopped parsley and the basil leaves. Serve hot with bread.
—*Melissa Rubel Jacobson*

MAKE AHEAD The flavored butter can be refrigerated for up to 1 week or frozen for up to 1 month.

WINE Ripe, luxurious Chardonnay.

SIZZLING SHRIMP SCAMPI

shellfish

Shrimp-and-Vegetable Tagine with Preserved Lemon

ACTIVE: 30 MIN; TOTAL: 2 HR 15 MIN
6 SERVINGS ● ●

¼ cup finely chopped flat-leaf parsley

3 tablespoons chopped cilantro, plus whole sprigs for garnish

2 tablespoons fresh lemon juice

1 tablespoon sweet paprika

1 teaspoon ground ginger

Small pinch of saffron threads, crumbled

⅓ cup extra-virgin olive oil

1½ pounds large shrimp—shelled and deveined, tails left on

2¼ pounds plum tomatoes—peeled, seeded and coarsely chopped

3 garlic cloves, minced

1½ teaspoons ground cumin

Salt and freshly ground pepper

3 large carrots, thinly sliced

1 large sweet onion, thinly sliced

4 large Red Bliss potatoes (about 1½ pounds), peeled and thinly sliced

1 red bell pepper, cut into thin strips

1 yellow bell pepper, cut into thin strips

½ preserved lemon, peel only, thinly sliced (see Note)

½ cup pitted green olives

---

buttery shrimp sauté

For a speedy seafood dinner, sauté shrimp and sugar snap peas in a mix of olive oil and butter and add a splash of white wine. When the shrimp are opaque, sprinkle with salt, lemon juice and chives; serve over buttered rice or orzo.

---

1. In a medium bowl, combine the parsley with the chopped cilantro, lemon juice, paprika, ginger, saffron and olive oil. Add the shrimp, toss to coat with the marinade and refrigerate for 2 hours.

2. Meanwhile, in a medium saucepan, combine the tomatoes with the garlic and cumin and season with salt and pepper. Simmer over moderate heat, stirring occasionally, until the tomatoes are broken down and slightly thickened, 10 minutes.

3. Spread the sliced carrots in a large enameled cast-iron casserole or Dutch oven and season lightly with salt and pepper. Add the onion, potatoes and bell peppers, lightly seasoning each layer with salt and pepper. Spread the tomato sauce on top. Cover and simmer over moderately low heat until the vegetables are just tender, about 20 minutes.

4. Add the preserved lemon peel slices and green olives to the casserole and arrange the shrimp on top in a single layer. Season with salt and pepper. Cover and cook over moderately low heat until the shrimp are pink and curled, about 3 minutes. Using a slotted spoon, transfer the shrimp to a plate. Raise the heat to moderate and bring the juices to a simmer. Cook the tagine uncovered, stirring once or twice, until the juices have evaporated, about 5 minutes; take care not to let the vegetables burn on the bottom. Transfer the vegetables to a large serving bowl and top with the cooked shrimp. Garnish with the cilantro sprigs and serve the tagine immediately.
—*Mourad Lahlou*

NOTE Preserved lemons are a Moroccan ingredient made by macerating whole lemons in lemon juice and salt until they're very soft. They're available at specialty food shops and kalustyans.com.

MAKE AHEAD The shrimp-and-vegetable tagine can be prepared through Step 3 and refrigerated overnight. Rewarm gently before proceeding.

WINE Fresh, fruity rosé.

Shrimp-and-Feta-Stuffed Zucchini

ACTIVE: 40 MIN; TOTAL: 1 HR 15 MIN
6 SERVINGS ●

2 tablespoons extra-virgin olive oil, plus more for brushing

1 large white onion, finely chopped

1 red bell pepper, finely chopped

½ fennel bulb, finely chopped

1 large garlic clove, very finely chopped

4 plum tomatoes, chopped

½ teaspoon crushed red pepper

Salt and freshly ground black pepper

¾ pound shelled and deveined large shrimp, finely chopped

2 tablespoons chopped parsley

2 tablespoons chopped dill

6 small round or oblong zucchini (2½ pounds), halved lengthwise

1½ cups crumbled feta (6 ounces)

1. Preheat the oven to 425°. In a skillet, heat the 2 tablespoons of olive oil. Add the onion, bell pepper, fennel and garlic; sauté over moderately high heat until tender, about 6 minutes. Add the tomatoes and crushed red pepper and cook, mashing, until thickened, about 5 minutes. Season with salt and black pepper. Remove from the heat; let cool slightly. Stir in the shrimp, parsley and dill.

2. Using a spoon, scoop out the flesh of the zucchini, leaving a ¼-inch shell all around. Rub with oil. Season the zucchini shells with salt and black pepper and stuff with the filling. Transfer to a lightly oiled roasting pan and roast for about 30 minutes, until the filling is cooked through and the zucchini is just tender.

3. Preheat the broiler and position a rack 6 inches from the heat. Top the stuffed zucchini with the feta and broil for 5 minutes, until the feta is melted and golden. Serve hot or at room temperature.
—*Ana Sortun*

WINE Fruity, light-bodied Beaujolais.

SHRIMP-AND-VEGETABLE TAGINE WITH PRESERVED LEMON

SHRIMP-AND-FETA-STUFFED ZUCCHINI

Shrimp Saganaki

TOTAL: 30 MIN
4 SERVINGS ● ●

2 tablespoons each of extra-virgin
   olive oil and canola oil
1 large onion, thinly sliced
6 plum tomatoes, coarsely chopped
Salt
Crushed red pepper
1½ pounds shelled and deveined large
   shrimp, halved lengthwise
½ cup pitted kalamata olives,
   coarsely chopped
¼ cup chopped fresh dill
3 ounces Greek feta cheese,
   crumbled
Crusty bread, for serving

In a large skillet, heat the oil until shimmering. Add the onion and cook over high
heat, stirring occasionally, until lightly
browned, 5 minutes. Add the tomatoes,
season with salt and red pepper and cook
until softened, crushing with the back of
a spoon, 5 minutes. Add the shrimp and
olives and cook, stirring occasionally, until
the shrimp are cooked, 3 minutes. Stir in
the dill and half of the feta; cook just until
hot, 1 minute. Sprinkle with the remaining
feta and serve with bread. —*Grace Parisi*
WINE Fruity, light-bodied Beaujolais.

Mama Chang's Stir-Fried Shrimp and Scallions

TOTAL: 30 MIN
4 SERVINGS ● ●

1½ pounds shelled and deveined
   large shrimp
3 garlic cloves, sliced
One 1-inch piece of fresh ginger,
   peeled and minced
1½ teaspoons crushed red pepper
1 large egg white

2 teaspoons cornstarch
¾ cup ketchup
½ cup low-sodium chicken broth
1 tablespoon sugar
1½ teaspoons freshly ground pepper
1½ teaspoons kosher salt
¼ cup canola oil
3 scallions, thinly sliced
½ cup coarsely chopped cilantro

1. In a large bowl, toss the shrimp with the
garlic, ginger, red pepper, egg white and
1 teaspoon of the cornstarch.

2. In a bowl, whisk the ketchup, broth, sugar,
pepper, salt and remaining cornstarch.

3. In a large skillet, heat the oil until shimmering. Add the shrimp and stir-fry over
high heat until they begin to turn pink. Add
the sauce and simmer until the shrimp
are cooked, 2 minutes. Stir in the scallions
and cilantro; serve. —*Joanne Chang*
WINE Dry, earthy sparkling wine.

● HEALTHY ● MAKE AHEAD ● VEGETARIAN ● STAFF FAVORITE

197

shellfish

Shrimp Fried Rice with Coconut and Pickled Onions

ACTIVE: 35 MIN; TOTAL: 1 HR 30 MIN

10 SERVINGS ● ●

- 3 cups long-grain rice (19 ounces)
- 5 cups water
- ½ cup finely shredded fresh or dried unsweetened coconut
- 1 small onion, cut into ½-inch dice
- 3 tablespoons rice vinegar

Salt

- 2 medium carrots, cut into ½-inch dice
- ½ cup plus 2 tablespoons vegetable oil
- 4 large eggs, beaten
- 2 large shallots, thinly sliced
- 1 pound medium shrimp, shelled and deveined

Freshly ground white pepper

- 4 cups coarsely chopped green cabbage (½ small head)
- 1 teaspoon crushed red pepper

One 10-ounce package frozen peas, thawed

- ¼ cup Asian fish sauce

1. In a large saucepan, rinse the rice, then drain it. Return the rice to the saucepan, add the water and bring to a boil. Cover the saucepan and cook the rice over low heat until the water is absorbed, about 15 minutes. Stir in the shredded coconut, cover and let stand off the heat for 10 minutes. Fluff the rice and spread it out on a large rimmed baking sheet. Let cool, then refrigerate, uncovered, until completely chilled, about 1 hour.

2. Meanwhile, in a small bowl, toss the onion with the vinegar and a large pinch of salt. Let stand for 10 minutes.

3. In a small saucepan of boiling water, cook the carrots until tender, about 6 minutes. Drain and set aside.

4. In a medium nonstick skillet, heat 1 tablespoon of the vegetable oil. Season the eggs with salt. Add them to the skillet and cook over moderate heat, stirring a few times, until just scrambled, about 1 minute. Transfer the eggs to a large plate.

5. Wipe out the skillet and heat 3 tablespoons of the vegetable oil in it. Add the sliced shallots and cook over moderately high heat, stirring frequently, until they're browned and crisp, about 2 minutes. Using a slotted spoon, transfer the shallots to a small bowl. Add the shrimp to the skillet and season with salt and white pepper. Cook over moderate heat, turning once, until just cooked through, about 2 minutes. Add the shrimp to the plate with the scrambled eggs.

6. Rub the cooked rice between your hands to separate the grains. In each of 2 large skillets, heat 3 tablespoons of vegetable oil. Add half of the cabbage and crushed red pepper to each skillet and stir-fry over moderately high heat until softened, about 3 minutes. Add half of the peas, carrots and pickled onion to each skillet and stir until hot.

7. Add half of the rice to each skillet along with the shrimp and eggs; toss over moderate heat until well mixed and heated through, 2 minutes. Remove from the heat and stir half of the fish sauce into the rice in each skillet. Season with salt and white pepper. Transfer the rice to a bowl, garnish with the fried shallots and serve.

—Chris Yeo

WINE Spicy American Gewürztraminer.

Curried-Shrimp Salad with Grilled Watermelon

ACTIVE: 35 MIN; TOTAL: 1 HR 35 MIN

4 FIRST-COURSE SERVINGS ●

Grilling watermelon gives it a terrific sweet-smoky flavor, but the key to charring it properly is to sprinkle it with sugar, which burns just a little on the fire. Here, Christopher Kostow (an F&W Best New Chef 2009) combines grilled watermelon with delicately curried shrimp and yogurt.

- 1 teaspoon curry powder
- ¼ cup plus 1 tablespoon extra-virgin olive oil
- 16 large shrimp (about ¾ pound), shelled and deveined
- 2 Kirby cucumbers (½ pound), cut into thin spears
- 2 tablespoons coarsely chopped mint
- 1 tablespoon fresh lime juice

Salt and freshly ground black pepper

- 1 pound red and yellow watermelons without the rinds, sliced into flat triangles

Sugar, for sprinkling

- 3 packed cups mâche
- ½ cup Greek-style whole-milk yogurt
- ¼ cup salted roasted pistachios, chopped

1. In a medium bowl, combine the curry powder and 1 tablespoon of the olive oil. Add the shrimp and toss to coat. Cover and refrigerate for 1 hour.

2. In another medium bowl, toss the cucumbers, mint and lime juice and season with salt and pepper. Cover and refrigerate.

3. Heat a grill pan. Sprinkle one side of each piece of watermelon with sugar. Grill on the sugared side over high heat until charred, about 2 minutes.

4. In a skillet, heat 2 tablespoons of the oil. Add the shrimp, season with salt and pepper and cook over moderate heat until white throughout, about 1½ minutes per side.

5. Add the mâche and the remaining 2 tablespoons of olive oil to the cucumbers and season with salt and pepper.

6. In a small bowl, season the yogurt with salt. Dollop the yogurt onto plates and top with the grilled watermelon and curried shrimp. Drizzle any curry oil from the skillet over the shrimp. Spoon the cucumber salad alongside, sprinkle with the pistachios and serve immediately.

—Christopher Kostow

WINE Fruity, soft Chenin Blanc.

shellfish

Barbecued Spiced Shrimp with Tomato Salad

 **TOTAL: 25 MIN**
8 SERVINGS ●

The big, bold Southwestern flavors in this shrimp seasoning—which includes pure ancho chile powder, sweet smoked paprika, cumin, cayenne pepper and brown sugar—epitomize star chef Bobby Flay's style. The seasoning mix would also be terrific on pork chops or beef tenderloin.

- ⅓ cup packed basil leaves, plus extra leaves for garnish
- ⅓ cup extra-virgin olive oil
- Kosher salt and freshly ground black pepper
- 2¼ teaspoons sweet smoked paprika
- 1½ teaspoons pure ancho chile powder
- 1½ teaspoons light brown sugar
- ½ teaspoon ground cumin
- ¼ teaspoon ground coriander
- ⅛ teaspoon cayenne pepper
- 24 jumbo shrimp, shelled and deveined
- 2 tablespoons canola oil
- 3 large yellow heirloom tomatoes (1½ pounds), sliced ¼ inch thick
- 1 small red onion, halved and thinly sliced

1. In a blender, puree the ⅓ cup of basil leaves with the olive oil until smooth. Season the oil with salt and black pepper.
2. Light a grill or preheat a grill pan. In a small bowl, mix the sweet smoked paprika with the pure ancho chile powder, light brown sugar, cumin, coriander, cayenne pepper, ½ teaspoon of salt and ¼ teaspoon of black pepper. Brush the shrimp with the canola oil and season all over with the spice mixture. Grill the shrimp over moderately high heat, turning once, until they are lightly charred and cooked through, about 4 minutes total.
3. Arrange the tomato and onion slices on a platter and drizzle with the basil oil.

Top with the shrimp, garnish with the remaining basil leaves and serve.
—*Bobby Flay*
MAKE AHEAD The basil oil can be refrigerated overnight. Bring to room temperature before serving.
WINE Bright, tart Barbera.

Indonesian-Style Shrimp Salad

 **TOTAL: 30 MIN**
6 SERVINGS

This recipe is based on *gado gado,* an Indonesian mix of crunchy vegetables in a sweet peanut dressing. F&W's Grace Parisi makes the dish more substantial by adding precooked shrimp; firm tofu would also be delicious here.

- ¼ cup plus 2 tablespoons creamy peanut butter
- ¼ cup plus 2 tablespoons unsweetened coconut milk
- 1½ tablespoons Asian fish sauce
- 1 teaspoon *sambal oelek* or Chinese chile-garlic sauce
- 1½ tablespoons fresh lime juice, plus lime wedges for garnish
- 2 teaspoons light brown sugar
- 3 carrots, coarsely shredded
- 1 seedless cucumber, peeled and cut into fine matchsticks
- 1 red or yellow bell pepper, cut into fine matchsticks
- 1 pound cooked large shrimp, shelled and halved lengthwise
- 2 romaine hearts, coarsely shredded
- Chopped scallions, chopped peanuts and cilantro leaves, for garnish

In a blender, combine the peanut butter with the coconut milk, Asian fish sauce, *sambal oelek,* lime juice and brown sugar and puree until smooth. Transfer the dressing to a large bowl. Add the shredded carrots, cucumber, bell pepper, shrimp and romaine and toss well. Garnish the salad with scallions, peanuts and cilantro and serve with lime wedges. —*Grace Parisi*

MAKE AHEAD The peanut dressing can be refrigerated for up to 5 days.
WINE Vivid, lightly sweet Riesling.

Poached Shrimp, Melon and Frisée Salad

ACTIVE: 35 MIN; TOTAL: 1 HR 15 MIN
8 FIRST-COURSE SERVINGS ●

To make the dressing for this pretty salad, Daniel Humm (an F&W Best New Chef 2005) reduces the shrimp-poaching liquid, which is flavored with coriander seeds, garlic, peppercorns and orange zest. The salad is wonderful as either a first course or a light main course.

- 2 small fennel bulbs, thinly sliced
- 1 small leek, white and tender green parts only, thinly sliced
- 3 garlic cloves
- 1 teaspoon fennel seeds
- 1 teaspoon coriander seeds
- 1 teaspoon black peppercorns
- Finely grated zest and juice of 1 medium orange
- 1 cup dry white wine
- 3 cups water
- Kosher salt
- 1½ pounds large shrimp, shelled and deveined
- 3 tablespoons extra-virgin olive oil
- 1 tablespoon white balsamic vinegar
- Piment d'Espelette (see Note)
- 1½ cups finely diced cantaloupe (½ pound)
- 1½ cups finely diced honeydew (½ pound)
- 1 small head of frisée, tender inner leaves only, chopped
- 1 tablespoon chopped tarragon

1. In a large saucepan, combine half of the sliced fennel with the leek, garlic, fennel seeds, coriander seeds, peppercorns, orange zest, orange juice, white wine, water and 2 teaspoons of kosher salt; bring to a boil. Simmer over low heat for 20 minutes. Let cool for 15 minutes.

BARBECUED SPICED SHRIMP WITH TOMATO SALAD

POACHED SHRIMP, MELON AND FRISÉE SALAD

2. Add the shrimp to the saucepan; cook over low heat until pink and curled, about 5 minutes. Remove from the heat and let the shrimp marinate in the warm liquid for 15 minutes. Using a slotted spoon, transfer the shrimp to a plate. Halve each shrimp lengthwise and refrigerate until cool. Strain the poaching liquid, reserving 1 cup.

3. In a small saucepan, boil the reserved poaching liquid over high heat until reduced to 2 tablespoons, 15 minutes. Transfer to a large bowl; whisk in the oil and vinegar. Season with salt and piment d'Espelette. Add the cantaloupe, honeydew, frisée, tarragon, shrimp and the remaining fennel. Season with salt and piment d'Espelette, toss and serve. —*Daniel Humm*

NOTE Piment d'Espelette, a smoky Basque chile powder, is available at specialty food stores.

WINE Full-bodied, rich Pinot Gris.

Shrimp-and-Vegetable Summer Rolls
ACTIVE: 40 MIN; TOTAL: 1 HR 15 MIN
8 FIRST-COURSE SERVINGS ●

- 2 cups shredded carrots
- 1 small red onion, thinly sliced
- ¾ cup plus 2 tablespoons unseasoned rice vinegar
- ½ cup sugar
- 2 garlic cloves, smashed
- 1 tablespoon Asian fish sauce

Sixteen 8-inch round rice papers

- 16 cilantro sprigs
- 1 head Boston lettuce, separated
- 1 pound cooked large shrimp, halved lengthwise
- 2 yellow bell peppers, cut into ¼-inch strips
- 3½ ounces bean thread vermicelli, soaked in hot water until pliable and drained well

1. In a bowl, toss the carrots and onion with ¼ cup plus 2 tablespoons of the vinegar and 2 tablespoons of the sugar. Let stand until the vegetables soften, 30 minutes. Drain.

2. In a glass bowl, mix the remaining vinegar and sugar with the garlic. Microwave at high power for about 30 seconds, until the sugar is dissolved. Stir in the fish sauce and set the dipping sauce aside to infuse for 30 minutes. Discard the garlic.

3. Meanwhile, soak 1 rice paper at a time in hot water until pliable, 10 seconds; transfer to a work surface. Set a cilantro sprig and lettuce leaf on the lower third of the rice paper and top with 3 shrimp halves. Top with some of the yellow pepper, vermicelli and pickled vegetables; roll tightly, folding in the sides. Repeat with the remaining ingredients. Halve the rolls and serve with the sauce. —*Melissa Rubel Jacobson*

WINE Light, fresh Pinot Grigio.

●HEALTHY ●MAKE AHEAD ●VEGETARIAN ●STAFF FAVORITE

shellfish

Chili Shrimp

TOTAL: 40 MIN
4 SERVINGS ●

2 pounds large shrimp, preferably head-on
2 tablespoons ketchup
2 tablespoons dry sherry
2 tablespoons Asian sweet chile sauce
2 tablespoons fresh lemon juice
2 tablespoons soy sauce
1 tablespoon sugar
3 tablespoons vegetable oil
2 medium jalapeños, seeded and minced
2 garlic cloves, minced
1 stalk of fresh lemongrass, tender inner white bulb only, very finely chopped
1 tablespoon minced fresh ginger
4 scallions, thinly sliced
¼ cup chopped cilantro
Steamed rice, for serving

1. Using scissors, cut down the back shell of each shrimp and remove the dark intestinal vein, leaving the shell intact. In a small bowl, combine the ketchup, sherry, chile sauce, lemon juice, soy sauce and sugar.
2. In a large skillet, heat 2 tablespoons of the vegetable oil. Add the deveined shrimp to the skillet and cook over high heat, turning once, until they start to curl and turn pale pink, about 2 minutes.

---

fast crab wraps

From chef Cathal Armstrong of Restaurant Eve in Alexandria, Virginia: Mix lump crab with mustard, mayonnaise and chopped scallion. Serve in lettuce leaves with extra-virgin olive oil and lemon juice.

---

3. Add the remaining 1 tablespoon of vegetable oil to the skillet with the minced jalapeños, garlic, lemongrass and ginger and cook, stirring, until fragrant, about 1 minute. Add the scallions and the ketchup mixture and stir-fry for 30 seconds. Stir in the cilantro. Spoon the shrimp onto plates and serve with the rice.
—*Rajat Parr*
WINE Vivid, lightly sweet Riesling.

Boiled Shrimp with Spicy Mayonnaise

TOTAL: 15 MIN
8 SERVINGS ●

2 very fresh organic egg yolks
1½ tablespoons Coleman's hot mustard powder
1 teaspoon fresh lemon juice
1 cup canola oil
Salt and freshly ground white pepper
1 tablespoon water
2 pounds medium shrimp, peeled and deveined

1. In a medium bowl, whisk together the egg yolks, mustard powder and lemon juice. Whisking constantly, slowly dribble in the canola oil. Season with salt and white pepper to taste. Whisk in the 1 tablespoon of water to thin out the mayonnaise if necessary.
2. Bring a large saucepan of water to a boil. Add the shrimp and boil until pink, about 3 minutes. Drain and let cool. Serve the shrimp with the spicy mayonnaise.
—*Eugenia Bone*
WINE Dry, light Champagne.

Red Wine–Braised Baby Octopus with Black Olives

ACTIVE: 1 HR; TOTAL: 1 HR 30 MIN
6 SERVINGS ●●
This octopus is gently simmered in a rich, robust red wine and tomato sauce until it's marvelously tender, then served on crunchy sourdough toasts.

3 tablespoons extra-virgin olive oil
1 large onion, cut into ½-inch dice
1 large carrot, cut into ½-inch dice
2 medium garlic cloves, very finely chopped
2 celery ribs, cut into ½-inch dice
¼ teaspoon crushed red pepper
1 bay leaf
One 14-ounce can chopped tomatoes
2 pounds baby octopus—cleaned, heads halved, tentacles quartered
Salt and freshly ground pepper
2 cups dry red wine, such as Syrah
1 cup pitted kalamata olives, rinsed
½ cup chopped parsley
6 slices of sourdough bread, toasted

1. In a medium enameled cast-iron casserole, heat 2 tablespoons of the oil. Add the onion, carrot, garlic, celery, crushed red pepper and bay leaf and cook over moderately high heat, stirring, until softened, about 8 minutes. Add the tomatoes and their juices and simmer for 2 minutes, until slightly reduced. Remove from the heat.
2. In a large skillet, heat 1½ teaspoons of the olive oil until shimmering. Add half of the octopus, season with salt and pepper and cook over high heat, stirring, until starting to brown, about 2 minutes. Scrape the octopus into the casserole. Repeat with the remaining 1½ teaspoons of olive oil and octopus. Add the red wine to the skillet and bring to a boil, scraping up the browned bits on the bottom. Pour the wine into the casserole.
3. Simmer the stew until the octopus is tender, 30 minutes. Add the olives and simmer for 5 minutes longer. Discard the bay leaf. Season the stew with salt and pepper and stir in the parsley. Set the sourdough toasts in shallow bowls, top with the octopus stew and serve immediately.
—*Emily Kaiser*
WINE Juicy, fresh Dolcetto.

Squid and Black-Eyed Pea Salad

ACTIVE: 20 MIN; TOTAL: 1 HR PLUS OVERNIGHT SOAKING

10 FIRST-COURSE SERVINGS ● ●

"Whenever you go to Spain, you always have beans," says chef-winemaker Gerald Hirigoyen, owner of the Basque restaurant Piperade in San Francisco and an F&W Best New Chef 1994. "And squid is everywhere in Basque country, where I grew up, and in California too." Hirigoyen combines earthy black-eyed peas (which are a kind of bean) and quickly boiled squid with red wine vinegar and fresh herbs to create a bright-flavored, satisfying first-course salad.

1½ cups dried black-eyed peas, soaked overnight and drained
Salt
1½ pounds cleaned squid— bodies cut into ½-inch rings, tentacles halved
¼ cup plus 2 tablespoons extra-virgin olive oil
¼ cup red wine vinegar
Freshly ground pepper
2 celery ribs, finely diced
¼ cup minced shallots
1 large tomato, finely diced
¼ cup finely chopped parsley
2 tablespoons chopped tarragon

1. In a large saucepan, cover the black-eyed peas with 2 inches of water and bring to a boil. Simmer over moderate heat until the peas are nearly tender, about 30 minutes. Season generously with salt and cook until tender, about 10 minutes longer. Drain the peas and let cool.

2. Bring a large saucepan of salted water to a boil and fill a large bowl with ice water. Add the squid to the boiling water and cook just until the pieces are firm, about 30 seconds. Drain and immediately transfer the squid to the ice water to cool thoroughly. Drain again and pat the squid dry with a clean towel.

3. In a large salad bowl, whisk the olive oil with the vinegar and season with salt and pepper. Add the squid, black-eyed peas, celery, shallots, tomato, parsley and tarragon. Toss the salad well and serve.
—Gerald Hirigoyen

MAKE AHEAD The dressed salad can be covered and refrigerated overnight. Toss the salad again just before serving.

WINE Fruity, light-bodied Beaujolais.

Crab, Apple and Watercress Salad with Walnut Vinaigrette

 TOTAL: 20 MIN
6 SERVINGS ● ●

Sweet-tasting lump crab is sold precooked, so it's perfect for a fast meal. F&W's Melissa Rubel Jacobson uses it here in a crunchy salad that gets a double dose of nutty flavor from walnuts and walnut oil.

2½ tablespoons white wine vinegar
1 small shallot, minced
2 teaspoons Dijon mustard
2 tablespoons walnut oil
2 tablespoons extra-virgin olive oil
Kosher salt and freshly ground pepper
2 bunches of watercress (about 14 ounces), thick stems discarded
1 pound jumbo lump crab, picked over and drained
2 celery ribs, thinly sliced
1 Granny Smith apple, cut into ½-inch dice
⅓ cup walnuts, coarsely chopped

1. In a bowl, whisk the vinegar with the shallot and mustard. Whisk in the walnut and olive oils and season with salt and pepper.

2. In a medium bowl, toss the watercress with 3 tablespoons of the dressing. In another medium bowl, gently toss the crab with the celery, apple, walnuts and the remaining dressing. Season with salt and pepper. Transfer the watercress to plates, top with the crab salad and serve.
—Melissa Rubel Jacobson

WINE Dry, fruity sparkling wine.

Steamed Clams in Verjus

  TOTAL: 30 MIN
4 SERVINGS ●

New Zealand chef Sara Simpson steams clams in verjus, a tart liquid pressed from unripe grapes; red vermouth would also add a wonderful zing.

¼ cup verjus or red vermouth
4 dozen littleneck clams, scrubbed
3 tablespoons extra-virgin olive oil
2 medium garlic cloves, very finely chopped
1 large shallot, very finely chopped
1 medium tomato, finely chopped
1 tablespoon chopped flat-leaf parsley
Salt and freshly ground black pepper

1. Preheat the oven to 300°. In a large, deep skillet, bring the verjus to a boil. Add the clams, cover and cook over high heat, shaking the pan occasionally. As the clams open, after about 4 minutes, transfer them to a deep, ovenproof platter. Discard any clams that do not open. Cover the platter with a clean damp kitchen towel and keep the clams warm in the oven. Reserve the clam cooking liquid in a bowl and wipe out the skillet.

2. Heat the olive oil in the skillet. Add the chopped garlic and shallot and cook over moderate heat, stirring, until the garlic and shallot are softened, about 4 minutes. Pour in the reserved clam cooking liquid, stopping before you reach the grit at the bottom. Boil over high heat until the liquid is reduced to 1 cup, about 5 minutes. Add the chopped tomato and parsley and season with salt and pepper. Pour the sauce over the clams and serve right away.
—Sara Simpson

SERVE WITH Crusty bread.

WINE Minerally, complex Sauvignon Blanc.

shellfish

Scallops with Grapefruit-Onion Salad

TOTAL: 25 MIN
8 FIRST-COURSE SERVINGS ●

Pickled pearl onions from a jar are usually relegated to cocktails, but in this ultra-simple recipe, F&W's Melissa Rubel Jacobson combines them with seared scallops and Ruby Red grapefruit.

4   Ruby Red grapefruits (about 2 pounds total)
3   tablespoons drained pickled cocktail onions
2   tablespoons parsley leaves
Freshly ground black pepper
24 sea scallops (about 2 pounds)
Kosher salt
1   tablespoon extra-virgin olive oil, plus more for drizzling

1. Using a very sharp paring knife, peel the grapefruits, carefully removing all of the bitter white pith that lies beneath the skin. Working over a bowl, carefully cut in between the membranes to release the grapefruit sections into the bowl. Discard all but 1 tablespoon of the grapefruit juice from the bowl (or put it to another use). Stir in the cocktail onions and parsley leaves and season with black pepper.
2. Pat the sea scallops dry with paper towels and season them all over with kosher salt. In a large nonstick skillet, heat the 1 tablespoon of olive oil until it is shimmering. Cook the scallops over moderately high heat, turning once, until they are browned and just cooked through, about 4 minutes total. Spoon the pickled-onion-and-grapefruit salad onto small plates and arrange the scallops around the salad. Drizzle each plate with a little olive oil and serve at once.
—*Melissa Rubel Jacobson*
MAKE AHEAD The grapefruit-onion salad can be prepared through Step 1, covered and refrigerated for up to 2 hours. Cook the scallops just before serving.
WINE Lively, tart Sauvignon Blanc.

Scallops with Chestnut Sauce and Crisp Sage

TOTAL: 40 MIN
4 FIRST-COURSE SERVINGS

2   tablespoons unsalted butter
1   thick slice of bacon (1 ounce), finely diced
1   medium leek, white and pale green parts only, coarsely chopped
2   tablespoons Cognac
1¼ cups chicken stock or low-sodium broth
1   cup vacuum-packed chestnuts
Salt and freshly ground pepper
2   tablespoons vegetable oil
8   large sea scallops (about 1 pound)
8   sage leaves

1. In a saucepan, melt 1 tablespoon of the butter. Add the bacon and cook over moderate heat until the fat has been rendered, about 4 minutes. Add the leek and cook, stirring occasionally, until softened, about 4 minutes. Add the Cognac and carefully ignite it. When the flames subside, add the chicken stock and chestnuts and bring to a boil. Simmer over moderate heat for 3 minutes. Transfer to a blender and puree. Return the chestnut sauce to the saucepan and season with salt and pepper.
2. In a large skillet, heat the vegetable oil. Season the scallops with salt and pepper. Add the sage leaves to the skillet and cook over moderately high heat, turning once, until crisp, about 1 minute. Using a slotted spoon, transfer the sage to a plate.
3. Add the scallops to the skillet and cook over high heat until starting to brown, about 1 minute. Reduce the heat to moderately high and cook the scallops until they're well glazed, about 1 minute. Turn the scallops and add the remaining 1 tablespoon of butter to the skillet. Continue cooking the scallops, basting with the butter, until browned and just cooked through, about 2 minutes longer.

4. Reheat the chestnut sauce and pour it into shallow bowls. Arrange the scallops in the sauce and garnish with the fried sage leaves. Serve right away. —*Rajat Parr*
MAKE AHEAD The chestnut sauce can be refrigerated overnight. Reheat gently.
WINE Dry, rich Champagne.

Clams with Pork and Golden Garlic

TOTAL: 30 MIN
4 SERVINGS ● ●

Ground pork and clams are a common combination in Chinese recipes. F&W's Marcia Kiesel sautés the two quickly with thin slivers of garlic, then adds black-bean chile sauce (available at some supermarkets and at Asian groceries) to create a fast, flavorful dish with deep, briny flavor and some heat.

3   tablespoons vegetable oil
4   large garlic cloves, very thinly sliced
¼ pound ground pork
½ cup dry white wine
40 littleneck clams, scrubbed
2   teaspoons Chinese black-bean chile sauce
4   scallions, thinly sliced
Rice, for serving

1. In a large skillet, heat the vegetable oil. Add the sliced garlic and cook over moderately low heat until golden brown, about 1 minute. With a slotted spoon, transfer the garlic to a plate.
2. Add the pork to the skillet and cook over high heat, breaking up the meat with a wooden spoon, until no pink remains, about 1 minute. Add the wine and clams; cover and cook until the clams open, about 3 minutes. As each clam opens, transfer it to a bowl. Stir the black-bean sauce into the juices in the skillet. Return the clams to the skillet along with the garlic and scallions and stir; serve with rice.
—*Marcia Kiesel*
WINE Fresh, fruity rosé.

CLAMS WITH PORK
AND GOLDEN GARLIC

SCALLOPS WITH
GRAPEFRUIT-ONION SALAD

shellfish

Chili Lobster

TOTAL: 1 HR

10 SERVINGS ●

To cut the prep here by 20 minutes, buy 1½ pounds of cooked shelled lobster meat instead of boiling the lobster yourself.

- 10 heads of baby bok choy
- Five 1½-pound live lobsters
- ¼ cup vegetable oil
- 6 garlic cloves, finely chopped
- 1 cup chicken stock or low-sodium broth
- ¾ cup ketchup
- 2 tablespoons *sambal oelek* (see Note)
- 1 large egg, lightly beaten
- Salt
- 1 small red bell pepper, cut into 1-inch-long strips

1. In a large pot of boiling water, cook the baby bok choy until it's bright green, about 1 minute. Using a slotted spoon, transfer to a large rimmed baking sheet and pat dry. Cover the baking sheet with foil.

2. Bring the pot of water back to a boil. Add the lobsters; cook until they're bright red all over, about 7 minutes. Transfer the lobsters to another large rimmed baking sheet and let cool slightly. Twist the tails off the bodies; crack the claws and knuckles and remove the meat. Using strong kitchen scissors, cut along the underside of the tail shells and remove the meat. Remove and discard the dark intestinal veins; cut the tails into 2-inch pieces. Arrange the lobster meat on the baking sheet, cover with a moistened kitchen towel and then cover tightly with foil.

3. Preheat the oven to 375°. In a medium skillet, heat the vegetable oil. Add the garlic and cook over moderately low heat until golden brown, about 4 minutes. Add the chicken stock, ketchup and *sambal oelek* and simmer over moderately high heat for 2 minutes. Add the egg and cook, stirring frequently, until the egg is fully incorporated and the sauce is thickened, about 30 seconds. Remove the sauce from the heat and season with salt, then transfer to a bowl.

4. Bake the covered lobster and bok choy for about 7 minutes, or until heated through. Mound the lobster meat on a large platter, arrange the bok choy alongside it and garnish with the red pepper strips. Serve at once, with the chile sauce. —Chris Yeo

NOTE *Sambal oelek*, a spicy Indonesian chile sauce, is available at Asian markets and specialty food stores.

MAKE AHEAD The boiled lobster and bok choy can be refrigerated overnight.

WINE Ripe, luxurious Chardonnay.

Seared Scallops with Pinot Gris Butter Sauce

ACTIVE: 25 MIN; TOTAL: 50 MIN

4 SERVINGS ●

- 2 tablespoons pine nuts
- 4 teaspoons extra-virgin olive oil
- 2 medium shallots, minced
- 2 cups Pinot Gris
- 2 thyme sprigs
- 1 cup fish stock
- 1 tablespoon heavy cream
- 1 stick unsalted butter, cut into ½-inch pieces and chilled
- 1 tablespoon minced chives
- Salt and freshly ground pepper
- 1 packed cup baby spinach
- 1 teaspoon lemon juice
- 2 tablespoons vegetable oil
- 16 large sea scallops
- ½ teaspoon Aleppo pepper flakes (optional)

1. In a skillet, toast the pine nuts over moderate heat until golden, 2 minutes; transfer to a plate to cool. Lightly crush the nuts.

2. In a medium saucepan, heat 1 teaspoon of the olive oil. Add the shallots and cook over moderate heat, stirring, until browned, 4 minutes. Add the wine and thyme; boil until reduced to ¼ cup, 15 minutes. Add the stock and boil until reduced to ¼ cup, about 9 minutes longer. Add the cream, bring to a boil and remove from the heat.

3. Strain the sauce into a saucepan. Whisk in the butter, 4 pieces at a time, until the sauce is thickened and smooth; set the pan over low heat as necessary to help melt the butter. Stir in the chives and season with salt and pepper. Remove from the heat.

4. In a medium bowl, toss the spinach with the lemon juice and the remaining olive oil; season with salt and pepper.

5. In the skillet, heat the vegetable oil. Season the scallops with salt and pepper, add to the skillet and cook over high heat, turning once, until browned but barely cooked through, 2 minutes per side. Transfer the scallops and spinach to plates. Garnish with the pine nuts and pepper flakes. Gently reheat the sauce, spoon on top and serve. —Hugh Acheson

WINE Full-bodied, rich Pinot Gris.

Grilled Scallops with Honeydew-Avocado Salsa

TOTAL: 30 MIN

4 SERVINGS ●

- Finely grated zest of 1 lime
- 2 tablespoons fresh lime juice
- 1 tablespoon extra-virgin olive oil, plus more for drizzling
- 1½ pounds honeydew melon, diced (2½ cups)
- 1 Hass avocado, diced
- Salt and freshly ground pepper
- 2 pounds large sea scallops

1. Light a grill. In a bowl, combine the lime zest and juice with the 1 tablespoon of oil. Gently fold in the diced honeydew and avocado; season with salt and pepper.

2. Drizzle the scallops with oil and season with salt and pepper. Grill over moderately high heat, turning once, until nicely charred and just cooked through, 3 to 4 minutes per side. Transfer the scallops to plates, spoon the salsa alongside and serve. —Marcia Kiesel

WINE Complex, aromatic Chenin Blanc.

CHILI LOBSTER

Spicy Lobster-Noodle Salad

TOTAL: 1 HR 15 MIN

10 SERVINGS ● ●

This cellophane-noodle salad, with creamy avocados, crunchy peanuts and a chile-honey dressing, is an excellent showcase for sweet Caribbean spiny lobsters, also known as rock lobsters. The recipe also works perfectly with easier-to-find Maine lobsters; they're more tender than spiny lobsters—and just as delicious.

- ¼ cup extra-virgin olive oil
- 4 large garlic cloves, very thinly sliced
- 2 large shallots, very thinly sliced

Salt
- 1 red bell pepper
- 1 fresh long red chile
- 3 tablespoons Asian fish sauce
- 3 tablespoons fresh lime juice, plus lime wedges for serving
- 2 tablespoons honey
- 1 tablespoon elderflower cordial (see Note)
- 1 teaspoon *sambal oelek* (see Note)
- ¼ teaspoon Asian sesame oil

Three 1½-pound live lobsters
One 3½-ounce package dried cellophane noodles

---

grilled bread and seafood

Stewed or steamed seafood is great over smoky grilled bread. Rub thick slices of day-old sourdough with a cut garlic clove, brush them with olive oil, grill both sides and serve at the bottom of the bowl.

- 2 large Hass avocados, cut into ½-inch chunks
- ¼ cup chopped salted roasted peanuts
- 2 tablespoons thinly sliced mint leaves
- 2 tablespoons thinly sliced cilantro leaves

1. Bring a large pot of water to a boil. In a small skillet, heat the olive oil. Add the garlic, shallots and ½ teaspoon of salt. Cook over moderately low heat, stirring occasionally, until the garlic and shallots are golden, about 7 minutes. Transfer to a medium bowl.

2. Roast the red bell pepper and fresh chile directly over a gas flame or under a pre-heated broiler, turning occasionally, until their skins are blistered and charred all over. Transfer to a plate and let cool. Peel the pepper and chile and discard the stems and seeds; cut into ¼-inch dice and transfer to the bowl with the shallot mixture. Add the fish sauce, lime juice, honey, elderflower cordial, *sambal oelek* and sesame oil and stir to combine. Season the chile-honey dressing with salt.

3. Add the lobsters to the boiling water headfirst and cook until bright red all over, about 6 minutes. Using tongs, transfer the cooked lobsters to a large rimmed baking sheet and let cool.

4. Crack the lobster claws and knuckles and remove the meat. Using scissors, cut along the underside of the tail shells and remove the meat. Remove and discard the dark intestinal veins from the tails. Cut the tails and claws into 1-inch chunks.

5. Bring a small saucepan of water to a boil. In a medium bowl, cover the cello-phane noodles with warm water and let stand until pliable, about 10 minutes. Drain the noodles. Using scissors, cut them into 3-inch lengths. Add the noodles to the saucepan and cook until al dente, about 1 minute. Drain the noodles and transfer to a large serving platter.

6. Scatter the lobster and avocados over the noodles. Drizzle with the chile-honey dressing. Garnish with the peanuts, mint and cilantro and serve the salad right away, with lime wedges.

—Jean-Georges Vongerichten

NOTE Elderflower cordial is a nonalcoholic drink sold at specialty food markets and online at chefswarehouse.com. *Sambal oelek,* an Indonesian chile sauce, is available at Asian markets and specialty shops.

MAKE AHEAD The cooked lobster meat and chile dressing can be refrigerated separately overnight.

WINE Fruity, low-oak Chardonnay.

Enchilado

ACTIVE: 25 MIN; TOTAL: 45 MIN

6 SERVINGS ●

Very different from the well-known Mexican enchilada, Cuban *enchilado* is a tomato-based seafood stew, typically made with shrimp and often served at dinner parties and on special occasions. The sauce, made with ketchup and tomato sauce, is sweet and tangy.

- ¼ cup plus 1 tablespoon extra-virgin olive oil
- 1 onion, finely chopped
- 2 garlic cloves, very finely chopped
- 1 medium green bell pepper, finely chopped

One 8-ounce can tomato sauce
One 4-ounce jar chopped pimientos with their juice
- ½ cup ketchup
- ½ cup dry white wine
- 1 tablespoon red wine vinegar
- 2 teaspoons Worcestershire sauce
- 1 bay leaf

Salt and freshly ground pepper
- 1½ pounds large shrimp, shelled and deveined
- 2 tablespoons chopped flat-leaf parsley

1. In a large saucepan, heat ¼ cup of the olive oil. Add the chopped onion, garlic and green bell pepper and cook over moderate heat, stirring occasionally, until softened, about 6 minutes. Add the tomato sauce, pimientos, ketchup, wine, vinegar, Worcestershire sauce and bay leaf and season with salt and pepper. Simmer the sauce over very low heat until it is thickened slightly, about 20 minutes.

2. In a large skillet, heat the remaining 1 tablespoon of olive oil until shimmering. Season the shrimp with salt and pepper and add them to the skillet. Cook over high heat, turning once, until the shrimp are lightly browned but not cooked through, about 3 minutes. Scrape the shrimp into the saucepan and simmer until they are pink and just cooked through, about 4 minutes longer. Discard the bay leaf. Transfer the stew to a serving bowl, garnish with the chopped parsley and serve. —*Lourdes Castro*

MAKE AHEAD The recipe can be prepared through Step 1 and refrigerated overnight. Rewarm before proceeding.

WINE Fresh, fruity rosé.

Italian Seafood Stew

photo, page 190

ACTIVE: 45 MIN; TOTAL: 1 HR 45 MIN

6 SERVINGS ● ●

In this luscious, tomato-rich seafood stew, New York chef Marco Canora cooks calamari slowly until it becomes supertender. While Canora sometimes varies the shellfish he uses here, he considers calamari essential to the success of the dish because it releases its liquid as it simmers, adding a huge amount of flavor to the sauce.

½ cup extra-virgin olive oil, plus more for drizzling
1 fennel bulb, cored and finely chopped
2 celery ribs, finely chopped
1 white onion, finely chopped
1 tablespoon dried oregano (preferably Sicilian)

Pinch of crushed red pepper
1½ pounds cleaned squid— bodies cut into ½-inch rings, tentacles halved
2 cups dry white wine
One 28-ounce can tomato puree
2 lemons—zest of one peeled in strips with a vegetable peeler, zest of the other finely grated
Salt and freshly ground black pepper
2 cups water
1 cup bottled clam broth
12 ounces mussels, scrubbed
12 ounces littleneck clams, scrubbed
12 ounces shelled and deveined large shrimp
12 ounces skinless striped bass fillet, cut into 2-by-1-inch pieces
2 tablespoons chopped parsley

1. In a very large, enameled cast-iron casserole or Dutch oven, heat the ½ cup of olive oil. Add the fennel, celery, onion, oregano and crushed red pepper and cook over moderate heat, stirring frequently, until the vegetables are softened, about 15 minutes. Add the squid and cook over moderately low heat for 15 minutes, stirring occasionally.

2. Stir in the wine and bring to a boil over moderately high heat. Cook until evaporated, about 20 minutes. Stir in the tomato puree and strips of lemon zest. Season with salt and pepper and cook over very low heat, stirring occasionally, until very thick, about 40 minutes.

3. Add the water and clam broth and bring to a boil. Remove and discard the lemon zest strips. Season the broth with salt and pepper. Add the mussels, clams and shrimp, cover and cook until most of the shells have opened, about 5 minutes. Add the striped bass and cook until opaque, about 2 minutes longer.

4. In a small bowl, combine the parsley with the grated lemon zest. Spoon the stew into deep bowls; sprinkle with the gremolata. Drizzle with oil; serve. —*Marco Canora*

SERVE WITH Garlic-rubbed toasts.
MAKE AHEAD The recipe can be prepared through Step 1 and refrigerated overnight. Reheat before proceeding.
WINE Fresh, minerally Vermentino.

Smoky Shellfish Stew with Herbs

TOTAL: 30 MIN
4 SERVINGS
1 tablespoon extra-virgin olive oil
1 pound large sea scallops (about 12)
Salt and freshly ground pepper
4 ounces thick-sliced bacon, diced
1 large shallot, minced
1 cup dry white wine
1 cup chicken stock or low-sodium broth
24 littleneck clams, scrubbed
½ cup frozen peas, thawed
2 tablespoons chopped mint
2 tablespoons chopped parsley
2 tablespoons snipped chives
Crusty bread, for serving

1. In a large skillet, heat the oil. Season the scallops with salt and pepper and cook over high heat, turning once, until browned, about 3 minutes total; transfer to a plate.

2. Add the bacon to the skillet and cook over high heat until browned, about 5 minutes. Add the shallot and cook, stirring, until softened, about 2 minutes. Add the wine and cook until reduced by half, scraping up any bits stuck to the pan, about 3 minutes. Add the stock and bring to a boil. Add the clams, cover and cook until most of them have opened, 5 to 8 minutes.

3. Stir in the peas, mint, parsley and chives. Add the scallops and any accumulated juices; cook until the scallops are heated through, about 2 minutes; discard any clams that don't open. Spoon the stew into bowls and serve with crusty bread. —*Seamus Mullen*

WINE Zippy, fresh Pinot Bianco.

GRILLED ASIAN EGGPLANT
WITH GINGER SAUCE (P. 224)

vegetables

Fantastic ideas for perfect
(and less-than-perfect) produce.

STIR-FRIED VEGETABLES WITH LEMONGRASS

VEGETABLE POTPIE WITH SWEET POTATO BISCUIT

Stir-Fried Vegetables with Lemongrass

 **TOTAL: 30 MIN**
4 SERVINGS ●

For this vegetarian Vietnamese stir-fry of asparagus, cauliflower and bell pepper, F&W's Marcia Kiesel substitutes soy sauce for the more traditional fish sauce. Lemongrass, basil and coconut milk make the dish fragrant and slightly sweet.

2 **large stalks of fresh lemongrass, tender inner white bulb only, thinly sliced**

3 **tablespoons vegetable oil**

3 **large shallots, thinly sliced**

1 **pound cauliflower, cut into 1-inch florets (4 cups)**

12 **asparagus spears, cut into 1-inch lengths**

½ **cup shredded carrots (about 2 medium)**

1 **red bell pepper, cut into 1-inch pieces**

¾ **cup water**

½ **cup unsweetened coconut milk**

3 **tablespoons soy sauce**

Freshly ground pepper

½ **cup chopped basil**

1 **cup mung bean sprouts**

Rice, for serving

1. In a mini food processor, finely chop the sliced lemongrass stalks.

2. In a large skillet, heat the vegetable oil. Add the lemongrass and shallots and stir-fry over high heat until the shallots are golden brown, about 2 minutes. Add the cauliflower, asparagus, carrots and red bell pepper along with ½ cup of the water; cover and cook over moderately high heat, stirring a few times, until the vegetables are crisp-tender, about 3 minutes. Stir in the coconut milk, soy sauce and the remaining ¼ cup of water and bring to a simmer. Remove from the heat and season with pepper. Stir in the basil and bean sprouts. Transfer the stir-fried vegetables to bowls and serve with rice.
—*Marcia Kiesel*

Vegetable Potpies with Sweet Potato Biscuits

ACTIVE: 45 MIN; TOTAL: 1 HR 45 MIN
8 SERVINGS ● ●

"At every gathering these days, there seems to be a vegetarian," says Renato Poliafito, co-owner of Baked in Brooklyn, New York, and Charleston, South Carolina. Stefania Rubicondo, the Brooklyn bakery's resident non-meat-eater, makes these individual pies with celery root, brussels sprouts and parsnips in a sage-infused sauce, then tops them with sweet potato biscuits.

1 pound parsnips, cut into
½-inch pieces
1 pound brussels sprouts,
halved lengthwise
½ pound pearl onions,
peeled and halved
(see Note)
1 medium head of cauliflower
(1½ pounds), cut into 1-inch
florets
1 large celery root (1½ pounds),
peeled and cut into ½-inch pieces
½ cup extra-virgin olive oil
20 sage leaves, plus 1 teaspoon
chopped sage
6 thyme sprigs, plus 1 teaspoon
chopped thyme
Salt and freshly ground pepper
2½ cups milk
¼ cup finely chopped
yellow onion
5 flat-leaf parsley sprigs
4 tablespoons unsalted butter
¼ cup all-purpose flour
½ cup heavy cream
Pinch of freshly grated nutmeg
Unbaked Sweet Potato Biscuits
(recipe follows)
1 large egg, beaten

1. Preheat the oven to 425°. In a large roasting pan, toss the parsnips, brussels sprouts, pearl onions, cauliflower florets and celery root with the olive oil. Add 6 of the sage leaves and 4 of the thyme sprigs and season with salt and pepper. Roast for about 30 minutes, stirring once or twice, until the vegetables are tender and lightly browned in spots. Discard the sage leaves and thyme sprigs. Lower the oven temperature to 375°.

2. Meanwhile, in a medium saucepan, combine the milk with the chopped onion, the parsley sprigs, 6 of the sage leaves and the remaining 2 thyme sprigs and bring to a simmer. Cover and let stand off the heat for 15 minutes. Strain the milk; rinse out the saucepan.

3. Melt the butter in the saucepan. Add the flour and cook over moderate heat, whisking, until golden, about 2 minutes. Add the strained milk to the saucepan, reduce the heat to low and whisk occasionally until very thick, about 10 minutes. Whisk in the chopped sage and thyme and the heavy cream and season with the nutmeg and salt and pepper. Fold the sauce into the roasted vegetables.

4. Spoon the vegetable mixture into eight large, 4-inch-wide ramekins and top with the unbaked Sweet Potato Biscuits. Brush the tops of the biscuits with the beaten egg and press the 8 remaining sage leaves onto the biscuits. Bake the potpies in the center of the oven for about 15 minutes, until the biscuits are golden and risen and the filling is bubbling. Let the potpies cool slightly; serve. —Stefania Rubicondo

NOTE To peel pearl onions, blanch them in a pot of boiling water for 1 minute. Let cool, then peel off the skins.

MAKE AHEAD The recipe can be prepared through Step 3 and refrigerated overnight. Return the vegetables to room temperature before baking.

SWEET POTATO BISCUITS
ACTIVE: 15 MIN; TOTAL: 1 HR 30 MIN
MAKES 8 BISCUITS ● ○

These flaky sweet potato biscuits make an attractive, dusky-orange topping for the vegetable potpies. Alternatively, they can be baked separately and served alongside roast meat and poultry or even eaten by themselves for breakfast.

One ½-pound sweet potato
1¾ cups all-purpose flour,
plus more for rolling
1 tablespoon light brown sugar
2½ teaspoons baking powder
½ teaspoon baking soda
1 teaspoon salt
7 tablespoons cold unsalted
butter, diced
⅓ cup buttermilk

1. Preheat the oven to 375°. Poke the sweet potato all over with a fork and bake for about 45 minutes, until tender. Peel and mash the potato. Set aside ¾ cup of the mashed potato and let cool completely; reserve the rest for another use. Raise the oven temperature to 425°.

2. In a food processor, pulse the 1¾ cups of flour with the brown sugar, baking powder, baking soda and salt. Add the butter and pulse until the mixture resembles coarse meal. Add the buttermilk and the ¾ cup of mashed sweet potato and pulse just until the dough comes together.

3. Turn the dough out onto a heavily floured work surface and knead 2 or 3 times, until smooth; the dough will be soft. Roll out the dough ¼ inch thick and cut out eight 4-inch rounds. Arrange the sweet potato biscuits on a parchment paper–lined baking sheet. Bake for about 15 minutes, until golden brown. Serve hot. —SR

MAKE AHEAD The unbaked Sweet Potato Biscuits can be frozen in a single layer on a baking sheet for up to 1 week.

Honey-and-Soy-Glazed Carrots
TOTAL: 35 MIN
8 SERVINGS ● ● ○ ●

Honey and soy turn these sautéed carrot sticks pleasingly sweet and salty, with a rich golden brown color around the edges.

2 pounds carrots, peeled and
cut into 2-by-½-inch sticks
2 tablespoons unsalted butter
2 tablespoons soy sauce
1½ tablespoons honey

1. Bring a large saucepan of salted water to a boil. Add the carrots and cook until tender, about 8 minutes. Drain.

2. In a large skillet, melt the butter. Stir in the carrots and soy sauce and cook over high heat until the carrots are browned in spots, 2 minutes. Stir in the honey and cook until the carrots are glazed, 2 minutes longer. Transfer to a platter; serve. —Peter Ting

vegetables

Pickled-Vegetable Salad with Soft-Boiled Eggs

TOTAL: 1 HR

4 SERVINGS ● ●

- 4 baby or small red beets, peeled and thinly sliced (see Note)
- 4 baby or small golden beets, peeled and thinly sliced
- 4 baby or small white turnips, peeled and thinly sliced
- 8 small radishes, thinly sliced
- 2 celery ribs, peeled and thinly sliced crosswise
- 1 fennel bulb—halved, cored and thinly sliced
- 3 tablespoons white balsamic vinegar
- 3 tablespoons extra-virgin olive oil

Salt and freshly ground pepper

- 4 large eggs

Four ½-inch-thick baguette slices, toasted

Fleur de sel, for sprinkling

1. Arrange the sliced vegetables in separate piles on 2 large rimmed baking sheets. In a small bowl, whisk the vinegar with the olive oil and season with salt and pepper. Drizzle the dressing over the vegetables and toss each pile separately. Let stand for at least 15 minutes or up to 1 hour.

2. Meanwhile, bring a medium saucepan of water to a boil. Carefully lower the eggs into the saucepan and reduce the heat to moderate. Simmer the eggs for 6 minutes. Pour off the hot water and gently shake the eggs in the pan to crack the shells. Fill the pan with cold water and let stand for 1 minute. Carefully peel the eggs. Reheat the peeled eggs for 2 minutes in 2 inches of simmering water. Drain and pat dry, then halve the eggs.

3. Arrange the vegetables on plates and top with the toasts and the soft-boiled eggs. Sprinkle the eggs and salads with fleur de sel and serve. —Barbara Lynch

NOTE Use a mandoline to cut the vegetables into thin slices.

Luxe Bubble and Squeak

TOTAL: 1 HR 30 MIN

8 SERVINGS ● ●

Traditionally made in England with mashed vegetables left over from a Sunday roast (here shaped into cakes and pan-fried), bubble and squeak allegedly gets its name from the sound the ingredients make in the skillet as they cook.

- 1 pound large red potatoes, peeled and cut into 2-inch chunks
- 4 medium turnips, peeled and quartered
- 1 small green cabbage, cored and quartered
- 1 pound brussels sprouts, trimmed and halved
- 2 large leeks, halved lengthwise
- 1½ tablespoons Worcestershire sauce
- ½ teaspoon celery seeds

Salt and freshly ground pepper

- ¼ cup vegetable oil, plus more for frying
- 4 tablespoons unsalted butter
- 1 pound chanterelle or cremini mushrooms, halved

All-purpose flour, for dusting

- 8 large eggs

1. In a large pot of simmering salted water, cook the potatoes and turnips until tender, about 15 minutes. Using a slotted spoon, transfer to a large bowl and mash. Add the cabbage, brussels sprouts and leeks to the pot; simmer until tender. Drain and chop. Add to the potato mixture with the Worcestershire and celery seeds; toss. Season with salt and pepper.

2. In a nonstick skillet, brown half of the vegetable mash in 2 tablespoons of the oil over high heat, stirring, 10 minutes; transfer to a baking sheet. Repeat with the remaining vegetables and 2 tablespoons of oil.

3. In the same skillet, melt the butter. Add the mushrooms and season with salt and pepper. Cover and cook over moderately low heat until tender, 8 minutes.

4. Form the mash into 16 patties and flour them; fry in the skillet in ¼ inch of oil over moderately high heat, turning once, until browned, 6 minutes. Transfer to plates.

5. Wipe out the skillet. Heat a thin layer of oil, add the eggs and cook until over-easy. Top the patties with the eggs, garnish with the mushrooms and serve. —Mark Hix

WINE Juicy, fresh Dolcetto.

Root-Vegetable Gratin

ACTIVE: 25 MIN; TOTAL: 2 HR 15 MIN

8 SERVINGS ● ● ●

- 2 large sweet potatoes, peeled
- 1 butternut squash neck (2¼ pounds) from a large butternut squash, peeled
- 1 medium rutabaga (2 pounds), peeled and halved lengthwise

Kosher salt and freshly ground pepper

- ½ cup low-sodium chicken broth
- ¼ cup heavy cream
- ¾ cup panko bread crumbs
- 1½ tablespoons extra-virgin olive oil

1. Preheat the oven to 375°. Using a mandoline, slice the potatoes and squash lengthwise ⅛ inch thick. Slice the rutabaga crosswise ⅛ inch thick.

2. Spray an 8-by-12-inch glass baking dish with cooking spray. Arrange half of the potatoes in the dish, overlapping them slightly; season with salt and pepper. Top with half of the rutabaga and the squash, seasoning each layer. Repeat the layering. Pour the broth over and around the vegetables.

3. Cover tightly with foil and bake for 1 hour, until the vegetables are almost tender when pierced. Remove the foil and pour the cream over the gratin. Bake for about 30 minutes longer, until the liquid has thickened.

4. Preheat the broiler. Mix the panko with the oil; season with salt and pepper; sprinkle over the gratin. Broil 3 inches from the heat for 2 minutes, until golden, rotating for even browning. Let stand for 10 minutes, then serve. —Melissa Rubel Jacobson

WINE Fruity, soft Chenin Blanc.

Spicy Brussels Sprouts with Mint

TOTAL: 25 MIN
4 TO 6 SERVINGS ● ●

The sweet-and-salty vinaigrette on these sprouts, bolstered by herbs and chiles, is a staple at David Chang's Manhattan restaurant Momofuku Ssäm Bar. The key to the dish is to almost burn the brussels sprouts; the charred flavor is irresistible.

2 tablespoons vegetable oil
½ cup Rice Krispies or other puffed rice cereal
¼ teaspoon *togarashi* (see Note on p. 26) or cayenne pepper
Kosher salt
¼ cup Asian fish sauce
2 tablespoons water
2 tablespoons sugar
1 tablespoon rice vinegar
1 tablespoon fresh lime juice
1 small garlic clove, minced
1 small red chile, minced
¼ cup chopped cilantro
2 tablespoons chopped mint
4 cups roasted or boiled brussels sprouts (about 2 pounds), halved lengthwise

1. In a large skillet, heat 1 tablespoon of the oil until shimmering. Add the Rice Krispies and *togarashi* and cook over high heat, stirring, until browned, about 30 seconds. Season with salt. Transfer to a plate and wipe out the skillet.

2. In a small bowl, combine the fish sauce, water, sugar, rice vinegar, lime juice, garlic and chile and stir until the sugar is dissolved. Add the cilantro and mint.

3. Add the remaining 1 tablespoon of oil to the skillet and heat until nearly smoking. Add the brussels sprouts; cook over high heat, stirring, until charred in spots and heated through, about 5 minutes. Transfer to a bowl and toss with the vinaigrette. Just before serving, sprinkle the Rice Krispies on top and serve right away.
—*David Chang*

Warm Spaghetti-Squash Salad

TOTAL: 40 MIN
8 SERVINGS ● ● ●

Mild spaghetti squash is delicious with potent ingredients like the olives and feta in this lemony salad, which makes a wonderful starter or side dish.

One 4-pound spaghetti squash, halved lengthwise and seeds scraped
1 cup sliced almonds (3 ounces)
½ cup chopped pitted green olives, such as Cerignola
½ cup thinly sliced scallion whites
½ teaspoon finely grated lemon zest
3 tablespoons fresh lemon juice
¼ cup plus 2 tablespoons canola oil
2 ounces Greek feta cheese, crumbled (¼ cup)
Kosher salt and freshly ground white pepper

1. Preheat the oven to 350°. Bring a large pot of water to a boil. Add the spaghetti squash and cook until it is al dente, about 12 minutes; drain. Place the spaghetti squash halves cut side down on a rack and let cool for 15 minutes.

2. Meanwhile, spread the sliced almonds on a pie plate and toast them in the oven for about 7 minutes, until lightly golden. In a mini food processor, combine the chopped olives with the sliced scallions, lemon zest, lemon juice and canola oil and pulse until finely chopped.

3. Working over a medium bowl and using a fork, scrape the cooked spaghetti squash into the bowl, separating the strands. Add the dressing along with the crumbled feta and toasted almonds and season with salt and white pepper. Toss the ingredients well and serve the squash salad warm.
—*Grace Parisi*

Braised Romaine with Toasted Almonds and Moscatel Syrup

TOTAL: 35 MIN
10 SERVINGS ●

Romaine hearts have a nice crunch—even when they're cooked. San Francisco chef-winemaker Gerald Hirigoyen creates a dressing for them with lightly sweet Moscatel vinegar (made from Moscatel grapes) that's reduced to a honeyed syrup; white balsamic is a less expensive substitute.

2 ounces almonds, chopped
¼ cup extra-virgin olive oil
2 large shallots, thinly sliced
2 large garlic cloves, thinly sliced
2 tablespoons unsalted butter
5 large romaine lettuce hearts, halved lengthwise
Salt and freshly ground pepper
1 cup chicken stock
¼ cup plus 2 tablespoons Moscatel vinegar or white balsamic vinegar
½ cup cilantro leaves

1. Preheat the oven to 375°. Spread the almonds on a pie plate and toast for about 7 minutes, until golden.

2. In a skillet, heat 2 tablespoons of the olive oil. Add the sliced shallots and garlic. Cook over moderate heat, stirring, until lightly browned; scrape into a large roasting pan. Add the butter and the remaining 2 tablespoons of olive oil to the skillet. Add the halved romaine hearts, cut side down, and cook over high heat until browned. Transfer the romaine to the roasting pan, cut side up; season with salt and pepper. Add the chicken stock to the skillet and bring to a boil; pour over the romaine. Cover the roasting pan with foil, transfer to the oven and braise for 10 minutes, until the romaine is crisp-tender. Transfer the lettuce to a platter and drizzle with some of the braising liquid.

3. In a skillet, boil the vinegar until reduced by half. Drizzle over the romaine, garnish with the almonds and cilantro and serve.
—*Gerald Hirigoyen*

roasting vegetables

F&W's **Melissa Rubel Jacobson** *roasts hearty winter vegetables until they're well-browned to bring out their sweet, earthy flavors. Creative additions like pecans and pomegranate seeds make these recipes special enough for the holiday table.*

Maple-Ginger-Roasted Vegetables with Pecans

ACTIVE: 30 MIN; TOTAL: 1 HR 30 MIN

12 SERVINGS ● ● ● ●

1½ cups pecans

4 medium carrots (¾ pound), peeled and sliced ¼ inch thick on the bias

2 large parsnips (1 pound), peeled and sliced ¼ inch thick on the bias

1 medium head of cauliflower (2½ pounds), cut into 1-inch florets

1 small butternut squash (2 pounds)—peeled, seeded and cut into 1-inch dice

1 pound brussels sprouts, halved

½ cup extra-virgin olive oil

¼ teaspoon freshly grated nutmeg

Kosher salt and freshly ground black pepper

2 tablespoons minced fresh ginger

⅓ cup pure maple syrup

1. Preheat the oven to 425°. Spread the pecans in a pie plate and toast until fragrant, about 6 minutes. Let cool.

2. In a large bowl, toss the carrots, parsnips, cauliflower, squash and brussels sprouts with the olive oil and nutmeg and season generously with salt and black pepper. Spread the vegetables on 2 large rimmed baking sheets and roast for 30 minutes, until the vegetables begin to brown. Scatter the pecans and ginger over the vegetables and drizzle with the maple syrup; toss well. Continue to roast the vegetables for 25 minutes longer, until they are tender and golden. Scrape the vegetables into a bowl and serve hot or at room temperature.

MAKE AHEAD The roasted vegetables can be kept at room temperature for up to 2 hours before serving.

TWO GREAT VARIATIONS

---

1 Spiced Vegetables with Pomegranate

Omit the pecans, ginger, syrup and nutmeg. Toss the vegetables with the olive oil, 1½ teaspoons smoked paprika, 1½ teaspoons cumin, ½ teaspoon coriander and ¼ teaspoon cayenne. Roast for 55 minutes, tossing halfway through. Toss the roasted vegetables with 1½ cups crumbled Mexican *cotija* or feta cheese and 1 cup pomegranate seeds before serving.

2 Roasted Vegetables with Fresh Herbs

Omit the pecans, ginger, syrup and nutmeg. Toss the vegetables with the olive oil and 10 sage leaves, 5 thyme sprigs and six 2-inch pieces of rosemary sprigs. Roast the vegetables on the baking sheets for about 55 minutes, tossing once halfway through, until they are tender and golden. Serve the roasted vegetables hot or at room temperature.

vegetables

Slow-Roasted Sweet Onions with "Licorice" Powder

ACTIVE: 30 MIN; TOTAL: 6 HR 30 MIN

12 SERVINGS ● ●

One of superchef Michel Bras's favorite garnishes is a sweet-savory combination of ground almonds, dehydrated olives and demerara sugar (a coarse, raw cane sugar with a subtle molasses flavor); the taste reminds him of licorice. Here it serves as a topping for buttery-soft, slow-roasted whole onions.

12 large sweet onions

½ cup oil-cured black olives, such as Thassos, pitted and chopped

½ cup whole blanched almonds, chopped

¼ cup demerara sugar

¼ cup poultry or veal demiglace (see Note)

¼ cup plus 2 tablespoons vegetable oil, such as grapeseed

3½ tablespoons red wine vinegar

Salt

1. Preheat the oven to 325°. Peel off the outer layers of the onions until each one is about 3 inches in diameter. Trim the root ends so the onions stand upright. Arrange the onions on a large rimmed baking sheet and cover with foil. Bake for about 4 hours, until they are partially softened.

2. Remove the foil and bake the onions in the upper third of the oven for 2 hours longer, rotating them occasionally, until they are very tender and richly browned outside. If the onions start to pop out of their skins, push them back in.

3. Meanwhile, spread the chopped olives on a microwave-safe plate. Microwave at high power for 12 minutes, until the olives are dehydrated but still plump; transfer to a food processor and pulse until finely chopped. Transfer the olives to a medium bowl and wipe out the food processor.

4. Pulse the almonds in the food processor until finely ground; transfer to a rimmed baking sheet and toss with the demerara

sugar. Bake in the same oven as the onions for about 6 minutes, stirring a few times, until golden and toasted. Let cool. Add the almonds to the olives and toss well.

5. In a saucepan, bring the demiglace to a boil. Transfer to a blender. Add the oil and vinegar and blend well. Season with salt.

6. Using a serrated knife, cut off the top fourth of each onion. Transfer the onions to plates. Spoon the vinaigrette on top and garnish with the almond-olive mixture. Serve right away. —*Michel Bras*

NOTE Demiglaces are available at specialty shops and dartagnan.com.

Roasted Cipollini Onions with Sherry Vinegar

ACTIVE: 30 MIN; TOTAL: 1 HR

4 SERVINGS ● ● ●

Roasted and glazed in sherry vinegar to bring out their natural sweetness, squat Italian cipollini onions are the perfect accompaniment to a thick steak. To make this simple dish more quickly, look for pre-peeled cipollini in the produce section of specialty food shops.

1½ pounds cipollini onions

¼ cup extra-virgin olive oil

1 tablespoon thyme leaves

1 teaspoon sugar

¼ cup plus 2 tablespoons sherry vinegar

Salt and freshly ground pepper

1. Preheat the oven to 425°. In a large pot of boiling, salted water, cook the cipollini until just tender, about 3 minutes. Drain and cool under cold running water. Trim and peel the onions and pat dry.

2. Transfer the onions to a large ovenproof skillet and stir in the oil, thyme, sugar and ¼ cup of the vinegar. Bring to a simmer over moderate heat. Cover the skillet with foil and roast the onions in the upper third of the oven for about 20 minutes, until soft. Remove the foil and roast the onions for about 10 minutes, basting a few times with the juices, until lightly glazed.

3. Transfer the skillet to the stove. Add the remaining 2 tablespoons of sherry vinegar and stir over moderate heat until the onions are richly glazed, about 2 minutes. Season with salt and plenty of pepper and serve. —*Matt Molina*

MAKE AHEAD The glazed onions can be refrigerated overnight. Reheat gently.

Leek Salad with Walnuts and Tomme de Brebis

TOTAL: 30 MIN

4 SERVINGS ● ● ● ●

Chef Armand Arnal of La Chassagnette, outside the southern French city of Arles, heightens the flavor of this salad with fresh toasted walnuts and shavings of the firm farmstead sheep's-milk cheese Tomme de Brebis.

4 medium leeks, halved lengthwise

1 cup walnuts

3 tablespoons extra-virgin olive oil

3 tablespoons red wine vinegar

Salt and freshly ground pepper

3 tablespoons very finely chopped chives

1 ounce firm sheep's-milk cheese, such as Tomme de Brebis, shaved with a vegetable peeler

1. Preheat the oven to 350°. Bring a large saucepan of salted water to a boil. Add the leek halves and simmer over moderately high heat until tender, 10 minutes. Drain the leeks and pat dry.

2. Spread the walnuts in a pie plate and bake for about 8 minutes, until golden brown. Let cool and coarsely chop.

3. In a small bowl, mix the olive oil with the red wine vinegar and season with salt and pepper. Arrange the leeks on a serving platter, cut side up. Drizzle with the vinaigrette and garnish with the chopped toasted walnuts, chopped chives and shaved cheese. Serve at room temperature. —*Armand Arnal*

WINE Light, crisp white Burgundy.

Broccoli à la Catalan

TOTAL: 45 MIN
4 SERVINGS ● ●

Napa chef Jeremy Fox combines broccoli and bell peppers in this hearty, Spanish-inspired salad studded with pine nuts and golden raisins.

- 4 red bell peppers
- 1 tablespoon pine nuts
- 1 tablespoon golden raisins
- 2 teaspoons sherry vinegar
- 1 tablespoon finely shredded mint leaves

Salt and freshly ground pepper

- 2 cups broccoli florets in ¾-inch pieces (from 1 bunch)
- 1 tablespoon extra-virgin olive oil

1. Preheat the oven to 450°. Arrange the bell peppers on a baking sheet and roast, turning once, until charred in spots and tender, about 25 minutes. Transfer the peppers to a bowl, cover with plastic wrap and let cool slightly.

2. Meanwhile, spread the pine nuts on a pie plate and toast just until golden, about 2 minutes. In a microwave-safe bowl, combine the raisins with 1 teaspoon of the vinegar and 2 tablespoons of water and microwave on high power for 30 seconds, just until the raisins are plump. Let cool, then drain the raisins.

3. Peel, seed and core the peppers, then cut into thin strips. Return the peppers to the bowl, stir in the mint and season with salt and pepper.

4. In a saucepan fitted with a steamer basket, bring 1 inch of water to a boil. Add the broccoli, cover and steam until crisp-tender, about 4 minutes; transfer to a bowl. Add the olive oil and the remaining 1 teaspoon of vinegar and toss. Stir in the raisins and nuts and season with salt and pepper.

5. Spread the peppers on a platter and top with the broccoli salad; serve right away.
—*Jeremy Fox*

SERVE WITH Crusty bread.

Broccoli Rabe with Black Olives and Lemon Zest

TOTAL: 30 MIN
4 SERVINGS ● ● ●

Two 1-pound bunches of broccoli rabe, thick stems discarded

- 2 tablespoons extra-virgin olive oil, plus more for drizzling
- 6 garlic cloves, minced
- ½ teaspoon crushed red pepper
- ½ cup pitted oil-cured black olives, chopped
- 1 teaspoon finely grated lemon zest

Salt

- 2 tablespoons freshly grated Parmigiano-Reggiano cheese

1. Cook the broccoli rabe in a large pot of boiling water until it is bright green, about 1 minute. Drain the rabe, reserving ½ cup of the cooking water.

2. In a large skillet, heat the 2 tablespoons of oil. Add the garlic and crushed red pepper and cook over moderately low heat until fragrant, about 1 minute. Add the broccoli rabe and the reserved cooking water, cover and simmer over moderately low heat until tender, about 10 minutes. Stir in the olives and lemon zest and season with salt. Transfer to a serving dish and drizzle with oil. Sprinkle with the cheese and serve.
—*Eugenia Bone*

Caponata with Kalamata Olives and Asiago Cheese

TOTAL: 1 HR 10 MIN
6 TO 8 SERVINGS ● ● ●

- ½ cup balsamic vinegar
- 1 tablespoon sugar
- 5 tablespoons extra-virgin olive oil
- 2 large eggplants (1½ pounds), cut into 1-inch dice

Salt and freshly ground pepper

- 2 medium zucchini (1 pound), cut into 1-inch dice
- 2 yellow squash (1 pound), cut into 1-inch dice
- 3 garlic cloves, thinly sliced
- 2 large celery ribs, peeled and cut into ½-inch dice
- 1 medium onion, cut into ½-inch dice
- 1 red bell pepper, cut into ½-inch dice

One 16-ounce can plum tomatoes, drained and chopped

- 1 cup pitted kalamata olives
- 2 tablespoons chopped parsley
- 2 tablespoons chopped oregano

One 3-ounce piece aged Asiago cheese, shaved into strips with a vegetable peeler (about ¾ cup)

Baguette slices, for serving

1. In a small saucepan, combine the vinegar with the sugar and boil over moderately high heat until reduced to 3 tablespoons, about 5 minutes. Let cool.

2. In a large nonstick skillet, heat 3 tablespoons of the olive oil until shimmering. Add the eggplant, season with salt and pepper and cook over moderately high heat, stirring, for 2 minutes. Reduce the heat to low and cook, stirring occasionally, until the eggplant is tender, 10 minutes. Transfer to a large bowl. Wipe out the skillet.

3. Add the remaining 2 tablespoons of oil to the skillet and heat until shimmering. Add the zucchini and yellow squash, season with salt and pepper and cook over moderate heat, stirring occasionally, until tender, about 7 minutes. Using a slotted spoon, transfer to the bowl with the eggplant.

4. Add the garlic, celery and onion to the skillet and cook over moderate heat, stirring occasionally, until softened slightly, about 5 minutes. Add the red bell pepper and cook until all of the vegetables are tender, about 4 minutes longer. Transfer to the bowl with the eggplant and squash.

5. Add the tomatoes, olives, parsley, oregano and balsamic syrup to the bowl and fold gently. Season the caponata with salt and pepper. Transfer to a clean bowl. Garnish with the Asiago cheese and serve with the baguette slices. —*Andres Barrera*

CAPONATA WITH KALAMATA OLIVES AND ASIAGO CHEESE   PAN-ROASTED CAULIFLOWER WITH PINE NUTS AND RAISINS

Pan-Roasted Cauliflower with Pine Nuts and Raisins

ACTIVE: 25 MIN; TOTAL: 1 HR 30 MIN
4 SERVINGS ● ● ○ ●

Master cook Paula Wolfert learned this recipe from the late Armenian cookbook author Arto Der Haroutunian. Cauliflower is caramelized with sugar on the stove, then baked with eastern Mediterranean ingredients: chopped tomatoes, plumped raisins and Marash red pepper flakes. Wolfert likes to cook with Spanish *cazuelas* (clay pots), but you can use any kind of flame-resistant pot or ovenproof skillet here.

- 2 tablespoons raisins (not golden)
- ¼ cup extra-virgin olive oil
- 1 head of cauliflower, cut into florets (4 cups)
- 1 teaspoon sugar
- 2 cups tomatoes—drained, peeled, seeded and chopped
- Pinch of crushed red pepper, preferably Marash (see Note)
- Salt and freshly ground black pepper
- 2 tablespoons pine nuts
- 1 garlic clove, finely chopped
- 2 tablespoons chopped parsley leaves
- 1½ tablespoons freshly squeezed lemon juice

1. Preheat the oven to 350°. In a small bowl, cover the raisins with water; let stand until softened, about 10 minutes. Drain.
2. Meanwhile, in a 10- to 12-inch *cazuela* or ovenproof skillet, heat the olive oil. Add the cauliflower florets and sugar and cook over moderately low heat, stirring occasionally, until the cauliflower starts to soften, about 10 minutes. Raise the heat to moderate and cook until the cauliflower is lightly browned, about 5 minutes longer.

Stir in the chopped tomatoes and crushed red pepper, season with salt and black pepper and cook until the tomatoes have begun to soften, about 5 minutes.
3. Add the raisins to the cauliflower along with ¼ cup hot water, the pine nuts and chopped garlic. Transfer the *cazuela* to the oven and bake the cauliflower for about 30 minutes, until it is very tender. Stir in the parsley and lemon juice and let stand at room temperature for 30 minutes. Serve the cauliflower warm.
—*Paula Wolfert*

NOTE Mild, earthy Marash red pepper flakes from Turkey are sold at Middle Eastern markets and online at vannsspices.com and zingermans.com.

MAKE AHEAD The cooked cauliflower can stand at room temperature for up to 4 hours. Rewarm the cauliflower in a 350° oven before serving.

vegetables

Parsley Salad with Pine Nuts and Lemon-Tahini Dressing

 TOTAL: 20 MIN
4 SERVINGS ● ● ●

Tahini, the creamy Middle Eastern sesame-seed paste, is the ingenious base for the dressing on this bold-flavored salad. The dressing would be terrific with any number of peppery greens, like escarole, watercress or celery leaves.

- ¼ cup pine nuts
- ¼ cup tahini paste, at room temperature
- 1½ tablespoons freshly squeezed lemon juice
- 1 small garlic clove, very finely chopped
- 2 tablespoons water
- Salt and freshly ground pepper
- 4 cups fresh flat-leaf parsley leaves, thick stems discarded (¾ pound)
- 4 scallions, thinly sliced crosswise

1. In a small skillet, toast the pine nuts over moderate heat, shaking the skillet occasionally, until the pine nuts are fragrant and golden brown, about 4 minutes. Transfer them to a plate and let cool.

---

fried shallots

Crisp and sweet, fried shallots are a perfect garnish for everything from steamed green beans to creamed spinach. To make them, use chef Chris Yeo's technique: In a small skillet, heat 2 inches of oil to 350°. Add shallot slices and fry until browned; transfer to paper towels to drain. Fried shallots can be kept at room temperature for up to 4 hours. Scatter them over dishes just before serving.

---

2. In a small bowl, blend the tahini with the lemon juice and finely chopped garlic. Stir in the water and season the tahini dressing with salt and pepper.
3. In a medium bowl, toss the parsley with the scallions and pine nuts. Add the tahini dressing and toss well. Transfer the salad to a serving bowl or plates and serve.
—*Andres Barrera*

Oven-Roasted Cauliflower Florets

 **ACTIVE: 10 MIN; TOTAL: 40 MIN**
4 SERVINGS ● ● ●

- One 2½-pound cauliflower, cut into 2-inch florets
- ⅓ cup extra-virgin olive oil
- Salt and freshly ground pepper
- 4 lemon wedges, for serving

Preheat the oven to 400°. On a large rimmed baking sheet, drizzle the cauliflower florets with the olive oil. Season them with salt and pepper and toss well. Roast for about 30 minutes, stirring occasionally, until the cauliflower is tender and golden brown. Transfer to plates, garnish with the lemon wedges and serve hot or at room temperature. —*Andres Barrera*
MAKE AHEAD The roasted cauliflower florets can stand at room temperature for up to 4 hours. Rewarm the cauliflower in a 350° oven before serving, if desired.

Stewed Okra and Tomatoes

 TOTAL: 25 MIN
4 SERVINGS ● ● ● ●

Cooking whole cumin seeds, turmeric and chile powder in oil brings out the spices' depth of flavor and adds complexity to this simple stewed okra-and-tomato dish.

- 2 tablespoons vegetable oil
- 2 garlic cloves, minced
- 1 small red onion, thinly sliced
- 1 teaspoon pure chile powder, such as ancho
- Pinch of cayenne pepper
- 1 teaspoon cumin seeds

- 1 teaspoon turmeric
- 1 pound okra, stemmed and sliced ½ inch thick
- 2 medium tomatoes, coarsely chopped
- ½ cup water
- Salt

1. In a medium skillet, heat the vegetable oil. Add the garlic and red onion and cook over moderate heat, stirring occasionally, until fragrant, about 3 minutes. Add the chile powder, cayenne, cumin seeds and turmeric and cook, stirring constantly, until fragrant, about 2 minutes.
2. Add the okra and cook for 2 minutes, tossing. Add the chopped tomatoes and cook over high heat until they release their juices, about 1 minute. Add the water, cover and cook, stirring occasionally, until the okra is just tender, about 5 minutes. Season with salt and serve.
—*Peggy Markel*
SERVE WITH Steamed basmati rice.
MAKE AHEAD The Stewed Okra and Tomatoes can be covered and refrigerated overnight. Reheat gently before serving.

Spicy Fried Okra with Crispy Shallots

 TOTAL: 30 MIN
10 SERVINGS ● ●

Okra is common in Singaporean cooking. At Straits Atlanta, chef Chris Yeo sautés the okra pods in hot oil until they're browned and crisp, then stir-fries them with chile sauce and pungent dried shrimp (widely available at Asian markets).

- Vegetable oil, for deep-frying
- 2 tablespoons dried shrimp
- 2 large shallots, thinly sliced
- 2 pounds okra, sliced diagonally ½ inch thick
- 3 tablespoons *sambal oelek* (see Note on p. 206)
- Salt
- ½ small red bell pepper, thinly sliced

PARSLEY SALAD WITH PINE NUTS   STEWED OKRA AND TOMATOES

1. In a large saucepan, heat 2 inches of vegetable oil to 350°. In a bowl, cover the dried shrimp with hot water. Let soak for 10 minutes. Drain and chop the shrimp.

2. Add the shallots to the oil and cook until browned and crisp, about 2 minutes. Using a slotted spoon, transfer to a plate.

3. Reheat the oil to 350°. Set a large rack over a baking sheet near the stove. Add the okra to the hot oil and fry until softened and bright green, about 1 minute. Using a slotted spoon, transfer the okra to the large rack.

4. Heat a large skillet. Add the okra and dried shrimp and stir-fry over high heat until hot, about 1 minute. Add the *sambal oelek* and toss to coat the okra. Remove the skillet from the heat and season the okra with salt. Transfer the okra to a large, shallow bowl. Top with the fried shallots and red pepper and serve. —*Chris Yeo*

Grilled Eggplant and Tomatoes with Parmesan-Basil Crumbs

TOTAL: 30 MIN

10 SERVINGS ● ●

Fresh bread crumbs are an underrated way of adding fabulous crunch to recipes. Here, Argentine chef Francis Mallmann uses bread crumbs tossed with chopped basil and lots of Parmigiano-Reggiano cheese to create a great topping for tender grilled vegetables.

 2 cups coarse fresh bread
    crumbs

Extra-virgin olive oil

 1 cup chopped basil
 ½ cup freshly grated Parmigiano-
    Reggiano cheese
 3 pounds eggplant, sliced
    lengthwise ½ inch thick

Salt and freshly ground pepper

 10 tomatoes, sliced 1 inch thick

1. Preheat the oven to 400°. Spread the fresh bread crumbs on a large rimmed baking sheet and drizzle with 1 tablespoon of olive oil; toss well. Bake for 8 minutes, until the bread crumbs are crisp and golden brown. Transfer the toasted bread crumbs to a medium bowl and toss with the chopped basil and grated Parmigiano-Reggiano cheese.

2. Light a grill. Brush the eggplant slices with oil; season with salt and pepper. Grill over moderate heat until charred and tender, about 2 minutes per side. Transfer the eggplant to a platter, fanning them out. Brush the tomatoes with oil and season with salt and pepper. Grill over moderate heat until charred and hot, about 1 minute per side.

3. Arrange the tomato slices over the eggplant and drizzle with oil. Sprinkle the bread crumbs over the top and serve right away. —*Francis Mallmann*

● HEALTHY   ● MAKE AHEAD   ● VEGETARIAN   ● STAFF FAVORITE

vegetables

Layered Eggplant, Zucchini and Tomato Casserole

ACTIVE: 30 MIN; TOTAL: 1 HR

6 SERVINGS ● ● ● ●

- 3 tablespoons extra-virgin olive oil, plus more for brushing
- 3 medium zucchini (1½ pounds), sliced lengthwise ¼ inch thick
- 2 long, narrow eggplants (1½ pounds), peeled and sliced lengthwise ⅓ inch thick
- Salt and freshly ground pepper
- 1 large shallot, minced
- 1 pound plum tomatoes, cut into ½-inch dice
- 3 ounces feta cheese, crumbled (¾ cup)
- ¼ cup chopped basil
- ⅓ cup *panko* or coarse dry bread crumbs

1. Preheat the oven to 425°. Oil 2 large rimmed baking sheets. Put the zucchini slices on one sheet and the eggplant on the other. Brush the slices all over with oil and season with salt and pepper. Arrange the slices on each sheet in a slightly overlapping layer. Bake for 15 minutes, until tender.

2. Meanwhile, in a large skillet, heat 2 tablespoons of the oil. Add the shallot and cook over moderate heat until softened, 3 minutes. Add the tomatoes and cook over high heat until slightly softened and bubbling, 1 minute. Season with salt and pepper.

3. Oil a shallow baking dish (about 10 by 15 inches). Lay half of the eggplant in the dish and spread one-fourth of the tomatoes on top. Scatter with half of the feta and basil. Layer half of the zucchini on top, followed by another fourth of the tomato and the remaining basil, eggplant and zucchini. Top with the remaining tomato and feta. Mix the *panko* with the remaining 1 tablespoon of oil; sprinkle over the casserole. Bake in the top third of the oven for 20 minutes, until bubbling and crisp. Let stand 5 minutes. Serve hot or warm. —*Marcia Kiesel*

WINE Fresh, fruity rosé.

Grilled Asian Eggplant with Ginger Sauce

photo, page 210

 TOTAL: 40 MIN

8 SERVINGS ● ● ●

F&W's Marcia Kiesel likes dressing up Asian eggplant with a vibrant fresh-ginger sauce that would also be good with steamed fish or poached chicken.

- ¼ cup water
- 1 tablespoon plus 1 teaspoon sugar
- ¼ cup plus 2 tablespoons finely grated fresh ginger
- ¼ cup unseasoned rice vinegar
- 1 teaspoon Asian sesame oil
- ½ cup vegetable oil, plus more for brushing
- Salt
- 8 Asian eggplants (2½ pounds), sliced lengthwise, then cut on the diagonal into 2-inch pieces and scored
- Purple basil leaves, for garnish (optional)

1. In a heatproof glass bowl, combine the water and sugar and microwave at high power for 10 seconds, until the sugar is dissolved. Add the grated ginger, vinegar, sesame oil and the ½ cup of vegetable oil and season the sauce with salt.

2. Set a large steamer basket in a large saucepan, add ½ inch of water and bring to a boil over moderately high heat. Steam the eggplant in batches, cut side down, until just tender, about 4 minutes.

3. Heat a grill pan. Lightly brush the eggplant pieces all over with vegetable oil. Grill over high heat until grill marks appear, about 30 seconds per side, then transfer to a serving platter. Spoon the ginger sauce over the eggplant. Garnish with the purple basil (if using) and serve.
—*Marcia Kiesel*

MAKE AHEAD The ginger sauce can be made up to 6 hours ahead and kept at room temperature.

Curried Eggplant with Chickpeas and Spinach

 ACTIVE: 15 MIN; TOTAL: 45 MIN

4 MAIN-COURSE SERVINGS

● ● ●

Canned chickpeas are often used in salads or hummus, but F&W's Grace Parisi roasts them here with eggplant, prewashed baby spinach and onion wedges to make a satisfying vegetarian main course.

- 2 large garlic cloves, minced
- Kosher salt
- 2 teaspoons Madras curry powder
- ½ cup vegetable oil
- 1 medium eggplant (about 1½ pounds), peeled and cut into ¾-inch pieces
- 1 large onion, cut into ½-inch wedges
- One 15-ounce can chickpeas, rinsed and drained
- ¼ cup finely julienned fresh ginger root
- Freshly ground pepper
- One 5-ounce bag baby spinach
- Warm naan and plain yogurt, for serving

Preheat the oven to 425°. On a work surface, use the side of a large knife to mash the garlic cloves to a paste with a pinch of kosher salt. In a large roasting pan, mix the garlic paste with the curry powder and vegetable oil. Add the eggplant pieces, onion wedges, chickpeas and julienned ginger root, season with salt and pepper and toss well. Spread the vegetables in an even layer in the pan and roast for about 30 minutes, stirring once or twice, until the eggplant and onion are completely tender. Stir in the baby spinach and roast just until wilted, about 2 minutes longer. Serve the curry with warm naan and plain yogurt.
—*Grace Parisi*

MAKE AHEAD The curry can be refrigerated overnight. Rewarm before serving.

WINE Full-bodied, rich Pinot Gris.

perfecting braised greens

F&W's **Marcia Kiesel** *boils kale before sautéing it—the key to making it tender. Currants, lemon and olives add big flavor to the sweet, silky leaves, as do the ingredients in the innovative variations; all three recipes would be fabulous with other hardy greens like dandelion or turnip greens.*

Kale with Currants, Lemon and Olives

TOTAL: 35 MIN
12 SERVINGS ● ●

- ½ cup dried currants
- 4 pounds kale, tough stems discarded
- 3 tablespoons unsalted butter
- 3 tablespoons extra-virgin olive oil
- 1 medium onion, thinly sliced
- ½ cup low-sodium chicken broth
- ½ cup pitted kalamata olives, thinly sliced
- Finely grated zest of 1 lemon
- 1 tablespoon fresh lemon juice
- Kosher salt and freshly ground black pepper

1. In a small bowl, cover the dried currants with hot water. Let stand until softened, about 5 minutes; drain.

2. Meanwhile, in a large pot of boiling water, cook the kale until tender, about 5 minutes, then drain. When the kale is cool enough to handle, gently squeeze out any excess water. Coarsely chop the kale.

3. In a large, deep skillet, melt the butter in the olive oil. Add the onion and cook over moderately low heat, stirring occasionally, until softened, about 7 minutes. Add the chicken broth and blanched kale and toss thoroughly. Cover and cook over moderate heat, stirring a few times, until the kale is hot and sizzling, about 3 minutes. Stir in the currants, olives, lemon zest and lemon juice and cook, stirring constantly, until heated through. Season with salt and pepper and serve.

MAKE AHEAD The kale can be covered and refrigerated overnight; reheat gently over moderate heat, adding a few tablespoons of chicken broth as necessary.

TWO GREAT VARIATIONS

1 Kale & Water Chestnuts in Curried Cream

Omit the currants, lemon zest and juice and olives. Blanch, drain and chop the kale as directed. In a small saucepan, reduce ¾ cup heavy cream over moderately low heat to ⅓ cup. In Step 3, add 4 teaspoons Madras curry powder to the softened onion in the skillet and cook until fragrant. Stir in the reduced cream and 8 ounces drained, sliced water chestnuts along with the chicken broth and kale. Cook, stirring, until heated through.

2 Kale with Shiitake Mushrooms

Omit the currants, lemon zest, lemon juice and olives. Blanch, drain and chop the kale as directed. Remove and discard the stems of 1 pound shiitake mushrooms. Thinly slice the shiitake caps and add them to the onion in the skillet in Step 3. Season with salt and black pepper and cook over moderately high heat until browned, about 8 minutes. Just before serving, stir in 3 tablespoons soy sauce and 2 teaspoons Asian sesame oil.

vegetables

Spinach Simmered in Yogurt

TOTAL: 25 MIN
4 SERVINGS ● ● ● ●

- 1 pound baby spinach, rinsed
- 2 tablespoons vegetable oil
- 3 garlic cloves, minced
- 2 small dried red chiles
- 1 teaspoon ground coriander
- 1 teaspoon turmeric
- 1 cup plain whole-milk yogurt

Salt

1. Heat a large skillet. Add one-third of the baby spinach and cook over moderately high heat, stirring, until wilted. Transfer the spinach to a colander. Repeat with the remaining spinach in 2 batches. Press all of the excess water out of the spinach and coarsely chop it.

2. Heat the vegetable oil in the same skillet. Add the garlic and chiles and cook over moderate heat until fragrant, 2 minutes. Add the coriander and turmeric and cook, stirring, until fragrant, 1 minute. Add the spinach and yogurt and cook over low heat, stirring, until the yogurt just begins to separate, 3 minutes. Season with salt and serve. —*Peggy Markel*

SERVE WITH Steamed basmati rice.

MAKE AHEAD The cooked spinach can be refrigerated overnight. Reheat gently.

Braised Red Cabbage with Caraway and Apple

ACTIVE: 30 MIN; TOTAL 1 HR 30 MIN
8 SERVINGS ● ● ●

- ¼ cup extra-virgin olive oil
- 1 medium onion, finely chopped
- 1 head of red cabbage (about 3 pounds), cored and shredded
- ½ cup dry red wine
- ½ cup cider vinegar
- 1 Golden Delicious apple—peeled, cored and cut into 1-inch pieces
- ¼ cup packed dark brown sugar
- 2 teaspoons caraway seeds
- 2 teaspoons mustard seeds

Salt and freshly ground pepper

In a large, deep skillet, heat the olive oil. Add the onion and cook over moderately low heat, stirring, until softened, about 6 minutes. Add the red cabbage and cook over moderate heat, stirring occasionally, until slightly wilted, about 10 minutes. Stir in the red wine and cook until evaporated. Add the cider vinegar and bring to a boil. Stir in the apple, brown sugar, caraway seeds and mustard seeds and season with salt and pepper. Cover, reduce the heat to low and cook, stirring occasionally, until the cabbage is tender, about 1 hour. Transfer to a bowl and serve. —*Luisa Weiss*

Roasted Radishes with Radish Greens

TOTAL: 30 MIN
8 SERVINGS ● ● ●

Gerard Craft (an F&W Best New Chef 2008) came up with this clever recipe one year when a local farmer had an abundance of radishes. Craft tried roasting them. The result: warm, crisp-tender radishes with delightfully bitter greens, which he finishes with butter and lemon.

- 3 bunches of small radishes with greens attached
- 2 tablespoons extra-virgin olive oil

Salt and freshly ground pepper

- 2 tablespoons unsalted butter
- 2 tablespoons fresh lemon juice

1. Preheat the oven to 500°. Trim the radishes and wash the greens; pat dry.

2. In a large ovenproof skillet, heat the oil until shimmering. Add the radishes, season with salt and pepper and cook over high heat, stirring occasionally, until lightly browned in spots, about 2 minutes. Transfer the skillet to the oven and roast the radishes for 15 minutes, until crisp-tender.

3. Return the skillet to the burner and stir in the butter to coat the radishes. Add the greens and cook over moderate heat until they are wilted, 2 minutes. Add the lemon juice and season with salt. Serve right away. —*Gerard Craft*

Cheese-Stuffed Grilled Peppers

TOTAL: 30 MIN
4 SERVINGS ● ● ●

Robert Perkins and John Lancaster, the wine directors at San Francisco's Boulevard restaurant, love making this snack at backyard barbecues using all types of medium-sized peppers: As the peppers blister, the cheese mixture tucked inside turns warm and gooey.

- 1 cup ricotta cheese (8 ounces)
- 1 cup cream cheese, at room temperature
- ½ cup freshly grated Parmigiano-Reggiano cheese

Salt and freshly ground pepper

- 4 Anaheim or Cubanelle peppers (see Note)
- 4 baby bell peppers
- 4 small poblano chiles

Extra-virgin olive oil, for rubbing the peppers

1. In a bowl, blend the ricotta with the cream cheese and Parmigiano-Reggiano. Season with salt and pepper.

2. Light a grill or heat a grill pan. Using a small, sharp knife, remove the stems from the peppers and reserve. Cut around inside the peppers to detach the membranes and remove the seeds. Using a butter knife, fill the peppers with the cheese mixture and reattach the tops of the peppers. Rub the peppers with olive oil.

3. Grill the peppers over moderately high heat, turning occasionally, until the peppers are blistered all over and the cheese filling is piping hot, about 7 minutes. Transfer the peppers to plates and serve.
—*John Lancaster and Robert Perkins*

NOTE Anaheim chiles are long, slender, mild green peppers; Cubanelle chiles have a similar shape but are lighter green and tend to be somewhat spicy.

MAKE AHEAD The cheese-filled peppers can be refrigerated overnight. Bring to room temperature before grilling.

CHEESE-STUFFED
GRILLED PEPPERS

vegetables

Oven-Roasted Tomatoes Stuffed with Goat Cheese

ACTIVE: 25 MIN; TOTAL: 1 HR 15 MIN

12 SERVINGS ● ○

For these buttery-soft roasted tomatoes, Alain Coumont (founder of the international bakery-café chain Le Pain Quotidien) boosts the flavor of the creamy goat cheese filling with garlic and basil. The result works both as a side dish or a main course with a salad and crusty bread.

- 12 medium tomatoes (3 pounds)
- 1²⁄₃ pounds fresh goat cheese
- 1 large egg, lightly beaten
- 2 medium garlic cloves, very finely chopped
- 2 tablespoons finely chopped fresh basil leaves
- 1 teaspoon kosher salt
- ¼ teaspoon freshly ground black pepper
- ¼ cup extra-virgin olive oil

1. Preheat the oven to 425°. Slice off the top ½ inch of each tomato and reserve the tops. Scoop out the tomato cores and seeds. Cut a very thin sliver off the bottom of each tomato to help them stand up straight. Arrange the tomatoes in a 9-by-13-inch glass or ceramic baking dish.
2. In a bowl, combine the goat cheese with the egg, garlic, chopped basil, salt, pepper

and 2 tablespoons of the olive oil. Spoon the goat cheese mixture into the tomatoes, mounding the filling ½ inch above the rim. Cover with the tomato tops and drizzle with the remaining 2 tablespoons of olive oil.
3. Bake the tomatoes for 35 minutes, until tender and browned in spots. Let stand for 15 minutes. Serve warm or at room temperature. —*Alain Coumont*
WINE Fresh, fruity rosé.

Grilled Corn with Mango-Habanero Butter

ACTIVE: 40 MIN; TOTAL: 1 HR 45 MIN

8 SERVINGS ● ○

Grilling guru Bobby Flay likes to cook corn on the cob with the husk tied back into a kind of handle. He soaks the bundle in cold water before it goes on the grill for two reasons: The moisture steams the kernels a little, making them tender, and prevents the husks from burning.

- 1 mango, peeled and coarsely chopped
- ¼ cup mango nectar
- 1 tablespoon honey
- ½ habanero chile, seeded
- 1½ sticks unsalted butter, softened
- 2 tablespoons packed cilantro leaves, chopped
- ½ teaspoon kosher salt
- 8 ears of corn

1. In a small saucepan, combine the chopped mango with the mango nectar, honey and habanero chile. Bring to a simmer and cook over moderate heat, stirring occasionally, until the mango is very soft, about 10 minutes. Transfer to a food processor and puree until smooth. Strain the mango puree into a small bowl and let cool, about 30 minutes.
2. Wipe out the food processor. Add the cooled mango puree along with the butter, chopped cilantro and salt and puree until smooth. Scrape the mango butter into a small bowl, cover and refrigerate until chilled, about 30 minutes.

3. Light a grill or preheat a grill pan. Pull the corn husks down to the base of the stalks, leaving the husks attached. Discard the corn silk. Using butcher string, tie back the husks. Fill a large bowl with cold salted water and submerge the ears of corn for about 10 minutes.
4. Drain the corn but don't pat dry. Grill the corn over moderate heat, turning occasionally, until tender and browned in spots, about 8 minutes. Transfer the corn to plates, spread with the mango-habanero butter and serve. —*Bobby Flay*
MAKE AHEAD The mango-habanero butter can be refrigerated for up to 2 weeks.

Mixed-Mushroom Strudel

ACTIVE: 30 MIN; TOTAL: 1 HR 30 MIN

6 SERVINGS ●

- 1½ sticks unsalted butter
- 2 pounds mixed mushrooms, such as white button, cremini and oyster, thinly sliced
- Salt and freshly ground pepper
- 1 onion, finely diced
- 3 tablespoons all-purpose flour
- 1½ cups mushroom or chicken broth
- 1 tablespoon chopped thyme
- 1 teaspoon finely grated lemon zest
- Eight 14-by-18-inch sheets of thawed phyllo dough

1. Preheat the oven to 350°. In a large skillet, melt 2 tablespoons of the butter. Add the sliced mushrooms and season with salt and pepper. Cover and cook over moderate heat, stirring a few times, until the mushrooms release their liquid, about 8 minutes. Uncover and cook, stirring occasionally, until the liquid has evaporated and the mushrooms are browned, about 8 minutes longer.
2. In another large skillet, melt 2 tablespoons of the butter. Add the onion and cook over moderate heat, stirring occasionally, until softened, about 7 minutes. Stir in the flour until incorporated, then

---

best grilled vegetable tip

Grillmeister-chef Tim Love of the Lonesome Dove Western Bistro in Fort Worth, Texas, chills scallions, zucchini, asparagus and other crunchy vegetables in a bowl of ice-cold water in the refrigerator for 30 minutes to ensure that they come off the grill especially moist and crisp.

gradually stir in the broth until smooth. Bring to a boil over moderately high heat and cook, stirring often, until thickened, about 2 minutes. Stir in the mushrooms, thyme and lemon zest. Remove from the heat and season with salt and pepper. Let cool completely.

3. In a small saucepan, melt the remaining 1 stick of butter. Line a large rimmed baking sheet with parchment paper. Place 1 phyllo sheet on the parchment and brush lightly with some of the melted butter. Top with the remaining phyllo, buttering each sheet as you go; reserve about 1½ tablespoons of the butter. Spoon the cooled mushroom filling onto a long side of the phyllo and carefully roll it up like a log, folding in the ends as you go. Shift the strudel to the center of the baking sheet, seam side down. Brush all over with the reserved melted butter. Bake for about 45 minutes, until the strudel is golden brown and crisp. Let rest for about 10 minutes, then slice and serve. —*Eugenia Bone*

MAKE AHEAD The strudel can be refrigerated for up to 2 days. Reheat to serve.

WINE Complex, elegant Pinot Noir.

Grilled Portobello Mushrooms with Tarragon-Parsley Butter

 TOTAL: 20 MIN
 4 SERVINGS ●

Much more than the sum of its two parts, New Zealand chef Sara Simpson's side dish of beefy grilled portobellos with herbed butter is satisfying enough to be a vegetarian main course.

- **4 tablespoons unsalted butter, softened**
- **1 tablespoon chopped tarragon leaves**
- **1 tablespoon chopped flat-leaf parsley**
- **Salt and freshly ground pepper**
- **8 medium portobello mushrooms, stemmed**
- **Extra-virgin olive oil, for brushing**

1. Light a grill. In a small bowl, blend the butter with the tarragon and parsley and season with salt and pepper.

2. Brush the portobello caps with olive oil and season with salt and pepper. Set the mushrooms on the grill, gills down, and cook over moderate heat, turning once, until tender and nicely charred, about 8 minutes. Dollop the tarragon-parsley butter over the gills and cook for about 1 minute longer, until the butter is melted. Transfer the grilled mushrooms to plates and serve right away. —*Sara Simpson*

MAKE AHEAD The herb butter can be refrigerated for up to 3 days. Bring to room temperature before proceeding.

Baby Zucchini Sauté with Mint

 TOTAL: 20 MIN
 10 SERVINGS ● ●

"I grow zucchini and end up with so much of it," says cookbook author Katie Lee. "Zucchini with lemon and mint is one of my favorite combos." Halved baby zucchini are pleasantly crisp-tender when sautéed, but the dish is equally delicious made with "adult" zucchini.

- **3 tablespoons extra-virgin olive oil**
- **1 large garlic clove, very finely chopped**
- **3 pounds baby zucchini, trimmed and halved lengthwise**
- **Salt and freshly ground pepper**
- **3 tablespoons fresh lemon juice**
- **⅓ cup chopped mint**

In a large skillet, heat the olive oil. Add the chopped garlic and cook over moderate heat, stirring, until it is fragrant but not browned, about 30 seconds. Add the baby zucchini halves, season with salt and pepper and cook over moderately high heat, stirring occasionally, until crisp-tender, about 8 minutes. Add the fresh lemon juice and transfer the zucchini to a serving bowl. Stir in the chopped mint and serve. —*Katie Lee*

Fried Zucchini Blossoms

 TOTAL: 30 MIN
 6 SERVINGS

Marco Canora, a Manhattan chef and restaurateur, grew up in New York's Hudson Valley with a fantastic vegetable garden that produced an abundance of zucchini. "I'd pick the flowers," he says, "then my mother would stuff them with any combination of things and fry them up in a simple *pastella*," a classic Italian batter of flour and water. Here Canora fills the blossoms with a mixture of anchovy fillets and fresh mozzarella before dipping them in sage-flecked batter and frying until crispy.

- **1½ cups all-purpose flour**
- **Salt**
- **2 tablespoons chopped fresh sage leaves**
- **1¾ cups ice water**
- **12 zucchini blossoms, stamens removed**
- **½ pound fresh mozzarella, cut into twelve ½-inch-wide, 1½-inch-long sticks**
- **6 anchovy fillets, halved**
- **Pure olive oil, for frying**

1. In a large bowl, combine the flour with a large pinch of salt and the chopped fresh sage leaves. Gradually whisk in the ice water until just blended.

2. Carefully open each zucchini blossom, place a piece of mozzarella and an anchovy half inside and twist the tops of the blossoms tightly to enclose the filling.

3. In a large saucepan fitted with a frying thermometer, heat ½ inch of the olive oil to 350°. Dip each stuffed blossom in the batter and allow the excess to drip back into the bowl. Fry 3 blossoms at a time, turning once, until crisp and golden, about 2 minutes per side. Drain on paper towels and season with salt. Serve right away. —*Marco Canora*

MAKE AHEAD The batter can be refrigerated for up to 2 hours. Stir the batter well before using.

vegetables

Maduros

TOTAL: 30 MIN
6 SERVINGS ●

When a plantain's peel turns dark brown, it's superripe and ready to be sliced and fried for the sticky-sweet Cuban side dish *maduros.* Cooking teacher Lourdes Castro recommends rolling the unpeeled plantains on the counter to soften the flesh, producing a more tender *maduro.*

- 2 cups vegetable oil, for frying
- 3 very ripe, black sweet plantains

1. In a large skillet, heat the oil. Place the plantains on a work surface and gently roll back and forth. Using a sharp knife, cut off the ends. Carefully peel and slice the plantains diagonally into 1-inch pieces.
2. Add half of the plantains to the oil; fry over moderate heat, turning occasionally, until browned, 5 minutes. Drain on paper towels. Repeat with the remaining plantains and serve. —*Lourdes Castro*

Tostones

TOTAL: 30 MIN
6 SERVINGS ●

Tostones are green plantains fried until crisp. Soaking the fried plantains in salted water before frying them a second time ensures that they are perfectly seasoned.

- 3 unripe, firm green plantains
- 3 cups vegetable oil, for frying

Salt

Lime wedges, for serving

1. Using a sharp knife, cut off the ends of the plantains. Score the skin of each plantain on four sides, then use your fingers to pry the skin loose. Cut the peeled plantains into 1-inch pieces.
2. In a large, deep skillet, heat the oil. Add the plantains and fry over moderate heat, turning occasionally, until lightly browned, about 5 minutes. Using a slotted spoon, transfer the plantains to paper towels to drain; let cool slightly. Using a mallet or the heel of your hand, smash each plantain to a ¼-inch thickness.

3. Fill a bowl with water and salt it liberally. Add the plantains and let soak for 1 minute; drain and transfer to paper towels to dry.
4. Heat the oil in the skillet. Fry the *tostones* again, turning, until crisp, 5 minutes. Transfer to paper towels; season with salt. Serve with lime wedges. —*Lourdes Castro*

Braised Baby Artichokes with Tomato Coulis

TOTAL: 1 HR
12 SERVINGS ● ● ●

- 2 lemons, halved
- 36 baby artichokes (3 pounds)
- ¼ cup extra-virgin olive oil
- 6 garlic cloves, quartered lengthwise
- 2 carrots, thinly sliced on the bias
- 1 medium onion, thinly sliced
- 1 tablespoon thyme leaves
- 2 bay leaves
- 1 teaspoon black peppercorns
- 1 teaspoon coriander seeds
- ¾ cup dry white wine
- ½ teaspoon salt

Fresh Tomato Coulis (recipe follows), for serving

1. Squeeze the lemons into a bowl of water. Working with 1 artichoke at a time, snap off the dark green outer leaves. Slice off all but 1 inch of the remaining leaves. Peel and trim the stems. Halve the artichokes, scrape out the chokes and soak in the lemon water.
2. In a large nonreactive skillet, heat the oil. Add the garlic, carrots, onion, thyme, bay leaves, peppercorns and coriander seeds; cook over moderately high heat until the onion begins to soften, 2 minutes.
3. Drain the artichokes and add them to the skillet. Cook until the onion is translucent, about 2 minutes longer. Add the wine and salt, cover and cook over moderate heat until the artichokes are just tender, about 10 minutes. Discard the bay leaves. Spoon the artichokes and their juices onto plates. Drizzle with the fresh Tomato Coulis and serve.

—*Alain Coumont*

TOMATO COULIS

TOTAL: 15 MIN
MAKES 1¼ CUPS ● ● ●

- 4 medium fresh tomatoes, quartered
- 4 oil-packed sun-dried tomatoes, drained
- 1 garlic clove
- 3 tablespoons extra-virgin olive oil
- 5 basil leaves

Pinch of crushed red pepper

Kosher salt and freshly ground black pepper

In the jar of a blender, puree the quartered fresh tomatoes with the drained sun-dried tomatoes, garlic clove, olive oil, basil leaves and crushed red pepper. Season with salt and black pepper. Refrigerate the coulis until ready to serve. —*AC*

Smoky Glazed Asparagus

ACTIVE: 15 MIN; TOTAL: 45 MIN
6 SERVINGS ● ● ●

Chef Nate Appleman (an F&W Best New Chef 2009) coats vegetables with a lemony, mayonnaise-based marinade before grilling them; the mayonnaise creates a beautifully blistered crust.

- ½ cup mayonnaise
- ¼ cup extra-virgin olive oil
- 3 tablespoons fresh lemon juice
- 1 garlic clove, crushed
- 1 tablespoon sweet smoked paprika
- 2 teaspoons kosher salt
- 1 teaspoon cumin seeds
- 1 pound thick asparagus, stalks peeled

1. Light a grill. In a shallow dish, whisk the mayonnaise with the oil, lemon juice, garlic, paprika, salt and cumin. Add the asparagus and toss; let stand for 30 minutes.
2. Grill the asparagus over moderately high heat, turning, until tender and blistered in spots, about 6 minutes; serve.

—*Nate Appleman*

SMOKY GLAZED ASPARAGUS

TOFU CASSEROLE

GRILLED TOFU WITH ASPARAGUS AND NORI VINAIGRETTE

Mustard-and-Mayonnaise-Glazed Asparagus

 ACTIVE: 15 MIN; TOTAL: 45 MIN

6 SERVINGS ● ●

¼ cup mayonnaise

¼ cup grainy mustard

¼ cup extra-virgin olive oil

3 tablespoons fresh lemon juice

1 teaspoon grated lemon zest

1 garlic clove, crushed

2 teaspoons kosher salt

2 teaspoons freshly ground pepper

1 pound thick asparagus, peeled

1. Light a grill. In a shallow dish, whisk the mayonnaise with the mustard, oil, lemon juice, lemon zest, garlic, salt and pepper. Add the asparagus and turn to coat. Let stand at room temperature for 30 minutes.

2. Grill over moderately high heat, turning, until tender and lightly blistered in spots, 6 minutes. Serve. —*Nate Appleman*

Grilled Tofu with Asparagus and Nori Vinaigrette

TOTAL: 50 MIN

4 SERVINGS ● ●

Top Chef culinary producer Lee Anne Wong plays with an array of Asian ingredients to create a wonderful marinade for firm tofu.

¼ cup rice vinegar

3 tablespoons white miso paste

2½ tablespoons soy sauce

1 tablespoon tahini paste

1 tablespoon agave nectar (see Note on p. 364)

2 teaspoons mirin

⅛ teaspoon Chinese five-spice powder

1 pound extra-firm tofu, drained and cut into 4 blocks

Vegetable oil

Three 7-by-8-inch sheets of toasted nori (seaweed), cut into strips

½ cup water

1 tablespoon honey

1 tablespoon fresh lemon juice

¼ teaspoon *sambal oelek* or other Asian chile paste (see Note on p. 206)

Salt and freshly ground black pepper

1 pound medium asparagus

1 teaspoon Asian sesame oil

¼ teaspoon crushed red pepper

2 teaspoons sesame seeds

½ cup cilantro leaves

1 large scallion, thinly sliced

1. Preheat the oven to 425°. In a medium baking dish, whisk 2 tablespoons of the vinegar, 2 tablespoons of the miso paste and 1½ tablespoons of the soy sauce with the tahini, agave nectar, mirin and five-spice powder until smooth. Add the tofu and turn to coat. Let stand for 30 minutes.

2. Meanwhile, in a blender, combine ¼ cup of vegetable oil with the nori, water, honey, lemon juice, *sambal oelek* and the remaining 2 tablespoons of rice vinegar, 1 tablespoon of miso and 1 tablespoon of soy sauce. Puree until smooth; season lightly with salt and black pepper. Refrigerate the vinaigrette.

3. On a baking sheet, toss the asparagus with the sesame oil; season with salt, black pepper and the red pepper. Roast for 10 minutes, until tender and browned.

4. Meanwhile, in a skillet, toast the sesame seeds over moderate heat until fragrant and lightly browned, 1 minute. Let cool.

5. Light a grill and brush with vegetable oil. Remove the tofu from the marinade and grill over moderate heat, turning once, until browned and heated through, 6 minutes. Cut each block into 3 slices.

6. Spoon some of the nori vinaigrette onto plates. Top with the asparagus and tofu. Sprinkle with the toasted sesame seeds, cilantro and scallion and serve.
—*Lee Anne Wong*
WINE Zippy, fresh Pinot Bianco.

Tofu Casserole

TOTAL: 30 MIN
4 SERVINGS ●

2 teaspoons instant dashi powder (see Note)
4 cups water
2 teaspoons finely grated ginger
¼ pound shiitake mushrooms, stemmed and caps thinly sliced
½ cup shelled edamame (3 ounces)
One 14-ounce package firm silken tofu, cut into 1-inch cubes
8 water chestnuts, thinly sliced
One 5-ounce bag baby spinach
2 tablespoons low-sodium soy sauce
2 tablespoons mirin
1 teaspoon fresh lemon juice
1 scallion, thinly sliced
4 teaspoons bonito flakes (optional; see Note)

In a large saucepan, bring the dashi and water to a simmer. Add the grated ginger, sliced shiitake, edamame, tofu and water chestnuts and simmer over moderate heat until the mushrooms are tender, about 5 minutes. Add the spinach, soy sauce, mirin and lemon juice and stir just until the spinach is wilted. Serve in bowls with the scallion and bonito flakes.
—*Takashi Yagihashi*
NOTE Instant dashi is a powdered base for the Japanese stock made from bonito (dried tuna flakes) and seaweed. Purchase it in the Asian section of supermarkets or from asianfoodgrocer.com.

Nori Hand Rolls with Kale and Green Beans
ACTIVE: 30 MIN; TOTAL: 1 HR 10 MIN
8 SERVINGS ● ●

¾ cup short-grain brown rice
1 tablespoon sugar
1 teaspoon kosher salt
3 tablespoons unseasoned rice vinegar
Four 8-by-7½-inch sheets of nori (seaweed), halved
4 teaspoons wasabi paste
16 green beans, blanched
8 large kale leaves, stemmed and blanched
4 scallions, halved lengthwise
½ cup low-sodium soy sauce
½ teaspoon Asian sesame oil

1. In a small saucepan, cover the brown rice with 1½ cups of water and bring to a boil. Cover and cook over low heat until the water has been absorbed, about 35 minutes. Transfer the cooked rice to a large bowl and fluff with a fork.

2. Meanwhile, in a small microwave-safe bowl, microwave the sugar and salt with 2 tablespoons of water at high power for 10 seconds, until the sugar is dissolved. Stir in 1 tablespoon of the rice vinegar. Sprinkle the vinegar mixture over the warm brown rice and stir well.

3. Lay a nori sheet on a work surface. Spread ¼ cup of the rice on the bottom half and spread ½ teaspoon of wasabi paste over the rice. Top with 2 green beans, 1 kale leaf and a halved scallion. Fold the nori over to form a cone or roll; set on a platter and repeat with the remaining nori and fillings.

4. In a bowl, stir the soy sauce and sesame oil with the remaining vinegar. Serve the rolls with the dipping sauce.
—*Marcia Kiesel*

Green Bean–and–Blood Orange Salad
TOTAL: 30 MIN
8 SERVINGS ● ● ●
"Blood oranges are part of my Sicily fascination," says Renato Poliafito of Baked in Brooklyn, New York, and Charleston, South Carolina. He uses them to add color and tang to green beans and reduces the juice with balsamic for the dressing.
Salt
2 pounds thin green beans
6 large blood oranges
¼ cup plus 2 tablespoons balsamic vinegar
1 tablespoon honey

1. Bring a large pot of salted water to a boil. Fill a large bowl with ice water. Cook the beans in the boiling water until bright green and al dente, about 5 minutes. Drain and immediately plunge the beans into the ice water. Drain again and pat dry.

2. Meanwhile, using a sharp knife, peel 4 of the oranges, removing all of the bitter white pith. Working over a bowl, cut in between the membranes to release the sections into the bowl. Zest one of the remaining oranges and juice both of them. Transfer the juice to a saucepan and add the vinegar and honey. Bring to a boil, then simmer over moderate heat until reduced to a syrup, 10 minutes. Season with salt.

3. Transfer the beans and oranges to a platter; drizzle the syrup on top. Garnish with the orange zest; serve. —*Renato Poliafito*

FIVE-SPICE-GLAZED SWEET POTATOES
WITH WALNUT TOFFEE (P. 240)

potatoes, grains & beans

Satisfying sides, healthy main courses
and excellent risottos for entertaining.

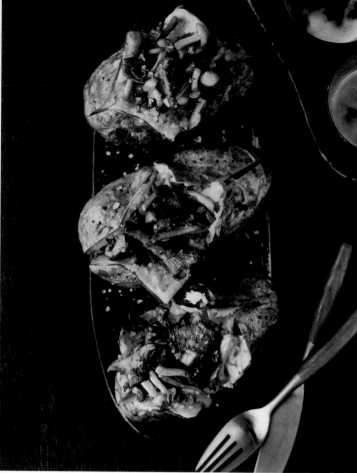

CRISP POLENTA WITH ROASTED CHERRY TOMATOES

BAKED POTATOES WITH WILD MUSHROOM RAGÙ

Crisp Polenta with Roasted Cherry Tomatoes

TOTAL: 45 MIN PLUS 2 HR CHILLING
8 SERVINGS ● ● ●

8½ cups water
6½ tablespoons extra-virgin olive oil
1 pound polenta (2¾ cups)
Kosher salt and freshly ground pepper
1½ pounds cherry tomatoes
on the vine
8 thyme sprigs
4 ounces fresh goat cheese,
crumbled

1. Lightly spray a 9-by-13-inch baking dish with cooking spray. In a large saucepan, bring the water and 2 tablespoons of the olive oil to a boil. Gradually whisk in the polenta and cook over low heat, whisking constantly, until thick, about 5 minutes; season with salt and pepper. Scrape the polenta into the baking dish and smooth the top. Cover the dish with plastic wrap and refrigerate until firm, 2 hours.

2. Preheat the oven to 375°. Line a rimmed baking sheet with parchment paper. Toss the tomatoes with 1½ tablespoons of the oil; season with salt and pepper. Arrange on the baking sheet and scatter the thyme on top. Roast for 20 minutes, until the tomatoes begin to burst; discard the thyme.

3. Meanwhile, turn the chilled polenta out onto a work surface and trim ½ inch off all sides. Cut the polenta into 8 rectangles. Heat a large nonstick skillet. Brush both sides of the polenta with the remaining 3 tablespoons of oil and season with salt. Working in 2 batches, cook the polenta over moderately high heat, turning once, until golden and crisp, 10 minutes. Transfer to plates and sprinkle with the goat cheese. Arrange the tomatoes over the polenta and serve. —*Melissa Rubel Jacobson*

Creamy Cheese Grits

TOTAL: 30 MIN
4 SERVINGS ● ●

Serve these luscious cheese grits in place of standard mashed potatoes.

5½ cups water
Salt
1½ cups stone-ground grits
2 tablespoons unsalted butter
⅓ cup freshly grated Parmigiano-
Reggiano cheese
Freshly ground pepper

In a medium saucepan, bring the water to a boil. Add a pinch of salt and gradually whisk in the grits. Cover and cook over low heat, whisking frequently, until the grits are thick, creamy and just tender, about 25 minutes. Stir in the butter and grated Parmigiano-Reggiano cheese, season with salt and pepper and serve hot.
—*Marcia Kiesel*

Spiced Millet Stew with Onions

ACTIVE: 20 MIN; TOTAL: 1 HR

4 SERVINGS ● ●

While researching a culinary tour in India, food guide Peggy Markel discovered this stew from the northwestern state of Rajasthan. Vibrantly flavored with spices and chiles, the dish has the texture of pleasantly grainy mashed potatoes.

- 1 cup millet (6 ounces)
- 3 tablespoons vegetable oil
- ½ teaspoon cumin seeds
- 3 medium onions, finely chopped
- 1 tablespoon minced garlic
- 3 cups water
- 1 cup plain whole-milk yogurt
- 2 teaspoons ground coriander
- ½ teaspoon turmeric
- ½ teaspoon crushed red pepper

Kosher salt

- 1 serrano or other green chile, seeded and minced
- 1 tablespoon chopped cilantro

1. In a large skillet, toast the millet over high heat, shaking the pan often, until slightly darkened, about 3 minutes. Transfer to a large plate to cool.

2. In a large saucepan, heat the vegetable oil. Add the cumin seeds and toast over high heat, shaking the pan, until fragrant, about 30 seconds. Add the onions; cook over moderate heat, stirring occasionally, until browned, about 20 minutes. Add the garlic and cook over moderate heat, stirring, until fragrant, about 3 minutes.

3. Add the millet and the water and bring to a boil. Cover and simmer over low heat, stirring, until the millet is just tender, about 20 minutes. Stir in the yogurt, coriander, turmeric, crushed red pepper and 1 teaspoon of salt and cook, stirring, until the yogurt is thickened slightly, about 4 minutes. Remove from the heat and season with salt. Transfer to a bowl, top with the chile and cilantro and serve right away.
—*Peggy Markel*

Baked Potatoes with Wild Mushroom Ragù

ACTIVE: 30 MIN; TOTAL: 1 HR 30 MIN

8 SERVINGS ●

F&W's Grace Parisi likes using a mix of shiitake, oyster, chanterelle and white button mushrooms for this succulent ragù to top baked potatoes, but any combination of wild mushrooms will work.

- 8 baking potatoes (4 pounds)
- ¼ cup plus 2 tablespoons canola oil, plus more for rubbing
- 2 tablespoons unsalted butter
- 4 pounds mixed wild mushrooms

Salt and freshly ground pepper

- 1 medium white onion, very finely chopped
- 4 medium garlic cloves, very finely chopped
- 1 cup dry white wine
- 1 cup beef stock or low-sodium broth
- 1 tablespoon chopped fresh tarragon leaves
- 2 teaspoons chopped fresh thyme leaves

1. Preheat the oven to 425°. Pierce the potatoes with a fork and rub with oil. Bake for 1 hour, or until tender when pierced.

2. Meanwhile, in a large, deep skillet, melt the butter in the oil. Add the mushrooms, season with salt and pepper and cook over high heat, stirring occasionally, until tender, 20 minutes. Add the onion and garlic and cook, stirring, until the mushrooms are deeply browned, 8 minutes. Add the wine and cook until evaporated. Stir in the stock, tarragon and thyme and bring to a boil. Season with salt and pepper.

3. Slit the potatoes and fluff the insides with a fork. Season with salt and transfer to plates. Spoon the mushroom ragù onto the potatoes and serve. —*Grace Parisi*

Rosemary-Roasted Potatoes

ACTIVE: 5 MIN; TOTAL: 50 MIN

8 SERVINGS ● ●

- 2½ pounds fingerling potatoes, halved lengthwise
- 3 tablespoons olive oil

Salt

- 2 rosemary sprigs

Preheat the oven to 400°. Arrange the potatoes in a roasting pan and toss with the olive oil. Season with salt and nestle the rosemary sprigs into the potatoes. Roast for 30 minutes, then flip the potatoes; they should be golden brown. If they stick, don't loosen them. After they cook a few minutes more, you'll be able to flip them over. Roast for another 15 minutes and serve. —*Eugenia Bone*

Rösti Potatoes

 ACTIVE: 15 MIN; TOTAL: 45 MIN

10 SERVINGS ● ●

Argentine chef Francis Mallmann's directions for making these Swiss potato cakes are very precise: Once they hit the griddle, cook them very slowly, and don't touch—except to flip them over—until they're done. That's the way to get a sensational crust.

2½ pounds baking potatoes, scrubbed
Extra-virgin olive oil, for frying
Salt

1. Heat a large griddle over moderately low heat or on a preheated grill. On a work surface, using a box grater, coarsely shred the potatoes into 10 fluffy piles—don't pat the piles down.

2. Add ⅛ inch of oil to the griddle and heat until shimmering. Carefully transfer the potato piles to the griddle, keeping them fluffy and evenly spaced. Season with salt. Cook over moderately low heat until well-browned and crisp on the bottom, 15 minutes. Turn the piles, adding another ⅛ inch of oil to the griddle. Cook for 15 minutes longer, until the potatoes are browned and crisp; season with salt and serve.
—*Francis Mallmann*

potatoes, grains & beans

Basque Steak Fries

TOTAL: 50 MIN

10 SERVINGS ●

Gerald Hirigoyen (an F&W Best New Chef 1994) tosses wedges of fried Yukon Gold potatoes with plenty of piment d'Espelette, a smoky Basque chile powder, to give the crispy potatoes a slightly spicy kick.

Eight 6-ounce Yukon Gold potatoes, cut into 1-inch-thick steak fries

Salt

1½ quarts vegetable oil, for frying

Piment d'Espelette or hot paprika

1. In a pot, cover the potatoes with cold water. Add a large pinch of salt. Bring to a simmer and cook the potatoes until nearly cooked through, 6 minutes. Drain, pat dry and let cool. Wipe out the pot.

2. In the same pot, heat the oil to 375°. Line a baking sheet with paper towels. Working in batches, fry the potatoes until deeply golden, 7 minutes per batch, then drain on the paper towels. Toss the fries with salt and piment d'Espelette; serve.
—*Gerald Hirigoyen*

Grandma's Crushed Potatoes

ACTIVE: 15 MIN; TOTAL: 1 HR 10 MIN

4 SERVINGS ● ●

2 pounds fingerling potatoes

Salt

1 teaspoon coriander seeds

½ teaspoon cumin seeds

¼ teaspoon turmeric

¼ teaspoon cayenne pepper

¼ cup vegetable oil

2 tablespoons chopped cilantro

1. Preheat the oven to 400°. In a pot, cover the potatoes with water. Add a large pinch of salt and bring to a boil. Cook over moderately high heat until barely tender, about 10 minutes. Drain and peel the potatoes.

2. In a small skillet, toast the coriander and cumin over moderately high heat until fragrant, about 1 minute. Transfer to a spice grinder and let cool, then grind to a powder and stir in the turmeric and cayenne.

3. Spread the potatoes on a large rimmed baking sheet and toss with the oil and then the spices. Season with salt and bake for 45 minutes, until tender and crisp. Using a fork, lightly crush the potatoes, then sprinkle with the cilantro and serve.
—*Rajat Parr*

Andouille–and–Sweet Potato Pie with Tangy Apple Salad

ACTIVE: 45 MIN; TOTAL: 2 HR 30 MIN

6 SERVINGS ●

1 pound small sweet potatoes, pierced with a fork

1 cup yellow cornmeal

1 cup all-purpose flour

Salt

1 stick plus 2 tablespoons cold unsalted butter, cubed

¼ cup plus 2 tablespoons ice water

1 tablespoon pure olive oil

½ pound andouille sausage, cut into 1-inch pieces

½ small onion, finely chopped

1 tablespoon minced garlic

½ teaspoon dried sage, crumbled

1 cup heavy cream

Freshly ground pepper

3 large egg yolks

Tangy Apple Salad (recipe follows), for serving

1. Preheat the oven to 350°. Wrap the sweet potatoes in foil and bake for 45 minutes, until soft. Let cool. Meanwhile, in a food processor, combine the cornmeal and flour with 1 teaspoon of salt. Add the cold butter cubes and pulse until the mixture resembles coarse meal. Add the ice water and pulse until the dough comes together. Turn the dough out onto a work surface and knead until smooth.

2. Lightly flour the work surface and roll out the dough to a 13-inch round about ¼ inch thick. Ease the dough into a 9-inch glass pie plate. Trim the overhang to 1 inch, then fold it under itself and crimp decoratively. Prick the bottom crust several times with a fork. Line the dough with foil and fill with pie weights. Bake for about 30 minutes, until the crust is barely set. Remove the foil and weights and bake for 10 minutes longer, until the crust is dry and very lightly browned.

3. Meanwhile, in a large skillet, heat the olive oil. Add the andouille sausage and cook over high heat, stirring occasionally, until it is lightly browned, about 5 minutes. Add the onion, garlic and dried sage and cook until the onion is softened, about 5 minutes. Let cool slightly.

4. Peel the sweet potatoes and transfer them to a food processor. Add the cream and puree until very smooth. Season with salt and pepper. Add the egg yolks and process until incorporated. Transfer the filling to a large bowl and stir in the andouille mixture. Scrape the filling into the crust and bake for about 45 minutes, until the custard is set. Let cool for 20 minutes, then cut the pie into wedges and serve with the Tangy Apple Salad. —*Donald Link*

MAKE AHEAD The pie can be refrigerated overnight. Rewarm before serving.

TANGY APPLE SALAD

 **TOTAL: 15 MIN**

6 SERVINGS ● ●

2 teaspoons cider vinegar

Pinch of sugar

¼ cup buttermilk

¼ cup vegetable oil

Salt and freshly ground pepper

2 large Granny Smith apples, peeled and cut into thin matchsticks

Two 6-ounce bunches of watercress, thick stems discarded

In a large bowl, whisk the cider vinegar with the sugar and buttermilk. Gradually whisk in the vegetable oil and season the cider dressing with salt and freshly ground black pepper. Add the apple matchsticks and watercress and toss to coat the salad. Serve the apple salad right away. —*DL*

perfecting mashed potatoes

The ideal mashed potatoes are ultrafluffy and smooth. F&W's **Grace Parisi**
likes mashing Yukon Gold potatoes, since they have a naturally creamy texture.
For contrast, she tops them with an irresistible tangle of sweet fried shallots.

Mashed Potatoes with Crispy Shallots

TOTAL: 45 MIN

12 SERVINGS ● ● ●

- 6 pounds Yukon Gold potatoes, peeled and quartered (see Note)
- 4 peeled garlic cloves
- 2 cups canola oil
- 6 large shallots, thinly sliced (1½ cups)
- 1 cup half-and-half
- 1½ sticks (12 tablespoons) unsalted butter

Kosher salt

1. In a large pot, cover the quartered potatoes and garlic cloves with cold water and bring to a boil. Simmer over moderate heat until the potatoes are tender when pierced with a fork, about 20 minutes.

2. Meanwhile, in a medium skillet, heat the canola oil until shimmering. Add the sliced shallots to the skillet in a single layer and cook over moderate heat, stirring frequently, until they are golden, about 15 minutes. Using a slotted spoon, transfer the shallots to a paper towel–lined plate to drain.

3. Drain the potatoes and garlic in a colander, shaking out the excess water. Add the half-and-half and butter to the pot and heat until melted. Remove from the heat. Press the potatoes and garlic through a ricer (or use a food mill or fine-mesh sieve) into the pot and season with salt. Stir and cook over moderate heat until very hot. Transfer the mashed potatoes to a bowl. Just before serving, sprinkle the shallots with salt and garnish the potatoes with the shallots.

NOTE Yellow-fleshed Yukon Gold potatoes are ideal for this recipe. They're available at most supermarkets.

MAKE AHEAD The mashed potatoes can be made earlier in the day and kept at room temperature; warm over moderate heat, stirring constantly. The fried shallots can be kept in an airtight container for up to 3 days; reheat in the oven if desired.

TWO GREAT VARIATIONS

1 Mashed Potatoes with Parmesan Cheese & Fresh Thyme

Omit the shallots. Make the mashed potatoes as directed. Stir 2 tablespoons thyme leaves and 1 cup freshly grated Parmigiano-Reggiano cheese into the mashed potatoes and garnish with thyme sprigs just before serving.

2 Mashed Potatoes with Butternut Squash

Omit the shallots. Mash 3 pounds potatoes with the garlic cloves. Peel and slice one 3-pound butternut squash ½ inch thick and roast in a 400° oven for about 25 minutes, until tender. Puree the squash in a food processor and stir the squash puree into the mashed potatoes.

potatoes, grains & beans

Five-Spice-Glazed Sweet Potatoes with Walnut Toffee

photo, page 234

ACTIVE: 20 MIN; TOTAL: 1 HR

10 TO 12 SERVINGS ● ●

- 6 pounds orange sweet potatoes or yams, peeled and cut into 2-inch chunks
- 1 cup light brown sugar
- 6 tablespoons unsalted butter
- 2 teaspoons Chinese five-spice powder
- ¼ teaspoon freshly grated nutmeg
- Salt
- Crunchy Walnut Toffee (recipe follows), coarsely chopped

1. Preheat the oven to 400°. Spread the sweet potato chunks in two 9-by-13-inch baking dishes. Add 1 cup of water to each dish, cover with foil and bake for about 25 minutes, until the sweet potatoes are barely tender. Pour off any remaining water from the baking dishes.

2. In a small saucepan, combine the brown sugar with the butter, five-spice powder and nutmeg and cook over moderate heat until the butter is melted and the mixture is bubbling, about 4 minutes. Pour the mixture over the potatoes, stir to coat and season with salt. Bake for 10 minutes, basting a few times, until the potatoes are tender and glazed. Sprinkle the walnut toffee over the potatoes; serve. —*Shawn McClain*

MAKE AHEAD The glazed sweet potatoes can be refrigerated overnight. Reheat before topping and serving.

CRUNCHY WALNUT TOFFEE

 ACTIVE: 10 MIN; TOTAL: 45 MIN

MAKES ABOUT 2 CUPS ● ●

- ½ cup sugar
- ¼ cup water
- 2 tablespoons light corn syrup
- 2 tablespoons unsalted butter
- ¼ teaspoon baking soda
- ¼ teaspoon salt
- 1 cup walnuts, coarsely chopped

Line a baking sheet with parchment paper. In a medium saucepan, combine the sugar, water, corn syrup and butter and bring to a simmer. Cook over moderate heat, swirling the pan a few times, until a light caramel forms, about 4 minutes. Stir in the baking soda and salt. Remove the pan from the heat and stir in the walnuts. Quickly spread the toffee on the prepared baking sheet as thinly as possible. Let cool completely. Break into pieces and serve. —*SM*

Cheesy Farro-and-Tomato Risotto

 TOTAL: 40 MIN

4 SERVINGS ● ● ●

- ¼ cup extra-virgin olive oil
- 1 small onion, finely chopped
- 3 garlic cloves, minced
- 1½ cups farro
- ¼ cup dry white wine
- 1 quart water
- 1 cup drained canned tomatoes, chopped
- ¼ cup freshly grated Parmigiano-Reggiano cheese
- Salt and freshly ground pepper
- 2 tablespoons sliced basil leaves

1. In a large saucepan, heat 3 tablespoons of the oil. Add the onion and cook over moderately high heat until softened, 2 minutes. Add the garlic and cook, stirring, until fragrant, 1 minute. Add the farro and stir until coated with oil, 1 minute. Add the wine and simmer until almost evaporated, 2 minutes. Lower the heat to moderate. Add 1 cup of the water and cook, stirring, until absorbed. Repeat with the remaining water, adding 1 cup at a time and stirring until the farro is just tender and suspended in a creamy sauce, 30 minutes total.

2. Stir in the tomatoes and bring to a boil over moderate heat. Off the heat, stir in the remaining 1 tablespoon of oil and the cheese. Season with salt and pepper. Garnish with basil and serve. —*Rajat Parr*

WINE Fresh, fruity rosé.

Summer Farro Salad

 **TOTAL: 30 MIN**

8 SERVINGS ● ● ● ●

New York City chef and cooking teacher Marco Canora says you can swap in any starch—like cubed bread or pasta—for the farro (a nutty Italian grain) in this recipe.

- ⅓ cup plus 2 tablespoons extra-virgin olive oil
- 1 small yellow onion, quartered
- 1 small carrot, halved
- 1 celery rib, halved
- 12 ounces farro (1¾ cups)
- 5 cups water
- Kosher salt
- 3 tablespoons red wine vinegar
- Freshly ground pepper
- ½ small red onion, thinly sliced
- 1 small seedless cucumber, halved lengthwise and thinly sliced crosswise
- 1 pint grape tomatoes, halved
- ¼ cup chopped fresh basil

1. In a large saucepan, heat 2 tablespoons of the olive oil. Add the quartered yellow onion and halved carrot and celery rib, cover the pan and cook over moderately low heat until the vegetables are barely softened, about 5 minutes. Add the farro and stir to coat with the oil. Add the water and bring to a boil. Cover the pan and simmer over low heat until the farro is barely tender, about 10 minutes; season with salt. Cover the pan and simmer until the farro is al dente, about 10 minutes longer. Drain the farro and remove and discard the onion, carrot and celery pieces. Let the farro cool completely.

2. In a large bowl, whisk the remaining ⅓ cup of olive oil with the red wine vinegar and season with salt and pepper. Fold in the cooled farro, sliced red onion, cucumber, grape tomatoes and chopped basil, season with salt and pepper and serve. —*Marco Canora*

SUMMER FARRO SALAD

Farro Salad with Squid and Chorizo

ACTIVE: 25 MIN; TOTAL: 1 HR 10 MIN
4 SERVINGS ● ● ●

- 1 cup farro
- ¼ cup extra-virgin olive oil
- 1 small red onion, finely chopped
- 2 ounces dry chorizo, skinned and sliced ¼ inch thick (½ cup)
- ¾ pound cleaned squid— bodies cut into ¼-inch rings, large tentacles halved

Salt

- 1 cup cherry tomatoes, halved
- 2 tablespoons chopped parsley
- 1 tablespoon chopped marjoram
- 1 tablespoon red wine vinegar

Freshly ground pepper

1. Bring a large saucepan of water to a boil. Add the farro, cover and simmer over low heat until al dente, about 45 minutes. Drain and transfer to a serving bowl.
2. In a large skillet, heat 2 tablespoons of the olive oil. Add the onion and cook over moderately high heat until softened, about 2 minutes. Stir in the chorizo and cook until sizzling, about 2 minutes. Add the squid and cook, stirring, until just white throughout, about 2 minutes. Season with salt.
3. Add the squid to the farro along with the cherry tomatoes, parsley, marjoram, vinegar and the remaining 2 tablespoons of olive oil. Season with salt and pepper, toss well and serve right away.
—David Swain

Bacon Quinoa with Almonds and Herbs

TOTAL: 40 MIN
4 SERVINGS ● ●

"Quinoa is a miracle food," says star chef Bruce Sherman (an F&W Best New Chef 2003). Native to the Andes Mountains, the protein-rich grain is now also grown in the U.S. Sherman tosses it with smoky bacon and toasted almonds to make a substantial side dish.

- ⅓ cup slivered almonds
- 1 teaspoon vegetable oil
- 2 thick slices of applewood-smoked bacon, cut into ¼-inch dice
- 1 small shallot, minced
- 1 cup quinoa, rinsed
- 2 cups chicken stock
- 1 sage sprig
- 1 tablespoon minced chives
- 1 tablespoon chopped parsley

Salt and freshly ground white pepper

1. Preheat the oven to 350°. Spread the almonds in a pie plate and toast in the oven until golden brown, 4 minutes; let cool.
2. In a medium saucepan, heat the oil. Add the bacon and cook over moderately high heat until the fat has rendered, about 2 minutes. Add the shallot and cook, stirring a few times, until softened but not browned, about 1 minute. Add the quinoa, stock and sage and bring to a boil. Cover and cook over low heat until the stock has been absorbed, about 17 minutes. Remove the quinoa from the heat and let stand, covered, for 5 minutes. Discard the sage and fluff the quinoa with a fork. Stir in the chives, parsley and toasted almonds. Season with salt and pepper and serve.
—Bruce Sherman

Lemony Quinoa Salad with Shaved Vegetables

ACTIVE: 25 MIN; TOTAL: 1 HR 25 MIN
4 SERVINGS ● ●

Jeremy Fox (an F&W Best New Chef 2008) tosses nutty-tasting quinoa with crunchy shaved vegetables for a refreshing salad loaded with vitamins and minerals.

- 8 large red radishes or 1 large watermelon radish
- 1 small black radish
- 1 medium carrot, peeled
- 1 medium fennel bulb, cored
- 1 cup quinoa, preferably red, rinsed and drained
- 2½ cups water

Finely grated zest of 2 lemons

Juice of 1 lemon

- 2 tablespoons vegetable oil

Salt and freshly ground pepper

1. Using a mandoline, thinly slice the radishes, carrot and fennel bulb. Transfer the shaved vegetables to a large bowl of ice water and refrigerate for about 1 hour, or until the vegetables are crisp.
2. Meanwhile, in a saucepan, bring the quinoa and water to a boil. Cover and cook over low heat until the water is absorbed and the quinoa is tender, 20 minutes. Let cool.
3. Drain and dry the shaved vegetables. In a bowl, combine the lemon zest and juice with the vegetable oil. Add the cooked quinoa and toss; season with salt and pepper. Serve the quinoa salad in bowls, topped with the shaved vegetables.
—Jeremy Fox

Quinoa Salad with Sugar Snap Peas

ACTIVE: 15 MIN; TOTAL: 40 MIN
6 SERVINGS ● ● ● ●

- ½ pound sugar snap peas
- 1½ cups quinoa, rinsed and drained
- ¼ cup plus 1 tablespoon extra-virgin olive oil
- 3 tablespoons white wine vinegar

Salt and freshly ground pepper

- ½ cup salted roasted pumpkin seeds
- ½ cup very finely chopped chives

1. In a small saucepan of boiling salted water, simmer the peas until bright green and crisp-tender, about 1 minute. Drain and spread out on a large plate to cool, then pat dry. Cut the peas on the diagonal into 1-inch pieces.
2. In a small saucepan, combine the quinoa with 2 cups of water and bring to a boil. Cover and cook over low heat until all of the water has evaporated and the quinoa is tender, about 15 minutes. Uncover and fluff the quinoa, then transfer to a large bowl and let cool to room temperature.

LEMONY QUINOA SALAD WITH SHAVED VEGETABLES

QUINOA WITH SUGAR SNAPS (AND BELL PEPPER SHOOTER, P. 74)

3. In a bowl, combine the oil and vinegar; season the dressing with salt and pepper. Add the peas to the quinoa along with the pumpkin seeds, chives and dressing; stir. Season with salt and pepper and serve at room temperature or lightly chilled. —*Marcia Kiesel*

MAKE AHEAD The salad can be refrigerated for up to 6 hours.

Black Bean–and–Quinoa Salad

ACTIVE: 30 MIN; TOTAL: 2 HR 45 MIN

8 SERVINGS ● ● ○

Boston chef and restaurateur Ken Oringer believes that chefs need to make a point of eating healthy dishes when they can, so he includes quinoa in his diet at least three times a week. Here he mixes the grain with black beans, onions and peppers to make a fun, hearty and very satisfying variation on prosaic five-bean salad.

12 ounces dried black beans, picked over and rinsed

Salt

1 cup quinoa, rinsed

3 tablespoons sherry vinegar

1 tablespoon soy sauce

1 tablespoon fresh lime juice

1 chipotle chile in adobo, very finely chopped

¼ cup plus 2 tablespoons extra-virgin olive oil

6 scallions, white and light green parts only, thinly sliced

1 small red onion, finely diced

1 medium yellow bell pepper, finely diced

¼ cup chopped cilantro

1. In a large saucepan, cover the black beans with cold water and bring to a boil. Cover the pot and let stand off the heat for about 1 hour.

2. Drain the beans. Return them to the pot and cover with 3 inches of water. Bring to a boil and simmer over low heat until tender, about 1 hour and 30 minutes; season generously with salt during the last 10 minutes. Drain and let cool.

3. Meanwhile, in a medium saucepan, combine the quinoa with 2 cups of water and a pinch of salt and bring to a boil. Cover the saucepan and simmer the quinoa over low heat until the water has been absorbed, about 15 minutes. Spread the quinoa on a plate and let cool.

4. In a large bowl, whisk the vinegar, soy sauce, lime juice and chipotle. Add the olive oil in a thin stream, whisking until blended. Add the black beans, quinoa, scallions, red onion, yellow pepper and cilantro. Season with salt, toss and serve. —*Ken Oringer*

MAKE AHEAD The bean-and-quinoa salad can be refrigerated overnight.

potatoes, grains & beans

Brown Rice Pilaf with Green Olives and Lemon

ACTIVE: 30 MIN; TOTAL: 1 HR 30 MIN

12 SERVINGS ● ●

Alain Coumont, founder of the bakery-café chain Le Pain Quotidien, makes this creamy (yet cream-free) rice dish with lemony Lucques olives and nutty Camargue red rice, but almost any green olive or short-grain brown rice would be delicious.

- 2 tablespoons extra-virgin olive oil, plus more for drizzling
- 2 medium onions, finely chopped
- 6 medium garlic cloves, minced
- 10 cups water
- 3 cups short-grain brown rice
- 1 thyme sprig
- 1 bay leaf

Kosher salt

- 1½ cups pitted small green olives, halved (6 ounces)
- ½ cup chopped flat-leaf parsley
- ¼ cup chopped basil, plus 24 basil leaves for garnish
- 3 tablespoons fresh lemon juice
- 1 tablespoon grated lemon zest

Freshly ground pepper

- 4 ounces aged goat cheese, shaved with a vegetable peeler

1. In a large saucepan, heat the 2 tablespoons of oil. Add the onions and garlic and cook over moderate heat, stirring occasionally, until softened, 8 minutes. Add the water, rice, thyme and bay leaf and bring to a boil for 1 minute. Remove from the heat, cover and let stand for 30 minutes.

2. Stir 1 tablespoon of salt into the rice. Cover and simmer over low heat, stirring occasionally, until most of the water has been absorbed, about 30 minutes. Remove from the heat; discard the bay leaf and thyme. Stir in the olives, parsley, chopped basil, lemon juice and lemon zest; season with salt and pepper. Spoon the rice into bowls. Drizzle with olive oil and garnish with the goat cheese and basil leaves; serve.

—*Alain Coumont*

Paella Valenciana

ACTIVE: 40 MIN; TOTAL: 1 HR 10 MIN

6 SERVINGS

- 3 tablespoons extra-virgin olive oil
- 1 large onion, thinly sliced
- 1 garlic clove, thinly sliced
- 3 whole chicken legs, split into thighs and drumsticks

Salt and freshly ground black pepper

- 3 ounces Spanish chorizo, finely diced
- 1 cup sliced piquillo peppers (from a 9-ounce jar)

One 15-ounce can large butter beans, drained and rinsed

- 5 cups chicken stock or low-sodium broth

Pinch of saffron threads, crumbled

- 2 cups arborio rice (15 ounces)
- ½ cup frozen baby peas
- 24 mussels, scrubbed and debearded (about 1 pound)
- 24 littleneck clams, scrubbed
- 6 jumbo shrimp in their shells, butterflied and deveined

1. In a large saucepan, heat 2 tablespoons of the olive oil. Add the sliced onion and garlic, cover and cook over low heat until they are softened, about 5 minutes. Uncover and cook, stirring occasionally, until the onion is lightly browned, about 5 minutes longer. Let cool slightly, then transfer the sautéed onion and garlic to a blender or food processor and puree until smooth, about 1 minute.

2. In a very large, deep skillet, heat the remaining 1 tablespoon of olive oil. Season the chicken legs with salt and black pepper, add to the skillet and cook over moderate heat, turning occasionally, until they are golden all over, about 12 minutes. Transfer the chicken legs to a plate.

3. Add the onion puree, diced chorizo, piquillo peppers and rinsed butter beans to the skillet and cook, stirring, until sizzling, about 2 minutes. Add the chicken stock and crumbled saffron, season with salt and bring to a boil. Stir in the rice. Nestle the chicken legs into the rice, cover and cook over moderately low heat until the rice is nearly tender, about 18 minutes. Add the peas, mussels, clams and shrimp, cover and cook until all the shellfish have opened and the chicken is cooked through, about 8 minutes. Let the paella rest for 5 minutes before serving.

—*Seamus Mullen*

MAKE AHEAD The onion puree can be refrigerated for up to 1 day. Bring to room temperature before using.

WINE Zesty, fresh Albariño.

Lemony Bulgur Salad with Shrimp and Spinach

ACTIVE: 15 MIN; TOTAL: 2 HR 10 MIN

6 SERVINGS ● ●

Bulgur (a quick-cooking form of whole wheat) is usually boiled before it's eaten, but for this terrific main-course salad, F&W's Melissa Rubel Jacobson simply softens it in warm tap water before tossing with baby spinach and precooked shrimp.

- 1½ cups coarse bulgur
- 1 teaspoon finely grated lemon zest
- ¼ cup fresh lemon juice
- 3 tablespoons chopped dill
- ½ cup extra-virgin olive oil
- 1 pound large cooked shrimp, shelled
- 3 cups baby spinach
- 4 radishes, thinly sliced
- 2 tablespoons pine nuts

Kosher salt and freshly ground pepper

1. In a bowl, cover the bulgur with warm tap water. Let stand until the grains are tender, about 2 hours. Drain well.

2. In a large bowl, whisk the lemon zest with the lemon juice and dill. Whisk in the olive oil. Add the bulgur, shrimp, spinach, radishes and pine nuts and toss to coat. Season with salt and pepper and serve.

—*Melissa Rubel Jacobson*

LEMONY BULGUR SALAD WITH SHRIMP AND SPINACH

BEAN, CORN AND SQUASH STEW

MAKE AHEAD The salad can be refrigerated for up to 1 day. Add the spinach, radishes and pine nuts just before serving.

Bean, Corn and Squash Stew

TOTAL: 50 MIN

4 SERVINGS ● ● ○ ○

In his excellent version of the traditional Chilean stew *porotos granados*, chef Alex Aguilera uses kidney beans in place of the customary cranberry beans, then folds in fresh basil and a swirl of paprika oil.

- 1 quart water
- One 1½-pound butternut squash—peeled, seeded and cut into 1-inch cubes
- 4 cups fresh corn kernels (cut from about 6 ears)
- One 19-ounce can kidney beans, drained
- ¾ cup chopped basil leaves
- ¼ cup plus 2 tablespoons vegetable oil
- 1 large onion, coarsely chopped
- 1 medium red bell pepper, coarsely chopped
- 1 medium green bell pepper, coarsely chopped
- 1 teaspoon ground cumin
- 1 teaspoon dried oregano
- 2 teaspoons hot paprika

Salt and freshly ground black pepper

1. In a large pot, bring the water to a boil with the squash and corn. Cover and simmer over moderately low heat until the squash is just tender, about 15 minutes. Add the kidney beans and cook until the beans are hot. Transfer 3 cups of the squash mixture to a blender along with some of the liquid and ½ cup of the basil; puree. Return the puree to the pot and keep the stew warm.

2. Meanwhile, in a large skillet, heat 2 tablespoons of the vegetable oil. Add the onion and bell peppers and cook over moderate heat, stirring occasionally, until the vegetables are softened, 8 minutes. Add the cumin, oregano and 1 teaspoon of the paprika and cook, stirring, until fragrant, about 4 minutes. Stir the vegetables into the stew and season with salt and pepper.

3. In a small saucepan, heat the remaining ¼ cup of oil. Add the remaining 1 teaspoon of paprika and cook over low heat until fragrant. Transfer to a small bowl.

4. Ladle the stew into bowls. Swirl in the paprika oil, sprinkle with the remaining ¼ cup basil and serve. —*Alex Aguilera*

MAKE AHEAD The bean stew can be prepared through Step 2 up to 2 days ahead. Rewarm, swirl in the paprika oil and sprinkle with the basil right before serving.

WINE Ripe, luxurious Chardonnay.

● HEALTHY ● MAKE AHEAD ○ VEGETARIAN ● STAFF FAVORITE

245

potatoes, grains & beans

Arroz Blanco

ACTIVE: 10 MIN; TOTAL: 35 MIN
6 SERVINGS ● ●

Cooking rice in garlicky olive oil and water—the Cuban way—makes it rich and fragrant. If you prefer, move the rice to the oven to finish the cooking: Bring the rice to a boil, place the covered pot in a 350° oven and cook for 30 minutes. Let stand for 5 minutes, then fluff with a fork and serve.

2 tablespoons extra-virgin olive oil
1 garlic clove, smashed
2½ cups water
1 teaspoon salt
1½ cups long-grain white rice, such as jasmine

In a large saucepan, heat the oil with the garlic over moderate heat and cook until the garlic is golden, about 2 minutes; discard the garlic. Add the water and salt to the saucepan and bring to a boil. Stir in the rice and return to a boil. Cover and simmer over very low heat until the rice is tender and the water is absorbed, 20 minutes. Let stand off the heat for 5 minutes, then fluff with a fork; serve. —*Lourdes Castro*

Porcini Risotto

TOTAL: 50 MIN
4 SERVINGS

1 ounce dried porcini mushrooms
2½ cups boiling water
3 cups chicken stock
Salt and freshly ground pepper
¼ cup extra-virgin olive oil
1 small shallot, minced
1 garlic clove, minced
1 cup arborio rice (7 ounces)
¼ cup dry white wine
1 small bay leaf
1 tablespoon unsalted butter
1 tablespoon mascarpone
1 cup freshly grated Parmigiano-Reggiano cheese (3 ounces)
1 pound fresh porcini or cremini mushrooms, thinly sliced
1 thyme sprig

1. In a heatproof bowl, soak the dried porcini in the boiling water until softened, 10 minutes. Drain, reserving 1 cup of the soaking liquid; rinse the mushrooms to remove any grit. Finely chop the porcini and reserve in a small bowl. Pour the soaking liquid into a medium saucepan, stopping before you reach the sediment at the bottom. Stir in the chicken stock and season with salt and pepper. Warm the stock over low heat.

2. In a large saucepan, heat 2 tablespoons of the oil until shimmering. Add the shallot and garlic and cook over moderate heat, stirring, until softened, 2 minutes. Add the rice and dried porcini and stir to coat. Add the wine and bay leaf and cook until the wine has evaporated. Add about one-fourth of the warm stock and cook over moderate heat, stirring constantly, until nearly absorbed. Continue adding the stock in batches, stirring constantly until the rice is al dente and suspended in a creamy sauce, about 20 minutes. Discard the bay leaf. Stir in the butter, mascarpone and cheese; season with salt and pepper and keep warm.

3. In a skillet, heat the remaining 2 tablespoons of oil. Add the fresh porcini and thyme; cook over high heat, stirring, until softened and golden, 8 minutes. Discard the thyme. Season the porcini with salt and pepper, spoon over the risotto and serve. —*Daniel Humm*

WINE Complex, elegant Pinot Noir.

Asparagus Risotto with Mint

TOTAL: 1 HR
4 SERVINGS

New Zealand chef Andy Glover cleverly flavors this risotto by cooking the rice in stock infused with mint sprigs and asparagus trimmings.

6 cups chicken stock or low-sodium broth
1¼ pounds medium asparagus—ends trimmed and reserved, spears sliced on the diagonal ¼ inch thick
4 mint sprigs, plus 2 tablespoons chopped mint leaves
2 teaspoons fennel seeds
2 tablespoons extra-virgin olive oil
1 small onion, finely diced
1 celery rib, finely diced
1½ cups arborio or *carnaroli* rice
½ cup dry white wine
2 tablespoons unsalted butter, softened
¼ cup freshly grated Parmigiano-Reggiano cheese, plus more for serving
Salt and freshly ground pepper

1. In a medium saucepan, combine the chicken stock with the asparagus ends and mint sprigs and bring to a boil. Reduce the heat to low, cover and keep hot.

2. In a large saucepan, toast the fennel seeds over high heat, stirring a few times, until fragrant, about 1 minute. Transfer the seeds to a mortar and let cool completely. Coarsely grind the seeds with a pestle.

3. In the same saucepan, heat the olive oil. Add the onion and celery and cook over moderate heat until softened, about 5 minutes. Add the rice and ground fennel and cook, stirring to coat the rice with oil. Add the wine and cook, stirring, until absorbed, about 2 minutes.

4. Add enough hot stock to just cover the rice and cook, stirring constantly, until the stock has been absorbed. Continue adding stock 1 cup at a time and cook, stirring constantly, until the rice is just tender, about 20 minutes total. Stir in the sliced asparagus and cook, adding more broth as necessary, until the asparagus is crisp-tender and the rice is al dente and bound in a creamy sauce, about 5 minutes longer.

5. Stir the butter into the risotto. Stir in the cheese and the chopped mint and season with salt and pepper. Spoon the risotto into bowls and serve, passing more cheese at the table. —*Andy Glover*

WINE Minerally, complex Sauvignon Blanc.

perfecting risotto

*F&W's **Grace Parisi** shares a simple, classic recipe for Milanese risotto infused with the traditional flavors of saffron and Parmesan. Then she offers three worldly, very different takes on this theme, with a hearty fennel-and-sausage variation, a seafood-filled version made creamy with mascarpone and a woodsy, deep-flavored mushroom risotto.*

Milanese Risotto

TOTAL: 30 MIN
6 SERVINGS ●

5½ cups chicken stock, preferably homemade, or low-sodium broth
2 tablespoons extra-virgin olive oil
1 small onion, finely chopped
Salt and freshly ground pepper
1½ cups arborio rice (10 ounces)
Pinch of saffron threads
½ cup dry white wine
½ cup freshly grated Parmigiano-Reggiano cheese
1 tablespoon unsalted butter
2 tablespoons chopped flat-leaf parsley

In a saucepan, bring the stock to a simmer; cover and keep warm over low heat. In a large saucepan, heat the oil. Add the onion, season with salt and pepper and cook over moderate heat, stirring, until softened, 5 minutes. Add the rice and cook for 1 minute, stirring to thoroughly coat. Crumble the saffron into the wine and add it to the rice. Cook, stirring, until the wine is absorbed. Add 1 cup of the stock to the rice and cook over moderate heat, stirring constantly, until nearly absorbed. Continue adding the stock ½ cup at a time, stirring, until it is nearly absorbed between additions. The risotto is done when the rice is al dente and suspended in a thick, creamy sauce, about 20 minutes total. Season the risotto with salt and pepper. Stir in the cheese, butter and parsley and serve immediately.

WINE Bright, tart Barbera.

THREE GREAT VARIATIONS

1 Fennel-and-Sausage Risotto

Make the risotto as directed, substituting pecorino for Parmigiano-Reggiano. In a large skillet, cook 1 pound crumbled sweet Italian sausage in 1 tablespoon olive oil over high heat until browned. Add 1 thinly sliced fennel bulb; cook until softened, 8 minutes. Stir the sausage and fennel into the risotto and serve.

WINE Juicy, fresh Dolcetto.

2 Creamy Seafood Risotto

Make the risotto as directed, substituting 3 cups clam juice and 2½ cups water for stock; omit the butter and cheese. In a skillet, cook 1 minced shallot in 1 tablespoon butter. Add ½ pound each chopped cooked shrimp and crabmeat; cook until hot. Add the seafood to the risotto, fold in ½ cup mascarpone and serve.

WINE Fresh, lively Soave.

3 Wild Mushroom & Red Wine Risotto

Make the risotto as directed, substituting red wine for white wine and omitting the saffron and butter. In a skillet, cook 1 minced shallot and 1 pound sliced wild mushrooms in 2 tablespoons butter over moderately high heat. Stir the mushrooms and shallot into the risotto and serve.

WINE Cherry-inflected, earthy Sangiovese.

potatoes, grains & beans

Armenian Rice

ACTIVE: 15 MIN; TOTAL: 1 HR

8 TO 10 SERVINGS

1½ sticks unsalted butter

3 ounces vermicelli or angel hair pasta, broken into 2-inch lengths (1 cup)

½ cup pine nuts

4 cups long-grain white rice

8 cups chicken stock, warmed

Kosher salt and freshly ground white pepper

⅓ cup thinly sliced mint leaves

In a large pot, melt the butter. Stir in the vermicelli and pine nuts and cook over high heat until golden brown, 3 minutes. Stir in the rice. Add the chicken stock, 1 teaspoon of salt and 1 teaspoon of white pepper. Cover and cook over low heat for 25 minutes, until the rice is tender and the stock has been absorbed. Uncover, fluff with a fork and cover again. Let stand for 20 minutes. Stir in half of the mint; season with salt and pepper. Transfer to a bowl, garnish with the remaining mint and serve. —*Lulu Powers*

Umbrian Lentil Stew with Olive-Oil-Fried Eggs

ACTIVE: 30 MIN; TOTAL: 1 HR 10 MIN

4 SERVINGS ● ●

Chef Matt Molina of L.A.'s Osteria Mozza uses small, brownish-green Umbrian lentils for this stew. "They have a rich, buttery flavor that's so comforting," he says.

2 tablespoons extra-virgin olive oil, plus more for frying

2 ounces thinly sliced prosciutto, very finely chopped

1 small carrot, peeled and coarsely chopped

1 small celery rib, coarsely chopped

½ small onion, finely diced

1 large garlic clove, very finely chopped

1½ teaspoons tomato paste

½ pound Umbrian lentils or green lentils (1¼ cups)

1 quart low-sodium chicken broth

Salt and freshly ground black pepper

4 large eggs

12 arugula leaves

Parmigiano-Reggiano cheese and aged balsamic vinegar, for serving

1. In a large saucepan, heat the 2 tablespoons of olive oil; add the finely chopped prosciutto and cook over low heat, stirring occasionally, until the prosciutto has rendered its fat.

2. In a food processor, finely chop the carrot and celery rib. Add the vegetables to the saucepan with the prosciutto along with the onion and garlic and cook, stirring, until the vegetables are softened, about 7 minutes. Add the tomato paste and stir over moderately high heat until shiny, about 1 minute. Add the lentils and 2½ cups of the chicken broth and bring to a boil. Simmer the lentils over low heat, stirring occasionally, until most of the broth has been absorbed, about 25 minutes. Add 1 more cup of the chicken broth and continue simmering until it has been absorbed, about 10 minutes. Add the remaining ½ cup of chicken broth and simmer until the lentils are tender and suspended in a creamy sauce, about 10 minutes longer. Season the lentil stew with salt and black pepper.

3. In a large nonstick skillet, heat a thin film of olive oil. Crack the eggs into the skillet, season them with salt and cook over moderately high heat until the edges of the egg whites are golden, the whites are just set and the egg yolks are still runny. Spoon the lentil stew into shallow bowls and top with the fried eggs and arugula leaves. Grate the Parmigiano-Reggiano cheese over the fried eggs and drizzle each serving with a little aged balsamic vinegar. Serve the lentil stew and eggs right away. —*Matt Molina*

MAKE AHEAD The lentil stew can be refrigerated overnight. Rewarm gently before proceeding with the recipe.

Beet Risotto

TOTAL: 1 HR

8 SERVINGS ●

7 cups chicken stock or 3½ cups low-sodium broth mixed with 3½ cups of water

4 tablespoons unsalted butter

¼ cup extra-virgin olive oil

1 large sweet onion, finely chopped

2 large beets (12 ounces each), peeled and coarsely shredded, plus thinly sliced beets for garnish

3 cups arborio rice (1¼ pounds)

6 ounces young pecorino cheese, freshly grated (1½ cups)

2 teaspoons poppy seeds, plus more for garnish

1. In a medium saucepan, bring the chicken stock to a simmer; cover and keep warm. In a medium enameled cast-iron casserole, melt the butter in the olive oil. Add the chopped sweet onion and cook over moderately high heat, stirring, until softened, about 5 minutes. Add the shredded beets and cook, stirring, until the pan is dry, about 12 minutes. Spoon half of the beets into a small bowl, leaving the remaining beets in the casserole.

2. Add the arborio rice to the casserole and cook, stirring, for 2 minutes. Add 1 cup of the warm chicken stock to the rice and cook over moderate heat, stirring, until the stock is nearly absorbed. Continue adding the warm chicken stock 1 cup at a time, stirring constantly, until the rice is al dente and a thick sauce forms, about 22 minutes total. Stir the reserved cooked beets, the grated pecorino cheese and the 2 teaspoons of poppy seeds into the risotto. Cook, stirring, until heated through; add a few tablespoons of water if the risotto is too thick. Spoon the beet risotto into shallow serving bowls. Garnish each serving with sliced beets and poppy seeds and serve the risotto right away. —*Grace Parisi*

WINE Dry, fruity sparkling wine.

BEET RISOTTO

Three-Lentil Dal

ACTIVE: 20 MIN; TOTAL: 1 HR 35 MIN

6 SERVINGS ● ● ●

A mix of lentils—earthy split peas, nutty *toor dal* (split pigeon peas) and creamy red lentils—adds complexity to this dish.

- ¾ cup yellow split peas (4 ounces)
- ¾ cup *toor dal* (dried split pigeon peas; 4 ounces)
- ¾ cup dried red lentils (4 ounces)
- 2 tablespoons vegetable oil
- 1 teaspoon cumin seeds
- 1 medium onion, cut into ½-inch dice
- 2 garlic cloves, minced
- 1 teaspoon ground coriander
- ½ teaspoon turmeric
- ¼ teaspoon cayenne pepper
- 1 large tomato, cut into ½-inch dice

Salt

- 1 tablespoon unsalted butter
- 2 tablespoons chopped cilantro

VEGETARIAN DINNER PARTY

Artichoke-and-Spinach Dip with Spiced Pita Chips, p. 18

· · · · · · · · · · · · · · · · ·

White Beans in Tomato Sauce, right

Giant Grilled Hunks of Bread, p. 255

Arugula-Fennel Salad, p. 48

Zippy, fresh Pinot Bianco

· · · · · · · · · · · · · · · · ·

Honeyed Fig Crostatas, p. 300

---

1. In a medium enameled cast-iron casserole, cover the yellow split peas, *toor dal* and red lentils with 1½ inches of water. Bring to a boil and simmer, uncovered, over low heat, stirring occasionally, until the red lentils and *toor dal* break down and the split yellow peas are tender, about 1 hour and 15 minutes.

2. In a large skillet, heat the oil until shimmering. Add the cumin and cook over moderate heat until darkened, 1 minute. Add the onion and garlic and cook, stirring, until golden brown, 6 minutes. Add the coriander, turmeric and cayenne and cook, stirring a few times, until fragrant, 2 minutes. Add the tomato and cook until softened, 3 minutes. Scrape the mixture into the dal and simmer over low heat, stirring occasionally, until the flavors are blended, 3 minutes. Season with salt. Stir in the butter and cilantro and serve.

—*Peggy Markel*

MAKE AHEAD The dal without the butter and cilantro can be refrigerated for up to 3 days. Reheat gently, adding water as necessary if the dal is too thick.

Quick White Bean Stew with Swiss Chard and Tomatoes

 TOTAL: 35 MIN

4 SERVINGS ● ● ● ●

Star restaurateur and winemaker Joe Bastianich uses white beans here, but he also loves making this recipe with chickpeas and large, flat *gigante* beans: "The bigger and creamier the beans are, the better."

- 2 pounds Swiss chard, large stems discarded and leaves cut crosswise into 2-inch strips
- ¼ cup extra-virgin olive oil
- 3 garlic cloves, thinly sliced
- ¼ teaspoon crushed red pepper
- 1 cup canned whole tomatoes, chopped

One 16-ounce can cannellini beans, drained and rinsed

Salt

1. Bring a saucepan of water to a boil. Add the chard and simmer over moderate heat until tender, 8 minutes. Drain the greens and gently press out excess water.

2. In the saucepan, heat the olive oil. Add the garlic and red pepper and cook over moderate heat until the garlic is golden, 1 minute. Add the tomatoes and bring to a boil. Add the beans and simmer over moderately high heat for 3 minutes. Add the chard and simmer over moderate heat until the flavors meld, 5 minutes. Season with salt and serve. —*Joe Bastianich*

White Beans in Tomato Sauce

ACTIVE: 30 MIN; TOTAL: 2 HR

6 SERVINGS ● ● ● ●

- 2 cups dried *zolfini* or cannellini beans, picked over and rinsed
- 1 sage sprig, plus ½ teaspoon chopped sage
- 2 garlic cloves, 1 minced
- 1 small bay leaf
- ¼ cup plus 2 tablespoons extra-virgin olive oil

Salt

- 1 cup canned tomato sauce

Freshly ground pepper

1. Cover the beans with 2 inches of water and bring to a boil. Cover and remove from the heat. Let stand for 1 hour, then drain.

2. Cover the beans with 4 inches of water. Add the sage sprig, whole garlic clove, bay leaf and 2 tablespoons of the oil. Bring to a boil; cook over moderately low heat for 30 minutes. Season with salt and cook for about 15 minutes longer, until tender; drain and discard the sage, garlic and bay leaf.

3. Meanwhile, in a medium, deep skillet, heat the remaining ¼ cup of oil. Add the chopped sage and the minced garlic and cook over moderate heat for 1 minute. Add the tomato sauce and bring to a simmer.

4. Add the beans to the skillet and cook, stirring, until saucy and thick, about 5 minutes. Season with salt and pepper and serve. —*Rolando Beramendi*

Frijoles Negros

ACTIVE: 30 MIN; TOTAL: 5 HR

6 SERVINGS ● ● ● ●

Their thick consistency and slightly sweet flavor make these black beans distinctly Cuban. The sweetness is nicely balanced with lots of crushed garlic and a hit of red wine vinegar. To check the beans for doneness, pinch one with your fingers: If it feels soft, it's ready.

- 1 pound dried black beans, picked over and rinsed

About 11 cups water

- 2 green bell peppers—1 cored and quartered, 1 finely chopped
- ½ cup extra-virgin olive oil
- 4 garlic cloves, crushed

Kosher salt

- 1 large onion, chopped
- ¼ teaspoon dried oregano
- 1 bay leaf
- 2 tablespoons sugar

Freshly ground pepper

- 2 tablespoons red wine vinegar
- 2 tablespoons dry white wine

1. In a large saucepan, combine the beans with 10 cups of water and the quartered green pepper and bring to a boil. Cover and remove from the heat. Let stand until the beans are softened, about 1 hour.

2. Return the beans to a boil and cook over very low heat until tender, 1½ to 2 hours. Discard the green pepper.

3. In a skillet, heat the oil. On a work surface, using the side of a large knife, mash the garlic to a paste with 1 teaspoon of salt; add to the skillet. Add the onion and chopped green pepper and cook over low heat, stirring, until softened, 8 minutes. Using a slotted spoon, add 1 cup of the beans to the skillet and mash to a paste.

4. Scrape the paste into the beans in the saucepan. Add the oregano, bay leaf, sugar, 2 teaspoons of salt and ½ teaspoon of pepper. Add the remaining 1 cup of water, or enough to just cover the beans, and cook for 1 hour, stirring occasionally. Add the vinegar and wine and cook, stirring frequently, until the beans are thick, about 15 minutes longer. Discard the bay leaf and serve. —Lourdes Castro

Spiced Chickpeas with Yogurt and Pine Nuts

 TOTAL: 30 MIN

4 SERVINGS ● ● ●

- 2 tablespoons extra-virgin olive oil
- 1 large onion, finely chopped
- 1 large garlic clove, minced
- ½ teaspoon ancho chile powder
- ½ teaspoon ground cumin
- ⅛ teaspoon ground turmeric

Pinch of cayenne pepper

One 15-ounce can chickpeas, drained

- 1 cup vegetable broth or water
- 1 tablespoon fresh lemon juice

Salt and freshly ground black pepper

- ¼ cup pine nuts
- 1⅓ cups plain fat-free Greek yogurt
- 1 tablespoon chopped mint

1. In a medium, deep skillet, heat the olive oil. Add the onion and garlic and cook over moderately high heat until softened, about 7 minutes. Stir in the chile powder, cumin, turmeric and cayenne and cook, stirring, for 1 minute. Add the chickpeas and broth and bring to a boil. Cover and simmer over moderately low heat for 15 minutes. Stir in the lemon juice and boil over moderately high heat, uncovered, until the liquid is thickened, about 3 minutes. Season with salt and pepper.

2. Meanwhile, in a small, dry skillet, toast the pine nuts over moderate heat, stirring, until golden, about 4 minutes.

3. Spoon the yogurt into shallow bowls. Top with the chickpeas, garnish with the mint and pine nuts and serve.
—Marisa May

MAKE AHEAD The spiced chickpeas can be prepared through Step 1 and refrigerated overnight. Reheat gently.

Chickpea Salad with Salami and Giardiniera Dressing

 TOTAL: 25 MIN

6 SERVINGS ●

The dressing for this reimagined antipasto is very smart and delicious: In place of vinegar or lemon juice, the salad gets tang from vinegary giardiniera vegetables (hot Italian pickled vegetables from a jar) that are combined with extra-virgin olive oil, capers and garlic.

- 1 cup giardiniera (stem the peperoncini), plus 2 tablespoons pickling liquid from the jar (see Note)
- ¼ cup plus 1 tablespoon extra-virgin olive oil
- 2 teaspoons capers, drained
- 1 small garlic clove, minced

Kosher salt and freshly ground black pepper

Two 15-ounce cans chickpeas, drained and rinsed

- ¼ pound sliced Genoa salami, halved and thinly sliced crosswise
- ¼ pound sliced provolone cheese, halved and thinly sliced crosswise
- 1 small head frisée (about 4 ounces), chopped
- 2 tablespoons thinly sliced basil leaves

1. In a food processor, combine the giardiniera vegetables with the pickling liquid, olive oil, capers and garlic and pulse until finely chopped. Season the dressing with salt and pepper.

2. In a large serving bowl, toss together the chickpeas, salami, provolone, frisée and basil. Add the dressing, toss to coat and serve right away.
—Melissa Rubel Jacobson

NOTE Giardiniera is available at supermarkets and Italian markets.

MAKE AHEAD The giardiniera dressing can be refrigerated for up to 3 days. The dressed salad can be refrigerated for up to 2 hours.

LEEK-AND-PECORINO PIZZA (P. 256)

breads, pizzas & sandwiches

New ways to elevate a brown-bag
lunch or casual dinner.

PULL-APART CHEESY ONION BREAD

JESSAMYN'S SEPHARDIC CHALLAH

Pull-Apart Cheesy Onion Bread

ACTIVE: 20 MIN; TOTAL: 1 HR 10 MIN
MAKES ONE 9-INCH LOAF ● ● ●

This cheesy onion bread is as fun to eat as monkey bread (balls of yeast dough that are baked in a pan together, then pulled apart at the table) but a lot less time-consuming to make. F&W's Grace Parisi spreads her buttery biscuit dough with a savory onion-Gruyère mixture, layers it sideways in a loaf pan, then bakes the bread until golden and fluffy.

1½ **sticks cold unsalted butter,**
    1 stick cubed
  1 **large onion, finely chopped**
  1 **tablespoon poppy seeds**
Kosher salt and freshly ground pepper
  3 **ounces Gruyère cheese,**
    coarsely shredded (1 cup)
  2 **cups all-purpose flour,**
    plus more for dusting
  2 **teaspoons baking powder**
  ½ **teaspoon baking soda**
  1 **cup buttermilk**

1. Preheat the oven to 425°. Butter a 9-by-4½-inch metal loaf pan. In a large skillet, melt the ½ stick of uncubed butter; pour 2 tablespoons of the melted butter into a small bowl and reserve. Add the chopped onion to the skillet and cook over moderate heat, stirring occasionally, until it is softened, about 8 minutes. Stir in the poppy seeds and season with salt and pepper. Scrape the onion mixture onto a plate and refrigerate for 5 minutes, until cooled slightly, then stir in the coarsely shredded Gruyère cheese.

2. Meanwhile, in a food processor, pulse the 2 cups of flour with the baking powder, baking soda and 1 teaspoon of salt. Add the stick of cubed butter and pulse until the butter cubes are the size of small peas. Add the buttermilk and pulse 5 or 6 times, just until a soft dough forms.

3. Turn the dough out onto a well-floured work surface and knead 2 or 3 times. Pat or roll the dough into a 2-by-24-inch rectangle. Spread the onion mixture on top of the bread. Cut the dough crosswise into 10 pieces. Stack 9 pieces onion side up, then top with the final piece onion side down. Carefully lay the stack in the prepared loaf pan and brush the top with the reserved melted butter.

4. Bake the loaf in the center of the oven for about 30 minutes, until it is golden and risen. Let the bread cool for at least 15 minutes before unmolding and serving.
—*Grace Parisi*

MAKE AHEAD The cooled, unmolded cheesy onion bread can be wrapped in plastic and stored at room temperature for up to 2 days. Rewarm before serving.

breads, pizzas & sandwiches

Jessamyn's Sephardic Challah

ACTIVE: 25 MIN; TOTAL: 3 HR 45 MIN PLUS COOLING

MAKES 2 ROUND LOAVES ● ● ●

Jessamyn Waldman, founder of Hot Bread Kitchen in Queens, New York, grew up in Canada eating challah, the Jewish Sabbath bread. Unlike the eggy challahs of the Ashkenazi Jews of Eastern Europe, this version comes from the Sephardic Jews of the Mediterranean, who flavor their challahs with caraway and anise. Many challahs are braided, but this one is twisted into a round, turban-shaped loaf.

- 3 tablespoons sesame seeds
- 1½ tablespoons caraway seeds
- 1½ tablespoons anise seeds
- 1 envelope active dry yeast
- 2 cups lukewarm water
- 5 cups bread flour
- 2½ tablespoons extra-virgin olive oil
- 2 tablespoons honey
- 1 tablespoon kosher salt
- Cornmeal, for dusting
- 2 large egg yolks

1. In a skillet, toast the sesame, caraway and anise seeds over moderate heat until fragrant, 2 minutes; transfer to a plate and let cool. In a small bowl, combine the yeast with 2 tablespoons of the water and let stand until thoroughly moistened, about 5 minutes.
2. In the bowl of a standing electric mixer fitted with the dough hook, combine the flour with the olive oil, the honey and the remaining water and mix at low speed until a very soft dough forms. Add the kosher salt, yeast mixture and all but 1 tablespoon of the seeds and mix at medium-low speed until the dough is supple and smooth, 10 minutes. Using oiled hands, transfer the dough to a large oiled bowl. Cover the bowl with plastic wrap and let stand in a draft-free spot until the dough is risen, 1 hour.
3. Lightly oil 2 small cookie sheets and dust them with cornmeal. Turn the dough out onto a lightly floured work surface and

press to deflate. Cut the dough in half and let rest for 5 minutes. Roll each piece into an 18-inch-long rope and let rest for 5 minutes longer, then roll each rope into a 32-inch rope. Beginning at the center and working outward, form each rope into a coil; tuck the ends under the coils.
4. Transfer each coil to a baking sheet and cover each loaf with a large, inverted bowl. Let stand for 1 hour, until the loaves have nearly doubled in bulk.
5. Preheat the oven to 400°. In a bowl, whisk the egg yolks with 1 tablespoon of water. Brush the egg wash over the loaves and let stand uncovered for 30 minutes. Brush with the egg wash once more and sprinkle with the reserved 1 tablespoon of seeds. Bake the loaves side by side in the center of the oven for 30 minutes, until they're golden and sound hollow when tapped on the bottom. Transfer the loaves to racks and let cool completely before slicing.
—*Jessamyn Waldman*

MAKE AHEAD The loaves can be wrapped in foil and refrigerated for up to 1 week.

Giant Grilled Hunks of Bread

 TOTAL: 10 MIN
4 SERVINGS ●

L.A. chef Matt Molina grills hunks of crusty peasant bread to serve with grilled steak; they're great for sopping up all the delicious juices. Molina prefers grilling fresh bread. "When the bread is doused with plenty of olive oil and cooked over high heat, its center becomes almost custardlike," he says.

- Four 3-inch-thick slices of peasant bread
- Extra-virgin olive oil, for brushing
- 2 large garlic cloves, peeled
- Maldon salt or other flaky sea salt

Light a grill. Generously brush the bread on both sides with olive oil. Grill over moderate heat until crisp and lightly charred, about 2 minutes per side. Rub both sides with the garlic cloves, season with salt and serve right away. —*Matt Molina*

Rosemary-Potato Focaccia Rolls

ACTIVE: 30 MIN; TOTAL: 3 HR

MAKES 12 ROLLS ● ● ●

- 1 envelope active dry yeast
- 2 cups lukewarm water
- 4¼ cups bread flour
- Extra-virgin olive oil
- 1 tablespoon sugar
- Kosher salt
- ½ pound small red-skinned potatoes, very thinly sliced
- 2 teaspoons chopped fresh rosemary

1. In the bowl of a standing electric mixer fitted with the dough hook, combine the yeast with 2 tablespoons of the water and let stand until moistened. Add the flour, ⅓ cup of olive oil, sugar, 2 teaspoons of salt and the remaining water; mix at medium speed until a soft, supple dough forms, 10 minutes. Transfer the dough to an oiled bowl, cover with plastic wrap and let stand in a draft-free spot for 1 hour.
2. Position racks in the upper and lower thirds of the oven and preheat the oven to 400°. Line 3 large rimmed baking sheets with parchment paper. On one of the sheets, toss the potatoes with the rosemary and ½ cup of olive oil and season with salt. Spread the potatoes in a single layer and bake until tender, 15 minutes. Let cool.
3. Turn the dough out onto an oiled surface and press to deflate. Cut the dough into 12 pieces and roll into balls; transfer to the remaining 2 baking sheets and brush with the oil used to roast the potatoes. Let stand in a draft-free spot until nearly doubled in bulk, 1 hour. Fan 3 potato slices on the top of each roll and brush with more oil.
4. Set a sheet pan in the bottom of the oven and fill with water to create steam. Bake the focaccia rolls for 30 minutes, until golden brown; shift the pans halfway through baking. Transfer the pans to racks and let the rolls cool completely.
—*Jessamyn Waldman*

breads, pizzas & sandwiches

Margherita Tortilla Pizzas

ACTIVE: 30 MIN; TOTAL: 1 HR 20 MIN

MAKES FOUR 10-INCH PIZZAS ●

Master chef Jacques Pépin makes quick pizzas with pita bread, *lavash* or flour tortillas. The possibilities are endless, from a simple Margherita to a white-clam pie inspired by the renowned Frank Pepe's Pizzeria Napolitana in New Haven, Connecticut. "The oven at Pepe's is heated with coal to over 2,000°," Pépin says. "While you can't duplicate that in your home oven, my tortilla version is quite good."

Four 10-inch flour tortillas

Extra-virgin olive oil

¼ cup freshly grated Parmigiano-Reggiano cheese

4 medium tomatoes (2 pounds)

Salt and freshly ground black pepper

1 pound fresh mozzarella, preferably buffalo, shredded (4 cups)

1 cup finely shredded fresh basil leaves

1. Set a pizza stone in the oven and preheat the oven to 500°, allowing at least 45 minutes for the stone to heat.

2. Brush both sides of one flour tortilla with olive oil. Place the tortilla on a lightly floured pizza peel and sprinkle the top with 1 tablespoon of the grated Parmigiano-Reggiano cheese. Thinly slice one of the tomatoes and arrange the slices on the tortilla. Season with salt and pepper and top with 1 cup of the mozzarella. Drizzle lightly with olive oil.

3. Slide the tortilla pizza onto the preheated pizza stone and bake for about 8 minutes, until the pizza is crisp on the bottom and the cheese is bubbling. Garnish with ¼ cup of the shredded fresh basil, cut the pizza into 8 wedges and serve right away. Repeat with the remaining tortillas, tomatoes, cheeses and basil.
—*Jacques Pépin*

WINE Zippy, fresh Pinot Bianco.

Leek-and-Pecorino Pizzas

photo, page 252

ACTIVE: 50 MIN; TOTAL: 1 HR 30 MIN

MAKES EIGHT 7-INCH PIZZAS ●

All-purpose flour, for dusting

1½ pounds pizza dough, cut into 8 pieces

¼ cup plus 2 tablespoons extra-virgin olive oil, plus more for brushing

2 large leeks, sliced ¼ inch thick

Salt and freshly ground pepper

¾ pound ground lamb

32 cherry tomatoes, halved

¼ pound truffled pecorino cheese, thinly sliced

1. Preheat the oven to 500°. Heat a pizza stone on the bottom of the oven for 45 minutes. (Alternatively, heat a large inverted baking sheet on the bottom rack of the oven for 5 minutes.)

2. On a lightly floured work surface, roll out each piece of dough to a 7-inch round. Oil 3 large baking sheets and place the dough rounds on the sheets. Cover with plastic wrap and let rest for 15 minutes.

3. Meanwhile, in a large skillet, heat ¼ cup of the olive oil. Add the sliced leeks, season with salt and pepper and cook over moderate heat, stirring occasionally, until softened, about 8 minutes; transfer the leeks to a plate. Add the remaining 2 tablespoons of olive oil to the skillet. Add the ground lamb, season the meat with salt and pepper and cook, breaking up the meat with a spoon, until no pink remains, about 5 minutes.

4. Generously flour a pizza peel. Place a dough round on the peel and brush with olive oil. Top with some of the leeks, lamb, tomatoes and pecorino cheese. Slide the dough round onto the hot stone or baking sheet and bake for about 4 minutes, until the pizza is bubbling and crisp. Repeat with the remaining ingredients and serve.
—*Marcia Kiesel*

WINE Ripe, juicy Pinot Noir.

Artichoke-and-Fontina Pizzas

TOTAL: 30 MIN PLUS OVERNIGHT MARINATING

MAKES TWO 10-INCH PIZZAS ●

Cookbook author Eugenia Bone marinates frozen artichokes overnight in olive oil with garlic, herbs and lemon juice before scattering them on these pizzas. You can also use store-bought marinated artichokes.

16 ounces frozen artichoke hearts, thawed and drained

1 cup plus 1 tablespoon olive oil

2 teaspoons fresh lemon juice

2 garlic cloves, smashed

2 thyme sprigs

2 rosemary sprigs

1 bay leaf

1 small dried red pepper

Salt

Cornmeal, for dusting

Two 8-ounce balls of store-bought pizza dough

2½ cups coarsely grated imported Fontina cheese

Freshly ground pepper

1. In a medium bowl, combine the artichoke hearts with 1 cup of the olive oil, the lemon juice, garlic, thyme, rosemary, bay leaf and chile pepper. Season with salt. Cover and refrigerate the artichokes overnight or for up to 3 days.

2. Preheat the oven to 425°. Dust a work surface with cornmeal and roll out each piece of pizza dough to a 10-inch round. Transfer to baking sheets. Drizzle the rounds with the remaining 1 tablespoon of olive oil. Bake for about 8 minutes, until the dough looks dry and bubbles appear on the surface. Remove from the oven.

3. Chop the artichokes into bite-size pieces; drain them on paper towels. Sprinkle the Fontina over the pizzas; distribute the artichokes over the cheese. Season with salt and pepper; return the pizzas to the oven. Bake for about 10 minutes, until the edges are browned. Serve hot. —*Eugenia Bone*

WINE Lively, tart Sauvignon Blanc.

SUMMER SQUASH PIZZA WITH GOAT CHEESE   PIZZA COOKS IN A CLAY OVEN

Summer Squash Pizza with Goat Cheese and Walnuts

ACTIVE: 25 MIN; TOTAL: 50 MIN

MAKES ONE 12-INCH PIZZA ●

Zucchini and yellow squash can both be mild in flavor, but nothing about this tangy, herby pizza is bland. The summer squash is sliced into slender coins, then roasted in a hot oven until it's lightly caramelized, bringing out its sweetness.

- 1 tablespoon extra-virgin olive oil, plus more for drizzling
- 1 medium garlic clove, very finely chopped

All-purpose flour, for dusting

- 6 ounces pizza dough

Pinch of crushed red pepper

Salt and freshly ground black pepper

- ½ small onion, thinly sliced
- ¼ cup shredded part-skim-milk mozzarella
- 1 teaspoon chopped summer savory
- ¼ pound summer squash, thinly sliced on a mandoline
- 2 ounces fresh goat cheese, crumbled
- 2 tablespoons chopped toasted walnuts

1. Preheat the oven to 500°. Preheat a pizza stone on the bottom of the oven for at least 45 minutes. (Alternatively, heat a large inverted baking sheet on the bottom rack of the oven for 5 minutes.) In a small bowl, combine the 1 tablespoon of olive oil with the finely chopped garlic and let stand. On a lightly floured work surface, roll out the pizza dough to form a 12-inch round, ¼ inch thick. Transfer the round to a lightly floured pizza peel.

2. Leaving a ½-inch border of dough, brush the round with the garlic oil and sprinkle with crushed red pepper, salt and black pepper. Scatter the onion slices over the round; top with the shredded mozzarella and chopped summer savory. Arrange the summer squash slices on top of the pizza in a single layer, overlapping them slightly. Dot the squash with the goat cheese.

3. Slide the summer squash pizza onto the preheated pizza stone and bake for about 5 minutes, until the bottom of the pizza crust is crisp and the squash slices are slightly browned on top. Carefully transfer the hot pizza to a work surface. Sprinkle the chopped toasted walnuts over the pizza and drizzle with olive oil. Cut the summer squash pizza into wedges and serve immediately.

—*Taylor Boetticher*

WINE Minerally, complex Sauvignon Blanc.

● HEALTHY   ● MAKE AHEAD   ● VEGETARIAN   ● STAFF FAVORITE

breads, pizzas & sandwiches

Mushroom–and–Goat Cheese Béchamel Pizzas

ACTIVE: 40 MIN; TOTAL: 1 HR 15 MIN

MAKES FOUR 9-INCH PIZZAS ● ●

To make these individual mushroom-topped pizzas extra luxe, chef Andres Barrera of Manhattan's City Winery spreads them with a velvety béchamel (a creamy white sauce of butter, flour and milk) enriched with goat cheese and seasoned with freshly grated nutmeg.

- 2 tablespoons unsalted butter
- 3 tablespoons all-purpose flour, plus more for dusting
- 1½ cups milk
- 2 ounces fresh goat cheese, thickly sliced

Freshly grated nutmeg

Salt and freshly ground black pepper

- 1 pound pizza dough
- 2 tablespoons extra-virgin olive oil, plus more for brushing
- 1 medium garlic clove, smashed
- 1 pound assorted fresh mushrooms, such as porcini, white button and stemmed shiitake, thinly sliced
- 1 teaspoon thyme leaves

---

easy pizza dough snacks

There are lots of things you can do with store-bought pizza dough. To make a flatbread: Roll out the dough 1 inch thick and drizzle with olive oil, minced garlic, Parmesan and parsley. Or, for a breakfast pastry, brush with melted butter and sprinkle with cinnamon sugar. Bake on a greased baking sheet at 450° until the dough is puffed and golden, about 10 minutes.

---

1. Preheat the oven to 500°. Preheat a pizza stone for 45 minutes or generously oil a large baking sheet. In a medium saucepan, melt the butter over moderate heat. Stir in the 3 tablespoons of flour until a paste forms. Gradually pour in the milk, whisking until smooth. Bring the béchamel sauce to a simmer over moderately high heat, whisking constantly, until thickened, about 4 minutes. Reduce the heat to low and cook, whisking often, until no floury taste remains, about 10 minutes. Remove from the heat and stir in the goat cheese until melted. Season the sauce with nutmeg, salt and pepper.

2. Cut the dough into 4 pieces. On a lightly floured work surface, roll out each piece to a 6-inch round. Dust them with flour; let rest until slightly puffed, 15 minutes.

3. Meanwhile, in a large skillet, heat the 2 tablespoons of olive oil. Add the smashed garlic clove and cook over moderate heat until golden, about 2 minutes. Add the mushrooms, cover and cook, stirring occasionally, until tender and browned, about 15 minutes. Discard the garlic. Season the mushrooms with salt and pepper and stir in the thyme leaves.

4. Roll out one of the dough rounds to form a 9-inch round. Transfer the round to the peel and brush the edge of the dough with olive oil. Spread ⅓ cup of the béchamel over the dough and scatter one-fourth of the mushrooms on top.

5. Transfer the mushroom–and–goat cheese pizza to the pizza stone and bake for about 5 minutes, until the edges of the crust are crisp and the béchamel is bubbling. Transfer the pizza to a work surface, cut into wedges and serve right away. Repeat with the remaining pizza dough, béchamel and sliced mushrooms.

—Andres Barrera

MAKE AHEAD The béchamel can be refrigerated for up to 2 days. Bring to room temperature before proceeding.

WINE Earthy, medium-bodied Tempranillo.

Green Olive–and–Garlic Pizza with Dough for Obsessives

ACTIVE: 45 MIN; TOTAL: 5 HR

MAKES FOUR 12-INCH PIZZAS ● ●

Andrew Green, wine director for the Bacchus Management Group (which includes Spruce in San Francisco), is obsessive about pizza: He kept journals on the different ways he tried making it until he hit on a crust that's a perfect balance of chewy and crispy. His ideal method involves preparing a batch of dough each day for three days, and blending some of the old dough into the new each time. The recipe here simplifies his fanatical crust-making method so that the pizza can be made in one day. To mimic the superhigh heat of a pizzeria, Green sets a baking stone inside his home oven, which he preheats to its highest temperature; he then finishes the pizza under the broiler.

DOUGH

- 1½ cups water
- 1 tablespoon Maldon salt (see Note)
- 1 teaspoon confectioners' sugar
- 1 package rapid-rise yeast
- 1 tablespoon extra-virgin olive oil, plus more for oiling the bowl
- 4 cups all-purpose flour, plus more for dusting

TOPPING

- 2 tablespoons extra-virgin olive oil, plus more for brushing
- 4 large garlic cloves, thinly sliced
- 20 green olives, preferably Castelvetrano, pitted and coarsely chopped (see Note)

Crushed red pepper, for sprinkling

Maldon salt and freshly ground black pepper

- 1 pound fresh mozzarella, sliced ⅛ inch thick

1. **MAKE THE DOUGH:** In a small saucepan, bring the water to 125°, using an instant-read thermometer to monitor the temperature. Stir in the Maldon salt and the confectioners' sugar until dissolved. Stir in the yeast and the 1 tablespoon of olive oil and let stand at room temperature until foamy, about 5 minutes.

2. In the bowl of a standing mixer fitted with the paddle attachment, mix the 4 cups of flour with the yeast mixture at low speed for 10 minutes. Let the pizza dough rest for about 10 minutes, then mix again at low speed for 10 minutes longer.

3. Lightly oil a large, warmed ceramic or glass bowl. Transfer the dough to the bowl, cover with a damp towel and let the dough stand in a warm place until doubled in bulk, about 2 hours.

4. On a lightly floured work surface, punch down the pizza dough and evenly divide it into 4 pieces.

5. Roll the pieces into balls. Dust the balls lightly with flour and set them on a large baking sheet about 6 inches apart. Cover the balls with lightly oiled plastic wrap and let stand for 2 hours.

6. Set a pizza stone in the middle rack of the oven and preheat at 500° for 1 hour.

7. **MAKE THE TOPPING:** In a small skillet, heat the 2 tablespoons of olive oil. Add the garlic and cook over low heat until golden brown, shaking the skillet a few times, about 4 minutes.

8. Five minutes before baking the pizzas, preheat the broiler. Lightly flour a pizza peel or rimless baking sheet. On a floured work surface, lightly roll out 1 ball of dough into an 8-inch round circle. Using your hands, stretch the dough into a thin 12-inch round. Transfer the dough to the peel. Lightly brush the dough with olive oil. Scatter one-fourth of the olives and garlic evenly over the dough. Sprinkle with a pinch of crushed red pepper and season with salt and black pepper. Arrange one-fourth of the mozzarella over the dough.

Slide onto the pizza stone. Broil for about 5 minutes, until the bottom crust is crisp and the top is bubbling. Transfer the pizza to a work surface and cut into wedges. Repeat with the 3 remaining pieces of dough and the toppings. Serve hot.
—*Andrew Green*

VARIATION Green also likes his pizza topped with cooked cubed pancetta, sautéed onions, halved figs and grated Fontina and Parmesan. He then garnishes the pie with arugula and a drizzle of olive oil.

NOTE Maldon salt is flaky and not as salty as table salt. If you don't have Maldon salt, substitute 2½ teaspoons of kosher salt in the dough. Castelvetrano olives, a Sicilian variety, are known for their mild, sweet flavor. Both Maldon salt and Castelvetrano olives are available at specialty food shops and some supermarkets.

WINE Fresh, lively Soave.

Squid Pizza with Saffron Aioli
TOTAL: 50 MIN

MAKES ONE 12-INCH PIZZA ●

Napa chef Michael Emanuel (an alumnus of Berkeley's Chez Panisse) tops this pizza with an irresistible mix of Provençal flavors: salty-sweet roasted squid, creamy aioli and crushed red pepper (French piment d'Espelette would also work well). Use the extra aioli as a dip for vegetables or a spread for sandwiches.

Pinch of saffron threads
  1 teaspoon water
  1 large egg yolk
  1 medium garlic clove,
      very finely chopped
  2 teaspoons fresh lemon juice
  ¾ cup plus 1 tablespoon
      extra-virgin olive oil, plus
      more for brushing
Salt
Cayenne pepper
  6 ounces cleaned squid—
      tentacles halved, bodies sliced
      crosswise ½ inch thick

Freshly ground black pepper
All-purpose flour, for dusting
  6 ounces pizza dough
Pinch of crushed red pepper
  ½ small red onion, very
      thinly sliced
  1 large plum tomato, diced
  1 teaspoon chopped fresh
      marjoram leaves
  1 tablespoon chopped flat-leaf
      parsley leaves

1. Preheat the oven to 500°. Preheat a pizza stone for 45 minutes. In a small bowl, crumble the saffron into the water; let steep for 5 minutes. In a blender or bowl, beat the egg yolk with the chopped garlic and 1 teaspoon of the fresh lemon juice. Gradually add the ¾ cup of olive oil, beating constantly, until very thick. Stir in the remaining 1 teaspoon of lemon juice and the saffron water and season the aioli with salt and cayenne pepper.

2. In a skillet, heat the remaining 1 tablespoon of olive oil until shimmering. Add the sliced squid, season with salt and black pepper and cook over high heat until just starting to whiten, 30 seconds. Transfer to a plate.

3. On a lightly floured work surface, roll out the pizza dough to a 12-inch round, ¼ inch thick. Transfer the round to a lightly floured pizza peel. Leaving a ½-inch border of dough, brush the round with olive oil and sprinkle with crushed red pepper, salt and black pepper. Scatter the onion slices over the round and top with the squid, tomato and marjoram.

4. Slide the pizza onto the hot stone and bake for about 5 minutes, until the bottom is crisp. Transfer to a work surface; drizzle with 3 tablespoons of the aioli. Reserve the remaining aioli for another use. Garnish the pizza with the parsley, cut into wedges and serve. —*Michael Emanuel*

MAKE AHEAD The saffron aioli can be refrigerated for up to 2 days.

WINE Dry, earthy sparkling wine.

breads, pizzas & sandwiches

Puff-Pastry Tomato Tarts

ACTIVE: 30 MIN; TOTAL: 1 HR 30 MIN

4 SERVINGS ●●

Norwegian chef Andreas Viestad's tarts have a flaky crust topped with tomatoes that become wonderfully sweet as they bake. Viestad likes to halve the tomatoes, but slicing them (as in this recipe) concentrates the flavor even more.

1½ pounds large heirloom
     tomatoes, cored
  2 teaspoons light brown sugar
Salt
All-purpose flour, for dusting
  ½ pound chilled all-butter
     puff pastry
  ¼ cup freshly grated Parmigiano-
     Reggiano cheese
  2 tablespoons unsalted butter,
     cut into small cubes
  1 tablespoon chopped basil

1. Preheat the oven to 400°. In a saucepan of boiling water, blanch the tomatoes until the skins start to curl, about 30 seconds; transfer to a plate and let cool. Peel the tomatoes. Halve them crosswise and squeeze out the seeds, then slice the tomatoes ½ inch thick. Sprinkle the tomatoes on both sides with the brown sugar and season with salt; transfer to a rack and let drain for about 30 minutes.

2. Meanwhile, line a large baking sheet with parchment paper. On a lightly floured work surface, roll out the puff pastry ⅛ inch thick. Using a 6-inch round plate as a template, cut out four 6-inch rounds. Transfer the rounds to the prepared baking sheet and freeze for 5 minutes. Bake the rounds for about 20 minutes, until they are golden brown and puffed.

3. Pat the tomato slices dry with paper towels. Sprinkle the pastry puffs with half of the grated cheese and arrange the sliced tomatoes in a circle in the center of each pastry round, leaving a ½-inch border. Dot the tomatoes evenly with the butter and sprinkle with the remaining cheese.

4. Bake the tarts for 10 minutes, then reduce the oven temperature to 350° and bake for 20 minutes longer, until the pastry is richly browned and the tomatoes have shrunken slightly. Let the tarts cool for at least 5 minutes, garnish with the basil and serve.
—Andreas Viestad

Palestinian Spinach Pies

ACTIVE: 30 MIN; TOTAL: 2 HR

MAKES TEN 5-INCH PIES ●●○○

These *fatayer* (spinach pies) from New York's Hot Bread Kitchen were inspired by a recipe from Palestinian-born baker Maha Ziadeh. The filling isn't flavored with feta, as it is in the more common Greek spinach pies. Instead, it's spiked with lemon and sumac, a tangy Middle Eastern spice. Ziadeh forms the pies into a triangle, but the half-moon shape here is simpler to make.

  1 cup plus 2 tablespoons
     all-purpose flour, plus more
     for dusting
  ½ cup whole wheat flour
  ½ teaspoon active dry yeast
  ⅔ cup lukewarm water
Salt
  ¼ cup plus 2 tablespoons
     extra-virgin olive oil
  1 medium onion, diced
  1 tablespoon ground sumac
     (see Note)
  2 teaspoons fresh lemon juice
Freshly ground pepper
Two 10-ounce packages frozen spinach,
     thawed and squeezed dry
  1 large egg, beaten

1. In the bowl of an electric mixer fitted with the dough hook, combine the 1 cup plus 2 tablespoons of all-purpose flour with the whole wheat flour, yeast, water, ½ teaspoon of salt and 3 tablespoons of the oil. Mix at medium speed until a soft, supple dough forms, about 10 minutes. Using oiled hands, transfer to an oiled bowl. Cover with plastic wrap and let the dough stand in a draft-free spot until slightly risen, about 1 hour.

2. Meanwhile, in a large skillet, heat the remaining 3 tablespoons of olive oil. Add the diced onion and cook over moderate heat until softened, about 7 minutes. Add the sumac and lemon juice and season with salt and pepper. Stir in the spinach and let cool completely.

3. Preheat the oven to 450° and line 2 baking sheets with parchment paper. Divide the dough into 10 pieces. Form each piece of dough into a ball, dust with flour and let stand for 10 minutes.

4. On a lightly floured surface, roll each ball of dough to a 5-inch round. Spread the spinach filling over half of each round, leaving a ½-inch border. Brush the rims with water and fold the dough over to enclose the filling; pinch the edges to seal.

5. Transfer the pies to the prepared baking sheets and brush the tops with the beaten egg. Bake for about 18 minutes, or until golden; shift the pans from top to bottom and front to back halfway through baking. Transfer the spinach pies to a platter and serve warm or at room temperature.
—Jessamyn Waldman

NOTE Sumac is a fruity, tangy spice made from dried ground berries. It is available at Middle Eastern markets and online from penzeys.com.

MAKE AHEAD The cooled pies can be tightly wrapped in foil and refrigerated overnight. Reheat in the foil in a 325° oven.

Prosciutto-Cheese and Squash-Pecorino Piadina

TOTAL: 1 HR 15 MIN

MAKES 8 PIADINA

Nate Appleman (an F&W Best New Chef 2009) describes *piadina*, the excellent flat-bread sandwiches, as "Italian quesadillas." Appleman cooks the flaky dough on a griddle until it's just crisp outside, then stuffs it with sumptuous combinations like tender roasted winter squash with pancetta, or prosciutto with stracchino cheese and peppery arugula.

PALESTINIAN SPINACH PIES

PROSCIUTTO-CHEESE AND SQUASH-PECORINO PIADINA

DOUGH

3½ cups all-purpose flour

½ teaspoon baking soda

2½ teaspoons kosher salt

1 cup solid vegetable shortening

¾ cup water

FILLINGS

One 3-pound butternut squash—
peeled, seeded and cut into
½-inch pieces (4 cups)

½ pound thickly sliced pancetta,
cut into 2-by-¼-inch matchsticks

3 tablespoons extra-virgin olive oil,
plus more for drizzling

Kosher salt and freshly ground pepper

4 ounces shaved
pecorino cheese

6 ounces thinly sliced prosciutto

½ pound stracchino or robiola
cheese, sliced

2 cups baby arugula

1. MAKE THE DOUGH: In a standing mixer fitted with the paddle, mix the flour with the baking soda and salt. Add the shortening and beat at low speed until the mixture resembles coarse meal. Gradually beat in the water on medium-low speed until the dough is smooth, about 3 minutes. Divide the dough into 8 pieces, cover with plastic wrap and let stand at room temperature for 30 minutes.

2. MEANWHILE, PREPARE THE FILLINGS: Preheat the oven to 400°. In a medium roasting pan, toss the butternut squash with the sliced pancetta, the 3 tablespoons of olive oil and a pinch each of salt and pepper. Roast for about 25 minutes, stirring occasionally, until the squash is tender and browned in spots and the pancetta is browned.

3. On an unfloured surface, roll out each piece of dough to an 8-inch round about ⅛ inch thick. Heat a griddle or cast-iron skillet. Cook the *piadina* one or two at a time over moderate heat, turning once, until lightly charred in spots and no longer doughy, 3 to 4 minutes. Transfer to a shallow bowl and cover with foil to keep warm while you cook the rest.

4. Arrange the *piadina* on a work surface. Top 4 of the *piadina* with the squash-pancetta mixture and pecorino and fold to close. Top the other 4 with the prosciutto, stracchino cheese and arugula. Drizzle lightly with olive oil, season with salt and pepper and fold to close. Serve the *piadina* immediately, either whole or cut into wedges. —Nate Appleman

MAKE AHEAD The *piadina* recipe can be prepared through Step 2 up to 4 hours ahead. Let the dough and squash stand at room temperature.

WINE Bright, tart Barbera.

● HEALTHY ● MAKE AHEAD ● VEGETARIAN ● STAFF FAVORITE

breads, pizzas & sandwiches

Asparagus-Cheese Tartines

TOTAL: 30 MIN
4 SERVINGS

These open-faced sandwiches with crisp asparagus, prosciutto and three layers of melted cheese are gooey and crunchy.

- 12 thin asparagus spears
- 1 tablespoon extra-virgin olive oil
- 2 large shallots, thinly sliced

Salt and freshly ground pepper

- 2 large plum tomatoes, sliced lengthwise ¼ inch thick

Four ¾-inch-thick slices of peasant or Pullman sandwich bread

- ¼ cup tapenade

Four ⅛-inch-thick slices each of Italian Fontina, fresh mozzarella and Gruyère cheese

- 4 very thin slices of prosciutto

Aged balsamic vinegar, for drizzling

1. Bring a large skillet of salted water to a boil. Add the asparagus and cook until crisp-tender, 2 minutes. Drain and transfer to a plate. Wipe out the skillet.

2. Add the oil and shallots to the skillet, season with salt and pepper and cook over moderate heat until softened, 4 minutes. Transfer the shallots to a plate. Add the tomatoes to the skillet, season with salt and pepper and cook over moderately high heat until lightly browned on one side, 2 minutes; transfer to the plate with the shallots.

3. Preheat the broiler. Arrange the bread on a baking sheet; toast in the broiler 3 inches from the heat, turning once, 2 minutes.

4. Spread the toasts with the tapenade and top with the sautéed shallots and sliced Fontina and mozzarella cheese. Broil the tartines 3 inches from the heat for 1 minute, until the cheese has melted. Top the tartines with the asparagus and drape with the Gruyère. Broil the tartines for 1 minute longer, until the Gruyère has melted. Top the tartines with the tomatoes and prosciutto, drizzle with the balsamic and serve right away. —*Lionel Vatinet*
WINE Tart, citrusy Riesling.

Tomato, Prosciutto and Gruyère Sandwiches

TOTAL: 30 MIN
4 SERVINGS ●

Swiss-born chef Daniel Humm's broiled cheese sandwiches make a terrific snack or a decadent lunch. The combination of bubbling hot Gruyère with white wine and kirsch, a cherry-flavored spirit, evokes a classic Swiss fondue.

Four 1-inch-thick slices of white bread

- 2 tablespoons extra-virgin olive oil
- 1 garlic clove
- 1 teaspoon dry white wine
- ½ teaspoon kirsch (optional)
- 2 ounces thinly sliced prosciutto
- 1 beefsteak tomato, peeled and thinly sliced

Salt

- ½ pound Gruyère cheese, thinly sliced

Freshly ground black pepper
Sweet paprika

1. Preheat the oven to 400°. Brush the bread slices on both sides with the olive oil and transfer to a baking sheet. Toast for 10 to 15 minutes, turning once, until the slices are golden and crisp on the outside but still soft inside. Rub the toast on one side with the garlic clove. In a small bowl, combine the white wine and kirsch and sprinkle lightly over the garlic-rubbed sides of the toast. Top with the sliced prosciutto and tomato and season lightly with salt. Top the open-faced sandwiches with the sliced Gruyère cheese.

2. Preheat the broiler. Broil the sandwiches as close to the heat as possible for about 3 minutes, watching closely and shifting the pan occasionally for even browning, until the Gruyère is bubbling. Sprinkle the open-faced sandwiches with black pepper and paprika and serve. —*Daniel Humm*
WINE Full-bodied, rich Pinot Gris.

Triple-Decker Baked Italian Cheese Sandwiches

ACTIVE: 30 MIN; TOTAL: 2 HR 45 MIN
8 SERVINGS ●

- 8 plum tomatoes, halved lengthwise
- ¼ cup extra-virgin olive oil

Kosher salt and freshly ground black pepper

- 1 teaspoon thyme leaves
- 2 white Pullman loaves— ends discarded, each loaf cut into twelve ½-inch-thick slices
- 1 pound sliced provolone cheese
- 1 pound Fontina cheese, coarsely shredded (about 5½ cups)
- ½ cup freshly grated Parmigiano-Reggiano cheese

1. Preheat the oven to 325°. On a large rimmed baking sheet, toss the halved tomatoes with 2 tablespoons of the olive oil and season with salt and pepper. Bake the tomatoes cut side up for 1½ hours, until soft and starting to brown. Sprinkle with the thyme leaves and bake for about 30 minutes longer, until the tomatoes are very tender and slightly shriveled but still juicy. Let cool.

2. Increase the oven temperature to 375°. Brush 16 bread slices with the remaining 2 tablespoons of olive oil; arrange 8 of the slices oiled side down on a large rimmed baking sheet. Top with the provolone and the unbrushed bread slices. Cover with the tomatoes, 4 cups of the Fontina and the remaining 8 bread slices, oiled side up. Press gently on the sandwiches and bake for about 15 minutes, until the bread is toasted and the cheese is melted.

3. Preheat the broiler. Toss the remaining Fontina with the grated Parmigiano-Reggiano cheese and sprinkle on the sandwiches. Broil the sandwiches 3 inches from the heat for about 1 minute, until the cheese is melted. Transfer to plates; serve.
—*Melissa Rubel Jacobson*
WINE Fresh, fruity rosé.

TRIPLE-DECKER BAKED ITALIAN
CHEESE SANDWICHES

Grilled Gruyère-and-Zucchini Sandwiches with Smoky Pesto

TOTAL: 30 MIN
4 SERVINGS ● ●

- 1 cup packed basil leaves
- 1 large garlic clove, coarsely chopped
- ½ teaspoon hot smoked paprika
- 3 tablespoons extra-virgin olive oil, plus more for brushing

Salt

- One 8-ounce zucchini, cut into 4 lengthwise slices
- 4 English muffins, preferably Bays, split
- 4 ounces Gruyère or Appenzeller cheese, cut into 8 thin slices

1. In a mini food processor, combine the basil, garlic and paprika and process until finely chopped. With the machine on, gradually pour in the 3 tablespoons of olive oil until blended. Season the pesto with salt.

2. Light a grill. Brush the zucchini slices with olive oil and season with salt. Grill over high heat until nicely charred and just tender, about 2 minutes per side. Cut each zucchini slice in half crosswise.

3. Grill the English muffins cut side down over low heat until just soft, about 30 seconds. Turn and grill until the muffins start to brown, about 1 minute. Spread the cut sides of the muffins with the pesto. Layer 1 slice of cheese, 2 zucchini pieces

---

best cheeses for panini

The best cheeses for pressed sandwiches are ones that melt superbly. Gruyère is a great choice for a nutty flavor, Fontina and Monterey Jack are mild and creamy, and Asiago and cheddar both lend a nice sharpness.

---

and 1 more slice of cheese on the bottom halves of each muffin. Close the sandwiches; brush the tops and bottoms with oil. Grill over low heat, turning, until they're crisp on the outside and the cheese is melted, about 4 minutes total. Cut the sandwiches in half and serve. —*Marcia Kiesel*
WINE Full-bodied, rich Pinot Gris.

Multigrain Grilled Cheese Sandwiches

ACTIVE: 20 MIN; TOTAL: 45 MIN
4 SERVINGS ●

- 4 plum tomatoes, halved lengthwise
- 2 tablespoons extra-virgin olive oil, plus more for brushing
- 1 tablespoon sherry vinegar
- 1 thyme sprig, plus 1 teaspoon thyme leaves

Salt and freshly ground black pepper
- 1 small clove garlic, very finely chopped
- 8 slices of multigrain bread
- ¾ cup shredded Manchego cheese
- ¾ cup shredded smoked cheddar cheese
- ¾ cup shredded Gouda cheese

1. Preheat the oven to 450°. In a bowl, toss the tomatoes with the 2 tablespoons of oil, the vinegar and the thyme sprig; season with salt and pepper. Arrange the tomatoes cut side down on a rimmed baking sheet and roast in the upper third of the oven for 10 minutes, until the skins begin to shrivel. Remove the skins. Turn the tomatoes over and roast for 10 minutes longer, until they are softened and lightly browned. Sprinkle with the chopped garlic and thyme leaves and season lightly with salt and pepper.

2. Preheat a panini press or grill pan. Arrange the bread slices in pairs and very lightly brush 1 side of each slice with oil. Turn the bread oiled side down and mound half of the cheeses on 4 of the slices. Top with the tomatoes, the remaining cheese

---

and the remaining bread, oiled side up. Grill until the bread is toasted and the cheese is melted. Cut the sandwiches in half and serve. —*Seamus Mullen*
WINE Fresh, fruity rosé.

Mexican Tortas with Black Beans and Chorizo

TOTAL: 30 MIN
4 SERVINGS

- 1 tablespoon vegetable oil, plus more for brushing
- ½ pound fresh Mexican chorizo, casings removed
- Two 15-ounce cans black beans, drained

Salt and freshly ground pepper
- 4 Mexican *bolillo* or *telera* rolls (see Note), or kaiser rolls, split
- 4 ounces fresh goat cheese, softened
- 1 Hass avocado, thinly sliced

Shredded romaine lettuce and sliced pickled jalapeños, for garnish

1. In a skillet, heat the 1 tablespoon of oil. Add the chorizo; cook over moderate heat, stirring, until meat is browned and no trace of pink remains, 10 minutes. Add the beans; mash well with a potato masher. Cook, stirring, until hot, 4 minutes. Season with salt and pepper, cover and keep warm.

2. Heat a griddle or large skillet over moderately high heat. Using your hands, pull out some bread from the centers of the rolls to create a small cavity. Brush the cut sides of the rolls with oil. Transfer the rolls, cut side down, to the griddle and cook until toasted, 2 minutes. Turn and cook 1 minute longer, until slightly crisp. Transfer to a work surface, cut side up.

3. Spread the tops of the *bolillo* rolls with the goat cheese. Spread the bottoms with 2 cups of the mashed black beans; reserve the remaining beans for another use. Top the beans with the avocado, lettuce and pickled jalapeños. Close the sandwiches, cut in half and serve. —*Rick Bayless*

NOTE *Bolillo* and *telera* rolls, the two classic breads for *tortas*, are 6-inch-long oval rolls similar to hoagies or soft baguettes; *telera* rolls are slightly flat. Both types of rolls are available at Latin supermarkets.

MAKE AHEAD The chorizo-and-black-bean filling can be refrigerated for up to 2 days. Reheat gently before using.

WINE Intense, fruity Zinfandel.

Lamb Pita Pockets with Tomato-Ginger Compote

ACTIVE: 45 MIN; TOTAL: 2 HR 30 MIN

6 SERVINGS ● ●

At Manhattan's City Winery, chef Andres Barrera slow-roasts lamb until tender, then stuffs it into warm pitas along with pickled red onions, feta cheese and a bright-flavored Tomato-Ginger Compote (also great on a burger or cheese plate).

Finely grated zest of 2 lemons

1 **tablespoon dried oregano**

2 **teaspoons freshly ground pepper**

1½ **teaspoons garlic powder**

1½ **teaspoons onion powder**

Kosher salt

Four 1-pound lamb shanks

2 **tablespoons extra-virgin olive oil**

1 **medium red onion, thinly sliced**

2 **tablespoons red wine vinegar**

½ **cup water**

6 **warmed pita breads, halved**

Tomato-Ginger Compote (recipe follows), for serving

4 **ounces feta cheese, crumbled (1 cup)**

1. Preheat the oven to 325°. In a small bowl, mix the lemon zest with the oregano, pepper, garlic powder, onion powder and 2 teaspoons of salt. Rub the mixture all over the lamb shanks.

2. In a large enameled cast-iron casserole, heat the olive oil. Add the lamb shanks and cook over moderately high heat, turning a few times, until browned all over, about

7 minutes. Cover and bake the shanks in the oven for about 2 hours, until they are very tender.

3. Meanwhile, in a medium bowl, toss the onion slices with the red wine vinegar; season with salt. Let stand at room temperature, tossing a few times, until softened, about 20 minutes.

4. Transfer the lamb shanks to a bowl. Set the casserole over high heat. Add the water and boil, scraping up the browned bits on the bottom. Pour the liquid into a small bowl and skim the fat from the surface.

5. Pull the the meat from the bones in large shreds, discarding the fat and gristle. Transfer the lamb to a bowl. Add the cooking juices and toss well. Season with salt.

6. Spoon the shredded lamb into the pita and spread a thick layer of the Tomato-Ginger Compote on top. Garnish with the pickled red onion and feta and serve.
—*Andres Barrera*

MAKE AHEAD The shredded lamb and pickled onion can be refrigerated separately for up to 2 days. Rewarm the lamb before assembling the sandwiches.

WINE Round, deep-flavored Syrah.

TOMATO-GINGER COMPOTE

ACTIVE: 15 MIN; TOTAL: 1 HR 30 MIN

MAKES 1½ CUPS ● ●

1 **quart water**

2 **pounds plum tomatoes, coarsely chopped**

½ **cup red wine vinegar**

½ **cup light brown sugar**

2 **teaspoons finely grated ginger**

1 **garlic clove, minced**

Salt

In a large saucepan, combine all of the ingredients except the salt and bring to a boil. Simmer over moderately low heat, stirring occasionally, until the compote has thickened and is reduced to 1½ cups, about 1 hour and 15 minutes. Let cool to room temperature and season with salt. Transfer to a jar and refrigerate. —*AB*

Za'atar Flatbreads with Cucumber-Yogurt Salad

ACTIVE: 30 MIN; TOTAL: 1 HR

6 SERVINGS ● ●

All-purpose flour, for dusting

12 **ounces pizza dough**

5 **ounces baby spinach**

½ **cup frozen baby peas, thawed**

1 **cup peeled, finely diced cucumber**

2 **tablespoons chopped parsley**

2 **tablespoons chopped mint**

2 **tablespoons chopped dill**

2 **teaspoons minced garlic**

One 17-ounce container Greek yogurt

1 **tablespoon fresh lemon juice**

½ **cup extra-virgin olive oil**

2 **cups shredded romaine lettuce**

Kosher salt

½ **cup za'atar spice mix (see Note)**

1. Preheat the oven to 450°. Heat a pizza stone on the bottom rack for 30 minutes, or preheat an inverted baking sheet.

2. On a lightly floured work surface, flatten the pizza dough into two 9-inch rounds about ¼ inch thick; transfer to 2 well floured pizza peels or inverted baking sheets. Let stand until slightly risen, 20 minutes.

3. Meanwhile, in a large saucepan, wilt the spinach with 1 tablespoon of water over high heat. Drain; rinse with cold water. Squeeze out and chop the spinach; transfer to a bowl. Add the peas and mash lightly with a fork. Stir in the cucumber, parsley, mint, dill and garlic. Stir in the yogurt, lemon juice and 2 tablespoons of oil. Fold in the romaine and season with salt.

4. In a bowl, combine the za'atar with the remaining oil and a generous pinch of salt.

5. Shake the pizza peel a few times to loosen the dough. Dust flour under any areas that stick. Spread the za'atar oil over the dough. Slide the rounds onto the hot stone and bake for 10 minutes, until golden and crisp. Transfer to a work surface, cut into wedges and serve with the salad. —*Ana Sortun*

NOTE Za'atar is available at Middle Eastern markets and penzeys.com.

● HEALTHY ● MAKE AHEAD ● VEGETARIAN ● STAFF FAVORITE

breads, pizzas & sandwiches

Focaccia Reubens

ACTIVE: 20 MIN; TOTAL: 50 MIN

4 SERVINGS

One ½-pound green cabbage,
    thinly sliced (4 cups)
  2 tablespoons cider vinegar
  1 tablespoon sugar
  ½ teaspoon kosher salt
Four 4-by-6-inch focaccia pieces, split
  ¼ cup ketchup
  ¼ cup mayonnaise
Eight ¼-inch-thick slices of Gruyère
    cheese (4 ounces)
  ½ pound thinly sliced corned beef
  2 tablespoons butter, softened

1. In a bowl, toss the cabbage with the vinegar, sugar and salt. Let stand, tossing occasionally, until softened, 30 minutes.
2. Heat a panini press or griddle. Arrange the focaccia on a work surface, cut side up. In a small bowl, combine the ketchup with the mayonnaise. Spread the dressing on the bottom halves of the focaccia. Set a slice of Gruyère on the dressing. Top with the corned beef, pickled cabbage and the remaining slices of Gruyère. Close the sandwiches and spread the outsides of the focaccia with the softened butter.
3. Add the sandwiches to the press and cook over moderate heat until the cheese has melted and the focaccia is crisp and golden, 6 minutes. Halve the sandwiches; serve right away. —*Dennis Leary*
WINE Ripe, juicy Pinot Noir.

Grilled Merguez Sandwiches with Caramelized Red Onions

TOTAL: 50 MIN

4 SERVINGS

  3 tablespoons extra-virgin olive oil
  2 red onions, sliced ¼ inch thick
Salt
  1 tablespoon honey
  1 tablespoon balsamic vinegar
Freshly ground pepper
Four 6-ounce merguez or fresh chorizo
    sausages, pricked with a fork

Four 6-inch pieces of baguette, split
    and toasted
 12 large cilantro sprigs
  4 lemon wedges, for serving

1. In a skillet, heat the oil. Add the onions, season with salt and cook over moderately high heat, stirring, for 5 minutes. Reduce the heat to moderate; cook, stirring occasionally, until softened, 10 minutes. Stir in the honey and vinegar; cook over low heat, stirring occasionally, until caramelized, 10 minutes. Season with salt and pepper.
2. Light a grill. Grill the sausages over moderate heat, turning occasionally, until nicely charred and cooked through, 15 minutes.
3. Set a sausage in each piece of baguette. Top with the onions and a few cilantro sprigs and close the sandwiches. Serve with lemon wedges. —*Andres Barrera*
WINE Intense, fruity Zinfandel.

Cuban Sandwiches with Tomato Jam

ACTIVE: 45 MIN; TOTAL: 5 HR

8 SERVINGS ●

One 7-pound bone-in pork butt
  ¼ cup pure olive oil, plus more
      for brushing
  1 tablespoon ground cumin
  1 tablespoon ground coriander
  1 tablespoon ground fennel
  2 teaspoons sweet paprika
  1 teaspoon cayenne pepper
Kosher salt
  2 red onions, cut into
      ½-inch rings
  ¼ cup mayonnaise
  ¼ cup Dijon mustard
  1 garlic clove, mashed to a paste
  8 soft hero rolls, split
  ½ pound sliced serrano
      ham or prosciutto
  ½ pound sliced Gruyère cheese
  4 dill or half-sour pickles,
      thinly sliced lengthwise
  ¼ cup sliced pickled jalapeños
Tomato Jam (recipe follows)

1. Preheat the oven to 350°. Set the pork in a roasting pan; rub with 2 tablespoons of the oil. In a bowl, combine the cumin, coriander, fennel, paprika, cayenne and 2 tablespoons of salt. Rub the spices over the pork; drizzle with the remaining 2 tablespoons of oil. Roast for 2 hours, then lower the oven temperature to 300°; roast for 2 hours longer, until an instant-read thermometer inserted in the thickest part of the meat registers 160°. Transfer to a board; let stand 30 minutes. Shred the meat.
2. Light a grill or preheat a grill pan. Brush the onions with olive oil and grill over high heat, turning occasionally, until softened and charred in spots, about 8 minutes.
3. In a bowl, combine the mayonnaise, mustard and garlic; spread on each roll. Top with the pork, ham, Gruyère, pickles, jalapeños, onions and Tomato Jam. Close the sandwiches; brush the outsides lightly with oil. Tightly wrap each sandwich in foil.
4. Set the sandwiches on the grill and top with a baking sheet and a brick or heavy can to press them. Grill over very low heat, turning once, until the cheese is melted and the bread crisp, 10 to 12 minutes. Unwrap; serve hot. —*Ken Oringer*
WINE Rustic, peppery Malbec.

TOMATO JAM

ACTIVE: 10 MIN; TOTAL: 1 HR 10 MIN

MAKES 1¼ CUPS ● ●

One 28-ounce can diced
    roasted tomatoes
  ¼ cup plus 2 tablespoons
      white wine vinegar
  ¼ cup sugar
  1 teaspoon mustard seeds
  ½ teaspoon curry powder
  ¼ teaspoon cinnamon
Pinch of ground cloves
Salt

In a large saucepan, combine all the ingredients; simmer gently over moderate heat, stirring occasionally, until thick and jam-like, 1 hour. Season with salt. —*KO*

GRILLED MERGUEZ SANDWICHES
WITH CARAMELIZED RED ONIONS

FOCACCIA REUBENS

breads, pizzas & sandwiches

Lavash Crackers

ACTIVE: 45 MIN; TOTAL: 2 HR

MAKES 36 CRACKERS ● ● ●

- 1 envelope active dry yeast
- 1¼ cups lukewarm water
- 4 cups bread flour
- ¼ cup extra-virgin olive oil
- 2 tablespoons honey

Kosher salt

Vegetable oil, for rubbing

- 1 tablespoon each of za'atar, sesame seeds and poppy seeds, for sprinkling (see Note)

1. In the bowl of a standing electric mixer, combine the yeast with 2 tablespoons of the water and let stand until moistened. Add the flour, olive oil, honey, 2 teaspoons of salt and the remaining water. Fit the mixer with the dough hook and mix on medium-low until a firm, supple dough forms, 15 minutes. Turn the dough out onto a floured surface and cut into thirds; let stand for 15 minutes.

2. Preheat the oven to 325°. Lightly coat the underside of three 12-by-15-inch rimmed sheet pans with vegetable oil. On a floured surface, roll out the dough to rectangles slightly larger than the pans, a scant ⅛ inch thick; if the dough springs back, let rest for a few minutes before rolling again. Drape each rectangle over the underside of each pan so it hangs over the edge.

3. Sprinkle each rectangle with water, then sprinkle with ½ teaspoon of salt and 1 tablespoon each of the za'atar and sesame and poppy seeds (1 flavor per tray). Leave the dough whole or, using a pastry wheel, cut it into twelve 3-by-5-inch pieces.

4. If you have 3 racks in your oven, bake 1 pan of lavash on each rack for 40 minutes, until browned and crisp; shift the pans halfway through baking. If you have 2 racks, bake in shifts for 35 minutes per batch. Transfer to racks to cool. Break the lavash as desired and serve. —*Jessamyn Waldman*

NOTE Za'atar, a Middle Eastern mix of sesame seeds, herbs and sumac, is available at specialty shops and penzeys.com.

Fig-and-Almond Bread Stuffing with Fennel

ACTIVE: 30 MIN; TOTAL: 1 HR 10 MIN

12 SERVINGS ●

- One 12-ounce loaf of peasant bread, cut into 1-inch cubes
- 5 ounces sliced almonds (1½ cups)
- 12 ounces dried Black Mission figs (2 cups), stemmed and chopped
- 2 tablespoons chopped sage
- 2 tablespoons chopped parsley
- 6 tablespoons unsalted butter, plus more for greasing
- 1 onion, finely chopped
- 3 celery ribs, finely chopped
- 2 large carrots, finely chopped
- 1 fennel bulb, cored and diced
- 2 garlic cloves, minced
- 1 tablespoon fennel seeds, chopped
- 8 large eggs, lightly beaten
- 2½ cups chicken stock or low-sodium broth

Salt and freshly ground pepper

1. Preheat the oven to 350°. Spread the bread on a large baking sheet and toast for about 15 minutes, stirring once, until slightly dry. Spread the almonds on another baking sheet and toast for 5 minutes, until lightly browned. Let the almonds cool, then lightly crush them. Transfer the bread and almonds to a large bowl and add the figs, sage and parsley.

2. In a large skillet, melt the 6 tablespoons of butter. Add the onion, celery, carrots, diced fennel bulb, garlic and fennel seeds and cook over moderate heat, stirring occasionally, until softened, 5 minutes. Let cool, then scrape the vegetables into the bread mixture. Stir in the eggs and stock and season with salt and pepper.

3. Butter a 9-by-13-inch baking dish. Spread the stuffing mixture in the dish and cover with foil. Bake for 30 minutes, until heated through. Uncover and bake for 10 minutes longer, until the top is lightly browned. Serve the stuffing hot. —*Shawn McClain*

Scallion Pancakes with Soy Dipping Sauce

TOTAL: 45 MIN

4 SERVINGS ● ●

Pizza dough is ideal for replicating this popular Chinese snack. The pancakes cook in only three minutes, until the edges are crispy and the centers are chewy. Eat them hot, right out of the skillet.

- 3 scallions—2 very finely chopped, 1 thinly sliced
- 1 tablespoon plus 1 teaspoon Asian sesame oil
- ½ teaspoon kosher salt
- ½ pound of pizza dough, at room temperature
- 2 tablespoons soy sauce
- 1 tablespoon water
- 2 teaspoons unseasoned rice vinegar
- ½ cup canola oil

1. In a small bowl, mix the finely chopped scallions with 1 tablespoon of the sesame oil and the salt. Cut the pizza dough in half. On a work surface, roll out each piece of pizza dough to a 10-by-6-inch rectangle. Spread the scallion and sesame oil mixture over the rectangles of dough, leaving a ½-inch border all around. Starting at a long edge, roll up each piece of dough and pinch to seal. Coil each roll of dough into a round and tuck the end under the coil. Cover and let stand for 15 minutes.

2. In a medium bowl, mix the sliced scallion with the remaining 1 teaspoon of sesame oil and the soy sauce, water and rice vinegar for the dipping sauce.

3. Roll each coil into an 8-inch round. (It's okay if some of the scallion mixture comes out of the coil; it will stick to the dough again as you roll out the pancakes.)

4. In a skillet, heat the canola oil until shimmering. Fry one scallion pancake at a time over moderately high heat, turning once, until golden, 3 minutes total. Drain on paper towels. Cut into quarters and serve with the dipping sauce. —*Joanne Chang*

perfecting stuffing

After tossing the ingredients and spreading them in a pan, F&W's **Melissa Rubel Jacobson** *chills her stuffing before baking. This ensures that the bread soaks up the liquid—key to a stuffing that's crisp on top and moist within.*

Bacon, Onion and Rye Bread Stuffing

ACTIVE: 30 MIN; TOTAL: 3 HR

12 SERVINGS ● ◉

One 9-inch-long loaf seeded rye bread, cut into 1-inch cubes

4 tablespoons unsalted butter

1 large sweet onion, such as Vidalia, halved and thinly sliced

1 celery rib, cut into ¼-inch dice

1 teaspoon chopped sage

1 teaspoon thyme leaves

½ pound piece of slab bacon, sliced ½ inch thick and cut into ½-inch dice

2½ cups chicken stock or low-sodium broth

1 egg

2½ teaspoons kosher salt

½ teaspoon freshly ground pepper

1. Preheat the oven to 375°. Lightly butter a 9-by-13-inch baking dish. On a large rimmed baking sheet, toast the rye bread cubes for about 15 minutes, tossing once halfway through, until lightly golden and dry. Transfer the bread to a large bowl.

2. In a skillet, melt the butter. Add the onion and celery; cook over moderate heat until tender, about 10 minutes. Add the sage and thyme and cook until fragrant, about 1 minute. Scrape into the bowl with the bread.

3. Wipe out the skillet. Add the bacon and cook over moderate heat until browned, about 10 minutes. Using a slotted spoon, transfer the bacon to the bowl with the bread. In a medium bowl, whisk the chicken broth with the egg. Pour over the bread mixture and add the salt and pepper. Toss until the liquid is absorbed. Scrape into the baking dish; cover with foil. Refrigerate for at least 1 hour or overnight.

4. Bake the stuffing for about 30 minutes, until hot throughout. Remove the foil and bake for about 30 minutes longer, until the top is lightly golden. Serve hot or warm.

TWO GREAT VARIATIONS

1 Shiitake Mushroom & Fresh Herb Stuffing

Replace the rye bread with one 21-inch baguette. Substitute a diced yellow onion for the Vidalia. Omit the bacon. Stem 1 pound shiitake mushrooms and thinly slice the caps. Cook the caps in 4 tablespoons butter until browned, 8 minutes; season with salt and pepper and add to the stuffing. Bake as directed.

2 Whole-Grain Bread Stuffing with Apples, Sausage & Pecans

Replace the rye bread with a 7-inch-round whole-grain loaf and the Vidalia with a diced yellow onion. Omit bacon. Cook 1 pound loose sweet Italian sausage with the onion. Toast and chop ¾ cup pecans; add with 1 diced Granny Smith. Bake as directed.

breads, pizzas & sandwiches

Vietnamese-Style Banh Mi Burgers

TOTAL: 30 MIN
4 SERVINGS

Is this an American take on a Vietnamese classic or a Vietnamese take on an American classic? Either way, these spicy burgers topped with Tabasco-spiked mayonnaise, slivers of crunchy pickled carrots and sprigs of cilantro are wonderful.

- 2 carrots, coarsely shredded
- ¼ cup unseasoned rice vinegar
- 1 tablespoon sugar
- ½ cup mayonnaise
- 2 tablespoons Tabasco
- 2 teaspoons tomato paste
- 1 garlic clove, minced
- Kosher salt and freshly ground pepper
- 1½ pounds ground beef chuck
- 1½ teaspoons curry powder
- 2 tablespoons vegetable oil
- 2 tablespoons unsalted butter, softened
- One 24-inch baguette, quartered crosswise and split
- 2 pickled jalapeños, thinly sliced
- 12 cilantro sprigs

1. Preheat the oven to 400°. In a small bowl, toss the carrots with the vinegar and sugar; let stand 10 minutes, then drain.
2. In a small bowl, whisk the mayonnaise with the Tabasco, tomato paste and garlic and season with salt and pepper.
3. Form the meat into four 6-inch-long oval patties about 1 inch thick. Season with the curry powder, salt and pepper. In a large skillet, heat the oil until shimmering. Cook the patties over moderate heat, turning once, until medium, about 12 minutes.
4. Spread the butter on the baguette. Set the bread cut side up on a baking sheet and bake for 5 minutes, until lightly toasted. Spread the mayonnaise on the bread and top with a burger patty, pickled carrots, jalapeño slices and cilantro. Close the sandwiches and serve hot. —*Joanne Chang*
WINE Vivid, lightly sweet Riesling.

Piquillo-Pepper Num Pangs

TOTAL: 35 MIN PLUS 1 HR PICKLING
4 SERVINGS ●

"People are more open to trying new things if the form is familiar," says Cambodian-born chef Ratha Chau. At Manhattan's Num Pang (Khmer for "bread"), he presents Southeast Asian flavors in the form of sandwiches. To save time, supplement store-bought pesto with chiles, lime juice and a little fish sauce instead of making the pesto in this recipe.

- 2 medium carrots, julienned
- 2 tablespoons cider vinegar
- 1 tablespoon sugar
- 3 packed cups Thai basil leaves
- 2 anchovy fillets, chopped
- 2 teaspoons fresh lime juice
- 1½ teaspoons Asian fish sauce
- 1 teaspoon crushed red pepper
- 2 garlic cloves—1 chopped, 1 whole
- ¼ cup extra-virgin olive oil
- Salt and freshly ground pepper
- Four 6-inch lengths of semolina baguettes or kaiser rolls, split
- 4 tablespoons unsalted butter
- Mayonnaise, for spreading
- Sriracha chile sauce, for drizzling
- One 6-ounce cucumber, thinly sliced lengthwise on a mandoline
- One 6-ounce jar piquillo peppers, drained
- 12 large cilantro sprigs

1. In a medium bowl, toss the carrots with the vinegar and sugar. Let stand at room temperature for 1 hour; stir occasionally.
2. In a food processor, combine the basil, anchovies, lime juice, fish sauce, crushed red pepper and chopped garlic; process to a paste. With the machine on, slowly pour in the olive oil and puree until blended. Season with salt and pepper. Let stand at room temperature for at least 30 minutes.
3. Preheat the broiler. Spread the cut sides of the baguettes with the butter. Toast the baguettes 3 inches from the heat. Rub the toasted sides with the garlic clove, spread with the mayonnaise and drizzle with the Sriracha. Arrange the cucumber, carrots and piquillo peppers on the bottoms and garnish with the cilantro. Spread the tops with the pesto and close the sandwiches. Cut in half and serve. —*Ratha Chau*
WINE Vivid, lightly sweet Riesling.

Oregon Tuna Melts

TOTAL: 25 MIN
4 SERVINGS

Approaching tuna-melt perfection, these sandwiches from Portland, Oregon, chef Tommy Habetz have the ideal tuna-to-cheese ratio. His smart idea: using balsamic vinaigrette in place of mayonnaise.

- Two 6-ounce cans albacore tuna
- ¼ cup finely diced red onion
- ¼ cup extra-virgin olive oil
- 1 tablespoon balsamic vinegar
- 1 tablespoon minced basil
- ½ teaspoon crushed red pepper
- Salt and freshly ground pepper
- 4 ciabatta rolls, split
- Dijon mustard and mayonnaise, for spreading
- Eight ¼-inch-thick slices of Swiss or cheddar cheese (6 ounces)
- Sixteen ⅛-inch-thick lengthwise slices of kosher dill pickle
- 2 tablespoons unsalted butter, softened

1. In a medium bowl, mix the tuna with the onion, olive oil, vinegar, basil and crushed red pepper. Season with salt and pepper.
2. Heat a panini press or griddle. Spread the cut sides of the rolls with mustard and mayonnaise and top with a slice of cheese. Spread the tuna salad on the bottoms and cover with the pickles. Close the sandwiches and spread the outsides of the rolls with the butter.
3. Add the sandwiches to the press and cook over moderate heat until the cheese is melted, about 6 minutes. Cut in half and serve. —*Tommy Habetz*
WINE Full-bodied, rich Pinot Gris.

OREGON TUNA MELTS

GORDITAS

CORN TORTILLAS

Tuna Bocadillos

 TOTAL: 45 MIN

4 SERVINGS ● ●

- 2 tablespoons extra-virgin olive oil, plus more for brushing
- 1 medium onion, finely chopped
- 2 leeks, white and tender green parts only, finely chopped
- 1 teaspoon chopped thyme
- ½ teaspoon dried marjoram

Salt and freshly ground pepper

- ½ teaspoon sugar
- 3 tablespoons sherry vinegar
- 1 carrot, finely diced

Two 8-ounce jars imported Spanish tuna in olive oil

Four 8-inch baguettes, split lengthwise

- 1 ripe tomato, halved crosswise
- 4 piquillo peppers, cut into thin strips

1. In a medium skillet, heat the 2 tablespoons of oil. Add the onion, leeks, thyme and marjoram. Season with salt and pepper. Cook over moderately low heat, stirring, until softened, 10 minutes. Add the sugar, sherry vinegar and carrot and cook over low heat just until the liquid has evaporated and the carrot is crisp-tender, about 5 minutes. Transfer to a bowl and refrigerate until cool, about 15 minutes.

2. Add the tuna and its oil to the vegetables, breaking the tuna into large flakes.

3. Preheat the broiler. Brush the cut sides of the baguettes with olive oil and toast slightly. Rub the cut sides of the tomato over the baguettes, leaving lots of pulp. Spoon the tuna salad onto the baguettes, top with the piquillos; serve. —*Alex Raij*

MAKE AHEAD The tuna salad can be refrigerated overnight.

WINE Fresh, fruity rosé.

Salmon Club Sandwiches

ACTIVE: 40 MIN; TOTAL: 2 HR

4 SERVINGS ●

- 2 tablespoons extra-virgin olive oil
- 1 medium onion, coarsely chopped
- 2 tablespoons tamarind concentrate
- 2 garlic cloves, coarsely chopped
- 2 dried chipotle chiles, stems and seeds discarded
- ¾ cup golden raisins
- ¼ cup tomato paste
- ¼ cup agave syrup (see Note)
- ½ teaspoon pure chile powder, such as ancho or pasilla

Salt and freshly ground pepper

Four skinless 4-ounce salmon fillets, halved crosswise

- 12 thin slices of whole wheat toast
- ¼ cup mayonnaise
- 1 cup arugula leaves
- 4 large slices of beefsteak tomato

1. In a saucepan, heat the oil. Add the onion and cook over moderate heat until softened. Add the tamarind, garlic, chipotles, raisins, tomato paste, agave and chile powder. Bring to a boil and simmer over low heat until thick, 20 minutes. Let cool, then puree in a blender. Season with salt and pepper.
2. Set the salmon in a large, shallow dish and season with salt and pepper. Coat with ½ cup of the sauce; refrigerate for 1 hour.
3. Light a grill and oil the grates. Grill the salmon over high heat, turning once and basting with another ½ cup of the sauce, until just cooked through, 4 minutes.
4. For each sandwich, use 3 slices of toast; spread each with 1 teaspoon of mayonnaise and layer with the arugula, tomato and fish. —Charles Dale

NOTE Sweet agave syrup, made from agave plants, is available at health-food stores.
WINE Ripe, juicy Pinot Noir.

Fried-Fish Sandwiches with Jalapeño-Spiked Tomatoes

TOTAL: 30 MIN
4 SERVINGS ●

2 cups all-purpose flour
Salt
2¼ cups club soda
1 teaspoon ground cumin
1 teaspoon dried oregano
1 teaspoon hot paprika
Four 6-ounce skinless haddock
    or hake fillets
Freshly ground pepper
2 medium tomatoes, thinly sliced
1 small yellow onion, thinly sliced
1 jalapeño, seeded and thinly sliced
¼ cup coarsely chopped cilantro
Vegetable oil, for frying
4 kaiser rolls, split and toasted
4 large Boston lettuce leaves

1. Fill a large bowl with ice water. In another bowl, whisk the flour with 1 teaspoon of salt. Whisk in the club soda until the batter is smooth. Set the bowl in the ice bath; let stand until chilled, 10 minutes.
2. Meanwhile, in a small bowl, combine the cumin, oregano and paprika. Season the fish with salt and pepper and sprinkle with the spice mixture. In a large bowl, gently toss the tomatoes with the onion, jalapeño and cilantro; season with salt.
3. In a large, deep skillet, heat 2 inches of vegetable oil to 350°. Place a rack over a rimmed baking sheet. Working with two at a time, dredge the fish fillets in flour, shaking off any excess. Dip the fillets in the batter and fry, turning once, until golden and cooked through, 4 minutes; transfer to the rack. Repeat with the remaining fish.
4. Arrange the rolls on a work surface, cut side up. Top the bottom halves with the lettuce, fish and tomato mixture. Close the sandwiches and serve. —Alex Aguilera
WINE Light, fresh Pinot Grigio.

Gorditas

TOTAL: 25 MIN
MAKES 10 GORDITAS
Crisp on the outside and soft within, these savory Mexican corn cakes are a great base for all types of toppings, from pulled pork to shredded chicken. For a more luscious gordita, fry the dough in lard or butter.

2 cups masa harina, preferably
    Bob's Red Mill (see Note)
1¼ cups water
¼ cup vegetable oil,
    plus more for frying
Shredded chicken, salsa, sour cream
    and cotija cheese, for serving

1. In a large bowl, mix the masa harina with the water and the ¼ cup of oil. Transfer the dough to a sheet of plastic wrap and roll into a 10-inch log; cut into 10 pieces. Using a 3-inch round biscuit cutter, mold the pieces into flat disks a scant ½ inch thick.
2. Heat a large griddle or comal (a round, flat griddle). Add the gorditas and cook over high heat, turning once, until lightly browned in spots, about 2 minutes per side. Using the back of a spoon, lightly press an indentation in the center of each gordita.
3. In a large skillet, heat ¼ inch of oil until shimmering. Add the gorditas and fry over high heat until golden and crispy, about 2 minutes per side; drain on paper towels. Top the indentations with chicken, salsa, sour cream and cheese and serve hot. —Jessamyn Waldman
NOTE Masa harina, lime-treated corn flour, can be found at bobsredmill.com.

Corn Tortillas

TOTAL: 30 MIN
MAKES 16 TORTILLAS ● ●

2 cups masa harina, preferably
    Bob's Red Mill (see Note, above)
1½ cups water
Shredded chicken, salsa, sour cream
    and cotija cheese, for serving

1. In a large bowl, combine the masa harina with the water and stir until moistened. On a sheet of plastic wrap, roll the dough into an 8-inch log and cut the log into 16 pieces. Roll each piece into a ball, transfer to a plate and cover loosely with plastic.
2. Heat a griddle or a comal (a flat, round griddle) until very hot. Line a basket or a wide, shallow bowl with a clean kitchen towel. Cut a sturdy, resealable plastic bag at the seams. Set 1 ball of dough between the sheets of plastic. Using a tortilla press, a skillet or a rolling pin, flatten the tortilla to a 5-inch round. Peel off the plastic and set the tortilla on the hot griddle.
3. Cook the tortilla over high heat until lightly browned in spots, about 1 minute. Flip and cook about 30 seconds longer. Wrap the cooked tortilla in the towel. Press, cook and wrap the remaining balls of dough, keeping the stack of tortillas covered. Serve the tortillas warm and wrap them around chicken, salsa, sour cream and cotija cheese. —Jessamyn Waldman
MAKE AHEAD The uncooked tortillas can be stacked between layers of wax paper and stored in a plastic bag in the refrigerator overnight. They can also be frozen for up to 1 month. Cook without thawing.

CINNAMON POLENTA
PANCAKES (P. 285)

breakfast & brunch

Wholesome or indulgent recipes
to start the day: sticky rolls, polenta
pancakes and more.

EGGS BAKED IN ROASTED-TOMATO SAUCE

SHERRIED MUSHROOMS WITH FRIED EGGS ON TOAST

Eggs Baked in Roasted-Tomato Sauce

ACTIVE: 15 MIN; TOTAL: 1 HR 15 MIN

4 SERVINGS ● ● ●

Marisa May, co-owner of New York City's SD26, likes breakfast dishes that sustain her throughout the day. One favorite: *uova al purgatorio,* eggs baked in an oregano-scented pureed tomato sauce.

1½ **pounds plum tomatoes,
      halved lengthwise**

2 **garlic cloves, smashed**

2 **tablespoons extra-virgin olive oil**

Salt and freshly ground pepper

1 **teaspoon chopped oregano leaves**

8 **large eggs**

2 **tablespoons freshly grated
      Parmigiano-Reggiano cheese**

1. Preheat the oven to 400°. In a roasting pan, toss the tomatoes and garlic with the oil and season with salt and pepper.

Arrange the tomatoes cut side up and roast for 15 minutes; turn and roast until soft, 20 minutes. Let cool, then scrape into a blender; puree. Stir in the oregano.
2. Set 4 shallow ovenproof bowls on a baking sheet. Strain the sauce into the bowls. Crack 2 eggs into each bowl and season with salt and pepper. Sprinkle the cheese over the eggs and bake for 15 minutes, until the whites are just set. Serve hot.
—*Marisa May*
SERVE WITH Toasted ciabatta bread.

Sherried Mushrooms with Fried Eggs on Toast

TOTAL: 35 MIN

4 SERVINGS ● ●

To make a fabulous topping for fried eggs, Napa chef Cindy Pawlcyn sautés mushrooms and onions with oloroso, the rich, nutty-tasting Spanish dry sherry.

2 **tablespoons extra-virgin
      olive oil, plus more for
      brushing**

¾ **pound mixed mushrooms,
      such as button and cremini,
      sliced ¼ inch thick**

Salt and freshly ground pepper

½ **small onion, thinly sliced**

¼ **cup dry sherry,
      such as oloroso**

**Four ½-inch-thick slices of
      rustic white bread**

2 **tablespoons unsalted butter**

4 **large eggs**

2 **tablespoons coarsely chopped
      flat-leaf parsley**

1. Preheat the oven to 400°. In a large skillet, heat the 2 tablespoons of olive oil until shimmering. Add the sliced mushrooms and season with salt and pepper. Cover and cook over moderate heat, stirring a few times, until the mushrooms are softened, about 4 minutes. Add the sliced onion, cover and cook, stirring occasionally, until the onion is softened and the mushrooms are browned, about 3 minutes longer. Add the sherry and cook until the liquid is almost evaporated, about 1 minute. Season the sherried mushrooms with salt and pepper. Remove the skillet from the heat, cover and set aside.

2. Arrange the bread slices on a large rimmed baking sheet and brush them with olive oil. Bake for about 6 minutes, until toasted. Transfer the toasts to plates.

3. In a large nonstick skillet, melt the butter over moderate heat. Crack the eggs one at a time into a small ramekin and then slip them carefully into the hot skillet. Cook the eggs, sunny-side up, until the egg whites are firm and the egg yolks are warmed yet still runny, about 5 minutes.

4. Spoon the sherried mushroom mixture onto the toasts and top each toast with one of the fried eggs. Garnish each fried egg with some of the chopped fresh parsley and serve right away.

—*Cindy Pawlcyn*

MAKE AHEAD The sherried mushrooms can be stored in a container in the refrigerator overnight. Reheat gently.

Eggs in Tomato Sauce

TOTAL: 20 MIN
4 SERVINGS ● ● ●

Mediterranean cooks make many versions of eggs poached in tomato sauce, but this one is slightly unusual because it involves gently folding the egg whites into the simmering sauce, almost like egg drop soup, to add substance. New York City chef Marco Canora got the idea from Fabio Picchi, owner of the legendary Cibrèo restaurant in Florence.

**Four 1-inch-thick slices of
    country bread**
¼ **cup extra-virgin olive oil,
    plus more for brushing**

4 **large eggs**
1 **small garlic clove,
    thinly sliced**
**Pinch of crushed red
    pepper flakes**
**One 14-ounce can whole tomatoes
    with their juices, crushed**
**Salt and freshly ground
    black pepper**
2 **teaspoons chopped fresh
    oregano leaves**

1. Preheat the broiler. Brush the bread slices on both sides with olive oil, arrange them on the baking sheet and broil for about 3 minutes, turning once, until the slices are golden and toasted. Place the toasts in 4 shallow bowls.

2. Arrange 5 small bowls on a counter. Crack the eggs: Reserve 2 of the whites in one of the bowls and 1 yolk in each of the other 4 bowls. Refrigerate the remaining 2 egg whites for another use.

3. In a medium nonstick skillet, heat the ¼ cup of olive oil with the sliced garlic clove and crushed red pepper. Cook over moderate heat until the sliced garlic is fragrant and golden, about 30 seconds. Add the crushed tomatoes and their juices, and season the sauce with salt and black pepper. Cook over high heat, stirring occasionally, until the tomato sauce is thickened, about 5 minutes.

4. Beat the egg whites with a fork and gently fold them into the simmering tomato sauce. Cook the sauce over moderately high heat just until the egg whites are set, about 1 minute. Using the back of a large spoon, make 4 indentations in the sauce. Slide an egg yolk into each indentation and cover the skillet. Cook over very low heat just until the egg yolks are warmed through but not set, about 1½ minutes. Spoon the tomato sauce and 1 egg yolk over each of the toast slices, garnish the eggs with the chopped fresh oregano leaves and serve right away.

—*Marco Canora*

Herb Frittatas with Minty Tomato Salad

TOTAL: 25 MIN
12 FIRST-COURSE SERVINGS ● ●

These frittatas are so thin and light, they're almost like crêpes. Alain Coumont, founder of the bakery-café chain Le Pain Quotidien, serves them with tomatoes and mint, but nearly any summer salad would work.

4 **large tomatoes, cored
    and diced**
¼ **cup coarsely chopped fresh
    mint, plus 3 dozen mint leaves
    for garnish**
**Kosher salt and freshly
    ground pepper**
1 **cup chopped flat-leaf
    parsley leaves**
3 **scallions, thinly sliced**
3 **medium garlic cloves, very
    finely chopped**
½ **teaspoon ground cumin**
2 **large eggs, lightly beaten**
¼ **cup extra-virgin olive oil**

1. Set a strainer over a bowl. In a medium bowl, toss the diced tomatoes with 2 tablespoons of the chopped mint and season with salt and pepper. Scrape the tomatoes into the strainer and let drain.

2. Meanwhile, in another bowl, toss the chopped parsley with the scallions, garlic, cumin and the remaining 2 tablespoons of chopped mint. Stir in the eggs and season with salt and pepper.

3. In a large cast-iron skillet, heat 2 tablespoons of the olive oil. Pour in half of the egg mixture and tilt the pan to spread it into a thin pancake. Cook over moderately high heat, turning once, until browned and crisp, about 4 minutes. Transfer the frittata to paper towels to drain. Repeat with the remaining 2 tablespoons of olive oil and egg. Cut the frittatas into wedges. Spoon the drained tomatoes alongside, garnish with the fresh mint leaves and serve the frittatas right away.

—*Alain Coumont*

breakfast & brunch

Frittata Sandwich

TOTAL: 50 MIN

4 SERVINGS ●

Tony Mantuano's Terzo Piano café at the Art Institute of Chicago offers modern, urban cooking. "It is more Milan than Florence," he says. Many dishes feature cheese from the amazing floor-to-ceiling *cave,* like this terrific frittata sandwich.

½ pound broccoli rabe

2 tablespoons extra-virgin olive oil

1 large garlic clove, smashed

5 ounces baby spinach (5 cups)

Salt and freshly ground black pepper

6 large eggs

¼ cup milk

4 ounces fresh mozzarella, cut into ½-inch cubes

Eight ¾-inch-thick slices of brioche, toasted

1. Preheat the oven to 350°. Bring a saucepan of water to a boil. Add the broccoli rabe and cook until softened, about 5 minutes. Drain and rinse under cold water. Pat dry and coarsely chop the broccoli rabe.

2. Heat the olive oil in a large ovenproof nonstick skillet. Add the garlic and cook over moderately high heat, stirring, until lightly browned, about 1 minute. Add the broccoli rabe and cook until lightly browned in spots, about 3 minutes. Add the spinach, season with salt and pepper and cook, stirring, until wilted, about 1 minute; discard the garlic.

3. In a medium bowl, whisk the eggs with the milk and season with salt and pepper. Add the mozzarella. Pour the eggs over the greens and shake the skillet gently to settle the mixture. Transfer the skillet to the oven and bake the frittata for about 20 minutes, or until set and puffed. Cut the frittata into quarters and sandwich between the slices of toasted brioche. Cut each sandwich in half and serve.

—*Tony Mantuano*

Corn Pudding

ACTIVE: 25 MIN; TOTAL: 1 HR 15 MIN

10 SERVINGS ● ●

"Some corn puddings are really dense," says cookbook author Katie Lee. "The egg whites here make this one lighter." The cornmeal in the recipe settles a bit in the bottom of the baking dish, almost creating a layer of corn bread under the moist, sweet corn pudding.

2 cups milk

½ cup heavy cream

4 medium ears of corn, shucked

1 tablespoon extra-virgin olive oil

1 medium sweet onion, finely chopped

1 stick unsalted butter

½ cup cornmeal

6 large eggs, separated

3 ounces sharp cheddar cheese, shredded (about 1 cup)

1 teaspoon plus a pinch of salt

½ teaspoon freshly ground black pepper

1. Preheat the oven to 350°. Butter a 10-by-15-inch baking dish. In a large saucepan, bring the milk and cream to a simmer over moderate heat. Add the corn, cover and cook over moderately low heat, turning a few times, until tender, about 10 minutes.

2. Meanwhile, in a medium skillet, heat the olive oil. Add the onion and cook over moderate heat until softened, about 8 minutes.

3. Transfer the corn to a plate and let cool. Remove the saucepan from the heat and swirl in the butter until melted. Let cool to room temperature. Using a serrated knife, cut the kernels off the cobs and add to the saucepan. Scrape the onion into the saucepan. Whisk in the cornmeal, egg yolks, cheddar, the 1 teaspoon of salt and the pepper.

4. In a large stainless steel bowl, beat the egg whites with the pinch of salt at high speed until firm peaks form. Fold the whites into the corn mixture and pour into the prepared baking dish. Bake for about 30 minutes, until the corn pudding is puffed and golden brown. Let the pudding rest for about 5 minutes before serving.

—*Katie Lee*

MAKE AHEAD The pudding can be prepared through Step 3 and refrigerated overnight. Bring to room temperature before proceeding.

Pea Tortilla with Mint and Yogurt

TOTAL: 20 MIN

10 SERVINGS ● ●

A Spanish *tortilla* is very similar to a frittata. Argentine chef Francis Mallmann makes this lovely spring version with Greek yogurt, chopped fresh mint and sweet baby peas, baked in the oven (preferably a wood-fired oven) until the eggs are just set. It's equally delicious served warm or at room temperature.

4 tablespoons unsalted butter

½ pound frozen baby peas—thawed, drained and patted dry

1½ cups plain Greek yogurt

8 large eggs

½ cup coarsely chopped mint

1 teaspoon kosher salt

¼ teaspoon freshly ground pepper

1. Preheat the broiler. In a large ovenproof nonstick skillet, melt the butter. Add the peas and cook over moderate heat until warm, about 3 minutes.

2. In a large bowl, beat ½ cup of the yogurt with the eggs, mint, salt and pepper until smooth. Pour the eggs over the peas and cook over moderately high heat until set on the bottom and around the edge, about 4 minutes. Transfer the skillet to the oven and broil 6 inches from the heat for about 3 minutes, until the top of the *tortilla* is set and lightly golden in spots. Slide the *tortilla* onto a plate, cut into wedges and serve with the remaining 1 cup of yogurt.

—*Francis Mallmann*

PEA TORTILLA WITH
MINT AND YOGURT

Bacon-and-Leek Quiches

ACTIVE: 45 MIN; TOTAL: 2 HR 30 MIN
MAKES TWO 10-INCH TARTS ● ●

CRUST

2½ cups all-purpose flour,
    plus more for dusting
½ teaspoon salt
1½ sticks cold unsalted
    butter, cubed
1 large egg yolk
¼ cup plus 3 tablespoons
    ice water

FILLING

1 pound thickly sliced bacon,
    cut into ½-inch dice
3 large leeks, white and
    tender green parts only,
    thinly sliced
1 teaspoon chopped fresh
    thyme leaves
Salt and freshly ground
    white pepper
8 ounces cave-aged Gruyère
    cheese, shredded
4 large eggs
2 large egg yolks
2½ cups heavy cream or
    half-and-half

1. MAKE THE CRUST: In a food processor, pulse the 2½ cups of flour with the salt. Add the butter and pulse until it is the size of small peas. Add the egg yolk and ice water and pulse until the pastry is moistened. Turn the pastry out onto a floured work surface and knead 2 or 3 times, just until smooth. Pat the pastry into 2 disks, wrap in plastic and refrigerate until firm, about 20 minutes.

2. Preheat the oven to 375°. On a lightly floured work surface, roll 1 disk of the pastry dough out to a 12-inch round. Gently ease the pastry round into a 10-inch fluted tart pan with a removable bottom without stretching the dough. Trim the excess and use it to patch any holes. Refrigerate the tart shell for 10 minutes. Repeat with the remaining pastry.

3. Line the tart shells with foil and fill with pie weights or dried beans. Bake the tart shells for 30 minutes, just until dry. Remove the foil and pie weights and bake the crusts for about 15 minutes longer, until they are dry and golden. Transfer the tart pans to 2 sturdy baking sheets.

4. MEANWHILE, MAKE THE FILLING: In a large skillet, cook the bacon over moderately high heat, stirring, until browned and crisp, about 7 minutes. Drain the bacon, leaving 1 tablespoon of the fat in the pan. Add the leeks and thyme to the skillet, season with salt and white pepper and cook over moderate heat, stirring occasionally, until the leeks are softened but not browned, about 5 minutes. Transfer to a bowl and let cool. Stir in the bacon and shredded cheese.

5. Divide the bacon-and-leek filling between the tart shells. In a bowl, whisk the eggs with the egg yolks and heavy cream. Season lightly with salt and white pepper. Pour the custard into the tart shells and bake for about 30 minutes, rotating the sheet halfway through for even baking, until puffed and lightly browned. Transfer the quiches to a rack and let cool for 15 minutes. Remove the rings, cut the quiches into wedges and serve.
—*Grace Parisi*

MAKE AHEAD The quiches can be covered and refrigerated overnight. Reheat the quiches gently before serving.

Welsh Rabbit

TOTAL: 30 MIN
8 SERVINGS ● ● ●

London chef and cookbook author Mark Hix says "rabbit," while other Brits say "rarebit"; whatever the pronunciation, these open-faced sandwiches are hard to resist. Thick slices of toasted country bread are topped with a blanket of melted extra-sharp English cheddar cheese seasoned with both Worcestershire sauce and Guinness stout.

1 cup Guinness stout
1 cup heavy cream
9 ounces extra-sharp cheddar
    cheese, shredded (3 cups)
4 large egg yolks
1½ tablespoons Worcestershire sauce
2 teaspoons dry mustard powder
Salt and freshly ground pepper
Eight ½-inch-thick slices of whole-
    grain country bread, toasted

1. Preheat the broiler. In a small saucepan, boil the stout over high heat until reduced to ½ cup, about 4 minutes. Add the cream and boil until reduced to ¾ cup, about 4 minutes. Scrape into a bowl and let cool to room temperature. Stir in the cheddar, egg yolks, Worcestershire sauce and dry mustard and season with salt and pepper.

2. Arrange the toasts on a large rimmed baking sheet. Spread the toasts with a ¼-inch-thick layer of the cheddar mixture. Broil 4 inches from the heat for about 2 minutes, until the topping is bubbling and browned around the edges. Serve right away. —*Mark Hix*

MAKE AHEAD The cheese mixture can be refrigerated overnight.

Orange-Cranberry Scones with Turbinado Sugar

ACTIVE: 15 MIN; TOTAL: 40 MIN
MAKES 8 SCONES ● ● ●

1½ cups all-purpose flour
¾ cup quick-cooking oats
2 teaspoons baking powder
½ teaspoon salt
5 tablespoons turbinado
    sugar (see Note)
6 tablespoons cold unsalted butter,
    cut into small cubes
½ cup dried cranberries
2 teaspoons grated orange zest
½ cup buttermilk, plus more
    for brushing

1. Preheat the oven to 425° and line a baking sheet with parchment paper. In a bowl, whisk the flour, oats, baking powder, salt

ORANGE-CRANBERRY SCONES WITH TURBINADO SUGAR

ORANGE POPOVERS

and 3 tablespoons of the sugar. Using a pastry blender or 2 knives, cut in the butter until the mixture resembles coarse meal. Mix in the cranberries and orange zest. Stir in the ½ cup of buttermilk until a stiff dough forms; knead until it just comes together.

2. On a floured surface, pat the dough into a ¾-inch-thick round and cut into 8 wedges. Brush with buttermilk. Sprinkle the remaining sugar on top. Transfer to the baking sheet and bake in the center of the oven for 17 minutes, until lightly browned. Transfer the scones to a rack and let cool slightly. Serve warm or at room temperature. —*Mani Niall*

SERVE WITH Preserves or jam.

NOTE Turbinado, a pale brown raw sugar, adds a great crunch when sprinkled on baked goods. It's sold as Sugar in the Raw in supermarkets and natural food stores, and at sugarintheraw.com.

Orange Popovers

 **ACTIVE: 10 MIN; TOTAL: 40 MIN**
MAKES 12 POPOVERS ●

F&W's Grace Parisi loves popovers, but baking them can be tricky: They don't always rise as they should. For these foolproof ones, Grace adds a bit of baking powder to the batter and chooses to use a regular (not nonstick) muffin tin, which helps keep the popovers from sinking.

- 3 **large eggs, at room temperature**
- 1 **tablespoon sugar**
- 1 **teaspoon finely grated orange zest**
- 1¼ **cups milk**
- 4 **tablespoons unsalted butter, melted**
- 1¼ **cups all-purpose flour**
- ½ **teaspoon baking powder**
- ½ **teaspoon salt**

1. Preheat the oven to 425°. In a large bowl, whisk the eggs with the sugar and grated orange zest. Whisk in the milk and 3 tablespoons of the melted butter. In another large bowl, whisk the flour with the baking powder and salt. Whisk the wet ingredients into the dry ingredients until only small lumps remain.

2. Brush the cups of a 12-cup muffin tin (preferably not nonstick) thoroughly with the remaining 1 tablespoon of melted butter and preheat the muffin tin in the oven for about 5 minutes; the butter will turn a nutty brown. Carefully fill the preheated muffin cups halfway with the popover batter. Bake the popovers for about 30 minutes, until they are risen and browned. Turn the popovers out onto a serving platter and serve them right away. —*Grace Parisi*

SERVE WITH Preserves or jam.

breakfast & brunch

Blueberry–Sour Cream Muffins

ACTIVE: 20 MIN; TOTAL: 50 MIN

MAKES 12 MUFFINS ● ●

TOPPING

½ cup light brown sugar

⅓ cup all-purpose flour

2 tablespoons unsalted butter, softened

1 teaspoon cinnamon

MUFFINS

1½ cups plus 1 tablespoon all-purpose flour

2 teaspoons baking powder

¼ teaspoon baking soda

½ teaspoon salt

1 large egg

¾ cup sugar

1 tablespoon unsalted butter, melted

1 rounded cup sour cream

1 teaspoon pure vanilla extract

¾ teaspoon finely grated lemon zest

1 rounded cup frozen blueberries

1. MAKE THE TOPPING: Preheat the oven to 375°. In a medium bowl, combine the brown sugar, flour, butter and cinnamon. Rub with your fingers to form coarse crumbs. Refrigerate until ready to use.

2. MAKE THE MUFFINS: Butter a 12-cup muffin pan. In a medium bowl, whisk the 1½ cups of flour with the baking powder, baking soda and salt. In a large bowl, using a hand-held mixer, beat the egg at medium speed until frothy. Add the sugar and melted butter and beat until pale yellow, 1 minute. Beat in the sour cream, vanilla and lemon zest until blended. Add the dry ingredients and beat at low speed until almost blended. In a bowl, toss the blueberries with the remaining 1 tablespoon of flour. Using a rubber spatula, fold the blueberries into the batter.

3. Fill the muffin cups three-fourths full of batter; sprinkle with the topping. Bake for 25 minutes, or until a cake tester comes out clean. Remove the muffins from the pan; let cool on a rack. —*Eugenia Bone*

Pecan-Maple Sticky Rolls

ACTIVE: 20 MIN; TOTAL: 45 MIN

MAKES 12 ROLLS ● ● ●

¾ cup whole pecans

2 cups all-purpose flour, plus more for dusting

¼ cup sugar

2 teaspoons baking powder

½ teaspoon baking soda

Pinch of salt

1½ sticks unsalted butter— 1 stick cubed and chilled, 4 tablespoons melted

1 cup buttermilk

1 teaspoon cinnamon

6 tablespoons pure maple syrup

1. Preheat the oven to 425°. Spread the pecans in a pie plate and toast for about 6 minutes, until fragrant; let cool slightly.

2. Meanwhile, spray a 12-cup muffin tin with cooking spray. In a food processor, pulse the 2 cups of flour with 2 tablespoons of the sugar, the baking powder, baking soda and salt. Add the cubed butter and pulse until it is the size of small peas. Add the buttermilk and pulse a few times, just until a soft dough forms. Turn the dough out onto a floured surface and knead 3 times. Pat or roll the dough into an 8-by-12-inch rectangle. Brush with 2 tablespoons of the melted butter.

3. In a small bowl, combine the remaining 2 tablespoons of sugar with the cinnamon and sprinkle all over the dough. Beginning at a long side, roll the dough into a tight cylinder and pinch the seam closed. Cut the dough into 12 slices.

4. Divide the maple syrup and the remaining 2 tablespoons of melted butter among the cups. Scatter the pecans in the cups and top with the dough pinwheels. Bake for about 18 minutes, until golden; place a baking sheet below to catch any drips. Invert a rack over the rolls and invert them onto the rack. Replace any pecans that get stuck in the cups and let cool for 5 minutes before serving. —*Grace Parisi*

Buttermilk-Parmesan Biscuits

ACTIVE: 25 MIN; TOTAL: 45 MIN

MAKES ABOUT 2 DOZEN BISCUITS ● ●

The key to making these biscuits light and flaky is working the dough as little as possible. Parmigiano-Reggiano gives them a great savory flavor.

4 cups all-purpose flour, plus more for dusting

1½ cups freshly grated Parmigiano-Reggiano cheese

2 tablespoons finely chopped fresh thyme

2 tablespoons baking powder

1 tablespoon kosher salt

1 teaspoon sugar

½ teaspoon baking soda

6 tablespoons vegetable shortening, chilled

6 tablespoons cold unsalted butter, cut into small pieces

1½ cups buttermilk, chilled

1. Preheat the oven to 425°. In a large bowl, whisk together the 4 cups of flour, the Parmigiano-Reggiano, chopped thyme, baking powder, salt, sugar and baking soda. Using a pastry cutter or 2 knives, cut in the chilled shortening and butter until the mixture resembles coarse meal. Add the buttermilk and mix gently until just incorporated.

2. On a floured work surface, using a rolling pin, gently roll out the dough to a 13-inch round about ½ inch thick. With a 2½-inch fluted biscuit cutter, cut out as many biscuits as possible. Transfer to 2 large baking sheets, leaving about 1 inch between biscuits. Gather the dough scraps, gently press them together and cut out 5 or 6 more biscuits.

3. Bake the biscuits for about 18 minutes, until they are golden brown and risen. Serve hot or warm. —*Shawn McClain*

MAKE AHEAD The biscuits can be kept at room temperature for up to to 3 hours; reheat before serving.

perfecting fruit jams

Small-batch jams are an easy way to join the DIY food revolution.
F&W's **Grace Parisi** *shares six super summer-fruit recipes.*

Fig Jam

TOTAL: 45 MIN PLUS COOLING

MAKES THREE ½-PINT JARS ● ●

- 2 pounds green or purple figs, stemmed and cut into ½-inch pieces
- 1½ cups sugar
- ¼ cup plus 2 tablespoons fresh lemon juice
- ½ cup water

1. In a large nonreactive saucepan, toss the fig pieces with the sugar and let stand, stirring occasionally, for about 15 minutes, until the sugar is mostly dissolved and the figs are juicy.

2. Add the lemon juice and water; bring to a boil, stirring until the sugar is completely dissolved. Simmer the fig jam over moderate heat, stirring occasionally, until the fruit is soft and the liquid runs off the side of a spoon in thick, heavy drops, about 20 minutes.

3. Spoon the jam into three ½-pint jars, leaving ¼ inch of space at the top. Close the jars and let cool to room temperature. Store the jam in the refrigerator for up to 3 months.

Peach Jam

ACTIVE: 40 MIN; TOTAL: 1 HR 40 MIN PLUS COOLING

MAKES THREE ½-PINT JARS ● ●

- 2½ pounds peaches—peeled, pitted and cut into ½-inch wedges
- 1½ cups sugar
- 2 tablespoons fresh lemon juice

1. In a nonreactive saucepan, toss the peaches with the sugar and let stand, stirring, until the sugar is mostly dissolved, 1 hour.

2. Add the lemon juice to the peaches and bring to a boil, stirring until the sugar is dissolved. Simmer over moderate heat, stirring occasionally, until the fruit is glassy and the liquid runs off the side of a spoon in thick, heavy drops, 20 to 25 minutes. Skim off any scum that rises to the surface of the jam.

3. Spoon the jam into three ½-pint jars, leaving ¼ inch of space at the top. Close the jars and let the jam cool to room temperature. Store the jam in the refrigerator for up to 3 months.

Mixed-Berry Jam

ACTIVE: 40 MIN; TOTAL: 1 HR 40 MIN PLUS COOLING

MAKES THREE ½-PINT JARS ● ● ●

- 1 pound strawberries, hulled and quartered
- 1½ cups sugar
- ½ lemon, seeded
- 1 pound mixed blueberries, blackberries and raspberries

1. In a large nonreactive saucepan, toss the strawberries with the sugar and let stand, stirring occasionally, until the sugar is mostly dissolved, about 1 hour.

2. Squeeze the lemon over the strawberries, add it to the saucepan and bring to a boil, stirring until the sugar is dissolved. Cook over moderately high heat, stirring, until the strawberries are just softened, 5 minutes. Add the mixed berries; cook over moderate heat until the liquid runs off the side of a spoon in thick, heavy drops, 20 to 25 minutes. Skim any scum that rises to the surface.

3. Discard the lemon; spoon the jam into three ½-pint jars, leaving about ¼ inch of space at the top. Close the jars and let cool to room temperature. Store in the refrigerator for up to 3 months.

THREE GREAT VARIATIONS

1 Fig Jam with Port

In the Fig Jam recipe, substitute white port for water; add a rosemary sprig with lemon juice; discard sprig before jarring.

2 Apricot Jam

In the Peach Jam recipe, replace the peaches with 2 pounds skin-on apricots, pitted and cut into ½-inch pieces.

3 Plum Jam

In the Mixed-Berry Jam recipe, substitute 2 pounds small plums, cut into ½-inch wedges; toss with sugar before cooking.

YOGURT-ZUCCHINI BREAD WITH WALNUTS

SOY MILK–ARBORIO RICE PUDDING WITH POACHED FIGS

Yogurt-Zucchini Bread with Walnuts

ACTIVE: 15 MIN; TOTAL: 1 HR 30 MIN PLUS COOLING

MAKES ONE 9-INCH LOAF ● ○

This moist, nutty bread is a terrific way to use up late-summer zucchini.

- 1 cup walnut halves (4 ounces)
- 2 cups all-purpose flour
- ½ teaspoon baking powder
- ½ teaspoon baking soda
- ½ teaspoon salt
- ¾ cup plus 2 tablespoons sugar
- 2 large eggs
- ½ cup vegetable oil
- ½ cup plain fat-free Greek yogurt
- 1 cup coarsely grated zucchini (from about 1 medium zucchini)

1. Preheat the oven to 325°. Butter and flour a 9-by-4½-inch metal loaf pan. Spread the walnut halves in a pie plate and toast them for about 8 minutes, until they are fragrant. Transfer the toasted walnuts to a cutting board and coarsely chop them, then freeze for 5 minutes to cool.

2. In a large bowl, whisk the flour with the baking powder, baking soda and salt. In a medium bowl, mix the sugar with the eggs, oil and yogurt. Add the wet ingredients to the dry ingredients along with the grated zucchini and toasted walnuts and stir until the batter is evenly moistened. Scrape the batter into the prepared pan and bake for about 1 hour and 10 minutes, until the loaf is risen and a toothpick inserted in the center comes out clean. Let cool on a rack for 30 minutes before unmolding and serving. —*Grace Parisi*

MAKE AHEAD The zucchini loaf can be wrapped tightly in plastic and kept at room temperature for up to 4 days, or frozen in plastic and foil for up to 1 month.

Soy Milk–Arborio Rice Pudding with Poached Figs

TOTAL: 1 HR

4 SERVINGS ● ● ○ ○

Restaurateur Joe Bastianich likes to reheat portions of this lightly sweet pudding for quick breakfasts.

FIGS

- ¼ cup ruby port
- 2 tablespoons sugar

Four 3-inch-long strips of orange zest

- 5 cloves
- 1 bay leaf
- 8 fresh figs, stemmed

PUDDING

- 1 cup water

Pinch of salt

- ½ cup arborio rice
- 2 cups plain soy milk
- 2 tablespoons honey
- 1 teaspoon pure vanilla extract

1. POACH THE FIGS: In a medium nonstick skillet, combine the port with the sugar, orange zest, cloves, bay leaf and 1 cup of water and bring to a boil. When the sugar dissolves, add the figs, stem end up, and simmer over low heat until the figs are almost completely tender, about 20 minutes. Add ¼ cup more water as needed if the liquid gets too syrupy. Discard the orange zest, cloves and bay leaf.

2. MEANWHILE, MAKE THE PUDDING: In a medium saucepan, bring the water to a boil with the salt. Add the rice and cook over low heat, stirring often, until most of the water has been absorbed, about 12 minutes. Stir in ⅓ cup of the soy milk and cook, stirring, until it is absorbed, about 3 minutes. Continue adding the soy milk ⅓ cup at a time and stirring constantly until it is absorbed between additions; after the soy milk is absorbed, the rice should be creamy and tender. Stir in the honey and vanilla.

3. Spoon the rice pudding into bowls. Top with the figs and some of the poaching syrup and serve right away.

—Joe Bastianich

MAKE AHEAD The poached figs can be refrigerated in their syrup overnight. Reheat gently, adding a bit more water as needed. The rice pudding can be refrigerated for up to 2 days. Reheat gently, adding more soy milk as needed.

Maple, Pear and Ricotta Parfaits

ACTIVE: 20 MIN; TOTAL: 1 HR 15 MIN

6 SERVINGS ● ● ●

These maple-infused poached pears can also be served separately with granola or creamy Greek yogurt.

- 2½ cups water
- ⅓ cup maple syrup
- 1 tablespoon fresh lemon juice
- Four 8-ounce firm but ripe Bartlett pears—peeled, cored and quartered
- 1 tablespoon sugar
- 1 tablespoon unsalted butter
- 1 teaspoon pure vanilla extract
- One 15-ounce container part-skim ricotta cheese
- ¼ cup unsalted roasted pistachios, coarsely chopped

1. In a large nonreactive saucepan, combine the water, maple syrup and lemon juice. Add the pears and simmer over moderately low heat, turning occasionally, until tender, about 35 minutes. Remove from the heat and let cool. Using a slotted spoon, transfer the poached pears to a work surface. Thinly slice the pears.

2. Bring the poaching liquid to a boil and stir in the sugar, butter and vanilla. Simmer over moderate heat until the liquid is reduced to ½ cup, 8 to 10 minutes.

3. In a bowl, whisk the ricotta until smooth; dollop a third of the cheese into 6 glasses. Top with half of the pears. Repeat with another dollop of ricotta and the remaining pears. Spoon the remaining ricotta on top; drizzle with the poaching liquid. Sprinkle with pistachios and serve. *—Marisa May*

Mom's Nutty Granola

TOTAL: 45 MIN PLUS COOLING

MAKES 7 CUPS ● ● ● ○

"I love this granola because I'm not a sweet breakfast person myself," says Jessamyn Waldman, founder of New York City's Hot Bread Kitchen. This recipe, from Waldman's mother, is more nutty than sweet.

- 3 cups old-fashioned rolled oats
- ½ cup unsalted roasted peanuts
- ½ cup unsalted roasted almonds
- ½ cup unsalted roasted pumpkin seeds
- ½ cup unsalted roasted sunflower seeds
- ¼ cup wheat germ
- 1 teaspoon salt
- 1 tablespoon hot water
- ¾ cup honey
- ½ cup vegetable oil
- ½ cup raisins

1. Preheat the oven to 325°. In a bowl, toss the oats, nuts, seeds and wheat germ. In a small bowl, dissolve the salt in the hot water. Whisk in the honey and oil. Stir the liquid into the nuts to coat thoroughly, then spread on a large rimmed baking sheet.

2. Bake the granola in the center of the oven for 40 minutes, stirring every 10 minutes, until nearly dry. Turn off the oven and prop the door open halfway; let the granola cool in the oven, stirring. Toss the granola with the raisins; store in an airtight container for up to 3 weeks. *—Jessamyn Waldman*

Cinnamon Polenta Pancakes

photo, page 274

TOTAL: 30 MIN

4 SERVINGS ● ●

The polenta (cornmeal) in these pancakes makes them especially satisfying.

- 1¼ cups all-purpose flour
- ¾ cup cornmeal
- 1 tablespoon sugar
- 1 teaspoon cinnamon
- 1 teaspoon baking powder
- ½ teaspoon baking soda
- Pinch of salt
- 1 cup low-fat buttermilk
- 2 large eggs, beaten
- ¼ cup olive oil
- ¼ cup water

1. In a large bowl, whisk the flour, cornmeal, sugar, cinnamon, baking powder, baking soda and salt. In a small bowl, whisk the buttermilk, eggs, olive oil and water. Whisk the wet ingredients into the dry ingredients, leaving small lumps.

2. Set a griddle or skillet over moderately high heat and spray it with vegetable oil spray. When the pan is hot, spoon in ¼-cup mounds of batter and spread to form 4-inch rounds. Cook the pancakes until the bottoms are browned and bubbles appear on the surface, 2 minutes. Flip and cook until browned on the bottom, 1 to 2 minutes. Serve warm. *—Marisa May*

SERVE WITH Berry compote.

● HEALTHY   ● MAKE AHEAD   ● VEGETARIAN   ● STAFF FAVORITE

WHITE PEACH TART (P. 302)

pies
& fruit
desserts

Recipes for every season, from a
wintry citrus parfait to a white peach tart
that's the essence of summer.

PEAR TARTE TATIN WITH RED WINE CARAMEL

MIXED-BERRY DUTCH BABY

Pear Tarte Tatin with Red Wine Caramel

ACTIVE: 30 MIN; TOTAL: 3 HR

8 TO 10 SERVINGS ● ●

Instead of apple pie, Chicago chef Shawn McClain ends his Thanksgivings with this stunning pear tarte Tatin. Because the recipe calls for store-bought puff pastry (McClain is a huge fan of Dufour's), it's quite easy to prepare.

- 2 **cups dry red wine**
- 2 **cinnamon sticks**
- ½ **cup sugar**
- ¼ **cup water**
- 2 **tablespoons unsalted butter**
- 1 **tablespoon pear liqueur (optional)**
- 5 **firm, ripe Bartlett pears— peeled, cored and halved**

One 14-ounce **sheet chilled all-butter puff pastry**

Crème fraîche, for serving

1. In a small saucepan, boil the wine with the cinnamon sticks over moderately high heat until reduced to ¼ cup, about 15 minutes. Discard the cinnamon sticks.

2. In a 12-inch skillet, combine the sugar and water. Cook over moderately high heat, swirling the pan occasionally, until a light amber caramel forms, about 5 minutes. Remove the skillet from the heat. Add the red wine syrup along with the butter and liqueur and cook to dissolve the hardened caramel, about 1 minute. Add the pear halves to the skillet and cook over low heat, turning occasionally, until the pears are tender and the pan juices are syrupy, about 20 minutes. Arrange the pears cut side up in the skillet with the thin ends pointing toward the center. Let cool for 30 minutes.

3. Preheat the oven to 375°. On a lightly floured work surface, roll out the puff pastry to a 13-inch square. Using the skillet lid as a template, cut out a 12-inch pastry round. Cut four 2-inch-long steam vents in the pastry and lay the round over the pears, tucking the edge into the skillet. Bake for about 1 hour and 10 minutes, until the pastry is deeply golden and risen. Let the tart cool in the skillet for about 15 minutes, then very carefully invert it onto a large plate. Cut into wedges and serve warm, with crème fraîche.

—*Shawn McClain*

Clay-Pot Tarte Tatin

ACTIVE: 45 MIN; TOTAL: 2 HR 45 MIN

8 SERVINGS ● ●

Stovetop-friendly ceramic flameware is perfect for preparing this tart, as an ordinary clay pot may not be able to withstand the heat required to caramelize the fruit. (A cast-iron skillet works well, too.) Cooked slowly before the tart is baked, the apples become tender, buttery and sweet.

10 Golden Delicious apples—
   peeled, cored and halved
Juice of 2 lemons
1 stick plus 2 tablespoons
   unsalted butter
¾ cup plus 1 tablespoon sugar
Pinch of salt
½ pound chilled all-butter
   puff pastry

1. Cut a thin slice from the stem ends of the apple halves so they will stand upright. In a large bowl, toss the apple halves with the lemon juice to coat thoroughly.

2. Set a 12-inch flameware or cast-iron skillet over low heat on a gas stove. (If using an electric stove, set the skillet over a heat diffuser.) Add the butter and heat until melted. Stir in the sugar and salt and cook for 5 minutes, until the sugar has dissolved but hasn't browned.

3. Pack the apple halves into the skillet, standing them upright in concentric circles. Cook over moderate heat until all but the tops of the apples are softened and their juices have formed a rich brown caramel, about 1 hour and 15 minutes. For even cooking, rotate the skillet 45 degrees about every 10 minutes. Lightly press down the apples with a spatula as they soften. Shake the skillet occasionally to prevent the apples from sticking.

4. Meanwhile, preheat the oven to 400°. On a lightly floured work surface, roll out the puff pastry to a 14-inch round about ⅛ inch thick. Prick the pastry all over with a fork. Refrigerate for 10 minutes.

5. Drape the pastry over the apples and tuck in the edge with a spoon. Bake for about 30 minutes, until the pastry is golden brown and cooked through. Remove the tarte Tatin from the oven and carefully invert it onto a large serving platter. Let cool for 10 minutes, then cut the tarte Tatin into wedges and serve warm.
—*Paula Wolfert*

SERVE WITH Vanilla ice cream, whipped cream or crème fraîche.

Mixed-Berry Dutch Baby

TOTAL: 35 MIN
6 TO 8 SERVINGS ●

A Dutch Baby, also known as a German pancake, is a mixture of eggs, flour and whole milk that's baked in a heavy skillet until it becomes puffy and golden. In this version, F&W's Grace Parisi folds in fresh raspberries and blackberries to create a wonderful summer dessert that's also great for breakfast.

3 large eggs
½ teaspoon finely grated
   lemon zest
⅓ cup granulated sugar
Pinch of salt
⅔ cup all-purpose flour
⅔ cup milk
2 cups fresh raspberries
2 cups fresh blackberries
4 tablespoons unsalted
   butter
Confectioners' sugar,
   for dusting

1. Preheat the oven to 425° and heat a 10-inch cast-iron skillet over moderate heat. In a medium bowl, whisk the eggs with the grated lemon zest, granulated sugar and salt until combined. Add the flour and milk and whisk until the batter is completely smooth. Gently stir 1 cup each of the fresh raspberries and blackberries into the pancake batter.

2. Melt the butter in the cast-iron skillet and add the berry pancake batter, gently spreading the fruit in the batter so that it is evenly distributed. Bake the Dutch Baby in the center of the oven for about 22 minutes, until the edge is browned and puffed and the center of the pancake is lightly browned in spots. Transfer the skillet to a trivet and use a fine-mesh sieve to dust the Dutch Baby with confectioners' sugar. Cut the pancake into wedges and serve immediately, with the remaining fresh raspberries and blackberries.
—*Grace Parisi*

Back-to-School Raspberry Granola Bars

ACTIVE: 15 MIN; TOTAL: 1 HR PLUS
3 HR COOLING
MAKES 16 BARS ● ● ●

New York City pastry chef Karen DeMasco's crumbly soft, jammy-sweet bars travel well, so they're ideal for school bake sales. She says, "They are quick to put together with pantry staples, and everyone seems to love them." They're delicious made with any flavor of jam, as well as the raspberry preserves called for here.

1 cup pecans, coarsely chopped
1½ cups all-purpose flour
1¼ cups old-fashioned rolled oats
⅓ cup granulated sugar
⅓ cup packed dark
   brown sugar
1 teaspoon kosher salt
½ teaspoon baking soda
1½ sticks unsalted butter, melted,
   plus more for greasing the pan
1 cup raspberry preserves

1. Preheat the oven to 350°. Butter an 8-inch square baking pan and line the bottom and sides with parchment paper. Spread the chopped pecans in a pie plate and toast in the oven for about 5 minutes, tossing halfway through, until lightly browned and fragrant. Let cool.

2. In a bowl, whisk the flour with the oats, both sugars and the salt, baking soda and pecans until evenly distributed. Using a wooden spoon, stir in the melted butter until thoroughly coated.

3. Press two-thirds of the oat mixture in an even layer on the bottom of the baking pan and spread all of the raspberry preserves over them. Sprinkle with the remaining third of the oat mixture.

4. Bake the bars for about 45 minutes, rotating the pan halfway through baking, until the top is golden brown. Transfer the pan to a wire rack and let the granola bars cool completely, about 3 hours. Cut into squares and serve. —*Karen DeMasco*

pies & fruit desserts

Warm Strawberry Crumb Cake

ACTIVE: 30 MIN; TOTAL: 2 HR 30 MIN

8 SERVINGS ● ● ●

Gerard Craft (an F&W Best New Chef 2008) tops spring's first strawberries with batter and bakes them until the fruit is warm and jammy and the cake is airy, with a delightfully crisp crust.

FILLING

3 pounds strawberries,
   hulled and halved (8 cups)

½ cup granulated sugar

2 tablespoons fresh
   lemon juice

2½ tablespoons cornstarch dissolved
   in 2½ tablespoons of water

1 vanilla bean, split and
   seeds scraped

CRUMB TOPPING

½ cup lightly packed
   light brown sugar

½ cup plus 2 tablespoons
   all-purpose flour

Pinch of salt

4 tablespoons cold unsalted
   butter, cubed

CAKE

2¼ cups all-purpose flour

1 tablespoon baking powder

¾ teaspoon salt

1 stick unsalted butter, softened

1¼ cups granulated sugar

3 large eggs

1½ teaspoons pure vanilla extract

¾ cup buttermilk

1. MAKE THE FILLING: Preheat the oven to 350°. In a large bowl, toss the strawberries with the sugar, lemon juice, cornstarch slurry and vanilla seeds and let stand until the berries release some of their juices, about 30 minutes. Pour the fruit filling into a 9-by-13-inch glass or ceramic baking dish set on a sturdy baking sheet.

2. MEANWHILE, MAKE THE CRUMB TOP-PING: In a medium bowl, mix all of the ingredients with your fingers until a coarse meal forms; press into small clumps.

3. MAKE THE CAKE: In a medium bowl, whisk the flour with the baking powder and salt. In a large bowl, using a handheld electric mixer, beat the butter with the sugar at medium-high speed until light and fluffy, about 3 minutes. Add the eggs, one at a time, beating well between additions. Beat in the vanilla extract and scrape down the bowl. Add the dry ingredients to the batter in 3 additions, alternating with the buttermilk.

4. Spoon the batter over the fruit filling, spreading it to the edge. Sprinkle with the crumb topping. Bake in the center of the oven for 1 hour and 15 minutes, until the fruit is bubbling, the crumb topping is golden and a toothpick inserted in the center of the cake comes out with a few moist crumbs attached. Transfer to a rack to cool slightly. Serve the crumb cake warm or at room temperature.

—Gerard Craft

VARIATION The fruit filling can also be made with a combination of blackberries, raspberries and blueberries.

SERVE WITH Vanilla ice cream.

MAKE AHEAD The crumb cake can be refrigerated overnight. Serve warm or at room temperature.

Cherry-Berry Pie

ACTIVE: 30 MIN; TOTAL: 4 HR 30 MIN
PLUS COOLING

MAKES ONE 10-INCH PIE ● ● ●

CRUST

2¼ cups all-purpose flour, frozen

2 teaspoons salt

14 tablespoons unsalted butter, cut
   into ½-inch cubes—9 tablespoons
   frozen, 5 tablespoons chilled

2 tablespoons red wine vinegar
   mixed with 6 tablespoons
   of ice water

FILLING

1 cup plus 1 teaspoon sugar,
   plus more for sprinkling

¼ cup quick-cooking tapioca

Pinch of salt

2 cups pitted sweet cherries

¾ pound raspberries (3 cups)

½ pound blueberries (1½ cups)

1 teaspoon all-purpose flour

2 tablespoons heavy cream

1. MAKE THE CRUST: In a food processor, pulse the flour and salt. Add the chilled butter and pulse until it's the size of small peas. Add the frozen butter and pulse until it's the size of small peas. Drizzle the vinegar mixture over the flour mixture. Pulse just until the dough starts to come together. Turn out onto a lightly floured surface and knead gently to form a smooth dough. Divide the dough in half and flatten into 2 disks. Wrap in plastic and refrigerate until firm, at least 2 hours.

2. On a lightly floured surface, roll out one disk of dough to a 12-inch round, ⅛ inch thick. Transfer to a 10-inch metal pie plate and freeze for 20 minutes. Roll out the remaining dough ⅛ inch thick. Transfer to a baking sheet and freeze for 20 minutes.

3. MAKE THE FILLING: In a small bowl, whisk 1 cup of sugar with the tapioca and salt. In another bowl, toss the cherries with the raspberries and blueberries. Sprinkle with the sugar mixture and toss gently.

4. Mix the flour and the remaining 1 teaspoon of sugar. Sprinkle in the crust; tap out the excess. Spoon the filling into the crust.

5. Using a fluted pastry wheel, cut the remaining dough into ¾-inch-wide strips. Arrange the strips across the pie in a lattice pattern. Trim the overhanging strips to ½ inch and press them to the crust. Pinch the rim between your fingers to flute it. Freeze the pie for 1 hour.

6. Preheat the oven to 400°. Brush the cream over the lattice crust and rim and sprinkle with sugar. Bake in the upper third of the oven for 1 hour, or until the crust is richly browned and the filling starts to bubble. If necessary, cover the pie with foil for the last 10 minutes of baking. Let cool on a rack until warm before serving.

—Paula Haney

CHERRY-BERRY PIE

pies & fruit desserts

Strawberries with Buttermilk Ice and Balsamic Vinegar

TOTAL: 20 MIN PLUS 3 HR FREEZING

4 SERVINGS ● ● ○ ○

Deanie Fox, pastry chef at Napa's Ubuntu restaurant and yoga studio, makes this fluffy granita with buttermilk, then spoons the creamy, tangy ice over lightly sweetened strawberries.

3½ tablespoons sugar

1½ tablespoons fresh lemon juice

1 cup low-fat buttermilk

1 pint strawberries, hulled and quartered

½ teaspoon finely grated lemon zest

1 teaspoon aged balsamic vinegar

4 tiny tarragon sprigs

1. In a bowl, whisk 1½ tablespoons of the sugar with ½ tablespoon of the lemon juice until the sugar is dissolved. Whisk in the buttermilk and pour into a shallow baking dish; freeze until firm, whisking the mixture every 30 minutes, about 3 hours.

2. In a bowl, toss the strawberries with the remaining 2 tablespoons of sugar and 1 tablespoon of lemon juice. Add the lemon zest and vinegar; let stand for 30 minutes. Spoon the berries and any juices into glasses. Using a fork, scrape the buttermilk ice into fluffy crystals and spoon over the strawberries. Garnish with the tarragon and serve. —Deanie Fox

healthy berry popsicles

Use a popsicle mold (or ice cube trays and popsicle sticks) to make creamy frozen yogurt pops: Stir strained berry preserves into whole-milk yogurt to taste; freeze in molds overnight. Run water over the molds to release pops.

Tomato-Raspberry Granita

ACTIVE: 10 MIN; TOTAL: 1 HR 20 MIN

4 SERVINGS ● ● ●

"One thing we often forget about tomatoes is that botanically, they are fruits, not vegetables," says Norwegian farmer-chef Andreas Viestad. For a light, refreshing dessert, he freezes chopped cherry tomatoes and raspberries to make a sweet, chunky granita. The flavors of the two fruits are surprisingly wonderful together.

1 cup raspberries, halved

½ pound cherry tomatoes, coarsely chopped

¼ cup sugar

2 teaspoons chopped mint

In a wide, shallow dish, toss the raspberries, tomatoes, sugar and mint and let stand at room temperature for 10 minutes, until the raspberries and tomatoes release their juices. Stir well. Smooth the mixture to an even layer, cover and freeze for about 1 hour, stirring a few times, until just frozen. Using a fork or spoon, break up the granita, scoop it into bowls and serve. —Andreas Viestad

Vanilla Zabaglione with Raspberries

ACTIVE: 30 MIN; TOTAL: 1 HR 30 MIN

10 SERVINGS ● ● ○

1 cup Marsala

1 cup sugar

1 vanilla bean, split and seeds scraped

1 dozen large egg yolks

1 cup heavy cream

2½ cups brandied cherries or Amaretto cherries

5 cups raspberries

1. In a saucepan, whisk the Marsala with the sugar and vanilla bean seeds and bring to a boil. Remove from the heat.

2. Meanwhile, bring a medium saucepan of water to a simmer; turn the heat to moderately low. Fill a large bowl with ice water. In a large stainless steel bowl, whisk or beat the egg yolks at low speed to break them up. Gradually add the hot Marsala mixture and beat until smooth.

3. Set the bowl over the simmering water without allowing the bowl to touch the water. Beat the egg yolk mixture until it is hot and foamy and leaves a ribbon trail when the beaters are lifted, about 10 minutes. Don't cook the zabaglione for too long, or it will curdle. Transfer the bowl to the ice water bath and let stand, whisking the zabaglione occasionally, until cooled. Cover and refrigerate for about 1 hour, until thoroughly chilled.

4. In another large stainless steel bowl, whip the cream to form firm peaks. Fold the whipped cream into the chilled zabaglione. Spoon the brandied cherries into rocks glasses or bowls. Top with the zabaglione, garnish with the raspberries and serve immediately. —Michael Emanuel

SERVE WITH Amaretti cookies.

MAKE AHEAD The zabaglione can be refrigerated overnight. Fold in the whipped cream just before serving.

Minted Watermelon Popsicles

TOTAL: 10 MIN PLUS 3 HR FREEZING

8 SERVINGS ● ● ○

These popsicles, made with lots of sweet watermelon and only a little sugar, can be frozen in special popsicle molds or in standard ice cube trays.

1½ pounds seedless watermelon without the rind, cut into 1-inch dice (about 4 cups)

2 tablespoons sugar

¼ cup mint leaves, minced

2 teaspoons grated lemon zest

Pinch of salt

In a blender, puree the watermelon with the sugar until smooth. Stir in the mint, grated lemon zest and salt. Pour the puree into 8 popsicle molds or 2 standard ice cube trays (insert popsicle sticks halfway through freezing) and freeze until hard, about 3 hours. —Joy Manning

STRAWBERRIES WITH BUTTERMILK ICE AND BALSAMIC

MINTED WATERMELON POPSICLES

Summer Blackberry Custards

ACTIVE: 15 MIN; TOTAL: 1 HR

12 SERVINGS ● ● ○

Alain Coumont, founder of the bakery-café chain Le Pain Quotidien, makes these ethereal, citrusy custards with blackberries. Try them with other berries or pitted cherries.

- 6 cups blackberries
    (2 pounds)
- 1½ cups whole milk
- ½ cup heavy cream
- 2 large eggs
- ¾ cup packed dark brown sugar
- ½ cup all-purpose flour
- 1 teaspoon pure vanilla extract
- 1 tablespoon fresh lemon juice
- ½ teaspoon finely grated
    orange zest

1. Preheat the oven to 450°. Spread ½ cup of the blackberries in each of twelve 4-ounce gratin dishes. Arrange the gratin dishes on 2 baking sheets.

2. In a bowl, whisk the milk with the cream, eggs, brown sugar, flour, vanilla, lemon juice and orange zest until smooth. Ladle ¼ cup of the custard into each dish; bake for about 15 minutes, until the centers are set. Transfer the custards to wire racks and let stand for 30 minutes. Serve.
—Alain Coumont

Lemon Sorbetto

 TOTAL: 10 MIN

8 SERVINGS ○

- 4 cups Spumante
- 2 pints frozen lemon sorbet

In a blender, combine half of the Spumante with half of the sorbet and blend just until the sorbet is soft but not liquefied—you're looking for a slushy texture. Pour into Champagne or parfait glasses and repeat with the remaining Spumante and sorbet. Serve the *sorbetto* with long sundae spoons and crisp cookies. —Eugenia Bone

Cucumber Frappés with Blackberries

 TOTAL: 15 MIN

4 SERVINGS ● ● ●

- 1 pint blackberries
- ¼ cup sugar
- 2 small seedless cucumbers—
    peeled, seeded and chopped
- 1 cup plain nonfat yogurt
- 1 cup ice cubes
- 2 tablespoons fresh lime juice
- 6 mint leaves

Pinch of salt

In a medium bowl, use a wooden spoon to lightly crush the blackberries with 1 tablespoon of the sugar. In a blender, combine the cucumbers, yogurt, ice cubes, lime juice, mint leaves, salt and the remaining 3 tablespoons of sugar and blend. Spoon the berries and their juice into glasses. Pour the frappé on top and serve right away. —Deanie Fox

● HEALTHY ● MAKE AHEAD ● VEGETARIAN ● STAFF FAVORITE

pies & fruit desserts

Blackberry Fool with Calvados

TOTAL: 30 MIN PLUS
OVERNIGHT MACERATING
8 SERVINGS ● ● ●

- 2 pounds blackberries (8 cups)
- 1 cup Calvados
- 2 cups heavy cream
- ½ cup sugar

1. Spread 4 cups of the blackberries in a shallow glass dish. Add the Calvados and stir gently to coat the berries. Cover and refrigerate overnight, stirring a few times.
2. The next day, in a food processor, combine the remaining 4 cups of blackberries with 1 tablespoon of the macerating liquid and pulse until coarsely pureed. Scrape the puree into a large bowl.
3. In another large bowl, whip the cream until soft peaks form. Gradually add the sugar and whip until firm. Scrape the whipped cream over the pureed blackberries and fold to blend. Using a slotted spoon, scoop the macerated blackberries into 8 tall glasses. Top with the blackberry whipped cream and serve. —*Peter Ting*
SERVE WITH Salted Shortbread Cookies (p. 339).
MAKE AHEAD The macerated blackberries can be refrigerated for up to 2 days.

Summer Berries with Cumin Meringues and Crème Fraîche

ACTIVE: 20 MIN; TOTAL: 4 HR 20 MIN
PLUS COOLING
4 SERVINGS ● ● ●

A touch of cumin gives these meringues an exotic earthiness.

- 3 large egg whites
- ⅛ teaspoon kosher salt
- ⅛ teaspoon cream of tartar
- ⅛ teaspoon finely ground cumin
- 1 cup sugar
- 4 cups (about 1½ pounds) mixed berries, such as raspberries, blackberries and quartered strawberries
- ¼ cup crème fraîche

1. Preheat the oven to 200°. Line a large baking sheet with parchment paper. In a medium stainless steel bowl, using a handheld mixer, beat the egg whites at medium speed until frothy. Add the kosher salt, cream of tartar and cumin and beat until the egg whites hold soft peaks. With the mixer running, gradually add the sugar, 1 tablespoon at a time, and continue to beat until firm, glossy peaks form. Drop the egg white mixture in evenly spaced 2-tablespoon-size mounds on the parchment paper–lined baking sheet.
2. Bake the meringues for 4 hours, until they are crisp but not browned. Let cool completely at room temperature. Serve the cumin meringues with the mixed fresh berries and crème fraîche.
—*Barbara Lynch*
VARIATION In place of the cumin, try making the meringues with ground coriander or cardamom.
MAKE AHEAD The baked meringues can be stored in an airtight container at room temperature overnight. Meringues get soggy in the refrigerator.

Blueberry-Almond Shortcakes with Crème Fraîche

ACTIVE: 45 MIN; TOTAL: 1 HR 45 MIN
8 SERVINGS ● ●

- ½ cup sliced almonds
- 2 cups all-purpose flour
- 1 cup almond flour (see Note)
- ½ cup cornmeal
- 1 tablespoon baking powder
- 1 teaspoon baking soda
- 1 teaspoon kosher salt, plus more for sprinkling
- ¾ cup sugar, plus more for sprinkling
- ¼ cup plus 2 tablespoons chilled vegetable shortening, cubed
- 4 tablespoons cold unsalted butter, cut into cubes, plus 1 tablespoon unsalted butter, melted
- 1 cup buttermilk
- 2½ cups blueberries (about 12 ounces)
- ¼ cup fresh orange juice
- 1 teaspoon grated orange zest
- 1 cup crème fraîche

1. Preheat the oven to 400°. Spread the almonds in a pie plate; toast for 6 minutes, until lightly golden and fragrant.
2. Line a large baking sheet with parchment. In a medium bowl, whisk the all-purpose flour with the almond flour, cornmeal, baking powder, baking soda, salt and ¼ cup of the sugar. Using a pastry blender or 2 knives, cut in the shortening and cold butter until they resemble peas. Add the buttermilk and stir until the dough is evenly moistened.
3. Transfer the dough to a lightly floured surface and pat into a 1-inch-thick round. Using a 3-inch biscuit cutter, stamp out 8 biscuits, patting the scraps back together as needed. Transfer the biscuits to the baking sheet and freeze for 30 minutes.
4. Brush the tops of the biscuits with the melted butter and sprinkle with sugar and kosher salt. Bake for about 18 minutes, until golden. Let stand until cool, 30 minutes.
5. Meanwhile, in another medium bowl, toss the blueberries with the remaining ½ cup of sugar, the orange juice and zest. Let stand until the sugar is dissolved, about 15 minutes. Transfer 1 cup of the blueberries to a food processor and puree until smooth. Scrape the puree into the blueberries in the bowl. Cover and refrigerate.
6. In another medium bowl, using an electric mixer, beat the crème fraîche at medium speed until thickened, about 30 seconds. Using a serrated knife, cut the biscuits in half horizontally and set the bottom halves on plates. Top with a dollop of crème fraîche, the blueberry compote and a few toasted almonds. Cover with the biscuit tops and serve. —*Barry Maiden*
NOTE Almond flour is simply ground blanched almonds. Look for it at specialty food stores and health-food stores.

BLACKBERRY FOOL WITH CALVADOS (AND
SALTED SHORTBREAD COOKIES, P. 339)

pies & fruit desserts

Honeyed Yogurt and Blueberry Tart with Ginger Crust

ACTIVE: 25 MIN; TOTAL: 1 HR 15 MIN
PLUS OVERNIGHT DRAINING

8 SERVINGS ● ● ●

- 10 whole graham crackers, broken into pieces
- ¼ cup crystallized ginger, minced
- 1 tablespoon sugar
- Pinch of salt
- 3 tablespoons unsalted butter, melted
- 1 large egg white
- 2 cups plain fat-free Greek yogurt, drained overnight
- 2 tablespoons honey
- 1½ cups blueberries (9 ounces)

1. Preheat the oven to 350°. Spray a 14-by-4½-inch rectangular fluted tart pan with a removable bottom with cooking spray. In a food processor, pulse the graham crackers with the crystallized ginger, sugar and salt until finely ground. Add the butter and egg white and pulse until the crumbs are evenly coated. Press the crumbs evenly over the bottom and up the sides of the tart pan. Bake for about 20 minutes, until the crust is lightly browned. Let cool completely.

2. In a bowl, mix the yogurt with the honey. Spread the yogurt in the crust and arrange the blueberries on top. Cut the tart in slices and serve. —*Melissa Rubel Jacobson*

Lemon-Blueberry Cheesecake Parfaits

ACTIVE: 1 HR; TOTAL: 4 HR

8 SERVINGS ● ● ●

SHORTBREAD

- 1¾ cups all-purpose flour
- ¼ cup plus 2 tablespoons cornmeal
- 1 teaspoon salt
- 2 sticks unsalted butter, at room temperature
- ¾ cup confectioners' sugar
- 2 teaspoons grated orange zest
- 1 teaspoon pure vanilla extract

BLUEBERRY COMPOTE

- 2 cups blueberries (12 ounces)
- ¼ cup granulated sugar
- ¼ cup water
- 1 teaspoon fresh lemon juice

CHEESECAKE CUSTARD

- 1 cup whole milk
- 5 tablespoons granulated sugar
- 4 large egg yolks
- 2½ tablespoons cornstarch
- 6 ounces cream cheese, at room temperature
- ¼ cup plus 2 tablespoons fresh lemon juice
- 1 teaspoon grated lemon zest, plus extra strips for garnish
- 1 teaspoon pure vanilla extract
- 1 cup heavy cream

1. MAKE THE SHORTBREAD: In a medium bowl, mix the flour with the cornmeal and salt. In a standing mixer fitted with the paddle, mix the butter with the confectioners' sugar at medium speed until creamy, about 2 minutes. Beat in the orange zest and vanilla. Add the flour mixture and beat at low speed until the dough just comes together. Pat the dough into a disk, wrap in plastic and refrigerate for 1 hour.

2. Preheat the oven to 350°. Line 2 large rimmed baking sheets with parchment paper. Unwrap the chilled shortbread dough and roll it out between 2 sheets of parchment paper to an 8-inch round (½ inch thick). Cut the dough into ½-inch-wide strips and transfer the strips to the baking sheets; leave 1 inch between each strip. Refrigerate the dough strips for 30 minutes, until chilled.

3. Bake the shortbread for about 20 minutes, until golden; rotate the pans halfway through for even baking. While the warm shortbread strips are still on the baking sheet, cut them into ½-inch cubes. Let cool, about 30 minutes.

4. MAKE THE BLUEBERRY COMPOTE: In a small saucepan, combine 1 cup of the blueberries with the sugar and water. Bring to a simmer and cook over moderate heat until the blueberries break down, about 5 minutes. Scrape the blueberry sauce into a blender, add the lemon juice and puree until smooth. Scrape the blueberry sauce into a bowl and fold in the remaining 1 cup of whole blueberries. Refrigerate until chilled, about 2 hours.

5. MEANWHILE, MAKE THE CHEESECAKE CUSTARD: In a medium saucepan, bring ¾ cup of the milk to a boil with 3 tablespoons of the sugar; remove from the heat. In a medium bowl, whisk the egg yolks with the cornstarch and the remaining ¼ cup of milk and 2 tablespoons of sugar. Gradually whisk the hot milk into the egg yolks, then pour the mixture into the saucepan and whisk constantly over moderate heat until thickened, about 2 minutes. Over low heat, whisk in the cream cheese, lemon juice, grated lemon zest and vanilla extract until smooth, about 1 minute. Scrape the cheesecake custard into a bowl. Press a piece of plastic wrap directly onto the surface of the custard and refrigerate until chilled, about 2 hours.

6. In a medium bowl, using an electric mixer, beat the cream to medium peaks. Fold the whipped cream into the chilled cheesecake custard until no streaks remain. Spoon the shortbread cubes and custard into bowls. Drizzle with the blueberry compote, garnish with the lemon zest strips and serve. —*Maggie Leung*

MAKE AHEAD The baked shortbread can be kept in an airtight container for up to 2 days. The assembled parfaits can be refrigerated for up to 1 day.

Apricot-and-Blueberry Tart

ACTIVE: 45 MIN; TOTAL: 4 HR 30 MIN
MAKES ONE 12-INCH TART ● ●
TART SHELL

- 3 tablespoons almond paste
- ¼ cup sugar
- ½ teaspoon salt
- 1 stick unsalted butter, softened

HONEYED YOGURT AND BLUEBERRY TART

LEMON-BLUEBERRY CHEESECAKE PARFAITS

All-purpose flour

1 large egg, lightly beaten

⅓ cup milk

FILLING

1⅓ cups milk

¼ vanilla bean, split, seeds scraped

⅓ cup sugar

2 large eggs

2 tablespoons cornstarch

2¾ pounds apricots, pitted and quartered

¾ pound blueberries (2 cups)

1. **MAKE THE TART SHELL:** In a standing mixer fitted with the paddle, blend the almond paste, sugar and salt with 3 tablespoons of the butter at medium speed until smooth. Beat in the remaining butter. Add 2 cups of flour and beat at low speed until just combined, then beat in the egg and milk. Scrape the dough onto a piece of plastic wrap and flatten into a disk. Wrap tightly; refrigerate for 2 hours, until firm.

2. Preheat the oven to 350°. On a lightly floured work surface, roll out the dough to a 14-inch round, ¼ inch thick; transfer to a 12-inch fluted tart pan with a removable bottom, pressing over the bottom and up the side without stretching. Trim any excess dough. Freeze the shell for 15 minutes.

3. Line the shell with foil and fill with pie weights or dried beans. Bake for 35 minutes, until the pastry is firm and starting to color. Remove the foil and weights and bake the shell for another 20 minutes, until golden and cooked through. If the rim starts to brown too quickly, cover with foil. Transfer the tart shell to a rack; let cool.

4. **MEANWHILE, MAKE THE FILLING:** In a medium saucepan, combine the milk with the vanilla bean and seeds and half of the sugar. Bring to a simmer over moderate heat, stirring. Remove from the heat. Remove the vanilla bean and reserve it for another use.

5. Fill a large bowl with ice water. In a medium heatproof bowl, whisk the eggs with the cornstarch and the remaining sugar until smooth. Gradually whisk in half of the hot milk. Pour the mixture into the saucepan and bring to a boil over moderate heat, whisking constantly, until the pastry cream is thickened, 3 minutes; scrape into a stainless steel bowl. Set the bowl in the ice bath and let stand, stirring often, until the pastry cream has cooled completely.

6. Spread the pastry cream in the shell in an even layer. Arrange the apricot quarters in four concentric circles, leaving a 1-inch gap between the second and third circles and a 2-inch round in the center of the tart. Fill in the spaces with the blueberries. Bake the tart for 50 minutes, until the apricots are tender. Let cool slightly. Unmold the tart, cut it into wedges and serve warm or at room temperature.

—*Michel Keller*

●HEALTHY ●MAKE AHEAD ●VEGETARIAN ●STAFF FAVORITE

pies & fruit desserts

Apricot, Almond and Brown Butter Tart

ACTIVE: 40 MIN; TOTAL: 3 HR 20 MIN

MAKES ONE 12-INCH TART ● ● ●

TART SHELL

- 2 cups all-purpose flour
- 1 tablespoon granulated sugar
- ½ teaspoon salt
- 1½ sticks (12 tablespoons) cold unsalted butter, cubed
- 5 tablespoons ice water
- ¼ teaspoon pure vanilla extract

FILLING

- ¾ cup slivered almonds
- 2 cups dry white wine
- 2 cups dried apricots (10 ounces)
- 1 stick unsalted butter
- 1 vanilla bean, split, seeds scraped
- 1¾ cups confectioners' sugar
- ¾ cup all-purpose flour
- 1 teaspoon salt
- 4 large eggs
- ¼ teaspoon pure almond extract

Sweetened whipped cream, for serving

1. **MAKE THE TART SHELL:** In a food processor, pulse the flour with the sugar and salt. Add the butter and pulse until the mixture resembles a coarse meal. Add the ice water and vanilla; pulse just until the dough comes together. Transfer to a lightly floured work surface; flatten into a disk. Wrap in plastic and refrigerate until firm, 1 hour.

2. Preheat the oven to 350°. On a lightly floured work surface, roll out the dough to a 15-inch round, ¼ inch thick. Transfer to a 12-inch fluted tart pan with a removable bottom; gently press it over the bottom and up the side. Trim any excess. Refrigerate for at least 20 minutes, until firm.

3. Line the tart shell with foil and fill with dried beans or pie weights. Bake for about 50 minutes, until the shell starts to brown around the edges. Remove the foil and weights and bake for about 25 minutes longer, until the shell is cooked through. Transfer to a rack and let cool. Lower the oven temperature to 325°.

4. **MAKE THE FILLING:** Spread the slivered almonds on a large rimmed baking sheet. Toast in the oven for about 6 minutes, until lightly browned. Let cool.

5. Meanwhile, in a medium nonreactive saucepan, bring the wine to a boil. Add the apricots, cover and simmer over moderate heat until plumped, about 10 minutes. Remove from the heat.

6. In a small skillet, cook the butter with the vanilla bean seeds over moderate heat until browned, about 4 minutes.

7. In a food processor, pulse the toasted almonds with the confectioners' sugar, flour and salt until finely ground. Add the eggs and pulse until just combined. Add the browned butter and the almond extract and pulse until smooth.

8. Drain the apricots and pat dry. Pour the almond filling into the tart shell. Nestle the apricots into the filling in concentric circles. Bake for about 50 minutes, until the filling is golden brown and set. Transfer to a rack to cool. Slice the tart into wedges and serve warm or at room temperature, dolloped with sweetened whipped cream.
—*Cindy Pawlcyn*

Apricot-and-Basil Shortbread Tart

ACTIVE: 30 MIN; TOTAL: 3 HR

6 SERVINGS ● ● ●

PASTRY CREAM

- 1 cup whole milk
- 5 tablespoons granulated sugar
- ¼ cup packed fresh basil leaves
- 2 large egg yolks
- 2½ tablespoons cornstarch
- 2 tablespoons unsalted butter

PASTRY

- 1 large hard-boiled egg yolk
- 1 stick plus 6 tablespoons unsalted butter
- ½ cup confectioners' sugar
- 1½ cups all-purpose flour
- ¼ cup potato starch
- 1¼ teaspoons kosher salt

TOPPING

- 6 apricots (1¼ pounds), halved
- 3 tablespoons granulated sugar
- ⅓ cup apricot jam, melted

1. **MAKE THE PASTRY CREAM:** In a saucepan, combine ¾ cup of the milk with the sugar and basil; bring to a simmer. Remove from the heat and let stand for 15 minutes. Remove the basil; squeeze any milk back into the pan.

2. In a bowl, whisk the remaining ¼ cup of milk with the yolks and cornstarch. Slowly whisk the yolk mixture into the warm milk; bring to a simmer over moderate heat, whisking constantly until very thick, 2 minutes. Remove from the heat and whisk in the butter until melted. Scrape into a bowl. Press plastic wrap directly on the surface and refrigerate until chilled, 2 hours.

3. **MAKE THE PASTRY:** Preheat the oven to 375°. Spray a 14-by-4½-inch rectangular tart pan with a removable bottom with nonstick cooking spray. In a standing mixer, beat the hard-boiled egg yolk with the butter and confectioners' sugar at medium speed until smooth, 2 minutes. Add the flour, potato starch and salt and beat at low speed until just combined. Using lightly floured hands, press the dough evenly over the bottom and up the sides of the tart pan. Refrigerate the crust for about 30 minutes, or until chilled.

4. Bake the crust for about 25 minutes, until golden. Cool on a rack for 1 hour.

5. **MAKE THE TOPPING:** Increase the oven temperature to 450°. Line a baking sheet with parchment paper. Arrange the apricot halves cut side up on the paper and sprinkle all over with the sugar. Roast for about 20 minutes, until tender and lightly browned. Cool completely, about 30 minutes.

6. Unmold the crust onto a serving plate and spread the cream evenly in the crust. Arrange the apricots on the cream, cut side down, and brush with the melted jam. Cut the tart crosswise into strips and serve.
—*Roy Shvartzapel*

APRICOT-AND-BASIL SHORTBREAD TART

pies & fruit desserts

Grilled Peaches and Plums with Mascarpone

TOTAL: 45 MIN

10 SERVINGS ● ●

Caramelizing plums and peaches on the grill brings out their natural sweetness; Argentine chef Francis Mallmann bastes them with butter and sugar to make them even more luscious. A dollop of cool mascarpone accompanies the warm fruit.

- 24 red or purple plums—halved and pitted, 4 plums thinly sliced
- 1 cup sugar
- 1 cup water
- 2 tablespoons fresh lemon juice
- 6 tablespoons unsalted butter, melted
- 10 peaches, halved and pitted

Mascarpone, for serving

1. Light a grill. In a medium saucepan, combine the sliced plums with ¾ cup of the sugar and the water and bring to a boil. Cover and simmer over moderately low heat until the plums are very soft, about 10 minutes. Transfer the plums to a food processor and puree until smooth. Scrape the plum sauce into a bowl, stir in the lemon juice and set aside.

2. In a small bowl, stir the melted butter with the remaining ¼ cup of sugar. Grill the halved plums and peaches over moderate heat, turning once, until the fruit is tender, about 6 minutes. Baste the plums and peaches with the butter and continue to grill, turning once and basting again, until caramelized and slightly charred, about 2 minutes longer.

3. Transfer the plums and peaches to plates and spoon the plum sauce on top. Dollop the mascarpone alongside and serve. —*Francis Mallmann*

MAKE AHEAD The plum sauce can be refrigerated for up to 2 days. Serve warm or at room temperature.

Plum Puff Dumplings

ACTIVE: 15 MIN; TOTAL: 45 MIN

6 SERVINGS ● ● ●

For her elegant interpretation of fruit Danish, F&W's Grace Parisi pinches plums into neat little puff pastry pockets.

All-purpose flour, for rolling

One 14-ounce package all-butter puff pastry, thawed and cold

- 5 large purple plums, cut into ½-inch wedges
- ¼ cup sugar, plus more for sprinkling
- 1½ teaspoons cornstarch
- ¼ teaspoon ground cardamom
- 1 large egg, beaten

Vanilla ice cream, for serving

1. Preheat the oven to 375° and line a large baking sheet with parchment paper. On a lightly floured work surface, roll out the puff pastry ⅛ inch thick. Cut the pastry into six 6-inch squares and transfer to the baking sheet; freeze for 5 minutes.

2. In a bowl, toss the plums with the ¼ cup of sugar and the cornstarch and cardamom. Spoon the fruit and juices onto the center of each puff pastry square. Working with 1 square at a time, bring up all 4 corners and pinch them together in the center. Pinch the seams closed at the bottom corners to trap any juices, leaving the tops open to vent steam. Brush the pastries with the egg and sprinkle with sugar. Bake in the center of the oven for about 30 minutes, until puffed and golden. Let cool slightly and serve with scoops of vanilla ice cream. —*Grace Parisi*

Honeyed Fig Crostatas

ACTIVE: 45 MIN; TOTAL: 2 HR 45 MIN

8 SERVINGS ● ○

- 2½ cups all-purpose flour
- ¼ cup plus 1 tablespoon sugar

Kosher salt

- 1½ sticks cold unsalted butter, cut into ½-inch pieces
- ¼ cup plus 3 tablespoons ice water
- 1½ pounds fresh green and purple figs, each cut into 6 wedges
- 5 teaspoons honey
- 1 teaspoon fresh lemon juice
- ¼ teaspoon fresh thyme leaves, plus small sprigs for garnish
- 1 egg beaten with 1 tablespoon of water

1. In a food processor, pulse the flour with the sugar and ½ teaspoon of salt. Add the cold pieces of butter and pulse until the butter is the size of peas. Add the water; pulse until the crostata dough just comes together. Pat the dough into a disk, wrap it well in plastic and refrigerate the disk for 30 minutes.

2. On a lightly floured surface, roll out the crostata dough ⅛ inch thick. Cut out eight 5-inch rounds, rerolling the scraps if necessary; transfer the rounds to a parchment paper–lined baking sheet and refrigerate them for 30 minutes.

3. Preheat the oven to 375°. In a bowl, toss two-thirds of the green and purple fig wedges with 3 teaspoons of the honey, the fresh lemon juice, thyme leaves and a pinch of salt. Arrange the fig wedges on the dough rounds, leaving a ½-inch border all around. Fold the edges over the figs and brush the dough with the egg wash. Chill for 30 minutes.

4. Bake the fig crostatas for about 35 minutes, rotating the baking sheet halfway through baking, until the crusts are golden. Let stand for 10 minutes.

5. Gently toss the remaining figs with the remaining 2 teaspoons of honey. Transfer the crostatas to plates, top with the figs and thyme sprigs and serve. —*Melissa Rubel Jacobson*

MAKE AHEAD The crostatas can be baked up to 6 hours ahead. Rewarm and top with the fresh figs before serving.

HONEYED FIG CROSTATAS

pies & fruit desserts

White Peach Tart

photo, page 286

ACTIVE: 30 MIN; TOTAL: 1 HR 50 MIN

8 SERVINGS ● ●

1½ cups all-purpose flour
¼   cup granulated sugar
½   teaspoon baking powder
½   teaspoon finely grated
     lemon zest
7   tablespoons unsalted
     butter, softened
1   large egg
1   large egg yolk
¼   cup plus 2 tablespoons
     peach preserves
3 to 4 firm white peaches,
     cut into ½-inch wedges
Confectioners' sugar, for dusting

1. Preheat the oven to 375° and position a rack in the lower third of the oven. In a food processor, combine the flour, granulated sugar, baking powder, grated lemon zest and softened butter and pulse to blend. Add the whole egg and egg yolk and process until a soft dough forms. Turn the dough out onto a work surface and knead just until it comes together. Press the dough evenly over the bottom and up the side of a 10½-inch fluted tart pan with a removable bottom.

2. Spread ¼ cup of the peach preserves on the tart dough and arrange the white peach wedges in concentric circles on top. Bake for 20 minutes, until the peach wedges are barely tender and the crust is still a bit pale. Brush the remaining 2 tablespoons of peach preserves over the peaches and bake for about 30 minutes longer, until the peach wedges are tender and the tart crust is golden. Immediately dust the tart with confectioners' sugar and let cool for at least 30 minutes before cutting into wedges and serving.

—*Marco Canora*

MAKE AHEAD The White Peach Tart can be made up to 8 hours in advance. Store at room temperature.

Roasted Peaches with Mascarpone Ice Cream

ACTIVE: 40 MIN; TOTAL: 3 HR 30 MIN

4 SERVINGS ● ●

ICE CREAM

4   large egg yolks
¾   cup plus 2 tablespoons sugar
2   cups whole milk
1   cup mascarpone (7 ounces)
½   teaspoon fresh lemon juice
Pinch of salt

PEACHES

2   cups dry white wine
2   tablespoons honey
1   cup water
¼   cup sugar
1   rosemary sprig
4   large, ripe but firm peaches—
     peeled, halved and pitted

1. MAKE THE ICE CREAM: In a large bowl, using a handheld mixer, beat the egg yolks with ¾ cup of the sugar at medium-high speed until fluffy, 3 minutes. In a saucepan, combine the milk with the remaining 2 tablespoons of sugar and bring to a simmer. Slowly beat the warm milk into the egg yolks at low speed. Scrape the custard into the saucepan. Cook over moderate heat, stirring constantly with a wooden spoon, until thick enough to coat the back of the spoon, about 5 minutes; don't let the custard boil.

2. Pour the custard into a bowl set in a larger bowl of ice water and whisk in the mascarpone, lemon juice and salt. Let stand until chilled, stirring occasionally, 30 minutes.

3. Pour the custard into an ice cream maker and freeze according to the manufacturer's instructions. Transfer the mascarpone ice cream to an airtight container and freeze until firm, at least 2 hours.

4. MEANWHILE, PREPARE THE PEACHES: In a large saucepan, combine the wine, honey, water and sugar and bring to a boil. Boil until reduced by half, about 30 minutes. Add the rosemary sprig and let stand for 10 minutes; discard the rosemary.

5. Preheat the oven to 350°. Arrange the peaches in an 8-by-11-inch baking dish. Pour the rosemary syrup on top and roast the peaches until tender, 40 minutes, basting and turning the peaches occasionally.

6. Scoop the mascarpone ice cream into bowls and top with the peach halves. Spoon the warm poaching liquid over the fruit and serve right away.

—*Daniel Humm*

MAKE AHEAD The ice cream can be frozen for up to 2 days.

Pan-Seared Apricots and Figs with Honey and Lavender

TOTAL: 25 MIN

12 SERVINGS ● ● ●

This simple dessert delivers a lot of flavor without a lot of work. Try it with any combination of summer fruits, such as plums, peaches or raspberries, or use thyme instead of lavender.

½   cup honey
2½ tablespoons fresh
     lemon juice
¼   teaspoon dried lavender
     blossoms
12 apricots, halved and pitted
18 fresh figs, halved lengthwise
12 mint sprigs, for garnish

1. In a large nonstick skillet, boil the honey with the lemon juice and dried lavender over high heat until it has reduced slightly, about 1 minute.

2. Arrange the apricot halves in the skillet, cut side down. Cook over high heat until just tender, about 2 minutes; turn and cook until softened, about 1 minute longer. Using a slotted spoon, transfer 2 apricot halves to each dessert plate.

3. Add the halved figs to the skillet and cook over high heat, turning once, until they are softened, about 2 minutes. Spoon the fig halves and pan juices over the apricots. Garnish the pan-seared fruit with the mint sprigs and serve at once.

—*Alain Coumont*

ROASTED PEACHES WITH
MASCARPONE ICE CREAM

PAN-SEARED APRICOTS AND FIGS
WITH HONEY AND LAVENDER

pies & fruit desserts

Buttermilk-Biscuit Peach Cobbler

ACTIVE: 40 MIN; TOTAL: 2 HR 45 MIN
8 SERVINGS ● ●

BISCUITS

- 2 cups all-purpose flour, plus more for dusting
- 2 tablespoons granulated sugar
- 2 teaspoons baking powder
- ½ teaspoon baking soda
- ½ teaspoon salt
- 7 tablespoons cold unsalted butter, cut into ½-inch cubes
- ¾ cup buttermilk
- 2 tablespoons heavy cream
- 1 tablespoon turbinado sugar, preferably Sugar in the Raw, or granulated sugar

5 natural sweeteners

Turbinado sugar Crunchy, light brown raw sugar that's good for baking and melting. $13 for 4 lbs; sugarintheraw.com.

Muscovado sugar Moist, richly flavored brown sugar. Look for the India Tree brand. $5.25 for 1 lb; dcimports.com.

Agave nectar Mild liquid sweetener made from agave plants. $23 for six bottles by Wholesome Sweeteners; amazon.com.

Jaggery Earthy cane sugar from India sold in dense clumps for grating. $7 for 7 oz; kalustyans.com.

Sorghum Mineral-rich syrup made from sorghum grain that's great on pancakes and biscuits. $8 for 6.75 oz; bourbonbarrelfoods.com.

COBBLER

- 1 cup pecans
- 10 peaches (4¾ pounds), pitted and cut into ½-inch slices
- ¼ cup light brown sugar
- 3 tablespoons granulated sugar
- 3 tablespoons cornstarch
- ¼ teaspoon cinnamon
- 1 teaspoon pure vanilla extract

WHIPPED CREAM

- 1¼ cups heavy cream
- ½ teaspoon cinnamon
- 1 teaspoon pure vanilla extract
- 2 tablespoons confectioners' sugar

1. MAKE THE BISCUITS: In a medium bowl, mix the 2 cups of flour, the granulated sugar, baking powder, baking soda and salt. Using a pastry blender or 2 knives, cut in the butter until it is the size of peas. Gently stir in the buttermilk until the dough just comes together.

2. Transfer the dough to a lightly floured surface and pat it into a ¾-inch-thick disk. Using a 2½-inch round biscuit cutter, stamp out 8 biscuits, patting the scraps together as needed. Transfer the biscuits to a parchment paper–lined baking sheet. Brush the tops with the cream and sprinkle with the turbinado sugar. Refrigerate the biscuits until chilled, about 30 minutes.

3. Preheat the oven to 450°. Bake the biscuits for about 15 minutes, until lightly golden; transfer to a rack to cool. Reduce the oven temperature to 375°.

4. MAKE THE COBBLER: Lightly butter an 8½-by-11-inch baking dish. Spread the pecans in a pie plate and toast in the oven for 8 minutes, until fragrant; let cool, then coarsely chop. In a bowl, toss the peaches, brown sugar, granulated sugar, cornstarch, cinnamon and vanilla. Fold in the pecans.

5. Spread the peaches in the prepared baking dish and cover with foil. Set the dish on a rimmed baking sheet and bake for 20 minutes, until the peaches begin to release their juices. Remove the foil and bake for about 30 minutes longer, stirring

once, until the peaches are bubbling. Arrange the biscuits over the fruit. Bake the cobbler for 5 minutes longer. Transfer to a rack to cool slightly.

6. MEANWHILE, MAKE THE WHIPPED CREAM: In a large bowl, combine all of the ingredients. Using an electric mixer, beat the cream at medium speed until softly whipped. Spoon the cobbler into shallow bowls, top with dollops of whipped cream and serve. —*Bobby Flay*

Peach-Gingersnap Crisp

TOTAL: 45 MIN
6 SERVINGS ● ●

- 4 tablespoons unsalted butter
- 6 large peaches (2½ pounds), peeled and cut into ½-inch wedges
- ¼ cup plus 2 tablespoons light brown sugar
- 2 tablespoons fresh lemon juice
- ¼ cup plus 2 tablespoons all-purpose flour

Pinch of salt

- 1 cup coarsely crushed gingersnaps

1. Preheat the oven to 400°. In a skillet, melt 2 tablespoons of the butter. Add the peaches and cook over high heat, stirring occasionally, until just softened, 8 minutes. Add ¼ cup of the brown sugar and the lemon juice and cook until the peaches are lightly caramelized, about 5 minutes; scrape into a 1½-quart baking dish.

2. Meanwhile, in a food processor, pulse the flour and salt with the remaining 2 tablespoons each of butter and light brown sugar until the mixture has the texture of coarse meal. Add the crushed gingersnaps and pulse 2 or 3 times, just to incorporate the cookies.

3. Press the topping into clumps and sprinkle over the peaches. Bake in the center of the oven for about 15 minutes, until the top is browned and the filling is bubbling. Let cool slightly, then serve. —*Grace Parisi*

BUTTERMILK-BISCUIT
PEACH COBBLER

pies & fruit desserts

White Chocolate–Citrus Parfait

ACTIVE: 1 HR; TOTAL: 2 HR

6 SERVINGS ● ●

LIME CURD

- 2 large eggs
- ¼ cup sugar
- 1½ teaspoons finely grated lime zest
- ¼ cup fresh lime juice
- 2 tablespoons sweetened condensed milk

MOUSSE

- 2 large eggs, separated
- 1¼ cups heavy cream
- 2 ounces white chocolate, chopped
- 2 teaspoons sugar
- ⅛ teaspoon cream of tartar
- Pinch of salt
- 2 teaspoons fresh lemon juice

CITRUS SALAD

- 1 cup fresh orange juice
- 1 tablespoon sugar
- 1 stalk of lemongrass, halved lengthwise and cut into 2-inch pieces
- Two ½-inch-thick coins of fresh ginger
- 2 teaspoons honey
- 1 tablespoon fresh lime juice
- ¼ teaspoon finely grated lime zest
- 1 tablespoon shredded mint
- 1 red grapefruit
- 2 navel oranges
- 1 tangerine

1. MAKE THE LIME CURD: Set a fine-mesh sieve over a bowl. In a small saucepan, cook the eggs, sugar, lime zest and juice over moderate heat, whisking constantly, until thickened, about 3 minutes. Strain the lime curd into the bowl and whisk in the condensed milk. Cover with plastic wrap and refrigerate for at least 1 hour, until chilled.

2. MAKE THE MOUSSE: Fill a large bowl with ice water. In a medium saucepan, cook the egg yolks with ¾ cup of the heavy cream over moderate heat, whisking constantly, until the mixture has the consistency of yogurt, about 5 minutes. Remove the saucepan from the heat and whisk in the chopped white chocolate. Scrape the white chocolate mixture into a medium bowl and set it in the large bowl of ice water to cool completely, stirring occasionally as the mixture cools.

3. In the bowl of an electric mixer fitted with the whisk attachment, beat the egg whites with the sugar, cream of tartar and salt until glossy, soft peaks form. Using a rubber spatula, gently fold the egg whites into the white chocolate mixture. In another medium bowl, beat the remaining ½ cup of heavy cream until it holds firm peaks. Gently fold the whipped cream into the white chocolate mixture along with the lemon juice. Cover the mousse with plastic wrap and refrigerate for 1 hour, or until chilled.

4. MAKE THE CITRUS SALAD: In a small saucepan, bring the fresh orange juice, sugar, lemongrass pieces and fresh ginger coins to a boil. Simmer over moderate heat until the juice has reduced to 3 tablespoons, about 10 minutes. Strain into a bowl and let cool. Whisk in the honey, lime juice, zest and mint.

5. Using a sharp knife, peel the citrus fruits, removing all of the bitter white pith. Working over a cutting board, cut in between the membranes to release the sections. Add to the orange dressing and toss.

6. Spoon the lime curd into 6 glasses. Using a slotted spoon, divide the citrus salad among the glasses and top each serving with some of the white chocolate mousse. Serve right away. —*Deanie Fox*

MAKE AHEAD The lime curd, white chocolate mousse and citrus salad can be refrigerated separately overnight.

Bourbon-Nectarine Ice Cream Sundaes with Pound Cake Croutons

TOTAL: 30 MIN

6 SERVINGS ●

This is an excellent grown-up version of an ice cream sundae, made with lush nectarines cooked in bourbon. The best part: the crisp, buttery pound cake croutons.

- 4 tablespoons unsalted butter
- 8 ounces homemade or store-bought all-butter pound cake, cut into ½-inch cubes
- 6 firm, ripe yellow nectarines, cut into thin wedges
- ½ cup light brown sugar
- ⅓ cup bourbon
- 1 tablespoon fresh lemon juice
- 2 pints vanilla ice cream

1. Preheat the oven to 375°. In a large skillet, melt 1 tablespoon of the butter. Add the pound cake cubes and toss to coat. Spread the buttered cubes on a rimmed baking sheet and bake for 15 minutes, until the cubes are toasted.

2. Meanwhile, wipe out the skillet. Add the remaining 3 tablespoons of butter and the nectarine wedges and cook over high heat, stirring occasionally, until the nectarines are slightly softened, about 5 minutes. Add the light brown sugar and stir until the sugar is melted. Remove the skillet from the heat. Add the bourbon and fresh lemon juice. Tilt the pan slightly away from you and carefully ignite the alcohol. Return to the burner and cook the fruit over moderate heat until the nectarines are softened and the bourbon sauce is slightly thickened, about 10 minutes.

3. Scoop the vanilla ice cream into ice cream bowls or glasses and spoon the warm nectarines and bourbon sauce on top. Garnish the sundaes with the pound cake croutons and serve right away. —*Grace Parisi*

BOURBON-NECTARINE ICE CREAM SUNDAES
WITH POUND CAKE CROUTONS

pies & fruit desserts

Lemon Ice Box Pie

TOTAL: 1 HR PLUS 7 HR COOLING
AND FREEZING
MAKES ONE 9-INCH PIE ● ● ●

Cookbook author David Guas's silken frozen pie was inspired by a dessert at Clancy's, one of Guas's favorite New Orleans neighborhood restaurants.

- 14 whole graham crackers, broken
- ¼ cup sugar
- ¼ teaspoon salt
- 6 tablespoons unsalted butter, melted
- Two 14-ounce cans sweetened condensed milk
- 1¼ cups fresh lemon juice
- 2 tablespoons finely grated lemon zest
- 8 large egg yolks

1. Preheat the oven to 325°. In a food processor, pulse the graham crackers with the sugar and salt until finely ground but not powdery. Add the butter and pulse until the crumbs are evenly moistened; transfer to a 9-inch springform pan and press into the bottom and two-thirds up the side. Set the pan on a rimmed baking sheet.

2. In a medium bowl, whisk the condensed milk with the lemon juice. In another bowl, using a handheld mixer, beat the lemon zest with the egg yolks until pale. Beat in the condensed milk mixture until smooth. Pour the filling into the crust.

3. Bake the lemon pie for about 25 minutes, until the edges are set and the center jiggles slightly when the pie is moved. Transfer the pan to a rack; let cool for 1 hour. Loosely cover the pie pan with plastic wrap and freeze the pie for at least 6 hours or overnight.

4. Wrap a warm, damp kitchen towel around the side of the springform pan to release the pie; remove the ring. Using a hot knife, slice the pie, transfer to plates and serve. —David Guas

SERVE WITH Whipped cream.

Toasted-Coconut Custard Tart

ACTIVE: 45 MIN; TOTAL: 3 HR 30 MIN
MAKES ONE 12-INCH TART ● ● ●

Celebrity chef Jean-Georges Vongerichten loves this tart recipe from his friend Maya Gurley (of Maya's Restaurant on the Caribbean island of St. Bart's). The soft custard filling and the caramelized shredded coconut topping have the creamy-crunchy texture of a coconut macaroon.

TART SHELL

- 2 cups all-purpose flour
- 1 teaspoon salt
- 1½ sticks cold unsalted butter, cut into ¼-inch cubes
- ¼ cup plus 1 tablespoon ice water

CUSTARD

- 2 large egg yolks
- 3 tablespoons all-purpose flour, plus more for dusting
- 1 vanilla bean, halved lengthwise, seeds scraped and bean reserved for another use
- 1¼ cups milk
- 3 cups finely shredded fresh coconut (6½ ounces)
- 1½ cups light brown sugar

Kiwi, Banana and Passion Fruit Salad (p. 310) and vanilla ice cream, for serving

Freshly ground white pepper

1. **MAKE THE TART SHELL:** In a large bowl, whisk the flour with the salt. Using a pastry cutter or 2 knives, cut in the cold cubes of butter until the mixture resembles coarse meal. Sprinkle with the ice water and stir lightly to form a dough. Wrap the dough in plastic and refrigerate for about 1 hour, until thoroughly chilled.

2. **MEANWHILE, MAKE THE CUSTARD:** In a medium saucepan, whisk the egg yolks with the 3 tablespoons of flour and the vanilla seeds until smooth. Gradually whisk in the milk. Cook over moderate heat, whisking constantly, until thickened, 5 minutes. Scrape the custard into a medium

bowl. Press a piece of plastic wrap directly onto the surface of the custard and let cool at room temperature until just warm.

3. Meanwhile, transfer the chilled tart dough to a lightly floured work surface and roll it out to a 15-inch round about ⅛ inch thick. Transfer the rolled dough to a 12-inch fluted tart pan with a removable bottom, gently pressing it into the bottom and up the side. Cut off any excess dough. Freeze the tart shell for about 20 minutes, until it is firm.

4. Preheat the oven to 350°. Line the tart shell with foil and fill with dried beans or pie weights. Bake the shell for about 40 minutes, until golden. Remove the foil and beans and bake for about 20 minutes longer, until the shell is golden brown and crisp. Transfer the tart pan to a rack and let cool completely.

5. Spread the custard in the tart shell in an even layer. In a large skillet, toss the shredded coconut with the brown sugar over moderately high heat, stirring, until the coconut shreds become translucent, about 2 minutes. Spread the shredded, sugared coconut over the custard in an even layer.

6. Bake the coconut custard tart for about 30 minutes, until the shredded coconut on top is richly browned. Transfer the tart pan to a rack and let cool to warm or room temperature. Unmold the tart onto a serving platter, then cut the tart into wedges and transfer to plates. Spoon the Kiwi, Banana and Passion Fruit Salad alongside. Serve with scoops of vanilla ice cream sprinkled lightly with freshly ground white pepper.
—Jean-Georges Vongerichten

MAKE AHEAD The unbaked tart shell can be frozen, wrapped in plastic, for up to 1 month. The cooled custard can be refrigerated overnight with a piece of plastic wrap pressed directly onto its surface. Bring the custard to room temperature before filling the tart shell.

perfecting pumpkin pie

Prebaking the crust makes for the ultimate pumpkin pie. F&W's **Grace Parisi** *also shares two clever variations on this classic: a towering chiffon pie, and a chocolate-swirled one.*

Classic Pumpkin Pie

ACTIVE: 20 MIN; TOTAL: 2 HR 30 MIN
PLUS COOLING
MAKES ONE 9-INCH PIE ● ● ●

All-Butter Pie Dough (recipe follows)
- 4 large eggs
- ¾ cup sugar
- 1 tablespoon cornstarch
- 2 teaspoons cinnamon
- ¼ teaspoon ground cloves

Pinch of salt
One 15-ounce can pumpkin puree
- ½ cup heavy cream

1. Preheat the oven to 350°. On a lightly floured surface, roll out the pie dough to a 13-inch round a scant ¼ inch thick. Fit the dough into a 9-inch glass pie plate and trim the overhang to ¾ inch. Fold the dough under itself and crimp decoratively; refrigerate the pie shell for 10 minutes.

2. Line the pie shell with foil and fill with pie weights or dried beans. Bake in the center of the oven until nearly set, about 25 minutes. Remove the foil and weights and bake until the crust is pale golden, about 10 minutes. Let cool slightly.

3. In a bowl, whisk the eggs with the sugar, cornstarch, cinnamon, cloves and salt until smooth. Whisk in the pumpkin, then the cream. Carefully pour the filling into the crust. Bake for about 45 minutes, until the custard is set (if the crust browns too fast, cover it with foil). Cool on a rack.

ALL-BUTTER PIE DOUGH
ACTIVE: 10 MIN; TOTAL: 40 MIN
MAKES DOUGH FOR 1 PIE ● ●

- 1¼ cups all-purpose flour

Pinch of salt
- 1 stick cold unsalted butter, cubed
- ¼ cup ice water

In a food processor, pulse the flour with the salt. Add the cubed butter and pulse until the butter is the size of peas. Drizzle in the water and pulse until the crumbs are moistened; turn out onto a work surface. Gather into a ball, flatten, wrap in plastic and refrigerate for 30 minutes.

TWO GREAT VARIATIONS

1 Pumpkin-Chiffon Pie
Fit the dough into a 10-inch glass pie plate. In Step 3, prepare the filling with just the 4 yolks and ½ cup of the sugar. Beat the 4 whites at medium-high speed until soft peaks form. Gradually add the remaining ¼ cup sugar; beat until glossy, 1 minute longer. Fold into the filling; bake as directed.

2 Chocolate-Swirled Pumpkin Pie
Finely chop 3 ounces of bittersweet chocolate. In a microwave-safe bowl, melt the chocolate; let cool. In Step 3, whisk the chocolate into 1 cup of the pumpkin filling. Pour the rest of the pumpkin filling into the crust. Dollop the chocolate filling on top and swirl it in with a butter knife. Bake as directed.

Kiwi, Banana and Passion Fruit Salad

TOTAL: 30 MIN
10 SERVINGS ● ●

While vacationing on the island of St. Bart's, superchef Jean-Georges Vongerichten created this sunny, sweet salad to accompany his Toasted-Coconut Custard Tart (p. 308) for a New Year's Day meal.

- 6 large, ripe passion fruit, halved (see Note)
- 2 tablespoons sugar
- 1 teaspoon fresh lemon juice

One 3-pound pineapple— peeled, cored and cut into 1-inch cubes

- 8 ripe kiwis, peeled and quartered lengthwise
- 3 medium bananas, cut into ¼-inch rounds
- 15 pitted prunes, halved

1. Set a fine sieve over a small saucepan. Working over the sieve, scoop the seedy pulp from 5 of the passion fruits. Press on the solids to extract as much juice as possible. Add the sugar to the juice in the saucepan and cook over moderate heat, stirring to dissolve the sugar, about 2 minutes. Transfer the passion fruit syrup to a medium bowl and stir in the lemon juice. Let cool. Scoop out the seedy pulp from the remaining passion fruit into the syrup and stir.

2. In a large serving bowl, toss the pineapple cubes with the quartered kiwis, banana rounds and halved prunes. Add the cooled passion fruit syrup, toss the ingredients until well distributed and serve the fruit salad right away.
—Jean-Georges Vongerichten

NOTE The color of a passion fruit's skin is not indicative of its ripeness. Whether green or purple, the sweetest passion fruits are those with thin skins and plenty of wrinkles.

MAKE AHEAD The passion fruit syrup can be refrigerated overnight.

Melon-and-Strawberry Salad with Spicy Lemongrass Syrup

ACTIVE: 20 MIN; TOTAL: 45 MIN
6 SERVINGS ● ●

Chiles add subtle heat to this exceptional fruit salad. Use any syrup left in the fruit bowl for cocktails: Mix a little of it into rum and pour the drink over ice.

- 2 plump lemongrass stalks, bruised and coarsely chopped
- 2 fresh hot red chiles, quartered lengthwise

Finely grated zest of 1 lime

- 1 cup sugar
- 1 pound strawberries, halved or quartered if large
- 1 pound cubed (¾-inch) peeled yellow or white-fleshed melon, such as Canary or Crenshaw
- 2 tablespoons slivered mint leaves
- 2 teaspoons minced crystallized ginger
- ½ cup crème fraîche

1. Set a medium bowl in a large bowl filled with ice. In a medium saucepan, combine the lemongrass, chiles, lime zest and sugar with 1 cup of water and bring to boil, stirring until the sugar is dissolved. Simmer until slightly thickened, about 8 minutes. Transfer to the ice water bath and let chill for 15 minutes.

2. In a large bowl, toss the strawberries with the melon and mint. Strain the cooled lemongrass syrup over the fruit and toss gently. Refrigerate just until slightly chilled.

3. In a bowl, stir the ginger into the crème fraîche. Spoon the fruit salad into bowls, top with a dollop of the ginger cream and serve.
—Grace Parisi

Passion Fruit Ice Cream Pie with a Ginger Crust

ACTIVE: 30 MIN; TOTAL: 3 HR
8 TO 10 SERVINGS ● ● ●

This isn't the kind of ice cream pie you'd make for a kid's birthday party. Instead of a plain cookie crust, F&W's Grace Parisi creates a crispy, chewy one with crumbled gingersnaps, chopped dried pineapple and candied ginger. And instead of the usual caramel or chocolate sauce on top, she prepares a delectable mix of dulce de leche and passion fruit nectar from the supermarket.

One 8-ounce box gingersnaps, lightly crushed

- 1 dried sweetened pineapple ring (1½ ounces), coarsely chopped
- 2 tablespoons coarsely chopped candied ginger
- 4 tablespoons unsalted butter, softened
- 1¼ cups dulce de leche (one 16-ounce jar)
- ½ cup passion fruit nectar (see Note)
- 3 pints vanilla ice cream, slightly softened
- ¼ cup salted roasted pistachios, coarsely chopped
- 2 tablespoons shredded sweetened coconut

1. In a food processor, combine the crushed gingersnaps with the pineapple, candied ginger and butter and process until fine crumbs form. Press the crumbs evenly over the bottom and 1 inch up the side of a 9-inch springform pan. Freeze until firm, about 10 minutes.

2. In a blender, blend the dulce de leche and passion fruit nectar until smooth.

3. Spread 1 pint of ice cream in the chilled crust. Using a very small ice cream scoop (2 tablespoons), scoop the remaining 2 pints of ice cream into the crust, leaving some nooks and crannies. Drizzle ¾ cup of the dulce de leche sauce over the ice cream, allowing it to pool in spots. Sprinkle with the pistachios and coconut and freeze until firm, at least 2½ hours.

4. Remove the ring and cut the pie into wedges. Serve the extra dulce de leche sauce at the table. —Grace Parisi

NOTE Look for passion fruit nectar at supermarkets, preferably the Looza brand.

PASSION FRUIT ICE CREAM
PIE WITH A GINGER CRUST

pies & fruit desserts

Roasted Bananas with Spiced Syrup and Candied Nuts

ACTIVE: 50 MIN; TOTAL: 1 HR 15 MIN

12 SERVINGS ● ●

CANDIED NUTS

1 cup sugar
⅓ cup water
⅔ cup roasted, skinned hazelnuts
⅓ cup unsalted pistachios

SPICED SYRUP

2 cups water
½ cup sugar
2 teaspoons cornstarch dissolved in
1½ tablespoons of water
½ teaspoon *ras el hanout* (see Note)

BANANAS

18 medium bananas, unpeeled
72 coffee beans (3 tablespoons)
Thirty-six 2-inch-long julienne strips of
candied orange peel (2 ounces)
2 vanilla beans, quartered and cut
into 1½-inch lengths
Four 1½-inch-long cinnamon sticks,
broken into shards

1. PREPARE THE CANDIED NUTS: Line a rimmed baking sheet with parchment paper. In a small saucepan, dissolve the sugar in the water and simmer over moderate heat until a rich brown caramel forms, 6 minutes. Add the nuts and stir to coat. Using a fork or slotted spoon, working quickly, transfer a few nuts at a time to the parchment paper and separate them. Let the nuts cool completely, 25 minutes.

2. MEANWHILE, MAKE THE SPICED SYRUP: In a small saucepan, boil the water with the sugar until reduced by one-fourth, 12 minutes. Scrape in the cornstarch slurry; simmer until the sauce thickens, 30 seconds. Remove from the heat; stir in the *ras el hanout*. Let cool to room temperature.

3. PREPARE THE BANANAS: Preheat the oven to 350°. Arrange the bananas on 2 large rimmed baking sheets. Using a skewer or paring knife, poke the bananas all over, about 1 inch deep and 1 inch apart. Stud the bananas with the coffee beans, orange

peel, vanilla beans and cinnamon sticks. Roast for 20 minutes, until very tender.

4. Halve 6 bananas crosswise. Spoon the syrup onto plates. Arrange a whole and halved banana on each plate. Garnish with candied nuts; serve warm. —*Michel Bras*

NOTE *Ras el hanout*, a Moroccan spice mix, is available at kalustyans.com.

Banana Pudding with Vanilla Wafer Crumble

TOTAL: 45 MIN PLUS 4 HR CHILLING

6 SERVINGS ● ● ●

5 large egg yolks
¼ cup cornstarch
½ cup plus 2 teaspoons sugar
Salt
2 cups whole milk
3 tablespoons banana liqueur
(optional)
2 tablespoons cold unsalted butter
plus 1 tablespoon melted butter
2 teaspoons pure vanilla extract
1 cup vanilla wafer cookies
(about 15), coarsely ground
¼ teaspoon cinnamon
2 bananas, coarsely chopped

1. In a medium bowl, whisk the egg yolks with the cornstarch, the ½ cup of sugar and ¼ teaspoon of salt. In a medium saucepan, bring the milk to a boil. Gradually whisk the milk into the egg yolk mixture until smooth. Transfer the pudding mixture to the saucepan and add the banana liqueur. Cook over moderate heat, whisking, until the pudding is thick, about 3 minutes. Scrape the pudding into a bowl and whisk in the cold butter and vanilla. Cover the surface of the pudding directly with plastic wrap and refrigerate until chilled, about 4 hours.

2. Preheat the oven to 325°. Line a baking sheet with parchment paper. In a bowl, combine the wafers, cinnamon, the remaining 2 teaspoons of sugar and a pinch of salt. Stir in the melted butter. Spread the crumble on the prepared baking sheet; bake for 15 minutes, until lightly browned. Let cool.

3. Spoon the bananas into bowls. Top with the pudding, sprinkle with the crumble and serve right away. —*David Guas*

Brown Butter Custard Pie with Cranberry Glaze

ACTIVE: 45 MIN; TOTAL: 2 HR 30 MIN

8 TO 10 SERVINGS ● ●

2 teaspoons plain powdered gelatin
Reserved browned butter solids from
Cinnamon Toast Crumb Crust
(recipe follows)
1 cup whole milk
⅓ cup light brown sugar
¼ teaspoon cinnamon
Kosher salt
¾ cup plus 2 tablespoons
heavy cream
¼ cup sour cream
Cinnamon Toast Crumb Crust
(recipe follows)
3½ ounces white chocolate,
coarsely chopped
2 tablespoons unsalted butter
½ cup mashed sweet potatoes
1 cup cranberry sauce,
pureed and strained

1. In a microwave-safe bowl, sprinkle the gelatin over 2 tablespoons of water and let stand until softened, 3 minutes. Microwave at high power for 10 seconds, until melted. In a microwave-safe measuring cup, microwave the reserved brown butter solids with the milk, sugar, ⅛ teaspoon of the cinnamon and a pinch of salt until warm. Whisk in the gelatin and refrigerate until set.

2. In a bowl, whisk ¾ cup of the cream and sour cream to soft peaks. Whisk the custard to loosen it, then fold into the whipped cream. Pour the custard into the crust; refrigerate for 30 minutes.

3. In a microwave-safe bowl, melt the white chocolate and butter. Add the sweet potatoes, the remaining 2 tablespoons of cream and ⅛ teaspoon of cinnamon and a pinch of salt; whisk until smooth. Transfer to a pastry bag fitted with a ½-inch plain tip and

refrigerate until chilled slightly, 15 minutes. Pipe 1-inch mounds around the edge of the pie. Refrigerate until set, 10 minutes.
4. Spread the cranberry puree evenly over the pie. Chill until set, at least 30 minutes. Cut into wedges; serve. —*Christina Tosi*

CINNAMON TOAST CRUMB CRUST
ACTIVE: 15 MIN; TOTAL: 1 HR
MAKES ONE 10-INCH CRUST ● ◐

- 2 sticks unsalted butter
- ½ cup sugar
- 1½ teaspoons kosher salt
- ½ teaspoon cinnamon
- 4 cups diced crusts and end pieces from 1 loaf of packaged white bread (10 ounces crusts)

1. Preheat the oven to 325°. In a saucepan, melt the butter. Cook over moderate heat, stirring, until the butter is golden brown, 8 minutes; strain into a heatproof measuring cup. Transfer the browned butter solids to a bowl and reserve for the Brown Butter Custard Pie.
2. Pour half of the melted butter into a bowl. Add the sugar, salt, cinnamon and bread; toss. Spread on a baking sheet; bake for 35 minutes, until golden. Let cool.
3. Rewarm the remaining melted butter; pour into a food processor. Add the croutons and pulse to fine crumbs; spoon into a 10-inch pie plate. Refrigerate for 5 minutes. Press the crumbs over the bottom and side of the pie plate; refrigerate until chilled and firm, about 15 minutes. —*CT*

Cranberry Panna Cotta
TOTAL: 30 MIN PLUS 2 HR CHILLING
8 SERVINGS ● ◐

- 1 cup fresh or frozen cranberries
- ¼ cup plus 2 tablespoons sugar
- 2 tablespoons water
- 3½ cups low-fat buttermilk
- 1 tablespoon plus ½ teaspoon unflavored powdered gelatin
- Plain low-fat yogurt and candied rose petals, for serving (see Note)

1. In a small saucepan, combine the cranberries with the sugar and water and bring to a boil. Simmer over moderate heat, stirring occasionally, until the cranberries soften, about 5 minutes. Mash the cranberries with the back of a spoon to make a thick sauce. Transfer the cranberry sauce to a large bowl and refrigerate, stirring often, until cool, about 15 minutes. Stir 3 cups of the buttermilk into the cranberry sauce.
2. In a small saucepan, sprinkle the gelatin over the remaining ½ cup of buttermilk. Let stand until the gelatin has dissolved, about 5 minutes. Heat the mixture over low heat, stirring a few times with a rubber spatula, until the buttermilk is just warm and the gelatin is melted, about 1½ minutes; fold into the cranberry mixture.
3. Pour the panna cotta into 8 glasses. Cover and refrigerate for about 2 hours, until they are set. Top each with a small dollop of yogurt and a few candied rose petals and serve. —*Marcia Kiesel*
NOTE Candied rose petals are available at markethallfoods.com.

Brown Butter–Cranberry Tart
ACTIVE: 40 MIN; TOTAL: 4 HR 40 MIN
MAKES ONE 10-INCH TART ● ◐
PASTRY

- 1½ cups all-purpose flour
- 2 tablespoons sugar
- ½ teaspoon salt
- 1 stick cold unsalted butter, cut into ½-inch pieces
- ¼ cup heavy cream
- 1 large egg yolk

FILLING AND TOPPING

- 1½ sticks unsalted butter
- 1 vanilla bean, split, seeds scraped
- 3 large eggs
- 2 cups plus 1 tablespoon sugar
- 1 teaspoon finely grated lemon zest
- ¼ cup all-purpose flour
- ¼ teaspoon salt
- 3½ cups fresh or frozen cranberries
- ¼ cup water

1. MAKE THE PASTRY: In a food processor, pulse the flour with the sugar and salt. Add the butter and pulse until it is the size of small peas. In a small bowl, whisk the cream with the egg yolk. Pour the cream mixture into the food processor and pulse until moist crumbs form. Turn the pastry out onto a work surface and pat into a disk. Wrap in plastic and refrigerate for about 30 minutes, or until chilled.
2. Preheat the oven to 375°. On a lightly floured work surface, roll out the pastry ⅛ inch thick. Fit the pastry into a 10-inch fluted tart pan with a removable bottom; trim the overhanging pastry. Patch any cracks with the pastry trimmings. Refrigerate for about 30 minutes, or until it is chilled.
3. Line the tart shell with foil and fill with pie weights or dried beans. Bake for about 25 minutes, until the rim is lightly golden. Remove the foil and weights and bake for about 10 minutes longer, until lightly golden all over. Set the tart pan on a baking sheet.
4. MEANWHILE, MAKE THE FILLING: In a small skillet, melt the butter with the vanilla bean and seeds. Cook over moderately high heat until the butter starts to turn golden and smells nutty, about 4 minutes. Remove from the heat and let cool for 5 minutes.
5. In a medium bowl, whisk the eggs with 1 cup plus 1 tablespoon of the sugar and the lemon zest. Strain the brown butter into the egg mixture and whisk until incorporated. Whisk in the flour and salt. Pour the filling into the tart shell and bake for about 25 minutes, until golden and set. Transfer to a rack to cool, about 2 hours.
6. In a saucepan, combine the remaining 1 cup of sugar with the cranberries and water. Bring to a simmer over moderately high heat and cook until the cranberries have just split and the sugar is dissolved, about 4 minutes. Scrape the cranberries into a bowl and refrigerate until cool, about 1 hour.
7. With a slotted spoon, arrange the cranberries on the tart; discard the liquid. Slice and serve. —*Katherine Thompson*

MILK-CHOCOLATE COOKIES
WITH MALTED CREAM (P. 330)

cakes, cookies & more

Chocolate cookies with malted cream,
a six-layer coconut cake and
other homey and showstopping sweets.

SPICED UPSIDE-DOWN APPLE BUNDT CAKE

GOAT CHEESE CHEESECAKE WITH HONEYED CRANBERRIES

Spiced Upside-Down Apple Bundt Cake

ACTIVE: 1 HR; TOTAL: 3 HR 30 MIN

MAKES 1 BUNDT CAKE ● ● ●

STREUSEL TOPPING

¼ cup pecan halves

2 tablespoons rolled oats

½ cup plus 1 tablespoon all-purpose flour

2 tablespoons packed light brown sugar

2 tablespoons granulated sugar

¾ teaspoon kosher salt

¼ teaspoon freshly ground pepper

⅛ teaspoon cinnamon

4 tablespoons unsalted butter, melted

CAKE

2¼ cups granulated sugar

1½ teaspoons cornstarch

½ teaspoon freshly grated nutmeg

½ teaspoon cinnamon

¼ teaspoon allspice

4 Granny Smith apples (2 pounds)—peeled, cored and cut into ½-inch dice

2 sticks plus 3 tablespoons unsalted butter, at room temperature

3 cups all-purpose flour

½ teaspoon baking soda

1 teaspoon kosher salt

1 cup buttermilk

¼ cup Calvados

½ teaspoon pure vanilla extract

2 teaspoons grated orange zest

3 large eggs

1. MAKE THE STREUSEL TOPPING: Preheat the oven to 325°. On a parchment paper–lined baking sheet, toast the pecans for 12 minutes, until lightly browned. Let cool. In a medium skillet, cook the oats over moderate heat, tossing, until fragrant and lightly toasted, about 4 minutes. Let cool.

2. In a food processor, pulse the flour with the pecans until the nuts are finely ground. Transfer to a bowl and stir in the oats, light brown sugar, granulated sugar, salt, pepper and cinnamon. Using a fork, stir in the butter until large clumps form. Spread the streusel on the baking sheet and bake for 25 minutes, until golden brown. Let cool.

3. MAKE THE CAKE: Increase the oven temperature to 350°. Generously butter and flour a 10-inch Bundt pan. In a bowl, combine ¼ cup of the sugar with the cornstarch, nutmeg, cinnamon and allspice. Add the apples and toss until thoroughly coated.

4. In a large skillet, melt 3 tablespoons of the butter. Add the apples and cook over moderately high heat, stirring, until almost tender, 6 minutes. Scrape onto a baking sheet; refrigerate until cool, 15 minutes.

5. In a medium bowl, whisk the flour with the baking soda and salt. In a measuring cup, mix the buttermilk with the Calvados and vanilla. In the bowl of a stand mixer fitted with the paddle, beat the remaining 2 sticks of butter and 2 cups of sugar with the orange zest at medium-high speed until fluffy, 2 minutes. Add the eggs one at a time, beating well between additions. At low speed, in 3 alternating additions, beat in the dry ingredients and buttermilk mixture; scrape down the bowl as necessary.

6. Spread the apples on the bottom of the Bundt pan. Scrape the cake batter over them and smooth the surface with a spatula. Bake in the center of the oven for 1 hour, until a toothpick inserted in the center of comes out clean. Let cool 5 minutes.

7. Set a rack on a baking sheet. Invert the cake onto the rack; scrape any apples stuck to the pan back onto the cake. While the apples are hot, pack the streusel topping over the top of the cake. Let stand until cool, 1 hour. Slice with a serrated knife and serve. —David Guas

SERVE WITH Whipped cream.

Goat Cheese Cheesecake with Honeyed Cranberries

TOTAL: 1 HR PLUS 5 HR 30 MIN CHILLING

8 TO 10 SERVINGS ●●○

Vegetable oil, for brushing

9 whole graham crackers, crushed
¼ cup light brown sugar
¼ teaspoon cinnamon
4 tablespoons unsalted butter, melted
10 ounces fresh goat cheese, softened
2 teaspoons fresh lemon juice
1½ cups heavy cream
⅓ cup plus ¼ cup granulated sugar
Julienned zest from 2 navel oranges
1 teaspoon Champagne vinegar
½ cup honey, preferably wildflower
1 cup cranberries (4 ounces)

1. Lightly brush a 9-inch springform pan with vegetable oil. In a food processor, pulse the graham crackers, brown sugar and cinnamon to fine crumbs. Add the butter and process until the crumbs are moistened. Press the crumbs over the bottom of the pan and refrigerate until firm, 30 minutes.

2. In a bowl, beat the cheese with the lemon juice until creamy. Add the cream; beat until very firm, 3 minutes. Add ⅓ cup of the granulated sugar; beat until smooth and slightly softened, 2 minutes. Pour the batter over the crust. Refrigerate until well chilled, at least 5 hours or preferably overnight.

3. In a saucepan of boiling water, simmer the orange zest over moderate heat for 10 minutes. Drain and return to the saucepan. Add the remaining ¼ cup of granulated sugar; stir over low heat until the sugar is melted and the zest glazed, 2 minutes. Stir in the vinegar; transfer to a small bowl.

4. Rinse and dry the saucepan. Add the honey and bring to a boil. Remove from the heat, stir in the cranberries and let cool.

5. Run a small, thin knife around the edge of the springform pan and remove the ring. Using a hot knife, trim the cake to a 6-inch square (serve the trimmings as snacks), then cut into 10 rectangles. Alternatively, cut the cake into wedges. Transfer to plates, garnish with the zest and cranberries and serve. —Timothy Hollingsworth

Almond-and-Candied-Orange Cake with Lemon Semifreddo

ACTIVE: 40 MIN; TOTAL: 2 HR 30 MIN

8 SERVINGS ●●○

SEMIFREDDO

1 cup heavy cream
2 large eggs, separated
½ cup granualated sugar
Finely grated zest of 2 lemons

CAKE

1 cup blanched almonds, coarsely chopped
1½ cups confectioners' sugar
⅓ cup all-purpose flour

Salt

2 tablespoons finely chopped candied orange peel
5 large egg whites
5 tablespoons melted unsalted butter, at room temperature
1 teaspoon pure orange extract

1. MAKE THE SEMIFREDDO: In a large, stainless steel bowl, beat the cream until softly whipped. Cover and refrigerate.

2. In a medium bowl, beat the egg whites until frothy, about 30 seconds. Beat in 5 tablespoons of the granulated sugar, 2 tablespoons at a time, beating until the whites are firm and glossy. In a small bowl, beat the egg yolks with the remaining 3 tablespoons of sugar until pale yellow and thick. Fold the yolk mixture and the lemon zest into the egg whites until just combined. Fold in the whipped cream. Scrape the mixture into a glass or ceramic bowl, cover with plastic wrap and freeze for about 2 hours, until the semifreddo is firm.

3. MEANWHILE, MAKE THE CAKE: Preheat the oven to 350°. Butter a 9-inch springform pan. Line the bottom with parchment paper and butter the paper; flour the pan, tapping out any excess. In a food processor, pulse the almonds until finely ground. Transfer the almonds to a medium bowl. Working over the bowl, sift the confectioners' sugar with the flour and ½ teaspoon of salt. Stir in the orange peel.

4. In a large bowl, using clean beaters, beat the egg whites with a pinch of salt until stiff peaks form. Sprinkle the almond mixture over the egg whites and fold just until incorporated. Fold in the butter and orange extract. Scrape the batter into the prepared pan and bake for about 35 minutes, until golden brown. Set the pan on a rack and let the cake cool. Unmold the cake and peel off the paper.

5. Cut the cake into wedges and transfer to plates. Top with scoops of semifreddo and serve. —Dale Gartland

SERVE WITH Orange sections or berries.

cakes, cookies & more

Great-Grandmother Pearl's Angel Food Cake with Peaches

ACTIVE: 30 MIN; TOTAL: 1 HR 30 MIN
PLUS COOLING
10 SERVINGS ● ●

Cookbook author Katie Lee likes to serves her great-grandmother's prize-winning cake with peaches because the cake sops up the fruit's juices nicely.

- 2 cups egg whites (from about 16 large eggs)
- 2 teaspoons cream of tartar
- ½ teaspoon salt
- 3 cups sugar
- 2 cups cake flour
- 1 teaspoon pure vanilla extract
- 1 teaspoon pure almond extract
- 5 peaches, sliced into thin wedges

Lightly sweetened whipped cream

1. Preheat the oven to 325°. In a standing electric mixer, beat the egg whites at medium speed until foamy. Add the cream of tartar and salt; beat to stiff peaks. Gradually beat in 2½ cups of the sugar, until smooth and glossy, about 4 minutes.

2. Transfer the egg whites to a wide bowl. Gradually sift the flour over the egg whites, gently folding it in with a spatula. Fold in the vanilla and almond extracts. Scrape the batter into a 10-inch angel food cake pan. Using a table knife, slice through the batter several times to release air bubbles. Tap the pan once or twice on a flat surface.

3. Bake in the center of the oven for 20 minutes. Increase the oven temperature to 350°; bake for about 35 minutes more, until a toothpick inserted in the center comes out clean. Invert the pan onto the neck of a wine bottle; let cool completely.

4. Meanwhile, toss the peaches with the remaining ½ cup of sugar; refrigerate, stirring occasionally, until juicy, at least 1 hour or up to 4 hours.

5. Run a thin-bladed knife around the side and tube of the pan. Unmold the cake onto a platter. Cut into wedges; serve with the peaches and whipped cream. —*Katie Lee*

Poppy Seed Cake

ACTIVE: 20 MIN; TOTAL: 2 HR PLUS
2 HR COOLING
MAKES ONE 8-INCH CAKE ● ● ●

Lauren Chattman, author of *Cake Keeper Cakes,* brings out the taste of the poppy seeds in this recipe by first soaking them in hot water, then lightly crushing them in a blender.

- ¾ cup poppy seeds
- 1⅓ cups all-purpose flour, plus more for dusting
- 2 teaspoons baking powder
- ¼ teaspoon salt
- 1¾ sticks (14 tablespoons) unsalted butter, softened
- 1 cup granulated sugar
- 4 large eggs
- 1 teaspoon pure vanilla extract
- 1 teaspoon pure almond extract

Confectioners' sugar, for dusting

1. In a saucepan, bring ½ cup of water to a boil. Remove from the heat, add the poppy seeds and cover. Let stand 1 hour. Scrape into a blender; pulse until lightly crushed.

2. Preheat the oven to 350°. Grease and flour an 8-inch square pan. In a bowl, whisk the 1⅓ cups of flour with the baking powder and salt. In a bowl, using a handheld mixer, beat the butter with the granulated sugar at medium-high speed until fluffy, 3 minutes. Add the poppy seed mixture; beat at medium speed until just combined. Add the eggs one at a time, beating well between additions. Beat in the vanilla and almond extracts. With a wooden spoon, stir in the flour mixture until just incorporated. Scrape into the pan.

3. Bake for 45 minutes, until the top is golden and a toothpick inserted into the center comes out clean. Let cool in the pan for 10 minutes, then invert onto a wire rack and let cool completely, about 2 hours. Dust with confectioners' sugar, cut into squares and serve. —*Lauren Chattman*

MAKE AHEAD The cake can be kept in an airtight container for up to 3 days.

Grilled Lemon Pound Cake with Peaches and Cream

ACTIVE: 30 MIN; TOTAL: 5 HR
10 SERVINGS ● ●

- 2 cups cake flour
- ¼ cup finely grated lemon zest (from 3 lemons)
- 1 teaspoon baking powder
- ½ teaspoon salt
- 2 sticks unsalted butter, at room temperature
- 2 cups sugar
- 6 large eggs, at room temperature
- ¼ cup whole milk
- ¼ cup fresh lemon juice
- 1 teaspoon pure vanilla extract

Vegetable oil, for brushing

- 4 large peaches, sliced into ½-inch wedges

Lightly sweetened whipped cream

1. Preheat the oven to 325°. Spray a 9½-by-5-inch loaf pan with nonstick cooking spray. In a medium bowl, whisk the cake flour with the lemon zest, baking powder and salt.

2. In a mixer fitted with the paddle, beat the butter and sugar at medium speed until pale and fluffy, 2 minutes. Scrape down the bowl. Add the eggs one at a time, beating well between additions. At low speed, beat in the flour mixture just until incorporated. Beat in the milk, lemon juice and vanilla, scraping down the bowl as necessary.

3. Scrape the batter into the prepared pan and bake for about 1 hour and 30 minutes, until the cake is golden and a toothpick inserted in the center comes out clean. Transfer the pan to a rack and let the cake cool for 20 minutes. Unmold the cake and let cool completely, about 3 hours.

4. Light a grill. With a serrated knife, cut the cake into 10 slices. Lightly oil the grate and grill the slices over moderate heat, turning once, until toasted, 2 minutes. Lightly oil the grate. Grill the peaches over moderately high heat until lightly browned and tender, 2 minutes. Serve the peaches over the cake, with whipped cream. —*Bryan Calvert*

cakes, cookies & more

Polenta Pound Cake with Mascarpone and Rosemary

ACTIVE: 25 MIN; TOTAL: 1 HR 45 MIN
10 SERVINGS ● ●

CAKE

1¾ cups cake flour, plus
      more for dusting

½ cup polenta

Pinch of salt

2 sticks unsalted butter, softened

½ cup sugar

6 large eggs, at room
      temperature

2 teaspoons pure vanilla extract

1 teaspoon fresh lemon juice

ROSEMARY SYRUP

½ cup honey

3 tablespoons water

2 rosemary sprigs

MASCARPONE

1 cup mascarpone,
      at room temperature

½ cup heavy cream

2 tablespoons sugar

½ vanilla bean, split lengthwise
      and seeds scraped

Fresh figs, sliced, for serving
      (optional)

1. MAKE THE CAKE: Preheat the oven to 325°. Butter and flour a 9-by-5-inch metal loaf pan. In a medium bowl, whisk the 1¾ cups of cake flour with the polenta and salt. In a large bowl, using an electric mixer, beat the softened butter with the sugar at medium-high speed until pale and fluffy, about 2 minutes. Add the eggs one at a time, beating well between additions. Beat in the vanilla extract and lemon juice. Gradually add the flour mixture to the egg mixture, beating the batter at low speed until just incorporated.

2. Scrape the batter into the prepared loaf pan and bake for about 1 hour, until a cake tester inserted in the center of the cake comes out with a few moist crumbs attached. Turn the pound cake out onto a rack and let it cool until warm.

3. MEANWHILE, MAKE THE ROSEMARY SYRUP: In a small saucepan, combine the honey with the water and rosemary sprigs and simmer over moderate heat for 2 minutes. Let the syrup cool to room temperature, about 15 minutes. Discard the rosemary sprigs. While the cake is still warm, lightly brush the top of the cake with some of the rosemary syrup.

4. MAKE THE MASCARPONE: In a medium bowl, whisk the mascarpone with the cream, sugar and vanilla bean seeds.

5. Using a serrated knife, cut the pound cake into thick slices and transfer to plates. Top each slice with a large dollop of mascarpone, drizzle with the remaining rosemary syrup and serve with sliced figs, if using. —*Eddie Russell*

MAKE AHEAD The polenta pound cake can be kept, covered, at room temperature for up to 2 days. The rosemary syrup and mascarpone can be refrigerated separately for up to 2 days.

Lemon–Poppy Seed Cake

ACTIVE: 20 MIN; TOTAL: 1 HR 30 MIN
MAKES ONE 9-INCH CAKE ● ●

Cookbook author Eugenia Bone adapted this recipe from one by the legendary baker Maida Heatter. Heatter's cake, called East 62nd Street Lemon Cake, was supposedly very popular among Manhattan socialites in the '70s.

2 tablespoons fine dry bread
      crumbs

1 cup all-purpose flour

½ cup plus 1 tablespoon
      cake flour

1 teaspoon baking powder

½ teaspoon salt

1 stick unsalted butter,
      softened

1 cup granulated sugar

2 large eggs

½ cup milk

Finely grated zest of 1 lemon

2 teaspoons pure lemon extract

2 tablespoons poppy seeds

1 cup confectioners' sugar

2 tablespoons freshly squeezed
      lemon juice

1. Preheat the oven to 350°. Butter a 9-inch round cake pan and dust with the bread crumbs; tap out any excess crumbs. In a medium bowl, whisk the all-purpose flour and cake flour with the baking powder and salt. In a large bowl, using a handheld electric mixer, beat the butter with the granulated sugar at medium-high speed until it is pale and fluffy. Beat in the eggs one at a time, beating well between additions. At low speed, in 2 alternating batches, beat in the dry ingredients and the milk. With a rubber spatula, fold in the lemon zest, lemon extract and poppy seeds.

2. Using a rubber spatula, scrape the batter into the prepared pan and bake for 30 minutes, until a cake tester inserted in the center of the cake comes out clean.

3. Carefully invert the cake onto a wire rack and let cool to room temperature. Transfer the cake to a serving plate.

4. In a medium bowl, stir the confectioners' sugar with the lemon juice to make a runny glaze. Using a spatula, spread the glaze over the cake, letting it run down the side. Cut into wedges and serve.
—*Eugenia Bone*

MAKE AHEAD The Lemon–Poppy Seed Cake can be stored in an airtight container at room temperature for up to 2 days.

Molasses-Gingerbread Cake with Mascarpone Cream

ACTIVE: 35 MIN; TOTAL: 1 HR 30 MIN
PLUS 2 HR COOLING
MAKES ONE 9-INCH CAKE ● ● ●

CAKE

2¼ cups all-purpose flour

1¾ teaspoons ground ginger

1 teaspoon cinnamon

1¾ teaspoons baking soda

½ teaspoon salt

¾ cup plus 2 tablespoons canola oil

LEMON–POPPY SEED CAKE

MOLASSES-GINGERBREAD CAKE WITH MASCARPONE CREAM

¾ cup plus 2 tablespoons
   dark brown sugar

½ cup plus 2 tablespoons molasses

¼ cup plus 2 tablespoons honey

2 eggs

1 teaspoon finely grated lemon zest

¾ cup boiling water

ORANGE CONFIT

1 orange, zest peeled with a
   vegetable peeler and sliced
   lengthwise into ⅛-inch strips

4 cups water

½ cup sugar

MASCARPONE CREAM

1 cup mascarpone,
   at room temperature

¾ cup heavy cream

¾ teaspoon finely grated
   orange zest

2 tablespoons confectioners' sugar

Pinch of salt

1. MAKE THE CAKE: Preheat the oven to 350°. Spray a 9-inch square baking pan with vegetable cooking spray. In a large bowl, combine the flour with the ground ginger, cinnamon, baking soda and salt. In a medium bowl, whisk the canola oil with the dark brown sugar, molasses, honey, eggs and finely grated lemon zest until smooth. Whisk the wet ingredients into the dry ingredients until just combined. Whisk in the boiling water. Scrape the batter into the prepared pan and bake for about 1 hour and 10 minutes, until a cake tester inserted in the center of the cake comes out clean. Set the pan on a wire rack and let the cake cool completely, about 2 hours.

2. MEANWHILE, MAKE THE ORANGE CONFIT: In a medium saucepan, combine the strips of orange zest with the water and sugar. Bring the liquid to a boil, stirring until the sugar has dissolved. Simmer rapidly over high heat until the liquid is syrupy and the orange zest is soft, about 30 minutes. Using a slotted spoon, transfer the orange confit strips to a plate to cool; discard the syrup.

3. MAKE THE MASCARPONE CREAM: In a large bowl, using an electric mixer at medium speed, beat the mascarpone with the cream, orange zest, confectioners' sugar and salt until soft peaks form.

4. Cut the molasses-gingerbread cake into squares and transfer to plates. Dollop the mascarpone cream on top, garnish with the orange confit and serve.
—*Katie Rosenhouse*

MAKE AHEAD The cake can be wrapped in plastic and kept at room temperature for up to 2 days. The orange confit can be stored in an airtight container at room temperature for up to 3 days.

● HEALTHY ● MAKE AHEAD ● VEGETARIAN ● STAFF FAVORITE   321

cakes, cookies & more

Nutella-Swirl Pound Cake

ACTIVE: 20 MIN; TOTAL: 2 HR PLUS
2 HR COOLING

MAKES ONE 9-INCH LOAF ● ● ●

Cookbook author Lauren Chattman makes this pound cake especially rich by swirling in the chocolate-hazelnut spread Nutella. She recommends serving the cake with coffee ice cream.

1½ cups all-purpose flour, plus
 more for dusting
 4 large eggs, at room temperature
 2 teaspoons pure vanilla extract
 ¾ teaspoon baking powder
 ¼ teaspoon salt
 2 sticks unsalted butter, softened
1¼ cups sugar
One 13-ounce jar Nutella

1. Preheat the oven to 325°. Lightly grease and flour a 9-by-5-inch loaf pan, tapping out any excess flour. In a glass measuring cup, lightly beat the eggs with the vanilla. In a medium bowl, whisk the 1½ cups of flour with the baking powder and salt.

2. In a large bowl, using a handheld mixer, beat the butter with the sugar at medium-high speed until fluffy, about 3 minutes. With the mixer at medium-low speed, gradually beat in the egg mixture until fully incorporated. Add the flour mixture in 3 batches, beating at low speed between additions until just incorporated. Continue to beat for 30 seconds longer.

3. Spread one-third of the batter in the prepared pan, then spread half of the Nutella on top. Repeat with another third of the batter and the remaining Nutella. Top with the remaining batter. Lightly swirl the Nutella into the batter with a butter knife. Do not overmix.

4. Bake the cake for about 1 hour and 15 minutes, until a toothpick inserted in the center comes out clean. Let cool in the pan for 15 minutes. Invert the cake onto a wire rack, turn it right side up and let cool completely, about 2 hours. Cut into slices and serve. —Lauren Chattman

Six-Layer Coconut Cake with Passion Fruit Filling

ACTIVE: 1 HR; TOTAL: 5 HR 45 MIN

8 TO 12 SERVINGS ● ●

This towering dessert is made up of layers of supermoist, almost puddinglike coconut cake spread with tangy passion fruit curd, then topped with whipped cream and crispy toasted coconut. The recipe is from Cynthia Wong, pastry chef at Cakes & Ale in Decatur, Georgia. The cake may look intimidating, but it's easy to make: "Just pop the layers out of the baking pans and slap them together," Wong says.

CAKE

4¼ cups all-purpose flour
2¼ cups sugar
 1 tablespoon plus 1½ teaspoons
 baking powder
 2 teaspoons kosher salt
 2 sticks unsalted butter, softened
1¼ cups unsweetened coconut milk
 ¾ cup water
 2 teaspoons pure vanilla extract
 6 egg whites

FILLING

 ¾ cup sugar
 ¼ cup cornstarch
 1 cup passion fruit nectar
 or puree
 4 egg yolks
 1 vanilla bean—split lengthwise,
 seeds scraped
 1 stick unsalted butter,
 cut into tablespoons

TOPPING

 2 cups large, unsweetened
 dried coconut flakes
 2 cups heavy cream
2½ tablespoons sugar

1. MAKE THE CAKE: Preheat the oven to 350°. Line the bottom of three 8-inch round cake pans with parchment paper rounds and spray the parchment with nonstick cooking spray.

2. In the bowl of an electric standing mixer fitted with the paddle attachment, combine the flour, sugar, baking powder and salt and mix at low speed. Mix in the softened butter, coconut milk, water and vanilla extract until smoothly combined. Scrape down the side of the bowl and beat the batter at high speed until very smooth, about 2 minutes.

3. In a medium bowl, using an electric mixer fitted with the whisk attachment, beat the egg whites until soft peaks form, about 2 minutes. Gently fold half of the egg whites into the batter with a rubber spatula until incorporated, then fold in the remaining whites until no streaks remain. Divide the cake batter evenly among the cake pans. Bake for about 45 minutes, until a toothpick inserted in the centers comes out clean. Cool the cakes in the pans on a rack for 15 minutes, then invert them and let cool completely, about 2 hours.

4. MEANWHILE, MAKE THE FILLING: In a medium saucepan, whisk the sugar and cornstarch. Whisk in the passion fruit nectar, egg yolks and vanilla seeds and cook over moderate heat, stirring constantly, until thick, 6 minutes. Remove from the heat; whisk in the butter, 1 tablespoon at a time, until incorporated. Scrape the filling into a glass bowl, press a sheet of plastic wrap on the surface and refrigerate until chilled, about 2 hours.

5. Using a serrated knife, cut each cake in half horizontally to create 6 layers. Set one layer on a cake plate. Spread with 6 tablespoons of the filling. Repeat with the remaining 5 cake layers and filling, ending with a layer of cake. Refrigerate until firm, 1 hour.

6. MEANWHILE, MAKE THE TOPPING: Spread the coconut on a large rimmed baking sheet. Bake for 5 minutes, stirring once, until lightly toasted. Let cool. In a large bowl, using an electric mixer, beat the cream with the sugar until medium-firm peaks form.

7. Frost the top and side of the cake with the whipped cream and coat with the coconut. Refrigerate for 1 hour before serving.
—Cynthia Wong

SIX-LAYER COCONUT CAKE
WITH PASSION FRUIT FILLING

cakes, cookies & more

Classic Carrot Cake with Fluffy Cream Cheese Frosting

ACTIVE: 40 MIN; TOTAL: 3 HR 30 MIN

8 TO 10 SERVINGS ● ● ●

Moist and not too sweet, this is the ultimate version of the 1970s favorite.

CAKE

- 1 cup pecans (4 ounces)
- 2 cups all-purpose flour
- 2 teaspoons baking powder
- 2 teaspoons baking soda
- 1 teaspoon cinnamon
- 1 teaspoon salt
- 1 cup vegetable oil
- ½ cup buttermilk
- 1½ teaspoons pure vanilla extract
- 4 large eggs
- 2 cups sugar
- 1 pound carrots, peeled and coarsely shredded

---

taste test: milk chocolate

Fruity, balanced, creamy and smooth, these milk-chocolate bars rated among the best:

365 Organic Well-rounded and fruity. $2 for 3 oz; wholefoodsmarket.com.

Dagoba Organic Milk Chocolate Balanced, with a lovely melt-in-the-mouth quality. $3 for 2 oz; dagobachocolate.com.

Hershey's Symphony Creamy and on the sweet side; a great value. $1.60 for 4.25 oz; hersheys.com.

Lindt Classic Recipe Smooth, with a delicate, caramel-like sweetness. $3.50 for 4.4 oz; lindt.com.

Valrhona Cao Grande Lait Made with organic beans. $3.80 for 3.5 oz; valrhona.com.

FROSTING

- 2 sticks unsalted butter, softened
- 1 pound cream cheese, softened
- 1 tablespoon pure vanilla extract
- 2 cups confectioners' sugar

1. Preheat the oven to 325°. Butter two 9-inch round cake pans; line the bottoms with parchment paper. Butter the parchment paper and flour the pans, tapping out the excess.

2. MAKE THE CAKE: Spread the pecans on a baking sheet and toast for 8 minutes, until fragrant. Cool and finely chop the pecans.

3. In a medium bowl, whisk together the flour, baking powder, baking soda, cinnamon and salt. In a small bowl, whisk the oil, buttermilk and vanilla. In a large bowl, using an electric mixer, beat the eggs and sugar at high speed until pale, 5 minutes. Beat in the liquid ingredients. Beat in the dry ingredients just until moistened. Stir in the carrots and pecans. Divide the batter between the pans and bake the cakes for 55 minutes to 1 hour, until springy and golden. Let the cakes cool on a rack for 30 minutes, then unmold the cakes and let cool completely.

4. MAKE THE FROSTING: In a large bowl, using an electric mixer fitted with the whisk attachment, beat the butter and cream cheese at high speed until light, about 5 minutes. Beat in the vanilla, then the confectioners' sugar; beat at low speed until incorporated. Increase the speed to high and beat until the frosting is light and fluffy, about 3 minutes.

5. Peel off the parchment paper and invert one cake layer onto a plate. Spread with a slightly rounded cup of the cream cheese frosting. Top with the second cake layer, right side up. Spread the top and side of the cake with the remaining frosting and refrigerate the cake until chilled, about 1 hour. Slice and serve. —*Jodi Elliot*

MAKE AHEAD The cream cheese–frosted carrot cake can be refrigerated for up to 1 day before serving.

Chocolate-Malt Stump de Noël

TOTAL: 1 HR 30 MIN PLUS OVERNIGHT CHILLING

16 SERVINGS ● ● ●

Matt Lewis and Renato Poliafito, co-authors of the *Baked* cookbook and owners of the bakeries of the same name in Brooklyn, New York, and Charleston, South Carolina, worked together to create this stupendous holiday dessert, a twist on the classic, elegant French *bûche de Noël* (so called because it looks like a log, or *bûche*). To make their stump, the duo roll up frosted cake strips to form an enormous round, then set the dessert on its side to look like a huge tree stump. It's much tastier than a traditional *bûche,* because the layers are made with less egg so they're less spongy. The cake is covered with a dark chocolate frosting; the filling is infused with Baked's signature flavor, malt (both malt powder and crushed malted milk balls).

- 1 cup all-purpose flour, plus more for dusting
- ¼ cup unsweetened cocoa powder, sifted
- ¼ teaspoon salt
- ¾ pound bittersweet chocolate, melted and cooled
- 2 tablespoons instant espresso powder dissolved in ¼ cup of hot water
- 1 dozen large eggs, at room temperature, separated
- 1⅓ cups sugar
- 1 tablespoon plus 1 teaspoon pure vanilla extract
- ¼ teaspoon cream of tartar
- 6 tablespoons unsalted butter, melted

Malted Buttercream and Dark Chocolate Buttercream (recipe follows)

Meringue mushrooms, candied cranberries and candied rosemary sprigs, for garnish (optional; see Note)

1. Preheat the oven to 350°. Butter two 12-by-17-inch rimmed baking sheets and line them with parchment paper, leaving a 1-inch overhang on all of the short sides. Butter the paper and dust with flour.

2. In a small bowl, whisk the 1 cup of flour with the cocoa and salt. In another small bowl, combine the chocolate and espresso. In the bowl of a standing electric mixer, combine the egg yolks with ⅔ cup of the sugar. Set the bowl over a pan of simmering water and whisk until the sugar is dissolved. Transfer the bowl to the mixer fitted with the whisk and beat at high speed until the yolks are pale and thick, about 5 minutes. Beat in the melted chocolate mixture along with the vanilla. Transfer to a large bowl.

3. Thoroughly wash and dry the mixer bowl and the whisk. Beat the egg whites with the cream of tartar on moderately high speed until soft peaks form. Gradually add the remaining ⅔ cup of sugar and continue beating at high speed until the whites are glossy, about 2 minutes longer. Whisk one-fourth of the egg whites into the cake batter, then fold in the remaining whites until no streaks remain.

4. In a small bowl, whisk the melted butter with ½ cup of the batter; fold this mixture into the batter. Working in 2 batches, sift the cocoa powder mixture over the batter and gently fold it in. Divide the batter between the prepared pans, spreading it out to fill the pans. Bake for about 18 minutes, until the cake feels springy and dry; shift the pans from top to bottom and front to back halfway through baking. Transfer the pans to racks to cool completely. Run the tip of a knife around the edges, cover with parchment paper and a baking sheet and invert; peel off the parchment on top.

5. Spread the Malted Buttercream over the cakes. Using a ruler, cut each cake precisely in half lengthwise, cutting through the paper; you should have four 6-by-17-inch strips of cake. Roll one strip into a tight coil, leaving the paper behind. Roll the 3 remaining cake strips around the coil in the same way to form a very wide, short jelly roll. Set the cake on a large plate, spiraled end up. Frost the outside of the cake with the Dark Chocolate Buttercream. Refrigerate until set, at least 8 hours. Decorate the cake with meringue mushrooms, cranberries and rosemary sprigs and serve, cutting the cake into wedges or horizontal slices.

—Matt Lewis and Renato Poliafito

NOTE Meringue mushrooms are available at 1-800-bakery.com.

MAKE AHEAD The chocolate stump cake can be refrigerated for up to 4 days. Let the cake stand at room temperature for 1 hour before serving.

MALTED BUTTERCREAM AND DARK CHOCOLATE BUTTERCREAM

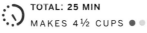

TOTAL: 25 MIN
MAKES 4½ CUPS ● ●

- 5 large egg whites, at room temperature
- 1½ cups sugar
- 1 teaspoon pure vanilla extract
- 4 sticks (1 pound) unsalted butter, at room temperature
- 4 ounces bittersweet chocolate, melted and cooled
- ¼ cup malt powder, dissolved in 2 tablespoons of hot water
- 12 malted milk balls, crushed

In the bowl of a standing electric mixer, combine the egg whites and sugar. Set the bowl over a pot of simmering water and whisk until the sugar is dissolved and the egg whites are just warm to the touch. Return the bowl to the mixer fitted with the whisk. Add the vanilla and beat the egg whites at high speed until firm and glossy, about 5 minutes. With the machine on, whisk in the butter a few tablespoons at a time. If the mixture begins to look curdled, continue to beat until smooth before adding more butter. Transfer 1½ cups of the buttercream to a bowl and whisk in the melted chocolate. Beat the dissolved malt powder into the remaining buttercream, then beat in the milk balls.

—ML and RP

MAKE AHEAD The buttercreams can be refrigerated, covered, overnight. Let return to room temperature before using.

Chocolate–Red Wine Cake

ACTIVE: 25 MIN; TOTAL: 1 HR 45 MIN
MAKES 1 BUNDT CAKE ● ● ●

A recipe in Anne Willan's 2001 *Cooking with Wine* inspired this fluffy, not-too-sweet cake, which has just enough wine in the batter to give it a slight boozy flavor.

- 2 cups all-purpose flour
- ¾ cup unsweetened cocoa powder (not Dutch process)
- 1¼ teaspoons baking soda
- ½ teaspoon salt
- 2 sticks unsalted butter, softened
- 1¾ cups granulated sugar
- 2 large eggs
- 1 teaspoon pure vanilla extract
- 1¼ cups dry red wine
- Confectioners' sugar, for dusting
- Whipped cream, for serving

1. Preheat the oven to 350°. Butter and flour a 12-cup Bundt pan. In a bowl, whisk the flour, cocoa powder, baking soda and salt.

2. In a large bowl, using a handheld electric mixer, beat the butter with the granulated sugar at medium-high speed until fluffy, 4 minutes. Add the eggs one at a time and beat until incorporated. Add the vanilla and beat for 2 minutes. Working in 2 batches, alternately fold in the dry ingredients and the wine, until just incorporated.

3. Scrape the batter into the prepared pan and bake for 45 minutes, until a toothpick inserted in the center comes out clean. Let the cake cool in the pan for 10 minutes, then turn it out onto a rack; let cool completely. Dust with confectioners' sugar and serve with whipped cream.

—Kristin Donnelly

cakes, cookies & more

Warm Double-Chocolate Brownie Cakes

ACTIVE: 20 MIN; TOTAL: 1 HR 15 MIN
MAKES 8 BROWNIE CAKES ● ●

Brownie meets cake in this dessert from Emily Luchetti, a cookbook author and the pastry chef at San Francisco's Farallon.

- 1 stick plus 2 tablespoons unsalted butter
- 5 ounces milk chocolate, chopped
- 3 tablespoons cake flour
- ⅓ cup all-purpose flour
- ½ cup unsweetened cocoa powder
- ½ teaspoon salt
- 2 large eggs
- ¾ cup sugar
- ½ teaspoon pure vanilla extract

Vanilla ice cream, for serving (optional)

1. Preheat the oven to 350°. Butter and flour 8 cups in a standard-size muffin pan. In a small saucepan, melt the butter. Add one-fifth of the milk chocolate and whisk until melted. Let cool slightly.

2. In a small bowl, whisk the cake flour with the all-purpose flour, unsweetened cocoa powder and salt. In a large bowl, using a handheld electric mixer, beat the eggs with the sugar at medium speed until pale and thick, about 5 minutes. Beat in the vanilla extract. Beat in the melted chocolate mixture and the dry ingredients in 3 additions, scraping down the bowl occasionally with a spatula. Stir in the remaining chopped chocolate.

3. Spoon the batter into the muffin cups and bake for about 22 minutes, until the cakes are risen and springy. Let the cakes cool in the muffin pan for 15 minutes, then turn them out onto a wire rack and let cool for 15 minutes longer. Serve warm, with ice cream. —*Emily Luchetti*

MAKE AHEAD The cooled brownie cakes can be stored in an airtight container at room temperature for up to 2 days. Rewarm before serving.

Warm Chocolate Cakes with Mascarpone Cream

TOTAL: 30 MIN
6 SERVINGS ● ●

- 8 ounces bittersweet chocolate, chopped, plus shavings for garnish (optional)
- 1½ sticks (6 ounces) unsalted butter
- 3 large eggs, plus 3 large egg yolks, at room temperature
- ½ cup sugar
- ¼ cup cake flour
- ½ cup heavy cream
- ½ vanilla bean, split and seeds scraped
- 2 tablespoons light brown sugar
- ½ teaspoon finely grated lemon zest
- 1 cup mascarpone (8 ounces)
- 1 teaspoon fresh lemon juice

About ½ cup brandied cherries or kirsch-soaked sour cherries

1. Preheat the oven to 375°. Coat six 6-ounce ramekins with butter and dust lightly with flour. Set the ramekins on a sturdy baking sheet. In a microwave-safe bowl, melt the chocolate with the butter; let cool.

2. In the bowl of a standing electric mixer fitted with the whisk, beat the eggs, yolks and sugar on high speed until pale and fluffy, about 4 minutes. Using a rubber spatula, gently fold in the chocolate, then fold in the cake flour just until no streaks remain.

3. Spoon the batter into the prepared ramekins and bake for 15 minutes, until the cakes have risen, the tops are dry and the centers are slightly jiggly. Let stand for 5 minutes.

4. In a bowl, beat the cream with the vanilla seeds, brown sugar and lemon zest until soft peaks form. Add the mascarpone and lemon juice and beat until blended.

5. Run the tip of a small knife around each cake to loosen it, then unmold onto plates. Spoon the mascarpone cream onto the cakes and garnish with the brandied cherries and chocolate shavings.
—*Hosea Rosenberg*

Milk-Chocolate-Frosted Layer Cake

ACTIVE: 45 MIN; TOTAL: 3 HR
MAKES ONE 9-INCH SQUARE LAYER CAKE ● ● ●

- 1¼ cups cake flour
- ¼ cup unsweetened cocoa powder
- ½ teaspoon baking powder
- 2 sticks unsalted butter
- ½ cup whole milk
- 6 large eggs, separated
- 1 cup sugar

Pinch of salt

- 1½ cups heavy cream
- 1½ pounds milk chocolate, finely chopped

Shaved milk chocolate, for garnish (optional)

1. Preheat the oven to 325°. Butter and flour two 9-inch square cake pans.

2. In a bowl, whisk the flour, cocoa and baking powder. In a saucepan, melt the butter in the milk over low heat. Transfer to a bowl and let cool slightly. Whisk in the egg yolks and ½ cup of the sugar. Add the dry ingredients and whisk until smooth.

3. In a bowl, beat the egg whites with the salt until soft peaks form. Gradually add the remaining ½ cup sugar; beat at medium-high speed until stiff and glossy. Fold the whites into the batter until no streaks remain. Divide the batter between the pans; bake for 25 minutes, until the cakes are springy and a toothpick comes out clean. Transfer to a rack; let cool completely.

4. Meanwhile, in a saucepan, bring the cream to a simmer. Put the chocolate in a heatproof bowl and pour the cream on top. Let stand for 3 minutes, then whisk until smooth. Let stand, stirring occasionally, until thick enough to spread, 1 hour.

5. Invert a cake layer onto a plate. Spread with 1 cup frosting. Top with the second layer; spread the remaining frosting over the top and sides. Let stand 30 minutes, cut into squares and garnish with chocolate shavings. —*Karina Gowing*

MILK-CHOCOLATE-FROSTED LAYER CAKE

cakes, cookies & more

Chocolate Soufflés

TOTAL: 30 MIN
6 SERVINGS ● ●

Chef and cookbook author Curtis Stone makes his soufflés with melted chocolate in addition to the usual cocoa powder, resulting in a deep, rich flavor. Since he uses just a tiny bit of butter and six egg whites, the soufflés are also delightfully light and fluffy.

- 1 tablespoon unsalted butter, softened
- ⅓ cup granulated sugar, plus more for coating the ramekins
- 4 ounces bittersweet chocolate, coarsely chopped
- ½ cup cold water
- ⅓ cup unsweetened cocoa powder
- 6 large egg whites, at room temperature

Confectioners' sugar, for dusting

1. Preheat the oven to 350°. Butter six 1-cup ramekins and coat with granulated sugar, tapping out the excess. Place the ramekins on a sturdy baking sheet.

2. In a large bowl set over a pan of simmering water, melt the chocolate. Off the heat, whisk in the water and cocoa until smooth. In another bowl, using a handheld electric mixer, beat the egg whites at medium-high speed until soft peaks form. Gradually beat in the ⅓ cup of granulated sugar and beat at high speed until firm and glossy, 1 minute. Fold one-fourth of the beaten egg whites into the chocolate mixture, then fold in the rest until no streaks of white remain.

3. Spoon the soufflé mixture into the ramekins and smooth the tops. Run the tip of your thumb around the inside rim of each ramekin to clean off any spills and to help the soufflés rise evenly.

4. Bake for 16 minutes, until very puffy and set around the edges. Dust with confectioners' sugar and serve. —*Curtis Stone*

MAKE AHEAD The recipe can be prepared through Step 3 and kept at room temperature for 1 hour before baking.

Chocolate Lava Cakes with Strawberries

ACTIVE: 25 MIN; TOTAL: 1 HR
10 SERVINGS ●

Atlanta chef Chris Yeo doesn't take credit for inventing this dessert—these individual cakes with molten centers appear on almost every restaurant menu in America. But his version is especially chocolaty, and made even better by the scoop of strawberry ice cream on top.

- 2 sticks (½ pound) unsalted butter, plus more for coating
- ¾ cup sugar, plus more for coating
- ¾ pound semisweet chocolate, chopped
- 6 large eggs
- ½ cup all-purpose flour

Strawberry ice cream and sliced strawberries, for serving

1. Preheat the oven to 425°. Butter ten 8-ounce ramekins and lightly coat them with sugar. Set the ramekins on a large rimmed baking sheet.

2. In a large bowl set over a saucepan of simmering water, melt the 2 sticks of butter and the semisweet chocolate until smooth, stirring a few times. Set the melted chocolate aside and keep warm; keep the saucepan of water simmering.

3. In another large bowl, whisk the eggs with the ¾ cup of sugar. Set the bowl over the simmering water and stir the eggs until warm. Remove the bowl from the heat. Using an electric mixer, beat the eggs at high speed until doubled in volume, about 5 minutes. Sift the flour over the chocolate mixture and gently fold in with a rubber spatula. Working in 2 batches, fold in the warm egg mixture.

4. Spoon the batter into the ramekins and bake for about 15 minutes, or until the cakes are set around the edges and wobbly in the centers. Remove the ramekins from the oven and let the chocolate cakes stand for 3 minutes.

5. Carefully invert the ramekins onto plates to unmold the chocolate cakes. Top each cake with a scoop of strawberry ice cream, spoon the sliced strawberries alongside and serve right away. —*Chris Yeo*

Chocolate-Hazelnut Baklava

ACTIVE: 1 HR; TOTAL: 2 HR 15 MIN
PLUS 4 HR COOLING
MAKES 24 PIECES ● ● ●

- 1 pound hazelnuts
- 12 ounces bittersweet chocolate, coarsely chopped
- 2⅔ cups sugar
- 1½ tablespoons cinnamon
- 1 pound phyllo dough
- 2 sticks unsalted butter, melted
- 2 cups water
- 1½ cups honey

1. Preheat the oven to 350°. Spread the nuts on a baking sheet and bake for 12 minutes, until the skins are blistered; let cool. Leave the oven on. Transfer the nuts to a towel and rub off the skins, then transfer to a food processor; pulse until coarsely chopped.

2. Add the chocolate, ⅔ cup of the sugar and the cinnamon to the food processor and pulse until the chocolate and nuts are finely chopped and the same size.

3. Unwrap the phyllo and cover with a sheet of plastic wrap. Generously butter a 9-by-13-inch metal baking pan. Butter and stack 8 sheets of phyllo. Trim the edges. Ease the stack into the pan. Sprinkle about 2 cups of the filling over the phyllo. Butter and stack 2 more phyllo sheets; fold them in half crosswise and place over the filling. Sprinkle on another 2 cups of the filling. Top with 2 more buttered, folded sheets and 2 cups of filling. Butter and stack 3 more phyllo sheets, fold them in half and place over the filling. Fold in the overhanging phyllo on top and brush generously with butter. Using a ruler and a sharp knife, cut the baklava (through the top and bottom) into 3-inch squares (there will be a bit left on one long side). Cut each square in half to make triangles.

4. Bake the baklava for 25 minutes, then lower the oven temperature to 300° and bake for 50 minutes longer, until golden. **5.** In a saucepan, bring the water, honey and the remaining 2 cups of sugar to a boil. Simmer over moderate heat for 10 minutes. Immediately ladle the hot syrup over the hot baklava and let stand until completely cool, at least 4 hours and preferably overnight. —*Ana Sortun*

MAKE AHEAD The baklava can be covered with foil and kept at room temperature for up to 2 days.

Warm Milk-Chocolate Croissant-Bread Pudding

ACTIVE: 15 MIN; TOTAL: 1 HR 30 MIN

12 SERVINGS ● ●

Roger Freedman, the chef at Rendezvous Bistro in Jackson Hole, Wyoming, created this indulgent recipe almost by accident: "I was making bread pudding at the Bistro and ran out of bread. I happened to have day-old croissants on the shelf, so I thought I'd give them a try. It turned out the croissants added a richness that bread wouldn't have." Freedman folds the pastries into a chocolate custard mixed with bits of chopped milk chocolate, then bakes everything in one big dish.

- 3 cups whole milk
- ½ vanilla bean, split and seeds scraped
- ¼ teaspoon salt
- ¾ pound milk chocolate, cut into ½-inch pieces
- 6 large eggs
- 6 large croissants (about 1 pound), cut into 1-inch pieces

Vanilla or coffee ice cream, for serving (optional)

1. Preheat the oven to 350°. In a medium saucepan, combine the whole milk with the vanilla bean and seeds and the salt and bring to a simmer. Cover and let the milk stand off the heat for 15 minutes. Discard the vanilla bean. Add half of the chopped milk chocolate to the warm milk and whisk until smooth. Let the milk and chocolate mixture cool for 15 minutes. Whisk in the eggs.

2. In a 9-by-13-inch baking dish, toss the croissant pieces with the remaining chopped milk chocolate. Pour the chocolate custard over the croissant pieces; press lightly to submerge them in the custard. Bake for 30 minutes, until the bread pudding is risen and set. Let cool slightly, then cut the chocolate bread pudding into squares and serve warm, with ice cream. —*Roger Freedman*

MAKE AHEAD The Warm Milk-Chocolate Croissant-Bread Pudding can be refrigerated overnight. Rewarm before serving.

Caramel-Pecan Bars

ACTIVE: 30 MIN; TOTAL: 2 HR 30 MIN

MAKES 16 BARS ● ● ●

These delightful nut bars, inspired by a recipe from Boston chef Ken Oringer's mother-in-law, are both gooey and crisp. Oringer sometimes adds a pinch of curry powder to the caramel because, he says, "I like for people to bite into these and wonder what the spice is. I love that element of surprise."

CRUST

- 2¼ cups all-purpose flour
- ½ cup granulated sugar
- ¾ teaspoon salt
- 1½ sticks cold unsalted butter, cut into cubes
- ¼ cup ice water
- 1 tablespoon distilled white vinegar

TOPPING

- 1½ sticks unsalted butter
- 1¼ cups light brown sugar
- ½ cup honey
- ½ teaspoon salt
- ¼ teaspoon curry powder (optional)
- 1 cup heavy cream
- 1 pound pecan halves

1. MAKE THE CRUST: In a food processor, pulse the flour with the granulated sugar and salt. Add the butter and process until the mixture resembles coarse meal. Sprinkle on the ice water and vinegar and process until the crumbs are evenly moistened. Turn the crumbs out onto a sheet of wax paper and knead just until the dough comes together. Pat the dough into a disk, wrap in plastic and refrigerate until slightly chilled, about 15 minutes.

2. Preheat the oven to 375°. Line the bottom of a 9-by-13-inch metal baking pan with parchment paper. Roll out the dough between 2 sheets of wax paper to an 11-by-15-inch rectangle ¼ inch thick. Trim the dough to a 9-by-13-inch rectangle and place it in the baking pan. Cut the remaining dough into ¾-inch-wide strips and press them up the sides of the pan to form a rim all around. Refrigerate the dough until firm, about 30 minutes.

3. Line the dough with parchment paper and fill with pie weights or dried beans. Bake for about 25 minutes, until the dough is just set. Remove the parchment paper and weights and bake the crust for about 12 minutes longer, until lightly golden and set. Let cool.

4. MAKE THE TOPPING: In a large saucepan, combine the butter, brown sugar, honey and salt and cook over moderate heat, stirring, until foamy and slightly thickened, about 10 minutes. Add the curry powder (if using) and cream and cook, stirring occasionally, until a candy thermometer inserted in the caramel registers 240° (soft ball stage), about 10 minutes longer. Add the pecans and cook for 2 minutes longer. Pour the filling over the crust, spreading it evenly. Bake for 15 minutes, until the crust is golden and the topping is bubbling. Let cool completely. Slide the parchment onto a cutting board. Cut into bars and serve. —*Ken Oringer*

MAKE AHEAD The bars can be kept at room temperature for up to 1 week.

cakes, cookies & more

Milk-Chocolate-Chip Cookies

ACTIVE: 30 MIN; TOTAL: 2 HR

MAKES 6 DOZEN COOKIES ● ●

- 2½ sticks unsalted butter, softened
- 1½ cups light brown sugar
- 1 cup plus 2 tablespoons granulated sugar
- 3 large eggs
- 1½ teaspoons pure vanilla extract
- 3 cups all-purpose flour
- 1½ teaspoons baking soda
- ½ teaspoon salt
- 1 pound milk-chocolate chips

1. In the bowl of a standing electric mixer fitted with the paddle, beat the butter, brown sugar, granulated sugar, eggs and vanilla at medium speed until light and fluffy, about 5 minutes. In a medium bowl, whisk the flour with the baking soda and salt. Add the dry ingredients to the mixer and beat at low speed until incorporated, scraping down the bowl occasionally. Stir in the chocolate chips. Cover and refrigerate the dough until chilled, about 1 hour.
2. Preheat the oven to 350° and line 2 large baking sheets with parchment paper. Scoop up 2-tablespoon-size clumps of the cookie dough and roll them into balls. Place the balls on the baking sheets about 3 inches apart (the cookies will spread quite a bit). Bake in the lower and middle thirds of the oven for about 17 minutes, until the cookies are lightly browned around the edges but still very soft in the centers; shift the pans from top to bottom and front to back halfway through baking. Slide the parchment onto racks and let the cookies cool. (Run the baking sheets under cold water between batches.) Repeat with the remaining dough. Serve the cookies warm or at room temperature. —*Tim Love*

MAKE AHEAD The cookies can be stored in an airtight container for up to 3 days.

Milk-Chocolate Cookies with Malted Cream

photo, page 314

ACTIVE: 30 MIN; TOTAL: 1 HR 30 MIN

MAKES ABOUT 30 COOKIES ● ● ●

COOKIES

- 1½ sticks unsalted butter, softened
- ½ cup light brown sugar
- ½ cup granulated sugar
- 6 ounces milk chocolate, melted and cooled slightly
- 1 tablespoon pure vanilla extract
- 1¾ cups all-purpose flour
- 2 tablespoons unsweetened cocoa
- 1 teaspoon baking soda
- ½ teaspoon salt

FILLING

- 1 stick unsalted butter, softened
- ½ cup chocolate malt powder, such as Ovaltine
- ½ teaspoon pure vanilla extract
- 2 cups confectioners' sugar

1. Preheat the oven to 350°. Line 2 baking sheets with parchment paper.
2. MAKE THE COOKIES: In a large bowl, using an electric mixer, beat the butter with the brown sugar and granulated sugar until smooth. Add the melted chocolate and vanilla and beat until smooth. In a small bowl, whisk the flour with the cocoa powder, baking soda and salt. Add the dry ingredients to the bowl and beat at low speed just until incorporated. Roll the dough between 2 sheets of parchment paper to a scant ¼-inch thickness and refrigerate until firm, about 15 minutes.
3. Using a 2-inch round cookie cutter, stamp out as many rounds as possible and transfer to the baking sheets, 1 inch apart. Gather the scraps and chill, with the cut-out rounds, for 10 minutes. Reroll the scraps and stamp out more rounds.
4. Bake the cookies in the lower and middle thirds of the oven for about 10 minutes, until dry and set; shift the pans halfway through baking. Transfer the cookies to a rack and let cool completely.

5. MAKE THE FILLING: In a bowl, using an electric mixer, beat the butter with the malt powder at medium speed until light, 3 minutes. Add the vanilla and confectioners' sugar and beat at low speed just until combined. Transfer the filling to a pastry bag fitted with a ½-inch plain tip. Arrange half of the cookies on a work surface, bottom side up, and pipe a 1-inch mound of filling onto each. Sandwich with the remaining cookies and serve. —*Matthew Rice*

Milk-Chocolate Tart with Pretzel Crust

ACTIVE: 45 MIN; TOTAL: 2 HR 45 MIN

PLUS 4 HR CHILLING

8 SERVINGS ● ● ●

CRUST

- 1 stick unsalted butter, softened
- 1¼ cups coarsely crushed thin pretzels (3½ ounces)
- ¾ cup confectioners' sugar
- ½ cup all-purpose flour
- 1 large egg
- 2 ounces bittersweet chocolate, melted

FILLING

- 1½ cups heavy cream
- ¾ pound milk chocolate, chopped

Maldon sea salt, crushed pretzels and crème fraîche, for serving

1. MAKE THE CRUST: In a mixer fitted with the paddle, beat the butter with ¾ cup of the pretzels and the confectioners' sugar at low speed until creamy. Beat in the flour and egg. Add the remaining ½ cup of pretzels, leaving some pieces intact. Flatten the dough between sheets of plastic wrap; refrigerate until chilled, 30 minutes.
2. Preheat the oven to 350°. Roll out the dough between the sheets of plastic wrap to a 12-inch round. Peel off the top sheet and invert the dough over a 10-inch fluted tart pan with a removable bottom. Press the dough into the corners and patch any tears. Trim the overhanging dough and refrigerate the shell for 30 minutes or until firm.

MILK-CHOCOLATE TART WITH PRETZEL CRUST

GIANDUJA TART WITH CHOCOLATE-COOKIE CRUST

3. Line the pastry shell with parchment paper and fill with pie weights. Bake for about 30 minutes, until nearly set. Remove the parchment and weights and bake for 10 to 15 minutes longer, until the tart shell is firm; cover the edge with foil if it darkens too much. Let the shell cool completely. Brush the melted chocolate over the bottom and up the side of the tart shell and refrigerate for 10 minutes, until set.

4. MEANWHILE, MAKE THE FILLING: In a medium saucepan, bring the cream to a simmer. Off the heat, add the milk chocolate and let stand for 5 minutes. Whisk until smooth. Transfer the filling to a bowl and let cool to room temperature, about 1 hour.

5. Pour the filling into the shell and refrigerate until set, at least 4 hours. Sprinkle lightly with sea salt and crushed pretzels. Cut into wedges, top with crème fraîche and serve. —*Colleen Grapes*

Gianduja Tart with Chocolate-Cookie Crust

ACTIVE: 30 MIN; TOTAL: 1 HR 20 MIN
PLUS 6 HR CHILLING

MAKES ONE 8-INCH TART ●

- 1¾ teaspoons unflavored gelatin
- 3 cups heavy cream
- 7 tablespoons sugar
- ½ pound gianduja chocolate, chopped (see Note)

Pinch of salt

- 8 ounces chocolate wafer cookies, broken into pieces
- 1 stick unsalted butter, melted
- ¾ cups blanched whole hazelnuts

1. In a bowl, sprinkle the gelatin over 1 tablespoon of water; let stand 5 minutes. In a saucepan, simmer the cream with 6 tablespoons of the sugar. Off the heat, stir in the gelatin until dissolved. Add the gianduja and salt; let stand until melted, 3 minutes.

Whisk until smooth. Scrape into a glass bowl, press plastic wrap onto the surface and let stand until cool, 1 hour.

2. Meanwhile, spray an 8-inch springform pan with nonstick cooking spray. In a food processor, pulse the cookies until fine; transfer to a bowl. Add the butter and the remaining tablespoon of sugar; stir to coat. Press the crumbs over the bottom of the pan; refrigerate until firm, 30 minutes.

3. Preheat the oven to 325°. Spread the hazelnuts on a baking sheet and toast for 12 minutes, until fragrant. Let cool.

4. Pour the filling over the crust; scatter the hazelnuts over the surface. Refrigerate, uncovered, until firm, about 6 hours.

5. Run a small hot knife around the edge of the tart. Unmold the tart, cut into wedges and serve. —*Tiffany MacIsaac*

NOTE Look for gianduja bars at specialty food shops.

cakes, cookies & more

Ganache-Stuffed Chocolate-Chip Cookies

ACTIVE: 45 MIN; TOTAL: 2 HR

MAKES 18 STUFFED COOKIES ● ● ●

COOKIES

- 1 cup walnuts
- 1 cup plus 2 tablespoons all-purpose flour
- 1 teaspoon baking soda
- ½ teaspoon salt
- 1 stick unsalted butter, at room temperature
- ½ cup packed light brown sugar
- ¼ cup granulated sugar
- ½ teaspoon pure vanilla extract
- 1 large egg
- 1 cup bittersweet chocolate chips

GANACHE

- 4 ounces bittersweet chocolate, chopped
- 5 tablespoons heavy cream
- 2½ tablespoons light corn syrup
- 2 tablespoons crème fraîche

1. MAKE THE COOKIES: Preheat the oven to 375°. Spread the nuts in a pie plate and toast for 8 minutes; let cool, then chop.

2. In a bowl, mix the flour, baking soda and salt. In the bowl of a mixer fitted with the paddle, cream the butter with the sugars and vanilla at medium speed, 1 minute. Beat in the egg. At low speed, beat in the dry ingredients. Beat in the walnuts and chocolate chips. Spoon level tablespoons of the dough onto 2 ungreased baking sheets, 2 inches apart. Refrigerate for 30 minutes.

3. MAKE THE GANACHE: Put the chocolate in a bowl. In a saucepan, bring the cream and corn syrup to a boil; pour over the chocolate and let stand for 1 minute. Whisk until smooth. Whisk in the crème fraîche. Refrigerate the ganache, stirring occasionally, until thick and spreadable, 1 hour.

4. Bake the cookies for 12 minutes, until golden; let cool on sheets for 2 minutes, then transfer to a rack to cool completely.

5. Sandwich the cookies with the ganache and serve. —Jessica Sullivan

Vanilla-and-Cider Panna Cottas with Spiced Ginger Cookies

ACTIVE: 30 MIN; TOTAL: 2 HR 30 MIN

PLUS 6 HR CHILLING

12 SERVINGS ● ●

- 3 cups whole milk
- 3 cups heavy cream
- ¾ cup plus 3 tablespoons sugar
- 2 plump vanilla beans, split and seeds scraped
- 3 cinnamon sticks, cracked
- 4 teaspoons powdered unflavored gelatin (from 2 envelopes)
- 3 cups apple cider

Spiced Ginger Cookies (recipe follows), for serving

1. In a large saucepan, combine the milk with the cream, ¾ cup of the sugar, the vanilla beans and seeds and cinnamon sticks and bring to a simmer. Remove from the heat, cover and let stand for 30 minutes. Strain the mixture through a fine sieve and return it to the saucepan.

2. In a small bowl, sprinkle 3 teaspoons of the gelatin over ¼ cup of cold water and let stand until softened, 2 minutes. Scrape the gelatin into the saucepan and whisk until dissolved. Transfer to a pitcher; pour about ½ cup into each of 12 small glasses. Refrigerate until chilled, at least 4 hours.

3. In a clean saucepan, boil the cider with the remaining 3 tablespoons of sugar until reduced to 1½ cups, about 15 minutes. Sprinkle the remaining 1 teaspoon of gelatin over 1 tablespoon of water and let stand until softened, about 2 minutes. Whisk the gelatin into the cider mixture until dissolved. Transfer the mixture to a pitcher and let cool completely (but don't let the gelatin set), about 30 minutes. Gently pour 2 tablespoons of the cider into each panna cotta over an inverted spoon; refrigerate until set, at least 2 hours. Serve with the ginger cookies. —Shawn McClain

MAKE AHEAD The panna cottas can be covered tightly in plastic wrap and refrigerated for up to 2 days.

SPICED GINGER COOKIES

ACTIVE: 30 MIN; TOTAL: 2 HR

MAKES 4 DOZEN COOKIES ● ●

Chicago chef Shawn McClain got the recipe for these crisp, spicy cookies from his former pastry chef, Elissa Narrow.

- 2¼ cups all-purpose flour
- 2 teaspoons baking soda
- 2 teaspoons ground ginger
- 1 teaspoon cinnamon
- ½ teaspoon salt
- ½ teaspoon ground allspice
- ¼ teaspoon freshly ground white pepper
- 2 sticks unsalted butter, softened
- ¼ cup granulated sugar
- ¼ cup light brown sugar
- 1 large egg
- ⅓ cup honey
- 1 cup turbinado or coarse sugar

1. In a medium bowl, whisk the flour with the baking soda, ginger, cinnamon, salt, allspice and white pepper. In a large bowl, using an electric mixer, beat the butter until creamy. Add the granulated sugar and the light brown sugar and beat at medium-high speed until light and fluffy, about 2 minutes. Beat in the egg and honey. Beat in the dry ingredients at low speed until combined. Transfer the dough to a sheet of plastic wrap, flatten into a disk and refrigerate until firm, about 30 minutes.

2. Preheat the oven to 350°. Line 3 baking sheets with parchment paper. Spread the turbinado sugar on a plate. Roll the dough into 1-inch balls and roll generously in the turbinado sugar. Transfer to the baking sheets about 1½ inches apart. Using a flat-bottomed glass, press each cookie to a 1½-inch round. Working with one baking sheet at a time, bake the cookies for 15 to 16 minutes, until they are deeply golden and the tops are cracked. Cool the baking sheets on wire racks. —Elissa Narrow

MAKE AHEAD The Spiced Ginger Cookies can be stored in an airtight container at room temperature for up to 3 days.

GANACHE-STUFFED CHOCOLATE-CHIP COOKIES

VANILLA-AND-CIDER PANNA COTTAS
WITH SPICED GINGER COOKIES

Crispy Chocolate Cookies

TOTAL: 45 MIN PLUS 2 HR CHILLING
MAKES 2½ DOZEN COOKIES ● ● ○

1½ cups all-purpose flour
½ cup granulated sugar
½ cup confectioners' sugar
¼ cup cornmeal
¼ cup unsweetened cocoa powder
½ teaspoon salt
¼ teaspoon baking soda
2 sticks cold unsalted butter,
    cut into ½-inch dice
1 teaspoon pure vanilla extract
1 ounce unsweetened chocolate,
    melted and cooled slightly

1. In a food processor, pulse the flour with both sugars and the cornmeal, cocoa, salt and baking soda. Add the butter and vanilla; pulse until the mixture resembles moist sand. Add the melted chocolate and pulse just until the dough comes together. Pat the dough into 2 disks, wrap in plastic and refrigerate until chilled, about 2 hours.

**BEST GIFT
COOKIES**

Caramel-Pecan
Bars, p. 329

Milk-Chocolate Cookies
with Malted Cream, p. 330

Chocolate-Gingerbread
Cookies, right

Jam-Filled Mezzaluna
Cookies, p. 338

Salted Shortbread
Cookies, p. 339

Chocolate Chip–Pretzel
Bars, p. 339

---

2. Preheat the oven to 325°. Line 2 large baking sheets with parchment paper. Roll out each disk of dough about ¼ inch thick between 2 sheets of parchment paper. Using a 2½-inch round cookie cutter, stamp out cookies as close together as possible. Transfer the rounds to the prepared baking sheets, placing them about 1 inch apart. Gather and reroll the scraps and stamp out more cookies.
3. Bake the cookies for about 18 minutes, until the tops are firm. Let cool completely on the baking sheets before serving.
—*Marilynn Brass and Sheila Brass*

No-Bake Chocolate–Peanut Butter Cookies

 TOTAL: 30 MIN
MAKES 18 COOKIES ● ○

These crumbly, ultra-peanutty cookies from F&W's Grace Parisi require only four ingredients: puffed-corn cereal, peanut butter cups, creamy peanut butter and chocolate sprinkles.

4 cups sweetened puffed-
    corn cereal, such as Corn Pops
    (4 ounces)
4 large peanut butter cups
    (3 ounces)
½ cup creamy peanut butter
About ¾ cup chocolate sprinkles

1. In a food processor, grind 3 cups of the corn cereal to a powder. Add the peanut butter cups and peanut butter and process until the mixture is glossy and comes together, about 2 minutes. Add the remaining 1 cup of corn cereal and process until the cereal is very finely chopped and the mixture just holds together; you should still see small flecks of cereal.
2. Roll the mixture into a 9-inch log and wrap in plastic. Roll the log back and forth until smooth. Unwrap the log and spread the chocolate sprinkles on the plastic wrap. Roll the log in the sprinkles, pressing to help them adhere. Wrap and refrigerate for 15 minutes.

3. Cut the log into 18 pieces and roll the edges in any leftover sprinkles. Serve.
—*Grace Parisi*
MAKE AHEAD The sliced cookies can be refrigerated for up to 5 days.

Chocolate-Gingerbread Cookies

ACTIVE: 1 HR; TOTAL: 5 HR
MAKES ABOUT 40 LARGE COOKIES
OR 20 SANDWICH COOKIES ● ● ○

These Christmas cookies combine chocolate with spicy gingerbread. "I was tired of basic gingerbread," says Matt Lewis, co-owner of Baked in Brooklyn, New York, and Charleston, South Carolina. "And my connection to chocolate is really deep." An added benefit of these cookies: The supple dough is easy to work with, and the scraps can be rerolled and cut.

COOKIES

3¼ cups all-purpose flour,
    plus more for dusting
⅓ cup unsweetened cocoa powder
1 tablespoon ground ginger
2 teaspoons cinnamon
1 teaspoon ground cloves
1 tablespoon baking soda
½ teaspoon baking powder
1 teaspoon salt
5 tablespoons unsalted butter,
    softened
⅓ cup solid vegetable shortening
½ cup packed dark brown sugar
1 large egg, at room temperature
½ cup molasses
2 ounces bittersweet chocolate,
    melted and cooled

ICING

1¼ cups confectioners' sugar
1 large egg white
1 teaspoon fresh lemon juice
Mascarpone Filling (recipe follows),
    optional

1. **MAKE THE COOKIES:** In a medium bowl, whisk the 3¼ cups of flour with the cocoa powder, ginger, cinnamon, cloves, baking

soda, baking powder and salt. In the bowl of a standing electric mixer fitted with the paddle, beat the softened butter with the vegetable shortening at medium speed until the mixture is smooth, about 30 seconds. Add the brown sugar and beat until fluffy, about 2 minutes.

2. Add the egg to the butter mixture and beat until incorporated. Beat in the molasses and then the melted bittersweet chocolate. Add the flour mixture in 3 batches, beating between additions. Divide the dough into 3 equal parts. Shape each part into a disk, then wrap each one in plastic wrap and refrigerate the cookie dough until chilled, about 2 hours.

3. Preheat the oven to 350°. Line 2 large baking sheets with parchment paper. On a lightly floured work surface, roll out 1 disk of dough ¼ inch thick. Using 4- to 5-inch cookie cutters, cut the dough into shapes and transfer to the prepared baking sheets. Reroll the dough scraps and cut out more cookies.

4. Bake the cookies for about 7 minutes, rotating the pans halfway through baking until the tops are dry. Let the cookies cool on the pans for 5 minutes, then transfer to wire racks to cool completely. Repeat the process with the remaining dough.

5. MAKE THE ICING: In a medium bowl, combine the confectioners' sugar with the egg white and lemon juice and whisk until the icing is completely smooth.

6. Scrape the Mascarpone Filling into a piping bag fitted with a medium tip. Turn half of the gingerbread cookies flat side up and pipe a thin layer of filling over the cookies. Top with the remaining cookies, flat side down.

7. Scrape the icing into a piping bag fitted with a very small tip. Decorate the cookies as desired. Let stand until the icing dries, about 30 minutes.
—Matt Lewis and Renato Poliafito

MAKE AHEAD The cookies can be kept in an airtight container for up to 5 days.

MASCARPONE FILLING
ACTIVE: 10 MIN; TOTAL: 2 HR
MAKES ABOUT 2 CUPS ● ●

This recipe turns Chocolate-Gingerbread Cookies into a deluxe sandwich cookie. Because the cookies aren't too sweet, the creamy, sugary mascarpone mixture complements them well.

- 1 **stick unsalted butter, softened**
- One 8-ounce container mascarpone **cheese, softened**
- 3 **cups confectioners' sugar, sifted**
- 1 **teaspoon pure vanilla extract**

In a bowl, beat the butter until smooth. Beat in the mascarpone cheese until combined. Add the sugar and vanilla and beat until smooth. Refrigerate the filling until it is slightly firm, about 2 hours.
—ML and RP

MAKE AHEAD The filling can be refrigerated for up to 1 day; let soften slightly at room temperature before using.

Chocolate Macarons
ACTIVE: 40 MIN; TOTAL: 1 HR 30 MIN
MAKES 2 DOZEN MACARONS ● ● ●

- 1¼ cups confectioners' sugar
- 1⅓ cups almond flour
  (see Note)
- 2½ tablespoons unsweetened
  Dutch-process cocoa powder
- 5 large egg whites,
  at room temperature
- ⅔ cup granulated sugar
- 2 tablespoons water
- ¼ cup heavy cream
- 1 teaspoon light corn syrup
- 1½ ounces bittersweet chocolate,
  coarsely chopped

1. Preheat the oven to 400° and position racks in the upper and lower thirds. Line 2 baking sheets with parchment paper.

2. In a large, wide bowl, using a large rubber spatula or handheld electric mixer, mix the confectioners' sugar with the almond flour and cocoa powder. Add 2 of the egg whites and mix until evenly moistened.

3. In a small saucepan, combine the granulated sugar with the water and bring to a boil; using a moistened pastry brush, wash down any crystals from the side of the pan. Boil over high heat until the syrup reaches 240° on a candy thermometer.

4. In another large bowl, using clean beaters, beat the remaining 3 egg whites until soft peaks form. With the mixer at high speed, carefully drizzle the hot sugar syrup over the egg whites and beat until the meringue is firm and glossy.

5. Stir one-fourth of the meringue into the almond-cocoa mixture. Using a rubber spatula, fold in the remaining meringue. Transfer the meringue to a pastry bag fitted with a plain ½-inch tip; pipe onto the prepared baking sheets in 1½-inch mounds, spacing them about 1 inch apart. Tap the sheets and let dry at room temperature for 15 minutes.

6. Transfer the meringues to the oven and immediately turn off the heat. Bake the meringues for 5 minutes. Turn the oven on to 400° again and bake the meringues for 8 minutes, until the meringues are puffed and the tops are firm and glossy. Transfer the baking sheets to racks and let the meringues cool completely.

7. Meanwhile, in a small saucepan, combine the cream with the corn syrup and bring to a boil. Remove from the heat. Add the chocolate and let stand until melted, about 5 minutes. Whisk until smooth. Transfer the ganache to a bowl and let cool to room temperature, whisking occasionally; it will become very thick.

8. Carefully peel the meringues off of the parchment paper. Spoon the ganache into a small pastry bag fitted with a ¼-inch tip. Alternatively, snip off a corner of a sturdy resealable plastic bag. Pipe the ganache onto the flat sides of half of the meringues. Top with the remaining meringues; serve.
—François Payard

NOTE Almond flour (finely ground blanched almonds) is available at supermarkets.

cakes, cookies & more

Raspberry Macarons

ACTIVE: 30 MIN; TOTAL: 1 HR 30 MIN
MAKES 20 MACARONS ● ◦

- 1 cup confectioners' sugar
- 1 cup almond flour
  (see Note on p. 335)
- 3 large egg whites,
  at room temperature
- ½ cup granulated sugar
- 2 tablespoons water
- 2 or 3 drops red food coloring
- ½ cup seedless raspberry jam

1. Preheat the oven to 400° and position racks in the upper and lower thirds. Line 2 baking sheets with parchment paper.
2. In a large, wide bowl, using a rubber spatula or handheld electric mixer, mix the confectioners' sugar and almond flour with 1 egg white until evenly moistened.
3. In a small saucepan, combine the granulated sugar with the water and bring to a boil; using a moistened pastry brush, wash down any crystals on the side of the pan. Cook over high heat until the syrup reaches 240° on a candy thermometer.
4. In another large bowl, using clean, dry beaters, beat the remaining 2 egg whites at medium-high speed until soft peaks form. With the mixer at high speed, carefully drizzle the hot sugar syrup over the whites and beat until firm and glossy. Beat in the food coloring until the meringue is bright pink.
5. Stir one-fourth of the meringue into the almond mixture. Using a rubber spatula, fold in the remaining meringue. Transfer the meringue to a pastry bag fitted with a plain ½-inch tip; pipe onto the prepared baking sheets in 1½-inch mounds, 1 inch apart. Tap the sheets and let dry for 15 minutes.
6. Transfer the meringues to the oven and immediately turn off the heat. Bake the meringues for 5 minutes. Turn the oven on to 400° again and bake the meringues for 8 minutes, until they are puffed and the tops are firm and glossy. Transfer the baking sheets to racks and let cool completely. Peel the meringues off of the parchment paper.

7. Spoon the jam into a small pastry bag fitted with a ¼-inch tip. Alternatively, use a sturdy resealable plastic bag and snip off a corner. Pipe the jam onto the flat sides of half of the meringues. Top with the remaining meringues and serve.
—*François Payard*

Vanilla-Scented Beignets

TOTAL: 1 HR
MAKES 50 BEIGNETS ● ◦

- 1 stick plus 1 tablespoon
  unsalted butter
- 1 cup water

Pinch of salt

- 1½ cups plus 1½ teaspoons
  granulated sugar
- 1 cup all-purpose flour
- 1 teaspoon pure vanilla extract
- 5 large eggs, at room
  temperature
- 1½ quarts vegetable oil,
  for frying

Confectioners' sugar, for dusting

1. In a saucepan, combine the butter, water, salt and 1½ teaspoons of the granulated sugar; bring to a boil. Remove from the heat. Add the flour and stir with a wooden spoon until combined. Return the saucepan to high heat and cook the dough, stirring, until very smooth, 1 minute. Transfer the dough to a bowl. Using a handheld electric mixer, beat in the vanilla, then beat in the eggs, one at a time.
2. In a saucepan, heat the oil to 375°. Line a baking sheet with paper towels. Scoop 10 scant tablespoons of the dough into the oil and fry, turning, until golden and puffed, 6 minutes. Transfer the beignets to the baking sheet and poke a small hole in the side of each to release steam. Repeat with the remaining dough.
3. Pour the 1½ cups of granulated sugar into a bowl. Toss the hot beignets in the sugar; transfer to a platter. Dust with confectioners' sugar and serve.
—*Gerald Hirigoyen*

Doughnut Holes with Raspberry Jam

ACTIVE: 35 MIN; TOTAL: 3 HR
8 SERVINGS ● ◦
STARTER

- ¾ teaspoon active dry yeast
- ¼ cup plus 1 tablespoon warm water
- ½ cup all-purpose flour

DOUGH

- ¾ teaspoon active dry yeast
- 2 tablespoons milk, warmed
- 1 cup plus 2 tablespoons flour
- 1 teaspoon salt
- 3 large egg yolks
- 2 tablespoons unsalted
  butter, melted
- 3 tablespoons sugar

JAM

- 1 pint red raspberries (12 ounces)
- 1½ cups sugar, plus more for coating

Vegetable oil, for frying

1. MAKE THE STARTER: In a medium bowl, dissolve the yeast in the water. Mix in the flour. Cover with plastic and let rise in a warm place until doubled in bulk, 1 hour.
2. MAKE THE DOUGH: In a standing mixer fitted with the dough hook, dissolve the yeast in the milk. Add the flour, salt, egg yolks, butter, sugar and the starter and mix until the dough forms a ball. Scrape the dough into a bowl, cover and let rise in a warm place until doubled in bulk, 1 hour.
3. MEANWHILE, MAKE THE JAM: In a saucepan, simmer the raspberries with the 1½ cups of sugar over moderate heat until thickened, about 25 minutes. Scrape the jam into a bowl and let cool for 1 hour.
4. Line a baking sheet with parchment paper. On a floured work surface, roll out the dough ½ inch thick. Stamp out 1-inch round doughnut holes as close together as possible. Reroll the scraps and repeat. Transfer to the baking sheet and cover with a damp cloth. Let stand for 15 minutes.
5. In a pan, heat 1 inch of oil to 325°. Fry holes until golden, 2 minutes. Drain; roll in sugar. Serve hot, with jam. —*Ginevra Iverson*

cakes, cookies & more

Jam-Filled Mezzaluna Cookies

ACTIVE: 45 MIN; TOTAL: 1 HR 30 MIN
PLUS 1 HR CHILLING

MAKES 14 TO 16 COOKIES ● ● ●

- 1½ cups pastry flour, plus
  more for dusting
- 2 tablespoons granulated sugar,
  plus more for sprinkling
- 1½ sticks (12 tablespoons)
  unsalted butter, cut into
  small pieces and chilled
- 1 tablespoon pure vanilla extract
- 1 large egg white
- ½ cup seedless raspberry or
  blackberry jam
- ½ cup sliced blanched almonds

Sifted confectioners' sugar, for dusting

1. In a bowl, whisk the 1½ cups of pastry flour with the 2 tablespoons of granulated sugar. Add the butter and, using a pastry blender, your fingers or 2 dinner knives, blend the butter into the flour until the mixture resembles coarse meal. Sprinkle on the vanilla and knead gently until a dough forms. Pat the dough into a disk, wrap in plastic and refrigerate until thoroughly chilled, at least 1 hour.

2. Preheat the oven to 350°. Line 2 large baking sheets with parchment paper and refrigerate. Cut the dough into 4 pieces. Working with 1 piece at a time and leaving the rest in the refrigerator, roll out the dough ⅛ inch thick on a lightly floured work surface. Using a 4-inch round biscuit cutter, stamp out as many rounds as possible; gather and reserve the scraps.

3. Brush the edges of each round with some of the egg white. Spoon 1 rounded teaspoon of jam onto one half of each round, leaving a ¼-inch border; fold the other half over. Using the tines of a fork, press the edges together to seal. Transfer the mezzalune to the chilled baking sheets, spacing them 2 inches apart. Repeat with the remaining 3 pieces of dough and filling, then repeat with the gathered scraps. Refrigerate for at least 10 minutes.

4. Brush the mezzalune with egg white, sprinkle with granulated sugar and top with a generous sprinkling of sliced almonds. Bake in the upper and lower thirds of the oven for about 40 minutes, until golden brown, switching the pans halfway through for even baking. Transfer the cookies to a rack to cool. Dust with confectioners' sugar and serve.
—Dahlia Narvaez

MAKE AHEAD The baked mezzaluna cookies can be stored at room temperature in an airtight container for up to 2 days or wrapped tightly in plastic and frozen for up to 2 weeks.

Passion Fruit Macarons

ACTIVE: 40 MIN; TOTAL: 1 HR 30 MIN

MAKES 20 MACARONS ● ● ●

Tangy-sweet and a beautiful bright yellow, these meringue sandwich cookies known as macarons have a creamy buttercream filling made with passion fruit puree and melted white chocolate.

- 1 cup confectioners' sugar
- 1 cup almond flour
  (see Note on p. 335)
- 3 large egg whites,
  at room temperature
- ½ cup plus 3 tablespoons
  granulated sugar
- 2 tablespoons water
- 3 or 4 drops yellow food coloring
- 2 teaspoons cornstarch
- ¼ cup passion fruit puree
- 1 tablespoon heavy cream
- 1½ ounces white chocolate,
  coarsely chopped
- 3 tablespoons unsalted butter

1. Preheat the oven to 400° and position racks in the upper and lower thirds. Line 2 baking sheets with parchment paper.

2. In a large, wide bowl, using a large rubber spatula or a handheld electric mixer, mix the confectioners' sugar and the almond flour with 1 of the egg whites until evenly moistened.

3. In a small saucepan, combine the ½ cup of granulated sugar with the water; bring to a boil. Using a moistened pastry brush, wash down any crystals from the side of the pan. Boil over high heat until the syrup reaches 240° on a candy thermometer.

4. In another large bowl, using clean beaters, beat the remaining 2 egg whites at medium-high speed until soft peaks form. With the machine at high speed, carefully drizzle the hot syrup over the whites; beat until firm and glossy. Beat in the food coloring until the meringue is bright yellow.

5. Stir one-fourth of the meringue into the almond mixture. Using a rubber spatula, fold in the remaining meringue. Transfer the meringue to a pastry bag fitted with a plain ½-inch tip; pipe onto the prepared baking sheets in 1½-inch mounds, spacing them about 1 inch apart. Tap the sheets and let dry for 15 minutes.

6. Transfer the meringues to the oven and immediately turn off the heat. Bake the meringues for 5 minutes. Turn the oven on to 400° again and bake for 8 minutes, until the meringues are puffed and the tops are firm and glossy. Transfer the baking sheets to racks; let cool completely.

7. Meanwhile, in a small saucepan, whisk the remaining 3 tablespoons of granulated sugar with the cornstarch. Whisk in the passion fruit puree and cream. Whisk over moderate heat until thick, about 4 minutes. Remove from the heat; whisk in the white chocolate until melted. Let cool slightly, then whisk in the butter. Let cool completely.

8. Carefully peel the meringues off of the parchment paper. Spoon the filling into a pastry bag fitted with a ¼-inch tip. Alternatively, use a sturdy resealable plastic bag and snip off a corner. Pipe the filling onto the flat sides of half of the meringues. Top with the remaining meringues and serve.
—François Payard

MAKE AHEAD The filled Passion Fruit Macarons can be stored in an airtight container at room temperature for up to 3 days.

Salted Shortbread Cookies

ACTIVE: 10 MIN; TOTAL: 50 MIN

MAKES 8 COOKIES ● ● ●

1¼ cups all-purpose flour
1 teaspoon salt
¼ cup sugar, plus more for sprinkling
1 stick unsalted butter, softened

1. Preheat the oven to 325°. Line a large rimmed baking sheet with parchment paper. In a large bowl, combine the flour with the salt and the ¼ cup of sugar. Using your fingers, rub in the butter until the mixture has the texture of sand. Gently knead the shortbread dough with your hands just until it comes together.

2. Transfer the dough to the parchment-lined baking sheet and press it into a 7-inch round about ⅓ inch thick. Prick the round of dough all over with the tines of a fork and lightly sprinkle the top with sugar. Using the blunt side of a large knife, score the round into 8 equal wedges. Bake the shortbread for 30 minutes, until pale golden brown and just cooked through. While the shortbread is still warm, cut through the score marks with a serrated knife to separate it into 8 wedges. Serve the Salted Shortbread Cookies warm or at room temperature. —Peter Ting

MAKE AHEAD The Salted Shortbread Cookies can be stored in an airtight container at room temperature for up to 3 days.

Pecan Shortbread Cookies

ACTIVE: 25 MIN; TOTAL: 2 HR 15 MIN

MAKES ABOUT 2½ DOZEN

COOKIES ● ● ●

New York City pastry chef and cookbook author Karen DeMasco beats the dough for these buttery pecan shortbread cookies with an entire vanilla bean; the oils in the pod add deep vanilla flavor. By rolling the dough in demerara sugar before slicing and baking the cookies, she makes them extra-crispy.

¾ cup pecans, coarsely chopped
1¼ sticks (10 tablespoons) unsalted butter, at room temperature
½ cup confectioners' sugar
½ vanilla bean, split lengthwise, seeds scraped
½ teaspoon pure vanilla extract
½ teaspoon kosher salt
1½ cups all-purpose flour
3 tablespoons demerara or turbinado sugar
1 large egg yolk, lightly beaten

1. Preheat the oven to 350°. Spread the pecans on a rimmed baking sheet and toast for about 6 minutes, until lightly browned and fragrant. Let cool.

2. In the bowl of a standing mixer fitted with the paddle, beat the butter with the confectioners' sugar, vanilla bean and seeds, vanilla extract and salt at medium speed until fluffy, about 3 minutes. Add the flour in 3 batches, beating at low speed until just incorporated. Discard the vanilla bean. Stir in the pecans.

3. Transfer the dough to a work surface and roll into a 1½-inch-thick log. Wrap the log in plastic or parchment paper and refrigerate for about 1 hour, until chilled.

4. Line 2 large rimmed baking sheets with parchment paper. Spread the demerara sugar on a platter. Brush the log with the egg yolk and roll in the sugar. Slice the log into ½-inch-thick rounds. Transfer the rounds to the prepared baking sheets, spacing them 1 inch apart.

5. Bake the shortbread cookies for about 20 minutes, until the edges are golden; rotate the baking sheets from top to bottom and front to back halfway through baking. Transfer the cookies to a wire rack and let stand until cooled completely, about 30 minutes, before serving. —Karen DeMasco

MAKE AHEAD The cookie dough can be frozen for up to 1 month.

Chocolate Chip–Pretzel Bars

ACTIVE: 15 MIN; TOTAL: 45 MIN

PLUS COOLING

MAKES 2 DOZEN 2-INCH BARS ● ● ●

These salty-sweet bars from F&W's Grace Parisi were inspired by the candy, snacks and cookies you'd send to a homesick child at summer camp.

2 cups all-purpose flour
1 teaspoon baking soda
½ teaspoon salt
1½ sticks unsalted butter, softened
1 cup light brown sugar
½ cup granulated sugar
2 large eggs
2 teaspoons pure vanilla extract
One 12-ounce bag bittersweet chocolate chips
1½ cups mini pretzels, coarsely chopped
2 tablespoons chocolate sprinkles

1. Preheat the oven to 350°. Line a 9-by-13-inch metal baking pan with parchment paper, allowing the paper to overhang by a couple of inches on the two long ends of the baking pan.

2. In a medium bowl, whisk together the flour, baking soda and salt. In a large bowl, using a handheld electric mixer, beat the butter with both sugars at medium speed until light, 1 minute. Beat in the eggs and vanilla extract. At low speed, beat in the dry ingredients. Stir in the chocolate chips and chopped mini pretzels.

3. Spread the batter in the pan and top with the sprinkles. Bake for 30 minutes, until golden; the center will still be a little gooey. Transfer the pan to a rack and let cool completely.

4. Run the tip of a knife around the side of the baking pan and carefully lift the bar out, using the overhanging parchment paper. Cut into 24 squares and serve. —Grace Parisi

MAKE AHEAD The bars can be stored in an airtight container at room temperature for up to 2 weeks.

cakes, cookies & more

Pecan Ice Cream Balls with Chocolate-Fudge Sauce

TOTAL: 45 MIN PLUS 3 HR FREEZING

10 SERVINGS ● ● ●

"This is a like a compact sundae," says cookbook author Katie Lee about the vanilla ice cream that she scoops into tennis-ball-size spheres, then rolls in toasted pecans. Sweetened condensed milk makes the warm chocolate-fudge sauce that she drizzles on top marvelously rich and creamy.

2½ pints vanilla ice cream

6 ounces pecans (2 cups)

One 12-ounce bag semisweet chocolate chips, or 12 ounces semisweet chocolate cut into chunks

One 14-ounce can sweetened condensed milk

4 tablespoons unsalted butter

1 teaspoon pure vanilla extract

1. Preheat the oven to 350°. Put the ice cream in the refrigerator until just softened, about 15 minutes. Line a baking sheet with wax paper and transfer it to the freezer.

2. Meanwhile, spread the pecans on a baking sheet and toast them until fragrant and browned, 8 minutes; transfer to a food processor and let cool completely. Coarsely chop the nuts and transfer to a pie plate.

best sundae topping

To top ice cream, F&W's Melissa Rubel Jacobson recommends a mix of salty, sweet and crunchy: Combine equal parts mini chocolate chips, chocolate sprinkles and chocolate cookie crumbs with coarsely chopped chocolate-covered coffee beans and coarsely chopped chocolate-covered pretzels.

3. Using a standard ice cream scoop, scoop a ½-cup portion of ice cream onto the pecans and roll into a ball, pressing lightly to help the nuts adhere. Transfer the ice cream ball to the prepared baking sheet in the freezer. Repeat with the remaining ice cream and pecans. Freeze the ice cream balls for at least 3 hours before serving.

4. Meanwhile, in a medium saucepan, combine the chocolate chips, condensed milk and butter and cook over low heat, stirring, until the chips are completely melted and the sauce is smooth. Remove from the heat and stir in the vanilla. Transfer the sauce to a pitcher.

5. Serve the ice cream in bowls or sundae cups and drizzle with the warm sauce.
—Katie Lee

Vietnamese Coffee Sundaes with Crushed Peanut Brittle

ACTIVE: 20 MIN; TOTAL: 40 MIN

4 SERVINGS ● ●

The Vietnamese love drinking superstrong iced coffee with copious amounts of sweetened condensed milk. Boston chef and restaurateur Joanne Chang created this simple ice cream sundae as a way to enjoy the same flavors.

1 cup plus 1 tablespoon sugar

½ cup water

1 cup unsalted roasted peanuts

½ teaspoon cinnamon

1 teaspoon kosher salt

¾ cup sweetened condensed milk

2 tablespoons instant coffee mixed with 1½ teaspoons of hot water

½ cup heavy cream

2 pints vanilla ice cream

1. Lightly grease a baking sheet. In a small saucepan, combine 1 cup of the sugar with the water and bring to a boil. Cook over moderately high heat, undisturbed, until an amber caramel forms, about 12 minutes. Remove the saucepan from the heat and stir in the roasted peanuts, cinnamon

and salt until the peanuts are evenly coated. Scrape the caramel mixture onto the prepared baking sheet and spread in an even layer. Let stand until the brittle is hardened, about 20 minutes.

2. Break off 4 medium-size pieces of the peanut brittle. Place the remaining brittle in a resealable plastic bag and roll with a rolling pin to crush the brittle into small pieces.

3. In a medium bowl, whisk the sweetened condensed milk with the dissolved instant coffee. In another medium bowl, using an electric mixer, beat the heavy cream with the remaining 1 tablespoon of sugar at high speed until softly whipped.

4. Scoop the ice cream into 4 bowls and drizzle with the milky coffee. Sprinkle with the crushed peanut brittle and top with a generous dollop of whipped cream. Garnish with the reserved pieces of peanut brittle and serve the sundaes at once.
—Joanne Chang

MAKE AHEAD Large chunks of the peanut brittle can be kept in an airtight container for up to 5 days.

Silky Chocolate Mousse with Peanut Butter Crunch

ACTIVE: 45 MIN; TOTAL: 4 HR

8 SERVINGS ● ●

Any chocolate and peanut butter lover will adore this elegant dessert from pastry chef Rachel Lansang-Hidalgo, formerly of Manhattan's Aureole. Lansang-Hidalgo tops a smooth milk-chocolate mousse with a roasted-peanut cream and crunchy cornflakes mixed with peanut butter, milk chocolate and peanuts.

PEANUT CREAM

¾ teaspoon unflavored gelatin

1 tablespoon water

1⅓ cups heavy cream

½ cup salted roasted peanuts, chopped

3 ounces white chocolate, chopped

VIETNAMESE COFFEE SUNDAE WITH CRUSHED PEANUT BRITTLE

SILKY CHOCOLATE MOUSSE WITH PEANUT BUTTER CRUNCH

MOUSSE

2¾ cups heavy cream

1½ pounds milk chocolate, chopped

3½ ounces unsweetened chocolate, chopped

½ cup sugar

3 tablespoons water

9 large egg yolks

CRUNCH

½ cup creamy peanut butter

2 ounces milk chocolate, chopped

2½ cups cornflakes, lightly crushed

¼ cup salted roasted peanuts, chopped

1. MAKE THE PEANUT CREAM: In a small bowl, sprinkle the gelatin over the water and let stand until softened, about 5 minutes. In a small saucepan, bring the heavy cream to a simmer with the chopped peanuts. Let the peanut cream stand off the heat for 15 minutes. Strain the peanut cream into a medium bowl; discard the chopped peanuts. Wipe out the saucepan, add back the cream and bring to a simmer. Off the heat, whisk in the gelatin and chopped white chocolate until melted. Transfer to a bowl and refrigerate the peanut cream until it is set, about 2 hours.

2. MEANWHILE, MAKE THE MOUSSE: In a small saucepan, heat the cream until steaming. Put the milk chocolate and unsweetened chocolate in a medium bowl and add the hot cream. Let stand until melted, then whisk until smooth; let cool. In another small saucepan, combine the sugar and water and bring to a boil, stirring until the sugar is dissolved.

3. In a large bowl, using an electric mixer, beat the egg yolks at high speed until smooth. Slowly pour in the hot sugar syrup while beating at high speed; be careful not to pour the syrup directly onto the beaters. Beat until the mixture is cool, pale and thick, about 5 minutes. Using a rubber spatula, fold in the chocolate mixture until no streaks remain. Cover the mousse with plastic wrap and refrigerate until chilled, about 1½ hours.

4. MAKE THE CRUNCH: Line a medium baking sheet with wax paper. In a medium microwave-safe bowl, melt the peanut butter and chocolate at high power at 30-second intervals, stirring, until smooth. Stir in the cornflakes and peanuts and spread the crunch on the baking sheet in a ½-inch layer. Freeze until firm, about 1½ hours. Chop into small pieces.

5. Spoon the mousse into 8 glasses or bowls and top each with a scoop of the peanut cream. Sprinkle with the peanut crunch and serve.

—*Rachel Lansang-Hidalgo*

● HEALTHY ● MAKE AHEAD ● VEGETARIAN ● STAFF FAVORITE

cakes, cookies & more

Frozen Chocolate-Chip Meringata

ACTIVE: 1 HR; TOTAL: 12 HR

8 TO 10 SERVINGS ● ● ●

Meringata (Italian for "meringue cake") is an elegant yet homey frozen dessert of whipped cream sandwiched between meringue rounds. Here, the *meringata* is sliced and served with a warm chocolate-espresso sauce.

- 6 large egg whites, at room temperature
- ½ teaspoon cream of tartar
- 1½ cups granulated sugar
- ½ teaspoon pure vanilla extract
- 2¼ cups heavy cream
- ¼ cup confectioners' sugar
- 1 pound bittersweet chocolate, finely chopped
- ¼ cup hot brewed espresso

1. Preheat the oven to 225° and position racks in the lower and middle thirds. Trace an 11-inch circle on the undersides of each of 2 sheets of parchment paper. Turn the paper over onto 2 large baking sheets.

2. In the bowl of a standing electric mixer fitted with the whisk, beat the egg whites with the cream of tartar at medium speed until foamy. Increase the speed to high and beat until soft peaks form. Add the granulated sugar 1 tablespoon at a time, beating for 5 seconds between additions. Add the vanilla and beat until the whites are stiff and glossy, about 4 minutes.

3. Transfer half of the meringue to a pastry bag fitted with a ½-inch plain round tip and pipe a ring of meringue just inside each drawn circle. Spoon the remaining meringue into the circles and spread it ½ inch thick. Bake the meringues for about 1½ hours, until very pale but dry. Turn off the oven, prop the door open slightly and let the meringues cool in the oven for at least 6 hours, until dry and crisp.

4. In a bowl, using an electric mixer, beat 2 cups of the cream with the confectioners' sugar until firm. Fold in one-fourth of the chocolate. Spread the cream over 1 round, spreading it to the edge. Top with the second round, pressing it lightly. Freeze until the cream is firm, about 4 hours.

5. Meanwhile, melt the remaining chocolate in a bowl set over a pan of simmering water. Off the heat, whisk in the remaining ¼ cup of cream and the espresso.

6. Using a serrated knife, cut the frozen cake into wedges and transfer to plates. Let stand for 10 minutes. Spoon some of the sauce on each wedge and serve.
—*Rolando Beramendi*

Milk-Chocolate Pots de Crème

TOTAL: 30 MIN PLUS 2 HR CHILLING

8 SERVINGS ● ● ●

Pot de crème ("pot of cream") is a traditional French custard typically served in a pot-shaped cup. This milk-chocolate version from Philadelphia pastry chef Frank Urso is supersilky and dense.

- 10 ounces milk chocolate, finely chopped
- 3 ounces bittersweet chocolate, finely chopped
- 1 cup milk
- 1 cup heavy cream
- ¼ cup sugar
- 5 large egg yolks

Crème fraîche and chocolate shavings, for garnish

1. In a large heatproof bowl, combine the milk and bittersweet chocolates.

2. In a medium saucepan, bring the milk, heavy cream and sugar to a boil, whisking constantly until the sugar is dissolved. In a medium heatproof bowl, whisk the egg yolks. Gradually whisk in half of the hot cream. Whisk the egg-and-cream mixture into the saucepan and cook over moderate heat, stirring with a wooden spoon, until the custard coats the back of the spoon, about 4 minutes. Pour the custard over the chocolate and let stand for 2 minutes, then stir until smooth.

3. Transfer the mixture to a blender and puree until very smooth, about 1 minute. Pour the mixture into eight 4-ounce ramekins and refrigerate until chilled, 2 hours.

4. Let the *pots de crème* stand at room temperature for 15 minutes. Garnish with crème fraîche and chocolate shavings and serve. —*Frank Urso*

Chocolate-Dipped Vanilla Caramels

ACTIVE: 30 MIN; TOTAL: 1 HR 30 MIN PLUS OVERNIGHT SETTING

MAKES ABOUT 7 DOZEN CARAMELS ● ● ●

- 2 sticks unsalted butter
- 2½ cups sugar
- 1 cup light corn syrup
- 1 cup heavy cream
- 1 vanilla bean, split, seeds scraped

Coarse sea salt, crumbled

- 1 pound bittersweet chocolate, melted (optional)

1. Line a 9-by-13-inch pan with foil; spray it with vegetable oil. In a heavy saucepan, melt the butter. Add the sugar, corn syrup and cream; bring to a boil, stirring until the sugar dissolves. Add the vanilla seeds. Cook over moderately low heat, stirring frequently, until a golden caramel forms and the temperature reaches 245° on a candy thermometer, 1 hour. Stir in 1 tablespoon of salt and scrape the caramel into the prepared pan. Let cool and set completely overnight.

2. Lightly oil a sheet of parchment paper and line 2 baking sheets with wax paper. Invert the caramel onto the parchment and peel off the foil. Using a sharp knife, cut the caramel into 1-inch-wide strips and then into 1-inch squares. Dip the squares into the chocolate, tap off the excess and transfer to the wax paper on the baking sheets. Sprinkle lightly with sea salt and refrigerate for 10 minutes. Alternatively, wrap the plain caramel squares in wax paper and tie with thread. —*Grace Parisi*

CHOCOLATE-DIPPED
VANILLA CARAMELS

cakes, cookies & more

Natilla

TOTAL: 30 MIN PLUS 3 HR CHILLING

6 SERVINGS ● ○

A direct descendant of the Spanish *crema catalana*, Cuban *natilla* is a rich, creamy egg custard made without the *crema*'s crispy sugar topping. It's sweet, thick, comforting and perfect for entertaining, because it can be prepared ahead completely. Adding eggs to the warm milk mixture can scramble them; to prevent that, add the milk mixture to the eggs very slowly in order to increase their temperature gradually.

- 4 cups whole milk
- One 2-inch strip of lemon zest
- 1 cinnamon stick
- ¼ teaspoon salt
- 1¼ cups granulated sugar
- 8 large egg yolks
- ¼ cup cornstarch dissolved in ¼ cup water
- 1 teaspoon pure vanilla extract
- Ground cinnamon, for garnish

1. In a large saucepan, combine the milk with the lemon zest, cinnamon stick and salt and bring to a simmer. In a large heatproof bowl, using a handheld electric mixer, beat the granulated sugar with the egg yolks at medium speed until they are pale, about 4 minutes. Beat in the cornstarch slurry. At low speed, gradually beat in half of the hot milk.

2. Pour the egg-and-milk mixture back into the saucepan and cook the custard over moderate heat, whisking constantly, for 18 minutes, until very thick. Whisk in the vanilla. Transfer the custard to a large bowl and discard the cinnamon stick and lemon zest. Press a piece of plastic wrap directly onto the surface of the custard and refrigerate until chilled, about 3 hours. Spoon the custard into 6 bowls, sprinkle with ground cinnamon and serve.
—*Lourdes Castro*

MAKE AHEAD The egg custard can be refrigerated for up to 3 days.

Creamy Caramel Pudding

TOTAL: 30 MIN PLUS 2 HR CHILLING

8 SERVINGS ● ● ○

This decadent-seeming pudding is low in fat and a good source of calcium.

- 1 quart 2-percent milk
- ¼ cup plus 3 tablespoons cornstarch
- 2 teaspoons pure vanilla extract
- Pinch of salt
- 2 cups sugar
- Nut brittle, for serving (optional)

1. In a small bowl, whisk ½ cup of the milk with the cornstarch, vanilla and salt until smooth. In a large saucepan, combine the sugar with ¼ cup plus 2 tablespoons of water and bring to a boil. Cook over moderately high heat, undisturbed, until a deep amber caramel forms, about 8 minutes. Remove from the heat. Very gradually whisk in the remaining 3½ cups of milk, ¼ cup at a time. Whisk over moderate heat until the caramel has dissolved. Simmer over moderately low heat until the mixture thickens slightly and deepens in color, about 10 minutes. Remove from the heat.

2. Gradually whisk the cornstarch mixture into the caramel. Cook over moderate heat, stirring, until the pudding is very thick, about 1 minute. Strain the pudding through a fine strainer set over a large measuring cup. Scrape into eight ½-cup ramekins and refrigerate until chilled, about 2 hours. Garnish with nut brittle, if desired. —*Melissa Rubel Jacobson*

MAKE AHEAD The pudding can be refrigerated for up to 2 days.

Classic Butterscotch Sauce

 TOTAL: 15 MIN

MAKES 2½ CUPS ● ○

- 1½ cups dark brown sugar
- ½ cup light corn syrup
- ¼ cup water
- 1 teaspoon kosher salt
- ¾ cup heavy cream
- 2 tablespoons Scotch whisky
- ½ teaspoon pure vanilla extract

In a heavy saucepan, combine the sugar, corn syrup, water and salt; cook to dissolve the sugar. Add the cream; simmer, stirring, until thickened, 10 minutes. Add the whisky and vanilla; simmer over low heat for 2 minutes. Let cool, then transfer to jars.
—*Grace Parisi*

MAKE AHEAD The sauce can be refrigerated for up to 3 months.

Chocolate-Almond Toffee

ACTIVE: 20 MIN; TOTAL: 1 HR

MAKES ABOUT 2 POUNDS ● ● ●

- 2 sticks unsalted butter
- 1½ cups sugar
- 2 tablespoons water
- 1 cup salted roasted almonds—
  - ¾ cup coarsely chopped,
  - ¼ cup finely chopped
- 1 tablespoon pure vanilla extract
- 1½ teaspoons coarse sea salt, crumbled
- ½ pound bittersweet chocolate, chopped

1. Line an 8-by-11-inch baking pan with foil. Spray the foil with oil. In a heavy saucepan, melt the butter. Stir in the sugar and water; bring to a boil. Wash down the side of the pan with a moistened pastry brush. Cook over moderate heat, stirring with a wooden spoon, until a deeply golden caramel forms and the temperature reaches 300° on a candy thermometer, 15 minutes; if the sugar and butter separate, stir vigorously to blend. Remove from the heat; add the coarsely chopped almonds, vanilla and salt. Scrape into the pan; cool for 10 minutes.

2. Sprinkle half the chocolate over the toffee; let stand until melted. Spread the chocolate; sprinkle with half the finely chopped almonds. Freeze for 10 minutes.

3. Invert the toffee onto a foil-lined baking sheet; peel off the foil backing. Melt the remaining chocolate. Spread over the top of the toffee; sprinkle with the remaining finely chopped almonds. Let cool, then break into shards. —*Grace Parisi*

Rice Brittle Crunch

ACTIVE: 15 MIN; TOTAL: 1 HR

MAKES ABOUT 3 CUPS ● ●

- 1 cup sugar
- 2 tablespoons light corn syrup
- 3 tablespoons water
- 1¾ cups toasted rice cereal, preferably Rice Krispies
- ¾ cup banana chips, coarsely chopped
- ½ cup salted roasted peanuts, coarsely chopped
- ¼ teaspoon baking soda

1. Line a rimmed baking sheet with parchment and spray the paper with nonstick cooking spray. In a medium saucepan, combine the sugar, corn syrup and water and bring to a boil over moderately high heat. Cook undisturbed until a deep amber caramel forms, about 7 minutes. Remove from the heat. Stir in the rice cereal, banana chips, peanuts and baking soda.

2. Quickly spread the brittle on the baking sheet, separating it into pieces as much as possible with a spatula. Let cool until hardened, about 45 minutes. Coarsely chop the brittle crunch or break it into clusters and serve.

—*Melissa Rubel Jacobson*

MAKE AHEAD The brittle can be stored in an airtight container for up to 3 days.

Sweet Sticky Rice with Mangoes and Sesame Seeds

ACTIVE: 25 MIN; TOTAL: 1 HR 35 MIN

8 SERVINGS ● ● ●

Most Thai dishes are best served at room temperature, including this creamy dessert: "If you chill it, it becomes rock-hard, but if you heat it up, it turns to mush," explains Andy Ricker, the chef at Pok Pok in Portland, Oregon. Many traditional recipes for sticky rice require steaming the grains for up to an hour, but for the supereasy adaptation here, Ricker cleverly suggests microwaving the rice for only about 15 minutes instead.

SAUCE

- 2 cups unsweetened canned coconut milk
- 1½ tablespoons sugar
- 1½ teaspoons kosher salt

RICE

- 2½ cups Thai sticky rice (1 pound)
- 1 cup unsweetened canned coconut milk
- ½ cup sugar
- 1 tablespoon kosher salt
- 2 mangoes—peeled, pitted and coarsely chopped
- 2 tablespoons toasted sesame seeds

1. MAKE THE SAUCE: In a medium saucepan, combine the coconut milk with the sugar and salt. Bring to a simmer and cook over moderate heat until thickened slightly, about 10 minutes. Transfer the mixture to a sauceboat and let cool to room temperature, about 1 hour.

2. MEANWHILE, PREPARE THE RICE: Place the sticky rice in a large, microwave-safe bowl and add cool water to cover; let soak for 1 hour.

3. Drain the soaked sticky rice and return it to the bowl. Add 2¼ cups of fresh water and cover the bowl with plastic wrap. Microwave the rice on high power for 5 minutes. Pull back the plastic wrap and stir the rice. Replace the plastic wrap and microwave the rice for another 5 minutes. Pull back the plastic wrap to stir the rice a second time. Replace the plastic wrap and microwave until the rice is just tender, about 3 minutes longer. Let stand, covered, for 5 minutes.

4. In a small saucepan, combine the coconut milk with the sugar and salt and bring to a simmer. Pour the hot coconut milk over the sticky rice, folding until just combined. Spoon the rice into bowls. Top with the mango and sesame seeds and serve, passing the sauce at the table.

—*Andy Ricker*

Rice Pudding with Poached Rhubarb

TOTAL: 1 HR PLUS 3 HR CHILLING

8 SERVINGS ● ●

RICE PUDDING

- 1 cup arborio rice
- 2½ cups whole milk
- 1 cup heavy cream
- ½ vanilla bean, split, seeds scraped
- ¾ cup sugar

POACHED RHUBARB

- 3 cups water
- 2 cups sugar
- 1 cup dry red wine or rosé
- 2 tablespoons fresh lemon juice
- 1 cinnamon stick
- ½ vanilla bean, split, seeds scraped
- 1 pound rhubarb, cut into 1-inch lengths

Small mint leaves, for garnish

1. MAKE THE RICE PUDDING: Fill a medium saucepan with water and bring to a boil. Add the rice and cook over high heat for 3 minutes. Drain the rice and return it to the saucepan. Add the milk, cream and the vanilla bean and seeds. Bring to a simmer; cook over low heat until the rice is very tender, about 25 minutes. Stir in the sugar; remove from the heat. Discard the vanilla bean. Scrape the pudding into a 9-by-13-inch glass dish, press a sheet of plastic wrap directly onto the surface of the pudding and refrigerate until chilled, about 3 hours.

2. MEANWHILE, MAKE THE POACHED RHUBARB: In a large saucepan, combine the water with the sugar, wine, lemon juice, cinnamon stick and the vanilla bean and seeds. Bring to a simmer and cook over moderate heat for 10 minutes. Add the rhubarb and simmer until tender, about 15 minutes. Pour the rhubarb and its poaching liquid into a glass or plastic bowl and refrigerate until chilled, about 3 hours.

3. Spoon the rice pudding into bowls. Using a slotted spoon, top with some of the rhubarb. Sprinkle with mint leaves and serve.

—*Krista Desjarlais*

JELLIED CRANBERRY SAUCE
WITH FUJI APPLE (P. 357)

sauces & condiments

Amazing vinaigrettes, salsas, pickles
and other great accompaniments.

CREAMY FETA VINAIGRETTE

ROMAINE SALAD (P. 352) WITH CAESAR-STYLE DRESSING

Creamy Feta Vinaigrette

 TOTAL: 5 MIN
MAKES ¾ CUP ● ○ ○

Pureeing feta cheese right into a vinaigrette makes the dressing smooth and luscious and ensures a little tang in every bite.

- 3 ounces feta cheese, preferably French, crumbled (¾ cup)
- 2½ tablespoons red wine vinegar
- 1 tablespoon water
- ½ teaspoon dried oregano
- ¼ cup plus 1 tablespoon extra-virgin olive oil

Kosher salt and freshly ground pepper

In a food processor, pulse the crumbled feta with the vinegar, water, oregano and oil until smooth. Season with salt and pepper. —*Melissa Rubel Jacobson*

SERVE WITH Grilled vegetables or shrimp, cucumber salad, spinach salad, tomato salad, potato salad.

Caesar-Style Dressing

 TOTAL: 5 MIN
MAKES ¾ CUP ●

This creamy, piquant dressing enriched with mayonnaise is perfect for anyone who is skittish about the raw eggs in a classic Caesar salad.

- ½ cup mayonnaise
- 2 oil-packed anchovies, drained
- 1 small garlic clove, chopped
- 1 tablespoon capers, drained
- 1 tablespoon fresh lemon juice
- 1 tablespoon water
- 1 teaspoon Dijon mustard
- 2 tablespoons freshly grated Parmigiano-Reggiano cheese

Kosher salt and freshly ground black pepper

In a food processor, combine the mayonnaise, anchovies, garlic, capers, lemon juice, water and mustard; process until smooth.

Add the cheese and pulse to blend. Season the dressing with salt and pepper. —*Melissa Rubel Jacobson*

SERVE WITH Romaine salad, crudités, potato salad, steamed broccoli, grilled chicken, salmon or tuna.

Ginger Vinaigrette

 TOTAL: 5 MIN
MAKES ⅔ CUP ● ○

F&W's Melissa Rubel Jacobson finds that the easiest way to peel fresh ginger for this punchy, Asian-inspired vinaigrette is to scrape it with the edge of a spoon. She then grates it on a Microplane zester (other fine graters work well, too).

- ¼ cup rice vinegar
- 1½ tablespoons sugar
- 1 tablespoon finely grated ginger
- ¼ cup vegetable oil

Kosher salt and freshly ground pepper

In a small bowl, mix the rice vinegar with the sugar and grated ginger until the sugar is dissolved. Whisk in the vegetable oil and season with salt and pepper.
—*Melissa Rubel Jacobson*

SERVE WITH Cabbage slaw, Chinese chicken salad, mixed green salad, grilled eggplant or tuna, summer rolls.

Honey-Lemon Dressing

 TOTAL: 5 MIN
MAKES ½ CUP ● ●

1 tablespoon plus 2 teaspoons fresh lemon juice
1 teaspoon finely grated lemon zest
1 tablespoon honey
½ teaspoon chopped thyme
¼ cup extra-virgin olive oil
Kosher salt and freshly ground pepper

In a small bowl, whisk the lemon juice with the lemon zest, honey and thyme. Whisk in the olive oil; season with salt and pepper.
—*Melissa Rubel Jacobson*

SERVE WITH Watercress salad, carrot salad, fennel salad, mixed green salad, citrus salad.

Sherry-Shallot Vinaigrette

ACTIVE: 5 MIN; TOTAL: 20 MIN
MAKES ⅓ CUP ● ● ●

Soaking thin shallot slices in sherry vinegar makes them deliciously pickle-like. For a tarter flavor, let the shallots soak for up to 2 hours.

1 large shallot, thinly sliced
1½ tablespoons sherry vinegar
Kosher salt and freshly ground pepper
¼ cup extra-virgin olive oil

In a small bowl, toss the shallot with the vinegar and season with salt and pepper. Let stand for 15 minutes, then whisk in the oil. —*Melissa Rubel Jacobson*

SERVE WITH Cucumber salad, sliced tomatoes, pasta salad, steak salad, steamed asparagus or green beans.

Roasted Poblano—Parsley Sauce

 TOTAL: 10 MIN
MAKES ABOUT 1 CUP ● ●

Ideal on grilled meats and roasted vegetables, this sauce is smoky (from roasted poblano chiles), salty (from pureed feta) and a little sweet (from parsley).

1 large poblano chile—roasted, skinned, seeded and chopped
2 cups packed flat-leaf parsley leaves
½ cup crumbled feta cheese
6 tablespoons vegetable oil
1 large garlic clove, minced
2 teaspoons freshly squeezed lime juice
Salt

In a food processor, pulse the poblano chile with the flat-leaf parsley, feta cheese, vegetable oil and garlic until pureed. Stir in the lime juice and season with salt.
—*Marcia Kiesel*

SERVE WITH Grilled bread, grilled meats, sliced tomatoes.

MAKE AHEAD The poblano-parsley sauce can be prepared, without the feta, lime juice and salt, and refrigerated overnight. Fold in the feta and add the lime juice and salt just before serving.

Roasted Poblano—Tomato Salsa with Marjoram

 **TOTAL: 30 MIN**
MAKES 3 CUPS ● ● ● ●

2 poblano chiles
One 28-ounce can whole tomatoes, drained
½ cup finely diced onion
¼ cup chopped cilantro
2 tablespoons chopped fresh marjoram
½ teaspoon ground cumin
1 teaspoon sugar
1 small pickled jalapeño, stemmed
Salt

1. Roast the poblanos directly over a gas flame, turning, until charred all over. Transfer the chiles to a bowl, cover with plastic wrap and let steam for 15 minutes.
2. Peel, core and seed the chiles and transfer to a blender. Add the tomatoes, onion, cilantro, marjoram, cumin, sugar and jalapeño and puree until smooth. Season with salt and serve. —*Tim Cushman*

MAKE AHEAD The poblano-tomato salsa can be refrigerated overnight.

Curried Apricot-and-Tomato Ketchup

TOTAL: 30 MIN PLUS 20 MIN COOLING
MAKES 1⅔ CUPS ● ●

1 teaspoon vegetable oil
½ cup coarsely chopped onion
1 teaspoon finely grated fresh ginger
1 garlic clove, minced
½ cup coarsely chopped dried apricots
1 large tomato—peeled, seeded and chopped
½ cup cider vinegar
½ cup water
¼ cup sugar
1 teaspoon Madras curry powder
Salt

In a medium saucepan, heat the vegetable oil. Add the onion, ginger and garlic and cook over low heat, stirring occasionally, until softened, about 10 minutes. Stir in the apricots, tomato, cider vinegar, water, sugar and curry powder. Simmer over moderately low heat until the apricots are soft, about 15 minutes. Scrape the contents of the saucepan into a blender and puree until smooth. Season the ketchup with salt and transfer to a bowl. Refrigerate until cool, about 20 minutes. Serve the ketchup at room temperature or chilled.
—*Grace Parisi*

SERVE WITH Sausages, chicken, ribs.

MAKE AHEAD The ketchup can be refrigerated for up to 2 weeks.

sauces & condiments

Avocado-and-Roasted-Tomatillo Salsa

TOTAL: 30 MIN
MAKES 3 CUPS ● ● ●

Pureeing avocados with roasted tomatillos, garlic, leek and jalapeño creates a tangy, guacamole-like dip that's excellent with tortilla chips.

- ½ pound tomatillos—husked, cored and quartered
- 3 garlic cloves, lightly smashed and peeled
- 1 jalapeño, stemmed and halved
- 1 leek, white part only, coarsely chopped
- 1 tablespoon vegetable oil
- 2 Hass avocados—peeled, pitted and coarsely chopped
- ¼ cup chopped cilantro
- 1 teaspoon sugar
- ½ teaspoon ground cumin
- ¼ cup finely chopped onion
- ½ teaspoon dried oregano, preferably Mexican, crumbled
- 1 tablespoon fresh lime juice

Salt

1. Preheat the oven to 425°. On a rimmed baking sheet, toss the quartered tomatillos, smashed garlic cloves, jalapeño halves and chopped leek with the vegetable oil and spread in a single layer. Roast the vegetables until lightly charred and softened, about 12 minutes. Transfer to a blender and let cool.

2. Add the chopped avocados, cilantro, sugar, ground cumin and ½ cup of water to the blender and puree until smooth. Add the chopped onion, dried oregano and fresh lime juice and pulse once or twice until all the ingredients are just incorporated. Transfer the salsa to a medium serving bowl and season with salt. Serve the salsa chilled or at room temperature.
—*Tim Cushman*

SERVE WITH Baked tortilla chips.

MAKE AHEAD The avocado-and-tomatillo salsa can be refrigerated overnight.

Minty Green Olive–Celery Salsa

TOTAL: 30 MIN
MAKES 2 CUPS ● ● ●

This bright, briny salsa is more like a crunchy tapenade. It's delicious over white fish like hake.

- 2 tablespoons extra-virgin olive oil
- 2 garlic cloves, lightly smashed and peeled
- 1 cup finely diced celery (3 ribs)
- 1 cup finely chopped pitted green olives (5 ounces)
- 2 tablespoons drained capers, chopped
- 2 tablespoons chopped mint

Freshly ground pepper

In a small skillet, heat the olive oil. Add the garlic cloves and cook over moderate heat until golden, about 2 minutes. Let the oil cool, then discard the garlic cloves. Transfer the garlicky oil to a bowl and add the diced celery, chopped green olives, capers and mint. Toss the salsa, season with freshly ground pepper and serve.
—*Tim Cushman*

Chopped-Olive Aioli

TOTAL: 15 MIN
MAKES 1 CUP ● ● ●

- 1 cup pitted green and black olives, chopped
- ¼ cup mayonnaise
- 2 scallions, finely chopped
- 2 tablespoons extra-virgin olive oil
- 2 tablespoons fresh lemon juice
- 1 tablespoon chopped capers
- 2 teaspoons chopped oregano
- 1 jalapeño, seeded and very finely chopped
- 1 garlic clove, finely chopped

In a medium bowl, fold together the chopped olives, mayonnaise, scallions, olive oil, lemon juice, capers, oregano, jalapeño and garlic until thoroughly combined. Serve the olive aioli right away.
—*Grace Parisi*

SERVE WITH Sausages, pork chops.

Smoky Pimiento Relish

TOTAL: 15 MIN
MAKES 2 CUPS ● ● ●

- ½ cup oil-packed sun-dried tomatoes, drained
- ¼ cup extra-virgin olive oil
- 3 canned chipotles in adobo, stemmed
- 1 garlic clove
- ½ teaspoon caraway seeds
- 1 cup roasted red peppers

Salt

In a food processor, pulse the tomatoes with the olive oil, chipotles, garlic and caraway seeds until finely chopped. Add the roasted peppers and pulse to a chunky puree. Season with salt and serve.
—*Grace Parisi*

SERVE WITH Sausages, steak, chicken.

Pickled Cucumber Relish

ACTIVE: 20 MIN; TOTAL: 1 HR 20 MIN
8 SERVINGS ● ● ●

Nothing could be simpler than this sweet-sour pickle of cucumbers marinated with Thai chiles and shallots in a white vinegar brine. It's an ideal accompaniment to coconut milk–based curries, fried fish cakes or grilled chicken.

- 2 cups warm water
- 1½ cups distilled white vinegar
- 1½ cups sugar
- 2 teaspoons kosher salt
- 6 Kirby cucumbers (1½ pounds), quartered lengthwise and thinly sliced crosswise
- 2 medium shallots, thinly sliced
- 2 Thai chiles, thinly sliced
- 2 tablespoons chopped cilantro

In a medium bowl, combine the water with the white vinegar. Add the sugar and salt, stirring to dissolve. Stir in the sliced cucumbers, shallots and Thai chiles. Cover and refrigerate the relish for at least 1 hour and up to 3 days. Stir in the chopped fresh cilantro just before serving.
—*Andy Ricker*

grilling sauce on a stick

When grilling a meal, chef **Robert Del Grande** *of RDG and Bar Annie in Houston threads ingredients for sauces onto skewers to cook alongside the meat. The blended sauces are smoky and superflavorful.*

Pineapple and Red Chile Salsa

TOTAL: 30 MIN

MAKES ABOUT 3 CUPS ● ● ●

- 1 small onion, quartered
- ½ pound plum tomatoes, halved lengthwise
- 4 garlic cloves, peeled
- ½ pound fresh pineapple, cut into 8 pieces
- 1 red bell pepper—stemmed, seeded and quartered
- 1 fresh long red chile, such as a cayenne or Holland chile—stemmed, seeded and quartered

Smoky Steak Sauce

TOTAL: 30 MIN

MAKES ABOUT 2½ CUPS ● ●

- 2 thick slices of bacon, halved crosswise and rolled into cylinders
- 1 small onion, quartered
- 1 portobello mushroom, stemmed and cap quartered
- 2 plum tomatoes, cored and halved lengthwise
- 4 pitted prunes
- 4 garlic cloves, peeled
- 1 large supple ancho chile, seeded and quartered

Creamy Green Chile and Avocado Sauce

TOTAL: 30 MIN

MAKES ABOUT 2¼ CUPS ● ● ●

- 1 firm Hass avocado—halved or quartered, pitted and skin left on for grilling; peel before blending
- 1 small onion, quartered
- 2 tomatillos—husked, cored and halved
- 4 garlic cloves, peeled
- 1 jalapeño—stemmed, seeded and quartered
- 1 poblano chile—stemmed, seeded and quartered

STEP ONE *Thread the ingredients onto skewers and grill.*

Brush the kebabs with oil and grill over high heat, turning occasionally, until the vegetables are charred in spots, about 15 minutes; let cool slightly. Remove the ingredients from the skewers and transfer them to a blender.

STEP TWO *Add the remaining ingredients.*

12 mint leaves	2 tablespoons white wine vinegar	¼ cup cilantro leaves
¼ cup water	2 tablespoons light brown sugar	¼ cup water
2 tablespoons fresh lime juice	½ cup water	2 tablespoons fresh lime juice

---

STEP THREE *Puree until smooth, then season with salt.*

SERVE WITH Grilled pork chops.
MAKE AHEAD The salsa can be refrigerated in an airtight container for up to 3 days.

SERVE WITH Grilled steak.
MAKE AHEAD The sauce can be refrigerated in an airtight container for up to 1 week.

SERVE WITH Grilled chicken.
MAKE AHEAD The sauce can be refrigerated in an airtight container for up to 2 days.

Basil Vinaigrette

TOTAL: 5 MIN
MAKES ⅓ CUP ● ●

- 1 small garlic clove
- 1 cup packed basil leaves, coarsely chopped
- ¼ cup extra-virgin olive oil
- 1½ tablespoons Champagne vinegar
- Pinch of crushed red pepper
- Salt and freshly ground black pepper

In a food processor, pulse the garlic clove until chopped. Add the coarsely chopped basil leaves and pulse until finely chopped. Add the olive oil, Champagne vinegar and crushed red pepper and process until the vinaigrette is smooth. Season with salt and black pepper.
—*Melissa Rubel Jacobson*

---

superfast salads

Watercress Salad with Toasted Pine Nuts made with **Honey-Lemon Dressing** (p. 349) Toss ¼ cup toasted pine nuts with 2 bunches of watercress and 1 thinly sliced Belgian endive. Add the dressing and toss to coat.

Romaine Salad with Grilled Sourdough Croutons made with **Caesar-Style Dressing** (p. 348) Brush 2 sourdough bread slices with olive oil and season with salt and pepper. Grill until toasted. Cut into croutons; toss with 2 hearts of romaine and the dressing.

Cabbage-and-Sesame Slaw made with **Ginger Vinaigrette** (p. 348) Toss 14 ounces coleslaw mix with the vinaigrette and 1 tablespoon toasted sesame seeds.

SERVE WITH Tomato salad, green bean salad, pasta salad, *panzanella* salad, grilled fish, chicken or lamb.

Fresh Herb-and-Tomato Salsa with Smoked Cheese

TOTAL: 20 MIN
MAKES 3 CUPS ● ●

Inspired by an Italian Caprese salad, this hearty tomato salsa is so chunky it could be eaten on its own with a fork, but it's also great with shredded chicken on a warm corn tortilla.

- 2 cups mixed yellow and red grape tomatoes, halved or quartered
- ½ cup finely diced smoked Gouda, smoked cheddar or smoked Monterey Jack cheese (2½ ounces)
- ¼ cup chopped cilantro
- 2 tablespoons shredded basil
- 2 tablespoons snipped chives
- Salt and freshly ground pepper

In a medium bowl, toss the tomatoes with the cheese, cilantro, basil and chives. Season with salt and pepper and serve.
—*Tim Cushman*

Chive-Sage Salt

TOTAL: 10 MIN
MAKES ABOUT 1 CUP ● ● ●

This bright green salt with minced chives and fried sage leaves is delicious rubbed on chicken or pork, sprinkled on roast potatoes or used as a dipping salt for radishes.

- 1 tablespoon extra-virgin olive oil
- ¼ cup sage leaves
- 1 cup minced chives
- 2 tablespoons kosher salt

In a small skillet, heat the olive oil. Add the sage leaves and cook over moderate heat, turning once, until crisp, about 2 minutes. Scrape the leaves and oil into a small bowl and let cool. Crumble the leaves. Add the chives and salt and stir to combine.
—*Marcia Kiesel*

SERVE WITH Grilled chicken or pork, roast potatoes, radishes, sliced tomatoes.
MAKE AHEAD The Chive-Sage Salt can be refrigerated for up to 1 week.

Spicy Red Chile Sauce

ACTIVE: 15 MIN; TOTAL: 45 MIN
MAKES 3 CUPS ● ● ●

Adapted from Eileen Yin-Fei Lo's *Mastering the Art of Chinese Cooking*, this sweet-hot sauce works with any fresh red chile.

- 1 pound fresh red jalapeño chiles
- 2 cups water
- 1¾ teaspoons salt
- 2½ tablespoons unseasoned rice vinegar
- 1½ tablespoons sugar

In a medium skillet, combine the red jalapeño chiles with the water and salt. Bring to a boil, cover and cook over moderately low heat until the chiles are tender, about 25 minutes. Stir in the rice vinegar and sugar, stirring until the sugar is dissolved. Let the mixture cool, then transfer to a blender. Puree the chiles with their liquid. Pour the red chile sauce into jars, cover and refrigerate. —*Eileen Yin-Fei Lo*

Quick Mustard Piccalilli

TOTAL: 10 MIN
MAKES ABOUT 2 CUPS ● ● ● ●

- ½ cup yellow mustard
- ¼ cup whole-grain mustard
- 2 tablespoons light brown sugar
- 1 large kosher dill pickle, finely diced (¾ cup)
- ¾ cup sauerkraut, rinsed and squeezed dry
- ½ cup lager beer
- ¼ cup chopped pickled cocktail onions

In a medium bowl, whisk the mustards with the brown sugar. Stir in the pickle, sauerkraut, lager and cocktail onions and serve.
—*Grace Parisi*

SERVE WITH Sausages, hot dogs.

BASIL VINAIGRETTE
(WITH HEIRLOOM TOMATOES)

FRESH HERB-AND-TOMATO SALSA
(WITH CHICKEN ON A TORTILLA)

sauces & condiments

Dill Pickles

TOTAL: 20 MIN PLUS
OVERNIGHT PICKLING
MAKES 1 QUART ● ● ○ ○

These incredibly simple pickles are flavored with exactly the right amount of chopped garlic and fresh dill along with such typical pickling spices as mustard, dill and coriander seeds. They are intensely crunchy and refreshing right out of the refrigerator after just a night of pickling.

- 1½ cups distilled white vinegar
- ¼ cup sugar
- 4 teaspoons kosher salt
- 1 teaspoon mustard seeds
- 1 teaspoon coriander seeds
- ¾ teaspoon dill seeds
- 2 cups hot water
- 2 pounds Kirby cucumbers, sliced ¼ inch thick
- ¾ cup coarsely chopped fresh dill
- 3 medium garlic cloves, coarsely chopped

1. In a large, heatproof measuring cup, combine the white vinegar, sugar, kosher salt, mustard seeds, coriander seeds and dill seeds with the hot water and stir until the sugar and salt are completely dissolved. Let the brine cool.

2. In a large bowl, toss the sliced cucumbers with the chopped fresh dill and garlic. Pour the cooled brine over the cucumber slices and stir gently to coat all the slices in brine. Place a small plate over the cucumbers to keep them submerged in the brine, then cover the bowl tightly with plastic wrap. Refrigerate the pickles overnight, stirring once or twice. Serve right away or transfer the pickles and their brine to an airtight quart container and store in the refrigerator. Serve the dill pickles cold. —*Bobby Flay*

MAKE AHEAD The dill pickles can be refrigerated with their brine in an airtight container for up to 1 week.

Sweet Pickle Relish

ACTIVE: 10 MIN; TOTAL: 30 MIN
MAKES 2 CUPS ● ● ○

- 1 teaspoon vegetable oil
- 1 cup finely chopped onion
- ¾ cup jalapeño pepper jelly
- ¼ cup cider vinegar
- 1 cup chopped bread-and-butter pickles
- ½ cup chopped sweet or hot pickled peppadew peppers (see Note)

Salt

In a medium saucepan, heat the vegetable oil. Add the onion and cook over low heat, stirring occasionally, until softened, about 10 minutes. Add the jalapeño jelly and cider vinegar and bring the liquid to a boil. Cook the mixture over moderate heat, stirring occasionally, until thickened, about 6 minutes. Let cool, then stir in the bread-and-butter pickles and pickled peppadews. Season with salt. —*Grace Parisi*

SERVE WITH Sausages, hot dogs.

NOTE Pickled peppadews are sweet, piquant South African peppers the size of cherry tomatoes. They're sold at specialty food stores and murrayscheese.com.

Pickled Red Onion

ACTIVE: 10 MIN; TOTAL: 30 MIN PLUS
OVERNIGHT PICKLING
MAKES ABOUT 1 CUP ● ● ○

- ½ cup dry red wine
- ½ cup balsamic vinegar
- ½ cup honey
- 1 bay leaf
- 1 teaspoon fennel seeds
- 1 teaspoon yellow mustard seeds
- ¼ teaspoon crushed red pepper
- 2 tablespoons extra-virgin olive oil
- 1 medium red onion, thinly sliced

Salt

1. In a small saucepan, combine the red wine with the balsamic vinegar, honey, bay leaf, fennel seeds, mustard seeds and crushed red pepper and bring to a boil over moderately high heat. Cover the saucepan and remove from the heat. Let the brine stand for 10 minutes.

2. In a medium skillet, heat the olive oil. Add the red onion slices, season with salt and cook over moderate heat, stirring the onion occasionally, until the slices are softened, about 6 minutes. Scrape the onion into a bowl.

3. Strain the brine over the onion and let cool to room temperature. Cover and refrigerate overnight. Bring to room temperature and serve in the brine. —*Shawn McClain*

SERVE WITH Chicken-Liver Mousse with Bacon and Apple (p. 14).

MAKE AHEAD The pickled onion can be refrigerated for up to 1 week.

Lemon Confit

TOTAL: 15 MIN PLUS 2 WEEKS' CURING
4 SERVINGS ● ○ ○

You can purchase jarred Moroccan preserved lemons at specialty food stores, but making your own is simple: The pleasantly pungent lemons, layered with salt and sugar, cure in the refrigerator for two weeks. Lemon confit is wonderful chopped and mixed into vinaigrettes or blended into butter and placed on broiled fish.

- 5 cups kosher salt
- 5 tablespoons sugar
- 6 lemons, quartered

In a large bowl, mix the salt with the sugar. Transfer half of the sugar-salt mixture to a medium bowl and add the lemons. Toss well. Pour a small layer of sugar-salt into a clean quart-size jar. Layer the lemons in the jar, covering them with the remaining sugar-salt as you go. Refrigerate the lemon confit for at least 2 weeks. To use, rinse the lemons well and use only the peel. —*Eric Ripert*

perfecting quick pickles

Following the example of pickle-obsessed chefs, F&W's **Grace Parisi** *creates three brines for everything from carrots to cauliflower.*

Spicy Dill Quick Pickles

TOTAL: 20 MIN PLUS OVERNIGHT BRINING

MAKES 2 QUARTS ● ● ○ ○

Vegetables (see below for preparation)

- 3 tablespoons kosher salt
- 2 tablespoons sugar
- 1¼ cups distilled white vinegar (5 percent acidity)
- 2 tablespoons coriander seeds
- 6 large garlic cloves, halved
- 4 to 6 long red or green hot chiles, halved lengthwise
- 16 dill sprigs

Pack vegetables into 2 clean 1-quart glass jars. In another jar, combine salt, sugar, vinegar, coriander and garlic. Shake to dissolve salt and sugar. Add 2 cups water; pour brine over vegetables. Tuck chiles and dill between vegetables. Add water to keep vegetables submerged. Close jars; refrigerate overnight or up to 1 month.

Winey-Briny Quick Pickles

TOTAL: 20 MIN PLUS OVERNIGHT BRINING

MAKES 2 QUARTS ● ● ○ ○

Vegetables (see below for preparation)

- 3 tablespoons kosher salt
- 1 tablespoon sugar
- 2 tablespoons mustard seeds
- ¼ cup tiny shallots, sliced lengthwise
- 1¼ cups white wine vinegar (6 percent acidity)
- 1½ cups dry white wine
- 24 small tarragon sprigs

Pack vegetables into 2 clean 1-quart glass jars. In another jar, combine the salt, sugar, mustard, shallots, vinegar and wine; shake until salt and sugar dissolve. Add 1 cup water; pour the brine over the vegetables. Tuck the tarragon between the vegetables. Add enough water to cover the vegetables and keep them submerged. Close jars; refrigerate overnight or up to 1 month.

Curry Quick Pickles

TOTAL: 20 MIN PLUS OVERNIGHT BRINING

MAKES 2 QUARTS ● ● ○ ○

Vegetables (see below for preparation)

- 3 tablespoons kosher salt
- 1 tablespoon sugar
- ½ cup thin matchsticks of fresh ginger
- 6 garlic cloves
- 1 teaspoon Madras curry powder
- 1¼ cups unseasoned rice vinegar (4.3 percent acidity)

Pack vegetables into 2 clean 1-quart glass jars. In another jar, combine the salt, sugar, ginger, garlic, curry powder and rice vinegar. Shake until the salt and sugar dissolve. Add 2 cups of water and pour the brine over the vegetables. Add enough water to cover the vegetables and keep them submerged. Close the jars and refrigerate the pickles overnight or for up to 1 month.

....

PICK YOUR PICKLE *For 1 quart, use 12 ounces vegetables.*

....

Asparagus Blanch trimmed asparagus spears in boiling water for 1 minute. Drain well, transfer to a plate and let cool.
Broccoli Stems Peel tough skin away and cut stems into slender sticks.

Carrot Sticks Blanch sticks in boiling water for 2 minutes, drain and cool.
Cauliflower Florets Cut into small florets. Blanch the florets in boiling water for 1 minute, drain and let cool.

Green Beans Steam beans for 2 minutes, transfer to a plate and let cool.
Kirby Cucumbers Quarter unpeeled cucumbers for pickle spears or slice them into thin rounds for pickle chips.

TANGY TOMATILLO-CUMIN SALSA (WITH SALMON)

A WINE-COUNTRY LUNCH

Fennel Mustard

ACTIVE: 10 MIN; TOTAL: 1 HR

MAKES 1 CUP ● ●

- 1 tablespoon vegetable oil
- 3 cups chopped fennel
- ½ cup white wine vinegar
- 1 tablespoon water
- 1 teaspoon dry mustard powder
- 2 teaspoons whole-grain mustard

Salt

In a skillet, heat the oil. Add the fennel, cover and cook over low heat, stirring occasionally, until softened, 25 minutes. Add the vinegar and cook, uncovered, until the fennel is tender, 15 minutes. Transfer to a blender. Add the water and mustard powder and puree. Scrape into a bowl and let cool. Stir in the whole-grain mustard and season with salt. Transfer to jars, cover and refrigerate. —*Thomas Keller*

SERVE WITH Roast pork.

Tangy Tomatillo-Cumin Salsa

TOTAL: 30 MIN PLUS CHILLING

MAKES 3 CUPS ● ● ●

The jalapeño in this tomatillo-based salsa can be either mild or fiery (depending on whether you leave in the seeds). Boston chef Tim Cushman prefers it fiery: "I like it when food is so spicy that it makes me sweat and cry," he says. Freshly ground and toasted cumin seeds add a depth of flavor that is especially good with salmon.

- 1 pound tomatillos, husked and cored
- 1 small onion, coarsely chopped
- 3 medium garlic cloves, smashed and peeled
- 1 jalapeño, stemmed and halved
- 2 teaspoons cumin seeds
- ½ cup chopped cilantro
- 1½ teaspoons sugar

Salt

1. In a large saucepan, cover the tomatillos, onion, garlic and jalapeño with water. Bring to a boil and simmer until the tomatillos just lose their bright green color, about 8 minutes. Drain, transfer the vegetables to a blender and let cool slightly.

2. In a small, dry skillet, toast the cumin seeds over moderate heat until fragrant, shaking the pan constantly, about 2 minutes. Transfer the seeds to a spice grinder and let cool slightly.

3. Grind the toasted cumin seeds to a powder and add the cumin to the blender along with the cilantro and sugar; puree the tomatillo mixture until smooth. Season the salsa with salt and refrigerate until cool. Serve the tomatillo salsa chilled. —*Tim Cushman*

MAKE AHEAD The Tangy Tomatillo-Cumin Salsa can be refrigerated in a covered container overnight.

Jellied Cranberry Sauce with Fuji Apple

photo, page 346

TOTAL: 20 MIN PLUS 3 HR CHILLING

12 SERVINGS ● ● ● ●

Cranberries need to be cooked for only a few minutes before they burst and form a sauce. To mold the sauce so it's slice-able, F&W's Melissa Rubel Jacobson adds diced apple, which is loaded with pectin, a natural gelling agent.

One 12-ounce bag fresh cranberries, plus more for garnish

1 large Fuji apple, peeled and cut into ½-inch dice

1 cup sugar

¾ cup water

Rosemary sprigs, for garnish

1. Line an 8-by-4-inch loaf pan with plastic wrap and spray the plastic wrap with nonstick cooking spray.

2. In a saucepan, combine the cranberries, apple, sugar and water. Bring to a boil; cook over moderately high heat, stirring frequently, until the cranberries are broken down and the sauce is very thick, 15 minutes. Scrape the sauce into the pan and refrigerate until chilled, 3 hours. Invert onto a serving plate; remove the plastic wrap. Garnish with fresh cranberries and rosemary sprigs. Slice with a serrated knife and serve. —*Melissa Rubel Jacobson*

Cranberry-and-Dried-Fruit Compote

TOTAL: 15 MIN PLUS 3 HR CHILLING

12 SERVINGS ● ● ●

One 12-ounce bag fresh cranberries

1¼ cups water

¾ cup golden raisins

⅔ cup sugar

½ cup dried cherries

½ cup quartered dried Black Mission figs

In a medium saucepan, combine the cranberries with the water, raisins, sugar, cherries and figs. Bring to a boil and cook over moderately high heat, stirring frequently, until the cranberries burst, about 6 minutes. Scrape the cranberry sauce into a bowl and refrigerate until chilled, about 3 hours. —*Melissa Rubel Jacobson*

MAKE AHEAD The cranberry compote can be kept in an airtight container in the refrigerator for up to 2 weeks. Serve the compote chilled or warm.

Cranberry, Clementine and Pumpkin Seed Conserve

TOTAL: 50 MIN PLUS 3 HR CHILLING

12 SERVINGS ● ● ● ●

3 clementines

1¼ cups sugar

1 cup water

One 12-ounce bag fresh cranberries

½ cup roasted pumpkin seeds

In a medium saucepan, cover the clementines with water. Bring to a simmer over moderately high heat until the skins soften, 8 minutes. Drain and coarsely chop the clementines. Wipe out the saucepan, then add the sugar, 1 cup water and the chopped clementines. Bring to a simmer over moderate heat until the clementine peel is sweet, 30 minutes. Add the cranberries and cook over moderately high heat, stirring frequently, until the cranberries burst, about 6 minutes. Scrape the cranberry sauce into a bowl and refrigerate until chilled, about 3 hours. Fold in the pumpkin seeds just before serving. —*Melissa Rubel Jacobson*

MAKE AHEAD The conserve can be kept in an airtight container in the refrigerator for up to 2 weeks. Serve chilled or warm.

Cranberry-Quince Chutney

TOTAL: 1 HR

MAKES 6 CUPS ● ● ●

1 tablespoon canola oil

1 small onion, very finely chopped

1 tablespoon minced ginger

1 garlic clove, minced

½ teaspoon ground allspice

1 star anise pod

1½ cups sugar

1 cup cider vinegar

1 cup water

3 quinces (8 ounces each)— peeled, cored and finely diced

1 Granny Smith apple—peeled, cored and finely diced

One 12-ounce bag cranberries

½ cup golden raisins

In a large saucepan, heat the canola oil. Add the onion, ginger, garlic, allspice and star anise and cook over moderate heat, stirring, until the onion is softened, about 5 minutes. Add the sugar, vinegar and water and bring to a simmer. Add the quince, apple, cranberries and raisins and cook over low heat, stirring occasionally, until thick and jammy, about 25 minutes. Discard the star anise. Serve the chutney warm or chilled. —*Shawn McClain*

MAKE AHEAD The chutney can be refrigerated for up to 2 weeks.

Fresh Blueberry Sauce

TOTAL: 10 MIN

MAKES 2¼ CUPS ● ● ●

This sauce is a splendid topping for ice cream. It can also be poured lightly on pound cake for a quick summer dessert.

1 pound fresh blueberries

⅓ cup sugar

1½ teaspoons fresh lemon juice

Pinch of salt

In a medium saucepan, mix the blueberries with the sugar. Cook over moderate heat until the blueberries begin to burst and release their liquid, about 5 minutes. Remove from the heat. Puree ½ cup of the blueberries and scrape back into the sauce. Stir in the fresh lemon juice and salt. Serve warm.

—*Melissa Rubel Jacobson*

MAKE AHEAD The Fresh Blueberry Sauce can be refrigerated for up to 2 days. Rewarm before serving.

WATERMELON-TEQUILA
COCKTAILS (P. 361)

beverages

Fabulous drinks, both alcoholic
and virgin, from some of
the world's best mixologists.

GINGER SHANDIES

SOUTHERN EXPOSURE

Hibiscus–Ginger Beer Zingers

TOTAL: 30 MIN

MAKES 12 DRINKS ● ● ●

  2 hibiscus tea bags
  4 cups boiling water
Cracked ice
Two to three 12-ounce bottles
    ginger beer
 12 pineapple slices, for garnish
 12 mint sprigs, for garnish

In a medium saucepan, steep the hibiscus tea bags in the boiling water until deep red, 25 minutes; discard the tea bags. Add ice to 12 glasses and fill each one halfway with the tea. Top off the drinks with ginger beer. Garnish each drink with a pineapple slice and a mint sprig and serve.
—*Marcia Kiesel*

MAKE AHEAD The steeped, cooled hibiscus tea can be refrigerated for up to 2 days before serving.

Ginger Shandies

TOTAL: 10 MIN

MAKES 6 DRINKS ●

  2 lemons, thinly sliced
     (6 slices reserved)
 18 small mint sprigs
Three 11.2-ounce bottles
    Hoegaarden or other Belgian
    white beer, chilled
One 12-ounce bottle ginger
    beer, chilled
Ice

1. In a large pitcher, combine the lemon slices and 12 mint sprigs. Slowly pour in the Hoegaarden and ginger beers. Stir gently to combine.
2. Fill 6 rocks glasses with ice and add one of the reserved lemon slices to each glass. Pour the shandy into the glasses, garnish with mint sprigs and serve.
—*Alison Attenborough and Jamie Kimm*

Southern Exposure

TOTAL: 10 MIN

MAKES 1 DRINK ● ●

  1 large celery rib
 1½ ounces gin
  ½ ounce simple syrup (see Note)
  ½ ounce fresh lime juice
 10 mint leaves, plus a sprig for garnish
Ice cubes

Finely grate the celery rib into a mesh strainer set over a bowl. Press on the pulp to extract the juice. Pour ¾ ounce of the juice into a shaker and add the gin, simple syrup, lime juice and mint leaves. Add a large handful of ice; close the shaker and shake vigorously. Strain into a chilled martini glass, garnish with the mint sprig and serve. —*Daniel Hyatt*

NOTE For 6 ounces of simple syrup, simmer ½ cup sugar with ½ cup water, stirring, until the sugar has dissolved.

Redhead in Bed

TOTAL: 25 MIN
MAKES 10 DRINKS ●

3 pounds strawberries, hulled and coarsely chopped

⅔ cup sugar

½ cup plus 2 tablespoons citrus vodka

¼ cup fresh lime juice

Ice

⅓ cup chilled Riesling

1. In a bowl, toss the strawberries with the sugar and let stand, stirring occasionally, until the strawberries release their juices, about 10 minutes.

2. In a blender, combine half each of the strawberries and their juices, the vodka and lime juice with 1 cup of ice and puree. Pour into a pitcher. Repeat with the remaining strawberries and juices, vodka and lime juice and 1 more cup of ice. Fill 10 collins glasses halfway with ice. Pour the drink into the glasses, top each with ½ tablespoon of Riesling and serve. —*Chris Yeo*

Fresh Tomato Bloody Marys

TOTAL: 25 MIN
MAKES 4 DRINKS ●

GARNISH

2 small celery ribs, minced

2 tablespoons minced onion

1 medium green heirloom tomato, such as Green Zebra, minced

½ teaspoon finely grated lemon zest

1 teaspoon fresh lemon juice

Salt

BLOODY MARY

1½ pounds chilled red tomatoes, coarsely chopped

½ cup chilled vodka

1 cup ice cubes

1 teaspoon tomato paste

½ small red chile, seeded and coarsely chopped

½ teaspoon celery salt

4 medium celery ribs and 4 thin green chiles (optional), for serving

1. PREPARE THE GARNISH: In a bowl, toss the celery with the onion, tomato, lemon zest and lemon juice; season with salt. Refrigerate while you make the drinks.

2. MAKE THE BLOODY MARY: In a blender, puree the tomatoes, vodka, ice, tomato paste, chile and celery salt; pour into glasses. Spoon the garnish on top, add a celery rib and chile to each glass and serve. —*Andreas Viestad*

Mark's Sidecar

TOTAL: 10 MIN
MAKES 1 DRINK ● ●

Sugar

Ice cubes

2 ounces Cognac

¾ ounce fresh lemon juice

½ ounce maraschino liqueur

½ ounce Angostura bitters

Moisten the rim of a martini glass and dip it in sugar. Fill a shaker with ice. Add the Cognac, lemon juice, maraschino liqueur and Angostura bitters; shake well. Strain into the glass and serve. —*Mark Mendoza*

Strawberry-Lemon Mojitos

TOTAL: 10 MIN
MAKES 4 DRINKS ● ●

8 lemon wedges

4 strawberries, plus 2 halved strawberries for garnish

24 mint leaves, plus 4 mint sprigs for garnish (optional)

Ice cubes plus crushed ice

8 ounces gold or aged rum

3 ounces fresh lemon juice

2 ounces prepared sugarcane syrup or agave nectar

In a cocktail shaker, muddle the lemon wedges with the whole strawberries and mint leaves. Add ice cubes and the rum, lemon juice and sugarcane syrup; shake well. Strain the mojitos into highball glasses filled with crushed ice. Garnish with the strawberry halves and mint sprigs and serve. —*Joaquin Simo*

Sparkling Mojito

TOTAL: 10 MIN
MAKES 1 DRINK ●

½ lime, cut into 4 pieces

¼ cup fresh mint leaves, torn, plus 1 mint sprig for garnish

1 tablespoon plus 1 teaspoon granulated sugar

Ice cubes

¼ cup (2 ounces) white rum

½ cup club soda, chilled

In a tall glass, muddle the lime with the mint leaves and sugar until the sugar is dissolved. Fill the glass with ice and stir in the rum and club soda. Garnish with the mint sprig and serve. —*Lourdes Castro*

Watermelon-Tequila Cocktails

photo, page 358

TOTAL: 25 MIN PLUS 2 HR CHILLING
MAKES 8 DRINKS ● ●

¼ cup water

¼ cup granulated sugar

8 cups diced seedless watermelon (1 pound)

¼ cup fresh lime juice

1¾ cups blueberries

¾ cup lightly packed fresh mint leaves, plus 8 sprigs for garnish

1¼ cups silver tequila

Ice cubes

1. In a small saucepan, bring the water to a simmer with the sugar and stir over moderate heat until the sugar is dissolved, about 1 minute; let the sugar syrup cool.

2. In a blender, puree the watermelon until smooth. Set a fine-mesh strainer over a bowl and strain the watermelon juice, pressing gently on the solids to extract as much juice as possible. Discard the pulp.

3. In a pitcher, combine the sugar syrup with the lime juice, blueberries and mint leaves. Lightly muddle the blueberries and mint. Add the watermelon juice and tequila. Refrigerate until chilled, about 2 hours.

4. Pour into tall ice-filled glasses. Garnish with the mint sprigs; serve. —*Bobby Flay*

Mango Alexanders

ACTIVE: 15 MIN; TOTAL: 35 MIN
MAKES 8 DRINKS ●

¾ cup water
¾ cup sugar
3 cups unsweetened coconut milk
½ cup fresh lime juice, plus
2 teaspoons finely grated
lime zest for garnish
2 cups mango vodka (see Note)
Ice

1. In a small saucepan, combine the water with the sugar. Bring to a simmer and cook over moderate heat until the sugar dissolves, about 1 minute. Transfer the sugar syrup to a small bowl and let stand until cool, about 20 minutes.
2. In a large pitcher, mix the coconut milk with the lime juice and sugar syrup. Pour in the vodka. Fill the pitcher with ice and stir until the mixture is chilled. Pour the mixture into martini glasses, sprinkle with the grated lime zest and serve.
—Andy Ricker

NOTE Mango vodka is sold in stores, but you can also make it at home: In a jar, combine 2 cups of vodka with 2 cups of diced fresh mango. Cover and refrigerate overnight or for up to 4 days. Strain, discarding the mango.

Mango-Peach Sangria

TOTAL: 30 MIN
4 SERVINGS ●

⅓ cup sugar
⅓ cup water
1 cup Grand Marnier
One 750-milliliter bottle Viognier
1 mango, chopped
2 peaches, cut into thin wedges
¼ cup mint leaves

In a saucepan, cook the sugar with the water until the sugar dissolves; transfer to a pitcher and refrigerate until cold, about 25 minutes. Stir in the Grand Marnier, Viognier, mango, peaches and mint; serve immediately. —John Besh

Philly Fish House Punch

TOTAL: 15 MIN PLUS 3 HR CHILLING
4 TO 6 SERVINGS ● ● ●

3 tablespoons confectioners' sugar
6½ ounces dark rum
4 ounces brandy
2 ounces peach schnapps
4 ounces cold brewed black tea
4 ounces fresh lemon juice
4 ounces cold water
Orange peels, for garnish

Set a funnel in a clean 750-milliliter bottle (such as a wine bottle) with a screw cap. Tap the confectioners' sugar into the bottle. Add the rum, brandy, schnapps, tea and lemon juice. Close the bottle and shake vigorously. Add the water and shake again. Seal and refrigerate until cold, about 3 hours. Serve the punch in the bottle, letting guests pour it into tumblers; garnish the drinks with orange peels.
—Tad Carducci and Paul Tanguay

Sparkling Pomegranate Punch

TOTAL: 15 MIN
10 TO 12 SERVINGS ● ●

This bubbly, sweet-tart punch combines sparkling wine, dessert wine and deep-red pomegranate juice.

3 tablespoons sugar
1 cup pomegranate juice
Two 750-milliliter bottles
sparkling wine, chilled
¾ cup late-harvest white wine,
such as late-harvest Riesling,
chilled
2 oranges, thinly sliced crosswise
1 cup diced fresh pineapple
¼ cup pomegranate seeds
Ice cubes, for serving

In a punch bowl, dissolve the sugar in the pomegranate juice, stirring vigorously. Add the sparkling wine and late-harvest white wine, then add the orange slices, diced pineapple and pomegranate seeds. Serve the pomegranate punch over ice cubes.
—Shawn McClain

Late-Harvest Wine and Campari Cocktails

TOTAL: 10 MIN PLUS 2 HR CHILLING
MAKES 10 DRINKS ● ●

When he's grilling for pleasure on a hot summer night, Argentine chef Francis Mallmann invariably has a cool cocktail in his free hand. The extra-refreshing one here combines sweet wine and the bitter Italian aperitif Campari.

3¾ cups sweet late-harvest
white wine, such as Riesling
2¼ cups fresh orange juice
1 cup Campari
Ice, for serving

In a large pitcher, mix the wine with the orange juice and Campari. Refrigerate until chilled, about 2 hours. Fill tall glasses with ice, pour the cocktail over the ice and serve. Francis Mallmann

Lime-and-Cucumber Frappé

TOTAL: 20 MIN
MAKES 1 DRINK ● ●

At the cozy Café Brújula in Oaxaca, Mexico, writers sit with their laptops and artists gather over drinks like this zingy blender-whirred frappé—a cold and frothy cucumber concoction.

2 tablespoons sugar
½ cup plus 2 tablespoons water
2 tablespoons fresh lime juice,
plus 1 lime wedge for garnish
One 2-inch piece of seedless
cucumber, peeled halfway
and coarsely chopped
4 ice cubes

1. In a microwave-safe cup, combine the sugar with the 2 tablespoons of water and microwave at high power for 15 seconds, until the sugar is dissolved; let cool.
2. In a blender, combine the sugar syrup with the lime juice, chopped cucumber, ice cubes and the remaining ½ cup of water; puree until frothy. Pour the frappé into a tall glass, garnish with the lime wedge and serve. —Kyle Dromgoole

SPARKLING POMEGRANATE PUNCH

LATE-HARVEST WINE
AND CAMPARI COCKTAILS

CAFÉ CUBANO

DOUBLE-CHOCOLATE HOT CHOCOLATE

Basil Limeade Slushies

TOTAL: 20 MIN
12 SERVINGS ●

A splash of soda water makes these tart slushies pleasingly bubbly. With a little rum, they'd also make great cocktails.

- 8 cups ice
- 4 cups water
- 3 cups fresh lime juice
- 3 cups lightly packed fresh basil leaves, plus basil sprigs for garnish
- 1½ cups sugar
- 1½ cups soda water

In a blender, working in batches, blend the ice with the water, lime juice, basil leaves and sugar until slushy. Pour the limeade into chilled glasses. Top each with 2 tablespoons of the soda water, garnish with the basil sprigs and serve.
—*Alain Coumont*

Iced Basil-and-Lemongrass Tea

ACTIVE: 15 MIN; TOTAL: 1 HR 45 MIN
6 SERVINGS ● ● ●

F&W's Marcia Kiesel uses whole strawberries or raspberries to give her chilled herb infusion a lovely pink hue.

- 3 large lemongrass stalks, coarsely chopped
- 1 cup chopped basil leaves and stems
- ½ cup chopped fresh mint leaves
- ⅓ cup tarragon leaves
- 4 whole berries, such as raspberries or strawberries, lightly crushed
- 2 quarts boiling water
- 3 tablespoons agave nectar or 2 tablespoons light honey (see Note)

Lime wheels, for garnish

Place the lemongrass, basil, mint, tarragon and berries in a large heatproof bowl. Add the boiling water, cover and let stand for 1½ hours. Strain into a pitcher and stir in the agave nectar. Pour into 6 ice-filled rocks glasses, garnish with the lime wheels and serve. —*Marcia Kiesel*

NOTE Agave nectar is a sweet syrup made from the core of the cactus-like agave plant. It's thinner than honey and dissolves more easily. Buy it at health-food stores.

Saffron Lassis

TOTAL: 10 MIN PLUS 1 HR CHILLING
2 SERVINGS ● ● ●

Lassis are ubiquitous in India; the shakes, made with yogurt or buttermilk, can be sweet or salty. The Imperial Hotel in New Delhi offers an extensive selection of lassis, including this sweet one, elegantly flavored with saffron.

Large pinch of saffron threads

3 tablespoons water

2 tablespoons sugar

1½ cups plain whole-milk yogurt

1. In a small bowl, crumble the saffron threads into 1 tablespoon of the water and let stand for 5 minutes.

2. Meanwhile, in a small, microwave-safe bowl, combine the remaining 2 tablespoons of water with the sugar and microwave for about 1 minute, stirring once or twice, until the sugar is completely dissolved. Transfer the bowl to the freezer until the syrup is cold, about 5 minutes.

3. In a bowl, whisk the yogurt with the saffron water and sugar syrup. Refrigerate, whisking a few times, until cold and brightly colored, about 1 hour. Pour the lassi into medium glasses and serve cold.

—*Peggy Markel*

Café Cubano

TOTAL: 20 MIN

6 SERVINGS

A well-made *café cubano* (Cuban coffee) has a sweet, frothy layer (called the *crema*) floating over strong espresso. Cooking teacher and cookbook author Lourdes Castro says you can't overbeat a *crema,* so stir it energetically.

Ground espresso

¼ cup sugar

Prepare a 6-serving stovetop espresso maker according to the manufacturer's directions and brew a pot of espresso. Put the sugar in a large glass measuring cup and add 1 tablespoon of the freshly brewed hot espresso. Using a small whisk, beat the sugar with the espresso until the *crema* is pale and thick and the sugar has almost completely dissolved, about 1 minute. Pour the remaining hot espresso over the *crema* and stir to combine. Let the foam rise to the top, then pour the Cuban coffee into espresso cups or small glasses and serve immediately.

—*Lourdes Castro*

Oaxacan Hot Chocolate

TOTAL: 15 MIN

4 TO 6 SERVINGS

Kyle Dromgoole, the owner of Café Brújula in Oaxaca, Mexico, got this simple spiced-hot-chocolate recipe from his wife's Oaxacan grandmother, who makes her own chocolate with local cacao and ground spices. Mexican cooks traditionally whip their hot chocolate with a wooden stirrer called a *molinillo,* but a wire whisk works just as well.

1 quart whole milk

3 tablets of Oaxacan or Mexican chocolate (10 ounces), chopped (see Note)

Ground cinnamon, for dusting

1. In a microwave-safe cup, heat the milk at high power for 5 minutes, until boiling.

2. Add the chopped chocolate to a 1½- to 2-quart heatproof pitcher. Pour the boiling milk over the chocolate and let stand for 1 minute. Mix the milk with the chocolate by rolling a whisk or wooden Mexican *molinillo* between the palms of your hands until the hot chocolate is smooth and slightly frothy, about 3 minutes. Pour into mugs, dust with cinnamon and serve. —*Kyle Dromgoole*

NOTE Mexican chocolate is quite sweet and somewhat grainy, since it's mixed with spices and sometimes ground nuts. Often sold in disks or tablets, it is available at Latin markets and some grocery stores.

Double-Chocolate Hot Chocolate

TOTAL: 10 MIN

2 SERVINGS

Matt Lewis and Renato Poliafito, the co-owners of Baked in Brooklyn, New York, and Charleston, South Carolina, firmly believe that homemade hot chocolate is superior to any commercial mix. They prepare theirs with bittersweet and milk chocolate and top it with marshmallows that they make and sell at their bakeries.

5 ounces bittersweet chocolate, coarsely chopped

2 ounces milk chocolate, coarsely chopped

½ cup boiling water

¾ cup whole milk

¼ cup heavy cream

2 tablespoons Jack Daniel's whiskey (optional)

Marshmallows, for serving

1. In a medium heatproof bowl, combine the bittersweet chocolate with the milk chocolate. Add the boiling water and let stand for 1 minute. Whisk the chocolate mixture until it is smooth.

2. In a small saucepan, bring the milk and cream just to a simmer. Add the chocolate mixture and whisk over moderate heat until hot. Remove the saucepan from the heat and add the whiskey. Pour the hot chocolate into demitasse cups or small mugs, garnish with marshmallows and serve. —*Matt Lewis and Renato Poliafito*

Hot Mulled Cider

ACTIVE: 15 MIN; TOTAL: 1 HR

8 SERVINGS ● ●

1 gallon apple cider

¾ cup dry white wine, such as Chardonnay

¼ cup honey

2 quince—peeled, cored and finely chopped

One 4-inch rosemary sprig

Two 3- to 4-inch cinnamon sticks, broken

4 cloves

1 star anise pod

½ teaspoon grated lemon zest

Combine the cider, wine, honey, quince, rosemary, cinnamon, cloves, star anise and lemon zest in a large saucepan and simmer over low heat for 45 minutes. Strain the mulled cider and discard the solids. Serve the mulled cider warm. —*Ken Oringer*

MAKE AHEAD The cider can be refrigerated overnight. Reheat before serving.

wine pairings

F&W's wine editor, **Ray Isle,** *has created the ultimate user-friendly guide to pairing wine and food. The glossary here, with descriptions of key wine varieties and advice on pairing specific bottles with specific recipes, is both flexible and focused.*

champagne & sparkling wines

Champagne, which is produced only in the Champagne region of France, is the greatest sparkling wine in the world—it's effervescent and lively, at the same time offering tremendous complexity and finesse. Champagnes are usually a blend of grapes, typically Pinot Noir and Chardonnay, often with a touch of Pinot Meunier as well. They range from dry (brut) to mildly sweet (demi-sec) to very sweet (doux). Different producers, or "houses," have different styles, too, ranging from light and delicate to rich and full-flavored. Many other countries also make sparkling wines. Those from North America tend to be more fruit-forward than most Champagnes. Cava, an inexpensive sparkler from Spain, often has an earthy character. Italy's Prosecco is also affordable, and popular for its engaging foaminess and hint of sweetness on the finish. Sparkling wines make great aperitifs, but they're also good throughout the meal, especially with shellfish and salty or spicy dishes.

DRY, LIGHT CHAMPAGNE
Nicolas Feuillatte Brut (France)
Pierre Peters Blanc de Blancs Brut (France)
Taittinger Brut La Française (France)

PAIRINGS
• Carrot Macaroni and Cheese, p. 86
• Boiled Shrimp with Spicy Mayonnaise, p. 202

DRY, RICH CHAMPAGNE
Bollinger Brut Special Cuvée (France)
Veuve Clicquot Brut Yellow Label (France)
Vilmart et Cie Grand Cellier (France)

PAIRINGS
• Salt-Crusted Tilapia with Lemongrass, p. 186
• Scallops with Chestnut Sauce and Crisp Sage, p. 204

DRY, FRUITY SPARKLING WINE
Domaine Chandon Blanc de Noirs (California)
Gloria Ferrer Sonoma Brut (California)
Mionetto Prosecco Brut (Italy)

PAIRINGS
• Pasta with Sizzled Sage, p. 82
• Hainan Chicken with Rice and Two Sauces, p. 100
• Cheese-Stuffed Chicken with Mustard Sauce, p. 115
• Lemony Spiced Tandoor Quail, p. 123
• Salt-Baked Trout, p. 184
• Grilled Quick-Brined Jumbo Shrimp, p. 193
• Crab, Apple and Watercress Salad, p. 203
• Beet Risotto, p. 248

DRY, EARTHY SPARKLING WINE
Gramona Gran Cuvee (Spain)
Jaume Serra Cristalino Brut NV (Spain)
Segura Viudas Brut Reserva (Spain)

PAIRINGS
• Panko-Coated Chicken Schnitzel, p. 96
• Miso-Ginger Chicken and Cabbage, p. 108
• Turkey Burgers with Spicy Pickle Sauce, p. 118
• Bluefish with Grape Leaves, p. 178
• Mama Chang's Stir-Fried Shrimp and Scallions, p. 197
• Squid Pizza with Saffron Aioli, p. 259

whites

ALBARIÑO & VINHO VERDE

The Albariño grape produces Spain's best white wines, fresh, lively bottlings that pair especially well with seafood—no surprise, as Albariño is grown in Galicia, where the fishing industry drives the economy. Mostly made in

wine pairings

stainless steel tanks without oak, Albariño has crisp flavors that suggest grapefruit and other citrus fruits, with a light mineral edge. Vinho Verde, or "green wine," from northern Portugal, often blends the Albariño grape (called Alvarinho there) with local varieties Loureiro and Trajadura. Bottled so young that it often has a lightly spritzy quality, Vinho Verde has a razor-sharp acidity and ocean freshness; it too is an ideal match for raw shellfish.

ZESTY, FRESH ALBARIÑO/VINHO VERDE
Casal Garcia Vinho Verde (Portugal)
Salneval Albariño (Spain)
Santiago Ruiz Rías Baixas (Spain)

PAIRINGS
- Mahimahi with Herbed White Wine Sauce, p. 180
- Fennel-Baked Sea Bass with Fennel Two Ways, p. 188
- Rosemary-Skewered Shrimp, p. 193
- Paella Valenciana, p. 244

WHITE BURGUNDY & CHARDONNAY

Chardonnay is grown in almost every wine-producing country in the world, and it's used to create wines in a wide range of styles. It is originally from France's Burgundy region, where the best white Burgundies are powerful and rich, with complex fruit flavors and notes of earth and minerals. More affordable Chardonnays from Burgundy—for instance, those simply labeled Bourgogne Blanc—are crisp and lively, with apple and lemon flavors. Chardonnays from America, Australia and Chile tend to be ripe and full-bodied, even buttery, with higher alcohol levels and vanilla notes from oak aging. Recently, however, more and more wine regions have been experimenting with fruity, fresh Chardonnays produced with very little or even no oak aging. Pair Chardonnays in the leaner Burgundian style with roasted chicken or seafood; the more voluptuous New World Chardonnays pair well with pasta dishes made with cream or cheese, with lobster or other rich seafood and with Asian dishes that include coconut milk.

LIGHT, CRISP WHITE BURGUNDY
Louis Latour Mâcon-Lugny (France)
Olivier Leflaive Bourgogne Blanc Les Sétilles (France)
William Fevre Chablis (France)

PAIRINGS
- Super-Crispy Fried Chicken, p. 97
- Mustard-Glazed Chicken with Bok Choy, p. 112
- Leek Salad with Walnuts and Tomme de Brebis, p. 218

RICH, COMPLEX WHITE BURGUNDY
Domaine Bouchard Père & Fils Beaune du Château Premier Cru (France)
Joseph Drouhin Beaune Clos des Mouches Blanc Premier Cru (France)
Lucien Le Moine Bourgogne Blanc (France)

PAIRINGS
- Chicken Breasts with Potatoes and Mashed Peas, p. 111

FRUITY, LOW-OAK CHARDONNAY
Chehalem INOX (Oregon)
Foxglove Edna Valley (California)
Kim Crawford Marlborough Unoaked (New Zealand)

PAIRINGS
- Roast Chicken with Tangerines, p. 96
- Honey–Soy Sauce Chicken with Mâche and Citrus, p. 104
- Mango-Glazed Turkey Breast, p. 122
- Spicy Lobster-Noodle Salad, p. 208

RIPE, LUXURIOUS CHARDONNAY
Beringer Napa Valley (California)
Hess Monterey (California)
Rosemount Estate Show Reserve Hunter Valley (Australia)

PAIRINGS
- Spinach-and-Ricotta Tortelli with Browned Butter, p. 84
- Roasted Herb Chicken with Morels and Watercress, p. 98
- Butter-Basted Chicken Skewers, p. 104
- Chicken with Walnuts, Leeks and Candied Lemon, p. 111
- Roast Turkey with Fried Sage and Pecans, p. 119
- Poached Salmon with Corn and White Wine Sauce, p. 175
- Grouper with Corn "Pudding" and Collard Greens, p. 188
- Sizzling Shrimp Scampi, p. 194
- Chili Lobster, p. 206
- Bean, Corn and Squash Stew, p. 245

CHENIN BLANC

Chenin Blanc is the star of France's Loire region, where it's used for complex Vouvrays and Savennières. Chenin has also proved to be at home in parts of California (particularly the little-known Clarksburg region), in Washington State and in South Africa, which produces some of the best-value white wines around—tart, medium-bodied whites with flavors of apple and peach. The more affordable South African, Californian and Washington versions are good with light fish or simple poultry dishes.

FRUITY, SOFT CHENIN BLANC

Hogue (Washington State)
Indaba (South Africa)
Man Vintners (South Africa)

PAIRINGS

- Chile-Brined Fresh Ham, p. 158
- Curried-Shrimp Salad with Grilled Watermelon, p. 198
- Root-Vegetable Gratin, p. 214

COMPLEX, AROMATIC CHENIN BLANC

Champalou Vouvray (France)
Domaine des Baumard Clos du Papillon (France)

PAIRINGS

- Chicken Paprikash, p. 109
- Chicken-and-Leek Pie, p. 114
- Stuffed Flounder with Frizzled Mint and Ginger, p. 180
- Grilled Scallops with Honeydew-Avocado Salsa, p. 206

GEWÜRZTRAMINER

One of the most easily identifiable grapes—the flamboyant aroma recalls roses, lychee nuts and spices such as clove and allspice—Gewürztraminer reaches its peak in France's Alsace region, producing full-bodied wines ranging from dry to quite sweet, with flavors of apricot, apple and baking spices. Gewürztraminer pairs well with Alsace cuisine—a tarte flambée made with ham and Gruyère, for instance. American Gewürztraminers tend to be less dense and unctuous, though they typically have a touch of sweetness on the finish and a delicate spiciness. Pair them with Asian food.

RICH ALSACE GEWÜRZTRAMINER

Hugel (France)
Trimbach (France)

PAIRINGS

- Grilled Red Curry Chicken, p. 103
- Roast Turkey with Jalapeño-Paprika Gravy, p. 119

SPICY AMERICAN GEWÜRZTRAMINER

Navarro Vineyards (California)
Thomas Fogarty Monterey (California)

PAIRINGS

- Salmon with Gingery Vegetables and Turmeric, p. 174
- Shrimp Fried Rice with Coconut and Pickled Onions, p. 198

GRÜNER VELTLINER

Grüner Veltliner, from Austria, has become a darling of American sommeliers, after decades of near obscurity in the United States. A refreshing, medium-bodied, peppery white wine with stone fruit flavors, it goes with everything from green salads to cold poached salmon to roasted chicken. The best Grüners can be expensive and have enormous aging potential.

PEPPERY, REFRESHING GRÜNER VELTLINER

Bründlmayer Kamptaler Terassen (Austria)
Hirsch Veltliner #1 (Austria)

PAIRINGS

- Zucchini Linguine with Herbs, p. 82
- Shrimp–and–Bok Choy Stir-Fry with Crispy Noodles, p. 193

PINOT BIANCO & PINOT BLANC

These are two names for the same grape; the first one is Italian and the second French. The French versions, from Alsace, are musky and creamy-textured; those from Italy have zippier acidity, with pear or soft citrus flavors. American Pinot Blancs are usually made in the French style. Pour Pinot Blancs with cheese-based dishes; Pinot Biancos go nicely with light foods like chicken breasts or flaky white fish.

ZIPPY, FRESH PINOT BIANCO

Abbazia di Novacella (Italy)
St. Michael-Eppan (Italy)

PAIRINGS

- Herb-Marinated Chicken Skewers with Harissa, p. 106
- Smoky Shellfish Stew with Herbs, p. 209
- Grilled Tofu with Asparagus and Nori Vinaigrette, p. 232
- Margherita Tortilla Pizzas, p. 256

CREAMY, SUPPLE PINOT BLANC

Hugel & Fils (France)
WillaKenzie Estate (Oregon)

PAIRINGS

- Chicken Salad with Zucchini, Lemon and Pine Nuts, p. 102
- Salt-Roasted Shrimp, p. 194

wine pairings

PINOT GRIGIO & PINOT GRIS

Pinot Grigio (from Italy) and Pinot Gris (from France's Alsace) are the same grape variety. Italian Pinots (and others modeled on them) tend to be light, simple wines with suggestions of peach and melon. These crisp, fresh whites are ideal as an aperitif or with light seafood or chicken breast dishes. Bottlings from Alsace are richer, with strong notes of almonds, spice and sometimes honey. American versions, mainly from Oregon, often tend more toward the Alsace style, and thus are mostly labeled Pinot Gris. They go well with creamy pastas or smoked foods.

LIGHT, FRESH PINOT GRIGIO
Hofstätter Joseph (Italy)
Meridian (California)
Tiefenbrunner (Italy)

PAIRINGS
- Rice-Noodle Salad with Chicken and Herbs, p. 93
- Pan-Roasted Salmon-and-Bread Salad, p. 176
- Pan-Seared Black Sea Bass with Endives, p. 188
- Shrimp-and-Vegetable Summer Rolls, p. 201
- Fried-Fish Sandwiches with Tomatoes, p. 273

FULL-BODIED, RICH PINOT GRIS
Domaines Schlumberger Les Princes Abbés (France)
Domaine Weinbach (France)
King Estate (Oregon)
MacMurray Ranch (California)

PAIRINGS
- Sour-Orange Yucatán Chickens, p. 98
- Roasted-Chicken-and-Potato Salad with Béarnaise, p. 100
- Chicken Salad with Piquillo Dressing, p. 112
- Turkey Breast with Ginger-Scallion Sauce, p. 120
- Cod with Artichokes and Chickpeas, p. 186
- Poached Shrimp, Melon and Frisée Salad, p. 200
- Seared Scallops with Pinot Gris Butter Sauce, p. 206
- Curried Eggplant with Chickpeas and Spinach, p. 224
- Tomato, Prosciutto and Gruyère Sandwiches, p. 262
- Grilled Gruyère-and-Zucchini Sandwiches, p. 264
- Oregon Tuna Melts, p. 270

RIESLING

Riesling is one of the great white grape varieties, and the style of the wines it produces varies dramatically by region. German Rieslings balance impressive acidity with apple and citrus fruit flavors, and range from dry and refreshing to sweet and unctuous. Alsace and Austrian Rieslings are higher in alcohol, which makes them more full-bodied, but they are quite dry, full of mineral notes. Australia's Rieslings (the best are from the Clare Valley) are zippy and full of lime and other citrus flavors. Those from Washington State tend to split the difference, offering juicy, appley fruit and lively acidity, with a hint of sweetness. Rieslings are extraordinarily versatile with food. As a general rule, pair lighter, crisper Rieslings with delicate (or raw) fish; more substantial Rieslings are good with Asian food, chicken, salmon and tuna.

TART, CITRUSY RIESLING
Banrock Station (Australia)
Leasingham Magnus (Australia)
Penfolds Eden Valley Reserve (Australia)

PAIRINGS
- Spicy Peanut Noodles, p. 93
- Chinese Chicken Salad, p. 101
- Spicy Asian-Chicken-Salad Lettuce Cups, p. 112
- Striped Bass with Sweet Carrots and Cider Glaze, p. 186
- Asparagus-Cheese Tartines, p. 262

VIVID, LIGHTLY SWEET RIESLING
Columbia Winery Cellarmaster's (Washington State)
J. Lohr Estates Bay Mist (California)
Weingut Selbach-Oster Estate (Germany)

PAIRINGS
- Soba Noodle Salad with Thai Red Curry Sauce, p. 92
- Updated Chicken Chow Mein, p. 112
- Thai Chicken, Zucchini and Tomato Curry, p. 113
- Chicken Curry with Squash, p. 114
- Thai Ground Pork Salad, p. 170
- Indonesian-Style Shrimp Salad, p. 200
- Chili Shrimp, p. 202
- Vietnamese-Style Banh Mi Burgers, p. 270
- Piquillo-Pepper Num Pangs, p. 270

FULL-BODIED, MINERALLY RIESLING
Domaine Marc Kreydenweiss Andlau (France)
Dr. Konstantin Frank (New York State)
Hiedler Heiligenstein (Austria)

wine pairings

PAIRINGS
- Sake-Steamed Halibut with Ginger and Cabbage, p. 180
- Shrimp and Mussels in Coconut Broth, p. 194

SAUVIGNON BLANC

Sauvignon's herbal scent and tart, citrus-driven flavors make it instantly identifiable. The best regions for Sauvignon are the Loire Valley in France, where it takes on a firm, minerally depth; New Zealand, where it recalls the tartness of gooseberries and, sometimes, an almost green, jalapeño-like note; California, where it pairs crisp grassiness and a melon-like flavor; and South Africa, particularly the Cape region, where it combines the minerality of France with the rounder fruit of California. Sauvignon Blanc teams well with light fish, shellfish, salads and green vegetables, and it's a perfect aperitif, too.

LIVELY, TART SAUVIGNON BLANC
Franciscan (California)
Geyser Peak Winery (California)
Honig (California)

PAIRINGS
- Glass Noodle Stir-Fry, p. 93
- Crisp Salmon with Avocado Salad, p. 178
- Spanish Mackerel Escabèche, p. 183
- Scallops with Grapefruit-Onion Salad, p. 204
- Artichoke-and-Fontina Pizzas, p. 256

MINERALLY, COMPLEX SAUVIGNON BLANC
Château de Sancerre Sancerre (France)
Concha y Toro Terrunyo (Chile)
Craggy Range Winery (New Zealand)

PAIRINGS
- Soy-Braised Turkey with Turkey Rice, p. 118
- Grouper with Cucumber Salad, p. 189
- Steamed Clams in Verjus p. 203
- Asparagus Risotto with Mint, p. 246
- Summer Squash Pizza with Goat Cheese, p. 257

SOAVE, VERDICCHIO & GAVI

These three light, usually inexpensive wines from Italy all match well with a wide range of foods. Soave, mostly made from the Garganega grape, is a fruity white that often has an almond note. Verdicchio, made from the grape of the same name, has a lemony zestiness. Gavi, made from a grape called Cortese, is typically tart, with

an aroma that suggests fresh limes. All three wines pair well with herby pasta sauces like pesto, white fish or fresh vegetable dishes.

FRESH, LIVELY SOAVE OR SIMILAR ITALIAN WHITE
Banfi Principessa Gavi (Italy)
Pieropan Soave Classico (Italy)
Villa Bucci Verdicchio (Italy)

PAIRINGS
- Whole Wheat Rigatoni with Roasted Vegetables, p. 78
- Fusilli alla Crazy Bastard, p. 82
- Penne with Asparagus, Sage and Peas, p. 84
- Tuna Scallopine with Parsley and Pomegranate p. 178
- Creamy Seafood Risotto, p. 247
- Green Olive–and–Garlic Pizza with Dough for Obsessives, p. 258

VERMENTINO

An up-and-coming white grape from the coastal regions of Italy, Vermentino marries vivacious acidity with stony minerality. The best Vermentinos come from very different parts of Italy—from Liguria in the north and from the island of Sardinia, off the central west coast. Drink Vermentino with seafood dishes of all kinds.

FRESH, MINERALLY VERMENTINO
Antinori (Italy)
Argiolas Costamolino (Italy)
Sella & Mosca La Cala (Italy)

PAIRINGS
- Spaghetti with Tomatoes and Capers, p. 80
- Angel Hair Pasta with Crab and Country Ham, p. 83
- Pasta with Smothered Broccoli Rabe and Olives, p. 88
- Lemon-Stuffed Grilled Branzino, p. 182
- Italian Seafood Stew, p. 209

VIOGNIER

Viogniers are seductive white wines, lush with peach and honeysuckle scents, a round, mouth-filling texture and little acidity. The Condrieu region in France's Rhône Valley produces the world's greatest Viogniers, and they can often be quite expensive; California and occasionally Australia have also had success with this grape. Viognier pairs well with grilled seafood; it's also a good match for most foods flavored with fruit salsas.

wine pairings

LUSH, FRAGRANT VIOGNIER

Alban Vineyards (California)

Cave Yves Cuilleron Condrieu (France)

Cono Sur (Chile)

PAIRINGS

- Chicken with Roasted Tomatoes and Cheesy Grits, p. 97
- Wine-Marinated Lamb Chops with Fennel Salad, p. 142
- Sesame-Crusted Tuna with Ginger Cream, p. 179

rosés

Rosé—that is, dry rosé—may be the world's most under-rated wine. Combining the light, lively freshness of white wines with the fruit and depth of reds, good rosés pair well with a remarkable range of foods, from delicate fish like sole to meats such as pork and veal. They also complement a range of ethnic cuisines—Chinese, Thai, Mexican and Greek. The best rosés, from southern France, are typically blends of grapes such as Syrah, Grenache, Cinsaut and Mourvèdre. Italy, Greece and Spain also produce terrific, refreshing rosés. American and Australian rosés, which tend to be fruitier and heavier, can also be very good.

FRESH, FRUITY ROSÉ

Crios de Susana Balbo (Argentina)

La Bargemone (France)

Muga (Spain)

PAIRINGS

- Linguine with Tomatoes, Baby Zucchini and Herbs, p. 79
- Crispy Baked Red Chile Chicken Wings, p. 107
- Turkey Burgers with Smoked Gouda, p. 118
- Warm Flank Steak Salad with Mint and Cilantro, p. 127
- Roast Beef Summer Rolls, p. 130
- Ginger-Beef Salad, p. 133
- Kogi Dogs, p. 152
- Pan-Roasted Pork Chops with Creamy Cabbage and Apples, p. 166
- Grilled Salmon with Preserved Lemon and Olives, p. 174
- Pomegranate-Glazed Salmon, p. 176
- Grilled Niçoise Tuna Steaks, p. 178
- Grilled Mackerel with Sicilian Caper-Tomato Salsa, p. 182
- Shrimp with Cheese-Grit Cakes and Bacon, p. 192
- Shrimp-and-Vegetable Tagine, p. 196
- Clams with Pork and Golden Garlic, p. 204
- Enchilado, p. 208
- Layered Eggplant, Zucchini and Tomato Casserole, p. 224

- Oven-Roasted Tomatoes Stuffed with Goat Cheese, p. 228
- Cheesy Farro-and-Tomato Risotto, p. 240
- Triple-Decker Baked Italian Cheese Sandwiches, p. 262
- Multigrain Grilled Cheese Sandwiches, p. 264
- Tuna Bocadillos, p. 272

reds

BARBERA

Barbera, which grows primarily in Italy's Piedmont region, mostly produces medium-bodied wines with firm acidity and flavors suggesting red cherries with a touch of spice. (Barrel-aged versions tend to be more full-bodied, and more expensive.) A great wine for pastas with meat- or tomato-based sauces, Barbera is also good with game and hard cheeses.

BRIGHT, TART BARBERA

C. G. Di Arie Sierra Foothills (California)

Coppo Camp du Rouss Barbera d'Asti (Italy)

Michele Chiarlo Barbera d'Asti (Italy)

PAIRINGS

- Creamy Buckwheat Pasta with Wild Mushrooms, p. 79
- Macaroni and Many Cheeses, p. 86
- Basic Meatballs, p. 151
- Roasted Pork Loin with Orange-Herb Sauce, p. 164
- Barbecued Spiced Shrimp with Tomato Salad, p. 200
- Milanese Risotto, p. 247
- Prosciutto-Cheese and Squash-Pecorino Piadina, p. 260

BEAUJOLAIS & GAMAY

Gamay, the grape of France's Beaujolais region, makes wines that embody everything that region is known for: light, fruity, easy-to-drink reds, ideal for a party or a picnic. Typically they are not aged in oak barrels and are released early (Beaujolais Nouveau, which appears on shelves little more than a month after the grapes are harvested, is the extreme example). Little Gamay is grown outside of Beaujolais, but what has been planted pairs well with the same foods as Beaujolais: light chicken dishes, salads, cheeses and charcuterie.

FRUITY, LIGHT-BODIED BEAUJOLAIS/GAMAY

Georges Duboeuf Beaujolais-Villages (France)

Jean-Paul Brun Terres Dorees (France)

Marcel Lapierre Morgon (France)

PAIRINGS
- Modern Turkey Tetrazzini, p. 90
- Shiitake-and-Scallion Lo Mein, p. 90
- Wasabi Flank Steak with Miso-Glazed Potatoes, p. 127
- Pork-and-Chile Stew, p. 160
- Pork-and-Tofu Stir-Fry, p. 166
- Scallion-and-Pecan-Crusted Catfish with Hominy, p. 184
- Shrimp-and-Feta-Stuffed Zucchini, p. 196
- Shrimp Saganaki, p. 197
- Squid and Black-Eyed Pea Salad, p. 203

CABERNET SAUVIGNON

Arguably the most significant red wine grape, Cabernet Sauvignon has traveled far beyond its origins in France's Bordeaux—it's now widely planted in almost every wine-producing country. Depending on climate, Cabernet can make either firm, tannic wines that recall red currants with a touch of tobacco or green bell pepper (colder climates) or softer wines that recall ripe black currants or black cherries (warmer climates). It almost always has substantial tannins, which help great Cabernets age for many years. The classic pairing with Cabernet is lamb, but it goes well with almost any meat—beef, pork, venison, even rabbit.

FIRM, COMPLEX CABERNET SAUVIGNON
Château de Pez (France)
St. Clement Napa Valley (California)
Wynns Coonawarra (Australia)

PAIRINGS
- Rib Eye Roast with Chestnuts and Brussels Sprout Leaves, p. 132
- Peppered Beef Tenderloin with Roasted Garlic–Herb Butter, p. 135
- Lamb Chops with Frizzled Herbs, p. 140
- Mustard-Crusted Lamb, p. 145
- Roast Veal with Marjoram, p. 171

RICH, RIPE CABERNET SAUVIGNON
Justin Vineyards & Winery (California)
Layer Cake Napa Valley (California)
Penley Estate Reserve (Australia)

PAIRINGS
- Korean Sizzling Beef, p. 128
- Beef Tenderloin with Pickled Onions, p. 132
- Meatballs with Peas, p. 150
- Beef Burgers with Peanut-Chipotle Barbecue Sauce, p. 152
- Pork Loin Roast with Herbs and Garlic, p. 166
- Pan-Roasted Veal Chops with Cabernet Sauce, p. 171

DOLCETTO

Though Dolcetto means "little sweet one," wines from this Italian grape are dry, grapey, tart, simple reds distinguished by their vibrant purple color and ebullient berry juiciness. Dolcettos should be drunk young, with antipasti, pastas with meat sauces or roasted poultry of any kind.

JUICY, FRESH DOLCETTO
Massolino Dolcetto d'Alba (Italy)
Parusso Dolcetto d'Alba Piani Noce (Italy)
Vietti Dolcetto d'Alba Tre Vigne (Italy)

PAIRINGS
- Summery Fettuccine Alfredo, p. 80
- Linguine with Red Cabbage, p. 80
- Potato Gnocchi with Butter and Cheese, p. 87
- Chilaquiles-Style Roasted Chicken Legs, p. 110
- Rabbit Stew with Olives and Rosemary, p. 149
- Meatball Spiedini, p. 151
- Spiced Pork Tenderloin with Honey Mustard, p. 165
- Red Wine–Braised Baby Octopus with Black Olives, p. 202
- Luxe Bubble and Squeak, p. 214
- Fennel-and-Sausage Risotto, p. 247

GRENACHE

When made well, Grenache produces full-bodied, high-alcohol red wines that tend to be low in acidity and full of black cherry and raspberry flavors. Grenache is often blended with other grapes to make dark, powerful reds in regions such as France's Châteauneuf-du-Pape or Spain's Rioja and Priorato. On its own in Australia and the United States, it can produce deeply fruity, juicy wines that go perfectly with grilled meats, sausages and highly spiced dishes.

JUICY, SPICY GRENACHE
Beckmen Vineyards Estate (California)
Bodegas Zabrin Garnacha de Fuego (Spain)
Yalumba Bush Vine (Australia)

wine pairings

PAIRINGS
- Grill-Smoked Whole Chicken, p. 100
- Chicken Thighs with Spicy Tomato-Pepper Sauce, p. 106
- Three-Ingredient Prime Rib Roast, p. 132
- Moroccan Spiced Lamb Patties with Peppers, p. 142
- Kibbe in Yogurt Sauce, p. 146
- Pork Souvlaki with Tzatziki, p. 160
- Apple-Glazed Barbecued Baby Back Ribs, p. 164
- Maple Sugar–Ginger Roast Pork, p. 164

MALBEC

Originally used as a blending grape in France's Bordeaux region, Malbec has found its true home in Argentina's Mendoza region. There, it produces darkly fruity wines with hints of black pepper and leather—like a traditional rustic country red, but with riper, fuller fruit. Malbecs are often very affordable, too, and go wonderfully with steaks and roasts, hearty stews and grilled sausages.

RUSTIC, PEPPERY MALBEC
Bodega Norton (Argentina)
Catena Zapata (Argentina)
Weinert (Argentina)

PAIRINGS
- Chicken Drumsticks with
  Asian Barbecue Sauce, p. 104
- Fajitas, p. 133
- T-Bone Churrasco a la Plancha, p. 136
- Chili with Guajillo and Ancho Chiles and Hominy, p. 155
- Braised Pork Shoulder with Chimichurri, p. 160
- Sausage-and-Pepper Heros, p. 170
- Cuban Sandwiches with Tomato Jam, p. 266

MERLOT

The most widely planted grape in France's Bordeaux region isn't Cabernet Sauvignon; it's Merlot. That's because Merlot blends so well with other grapes, and also because Merlot's gentle succulence and plummy flavors have gained favor as worldwide tastes have shifted toward fruitier, easier-drinking wines. Good Merlots are made in France, Italy, Chile, the United States and Australia, and all of them tend to share supple, velvety tannins and round black cherry or plum flavors. Merlot pairs beautifully with many foods—try it with pâtés or other charcuterie, pork or veal roasts, rich, cheesy gratins and even hamburgers.

LIVELY, FRUITY MERLOT
Columbia Crest Grand Estates (Washington State)
Francis Coppola Diamond Collection (California)
Hardys Stamp of Australia (Australia)

PAIRINGS
- Hanger Steak with Herb-Nut Salsa, p. 126
- Middle Eastern Lamb Skewers, p. 146
- Meat Loaf with Mustard Seeds and White Pepper, p. 150

DEEP, VELVETY MERLOT
Avignonesi Desiderio (Italy)
L'Ecole No 41 (Washington State)
Paloma (California)

PAIRINGS
- Chicken Smothered in Gravy, p. 101
- Cornish Hens with Plum-and-Leek Stuffing, p. 122
- Hanger Steak with Warm Bulgur Salad, p. 127
- Beef Stroganoff, p. 133
- Grilled Skirt Steaks, p. 136
- Cheddar BLT Burgers, p. 154
- Garlic-Rubbed Pork Shoulder with Vegetables, p. 159

NEBBIOLO, BAROLO & BARBARESCO

Nebbiolo is the greatest grape of Italy's Piedmont. And if you ask a farmer, it is unquestionably one of the most difficult to grow. Certainly it is formidable, with fierce tannins and acidity, but it is also gloriously scented—"tar and roses" is the classic description—and has a supple, evocative flavor that lingers on the tongue. Those flavors are more substantial and emphatic in Barolos and more delicate and filigreed in Barbarescos, the two primary wines from Piedmont. Pour good Nebbiolo with foods such as braised short ribs, beef roasts, bollito misto and anything that involves truffles.

COMPLEX, AROMATIC NEBBIOLO
Borgogno Barolo (Italy)
Pio Cesare Barolo (Italy)
Produttori del Barbaresco Barbaresco (Italy)

PAIRINGS
- Pappardelle with Veal Ragù, p. 86
- Duck Breast with Fig Sauce, p. 116
- Focaccia-Stuffed Squab with Bean Stew, p. 122
- Garlic Salt–Crusted Bistecca, p. 131
- Grilled Porterhouse Steak with Summer Vegetables, p. 135
- Rabbit Ragout with Soppressata and Pappardelle, p. 149

wine pairings

PINOT NOIR & RED BURGUNDY

Pinot Noir probably inspires more rhapsodies—and disappointments—among wine lovers than any other grape. When it's good, it's ethereally aromatic, with flavors ranging from ripe red berries to sweet black cherries, and tannins that are firm but never obtrusive. (When bad, unfortunately, the wine is acidic, raspy and bland.) The greatest Pinot Noirs come from France's Burgundy region, age-worthy wines that are usually quite expensive. More affordable and typically more fruit-forward Pinots can be found from California and Oregon as well as New Zealand, Chile and Australia. Pinot Noir pairs well with a wide range of foods—fruitier versions make a great match with salmon or other fatty fish, roasted chicken or pasta dishes; bigger, more tannic Pinot Noirs are ideal with duck and other game birds, casseroles or stews such as beef bourguignon.

RIPE, JUICY PINOT NOIR
A to Z (Oregon)
Au Bon Climat Santa Barbara County (California)
DeLoach Russian River Valley (California)

PAIRINGS
- Stir-Fried Udon Noodles, p. 92
- Fried Chicken Liver, Bacon and Tomato Salad, p. 102
- Grilled Chicken Breasts with Sautéed Mushrooms, p. 115
- Coriander-Crusted Duck Breasts, p. 116
- Roast Turkey with Lemon and Chives, p. 119
- Herb-Roasted Turkey with Gravy, p. 120
- Grilled Beef-Tenderloin Skewers with Red Miso, p. 126
- Vaca Frita, p. 128
- Shepherd's Pie, p. 155
- Juicy Buttermilk Pork Chops, p. 168
- Black-Sesame Salmon Balls, p. 175
- Salmon with Andouille Sausage and Green Olives, p. 175
- Leek-and-Pecorino Pizzas, p. 256
- Focaccia Reubens, p. 266
- Salmon Club Sandwiches, p. 272

COMPLEX, ELEGANT PINOT NOIR
Faiveley Nuits-St-Georges (France)
Palliser Estate (New Zealand)
Scherrer (California)

PAIRINGS
- Chicken, Wild Mushroom and Roasted-Garlic Sauté, p. 107
- Grilled Spiced Duck Breasts with Blackberries, p. 115
- Braised Duck with Pinot Noir, Tomatoes and Grapes, p. 116

- Tamarind Beef, p. 130
- Grilled Beef with Cauliflower-Broccoli Hash, p. 134
- Chopped Lamb Steak with Garlicky Spinach, p. 142
- Grilled Pork Rib Roasts with Green Beans, p. 161
- Sausage, Bread and Chicken Liver Spiedini, p. 171
- Salmon with Shiitake and Red Wine Sauce, p. 176
- Grilled Halibut with Fingerlings and Tomato Butter, p. 182
- Mixed-Mushroom Strudel, p. 228
- Porcini Risotto, p. 246

RIOJA & TEMPRANILLO

Tempranillo, the top red grape of Spain, is best known as the main component in red Rioja, where it contributes earthy cherry flavors and firm structure. It is also used in almost every other region of Spain, and generally produces medium-bodied, firm reds suitable for meat dishes of all kinds, particularly lamb.

EARTHY, MEDIUM-BODIED TEMPRANILLO
Bodegas Montecillo Reserva (Spain)
Marqués de Cáceres Crianza (Spain)
Torres Celeste (Spain)

PAIRINGS
- Chicken Sofrito, p. 108
- Chicken Legs with Roasted Garlic–Ancho Sauce, p. 110
- Flank Steak with Corn, Tomato and Asparagus, p. 128
- Grilled Steak Tacos with Avocado Salsa, p. 138
- Herbed Roast Leg of Lamb, p. 145
- Lamb Skewers with Salsa Verde, p. 148
- Cocoa-and-Chile-Rubbed Pork Chops, p. 168
- Mushroom–and–Goat Cheese Béchamel Pizzas, p. 258

SANGIOVESE

Sangiovese is primarily known for the principal role it plays in Tuscan wines such as Chianti, Brunello and Carmignano, though these days it is also being grown in the United States and Australia. Italian Sangioveses have vibrant acidity and substantial tannins, along with fresh cherry fruit and herbal scents. New World versions tend toward softer acidity and fleshier fruit. Pair Sangioveses with rare steaks, game birds (or wild boar), rich chicken or mushroom dishes or anything with tomato sauce.

CHERRY-INFLECTED, EARTHY SANGIOVESE
Castello Banfi Col di Sasso (Italy)
Castello di Monsanto Chianti Classico Riserva (Italy)
Di Majo Norante (Italy)

wine pairings

PAIRINGS
- Bucatini Carbonara, p. 78
- Red Wine Spaghetti with Walnuts and Parsley, p. 80
- Corn, Chicken and Beef Gratins, p. 114
- Beef Tenderloin with Aromatic Thai Spices, p. 130
- Balsamic-and-Rosemary-Marinated Steak, p. 135
- Supersize Meatballs, p. 151
- Wild Mushroom and Red Wine Risotto, p. 247

SYRAH & SHIRAZ

Probably no other grape scores higher on the intensity meter than Syrah. It's the marquee grape of France's Rhône Valley, where it makes full-bodied, smoky, powerful reds with hints of black pepper. It has also become the signature grape of Australia, where it's known as Shiraz, and typically produces fruitier, less tannic wines marked by sweet blackberry flavors and occasionally fresh espresso notes. American Syrahs lean more toward the Australian mold, thanks to California's similarly moderate weather; there are a few very good, earthy Syrahs coming from South Africa, too, particularly from the Stellenbosch subregion. Barbecued foods with a smoky char pair nicely with Syrah, as do lamb, venison and game birds.

INTENSE, SPICY SYRAH OR SHIRAZ
Delas Les Launes Crozes-Hermitage (France)
Dunham Cellars (Washington State)
M. Chapoutier La Sizeranne Hermitage (France)

PAIRINGS
- Greek Baked Pasta, p. 88
- Braised Lamb Shanks with Garlic and Indian Spices, p. 139
- Vadouvan-Spiced Leg of Lamb, p. 145
- Cumin-Spiced Burgers with Harissa Mayo, p. 152
- Pan-Seared Pork with Green Peppercorn Sauce, p. 168

ROUND, DEEP-FLAVORED SYRAH OR SHIRAZ
d'Arenberg The Footbolt (Australia)
Qupé Central Coast (California)
Torbreck Woodcutters (Australia)

PAIRINGS
- Chicken Shawarma with Green Beans and Zucchini, p. 108
- Paprika-Rubbed Tenderloin with Citrus-Mustard Butter, p. 134
- Syrah-Braised Lamb with Olives, Cherries and Endives, p. 138

- Slow-Roasted Lamb with Almond-Mint Pesto, p. 140
- Grilled Lamb Chops with Roasted Garlic, p. 144
- Cumin-Rubbed Leg of Lamb with Black Olive–Yogurt Sauce, p. 144
- Lamb Pita Pockets with Tomato-Ginger Compote, p. 265

FRUITY, LUSCIOUS SYRAH OR SHIRAZ
Oxford Landing (Australia)
Porcupine Ridge (South Africa)
Woop Woop (Australia)

PAIRINGS
- Syrah-Braised Short Ribs, p. 138
- Spicy Lamb Shish Kebabs, p. 148
- Asian Meatball Wraps, p. 151
- Asian Spiced Pork Shoulder, p. 159
- Honey-Glazed Baby Back Ribs, p. 162
- Spicy and Sticky Baby Back Ribs, p. 162
- Pork Belly with Buckwheat Spaetzle and Collards, p. 169

ZINFANDEL

Though Zinfandel is descended from the Croatian grape Crljenak, the wine it produces is entirely Californian in character. The California wine country's warm, easygoing weather gives Zinfandel a jammy, juicy fruitiness (except when it's made into dull, lightly sweet white Zinfandel). Typically high in both alcohol and flavor—boysenberries with a touch of brambly spiciness—Zinfandel is the perfect cookout wine, great with grilled burgers, sausages or chicken, or even chips and dip.

INTENSE, FRUITY ZINFANDEL
Bogle Vineyards Old Vine (California)
Ravenswood Lodi (California)
Seghesio Family Vineyards Sonoma (California)

PAIRINGS
- Rigatoni with Spicy Italian Salami, Cherry Tomatoes, Olives and Capers, p. 82
- Pan-Roasted Chicken Breasts with Mole Negro, p. 110
- Coriander-Dusted Roast Beef, p. 133
- Chipotle-Marinated Flatiron Steak with Avocado-Corn Relish, p. 136
- Yogurt-Marinated Lamb Kebabs with Lemon Butter, p. 148
- Green-Chile Bacon Burgers with Goat Cheese, p. 150
- Mo's Sticky Ribs, p. 162
- Mexican Tortas with Black Beans and Chorizo, p. 264
- Grilled Merguez Sandwiches with Red Onions, p. 266

15 rules for perfect pairings

F&W's **Ray Isle** *created pairing principles for the world's most important wines, then the F&W Test Kitchen came up with stellar recipes to match.*

1 Champagne is perfect with anything salty.

Most dry sparkling wines, such as brut Champagne and cava, have a faint sweetness that makes them extra-refreshing with salty foods.

CRISPY UDON NOODLES WITH NORI SALT (P. 12)

2 Sauvignon Blanc goes with tart dressings and sauces.

Tangy dressings and sauces won't overwhelm zippy white wines like Sauvignon Blanc, Vinho Verde from Portugal and Verdejo from Spain.

SCALLOPS WITH GRAPEFRUIT-ONION SALAD (P. 204)

3 When a dish has lots of fresh herbs, drink a Grüner Veltliner.

Austria's Grüner has a citrus-and-clover scent that's lovely with herb-rich dishes. Spain's Albariño and Italy's Vermentino are great too.

ZUCCHINI LINGUINE WITH HERBS (P. 82)

4 Pinot Grigio pairs with light fish dishes.

Light seafood dishes take on more flavor when matched with equally delicate whites, like Pinot Grigio from Italy or Chablis from France.

SEAFOOD TOSTADA BITES (P. 24)

5 For fatty fish or fish in a rich sauce, look to Chardonnay.

Silky whites, such as Chardonnays from California, Chile or Australia, are delicious with fish like salmon or any kind of seafood in a lush sauce.

SIZZLING SHRIMP SCAMPI (P. 194)

6 Pair sweet & spicy dishes with off-dry Riesling.

The slight sweetness of many Rieslings, Gewürztraminers and Vouvrays helps tame the heat of spicy Asian and Indian dishes.

THAI GREEN SALAD WITH DUCK CRACKLINGS (P. 52)

7 Moscato d'Asti loves fruit desserts.

Slightly sweet sparkling wines such as Moscato d'Asti and demi-sec Champagne emphasize the fruit in the dessert, not the sugar.

HONEYED FIG CROSTATAS (P. 300)

8 Rosé Champagne is great with dinner, not just hors d'oeuvres.

Although most people drink sparkling rosé with hors d'oeuvres, these wines have the depth of flavor to go with a wide range of main courses.

BEET RISOTTO (P. 248)

9 For rich, cheesy dishes, try a dry rosé.

Some cheeses go better with white wine, some with red; yet almost all pair well with dry rosé, with its balance of acidity and fruit.

TRIPLE-DECKER BAKED ITALIAN CHEESE SANDWICHES (P. 262)

10 Pinot Noir is great for dishes with earthy flavors.

Ingredients like mushrooms and truffles taste great with Pinot Noir and Dolcetto, which are light-bodied but full of savory depth.

LEEK-AND-PECORINO PIZZAS (P. 256)

11 Old World wines and Old World dishes are usually good together.

The flavors of foods and wines that have grown up together over the centuries—in Tuscany, for instance are almost always a good fit.

PAPPARDELLE WITH VEAL RAGÙ (P. 86)

12 Malbec won't be overshadowed by sweet-spicy barbecue sauces.

Malbec, Shiraz and Côtes-du-Rhône are big and bold enough to drink with foods that are brushed with heavily spiced barbecue sauces.

CHICKEN DRUMSTICKS WITH ASIAN BARBECUE SAUCE (P. 104)

13 For pâtés, mousses and terrines, pour a Zinfandel.

The words *rustic* and *rich* describe chicken-liver mousse as much as they do wines like Zinfandel, Italy's Nero d'Avola and Spain's Monastrell.

CREAMY CHICKEN-LIVER MOUSSE (P. 14)

14 Juicy red meat is fabulous with Cabernet Sauvignon.

California Cabernet, Bordeaux and Bordeaux-style blends are terrific with steaks or chops: Their tannins refresh the palate after each bite.

KOREAN SIZZLING BEEF (P. 128)

15 Match highly spiced dishes with Syrah.

For heavily seasoned meat, look for a red with spicy notes, like Syrah from Washington, Cabernet Franc from France and Xinomavro from Greece.

CUMIN-SPICED BURGERS WITH HARISSA MAYO (P. 152)

recipe index

a

almonds

Almond-and-Candied-Orange Cake with Lemon Semifreddo, 317

Apricot, Almond and Brown Butter Tart, 298

Bacon Quinoa with Almonds and Herbs, 242

Bitter Greens with Almonds and Goat Cheese, 42, **43**

Blueberry-Almond Shortcakes with Crème Fraîche, 294

Braised Romaine with Toasted Almonds and Moscatel Syrup, 216

Chocolate-Almond Toffee, 344

Chocolate Macarons, 335

Fig-and-Almond Bread Stuffing with Fennel, 268

Jam-Filled Mezzaluna Cookies, 338

Mom's Nutty Granola, 285

Passion Fruit Macarons, 338

Raspberry Macarons, 336

Slow-Roasted Lamb Shoulder with Almond-Mint Pesto, 140

Tangy Red-Pepper-and-Nut Dip, 19

White Gazpacho, 74

anchovies

Caesar-Style Dressing, 348, **348**

Creamy Anchovy Rouille, 70

Crisp Escarole Salad with Garlicky Anchovy Dressing, 44

Tomato-and-Anchovy Salad with Garlic Cream, 42, **43**

apples + apple cider

Braised Red Cabbage with Caraway and Apple, 226

Chicken-Liver Mousse with Bacon and Apple, 14

Clay-Pot Tarte Tatin, 288

Crab, Apple and Watercress Salad with Walnut Vinaigrette, 203

Hot Mulled Cider, 365

Jellied Cranberry Sauce with Fuji Apple, **346,** 357

Lemony Waldorf Salad, 54, **54**

Pan-Roasted Pork Chops with Creamy Cabbage and Apples, 166

Spiced Upside-Down Apple Bundt Cake, 316, **316**

Tangy Apple Salad, 238

Waldorf Chicken Salad, 54

Whole-Grain Bread Stuffing with Apples, Sausage and Pecans, 269

apricots

Apricot, Almond and Brown Butter Tart, 298

Apricot-and-Basil Shortbread Tart, 298, **299**

Apricot-and-Blueberry Tart, 296

Apricot Jam, 283

Curried Apricot-and-Tomato Ketchup, 349

Grilled Apricot, Arugula, and Goat Cheese Salad, 46

Pan-Seared Apricots and Figs with Honey and Lavender, 302, **303**

artichokes

Artichoke-and-Fontina Pizzas, 256

Artichoke-and-Spinach Dip with Spiced Pita Chips, 18

Artichoke Custards with Fava Bean Sauce, 17

Braised Baby Artichokes with Tomato Coulis, 230

Cod with Artichokes and Chickpeas, 186, **187**

arugula

Antipasto Salad, 41

Arugula-Fennel Salad, 48, **49**

Asian Pear–Arugula Salad with Goat Cheese, 46

Bitter Greens with Almonds and Goat Cheese, 42, **43**

Butternut Squash Salad with Hazelnuts, 50

Grilled Apricot, Arugula and Goat Cheese Salad, 46

Mustard-Glazed Chicken with Arugula and Bok Choy, 112, **113**

Pan-Fried Scamorza with Arugula Salad and Two Pestos, 34

Roasted-Chicken-and-Potato Salad with Béarnaise Dressing, 100

Asian Pear–Arugula Salad with Goat Cheese, 46

asparagus

Asparagus-and-Ricotta Toasts, 22

Asparagus-Cheese Tartines, 262

Asparagus Risotto with Mint, 246

Crab, Avocado, and Asparagus Salad, 51

Curry Quick Pickles, 355, **355**

Grilled Tofu with Asparagus and Nori Vinaigrette, 232, **232**

Mustard-and-Mayonnaise-Glazed Asparagus, 232

Penne with Asparagus, Sage and Peas, 84, **85**

Smoky Glazed Asparagus, 230, **231**

Spicy Dill Quick Pickles, 355, **355**

Stir-Fried Vegetables with Lemongrass, 212, **212**

Winey-Briny Quick Pickles, 355, **355**

avocados

Avocado, Grapefruit and Hearts of Palm Salad, 55

Avocado-and-Onion Salad, 54, **54**

Avocado-and-Roasted-Tomatillo Salsa, 350

Cheese-Topped Guacamole, 20, **21**

Chipotle-Marinated Flatiron Steak with Avocado-Corn Relish, 136

Crab, Avocado and Asparagus Salad, 51

Crab-and-Avocado Toasts, 22

Creamy Green Chile and Avocado Sauce, 351, **351**

Crisp Salmon with Avocado Salad, **172,** 178

Curried Tofu-and-Avocado Dip with Rosemary Pita Chips, 18

Grilled Scallops with Honeydew-Avocado Salsa, 206

recite index

recipe index

recipe index

recite index

recipe index

recipe index

recipe index

recipe index

recipe index

recipe index

recipe index

t

recipe index

V

W

contributors

Matthew Accarrino is the chef at SPQR in San Francisco.

Hugh Acheson, an F&W Best New Chef 2002, is the chef at Five & Ten and the owner of Gosford Wine, both in Athens, Georgia.

Laura Adrian is the co-chef and co-owner of Hidden Kitchen, a restaurant and supper club in Paris.

Alex Aguilera is the chef at Liguria wine bar in Santiago, Chile.

Tom Aikens is the chef and owner of Tom's Kitchen and the Michelin-starred Tom Aikens, both in London.

Nate Appleman, an F&W Best New Chef 2009, is a partner with restaurateur Keith McNally in the forthcoming Pulino's Bar and Pizzeria in New York City.

Armand Arnal is the chef at La Chassagnette outside Arles, France.

Alison Attenborough is a New York–based chef, food stylist and recipe developer and the co-author of *Williams-Sonoma Cooking for Friends.*

Andres Barrera is the chef at City Winery in New York City.

Joe Bastianich co-owns six restaurants in New York, three in Las Vegas and two in Los Angeles with partner Mario Batali. He is also the co-founder of two wineries in Italy and co-author of *Vino Italiano.*

Rick Bayless, an F&W Best New Chef 1988, is the chef and owner of Frontera Grill, Topolobampo and Xoco, all in Chicago. He is also the host of the PBS series *Mexico—One Plate at a Time,* the author of numerous cookbooks and the founder of Frontera Foods.

Rolando Beramendi is the founder and vice president of Manicaretti Imports in Oakland, California.

John Besh, an F&W Best New Chef 1999, is the chef and owner of Restaurant August, Besh Steak and Lüke, all in New Orleans, and La Provence in Lacombe, Louisiana. He is also the author of *My New Orleans: The Cookbook.*

Michael Black is the co-chef and co-owner of Sebo in San Francisco.

Taylor Boetticher is the co-owner of the Fatted Calf Charcuterie in Napa.

Eugenia Bone is the author of several books; her most recent is *Well Preserved.*

Michel Bras is the Michelin-starred chef and owner of three restaurants, including his flagship, Michel Bras, in Laguiole, France.

Marilynn Brass and her sister, **Sheila Brass,** are the authors of *Heirloom Cooking with the Brass Sisters* and *Heirloom Baking with the Brass Sisters.*

David Bull, an F&W Best New Chef 2003, is the chef at Bolla in the Stoneleigh Hotel in Dallas.

Bryan Calvert is the chef and co-owner of James in Brooklyn, New York.

Marco Canora is the chef and co-owner of Hearth, Insieme and Terroir in New York City and the author of *Salt to Taste.*

Tad Carducci is a member of the beverage consulting firm Tippling Bros. and beverage director at Apothecary Bar and Lounge in Philadelphia.

Lourdes Castro is the director of the Biltmore Culinary Academy in Coral Gables, Florida, and the author of *Simply Mexican* and *Eat, Drink, Think in Spanish.*

Bryan Caswell, an F&W Best New Chef 2009, is the chef at Reef in Houston.

David Chang, an F&W Best New Chef 2006, is the chef and owner of four Manhattan restaurants, including his flagship, Momofuku Noodle Bar. He is also the co-author of *Momofuku.*

Joanne Chang is the co-owner of Myers + Chang restaurant and the owner of Flour Bakery, both in Boston.

Lauren Chattman is the author of many cookbooks, including *Instant Gratification* and *Cake Keeper Cakes.*

Ratha Chau is the chef and owner of Kampuchea and Num Pang in New York City.

Roy Choi is the chef and owner of Kogi BBQ Trucks and Kogi at the Alibi Room in Los Angeles.

Eric Chopin is the chef at the Mansion on Peachtree hotel in Atlanta.

Tom Colicchio, an F&W Best New Chef 1991, is the chef and owner of Craft, Craftbar and Craftsteak, with locations throughout the country, and 'wichcraft in New York City. He is also the head judge on Bravo's *Top Chef.*

Charlie Collins is the chef and owner of the restaurant at Panamonte Inn & Spa in Boquete, Panama.

Alain Coumont is the founder of the bakery-café chain Le Pain Quotidien, with more than 100 locations in over 15 countries.

contributors

Gerard Craft, an F&W Best New Chef 2008, is the chef and owner of Niche and Taste by Niche, both in St. Louis.

Tim Cushman, an F&W Best New Chef 2008, is the chef and co-owner of O Ya in Boston.

Charles Dale, an F&W Best New Chef 1995, is the chef at Terra restaurant at the Encantado resort in Santa Fe, New Mexico.

Robert Del Grande is the chef and co-owner of RDG and Bar Annie, both in Houston.

Karen DeMasco is the pastry chef at Locanda Verde in New York City and the author of *The Craft of Baking*.

Krista Desjarlais is the chef and owner of Bresca in Portland, Maine.

Fred Donnelly is the chef and owner of Mo Gridder's in the Bronx, New York.

Kristin Donnelly is an associate food editor at F&W.

Vinny Dotolo, an F&W Best New Chef 2009, is the co-chef and co-owner of Animal in Los Angeles.

Celestino Drago, an F&W Best New Chef 1993, is the chef and owner of five California restaurants, including his flagship, Drago Ristorante, in Santa Monica.

Kyle Dromgoole is the owner of Café Brújula in Oaxaca, Mexico.

Randolph Dudley is a graphic designer and a chef for The FourCoursemen supper club in Athens, Georgia.

Jodi Elliot was the pastry chef at the Urban Farmer in Portland, Oregon.

Michael Emanuel is a private chef in Napa Valley.

Kelly English, an F&W Best New Chef 2009, is the chef and owner of Restaurant Iris in Memphis.

Ryan Farr is the butcher and owner of 4505 Meats in San Francisco.

Josh Feathers is the corporate chef at Blackberry Farm resort in Walland, Tennessee.

Raul Molina Fernandez is the chef at Emiliano Garcia's Casa Montana in Valencia, Spain.

Bobby Flay is the chef and owner of five restaurants, including Mesa Grill, with outposts in New York City, Las Vegas and the Bahamas. He also owns Bobby's Burger Palace, with four locations in the Northeast, and stars on Food Network's *Boy Meets Grill, Throwdown!* and *Iron Chef America.*

Deanie Fox is the pastry chef at Ubuntu in Napa.

Jeremy Fox, an F&W Best New Chef 2008, is the chef and co-owner of Ubuntu in Napa.

Roger Freedman is the chef at Rendezvous Bistro in Jackson Hole, Wyoming.

Mark Fuller, an F&W Best New Chef 2009, is the chef and co-owner of Spring Hill in Seattle.

Dale Gartland is the chef at the Farm at Cape Kidnappers resort in Hawke's Bay, New Zealand.

Andy Glover is the chef at Mission Estate Winery in Hawke's Bay, New Zealand.

Suzanne Goin, an F&W Best New Chef 1999, is the chef and co-owner of A.O.C., Lucques and Tavern and co-owner of the Hungry Cat, all in Los Angeles. She is also the author of *Sunday Suppers at Lucques.*

Karina Gowing is the bakery manager at Me & Ollie's in Portsmouth, New Hampshire.

Meg Grace is the chef and co-owner of The Redhead in New York City.

Colleen Grapes is the pastry chef at The Harrison in New York City.

Andrew Green is the wine director for the Bacchus Management Group in California, which includes Spruce restaurant in San Francisco.

David Guas is the owner of Damgoodsweet consulting group and co-author of the cookbook *DamGoodSweet.*

Tommy Habetz is the chef at Bunk in Portland, Oregon.

Paula Haney is the chef and owner of Hoosier Mama Pie Company in Chicago.

Angela Hartnett is a Michelin-starred chef at York & Albany in London.

Helen Jane Hearn is a co-founder of the national cheese-tasting club Cheesewhizzes based in St. Helena, California.

Anissa Helou, a London-based Syrian-Lebanese cookbook writer, leads culinary tours around the world.

Maria Hines, an F&W Best New Chef 1995, is the chef and owner of Tilth in Seattle.

Gerald Hirigoyen, an F&W Best New Chef 1994, owns the Basque restaurant Piperade in San Francisco. He also makes wine in Montsant, Spain.

Mark Hix is the chef and owner of Hix Oyster and Chop House in London.

Timothy Hollingsworth is the chef de cuisine at the French Laundry in Napa Valley.

Linton Hopkins, an F&W Best New Chef 2009, is the chef at Restaurant Eugene and Holeman and Finch, both in Atlanta.

Daniel Humm, an F&W Best New Chef 2005, is the chef at Eleven Madison Park in New York City.

contributors

Daniel Hyatt is the bar manager at Alembic Bar in San Francisco.

Ginevra Iverson is the chef and owner of Restaurant Eloise in Sebastopol, California.

Melissa Rubel Jacobson is F&W's senior associate recipe developer and the associate food editor for F&W Cookbooks.

Emily Kaiser is an associate food editor at F&W.

Michel Keller is the former pastry chef and owner of Restaurant du Village in Chester, Connecticut.

Thomas Keller, an F&W Best New Chef 1988, is the chef and owner of nine restaurants, including the French Laundry and Bouchon in Napa Valley and Per Se in New York City. He is the author of several cookbooks, most recently *Ad Hoc at Home*.

Kelsie Kerr, an F&W Best New Chef 1997, runs the cooking school at Cavallo Point Lodge in Sausalito, California.

Marcia Kiesel is the F&W Test Kitchen supervisor and co-author of *The Simple Art of Vietnamese Cooking*.

Jamie Kimm is a personal chef and food stylist as well as the co-author of *Williams-Sonoma Cooking for Friends*.

Christopher Kostow, an F&W Best New Chef 2009, is the chef at Meadowood Napa Valley in St. Helena, California.

Mourad Lahlou is the chef and owner of Aziza in San Francisco.

John Lancaster is the wine director at Boulevard in San Francisco.

Rachel Lansang-Hidalgo was the pastry chef at Aureole in New York City.

Dennis Leary is the chef and owner of The Sentinel in San Francisco.

Katie Lee is the author of *The Comfort Table* and *The Comfort Table: Recipes for Everyday Occasions*.

Joseph Lenn is a chef at Blackberry Farm resort in Walland, Tennessee.

Maggie Leung was the pastry chef at Lark Creek Inn in Larkspur, California.

Matt Lewis co-owns Baked in Brooklyn, New York, and Charleston, South Carolina. He is also the co-author of *Baked: New Frontiers in Baking*.

Paul Liebrandt, an F&W Best New Chef 2009, is the chef and co-owner of Corton in New York City.

Chris Lilly is the chef at Big Bob Gibson Bar-B-Q in Decatur, Alabama, as well as the author of *Big Bob Gibson's BBQ Book: Recipes and Secrets from a Legendary BBQ Joint*.

Donald Link is the chef and owner of Herbsaint and Cochon in New Orleans and the author of *Real Cajun: Rustic Home Cooking*.

Anita Lo, an F&W Best New Chef 2001, is the chef and owner of Annisa restaurant and chef-partner of Rickshaw Dumpling Bar, both in New York City.

Giorgio Locatelli is the Michelin-starred chef at Locanda Locatelli in London and a consulting chef for the Hotel Missoni Edinburgh.

Tim Love is the chef and owner of Lonesome Dove Western Bistro and Love Shack, both in Fort Worth, Texas.

Emily Luchetti is a cookbook author and the pastry chef at Farallon and Waterbar in San Francisco. Among her cookbooks are *A Passion for Desserts* and *Classic Stars Desserts*.

Barbara Lynch, an F&W Best New Chef 1996, is the chef and owner of four Boston restaurants, including No. 9 Park.

She also owns two bars, a butcher shop and a catering company in Boston.

Tiffany MacIsaac is the pastry chef at Birch & Barley in Washington, DC.

Lachlan Mackinnon-Patterson, an F&W Best New Chef 2005, is the chef and co-owner of Frasca Food and Wine in Boulder, Colorado.

Barry Maiden, an F&W Best New Chef 2009, is the chef and owner of Hungry Mother in Cambridge, Massachusetts.

Francis Mallmann is the owner of three South American restaurants, including his flagship, 1884, in Mendoza, Argentina. He is also the author of *Seven Fires: Grilling the Argentine Way*.

Joy Manning is *Philadelphia* magazine's restaurant critic and the co-author of *Almost Meatless*. She also writes the blog *What I Weigh Today*.

Tony Mantuano is the chef and owner of Spiaggia and the Art Institute's Terzo Piano in Chicago and co-author of *The Spiaggia Cookbook* and *Wine Bar Food*.

Joe Marcos is the chef de cuisine at Pizzeria Mozza in Los Angeles.

Peggy Markel owns an international culinary tour company, Peggy Markel's Culinary Adventures.

Gonzalo Martinez is the chef at Sazón, the school at Casa de Sierra Nevada in San Miguel de Allende, Mexico.

Marisa May co-owns SD26 in New York City.

Shawn McClain is the chef and owner of Spring and Green Zebra, both in Chicago.

Mark Mendoza is the sommelier at Sona in Los Angeles.

Rosita Missoni is the founding designer of the Italian fashion company Missoni and an avid home cook.

Matt Molina is the chef at Osteria Mozza and Pizzeria Mozza in Los Angeles.

Seamus Mullen is the chef and co-owner of Boqueria in New York City.

Wade Murphy is the chef at Lisloughrey Lodge in Cong, Ireland.

David Myers, an F&W Best New Chef 1993, is the chef and owner of Sona in Los Angeles.

Tom Mylan is the butcher at the Meat Hook in Brooklyn, New York. He teaches classes in butchering.

Nirmala Narine is the author of *Nirmala's Edible Diary*.

Elissa Narrow is a chef-instructor at the Illinois Institute of Art Chicago.

Dahlia Narvaez is the pastry chef at Mozza in Los Angeles.

Gina Neely and her husband, **Patrick Neely,** co-star on Food Network's *Down Home with the Neelys*. They also co-own Neely's Bar-B-Que in Memphis.

Justin Neidermeyer is the former chef and owner of Spinasse in Seattle.

Andrea Nguyen is a food writer, researcher and teacher specializing in Asian cultures. She is also the author of *Into the Vietnamese Kitchen* and *Asian Dumplings*.

Mani Niall is the owner of Mani's Bakery Café in Los Angeles and the author of *Baked, Covered in Honey* and *Sweet!*

Andy Nusser is the chef at Mario Batali's Tarry Lodge in Port Chester, New York.

Patrick O'Connell is the chef and co-owner of the Inn at Little Washington in Washington, Virginia.

Kevin O'Connor is the former wine director at Spago Restaurant in Beverly Hills.

Alejandro Ruíz Olmedo is the chef at Casa Oaxaca in Oaxaca, Mexico.

Ken Oringer is the chef and owner of six Boston area restaurants: Clio, Uni, Toro, La Verdad, KO Prime and, most recently, Coppa.

Doris Esther Ayola Orozco is a chef at Escape to Shape in Cartagena, Colombia.

Matt Palmerlee is a chef for The FourCoursemen supper club and co chef at Farm 255, both in Athens, Georgia.

Grace Parisi is F&W's Test Kitchen senior recipe developer and the author of *Get Saucy*.

Rajat Parr is the sommelier and partner at RN74 in San Francisco as well as the wine director of chef Michael Mina's restaurant group. He also owns his own wine label, Parr Selections.

Cindy Pawlcyn is the chef and owner of Mustards Grill, Cindy's Backstreet Kitchen and Go Fish, all in Napa Valley.

François Payard is the owner of Payard Patisserie & Bistro in Las Vegas, Tokyo, Yokohama, Seoul and São Paulo, and François Chocolate Bar in New York City. His most recent cookbook is *Chocolate Epiphany*.

Mark Peel is the chef and owner of Campanile and the co-owner of Tar Pitt, both in Los Angeles. He is also the co-author of *New Classic Family Dinners*.

Jacques Pépin is an F&W contributing editor, master chef, television personality, cookbook author and the dean of special programs for the French Culinary Institute in New York City.

Braden Perkins is the co-chef and co-owner of Hidden Kitchen, a restaurant and supper club in Paris.

Robert Perkins is the wine director at Boulevard in San Francisco.

Renato Poliafito co-owns Baked in Brooklyn, New York, and Charleston, South Carolina. He is also the co-author of *Baked: New Frontiers in Baking.*

Naomi Pomeroy, an F&W Best New Chef 2009, is the chef at Beast in Portland, Oregon.

Lulu Powers is a Los Angeles–based caterer and cookbook author. Her new cookbook is *Lulu Powers Food to Flowers: Simple, Stylish Food for Easy Entertaining.*

Alex Raij is the chef and owner of Txikito in New York City.

Matthew Rice was the pastry chef at Niche in St. Louis.

Andy Ricker is the chef and owner of Pok Pok in Portland, Oregon.

Eric Ripert is the chef and co-owner of Le Bernardin in New York City and the culinary director of Westend Bistro in Washington, DC, and 10 Arts in Philadelphia. He is also the co-author of three cookbooks, most recently *On the Line: Inside the World of Le Bernardin.*

Hosea Rosenberg, the winner of *Top Chef* Season 5, was the chef at Jax Fish House in Boulder, Colorado.

Katie Rosenhouse is the pastry chef at Olana in New York City.

Stefania Rubicondo is a baker at Baked in Brooklyn, New York.

Eddie Russell is the co-chef at Farm 255 and a chef for The FourCoursemen supper club, both in Athens, Georgia.

Damien Schaefer is a graphic designer and a chef for The FourCoursemen supper club in Athens, Georgia.

Bruce Sherman, an F&W Best New Chef 2003, is the chef and owner of North Pond in Chicago.

contributors

Jon Shook, an F&W Best New Chef 2009, is the co-chef and co-owner of Animal in Los Angeles.

Roy Shvartzapel is the pastry chef at Cyrus in Healdsburg, California.

Joaquin Simo is a bartender at Death & Co. in New York City and the deputy editor of F&W's annual *Cocktails* book.

Kerry Simon is the chef and co-owner of Simon and CatHouse, both in Las Vegas, Simon LA in Los Angeles and Impala in San Francisco.

Sara Simpson is the chef at Terroir restaurant at Craggy Range, a winery in Hawke's Bay, New Zealand.

Clint Sloan is the sommelier at McCrady's in Charleston, South Carolina.

Michael Solomonov is the chef and co-owner of Zahav in Philadelphia.

Ana Sortun is the chef and owner of Oleana and Sofra in Cambridge, Massachusetts. She is also the author of *Spice.*

Frank Stitt owns three restaurants in Birmingham, Alabama, including his flagship, Bottega. He is also the author of *Frank Stitt's Bottega Favorita* and *Frank Stitt's Southern Table.*

Curtis Stone is the star of TLC's *Take Home Chef* and the author of *Relaxed Cooking with Curtis Stone.*

Patrick Stubbers is a chef for The FourCoursemen supper club and a sous-chef at The National, both in Athens, Georgia.

Caroline Styne is the co-owner and sommelier of Lucques and A.O.C. in Los Angeles.

Jessica Sullivan is the pastry chef at Boulevard in San Francisco.

Mark Sullivan, an F&W Best New Chef 2002, is the chef and co-owner of Village Pub and Spruce, both in San Francisco.

Bernie Sun is the corporate beverage director of Jean-Georges Vongerichten's restaurant group, Jean-Georges Management LLC, in New York City.

David Swain is the chef at Fino in Willunga, Australia.

Paul Tanguay is a member of the beverage consulting firm Tippling Bros. and beverage director at Apothecary Bar and Lounge in Philadelphia.

Katherine Thompson is the pastry chef at Dell'anima and L'Artusi in New York City.

Peter Ting is a London-based ceramicist and serious home cook.

Christina Tosi is the pastry chef for the Momofuku restaurants in New York City.

Laurent Tourondel is the chef and co-owner of BLT restaurants worldwide.

Silvio Ursini is the chef and owner of Osteria Tornabuoni in Tuscany and Obikà restaurants worldwide.

Frank Urso is the pastry chef at Barclay Prime in Philadelphia.

Lionel Vatinet is the baker and owner of Le Farm Bakery in Cary, North Carolina.

Andreas Viestad is a Norwegian chef, food writer, celebrity farmer and the host of the PBS cooking show *Perfect Day.*

Jean-Georges Vongerichten, an F&W contributing editor, is the chef and co-owner of restaurants around the world, including Jean Georges in New York City. He is the author of four cookbooks; the most recent is *Asian Flavors of Jean-Georges.*

Jessamyn Waldman is the founder of Hot Bread Kitchen in Queens, New York.

Natalie Wassum is a co-founder of the national cheese-tasting club Cheesewhizzes based in St. Helena, California.

Luisa Weiss is an editor at Stewart, Tabori & Chang. She edited *Baked: New Frontiers in Baking.*

Tristan Welch is the chef at Launceston Place in London.

Michael White is the chef and co-owner of the New York City restaurants Alto, Convivio and Marea.

Robert Wiedmaier is the chef and owner of Brabo in Alexandria, Virginia.

Paula Wolfert is an authority on Mediterranean cooking and an F&W contributing editor. She is the author of numerous cookbooks; her most recent is *Mediterranean Clay Pot Cooking.*

Cynthia Wong is the pastry chef at Cakes & Ale in Decatur, Georgia.

Lee Anne Wong was a contestant on the first season of Bravo's *Top Chef* and the culinary producer for the show's fifth season.

Takashi Yagihashi, an F&W Best New Chef 2000, is the owner of Okada restaurant in Las Vegas and Noodles by Takashi Yagihashi in Chicago. He is also the author of *Takashi Noodles.*

Chris Yeo is the chef-owner of five restaurants, including Straits Atlanta, where he is a partner with the rapper Ludacris.

Eileen Yin-Fei Lo is the author of numerous cookbooks, including *Mastering the Art of Chinese Cooking.*

Nathanial Zimet is the chef and owner of Boucherie in New Orleans.

photographers

measurement guide

Basic Measurements

GALLON	QUART	PINT	CUP	OUNCE	TBSP	TSP	DROPS
1 gal	4 qt	8 pt	16 c	128 fl oz			
½ gal	2 qt	4 pt	8 c	64 fl oz			
¼ gal	1 qt	2 pt	4 c	32 fl oz			
	½ qt	1 pt	2 c	16 fl oz			
	¼ qt	½ pt	1 c	8 fl oz	16 tbsp		
			⅞ c	7 fl oz	14 tbsp		
			¾ c	6 fl oz	12 tbsp		
			⅔ c	5⅓ fl oz	10⅔ tbsp		
			⅝ c	5 fl oz	10 tbsp		
			½ c	4 fl oz	8 tbsp		
			⅜ c	3 fl oz	6 tbsp		
			⅓ c	2⅔ fl oz	5⅓ tbsp	16 tsp	
			¼ c	2 fl oz	4 tbsp	12 tsp	
			⅛ c	1 fl oz	2 tbsp	6 tsp	
				½ fl oz	1 tbsp	3 tsp	
					½ tbsp	1½ tsp	
						1 tsp	60 drops
						½ tsp	30 drops

U.S. to Metric Conversions

The conversions in the first three columns are approximations. For more precise conversions, use the formulas to the right.

VOLUME			WEIGHT			TEMPERATURE			CONVERSION FORMULAS
1 tsp	=	5 ml	1 oz	=	28 g	475°F	=	246°C	tsp x 4.929 = ml
1 tbsp	=	15 ml	¼ lb (4 oz)	=	113 g	450°F	=	232°C	tbsp x 14.787 = ml
1 fl oz	=	30 ml	½ lb (8 oz)	=	227 g	425°F	=	218°C	fl oz x 29.574 = ml
¼ c	=	59 ml	¾ lb (12 oz)	=	340 g	400°F	=	204°C	c x 236.588 = ml
½ c	=	118 ml	1 lb (16 oz)	=	½ kg	375°F	=	191°C	pt x .473 = L
¾ c	=	177 ml				350°F	=	179°C	qt x .946 = L
1 c	=	237 ml	LENGTH			325°F	=	163°C	oz x 28.35 = g
1 pt	=	½ L	1 in	=	2.5 cm	300°F	=	149°C	lb x .453 = kg
1 qt	=	1 L	5 in	=	12.7 cm	275°F	=	135°C	in x 2.54 = cm
1 gal	=	4 L	9 in	=	23 cm	250°F	=	121°C	(°F−32) x .556 = °C